Frommer's®

Austria

13th Edition

by Darwin Porter & Danforth Prince

Here's what the critics say about Frommer's:

"Amazingly easy to use. Very portable, very complete."
—BOOKLIST

"Detailed, accurate, and easy-to-read information for all price ranges."
—GLAMOUR MAGAZINE

"Hotel information is close to encyclopedic."
—DES MOINES SUNDAY REGISTER

"Frommer's Guides have a way of giving you a real feel for a place."
—KNIGHT RIDDER NEWSPAPERS

Wiley Publishing, Inc.

Published by:

WILEY PUBLISHING, INC.

111 River St.
Hoboken, NJ 07030-5774

ISBN 978-0-470-39897-5
Editor: Ian Skinnari
Production Editor: Eric T. Schroeder
Cartographer: Elizabeth Puhl
Photo Editor: Richard Fox
Production by Wiley Indianapolis Composition Services

Front cover photo: Springtime in the Austrian Alps
Back cover photo: Mozart's House in Salzburg

For information on our other products and services or to obtain technical support, please contact our Customer Care Department within the U.S. at 800/762-2974, outside the U.S. at 317/572-3993 or fax 317/572-4002.

Wiley also publishes its books in a variety of electronic formats. Some content that appears in print may not be available in electronic formats.

Manufactured in the United States of America

5 4 3 2 1

CONTENTS

4 SUGGESTED AUSTRIAN ITINERARIES 70

5 SETTLING INTO VIENNA 83

6 EXPLORING VIENNA 138

7 LOWER AUSTRIA 184

8 BURGENLAND 205

AUSTRIA CONTENTS

9 SALZBURG: CITY OF MOZART 218

10 LAND SALZBURG 267

11 UPPER AUSTRIA 303

12 INNSBRUCK & TYROL: THE BEST OF SCENIC AUSTRIA 337

13 VORARLBERG 404

14 CARINTHIA 431

15 STYRIA 452

APPENDIX A: FAST FACTS, TOLL-FREE NUMBERS & WEBSITES 481

APPENDIX B: LANGUAGE LESSONS 488

INDEX 491

LIST OF MAPS

AN INVITATION TO THE READER

In researching this book, we discovered many wonderful places—hotels, restaurants, shops, and more. We're sure you'll find others. Please tell us about them, so we can share the information with your fellow travelers in upcoming editions. If you were disappointed with a recommendation, we'd love to know that, too. Please write to:

Frommer's Austria, 13th Edition
Wiley Publishing, Inc. • 111 River St. • Hoboken, NJ 07030-5774

AN ADDITIONAL NOTE

Please be advised that travel information is subject to change at any time—and this is especially true of prices. We therefore suggest that you write or call ahead for confirmation when making your travel plans. The authors, editors, and publisher cannot be held responsible for the experiences of readers while traveling. Your safety is important to us, however, so we encourage you to stay alert and be aware of your surroundings. Keep a close eye on cameras, purses, and wallets, all favorite targets of thieves and pickpockets.

ABOUT THE AUTHORS

As a team of veteran travel writers, **Darwin Porter** and **Danforth Prince** have produced titles for Frommer's including guides to Italy, France, the Caribbean, England, and Germany. A film critic, columnist, and broadcaster, Porter is also a Hollywood biographer. Recent releases by Darwin include *Brando Unzipped,* documenting the private life of Marlon Brando, and *Jacko: His Rise and Fall,* the first complete biography ever written on the tumultuous life of Michael Jackson. Prince was formerly employed by the Paris bureau of the *New York Times* and is today the president of Blood Moon Productions and other media-related firms. Porter and Prince's latest non-travel-related venture, jointly co-authored and published in 2008 by Blood Moon, is *Hollywood Babylon—It's Back!,* which one critic described as "the hottest compilation of inter-generational scandal in the history of Hollywood."

FROMMER'S STAR RATINGS, ICONS & ABBREVIATIONS

Every hotel, restaurant, and attraction listing in this guide has been ranked for quality, value, service, amenities, and special features using a **star-rating system.** In country, state, and regional guides, we also rate towns and regions to help you narrow down your choices and budget your time accordingly. Hotels and restaurants are rated on a scale of zero (recommended) to three stars (exceptional). Attractions, shopping, nightlife, towns, and regions are rated according to the following scale: zero stars (recommended), one star (highly recommended), two stars (very highly recommended), and three stars (must-see).

In addition to the star-rating system, we also use **seven feature icons** that point you to the great deals, in-the-know advice, and unique experiences that separate travelers from tourists. Throughout the book, look for:

Finds	Special finds—those places only insiders know about
Fun Facts	Fun facts—details that make travelers more informed and their trips more fun
Kids	Best bets for kids and advice for the whole family
Moments	Special moments—those experiences that memories are made of
Overrated	Places or experiences not worth your time or money
Tips	Insider tips—great ways to save time and money
Value	Great values—where to get the best deals

The following **abbreviations** are used for credit cards:

AE	American Express	DISC	Discover	V	Visa
DC	Diners Club	MC	MasterCard		

FROMMERS.COM

Now that you have this guidebook to help you plan a great trip, visit our website at **www.frommers.com** for additional travel information on more than 4,000 destinations. We update features regularly to give you instant access to the most current trip-planning information available. At Frommers.com, you'll find scoops on the best airfares, lodging rates, and car rental bargains. You can even book your travel online through our reliable travel booking partners. Other popular features include:

- Online updates of our most popular guidebooks
- Vacation sweepstakes and contest giveaways
- Newsletters highlighting the hottest travel trends
- Podcasts, interactive maps, and up-to-the-minute events listings
- Opinionated blog entries by Arthur Frommer himself
- Online travel message boards with featured travel discussions

What's New in Austria

While Austria's imperial monuments and scenic wonders remain eternal, here are some of the latest developments that might affect your trip.

VIENNA **Accommodations** With its young, modern, and chic design, **Falkensteiner Hotel Am Schottenfeld,** Schottenfeldgasse 74 (✆ **01/526-5181**), is perhaps the most dramatically lit hotel in Vienna. The Falkensteiner offers elegant rooms of contemporary comfort and tasteful appointments, along with marble-floored bathrooms. It's filled with thoughtful extras from its kids' club to its Turkish bath.

Dining A hot new dining choice for Vienna, drawing the serious foodie, is **Dining Room,** Maygasse 31 (✆ **01/804-8586**), where reservations are imperative because the restaurant can only accommodate 12 diners. The setting for some of the finest international cuisine served in Vienna is a private home, an intimate little hideaway that is the address of the owner and chef, Angelika Apfelthaler. She prepares each meal herself and often dedicates her dinners to a special theme, perhaps Moroccan nights.

Attractions In late 2008, Vienna's public transport authorities will unveil new connections on Vienna's famous Ring Boulevard, which, for the first time, will be linked to the heart of the city and many of the most visited tourist attractions of the First District. However, the entire round of the Ring Boulevard will not be changed.

The new line will link all the major sights along the Ring, including the Burgtheater, City Hall, Parliament, and the Fine Art and Natural History museums, along with the Vienna State Opera. A new line 2 will run not only to the Hofburg, but also to the Stadpark, MAK (Museum of Applied Art), the Urania, and Schwedenplatz.

The famed **Lippizzaner Museum,** in the Hofburg Palace, has closed due to lack of funding. The museum, a favorite of horse lovers, traced the history of the **Spanish Riding School** (p. 144), which still remains open in spite of money problems.

Shopping For art lovers, a unique shopping adventure can be found at **M-ARS,** 9 Westbahnstrasse (✆ **01/890-5803**). This is a "supermarket," stocked not with groceries but with works of art. You can literally take a shopping cart around with you. Rest assured that many works of art begin at only $15. More than 1,000 paintings, sculptures, and photographs—the work of some 50 artists—are on sale.

After it received international publicity, **Gegenbauer,** Gegenbauer 14, Naschmarkt (✆ **01/604-1088**), is attracting gourmets from around the world. It offers the greatest collection of artisan vinegars in Austria, some 50 in all, plus 20 specialty oils. It's been in business since 1929, although only in 2008 did it become recognized for its rare offerings such as tomato vinegar. You can even purchase vinegar that's made from beer.

After Dark More and more club-goers are flocking to the **Babenberger Passage,** Ringstrasse at Babenbergerstrasse (✆ **01/961-8800**), the most futuristic club in Vienna, evoking a spaceship. There's dancing in a romantically contemporary bar, and the bartenders serve some of the best cocktails in Vienna.

Installed in a cavernous underground station, **Club Cavina,** Josefstadtstrasse 84/Stadtbahnbogen (✆ **01/406-4322**), presents live music. It's one of the hippest clubs in Vienna, attracting artsy types.

LOWER AUSTRIA **Dining** In the former imperial city of Wiener Neustadt, **Gastube Stachl,** Lange Gasse 20 (✆ **02622/25221**), has moved up the culinary scale and is now cited as the best place to dine within the city. It lies in the heart of town in an all-pedestrian zone. Its chefs prepare a Continental cuisine that has the old Austrian favorites, such as Wiener schnitzel, but also does more modern dishes such as strips of marinated salmon with pesto sauce.

SALZBURG **Accommodations** On the outskirts of the city at Gersberg, **Romantic Hotel Die Gersberg,** Gersberg 37 (✆ **0662/641257**), has been restored and now is one of the most atmospheric places to stay in the region. Only a 15-minute drive from the center of Salzburg, it dates from the 16th century, when it began life as a farmstead. From a summer garden to a blazing fireplace in winter, it has all the charm of yesterday, along with modern comforts.

Dining The chic **Hotel Bristol,** Makartplatz 4 (✆ **0662/873557**), has opened the trendy Polo Lounge, serving a first-rate cuisine, mainly Austrian, Italian, and international. The venue is stately and baronial, with large-scale oil paintings, and the meticulous cooking is equally opulent.

Strassewirt, Leopoldkronestrasse 39 (✆ **0662/826391**), is the latest first-class restaurant to burst onto the scene, lying a 10-minute walk south of the historic core of Salzburg. Occupying three indoor dining rooms and a well-landscaped garden, it lies in a renovated building 2 centuries old. Market-fresh menu items celebrate the cuisine and the agrarian bounty of Austria, including lamb from nearby mountains.

Attractions Salzburg has opened a number of new museums lately, including a series of attractions in the **Salzburg Museum/Neue Residenz,** which was built in the 1600s to house overflow guests from Prince-Archbishop Wolf Dietrich's palace. The entrance is on Mozartplatz 1 (✆ **0662/620808-700**). Some of the highlights of this new museum are rare archaeological treasures once housed in the Museum Carolino Augusteum, including Hallstatt Age relics, paintings by Old Masters, and Gothic panel art.

LAND SALZBURG **Accommodations** In the old spa town of Badgastein, once patronized by Kaiser Wilhelm I and Otto von Bismarck, the landmark hotel, **Elisabethpark,** has come under new ownership at its address at Franz-Josef-Strasse 5 (✆ **06434/25510**). New owners have vastly improved the hotel, which was pretty good to begin with. Two hotel shuttle buses now take you to and from the train station.

Dining A chic a-la-carte restaurant and wine bar, **Prälatur** is among the most elegant places to dine in town, with its traditional and innovative specialties. **Sisi,** named after the ill-fated empress, is a traditional Austrian coffeehouse with various specialty coffees and a large selection of the most delicious cakes and pastries in town.

UPPER AUSTRIA **Accommodations** In the provincial capital of Linz, **Drei Mohren,** Promenade 17 (✆ **0732/772626-0**), has been so vastly improved that it is now rated four stars by the government (the smallest hotel in the area with such a high rating). It has only 25 units, which makes it a boutique hotel. The atmosphere is intimate, the service topnotch. The rooms are spread across three restored buildings from the 16th century, which have been considerably modernized.

Dining Herberstein, Alstadt 10 (© **0732/786161**), may be in a historic building in the old town, but it has improved its menu and its setting so much that it is now one of the most stylish dining venues in the city. It has both an inviting courtyard and a lively bar scene, and its fusion cuisine, both Austrian and Asian, makes Herberstein come out at the top of the heap.

INNSBRUCK Dining In the capital of the Tyrol, **Lichtblick,** Maria-Theresienstrasse 18 (© **0512/566550**), occupies the seventh floor of the Rathausgalerie in the center of town. An international restaurant, a chic dining spot has been installed here, with vistas over the Alstadt or old city. Market-fresh ingredients are used to concoct a sublime cuisine, and there is also the adjoining Café Bar Lounge 360, which is the most dramatic place at which to have a drink in Innsbruck.

VORALBERG Accommodations In this far-western province, the city of Feldkirch makes an ideal stopover. Recent improvements in its rooms and cuisine are drawing more discerning visitors to **Landgasthof Schäfle** at Naflastrasse 3 at Feldkirch-Altenstadt (© **05522/72203**). Here you can rent a cozy, comfortably furnished bedroom or dine on a superb Austrian and continental cuisine. In fair weather, tables are placed in the manicured garden. The hotel is good value in expensive Austria, with double bedrooms costing 90€ ($144), or a fixed-price menu going for 15€ ($24).

CARINTHIA Accommodations In the capital city of the province, Klagenfurt, **Das Salzamt Palais Hotel Landhaus,** Landhaushof 3 (© **0463/590959**), has opened in a restored Renaissance palace in the heart of the city. Originally, the building was a former town salt tax office, but today it offers lushly decorated bedrooms, luxurious bathrooms (some with whirlpool baths), and heavenly beds. Personal service is a hallmark of this boutique hotel, as there are only 27 units.

Another small boutique hotel, a pocket of posh, has opened. It's **Palais Porcia,** Neuereplatz 13 (© **0463/511590-30**), in a restored former town palace dating from the 18th century and once belonging to the Italian princes of the House of Porcia. Bedrooms are stylish with baroque embellishments and Biedermeier antiques. Four-poster beds and antique art add to the charm.

STYRIA Dining In the capital of the province, the city of Graz, Arnold Schwarzenegger's hometown, the **Sacher** restaurant and cafe has opened at Herrengasse 6 (© **0316/8005-0**) and has immediately become a chic rendezvous stopover. With a classic Austrian menu, chefs turn out such long-enduring favorites as *tafelspitz* (boiled beef) and Wiener schnitzel. Of course, they also make the famed Sacher torte, a chocolate lover's fantasy dessert.

1 The Best of Austria

There's so much to do in Austria, from exploring historic castles and palaces to skiing some of the world's finest alpine slopes. All the choices you'll have to make when planning your trip can be a bit overwhelming. We've tried to make your task easier by compiling a list of our favorite experiences and discoveries. In the following pages you'll find the kind of candid advice we'd give our close friends.

1 THE BEST TRAVEL EXPERIENCES

- **Skiing in the Alps:** Skiing is the Austrian national sport and the reason thousands of visitors come to Austria. The country abounds in ski slopes, and you'll find the best ones in Tyrol, Land Salzburg, and Vorarlberg, although most parts of Carinthia, Western Styria, and Lower Austria also have slopes. The season lasts from late November to April, depending on snow conditions. At 1,739m (5,705 ft.), the Obertauern region extends its ski season until May. Daredevils can ski glaciers at 3,355m (11,010 ft.), even in summer. See "The Best Ski Areas," later in this chapter.
- **Feasting on the "Emperor's Dish,"** ***Tafelspitz:*** Get a taste for typical Austrian cuisine with the fabled *tafelspitz* (boiled beef dinner), favored by Emperor Franz Josef. It might sound dull, but *tafelspitz* is far from bland. Boiled to a tender delicacy, the "table end" cut is flavored with spices, including juniper berries, celery root, and onions. An apple-and-horseradish sauce further enlivens the dish, which is usually served with fried, grated potatoes. The best *tafelspitz* is served in Vienna, where the chefs have been making the dish for decades. See chapter 5.
- **Listening to Mozart:** It's said that at any time of the day or night in Austria, someone, somewhere is playing the music of Wolfgang Amadeus Mozart. You might hear it at an opera house; a church; a festival; an open-air concert; or, more romantically, in a Belle Epoque cafe, performed by a Hungarian orchestra. Regardless, "the sound of music" drifting through Vienna is likely the creation of this child prodigy. Try to hear Mozart on his home turf, especially in Vienna and Salzburg. See chapters 6 and 9.
- **Watching the Lipizzaner Stallions (Vienna):** Nothing evokes the heyday of imperial Vienna more than the Spanish Riding School. The sleek white stallions and their expert riders demonstrate the classic art of dressage in choreographed leaps and bounds. The stallions are the finest equestrian performers on earth. You can watch the performances, but you'll need to make reservations 6 to 8 weeks in advance. See p. 144.
- **Cruising the Danube (Donau):** Johann Strauss took a bit of poetic license in calling the Donau "The Blue Danube," as it's actually a muddy-green color. But a Danube cruise is the highlight of any Austrian vacation. The legendary DDSG, Blue Danube Shipping Company, Handelskai 265, A-1020 Vienna (✆ **01/588800;** www.ddsg-blue-danube.at), offers 1-day trips. On

board, you'll pass some of the most famous sights in eastern Austria, including Krems and Melk. See "Cruising the Danube," p. 165.

- ***Heurigen* Hopping in the Vienna Woods:** *Heurigen* are rustic wine taverns that celebrate the arrival of each year's new wine *(heuriger)* by placing a pine branch over the door. Austrians rush to these taverns to drink the new local wines and feast on a country buffet. Some *heurigen* have garden tables with panoramic views of the Danube Valley, whereas others provide shaded, centuries-old courtyards where revelers can enjoy live folk music. Try the red wines from Vöslau, the Sylvaner of Grinzing, or the Riesling of Nussberg, while listening to a *Schrammelmusik* quartet and all the revelers singing *"Wien bleibt Wein"* ("Vienna loves wine"). See "The Wienerwald (Vienna Woods)" in chapter 7.
- **Reliving *The Sound of Music:*** In 1964, Julie Andrews, Christopher Plummer, and a gaggle of kids imitating the von Trapp family filmed one of the world's great musicals. The memory of that Oscar-winning movie lingers on, as a steady stream of visitors head to Salzburg just to take *The Sound of Music* tour. You visit the Nonnberg Abbey and that little gazebo where Rolf and Liesl danced in the rain. There's also a stop at the Felsenreitenschule (Rock Riding School), where the von Trapps gave their final performance. See p. 257.
- **Driving on Top of the World on the Grossglockner Road (Land Salzburg):** For the drive of a lifetime, you can take Europe's longest and most panoramic alpine highway, with hairpin turns and bends around every corner. It begins at Bruck an der Grossglocknerstrasse at 757m (2,484 ft.); continues through the Hochtortunnel, where the highest point is 2,507m (8,225 ft.); and ends in the province of Carinthia. The mountain part of the road, stretching some 22km (14 miles), often at 1,983m (6,506 ft.), has a maximum gradient of 12%. You can drive this stunning engineering feat from mid-May to mid-November, although the road is safest from mid-June to mid-September. The views are among the greatest in the world, but keep your eyes on that curvy road! See section 6 in chapter 10, "Land Salzburg."
- **Exploring the Alps:** There are few places in the world that are as splendid as the limestone chain of mountains shared between Austria and Bavaria. Moving toward the east, the Alps slope away to the Great Hungarian Plain. The Austrian Alps break into three chains, including the High or Central Alps, the Northern Limestone Alps, and the Southern Limestone Alps. In the west, you discover fairy-tale Tyrolean villages, the Holy Roman Empire attractions of Innsbruck, and some of the world's greatest ski resorts, including St. Anton, Zürs, Lech, and Kitzbühel. Filled with quaint little towns, the Eastern Alps sprawl across the Tyrolean country, West Styria, and Land Salzburg. Castles and stunning views await you at every turn. See chapters 10, 12, 13, and 15.

2 THE MOST ROMANTIC GETAWAYS

- **Hof bei Salzburg (Land Salzburg):** Lying on Lake Fuschl (Fuschlsee), this chic resort is only a 15-minute ride from Salzburg; it boasts a breathtaking alpine backdrop of blue clear-but-chilly waters, mountains, and evergreen forests. Based here, you can also easily get to Fuschlsee, Wolfgangsee, and Mondsee. The town offers some romantic places to stay, notably the **Hotel Schloss**

Fuschl (✆ **06229/22530;** www.starwoodhotels.com). See p. 300.

- **St. Wolfgang (Upper Austria):** On the Wolfgangsee, one of Austria's loveliest lakes, St. Wolfgang lies in the mountains of the Salzkammergut. It's the home of the **White Horse Inn** (✆ **06138/23060;** www.weissesroessl.at), which served as the setting for Ralph Benatzky's operetta of the same name. Lying 50km (32 miles) east of Salzburg, the resort is a summer paradise, with lakefront beaches and cafes, hiking opportunities in all directions, and skiing in winter. See section 3, "St. Wolfgang & Bad Ischl," in chapter 11.
- **Mutters (Tyrol):** On a sunny plateau above Innsbruck, this little resort has been called the most beautiful village in Tyrol (quite a compliment). Mutters, a central base of the 1964 and 1976 Olympics, attracts visitors year-round. The most romantic place to stay is the **Hotel Altenburg** (✆ **0512/548524;** www.altenburg.com), which was a restaurant in 1622 and later a farmhouse before it converted into an elegant hotel. See p. 370.
- **Stuben (Vorarlberg):** The rich and famous might flock to Vorarlberg's stellar ski resorts, Zürs or Lech, but we think you should sneak away to the little village of Stuben, 10km (6 miles) north of Lech on the west side of the Arlberg Pass. A way station for alpine travelers for centuries, Stuben was the birthplace of the great ski instructor Hannes Schneider. In winter, you can take a horse-drawn sleigh from Lech to Stuben. Once here, stay at **Hotel Mondschein** (✆ **05582/511;** www.mondschein.com), a 1739 house converted to a hotel. See p. 413.
- **Pörtschach (Carinthia):** Many wealthy Viennese have lavish summer homes in this resort town on the northern perimeter of Lake Wörther. Known for its lakeside promenade, it attracts a sports-oriented crowd who want to hike, play golf, ride, sail, water-ski, or just enjoy scenic drives through the countryside. Lake Wörther is Carinthia's largest alpine lake, yet its waters are warm, often going above 27°C (80°F) in summer. We recommend staying and dining at the romantic **Hotel Schloss Leonstain** (✆ **04272/2816;** www.leonstain.at), where Johannes Brahms composed his Violin Concerto and Second Symphony.
- **Bad Aussee (Styria):** An old market town and spa, in the "green heart" of the Salzkammergut, Bad Aussee is 80km (50 miles) southeast of Salzburg. In the Valley of Traun, it's set against the backdrop of Totes Gebirge and the Dachstein massif. June is a lovely time to visit, when fields of narcissus burst into bloom. Bad Aussee lies only 5km (3 miles) north of the lake, Altausee, and is situated in one of the most beautiful parts of Austria. Long known as a summer spa resort, it's also developing into a winter ski center. The best place to stay is the **City Hotel Erzherzog Johann** (✆ **03622/52507;** www.erzherzog-johann.com). See section 4, "Bad Aussee," in chapter 15.

3 THE BEST CASTLES & PALACES

- **Schönbrunn Palace (Vienna):** This palace of 1,441 rooms was the summer residence of the powerful Hapsburg family. The great baroque architect J. B. Fischer von Erlach modeled his plans on Versailles, though he ultimately surpassed the French palace in size. Even so, Maria Theresia spoke of the palace as "cozy," where she could retreat with her many children and paint watercolors or work on her embroidery. The Hapsburg dynasty came to an end here when Karl I signed his Act of Abdication on November 11, 1918. See p. 151.

- **Hofburg (Vienna):** The winter palace of the Hapsburgs, Hofburg was the seat of an imperial throne that once governed the mighty Austro–Hungarian Empire. The sprawling palace reads like an architectural timeline of the Hapsburg family, dating from 1279 with subsequent additions continuing until 1918. Today the Hofburg houses everything from the offices of the president of Austria to the Spanish Riding School with its Lipizzaner stallions—even the Vienna Boys' Choir. See chapter 6.
- **Österreichische Galarie Belvedere (Belvedere Palace; Vienna):** On a slope above Vienna, this palace was designed by Johann Lukas von Hildebrandt, the last major architect of the baroque in Austria. Belvedere served as a summer home for Prince Eugene of Savoy, the country's greatest military hero. The palace was a gift from the imperial throne in recognition of the prince's military achievements, although he was (at the time) richer than the Hapsburgs. Not exactly pleased with his "gift," the hero made stunning baroque additions and improvements. As a collector and patron of the arts, he filled the palace with objets d'art. See p. 150.
- **Schloss Esterházy (Eisenstadt):** This castle in Eisenstadt, capital of Burgenland, was the seat of the Esterházy princes, a great and powerful Hungarian family who helped the Hapsburgs gain control of Hungary. The seat of their power was built around an inner courtyard and designed by Carlone, the Italian architect. Work started on the castle in 1663, but the design was subsequently altered over the years and later received the baroque treatment. The family invited Haydn here to work on his music, and in the Haydnsaal, the great composer conducted an orchestra for the family's entertainment. See p. 207.
- **Residenz (Salzburg):** The seat of the Salzburg prince-bishops, this opulent palace dates from 1120. Over the years, newer palaces were added to form an ecclesiastical complex. On the palace's second floor is a 15-room art gallery filled with the works of 16th- to 18th-century European masters. You can also walk through more than a dozen richly decorated staterooms. The Residenz fountain, which dates from the 1660s, is one of the largest and most impressive baroque fountains north of the Alps. See p. 251.
- **Hofburg (Innsbruck):** This imperial palace, built in the 14th to 16th centuries, was the seat of Emperor Maximilian I. In the 18th century, Empress Maria Theresia made major structural changes, giving it a rococo appearance; the Giant's Hall is an architectural marvel of 18th-century Austrian architecture. In the palace's main hall hangs a portrait of Maria's famous youngest daughter, Marie Antoinette—with her head. See p. 347.

4 THE BEST CATHEDRALS & ABBEYS

- **Domkirche St. Stephan (Vienna):** Crowned by a 137m (450-ft.) steeple, St. Stephan's, the Cathedral of Vienna, is one of Europe's great Gothic structures. The Austrian writer Adalbert Stifter claimed that its "sheer beauty lifts the spirit." The Viennese regard this monument with great affection, calling it *Der Steffl.* Intricate altar pieces, stone canopies, and masterful Gothic sculptures are just some of the treasures that lie within. Climb the spiral steps to the South Tower for a panoramic view of the city. See p. 145.

- **Melk Abbey (Melk):** This abbey church, situated on a promontory above the Danube, is one of the world's finest baroque buildings. Melk figures in the *Nibelungenlied,* the great German epic poem, as well as Umberto Eco's best-selling *The Name of the Rose.* The view from here is one of the most panoramic in a country known for its views. This baroque masterpiece has burned many times, the first time in 1297 and then in 1683 and 1735, but each time it has risen from the ashes. After a 1947 fire, the golden abbey church was restored yet again, including the regilding of statues and altars with gold bullion. See p. 203.
- **Salzburger Dom (Salzburg):** World renowned for its 4,000-pipe organ, this cathedral is the "most perfect" Renaissance structure in the Germanic countries, with a rich baroque interior and elaborate frescoes. It towers 76m (249 ft.) into the air and holds 10,000 worshippers. The present cathedral was consecrated with great ceremony in 1628, although records show a cathedral on this spot since the 8th century. In 1756, Mozart was baptized in the Romanesque font. See p. 252.
- **Abbey of St. Florian (St. Florian, Near Linz):** Austria's largest abbey is a towering example of the baroque style. On a site occupied by the Augustinians since the 11th century, the present structure was constructed mainly from 1686 to 1751. Honoring a 4th-century Christian martyr and saint, the abbey has as its chief treasure the Altdorfer Gallery, whose most valuable pictures are those by Albrecht Altdorfer, master of the Danubian school. Anton Bruckner, Austria's greatest composer of church music in the 1800s, became the organist at St. Florian as a young man and composed many of his masterpieces here. See p. 309.

5 THE BEST MUSEUMS

- **Kunsthistorisches Museum (Vienna):** This art gallery, across from Hofburg Palace, houses the stellar art collection of the Hapsburg dynasty. It's especially strong in the Flemish, Dutch, and German schools, with works ranging from Rubens and Dürer to Pieter Bruegel the Elder and Van Dyck. Also strong are the Italian, Spanish, and French collections, with works by Veronese, Caravaggio, and Tintoretto. See p. 147.
- **MuseumsQuartier (Vienna):** Vienna launched its new millennium with one of the major cultural centers to open in Middle Europe in some 2 decades. Architecturally stunning, this complex contains a treasure trove of art, being especially strong in modern works. The three major museums to visit here are Kunsthalle Wien, Leopold Museum, and MUMOK (Museum of Modern Art Ludwig Foundation). See p. 144.
- **Mozart's Geburtshaus (Salzburg):** Music pilgrims flock to see the typical old burgher's house where Mozart was born. You can still see many of his childhood belongings, including a lock of his hair, his first viola, and a pair of keyboard instruments. Mozart's first violin is also displayed. Even at the age of 4, he was a musical genius. See p. 252.
- **Mauthausen (Upper Austria):** The most unusual and horrifying museum in Austria lies 29km (18 miles) down the Danube from Linz. Mauthausen was a notorious concentration camp, used in World War II for the slaughter of Austria's Jews. It's estimated that

some 200,000 victims were killed here. Visitors today can bear witness to this scene of holocaust. See p. 317.

- **Tiroler Volkskunst–Museum (Innsbruck):** In an abbey with 16th-century origins, this museum of popular art contains Austria's most impressive collection of Tyrolean artifacts. You'll see everything from mangers to monumental stoves. The collections sweep from the Gothic decorative style through the Renaissance to the rich and opulent baroque era. The first floor contains models of Tyrolean houses. See p. 348.
- **Landeszeughaus (Graz):** This armory, built between 1642 and 1645, displays 3 centuries of weaponry, one of Europe's great collections. Here you'll see some 30,000 harnesses, coats of mail, helmets, swords, pikes, and muskets of various kinds, along with pistols and harquebuses. There are richly engraved and embossed jousting suits and a parade of armor. See p. 461.
- **Österreichisches Freilichtmuseum (Outside Graz):** Just 16km (10 miles) from Graz, in a wooded valley, is one of Austria's great open-air museums. This museum of vernacular architecture, spread across 50 hectares (120 acres), features some 80 rural homes with ancillary buildings that have been reassembled. The site presents an excellent overview of the country's rural heritage, from a Carinthian farmstead to alpine houses from the Tyrol. See p. 463.

6 THE BEST HISTORIC TOWNS

- **Krems (Lower Austria, Outside Vienna):** In the eastern part of the Wachau, on the river's left bank, this 1,000-year-old town incorporates the little village of Stein, with narrow streets terraced above the river. Many houses date from the 16th century. See p. 198.
- **Wels (Upper Austria):** Even in Roman times, Wels, on the left bank of the Traun River, was a flourishing town. Emperor Maximilian I died here in 1519. Its parish church has a 14th-century chancel with a tower from 1732. Across from the church is the house of Salome Alt, the notorious mistress of Prince-Archbishop Wolf Dietrich of Salzburg, who bore him 15 children. See section 6, "Wels," in chapter 11.
- **St. Christoph (Tyrol):** St. Christoph, the mountain way station of St. Anton in Tyrol, sits at an elevation of 1,784m (5,853 ft.). It was a famous settlement on the road to the Arlberg Pass, and was the site of a fabled hospice established in 1386. Members patrolled the pass looking for frozen bodies and assisting wayfarers in trouble. See p. 378.
- **Lienz (East Tyrol):** Not to be confused with Linz in Upper Austria, Lienz, with an *e,* is the capital of remote East Tyrol. Set at the junction of three valleys, this colorful town stretches along the banks of the Isel River. In summer, mountain climbers use it as a base to scale the Dolomites. The town is presided over by Schloss Bruck, the fortress of the counts of Gorz. See p. 400.
- **Mariazell (Styria):** Pilgrims come here to see the Mariazell Basilica, dating from the early 1200s, and its trio of prominent towers. Both Fischer von Erlachs, senior and junior, the famed baroque architects, helped transform the church. The Chapel of Grace inside is the national shrine of Austria, Hungary, and Bohemia. If you're exploring Styria, this old town, both a winter playground and a summer resort, is worth a stop. See section 3, "Mariazell," in chapter 15.

7 THE BEST OUTDOOR ADVENTURES

Skiing is the name of the game in Austria. See section 8, below, for a list of the best ski areas.

- **Biking Along the Danube:** The Lower Danube Cycle Track is a biker's paradise. The most exciting villages and stopovers along the Danube, including Melk and Dürnstein, are linked by a riverside bike trail between Vienna and Naarn. As you pedal along, you'll pass castles, medieval towns, and latticed vineyards. You can rent bikes from the train or ferry stations, and all tourist offices provide route maps. See chapter 6.
- **Ballooning over Styria:** Styria has some of the best alpine ballooning in Europe, as experienced by participants who have sailed over the alpine ranges of the Salzkammergut and a steppelike landscape that evokes the Great Hungarian Plain. A typical ballooning excursion will cross river valleys, mountain peaks, glaciers, and vineyards. For outfitters, see p. 452.
- **Canoeing & Rafting in the Salzburg Alps (Land Salzburg):** Known for their beautiful alpine lakes and roaring whitewater streams, the lakes in and around Salzburg are some of the most ideal in Europe for canoeing, rafting, and kayaking. Waters aren't polluted and powerboats are restricted, making these safe and idyllic adventures. See p. 268.
- **Hiking in the Zillertal Alps (Tyrol):** This mountain paradise is the best place to hike in Western Austria. Instead of roads, you'll find footpaths winding through the scenic Zillertal Valley, east of Innsbruck. Alpine guides lead you to some of the most panoramic scenery you've ever seen. This alpine world is yours as you hike across mountain trails or ascend on lifts to higher elevations. You can even find year-round skiing at Tuxer Gletscher, a glacier. See section 7, "The Ziller Valley," in chapter 12.
- **Traversing Ice Age Valleys:** No scenic thrill in all of Europe quite matches that available in the Hohe Tauern National Park, Europe's largest national park. Part of the Austrian Central Alps, the Hohe Tauern range cuts across Land Salzburg, Tyrol, and Carinthia. Molded during the Ice Age, these valleys are filled with pastureland, alpine heaths, vast expanses of snow and ice, forested bulwarks, fields of rock, and gargantuan alluvial and mudflow cones. The park is also home to numerous nearly extinct species. Much of this vast and remote area has never been explored, but parts are accessible by car or government-owned Bundesbus (the route goes from Böckstein to Badgastein and from Zell am Ziller to Krimml). You can get car or bus information from the local tourist office. See chapter 10.

8 THE BEST SKI AREAS

- **Innsbruck:** Tyrol's capital Innsbruck is set against a scenic backdrop of high mountain peaks, with good skiing in virtually all directions. Two Olympic Winter Games have been staged in the Innsbruck area. It's somewhat inconvenient to get to the slopes, but it's worth the effort. There are five ski resorts around Innsbruck. Hungerburg is the local favorite, because a funicular from the city heads directly to the base station at Höch Innsbruck at 300m (984 ft.). Nearby Igls also enjoys great favor, with its extensive slopes under the

Patscherkofel peak. Although it's the farthest from Innsbruck, Axamer Lizum offers the most extensive all-around skiing. Good snow conditions are generally the rule. See chapter 12.

- **St. Anton am Arlberg:** This picture-postcard Tyrolean village sits at 1,304m (4,278 ft.), although its upper slopes climb to more than 2,801m (9,190 ft.). Massive snowfalls attract intermediate and expert skiers from all over. St. Anton lies at the eastern base of the Arlberg Pass. St. Christoph, 10km (6 miles) west, lies almost on the Arlberg Pass and is another chic winter enclave. Four major ski areas at St. Anton (Galzig, Valluga, St. Christoph, and Gampen/Kapall) form one big ski circuit. See p. 371.
- **Seefeld (Tyrol):** Seefeld is one of the major international ski resorts of Europe, and hosted the Nordic events for the 1964 and 1976 Olympic Winter Games and the 1985 Nordic Ski World Championships. On a sunny plateau at 1,052m (3,451 ft.), it has prime skiing conditions and a network of surface lifts, chairlifts, and cable cars that appeal to skiers of all levels. In addition, there are 200km (124 miles) of prepared cross-country tracks. Seefeld is also known for its other winter sports, including curling and outdoor skating. See section 6, "Seefeld," in chapter 12.
- **Kitzbühel:** This home of the world's original lift circuit is a medieval walled city and regal resort that, in the 1960s, blossomed into a premier international spot. Visitors flock here in winter to ski forested trails and broad alpine ridges. The Hahnenkamm ski circus has more than 50 lifts at elevations of 800 to 2,000m (2,625–6,566 ft.). The main season runs from Christmas to mid-March. See section 8, "The Kitzbühel Alps," in chapter 12.
- **Lech & Zürs:** In Vorarlberg, these neighboring resorts feature the best skiing in Austria. They are also among Europe's most exclusive ski resorts, drawing a chic crowd. Both resorts cater to novice and intermediate skiers with broad boulevards winding between peaks and runs that fall straight back to the resorts. The resorts also offer high altitudes and good snow conditions, plus a high-tech lift system. Huge chunks of skiable terrain above both resorts provide a 20km-long (12-mile) circuit with generally superior ski conditions. See p. 406 for Lech; p. 413 for Zürs.

9 THE BEST LAKE RESORTS & SPAS

- **Baden bei Wien (Lower Austria):** Developed by the ancient Romans, and then studded with ocher-colored Biedermeier buildings during the early 19th century, this was once known as the "dowager empress" of Austrian spas. Today, frequent chamber concerts and elaborate flowerbeds keep the aura of old-fashioned grandeur alive. See section 2, "The Spa Town of Baden bei Wien," in chapter 7.
- **Bad Hofgastein (Land Salzburg):** A select annex of the larger, better-known resort of Badgastein, Bad Hofgastein appeals to anyone in search of peace, healing, and quiet. Civic architecture and hotels are appropriately grand and solemn. See section 3, "Bad Hofgastein," in chapter 10.
- **Badgastein (Land Salzburg):** This is Austria's premier spa, with a resort industry dating from the 1400s. Hotels are almost universally excellent, offering the densest concentration of fine lodgings in Land Salzburg. See chapter 10.
- **St. Wolfgang (Upper Austria):** The landscapes around this lake are so lovely that they served as the setting for the

popular musical work *The White Horse Inn,* by Ralph Benatzky. Adjacent to the grander and somewhat more formal resort of Bad Ischl, St. Wolfgang offers ample options for outdoor diversions. See chapter 11.

- **Bad Ischl (Upper Austria):** For more than 60 years, Franz Josef selected Bad Ischl as the summer holiday seat of the Hapsburg Empire. No other Austrian resort captures the glamour of the long-departed empire quite like this one. See chapter 11.
- **Pörtschach (Carinthia):** This is the premier resort in Carinthia, the south-easterly Austrian province bordering the edge of Slovenia, and the site of dozens of fine villas.
- **Velden (Carinthia):** The region's most sophisticated resort, Velden is the heart of the so-called "Austrian Riviera." Despite the traffic, it offers a convenient combination of bucolic charm and Viennese style. See p. 444.
- **Villach (Carinthia):** The second-largest town in the province, it's the gateway to Austria's lake district, northeastern Italy, and Slovenia. The nearby village of Warmbad-Villach offers warm springs, favored by the ancient Romans. See section 4, "Villach," in chapter 14.
- **Bad Gleichenberg (Styria):** Set within one of the most undiscovered regions of Austria, near the Slovenian border, this is the most important summer spa in Styria. It stands among rolling hills and vineyards, and is an area rich in history, natural beauty, and imperial nostalgia. See section 2, "Bad Gleichenberg," in chapter 15.
- **Bad Aussee (Styria):** Lying at the junction of two tributaries of the region's most important river, Bad Aussee is known for its verdant beauty, healthful waters, and bracing climate. It's also the center of a network of hiking and cross-country ski trails. See section 4, "Bad Aussee," in chapter 15.

10 THE BEST LUXURY HOTELS

- **Goldener Hirsch** (Salzburg; ✆ **800/325-3535** in the U.S., or 0662/8084; www.starwoodhotels.com): For some 6 centuries, this mellow old hostelry has been welcoming guests to its patrician precincts. With the city's best and most professional staff, the Goldener Hirsch is the finest hotel in Salzburg. In the Old Town, near Mozart's birthplace, the building is a historical monument, rich in legend and lore. Although rooms vary, all are furnished with antiques, in traditional taste, but have modern plumbing and appointments. See p. 226.
- **Hotel Bristol** (Vienna; ✆ **888/625-5144** in the U.S., or 01/515160; www.westin.com/bristol): Facing the Staatsoper, this classic six-story building is a Viennese symbol of luxury and class. It ranks with the Imperial as the city's most glamorous hotel. The luxuriously appointed and often exquisite rooms boast a cornucopia of amenities. Velvet and silk, chandeliers, and double doors adorn the place, and the ever-attentive, gracious staff adds to the allure. See p. 99.
- **Hotel Grüner Baum** (Badgastein; ✆ **06434/25160**; www.grunerbaum.com): A veritable village has grown up around this converted hunting lodge. The family-run hotel has sheltered everybody from Toscanini to the shah of Iran. Scattered chalets house some of the finest rooms at this fashionable spa—each in the typical alpine style. The hospitality is unequaled in the area. See p. 330.

- **Hotel Imperial** (Vienna; ✆ **800/325-3589** in the U.S., or 01/501100; www.luxurycollection.com/imperial): Once a ducal palace, and now Vienna's most glamorous hotel, the Imperial is a landmark 2 blocks east of the Staatsoper. Built in 1869, it's Austria's official "guesthouse," often hosting visiting musicians (Wagner stayed here long ago). A wealth of antiques adorns the gracious public areas, and everything is gilt-edged, from the polished marble to the glittering chandeliers. Opulently appointed rooms vary in size but are generally regal. See p. 100.
- **Hotel Schloss Dürnstein** (Dürnstein, along the Danube; ✆ **02711/212;** www.schloss.at): Near the medieval village in Wachau, this fairy-tale castle is perched above a bend in the river. Above the hotel are the ruins of a castle where Richard the Lion-Hearted was imprisoned. This exquisite gem of a hotel brims with history, glamour, art, and fantasy. See p. 202.
- **Hotel Schloss Fuschl** (Hof bei Salzburg; ✆ **06229/22530;** www.starwoodhotels.com): East of Salzburg, this medieval castle and its outbuildings have origins dating from 1450. Everybody from Eleanor Roosevelt to Khrushchev has stayed in this rich, lush setting of oriental rugs, antiques, fine art, and vaulted ceilings. Diners sit on a terrace taking in panoramic lake and alpine views. The spacious rooms are beautifully furnished and well maintained. Sports lovers feel at home with a 9-hole golf course, indoor pool, and Turkish bath and sauna. See p. 300.
- **Grand Hotel** (Zell am See; ✆ **06542/788-0;** www.grandhotel-zellamsee.at): Three "grand hotels" have stood on this site over the years, and the latest incarnation is the grandest of them all. Windows open onto incredible views of the lake and the Alps. Flanked by pillars, the glassed-in pool also offers lake views, and the hotel has an array of facilities ranging from a gym to a sauna. The contemporary rooms, which vary in size and design, are the best in town. See p. 297.
- **Romantik Hotel Post** (Villach; ✆ **04242/261010;** www.romantik-hotel.com): With architectural origins from 1500, this is the most fabled hotel in Carinthia. A hotel since the 1730s, it's a cozy and charming retreat on the town's main square. A pianist plays on the terrace in summer. Rooms are richly furnished, often with oriental rugs on parquet floors, including the suite where Emperor Charles V once slept in the 1500s. A solarium, gym, and sauna keep the hotel up to date. See p. 449.

11 THE BEST AFFORDABLE HOTELS

- **Hotel Alte Post-Wrann** (Velden; ✆ **04274/2141;** www.wrann.at): In the sophisticated summer resort of Carinthia, at the western end of the Wörther See, this is an ideal choice for an "Austrian Riviera" vacation. Once the headquarters of a postal route station, it was long ago renovated, enlarged, and turned into this welcoming hotel. Rooms are sunny and traditionally furnished. The restaurant, with its massive ceiling beams, is very good. There's also a Viennese-style *heurige* (rustic wine tavern) serving the finest local wines. See p. 445.
- **Hotel Auersperg** (Salzburg; ✆ **0662/889440;** www.auersperg.at): A traditional family-run hotel with generously sized rooms, this charmer has an old-fashioned atmosphere but is still beautifully maintained, from its antiques-filled drawing room to its convivial library

bar. It's a warm, inviting, and cozy place to base yourself in the city of Mozart. See p. 230.

- **Hotel Goldener Adler** (Innsbruck; ✆ **0512/571111;** www.goldeneradler.com): This hotel, which has hosted everyone from Goethe to Paganini, has a history spanning 6 centuries. Genuine art decorates the public areas, and the four dining rooms (including a Tyrolean cellar) are local favorites for eating and drinking. Rooms vary in size but are nicely appointed, with Tyrolean touches. The place isn't luxurious, but it's historic and comfortable. See p. 353.
- **Hotel Kaiserin Elisabeth** (Vienna; ✆ **01/515260;** www.kaiserinelisabeth.at): Lots of famous folks, from Wagner to Franz Liszt, have stayed in this building, which dates from the 14th century. It manages to be stately and homey at the same time. Public areas are richly furnished with oriental rugs, a dome skylight, and marble floors. The most desirable rooms are furnished in a neo-baroque style with parquet floors. See p. 102.
- **Hotel-Restaurant Sänger Blondel** (Dürnstein; ✆ **02711/253;** www.saengerblondel.at): Along the Danube sits this charmingly old-fashioned place, painted a bright lemon and accented with green shutters. It's named for the faithful minstrel who searched the countryside for the imprisoned Richard the Lion Hearted. Today guests are housed in traditionally styled and cozy rooms; if your windows are open, you can sometimes hear zither music drifting in from the courtyard. See p. 201.
- **Hotel Seehof** (Goldegg; ✆ **06415/8137-0;** www.seehof-goldegg.com): This hotel, on a small alpine lake south of Salzburg, dates from 1449. Rustic artifacts and local painted furnishings add to its old-fashioned charm. In summer, guests can enjoy the outdoor terrace, but in winter, they come here for skiing. The hotel rents ski equipment and directs guests to the nearby slopes. See p. 273.
- **Romantik Hotel Traube** (Lienz; ✆ **04852/64444;** www.tiscover.at/romantikhotel-traube): Deep in the heart of East Tyrol, this classic hotel, rebuilt after World War II damage, is the most desirable in this remote and offbeat part of Austria. Its prices are reasonable, and the hotel also offers the best restaurant in East Tyrol. Open your window, see the mountains, and imagine you're Julie Andrews. See p. 402.
- **Schlosshotel Freisitz Roith** (Gmunden; ✆ **07612/64905;** www.oberoesterreich.at/schlosshotel): Built as a summer house by the Hapsburg Emperor Rudolf II in 1597, this castle hotel, in one of the most popular summer resorts in the Salzkammergut, is now open to the masses. Converted into a hotel in 1965, it's a winning combination of a baroque private residence and a Victorian hotel. See p. 332.

12 THE BEST RESTAURANTS

- **Europastüberl** (Innsbruck; ✆ **0512/593-01**): Head here for spectacular food served among meticulously re-created traditional Tyrolean decor. As business travelers and corporate bigwigs know, its setting manages to be simultaneously rustic and sumptuous. See p. 356.
- **Fabios** (Vienna; ✆ **01/532-2222**): This is the most sought-after table in Vienna today, attracting the city's glitterati, who rave about the chef's finely honed Mediterranean and international cuisine. Precise, inventive fare is served here, celebrating the bounty of Austria and neighboring Italy. See p. 121.

- **Goldener Hirsch** (Salzburg; ✆ **0662/80840**): Hospitality has been served up within its thick walls since 1407, but today the victuals are vastly improved, and the clientele is a little more refined. Few other places are as elegant, and during the Salzburg Music Festivals, this is definitely the place to be. The chef prefers the *grand bourgeois* tradition, and prepares meals with both a jeweler's precision and a poet's imagination. See p. 237.
- **Maria Loretto** (Klagenfurt; ✆ **0463/24465**): This is the premier restaurant in the capital of Carinthia, site of Austria's summer lake district. A specialist in seafood, the restaurant hauls in raw ingredients from the Mediterranean and Atlantic, and its chefs fashion them into delectable platters. See p. 438.
- **Restaurant Ferwall** (St. Anton; ✆ **05446/3249**): Set in the high Alps near the Arlberg Pass, this place attracts some of the most discerning palates in Europe. Since 1972, the restaurant has been serving some of the finest fare in Tyrol, with a traditional Austrian and international menu taking on innovative modern twists. The restaurant celebrates Tyrolean country life. See p. 376.
- **Sacher Hotel Restaurant** (Vienna; ✆ **01/514560**): A celebrity favorite since the days of the Empire, this is the home of one of the world's most famous pastries, the Sachertorte. Against a flaming scarlet background, you can enjoy dishes that pleased emperors—notably Vienna's famous *tafelspitz,* the most savory and herb-flavored boiled beef you'll ever taste. Come dressed to the nines and prepare to enjoy a banquet fit for a king. See p. 120.

13 THE BEST DINING BARGAINS

- **Auerhann** (Zug; ✆ **05583/275414**): Warm, woodsy, and permeated with the aroma of good food and a convivial hubbub from the other tables, this inexpensive restaurant is in a building erected during the 1600s. Its three types of fondue and its fresh trout from nearby streams are among the best in the province. See p. 411.
- **Gulaschmuseum** (Vienna; ✆ **01/5121017**): Imagine a "museum" devoted to goulash. Here you can find 15 varieties of this savory kettle of goodies inspired by neighboring Hungary, once part of the Austro–Hungarian Empire. Each dish is redolent with the taste of paprika, Hungary's national spice. There's even an all-vegetarian version. See p. 127.
- **Herzl Tavern** (Salzburg; ✆ **0662/8084889**): Owned by the city's most glamorous hotel, the super-expensive Goldener Hirsch, the Herzl—in the center of town—is frequented by some of Europe's most celebrated musicians, who for some reason always demand the finest in cuisine. Here they get hearty food prepared in a traditional style and made with only the finest ingredients. See p. 240.
- **Hirschen-Stuben** (Innsbruck; ✆ **0512/582979**): This charming restaurant, in a restored 17th-century house, is known for its good Austrian and Italian cuisine served at affordable prices. From stewed deer to the best of alpine lake fish, this one is a winner. See p. 359.
- **Landhaus-Keller** (Graz; ✆ **0316/830276**): In a historic building with outdoor tables in summer, this cellar serves some of the best local specialties, many based on old recipes handed

down from generation to generation. It's hearty drinking and dining here. See p. 467.

- **Plachutta** (Vienna; ✆ **01/5121577**): The Viennese are fanatical about their *tafelspitz* the way Italian chefs are firm in their standards for tomato sauce, or American Southerners insist that theirs is the only true fried chicken. No place in all of Austria serves better *tafelspitz* than Plachutta, which produces 10 different variations. See p. 121.
- **Restaurant Wirt am Berg** (Wels; ✆ **07242/45059**): With a pedigree dating from 1630, Wirt am Berg boasts a vast wine cellar and flavorful food. Its modest prices draw diners from as far away as Munich. See p. 335.
- **Weinhaus Attwenger** (Bad Ischl; ✆ **06132/23327**): Some parts of it, built in 1540, were already well established when 19th-century composers Bruckner and Léhar adopted it as one of their preferred wine houses. See p. 326.

14 THE BEST CLASSIC CAFES

- **Café Bazar** (Salzburg; ✆ **0662/874278**): This cafe has been a local favorite since 1906, enjoying a palatial pink stucco setting across the river from the Old Town. It's been fashionable since the days of Franz Josef and the menu never changes—only the prices. See p. 238.
- **Café Demel** (Vienna; ✆ **01/5351717**): This most famous cafe in Vienna has a long-standing feud with the Sacher Hotel as to who has the right to sell the legendary and original Sachertorte. Demel claims that the chef who invented the torte left the Sacher to work for Demel, bringing his recipe with him. See p. 130.
- **Café Frauenschuh** (Mondsee; ✆ **06232/2312**): Deliciously loaded with every imaginable kind of high-calorie pastry, this time-honored place is a cliché of old-fashioned Austrian charm. See p. 322.
- **Café Imperial** (Vienna; ✆ **01/50110389**): Owned and operated by a grand hotel, this cafe was once a favorite of composer Gustav Mahler. Now it's favored by a chic local lunchtime crowd and offers "the most regal" cup of coffee, pastry, or glass of wine in town. See p. 131.
- **Café Landtmann** (Vienna; ✆ **01/241000**): The newspapers it provides for its patrons are tattered by the end of every day, and a haze of smoke evokes the back-room machinations of a meeting of political cronies from another era. Sigmund Freud claimed it as his favorite cafe; and after your first 15 minutes inside, you might, too. See p. 131.
- **Café Munding** (Innsbruck; ✆ **0512/584118**): Plushly decorated and upholstered, this cafe offers a setting from 1720, torrents of Tyrolean color, unusual murals, and platters of food followed by a scrumptiously fattening array of creamy pastries. See p. 363.
- **Café Tomaselli** (Salzburg; ✆ **0662/844488**): Established in 1705, it provides a rich atmosphere as well as delectably fattening pastries and endless cups of coffee. See p. 236.
- **Konditorei Zauner** (Bad Ischl; ✆ **06132/2331020**): It's the oldest pastry shop in Austria and the emporium that satisfied the long-ago sugar cravings of such Hapsburg monarchs as Franz Josef. Today, it trades heavily on the aristocratic associations of yesteryear, attracting droves of tourists to its baroque-inspired setting in the resort's center. See p. 327.

2

Austria in Depth

When most people think of Austria, they imagine Vienna in its heyday, a glittering city of romance and gaiety, enchanting waltzes, luscious pastries, the operetta, and the Danube (and no one conjures up these images of 19th-century Vienna more than Johann Strauss, Jr., of "Blue Danube Waltz" fame). But there's another side to Austria: the spirit of the mountains. You'll find this especially in Tyrol, a land of rugged individuality and independence, where previous generations eked out an existence amid a mountainous terrain and harsh climate.

Austria's capital, Vienna, the royal seat of the Hapsburgs for 600 years, has always stood out as a center of art and music, as well as architecture. Visitors today will find a newer and brighter Vienna, a city with more *joie de vivre* than it's had since before World War II. It's still the city where the music never stops. In spite of two world wars, much of the empire's glory and grandeur remain. Its treasures now stock the museums, and its palaces are open to visitors. Vienna has been called an "architectural waltz"—baroque buildings, marble statues, lovely old squares, grand palaces, and famous concert halls are all still here, as if the empire were still flourishing. In fact, to understand Austria is to grasp the meaning of baroque—though in this sense it's not merely an architectural style, but a defining characteristic of the people: flamboyant, theatrical, and extravagant.

When it comes to politics, however, Austria is deeply polarized. The establishment of the far-right Freedom Party in 2000, pushing what critics considered an anti-EU and anti-immigrant platform, brought Austria worldwide condemnation. In contrast, many citizens of Vienna, and Austria in general, are among the most liberal, advanced, well informed, and tolerant on earth.

As one example of the more left-wing Austria, environmental awareness is on the rise. Recycling is more evident than in any other European country, with recycling bins a common sight on city streets. Another highly visible example is the low-cost public housing, called *Gemeindebauten;* it's estimated that about a third of the population of Vienna lives in government-owned apartments.

Birthplace of Mozart, Freud, Hitler, and the Wiener schnitzel, Austria defies easy categorization. As Wolfgang Seipel, who waits tables in a local cafe, told us, "We have our guilt, the famous Viennese schizophrenia. We've condoned atrocities, and there have been some embarrassing Nazi revelations. If Freud were still with us, I'm sure he'd wear out a couch every month. But in spite of it all, Vienna still knows how to show you a hell of a good time."

Austria and its people are moving deeper into the new millennium. But to appreciate its present more deeply, it's necessary to look back at its rich classical, culinary, and historical legacy. In this chapter you'll be introduced to a delightful people, the Austrians, as we briefly discuss, among other things, their history, art, famous citizens, music, food, and folklore.

Austria is a parliamentary democracy, and the head of the state is the federal president. The country's main legislative bodies are the houses of the Nationalrat and the Bundesrat. Together they form what is known as the federal assembly. The federal government is headed by a chancellor, who, along with cabinet members, conducts any government affairs that are not the responsibility of the president.

In today's government, personal liberty is guaranteed, and the federal constitution prohibits discrimination on the grounds of sex, birth, class, religion, race, status, or language.

Vienna today stands at the crossroads of Europe, just as it did in the heyday of the Austro-Hungarian Empire. During the Cold War, the government pretended to maintain neutrality, which it did not possess, as Austrian leaders feared the return of the Russians, who left peacefully in 1955. Since the collapse of the Iron Curtain, Austria has been moving toward greater cooperation and unity with the Western powers. However, at the turn of the millennium, an estrangement between Austria and its EU neighbors moved dangerously close to the brink, when the European Union temporarily imposed sanctions on Austria—due to what was viewed as a "dangerous" tilt to the right in 1999—when the so-called Freedom Party won 27% of the vote in national elections. The party was anti-immigration, blaming foreigners for many of the country's ills, ranging from rising crime to an increase in drug abuse.

But in October of 2006, Austria's opposition Social Democrats won nationwide elections, swinging the country to the center-left after more than 6 years of influence by the extreme right. Immigration was a central theme in the campaign; the far right wants to reduce the number of foreigners in Austria by 30%—as of 2008, 16% of Vienna's residents claim some place other than Austria as their birthplace, with most immigrants hailing from Turkey, the former Yugoslavia, Poland, and even Germany. The Social Democrats, on the other hand, promised to lower the number of unemployed and reduce salary differences between men and women.

Politics aside, a slight downward drift in tourism is blamed on the daunting prices in Austria. As a cafe owner told us, "We

Did You Know . . . ?

- Vienna, once "the capital of the musical world," lost interest in Mozart and didn't appreciate the talents of such composers as Schubert.
- Seventy percent of Austria is covered by the mountains and foothills of the Alps.
- The young artist Adolf Hitler was rejected from the Viennese Academy.
- After the 1683 siege of Austria, the retreating Turks left behind sacks of coffee, giving birth to the Viennese coffeehouse.
- The first woman to win the Nobel Peace Prize was a Viennese aristocrat, Baroness Bertha von Suttner, who received the award in 1905 for her book *Lay Down Your Arms.*

must change our attitudes from complacency and haughtiness to service with a smile. We're going to have to not only improve service but drop prices to bring the world back to our door."

As a center of European culture, Vienna has more than 100 art museums, attracting eight million visitors annually. In 2001, Vienna was designated a UNESCO World Heritage Site, ranking third in the world in terms of quality of life.

As a world capital, Vienna rivals Geneva in being the seat of a number of United Nations offices and various international institutions, including the all-important Organization of Petroleum Exporting Countries (OPEC). Vienna is also the seat of a number of charitable organizations, including SOS Children's Villages, founded in 1949. Today this organization serves 132 countries and territories worldwide.

Meanwhile, record warmth in recent years—with autumn temperatures in Austria prevailing even in winter—has brought home the profound threat of a climate change in the country's ski industry.

Climatologists in Vienna announced in 2008 that the warming trend will be drastic by 2020. In reports filed, these experts said that the Austrian Alps are warming twice as fast as the average in the rest of the world. They claimed that in 1980, 75% of alpine glaciers were advancing. By 2008, 90% were retreating.

2 LOOKING BACK AT AUSTRIA

Austria's history has been heavily influenced by its location along the Danube. Its position at the crossroads of three great European cultures—Roman, Germanic, and Slavic—transformed the country into a melting pot, and more often than not, a battlefield.

By 100 B.C., the Romans had begun making military excursions into Austria; by 15 B.C., they had conquered the entire country. Valued as an alpine outpost of the frontier, it remained under the control of Rome for more than 500 years. Roads were built, vineyards and wine making introduced, and Roman law instituted. The spread of Christianity began around A.D. 300.

The decline of Roman power was speeded by the arrival of Germanic tribes. The region was eventually taken over by the Bavarians from the northwest, under Frankish leadership. When Charlemagne became king of the Franks in A.D. 768, he established peace with his sword and achieved a more civilized culture.

After Charlemagne's death, the region again became a battleground, with a staggering number of claimants. The Babenbergs eventually came out on top, and ruled over Austria from 976 to 1246. This royal family realized that territory could better be gained by treaty, inheritance, marriage, and politics than through war, so the region grew, and farms, towns, and cities thrived. By the end of the 10th century, the region was already being mentioned as Ostarrichi, which evolved into the German name, Österreich (Austria).

THE HAPSBURG REIGN

After the Babenberg dynasty died out, Rudolph I was crowned in 1273, inaugurating the Hapsburg era, which would last more than 600 years. The Hapsburgs saw their fortunes rise and fall as Holy Roman Emperors and rulers of Austria, Hungary, Germany, Bohemia, Italy, Belgium, Spain, the Netherlands, and other territories; their troops were involved in every conflict that erupted in Europe, and neighboring nations moved from ally to adversary and back again. During the Hapsburg rule, there were 20 emperors and kings, and there was a time, at the height of their

IMPRESSIONS

Little Austria, a torso from which all foot limbs have been amputated, is running merrily about in its self-propelled invalid chair.

—Arthur Koestler, "The Lion and the Ostrich," *Encounter* (1963)

dynastic influence, when the sun never set on the Hapsburg Empire.

Austria emerged as a major European power after the defeat of the Turks, who had moved westward to lay siege to Vienna in 1683. This crucial battle helped determine the course of European history. The Treaty of Karlowitz in 1699 brought most of Hungary under Hapsburg domination, and the Hungarian throne was made a hereditary possession of the Hapsburgs (the union of Austria and Hungary lasted until 1918).

When Emperor Charles VI died without male heirs, the Austrian Hapsburg dynasty was threatened. The Pragmatic Sanction of 1720 allowed the Hapsburg empire to pass to a female heir, and set the stage for one of the greatest and most famous reigns in history, that of Maria Theresa, who ruled from 1740 to 1780. During her reign, moderate reforms were carried out, including a streamlining of the political system. The empress, although a Catholic, also limited the power of the clergy. In 1773 she initiated public education throughout her empire.

Joseph II, son of Maria Theresa, was called "The Enlightened Despot"; he continued his mother's work with a more radical approach. However, two significant changes were his: the abolition of serfdom and the introduction of complete freedom of religion.

Napoleon, of course, played his part on the stage of Austrian history: French victories brought about the loss of Lombardy, Tuscany, provinces on the Rhine, Italian provinces, Bavaria, Baden, and Württemberg.

Under the leadership of Prince von Metternich as foreign minister, and later chancellor, of Austria after the abdication of Napoleon, many of the Polish and Italian territories lost during this tumultuous era were regained at the Congress of Vienna in 1814 to 1815. But Austria never regained its previous power, and it began a slow decline that culminated in the breakup of the empire following World War I.

After the collapse of the Central Powers—Austria-Hungary, Germany, Turkey, and Bulgaria—at the end of World War I, the last Hapsburg was forced to abdicate the throne on November 11, 1918. The monarchy was dissolved; Austria and Hungary became separate republics, while other lands were lost to Italy, Romania, Poland, and the newly formed Yugoslavia and Czechoslovakia.

ANSCHLUSS & WORLD WAR II

Austria, along with most of Europe, shared in the political turmoil "between the wars." Political violence became a sad fact of life. Engelbert Dollfuss launched a conservative government in 1932, but he was assassinated by Austrian Nazis in 1934.

After Adolf Hitler took power in 1933 in Germany, Austrian Nazis campaigned, even demanded, unification with Germany. Dollfuss was succeeded by Kurt Schuschnigg, and he faced major opposition from the Nazis in trying to maintain Austrian independence. As Hitler's troops massed on the Austrian frontier, Schuschnigg resigned in 1938.

Germany invaded Austria on March 12 of that year; *Anschluss* (union with Germany) was proclaimed. In effect, Austria had become a province of the Third Reich. The thousands of Austrians who turned out on March 14, 1938, to cheer Nazi troops as they marched triumphantly into Vienna must have had second thoughts by 1945. Austria paid a terrible price for its participation with Germany in World War II.

On April 13, 1945, Allied forces liberated Austria and a republic was reestablished. Austria was divided into four zones of occupation, each controlled by one of the Allied powers—the United States, the Soviet Union, Britain, and France. Vienna was jointly administered by all four powers (as was Berlin in neighboring Germany). U.S. aid helped to stabilize the war-torn economy.

POSTWAR AUSTRIA

Occupation forces withdrew in 1955, marking the beginning of coalition governments and a stable economy. The Soviets returned property that in 1945 had been seized as German assets. Austria was given back major industrial plants, oil fields and installations, and the assets of the Danube Steamship Company, in return for money and goods as reparations to the Russians.

In the Austrian State Treaty, a peace treaty signed by the United States, Britain, France, and the Soviet Union in 1955, Austria was recognized as a sovereign, independent, and democratic state, with the four powers declaring that they would respect its independence and territorial integrity. The pre-1938 frontiers were guaranteed, political or economic union with Germany was prohibited, human rights and the rights of the Slovene and Croat minorities and of democratic institutions were pledged, and all National Socialist and Fascist organizations were dissolved.

Although not mentioned in the treaty, the Allied powers also guaranteed Austrian neutrality. The Austrian federal government passed a constitutional law declaring the country's permanent neutrality and stating that Austria would never again accede to any military alliances nor permit the establishment of military bases by foreign states on its territory.

RECENT HISTORY

The world paid Austrian politics little attention until 1986, when Kurt Waldheim, former secretary general of the United Nations, was elected president of Austria, a largely ceremonial post. It was revealed that he had been an officer in the Nazi army and had countenanced the deportation of Jews to extermination camps. The United States declared him persona non grata. Many Austrians defiantly stood by Waldheim, declaring that they would not let world opinion dictate their choice of a president. Other Austrians were deeply embarrassed by Waldheim's election.

Waldheim was forbidden to seek reelection; and, in May 1992, Thomas Klestil, a career diplomat, was elected president. His candidacy was supported by the Austrian People's Party, representing the center of the political spectrum in Austria.

In the 1990s, Austria was at the crossroads of upheaval, war, and change. To its east, Hungary was the first country to dismantle a once heavily fortified frontier—called the beginning of the "Iron Curtain" during the Cold War. To the south, Yugoslavia was split apart with war, and new countries emerged, including Slovenia, which shares Austria's southern border. Since 1989, Austria has become either the final or the first destination of Balkan refugees and waves of emigrants from Eastern Europe, and this has led to inevitable tensions. Austria's admission into the European Union was a slow and laborious process, initiated in 1972 and finally completed in 1995. Since the last World War, Viennese and Austrian politics have been dominated by the moderate

Impressions

Austria is Switzerland, speaking pure German and with history added.

—J.E. Morpugo, *The Road to Athens* (1963)

policies of the Social Democrats, who have at times shared power with the more right-wing proponents, the ÖVP (Austrian People's Party).

Early in 1997, Franz Vranitzky, the chancellor of Austria, announced his retirement. "Ten years are a sufficient spell" for a job, claimed the man who took Austria into the European Union and was the first leader to acknowledge guilt for the country's Nazi past.

In 1998, as part of an ongoing effort to lay the past to rest, Austrian officials agreed to return to their rightful owners art confiscated by the Nazis. The Austrian minister of culture, Elisabeth Gehrer, said she wanted to correct what she termed "immoral decisions" made at the end of World War II. This bold move sent reverberations throughout the museum world of Europe and the U.S.

In 2002, Austria faced one of its worst major disasters in decades. Along with its Central European neighbors, such as Germany, Austria suffered crippling floods as the banks of the Danube overflowed. Billions of euros in damage were done to homes, farms, buildings, and businesses, a nightmare for the insurance industry.

In 2004, Elfriede Jelinek, the controversial feminist writer and outspoken critic of the far-right Freedom Party, won the Nobel Prize for literature. On another front, Charles I, the last Hapsburg to rule as emperor, was beatified by the pope.

But it was news of an expat Austrian, a citizen of Graz, that made the biggest headlines in both Vienna and the country itself in 2004. Their homegrown son, muscleman/movie star Arnold Schwarzenegger, swept into the governor's office in California in a recall vote. Even though he's married to a Kennedy, Maria Shriver, Schwarzenegger is a Republican, and lent the prestige of his name in the campaign of George W. Bush for reelection. For his efforts, he told a stunned nation, he was denied sex for 2 weeks.

3 VIENNA'S ART & ARCHITECTURE

Austria's location at the crossroads of the Germanic, Mediterranean, and Eastern Europe worlds contributed to a rich and varied artistic heritage.

The country is best known for the splendor of its baroque and rococo palaces and churches. It also contains a wealth of internationally renowned Gothic and modern architecture.

ART

Early Ecclesiastical Art

Most art in the early medieval period was church art. From the Carolingian period, the only survivors are a handful of **illuminated manuscripts** now in Vienna's National Library. The most famous is the *Cutbercht Evangeliar* from around 800, a richly illuminated copy of the four gospels.

The Romanesque period reached its peak between 1000 and 1190. Notable from this time is the Admont Great Bible, crafted around 1140, one of the prized treasures of Vienna's National Library. In 1181, the famous goldsmith Nicolas de Verdun produced one of the finest **enamel works** in Europe for the pulpit at Klosterneuburg Abbey. Verdun's 51 small panels, crafted from enamel and gold, depict scenes from the religious tracts of the Augustinians. After a fire in the 1300s, the panels were repositioned onto an altarpiece, known as the Verdun Altar at Klosterneuburg, where they can be seen today.

The Gothic Age

The Gothic age in Austria is better remembered for its architecture than its painting and sculpture. Early Gothic sculpture was influenced by the **Zachbruchiger Stil** (zigzag style), identified by vivid angular outlines of forms against contrasting backgrounds. The era's greatest surviving sculptures date from around 1320 and include the *Enthroned Madonna of Klosterneuburg* and the *Servant's Madonna,* showcased in Vienna's St. Stephan's Cathedral.

By the late 1300s, Austrian sculpture was strongly influenced by Bohemia. The human form became elongated, exaggerated, and idealized, often set in graceful but unnatural S curves. Wood became increasingly popular as an artistic medium and was often painted in vivid colors. A superb example of **Gothic sculpture** is the *Servant's Madonna* in St. Stephan's Cathedral. Carved around 1320, it depicts Mary enthroned and holding a standing Christ child.

From the Renaissance to the 18th Century

During most of the Renaissance, Vienna was too preoccupied with fending off invasions, sieges, and plagues to produce the kind of painting and sculpture that flowered in other parts of Europe. As a result, in the 17th and 18th centuries, Vienna struggled to keep up with such cities as Salzburg, Munich, and Innsbruck.

Most painting and sculpture during the baroque period was for the enhancement of the grandiose churches and spectacular palaces that sprang up across Vienna. Artists were imported from Italy; one, **Andrea Pozzo** (1642–1709), produced the masterpiece *The Apotheosis of Hercules,* which appears on the ceilings of Vienna's Liechtenstein Palace. Baroque painting emphasized symmetry and unity, and *trompe l'oeil* was used to give extra dimension to a building's sculptural and architectural motifs.

The first noteworthy Austrian-born baroque painter was **Johann Rottmayr** (1654–1730), the preferred decorator of the two most influential architects of the age, von Hildebrandt and Fischer von Erlach. Rottmayr's works adorn some of the ceilings of Vienna's Schönbrunn Palace and Peterskirche. Countless other artists contributed to the Viennese baroque style. Notable are the frescoes of **Daniel Gran** (1694–1754), who decorated the Hofbibliothek. He also has an altarpiece in the Karlskirche.

Vienna, as it emerged from a base of muddy fields into a majestic fantasy of baroque architecture, was captured on the canvas in the landscapes of **Bernardo Bellotto** (1720–80), nephew and pupil of the famous Venetian painter Canaletto. Brought to Vienna at the request of Maria Theresa, Bellotto managed to bathe the city in a flat but clear light of arresting detail and pinpoint accuracy. His paintings today are valued as social and historical as well as artistic documents.

Dutch-born, Swedish-trained **Martin van Meytens** (1695–1770), court painter to Maria Theresa, captured the lavish balls and assemblies of Vienna's aristocracy. His canvases, though awkwardly composed and overburdened with detail, are the best visual record of the Austrian court's balls and receptions. In 1730, van Meytens was appointed director of Vienna's Fine Arts Academy.

Sculptors also made their contribution to the baroque style. **Georg Raphael Donner** (1693–1741) is best known for the remarkable life-size bronzes of the Fountain of Providence in the Neuer Markt. **Balthasar Permoser** (1651–1732) is responsible for the equestrian statues of

Prince Eugene of Savoy in the courtyard of the Belvedere Palace. The famous double sarcophagus in the Kapuzinerkirche, designed for Maria Theresa and her husband, Francis Stephen, is the masterpiece of **Balthasar Moll** (1717–85).

Equally influential was **Franz Xaver Messerschmidt** (1737–83), the German-trained resident of Vienna, who became famous for his portrait busts. His legacy leaves accurate and evocative representations of Maria Theresa, her son Joseph II, and other luminaries.

The Revolt from "Official Art"

In rebellion against "official art," a school of **Romantic Realist** painters emerged, drawing on biblical themes and Austrian folklore. Scenes from popular operas were painted lovingly on the walls of the Vienna State Opera. The 17th-century Dutch masters influenced landscape painting.

Georg Waldmüller (1793–1865), a self-proclaimed enemy of "academic art" and an advocate of realism, created one of the best pictorial descriptions of Viennese Biedermeier society in his *Wiener Zimmer* (1837). More than 120 of his paintings are on display at the Upper Belvedere museum.

Another realist was **Carl Moll** (1861–1945), whose graceful and evocative portrayals of everyday scenes are prized today. **Joseph Engelhart** (1864–1941) was known for his voluptuous renderings of Belle Epoque coquettes flirting with Viennese gentlemen.

The Secessionist Movement

Young painters, decorators, and architects from Vienna's Academy of Fine Arts founded the Secessionist Movement (Sezessionstil) in 1897. The name captures their retreat (secession) from the Künstlerhaus (Vienna Artists' Association), which they considered pompous, sanctimonious, artificial, mediocre, and mired in the historicism favored by Emperor Franz Joseph. Their artistic statement was similar to that of the Art Nouveau movement in Paris and the Jugendstil movement in Munich.

The Secessionist headquarters, on the Friedrichstrasse, at the corner of the Opernring, was inaugurated in 1898 as an exhibition space for avant-garde artists. Foremost among the group was **Gustav Klimt** (1862–1918), whose work developed rapidly into a highly personal and radically innovative form of decorative painting based on the sinuous curved line of Art Nouveau. His masterpieces include a mammoth frieze, 33m (110 ft.) long, encrusted with gemstones, and dedicated to Beethoven. Executed in 1902, it's one of the artistic focal points of the Secessionist Pavilion. Other pivotal works include *Portrait of Adèle Bloch-Bauer* (1907), an abstract depiction of a prominent Jewish Viennese socialite. Its gilded geometric form is reminiscent of ancient Byzantine art.

The Modern Age

Klimt's talented disciple was **Egon Schiele** (1890–1918). Tormented, overly sensitive, and virtually unknown during his brief lifetime, he is now considered a modernist master whose work can stand alongside that of van Gogh and Modigliani. His works seem to dissolve the boundaries between humankind and the natural world, granting a kind of anthropomorphic humanity to landscape painting. One of his most disturbing paintings is the tormented *The Family* (1917), originally conceived as decoration for a mausoleum.

Modern sculpture in Vienna is inseparable from the international art trends that dominated the 20th century. **Fritz Wotruba** (1907–75) introduced a neo-cubist style of sculpture. Many of his sculptural theories were manifested in his Wotruba Church (Church of the Most Holy Trinity), erected toward the end of his life in Vienna's outlying 23rd District. Adorned with his sculptures and representative of his architectural theories in general, the building is an important sightseeing and spiritual attraction.

Oskar Kokoschka (1886–1980) was one of Vienna's most important contemporary painters. Kokoschka expressed the frenzied psychological confusion of the years before and after World War II. His portraits of such personalities as the artist Carl Moll are bathed in psychological realism and violent emotion.

ARCHITECTURE

Gothic

Although Vienna holds no remains of early medieval buildings, a number of Gothic buildings rest on older foundations. During the 1300s, ecclesiastical architecture was based on the Hallenkirche (hall church), a model that originated in Germany. These buildings featured interiors that resembled enormous hallways, with nave and aisles of the same height. The earliest example of this style was the choir added in 1295 to an older Romanesque building, the abbey church of Heiligenkreuz, 15 miles west of Vienna.

The most famous building in the Hallenkirche style was the first incarnation of St. Stephan's Cathedral. Later modifications greatly altered the details of its original construction, and today only the foundations, the main portal, and the modestly proportioned western towers remain. Much more dramatic is the cathedral's needle-shaped central spire, completed in 1433, which still soars high above Vienna's skyline. St. Stephan's triple naves, each the same height, are a distinctive feature of Austrian Gothic. Other examples of this construction can be seen in the Minorite Church and the Church of St. Augustine.

During the late 1400s, Gothic architecture retreated from the soaring proportions of the Hallenkirche style, and focus turned to more modest buildings with richly decorated interiors. Stone masons added tracery (geometric patterns) and full-rounded or low-relief sculpture to ceilings and walls. Gothic churches continued to be built in Austria until the mid-1500s.

From Gothic to Baroque

One of the unusual aspects of Vienna is its lack of Renaissance buildings. The Turks besieged Vienna periodically from 1529 until the 1680s, forcing planners to use most of their resources to strengthen the city's fortifications.

Although Vienna itself has no Renaissance examples, Italian influences were evident for more than a century before baroque gained a true foothold. Late in the 16th century, many Italian builders settled in the regions of Tyrol, Carinthia, and Styria. In these less-threatened regions of Austria, Italian influence produced a number of country churches and civic buildings in the Renaissance style, with open porticoes, balconies, and loggias.

The Flowering of the Baroque

The 47-year rule of Leopold I (1658–1705) witnessed the beginning of the golden age of Austrian baroque architecture. Italian-born Dominico Martinelli (1650–1718) designed the **Liechtenstein Palace,** built between 1694 and 1706 and inspired by the Renaissance-era Palazzo Farnese in Rome.

Austria soon began to produce its own architects. **Johann Bernhard Fischer von Erlach** (1656–1723) trained with both Bernini and Borromini in Rome. His style was restrained but monumental, drawing richly from the great buildings of antiquity. Fischer von Erlach knew how to transform the Italianate baroque of the south into a style that suited the Viennese. His most notable work is the **Karlskirche,** built in 1713. He also created the original design for Maria Theresa's **Schönbrunn Palace.** He had planned a sort of super-Versailles, but the project turned out to be too costly. Only the entrance facade remains of Fischer von Erlach's design. The **Hofbibliothek (National Library),** on Josephsplatz, and the **Hofstalungen** are other notable buildings he designed.

Fischer von Erlach was succeeded by another great name in the history of architecture: **Johann Lukas von Hildebrandt** (1668–1745). Von Hildebrandt's design for Prince Eugene's **Belvedere Palace**—a series of interlocking cubes with sloping mansard-style roofs—is the culmination of the architectural theories initiated by Fischer von Erlach. Other von Hildebrandt designs in Vienna include the **Schwarzenberg Palace** (now a hotel) and **St. Peter's Church.**

The **rococo style** developed as a more ornate, somewhat fussier progression of the baroque. Gilt stucco, brightly colored frescoes, and interiors that drip with embellishments are its hallmarks. Excellent examples include the **Abbey of Dürnstein** (1731–35) and **Melk Abbey,** both in Lower Austria. One of the most powerful proponents of rococo was Maria Theresa, who used its motifs so extensively within Schönbrunn Palace during its 1744 renovation that the school of Austrian rococo is sometimes referred to as "late-baroque Theresian style."

In response to the excesses of rococo, architects eventually turned to classical Greece and Rome for inspiration. The result was a restrained neoclassicism that transformed the skyline of Vienna and lasted well into the 19th century. The dignified austerity of Vienna's **Technical University** is a good example.

Eclecticism & Vienna's Ring

As Austria's wealthy bourgeoisie began to impose their tastes on public architecture, 19th-century building grew more solid and monumental. The neoclassical style remained the preferred choice for government buildings, as evidenced by Vienna's **Mint** and the **Palace of the Provincial Government.**

The 19th century's most impressive Viennese architectural achievement was the construction of the **Ringstrasse** (1857–91). The medieval walls were demolished, and the Ring was lined with showcase buildings. This was Emperor Franz Joseph's personal project and his greatest achievement. Architects from all over Europe answered the emperor's call, eager to seize the unprecedented opportunity to design a whole city district. Between 1850 and the official opening ceremony in 1879, the Ring's architecture became increasingly eclectic: French neo-Gothic (the Votivkirche), Flemish neo-Gothic (the Rathaus), Greek Revival (Parliament), French Renaissance (Staatsoper), and Tuscan Renaissance (Museum of Applied Arts). While the volume of traffic circling Old Vienna diminishes some of the Ring's charm, a circumnavigation of the Ring provides a panorama of eclectic yet harmonious building styles.

Secessionist & Political Architecture

By the late 19th century, younger architects were in rebellion against the pomp and formality of older architectural styles. In 1896, young **Otto Wagner** (1841–1918) published a tract called *Moderne Architektur,* which argued for a return to more natural and functional architectural forms. The result was the establishment of **Art Nouveau (Jugendstil,** or, as it applies specifically to Vienna, **Sezessionstil**). The Vienna Secession architects reaped the benefits of the technological advances and the new building materials that became available after the Industrial Revolution. Wagner, designer of Vienna's **Kirche am Steinhof** and the city's **Postsparkasse** (Post Office Savings Bank), became a founding member of the movement.

Joseph Hoffman (1870–1955) and **Adolf Loos** (1870–1933) promoted the use of glass, newly developed steel alloys, and aluminum. In the process, they discarded nearly all ornamentation, a rejection that contemporary Vienna found profoundly distasteful and almost shocking. Loos was particularly critical of the buildings adorning

Impressions

I left Austria with feelings of utter disgust and dislike. They are a stupid, stolid, disobliging grasping lot. There is no place in the world where you pay so high and get so little, even of common politeness, in return, as in Germany.

—Lilian Leland, *Travelling Alone, A Woman's Journey Round the World,* 1890

the Ringstrasse. His most controversial design is the **Michaelerplatz Building.** Sometimes referred to as "the Loos House," it was erected on Michaelerplatz in 1908. The streamlined structure was bitterly criticized for its total lack of ornamentation and its similarities to the "gridwork of a sewer." According to gossip, the emperor found it so offensive that he ordered his drivers to avoid the Hofburg entrance on Michaelerplatz altogether.

Architectural philosophies were also affected during the "Red Vienna" period by the socialist reformers' desire to alleviate public housing shortages, a grinding social problem of the years between world wars. The Social Democratic Party began erecting "palaces for the people." The most obvious example is the **Karl-Marx-Hof** (Heiligenstadterstrasse 82–92, A-1190), which includes 1,600 apartments and stretches for more than half a mile.

To the Present Day

After World War II, much of Vienna's resources went toward restoring older historic buildings to their prewar grandeur. New buildings were streamlined and functional; much of Vienna today features the same kind of neutral modernism you're likely to find in postwar Berlin or Frankfurt.

Postmodern masters, however, have broken the mold of the 1950s and 1960s. They include the iconoclastic mogul Hans Hollein, designer of the silvery, curved-sided **Haas Haus** (1990) adjacent to St. Stephan's Cathedral. The self-consciously avant-garde **Friedensreich Hundertwasser** is a multicolored, ecologically inspired apartment building at the corner of Löwengasse and Kegelgasse that appears to be randomly stacked.

Lately, **Hermann Czech** has been stirring architectural excitement, not so much by building new structures as developing daring interiors for boutiques and bistros; examples are the **Kleines Café** (Franziskanerplatz 3) and **Restaurant Salzamt** (Ruprechtsplatz 1).

4 THE LAY OF THE LAND

The varied and complicated character of Austria's terrain has divided the country into a number of natural regions. Today, most of these areas enjoy some degree of self-government as well as rich and deeply ingrained local traditions.

Except for the fertile valleys of the Danube and the section of eastern and southeastern Austria that borders on Moravia and the great Hungarian plain, almost three-quarters of the country is mountainous. The country's average height above sea level is 915m (3,000 ft.). Austria marks the eastern terminus of the Alps, which cover about two-thirds of the country's surface. The remaining mountainous third is geologically distinct—part of the ancient granite mass of the Bohemian massif.

The Wild Alps

Many alpine animals such as the lynx, otter, and alpine ibex have all but disappeared during this century in the Alps. Other animals are endangered, including wildcats, susliks, certain nesting birds, toads, and fish.

An effort to reintroduce species eradicated from their habitat by hunters and ranchers has been an unqualified success. Brown bears have been sighted in increased abundance over recent years, along with migrating elk. Although wolves have not reemerged since being killed off in the 1950s by ranchers, the deer and stag population has enjoyed such exponential growth that in some regions hunting has become necessary to keep the population and natural balance in check.

Other species continue to thrive in the alpine environment. Unobtrusive hikers will find the Alps teeming with creatures. You might behold the chamois gracefully bounding up alpine trees or watch a golden eagle in circling flight above. The griffon vulture's 9-foot wingspan may intimidate even the most seasoned hiker. A hiker might even be befriended by a marmot or an alpine chough basking in a sunny meadow. (But if you threaten the gentle marmot, you might learn why it's nicknamed the whistle pig.) The hill country and lower mountain ranges are often home to badgers, martens, and hares. Hedgehogs are rare, one of the endangered species of rodents.

Ornithologists have a field day in the Alps, as the breadth of birds is immense. Great white herons guide you down the Danube like a teasing trail of gingerbread crumbs; they pause for respite along the banks long enough for you to catch up to them by riverside trail, only to depart in flight to another sanctuary 20m (66 ft.) downstream. Storks, marsh warblers, gray geese, spoonbills, and terns can also be spotted. A bird-watcher might sight a diving blue kingfisher, particularly its extended underwater search for insects below ripples of streams and rivers. The distinctive red-and-black wings of the gray alpine wall creeper set it apart from the cliff faces it ascends. The spotted woodpecker, the goldfinch, the redstart, the thrush, and the blue lit sing for wintertime food from nearby human settlements, but the finch, the lark, and the song thrush save their voices for spring. Keen eyes only will spot falcons, buzzards, and other birds of prey. When hiking at night, don't forget nocturnal birds like the tawny owl.

Geologists divide the alpine regions of Austria into the central, southern, and northern districts. All three are quite naturally beautiful. The highest peaks and longest glaciers are in the central region, in the region of the Ötztal; Silvretta; the Stubai Alps; and the Hohe Tauern, site of the country's most powerful glaciers.

A large belt along the eastern slopes of the Grossglockner and a section of the Schobergruppe Massif have been earmarked as the Hohe Tauern National Park, which features some of the most dramatic landscapes in the country. Lakes, forests, and alpine pastures—set against a backdrop of powerful and protecting glaciers—riddle the park. These glaciers advanced north at least 10,000 years ago, spreading across the Bavarian plateau, almost to the border of what today is the city of Munich. All this glacier movement created natural amphitheaters called "cirques." They also formed what geologists call "hanging valleys," which are marked by towering waterfalls.

The creation of national parks has helped conserve valuable biotopes—high-altitude forests, water marshes, and the specialized plant life of steep cliffs and mountain banks. The parks protect this fauna from the detrimental effects of mass tourism yet keep them accessible to respectful admirers. Water lilies, flowering meadow shrubs, patches of moss and fern that grow in the dank darkness of forests, the snowdrop, and the pink hues of meadow saffron, even the gorgeous colors of the mountain rose and gentian—which punctuate the flowering alpine meadows—are finest in their natural setting, not wilting in some makeshift bouquet. On the contrary, bluebells, pinks, cornflowers, buttercups, daisies, and primroses blossom in such abundance that they can be picked at will.

The season for mountain wildflowers varies depending on spring temperatures and snowpack; expect most to have blossomed by the end of July or early August. In autumn, the perennial changing of the leaves is another colorful and splendid sight. If you're interested in learning more about high altitude flora, visit an alpine garden or walk down an instructional guided path.

You might even find a snack along the way, in the form of a wild berry or mushroom (but be careful, as some varieties are poisonous). Wild raspberries, strawberries, bilberries, blackberries, cranberries, flap mushrooms, chanterelles, and parasol mushrooms quell a hiker's hunger with astonishingly favorable tastes, particularly when hand-picked, but can be easily confused with inedible or poisonous varieties.

Nearly half of the vegetation is remnants of deciduous forests, such as mixed mountain forests. Most alpine forests consist of conifers, including the spruce, the larch (the only European conifer to lose its needles in winter), the Austrian pine (with a darkly fissured bark), and the arolla pine, with upward curving branches that evoke candelabra.

Nearly a third of the vegetation sprouts on rock debris and in alpine meadows. A mixed mountain forest thrives below 1,372m (4,500 ft.), whereas a coniferous forest exists at an altitude of 1,678m (5,500 ft.). Above that, wind-dwarfed bushes and alpine meadows predominate.

In spring, summer, and autumn, many different rare species of plants flower. They don't live long once picked, so please leave them for the next person to enjoy. The flora coexist with a variety of alpine animals such as the chamois, ibex (reintroduced in 1930), marmot, snow hare, alpine salamander, golden eagle, ptarmigan, black grouse, capercaillie, alpine chough, black woodpecker, and three-toed woodpecker. Other animals, such as the wolf, lynx, bear, and golden vulture, once thrived in the Alps but have not survived.

After its mountains, Austria's great defining feature is the Danube. With the exception of a handful of streams in the country's west that flow to the Rhine, and a few in the north that empty into the Moldau (a tributary of the Elbe), all of Austria's creeks, streams, and rivers empty into the Danube. This, Europe's longest river, originates in Germany's Black Forest and enters Austria near Passau. A few miles from the Austrian border the Danube is joined by the Inn River (from which comes the name Innsbruck); the water provided by this great tributary, which flows from the Bernina and the Tauern Alps, is what makes the Danube navigable. One of the most important watercourses in European history, the Danube runs west to east across the Vienna basin, as the fertile plains of central Austria are called. The river bisects both Vienna and Budapest (capital of Austria's historic partner, Hungary) and links together in navigable form many towns and settlements of south-central Europe.

Austria is also graced with many freshwater lakes that are beautiful and draw sports enthusiasts to their shores.

5 AUSTRIA IN POPULAR CULTURE: BOOKS, FILM & MUSIC

BOOKS

History

The Austrians: A Thousand-Year Odyssey, Gordon Brook-Shepherd: Historian Brook-Shepherd looks at Austria's long history to explain its people: who they are, how they got there, and where they're going.

Fin-de-Siecle Vienna: Politics and Culture, Carl E. Schorske: This landmark book takes you into the political and social world of Vienna during the late 19th and early 20th centuries.

A Nervous Splendor: Vienna 1888–1889, Frederic Morton: Morton uses the mysterious deaths of Archduke Rudolf and Baroness Marie Vetsera at Mayerling as a point of departure to capture in detail the life of Imperial Vienna at its glorious height.

The Hapsburgs: Embodying Empire, Andrew Wheatcroft: Here is the full sweep of the Hapsburg dynasty, from the Middle Ages to the end of World War I, focusing on such remarkable personalities as Rudolph I, Charles V, Maria Theresia, and Franz Josef I.

Art, Architecture & Music

J. B. Fischer von Erlach, Hans Aurenhammer: This entertaining volume illuminates the life, times, and aesthetic vision of the court-appointed architect who transformed the face of 18th-century Vienna and Salzburg.

Vienna 1900: Art, Architecture, and Design, Kirk Varnedoe: During the late 19th century, Vienna's artistic genius reached dazzling heights of modernity. These movements are explored in this appealing primer.

On Mozart, Anthony Burgess: Set in heaven, amid a reunion of the greatest composers of all time, this controversial book creates debates about music that never occurred but should have. Condemned by some critics as gibberish and praised by others as brilliant and poetic, Burgess's work is highly recommended for musical sophisticates with a sense of humor.

Music and Musicians in Vienna, Richard Rickett: Few countries in Europe pride themselves as thoroughly as Austria does for its music. This brief, wisely created volume offers a broad overview of the country's musical heritage. It makes a good introduction to the subject.

Biography

Freud: A Life for Our Times, Peter Gay: Gay's biography is a good introduction to the life of one of the seminal figures of the 20th century. Freud, of course, lived in Vienna until he fled from the Nazis in 1938, settling with his sofa in London.

Haydn: A Creative Life in Music, Karl and Irene Geiringer: This is the best biography of composer Franz Josef Haydn, friend of Mozart, teacher of Beethoven, and court composer of the Esterházys.

Mozart: A Cultural Biography, Robert W. Gutman: Music historian Gutman places Mozart squarely in the cultural world of 18th-century Europe.

Empress Maria Theresia (Harper & Row), Robert Pic: The life and times of the greatest, most colorful Hapsburg monarch is richly treated in this engrossing biography.

FILM

Though Austrians have played a major role in world cinema, most film artists made their movies in such places as Berlin or Hollywood. Austrians who went on to international film fame have included Erich von Stroheim, Josef von Sternberg (who masterminded the career of Marlene Dietrich), G. W. Pabst, Max Reinhardt, Richard Oswald, Curt Jurgens, Hedy Lamarr, Maximilian Schell, and the great actress Elizabeth Bergner.

Among the distinguished directors who hailed from Austria, Billy Wilder made some of the most classic Hollywood pictures of all time, such as *Sunset Blvd.* (1950) with Gloria Swanson and *Some Like It Hot* (1959) with Marilyn Monroe. Fred Zinnemann directed 21 feature films, including *The Men* (1949), *High Noon* (1951), and *Julia* (1976).

A first-rate film that hauntingly evokes life in postwar Vienna is *The Third Man* (1949), starring Joseph Cotten and Orson Welles. And who could visit Austria without renting a copy of *The Sound of Music* (1965)? The film won several Academy Awards, including Best Picture. Starring Julie Andrews, it was filmed in the lovely city of Salzburg.

Fritz Lang (1890–1976) was an Austrian-born film director whose success was proven in Europe before his eventual naturalization as a U.S. citizen. Often criticized for his persistent emphasis on fatality and terror, his films were hailed for their intellectualism and visual opulence. In Europe, especially Germany, his films included *Metropolis* (1924), whose stark portrayal of automated urban life has been praised as revolutionary, and, on the eve of the rise to power of the Nazi regime, the eerily clairvoyant *Das Testament des Dr. Mabuse* (1933). Welcomed into Hollywood by the avant-garde, he directed sometime-successful films which included *Fury* (1936), *Western Union* (1941), *Clash by Night* (1952), and *Rancho Notorious* (1952).

Erich von Stroheim (1886–1957) was the pseudonym of Oswald von Nordenwald. He was one of the most innovative and exacting film directors in the history of cinema. Born in Vienna, he served in the Hapsburg cavalry before rising within the ranks of Berlin's golden age of silent films. After immigrating to Hollywood in 1914, he worked for legendary director D. W. Griffith, eventually becoming noted for his minute realism and his almost-impossible demands on the actors and resources of Hollywood. As a director, his most legendary films were *Blind Husbands* (1919), *Foolish Wives* (1922), the epic masterpiece *Greed* (1928), and the spectacularly expensive flop that almost ended Gloria Swanson's film career, *Queen Kelly* (1928). As an actor, his most famous roles were as stiff-necked but highly principled Prussian military officers (often wearing monocles) in such films as Jean Renoir's *Grand Illusion* (1937). Most young movie fans know him for what he called "the dumb butler part" in Billy Wilder's 1950 classic, *Sunset Blvd.*

Hedy Lamarr (1913–2000), born in Vienna, was a plump little baby girl who rose out of Austria to become one of the shining lights in MGM mogul Louis B. Mayer's cavalcade of stars. She was, at least in the 1940s, acclaimed as "the most beautiful woman of the century." Achieving world notoriety by her nude scenes in *Ecstasy,* she later played opposite such stars as Clark Gable and made such films as *White Cargo* and the epic Cecil B. DeMille extravaganza *Samson and Delilah.*

Although Mayer considered Lamarr "beautiful but stupid," her stunning face concealed an inventive mind. In 1942, while filming *White Cargo,* she came up with an idea for radio control torpedoes, in itself not a new idea. But her concept for "frequency hopping" was innovative and was two decades ahead of its time. The Navy turned a deaf ear to her invention. However, in 1957 the concept was picked up and, in time, became a primary tool for secure military communications. Regrettably, Lamarr let her patent expire, and she never gained any royalties from her invention. Her declining years were marked by tragedy, including arrests for shoplifting.

A more recent Austrian actor to achieve world fame is **Klaus Maria Brandauer,** who appeared in *Russia House* and *White Fang.* Born in 1944 in Austria, this pudgy, balding, and short actor—not your typical leading man—is best remembered in America as the villain in the James Bond thriller *Never Say Never Again* and as the husband of Meryl Streep in *Out of Africa,* for which he was nominated as best supporting actor in 1985.

Some film critics have hailed Austria today as "the world capital of feel-bad cinema." The most internationally known director of this movement is **Michael Haneke,** who came to prominence with *The Seventh Continent* in 1989. He had a great hit in *The Piano Teacher* in 2001, which was set in the world of Viennese high culture.

The Austrian actor—now a governor—whose name is most instantly recognizable around the world today is, of course, **Arnold Schwarzenegger,** the son of a policeman from Graz who became a multimillionaire superstar in America. He turned his body-building career into a world class action star, going from The Terminator to Governator.

MUSIC

Music is central to Viennese life. From the concertos of Mozart and Johann Strauss's waltzes to opera and folk tunes, the Viennese are surrounded by music—and not only in the concert hall and opera house, but at the *heurige* as well. The works of the musicians mentioned below are available on classical CDs.

The Classical Period

The classical period was a golden age in Viennese musical life. Two of the greatest composers of all time, Mozart and Haydn, worked in Vienna. Maria Theresa herself trilled arias on the stage of the Schlosstheater at Schönbrunn, and she and her children and friends often performed operas and dances.

Classicism's first great manifestation was the development of *Singspiele,* a reform of opera by **Christoph Willibald Ritter von Gluck** (1714–87). Baroque opera had become overburdened with ornamentation, and Gluck introduced a more natural musical form. In 1762, Maria Theresa presented Vienna with the first performance of Gluck's innovative opera *Orpheus and Eurydice.* It and *Alceste* (1767) are his best-known operas, regularly performed today.

Franz Joseph Haydn (1732–1809) is the creator of the classical sonata, which is the basis of classical chamber music. Haydn's patrons were the rich and powerful Esterházy family, whom he served as musical director. His output was prodigious. He wrote chamber music, sonatas, operas, and symphonies. His strong faith is in evidence in his oratorios; among the greatest are *The Creation* (1798) and *The Seasons* (1801). He also is the composer of the Austrian national anthem (1797), which he later elaborated in his quartet, Opus 76, no. 3.

The most famous composer of the period was **Wolfgang Amadeus Mozart** (1756–91). The prodigy from Salzburg charmed Maria Theresa and her court with his playing when he was only 6 years old. His father, Leopold, exploited his

Fun Facts Shall We Waltz?

Dictionaries define the waltz as a form of "round dance," but anyone who has ever succumbed to its magic invariably defines it as pure enjoyment, akin to falling in love—a giddy, romantic spinning associated with women in long gowns, men in formal clothing, and elaborate ballrooms.

Many people think that the Strausses—father and son—actually invented the dance. However, the waltz has roots throughout Europe and began its life in theaters and inns. Fashionable hostesses considered it vulgar. At court, highly stylized dances, such as the minuet and the gavotte, were the rule. The waltz, gaining propriety in the second half of the 18th century, brought a greater naturalism and zest to grand parties with its rhythmic lilt and uninhibited spinning.

A violinist and composer of dance music, Johann Strauss the Elder (1804–49) introduced his famous *Tauberlwalzer* in Vienna in 1826. As a dance musician for court balls, he became indelibly associated with the social glitter of the Austrian court. His fame grew to such an extent that he began a series of tours (1833–40) that took him to England, where he conducted his music at Queen Victoria's coronation.

His famous son, Johann Strauss the Younger, was "the King of the Waltz." He formed his own dance band and met with instant success. He toured Europe and even went to America, playing his waltzes to enthusiastic audiences. By 1862, he relinquished the leadership of his orchestra to his two brothers and spent the rest of his life writing music. He brought the waltz to such a high degree of technical perfection that eventually he transformed it into a symphonic form in its own right.

The waltz lives on today in his most famous pieces, "The Blue Danube" (1867), "Tales from the Vienna Woods" (1868), "Weiner Blut," and the "Emperor Waltz." His genius ushered in the "golden age of operetta." Every New Year's Eve, the Vienna State Opera schedules a splendid performance of perhaps the best beloved of his operettas, *Die Fledermaus* (1874). The heritage of "the Waltz King" forms a vital part of Austria's cultural self-image.

son's talent—"Wolferl" spent his childhood touring all over Europe. Later he went with his father to Italy, where he absorbed that country's fertile musical traditions. Leaving Salzburg, he settled in Vienna, at first with great success. His influence effected fundamental and widespread changes in the musical life of the capital. Eccentric and extravagant, he was unable to keep patronage or land any lucrative post; he finally received an appointment as chamber composer to the emperor Joseph II at a minimal salary. Despite hard times, Mozart refused the posts offered him in other cities, possibly because in Vienna he found the best of all musical worlds—the best instrumentalists, the finest opera, the most talented singers. He composed more than 600 works in practically every musical form known to the time; his greatest compositions are unmatched in beauty and profundity. He died in poverty, buried in a pauper's grave in Vienna, the whereabouts of which are uncertain.

The Romantic Age

Franz Schubert (1797–1828), the only one of the great composers born in Vienna, was of the Biedermeier era and the most Viennese of musicians. He turned *lieder,* popular folk songs often used with dances, into an art form. He was a master of melodic line, and he created hundreds of songs, chamber music works, and symphonies. At the age of 18, he showed his genius by setting the words of German poet Goethe to music in *Margaret at the Spinning Wheel* and the *Elf King.* His *Unfinished Symphony* remains his best-known work, but his great achievement lies in his chamber music and song cycles.

The 19th Century

After 1850, Vienna became the world's capital of light music, exporting it to every corner of the globe. The **waltz,** originally developed as a rustic Austrian country dance, was enthusiastically adopted by Viennese society.

Johann Strauss (1804–49), composer of more than 150 waltzes, and his talented and entrepreneurial son, **Johann Strauss the Younger** (1825–99), who developed the art form further, helped spread the stately and graceful rhythms of the waltz across Europe. The younger Strauss also popularized the operetta, the genesis of the Broadway musical.

The tradition of Viennese light opera continued to thrive, thanks to the efforts of **Franz von Suppé** (1819–95) and Hungarian-born **Franz Lehár** (1870–1948). Lehár's witty and mildly scandalous *The Merry Widow* (1905) is the most popular and amusing light opera ever written.

Vienna did not lack for important serious music in the late 19th century. **Anton Bruckner** (1824–96) composed nine symphonies and a handful of powerful masses. **Hugo Wolf** (1860–1903), following in Schubert's footsteps, reinvented key elements of the German lieder with his five great song cycles. Most innovative of all was **Gustav Mahler** (1860–1911). A pupil of Bruckner, he expanded the size of the orchestra, often added a chorus or vocal soloists, and composed evocative music, much of it set to poetry.

The New Vienna School

Mahler's musical heirs forever altered the world's concepts of harmony and tonality, and introduced what were then shocking concepts of rhythm. **Arnold Schoenberg** (1874–1951) expanded Mahler's style in such atonal works as *Das Buch der Hangenden Garten* (1908) and developed a 12-tone musical technique referred to as "dodecaphony" (*Suite for Piano,* 1924). By the end of his career, he pioneered "serial music," series of notes with no key center, shifting from one tonal group to another. **Anton von Webern** (1883–1945) and **Alban Berg** (1885–1935), composer of the brilliant but esoteric opera *Wozzeck,* were pupils of Schoenberg's. They adapted his system to their own musical personalities.

Finally, this discussion of Viennese music would not be complete without mention of the vast repertoire of folk songs, Christmas carols, and country dances that have inspired professional musicians and ordinary folk alike for generations. The most famous Christmas carol in the world, ***"Stille Nacht, Heilige Nacht"*** ("Silent Night, Holy Night"), was composed and performed for the first time in Salzburg in 1818 and heard in Vienna for the first time that year.

6 EATING & DRINKING IN AUSTRIA

It's pointless to argue whether a Viennese dish is of Hungarian, Czech, Austrian, Slovenian, or even Serbian origin. Personally, we've always been more interested in taste. Our palates respond well to *Wienerküche* (Viennese cooking), a centuries-old blend of foreign recipes and homespun concoctions. Viennese cooking tends to be rich and heavy, with little regard for cholesterol levels.

FROM WIENER SCHNITZEL TO SACHERTORTE

Of course everyone knows Wiener schnitzel, the breaded veal cutlet that has achieved popularity worldwide. The most authentic local recipes call for the schnitzel to be fried in lard, but everyone agrees on one point: The schnitzel should have the golden-brown color of a Stradivarius violin.

Another renowned meat specialty is boiled beef, or *tafelspitz,* said to reflect "the soul of the empire." This was Emperor Franz Joseph's favorite dish. For the best, try it at Hotel Sacher; if you're on a budget, then order *tafelspitz* at a *beisl,* cousin of the French bistro.

Roast goose is served on festive occasions, such as Christmas, but at any time of the year you can order *eine gute fettgans* (a good fat goose). After such a rich dinner, you might want to relax over some strong coffee, followed by schnapps.

For a taste of Hungary, order a goulash. Goulashes (stews of beef or pork with paprika) can be prepared in many different ways. The local version, *Wiener gulasch,* is lighter on the paprika than most Hungarian versions. And don't forget *gulyassuppe* (a Hungarian goulash soup), which can be a meal in itself.

Viennese pastry is probably the best in the world, both rich and varied. The familiar strudel comes in many forms; *apfelstrudel* (apple) is the most popular, but you can also order cherry and other flavors. Viennese cakes defy description—look for *gugelhupf, wuchteln,* and *mohnbeugerl.* Many of the *torten* are made with ground hazelnuts or almonds in the place of flour. You can put whipped cream on everything. Don't miss *rehruken,* a chocolate "saddle of venison" cake that's studded with almonds.

Even if you're not addicted to sweets, there's a gustatory experience you mustn't miss: the Viennese Sachertorte. Many gourmets claim to have the authentic, original recipe for this "king of tortes," a rich chocolate cake with a layer of apricot jam. Master pastry baker Franz Sacher created the Sachertorte for Prince von Metternich in 1832, and it is still available in the Hotel Sacher. Outstanding imitations can be found throughout Vienna.

COFFEE

Although it might sound heretical, Turkey is credited with establishing the famous Viennese coffeehouse. Legend holds that Turks retreating from the siege of Vienna abandoned several sacks of coffee, which, when brewed by the victorious Viennese, established the Austrian passion for coffee for all time. The first *kaffeehaus* was established in Vienna in 1683.

In Vienna, *Jause* is a 4pm coffee-and-pastry ritual that is practiced daily in the city's coffeehouses. You can order your coffee a number of different ways—everything from *verkehrt* (almost milk pale) to *mocca* (ebony black). Note that in Vienna, only strangers ask for *einen kaffee* (a coffee). If you do, you'll be asked what kind you want. Your safest choice is a large or small *brauner*—coffee with milk. *Kaffee mit schlagobers* (with whipped cream) is perfect for those with a sweet tooth. You can even order *doppelschlag* (double whipped cream).

BEER, WINE & LIQUEURS

Vienna imposes few restrictions on the sale of alcohol, so except in alcohol-free places, you should be able to order beer or wine with your meal—even if it's 9am. Many Viennese have their first strong drink in the morning, preferring beer over coffee to get them going.

In general, **Austrian wines** are served when new, and most are consumed where they're produced. We prefer the white wine to the red. More than 99% of all Austrian wine is produced in vineyards in eastern Austria: principally Vienna, Lower Austria, Styria, and Burgenland. The most famous Austrian wine, Gumpoldskirchen, which is sold all over Vienna, comes from Lower Austria, the country's largest wine producer. At the heart of the Baden wine district of Sudbahnstrecke is the village of Gumpoldskirchen, which gives the wine its name. This white wine is heady, rich, and slightly sweet.

Located in an outer district of Vienna, Klosterneuburg, an ancient abbey on the right bank of the Danube, produces the finest white wine in Austria. Monks have made Klosterneuburger at this monastery for centuries. The Wachau district, west of Vienna, also produces some fine delicate wines, including Loibner Kaiserwein and Duernsteiner Katzensprung, which are fragrant and fruity.

By far the best red wine—on this there is little disagreement—is Vöslauer, from Vöslau. It's strong but not quite as powerful as Gumpoldskirchen and Klosterneuburger. From Styria comes Austria's best-known rosé, Schilcher, which is slightly dry, fruity, and sparkling.

Because many Viennese visiting the *heurigen* outside the city didn't want to get too drunk, they started diluting the new wine with club soda or mineral water. Thus the spritzer was born. The mix is best with a very dry wine.

In all except the most deluxe restaurants, it's possible to order a carafe of wine, *offener Wein,* which will be much less expensive than a bottle.

Austrian beers are relatively inexpensive and quite good, and they're sold throughout Vienna. Vienna is home to what we believe is the finest beer in the region, Schwechater. Gösser, produced in Styria, is one of the most favored brews and comes in both light and dark. Adambräu, another native beer, is also sold in Vienna's bars and taverns, along with some lighter, Bavarian-type beers such as Weizengold and Kaiser. For those who prefer the taste without the alcohol, Null Komma Josef is a local alcohol-free beer.

Two of the most famous and favored **liqueurs** among Austrians are *slivovitz* (a plum brandy that originated in Croatia) and *barack* (made from apricots). Imported whisky and bourbon are likely to be lethal in price. When you're in Vienna, it's a good rule of thumb to drink the "spirit of the land."

The most festive drink is ***Bowle*** (pronounced *bole*), which is often served at parties. It was first made for us by the great Austrian chanteuse Greta Keller, and we've been devotees ever since. She preferred the lethal method of soaking berries and sliced peaches overnight in brandy, adding three bottles of dry white wine, and letting it stand for another 2 to 3 hours. Before serving, she'd pour a bottle of champagne over it. In her words, "You can drink it as a cocktail, during and after dinner, and on . . . and on . . . and on!"

THE HEURIGEN

In 1784, Joseph II decreed that each vintner in the suburbs of Vienna could sell his own wine right on his doorstep. A tradition was born that continues today. *Heurig* means "new wine" or, more literally, "of this year."

The *heurigen,* or wine taverns, lie on the outskirts of Vienna, mainly in Grinzing. In summer, in fair weather, much of the drinking takes place in vine-covered gardens. In some old-fashioned places, on a nippy night, you'll find a crackling fire in a flower-bordered ceramic stove. There's likely to be a Gypsy violinist, an accordionist, or perhaps a zither player entertaining with Viennese songs. Most *heurigen* are rustic, with wooden benches and tables, and it's perfectly acceptable to bring your own snacks. But today, many are restaurants, serving buffets of meats, cheeses, breads, and vegetables. ***Beware:*** The wine is surprisingly potent, in spite of its innocent taste.

3

Planning Your Trip to Austria

This chapter is devoted to the where, when, and how of your trip—the advance-planning issues required to get it together and take it on the road.

1 VISITOR INFORMATION

TOURIST OFFICES Contact the **Austrian National Tourist Office,** P.O. Box 1142, New York, NY 10108-1142 (✆ **212/944-6880;** www.austria-tourism.com). In Canada, you'll find offices at 2 Bloor St. E., Suite 3330, Toronto, ON M4W 1A8 (✆ **416/967-3381**). In London, contact the office at 14 Cork St., W1X 1PF (✆ **0845/101-1818**).

Dispensing information for the entire country, the **Austrian National Tourist Office** is at Margaretenstrasse 1, A-1040 Vienna (✆ **0810/10181818**). However, it cannot make reservations for you. As you travel throughout the towns and villages of Austria, you'll see signs emblazoned with a fat **i** (for information) in front of the local tourist office, where you can obtain maps and might even get assistance in finding a hotel if you arrive without a reservation. You might also want to ask for the free English-language booklet ***Art and Architecture in Austria,*** which lists examples and photos of Austria's most renowned architectural sites.

WEBSITES To begin your exploration of Austria, check out the sites for the **Austrian National Tourist Office** (www.austria.info.at), **Tourist-Net: Austria** (www.tourist-net.co.at), **Vienna Tourist Board** (www.info.wien.at), and **Mozart Concerts** (www.mozart.co.at).

MAPS Some of the most useful maps for touring the countryside include Michelin's *Austria* (no. 426) and Freytag & Berndt's *Autokarte Austria.* Even more detailed is Freytag & Berndt's *Grosse Strassen Karten,* which covers Austria in three separate breakdowns, with the enlargement of certain regions of Land Salzburg available on a fourth. Some visitors find it more convenient to buy these same four maps in the form of the 12-page atlas, *Grosser Auto Atlas Österreich.* It includes helpful blowups of the centers of many of the country's large- and medium-size cities.

Freytag & Berndt also publish detailed maps (in either atlas or foldaway form) of Greater Vienna. Maps of Vienna's public transport system are available from the city's tourist offices.

Hill-climbers and trekkers appreciate Freytag & Berndt's detailed topographical maps known as the *Wanderkarten (W.K.).* The company also publishes hiking maps of specific regions, including the Carinthian lakes.

Most of the maps mentioned above are available in bookstores throughout Austria and in larger bookstores in the rest of Europe and North America. Freytag & Berndt's shops are at Kohlmarkt 9, in Vienna, and at Wilhelm-Greil-Strasse 15, in Innsbruck.

If you'd like a map before your trip to plan your itinerary, you can obtain one from Rand McNally, Michelin, or AAA. These are sold at bookstores all over America. Rand McNally also has an online store: **www.randmcnally.com.** The U.S. headquarters of Michelin is at P.O. Box 19008, Greenville, SC 29602 (✆ **800/423-0485**). **AAA (the American Automobile Association;** ✆ **212/757-2000** or 800/222-1134; www.aaa.com) publishes a regional map of Austria that's available free to members at most AAA offices throughout the United States.

2 ENTRY REQUIREMENTS

PASSPORTS

Citizens of the United States, Canada, the United Kingdom, Australia, Ireland, and New Zealand need only a valid passport to enter Austria. No visa is required. Safeguard your passport in an inconspicuous, inaccessible place such as a money belt. If you lose it, visit the nearest consulate of your native country as soon as possible for a replacement. It's always a good idea to have a photocopy of your passport to expedite replacement.

CUSTOMS

What You Can Bring into Austria

Visitors who live outside Austria in general are not liable to pay duty on personal articles brought into the country temporarily for their own use, depending on the purpose and circumstances of each trip. Customs officials have great leeway here. Likewise, travelers 17 years of age and older may carry up to 200 cigarettes, 50 cigars, or 250 grams of tobacco plus 1 liter of distilled liquor and either 2 liters of wine or 3 liters of beer duty-free.

What You Can Take Home from Austria

Returning U.S. citizens who have been away for 48 hours or more are allowed to bring back, once every 30 days, $800 worth of merchandise duty-free. You'll be charged a flat rate of 10% duty on the next $1,000 worth of purchases. Be sure to have your receipts handy. On gifts, the duty-free limit is $200. For more specific guidance, contact the **Customs & Border Protection (CBP)** (✆ **877/287-8667;** www.cbp.gov), and request the free pamphlet "Know Before You Go." For a clear summary of Canadian rules, request the booklet *I Declare* from **Canada Border Services Agency** (✆ **800/461-9999** in Canada, or 204/983-3500; www.cbsa-asfc.gc.ca). If you're a citizen of the United Kingdom, contact **HM Revenue Customs** (✆ **0845/010-9000;** www.hmrc.gov.uk). Australian citizens should contact the **Australian Customs Service** (✆ **1300/363263** in Australia; www.customs.gov.au). New Zealanders should contact **New Zealand Customs Service** (✆ **0800/428-786** or 04/473-6099; www.customs.govt.nz).

3 WHEN TO GO

Vienna experiences its high season from April to October, with July, August, and the main festivals being the most crowded times. Bookings around Christmastime are also heavy, as many Austrians visit their capital during this festive time. Always arrive with reservations during peak seasons. During the off-season, hotel rooms are generally plentiful and less expensive, and there is less demand for tables in the more popular restaurants.

CLIMATE

In Austria, the temperature varies greatly depending on your location. The national average ranges from a low of 9°F (–13°C) in January to a high of 68°F (20°C) in July. However, in Vienna, the January average is 32°F (0°C); for July, it's 66°F (19°C). Snow falls in the mountainous sectors by mid-November. Road conditions in winter can be very dangerous in many parts of the country. The winter air is usually crisp and clear, with many sunny days. The winter snow cover lasts late December through March in the valleys, November through May at about 1,830m (6,004 ft.), and all year at 2,592m (8,504 ft.) or higher. The ideal times for visiting Vienna are spring through fall. Even in spring and fall, there are many mild, sunny days. By the end of July, alpine wildflowers are in full bloom.

Vienna's Average Temperature & Rainfall

	Jan	Feb	Mar	Apr	May	June	July	Aug	Sept	Oct	Nov	Dec
Temp. (°F)	30	32	38	50	58	64	68	70	60	50	41	33
Temp. (°C)	–1	0	4	10	14	18	20	21	16	10	5	0
Rainfall (in.)	1.2	1.9	3.9	1.3	2.9	1.9	.8	1.8	2.8	2.8	2.5	1.6

Salzburg's Average Temperature & Rainfall

	Jan	Feb	Mar	Apr	May	June	July	Aug	Sept	Oct	Nov	Dec
Temp. (°F)	28	35	37	45	55	64	68	67	60	50	39	33
Temp. (°C)	–2	2	3	7	13	18	20	19	16	10	4	0
Rainfall (in.)	2.5	2.6	2.8	3.5	5.3	6.8	7.5	6.4	3.6	2.9	2.7	2.7

Innsbruck's Average Temperature & Rainfall

	Jan	Feb	Mar	Apr	May	June	July	Aug	Sept	Oct	Nov	Dec
Temp. (°F)	30	39	52	59	68	73	77	75	70	59	45	36
Temp. (°C)	–1	4	11	15	20	23	25	24	21	15	7	2
Rainfall (in.)	3.4	2.5	3.2	4.1	4.5	5.4	5.8	5.3	4.2	3.5	3.3	3.7

AUSTRIA CALENDAR OF EVENTS

For more information about these and other events, contact the various tourist offices throughout Austria. For an exhaustive list of events beyond those listed here, **check http://events.frommers.com**, where you'll find a searchable, up-to-the-minute roster of what's happening in cities all over the world.

January

New Year's Eve/New Year's Day. Vienna's biggest night is launched by the famed concert of the Vienna Philharmonic Orchestra. The New Year also marks the beginning of **Fasching,** the famous Vienna Carnival season, which lasts through Shrove Tuesday (Mardi Gras). For tickets and information, contact the Wiener Philharmoniker, Bösendorferstrasse 12, A-1010 Vienna (© **01/5056525;** www.wienerphilharmoniker.at). The concert is followed by the **Imperial Ball** in the Hofburg. For information and tickets, contact the Hofburg Kongresszentrum, Hofburg, Heldenplatz, A-1014 Vienna (© **01/587/3666;** www.hofburg.com).

Berg Isel Ski Jumping Competition, Innsbruck. One of the country's most daredevil ski-jump competitions kicks off the new year at a platform built for the 1964 Olympics. First week in January.

Hahnenkamm World Cup Ski Race, Kitzbühel. Since 1931, this major sporting event has drawn world-class skiers from around the globe to compete for the prestigious World Cup. Skiers compete over 2 days, but the whole town parties for a week. Tickets are available at the gate. For information, contact the Kitzbühel Tourist Office (✆ **05356/777;** www.kitzbuehel.com). Mid-January.

Eistraum (Dream on Ice). During the coldest months of Austrian winter, the monumental plaza between the Town Hall and the Burgtheater is flooded and frozen; lights, loudspeakers, and a stage are hauled in, and the entire civic core is transformed into a gigantic ice-skating rink. Sedate waltz tunes accompany the skaters during the day, and DJs spin rock, funk, and reggae after the sun goes down. Around the rink, dozens of kiosks sell everything from hot chocolate and snacks to wine and beer. For information, call ✆ **01/4090040,** or visit **www.wienereistraum.com**. Last week of January to mid-March.

Mozart Week, Salzburg. This festival features opera, orchestral works, and chamber music. Get tickets at the Mozarteum, Schwarzstrasse 26, A-5024 Salzburg (✆ **0662/873154;** www.mozarteum.at). Late January to early February.

February

Opera Ball. On the last Thursday of the Fasching, Vienna's high society gathers at the Wien Staatsoper for the grandest ball of the Carnival season. The evening opens with a performance by the Opera House Ballet. You don't need an invitation, but you do need to buy a ticket, which, as you might guess, isn't cheap. For information, contact the Vienna Opera House directly (✆ **01/51444-2250;** www.staatsoper.at).

Ski Festival. Gaschurn, in the heart of Vorarlberg (9.6km/6 miles from Schruns), is the resort that lies closest to the downhill runs of the Silvretta-Nova subdivision of the Montafon Valley. It's the site of a 1-week ski festival sponsored by the Belgian-Austrian chocolate manufacturer Suchard. The men's and women's events are the Montafon Valley's most important ski competition. For information, contact the Vorarlberg Tourist Office (✆ **05574/425250;** www.vorarlberg.cc). Late February to early March.

March

Bregenz Spring Festival. The Vienna Symphony Orchestra usually appears at these concerts, which usher in the greening of the surrounding Alps. For information, contact the Bregenz Festival, Plaz der Wiener Symphoniker 1, A-6900 Bregenz (✆ **0557/4076;** www.bregenzerfestspiele.com). First 3 weeks of March.

Vienna Spring Festival. The festival has a different central theme every year, but you can always count on music by the world's greatest composers, including Mozart and Brahms, at the Konzerthaus. The booking address is Karlsplatz 6, Lothringerstrasse 20, A-1030 Vienna (✆ **01/242002;** www.konzerthaus.at). Mid-March through the first week of May.

May

International Music Festival. This traditional highlight of Vienna's concert calendar features top-class international orchestras, distinguished conductors, and classical greats. You might hear Beethoven's *Eroica* as it was meant to be played, Mozart's *Jupiter* Symphony, and perhaps Bruckner's *Romantic.* The list of conductors and orchestras reads like a who's who of the international world of music. The venue and booking address is Wiener Musikverein, Bösendorferstrasse 12, A-1010 Vienna (✆ **01/5058190;** www.musikverein-wien.at).

Early May through the first 3 weeks of June.

Vienna Festival. An exciting array of operas, operettas, musicals, theater, and dances are performed. New productions of treasured classics are presented alongside avant-garde premieres, all staged by internationally prominent directors. In addition, celebrated productions from renowned European theaters offer guest performances. Anticipate such productions as Mozart's *Così fan tutte,* Monteverdi's *Orfeo,* and Offenbach's *La Vie Parisienne.* For bookings, contact Wiener Festwochen, Lehárgasse 11, A-1060 Vienna (© **01/5892222;** www.festwochen.at). The second week of May until mid-June.

June

Danube Lower Austria Festival, along the Danube River, in various locations and at St. Pölten, the state capital. Dance, theater, music, art, poetry, and ecology are presented at a number of venues, including a riverboat. Mid-June to mid-July.

Midsummer Night Celebration. This celebration is held all over Austria, with bonfires and folkloric events. The liveliest observances are in the Tyrolean valley towns and in the Wachau region along the Danube in Austria. June 20.

Styriarte Graz. This grand annual cultural celebration features a different theme every year. For tickets and information, contact Styriarte Graz, Palais Attems, Sackstrasse 17, A-8010 Graz (© **0316/8129410;** www.styriarte.com). Late June to mid-July.

Vienna Jazz Festival. This is one of the world's top jazz events, using the Vienna State Opera as its central venue. The program calls for appearances by more than 50 international and local stars. For information and bookings, contact the Verein Jazz Fest Wien, Lammgasse 12 (© **01/[illegible];** [illegible] org). Late June to mid-July.

July

Vienna Summer of Music. This premier event fills the cultural calendar with concerts at City Hall, Schönbrunn Palace, and many landmark homes of great 19th-century Viennese musicians. Densely packed with musical options, the festival often features a series of different musical events on any given night. For tickets, schedules, and information, contact the Wiener Musiksommer, Laudongasse 4, A-1010 Vienna (© **01/400084722**). July 1 to late August.

Festival of Early Music, Innsbruck. Everything from baroque operas to recitals featuring historical instruments characterizes this annual event. Concerts are presented at the Hofburg, the Tyroler Landestheater, and the Castle Ambras. For tickets and information, contact the Innsbruck Festival, Burggraben 3, A-6020 Innsbruck (© **0512571032;** www.altemusik.at). Mid-July into August.

Bregenz Summer Festival. The cultural highlight of the summer is the appearance once again of the Vienna Symphony Orchestra. For information, contact the Bregenz Tourist Office, Plaz der Wiener, Symphoniker 1, A-6900 Bregenz (© **05574/407;** www.bregenzerfestspiele.com). Mid-July to mid-August.

Salzburg Festival. Since the 1920s, this has been one of the premier cultural events of Europe, sparkling with opera, chamber music, plays, concerts, appearances by world-class artists, and many other cultural presentations. Always count on stagings of Mozart operas. Performances are held at various venues throughout the city. For tickets, write several months in advance to the Salzburg Festival, Postfach 140, A-5010 Salzburg (✆ **0662/8045500;** www.salzburgfestival.at). Late July to late August.

Summer Stage, Vienna. Along the quays of the Donau Inlet, adjacent to the Friedensbrücke, midsummer is celebrated by hundreds of the young, the upwardly mobile, and the trendy who converge on the periphery of the city to enjoy the night air and one another's company. Temporary stages present everything from performance art to live music. Adding to the revelry are the 20 or so seasonal bars that open their doors to the milling summer crowd every night from 5pm to 2am. July and August.

Music Film Festival. Opera, operetta, and masterful concert performances captured on celluloid are enjoyed free under a starry sky in front of the neo-Gothic City Hall on the Ringstrasse. Programs focus on works by Franz Schubert, Johannes Brahms, or other composers. For more information, contact Ideenagentur Austria, Opernring 1R, A-1010 Vienna (✆ **01/40008100;** www.wien-event.at). Mid-July to mid-September.

September

Haydn Days, Eisenstadt, in Burgenland. Held in Eisenstadt, where Haydn lived for 40 years, this festival presents the composer's trios, quartets, symphonies, operas, and choral works. Venues include the Esterházy castle, local churches, and even the city's public parks. For tickets and information, contact the Burgenlandische Haydn Festspiele, Schloss Esterházy, A-7000 Eisenstadt (✆ **02682/61866;** www.haydnfestival.at). Early to mid-September.

International Bruckner Festival, Linz. This month-long festival features concerts, theatrical presentations, art exhibits, and fireworks. For tickets and information, contact Festspiele, Untere Donaulände 7, A-4010 Linz (✆ **0732/76122124;** www.brucknerhaus.linz.at). Mid-September to early October.

October

Viennale. This film festival shows everything from the most daringly avant-garde to golden oldies of the (mostly European) silver screen. Check the program to see which films will be in English or have English subtitles. For tickets and information, contact the Wiener Festwochen Viennale, Stiftgasse 6, A-1070 Vienna (✆ **01/5265947;** www.viennale.at). Throughout October.

Wien Modern, in its 22nd year in 2009, was founded by Claudio Abbado and is devoted to the performance of contemporary works in music. The emphasis is not just on Austrian composers—it has included works from Scandinavian and Baltic countries, Iceland, Romania, Portugal, and other nations. Some of the composers make live appearances and discuss their compositions. Concerts usually last 1½ to 2 hours. Performances are at Verein Wien Modern, Lothringerstrasse 20 (✆ **01/242000**), but the booking phone number is (✆ **01/242002;** www.konzerthaus.at). Late October to late November.

November

Vienna Schubert Festivale. This all-Schubert celebration marks its 27th annual observance in 2009. For information, contact Wiener Musikverein, Karlsplatz 6, A-1010 Vienna (✆ **01/5058190;** www.musikverein-wien.at). Third week of November.

December

Christkindlmarkt. Look for pockets of folkloric charm (and, in some cases, kitsch) associated with the Christmas holidays. Small outdoor booths, known as Christkindlmarkt—usually adorned with evergreen boughs, red ribbons, and, in some cases, religious symbols sprout up in clusters around Vienna. They're selling old-fashioned toys, *Tannenbaum* (Christmas tree) decorations, and gift items. Food vendors will also be nearby offering sausages, cookies and pastries, roasted chestnuts, and *kartoffel* (sliced and roasted potato slices). The greatest concentrations of these open-air markets can be found in front of the Rathaus, in the Spittelberg Quarter (7th District), at Freyung, the historic square in the northwest corner of the Inner City. Late November to New Year's.

4 GETTING THERE & GETTING AROUND

GETTING TO AUSTRIA

Although Vienna is serviced by a number of European airlines, most flights coming from the Western Hemisphere require a transfer in other European cities such as London or Frankfurt.

If you're planning to travel to western Austria—Innsbruck, Salzburg, Tyrol, Vorarlberg, and parts of Land Salzburg—keep in mind that these destinations are closer to Munich than to Vienna. It might be easier to fly to Munich and then rent a car or take a train to your final destination.

Also, if your destination lies somewhat off the beaten track, note that more connections are possible into the secondary airports of Austria from Frankfurt than from any other non-Austrian city. These connections are usually made by Lufthansa, Austrian Airlines, or Tyrolean Air, or on flights maintained cooperatively by some combination of those three.

Most flights from London to Vienna depart from London's Heathrow Airport. The flight takes 2 hours and 20 minutes.

By Plane

From the U.S., you can fly directly to Vienna on **Austrian Airlines** (© **800/843-0002** in the U.S. and Canada; www.austrianair.com), the national carrier of Austria. There's nonstop service from New York to Vienna (approx. 9 hr.) and from Washington and Toronto to Vienna.

British Airways (© **800/AIRWAYS** in the U.S. and Canada; www.britishairways.com) provides excellent service to Vienna. Passengers fly first to London—usually nonstop—from 23 gateways in the U.S., five in Canada, two in Brazil, and one each in Bermuda, Mexico City, and Buenos Aires. From London, British Airways has two to five daily nonstop flights to Vienna from either Gatwick or Heathrow airports.

Flights on **Lufthansa** (© **800/645-3880** in the U.S. and Canada; www.lufthansa.com), the German national carrier, depart from North America frequently for Frankfurt and Düsseldorf, with connections to Vienna.

American Airlines (© **800/433-7300** in the U.S. and Canada; www.aa.com) funnels Vienna-bound passengers through gateways in Zurich or London.

If you're traveling from Canada, you can usually connect from your hometown to **British Airways** (© **800/AIRWAYS** in Canada; www.britishairways.com) gateways in Toronto, Montreal, and Vancouver. Separate nonstop flights from both Toronto's Pearson Airport and Montreal's Mirabelle Airport depart every day for London, and flights from Vancouver depart for London three times a week. In London, you can stay for a few days (arranging discounted hotel accommodations through the British Airways tour desk) or head directly to Vienna on any of the two to five daily nonstop flights from either Heathrow or Gatwick.

There are frequent flights between London and Vienna, the majority of which

Security Measures

Because of increased security measures, the Transportation Security Administration has made changes to the prohibited items list. All liquids and gels—including shampoo, toothpaste, perfume, hair gel, suntan lotion, and all other items with similar consistency—**are limited** within your carry-on baggage and the security checkpoint. Check the **Transportation Security Administration** site, **www.tsa.gov**, for the latest information.

depart from London's Heathrow Airport. Flight time is 2 hours and 20 minutes.

Austrian Airlines (✆ **0870/124-2625** in London; www.austrianair.com) has four daily nonstop flights into Vienna and two daily nonstop flights to Innsbruck from Heathrow. **British Airways** (✆ **0870/850-9850** in London; www.britishairways.com) surpasses that, offering three daily nonstop flights from Heathrow and two from Gatwick, with easy connections through London from virtually every other part of Britain.

By Car

If you're traveling from continental Europe and don't want to fly, there are several other options for getting to Austria. If you're coming over from Britain and have arrived at a Channel port in France, by either ferry or the Chunnel, Vienna is about 1,285km (799 miles) away; Salzburg is about 1,030km (640 miles). It's faster to travel on the motorways going through Frankfurt, Cologne, Passau (Germany), and Linz (Austria). One of the main roads into Austria is the Autobahn from Munich via Salzburg to Vienna. From Switzerland, the main arteries are via Feldkirch to Innsbruck (capital of Tyrol), or from Basel via Karlsruhe to Munich and then on the busy Autobahn to either Salzburg or Vienna.

By Train

If you plan to travel a lot on the European or British railroads on your way to or from Vienna, you'd do well to secure the latest copy of the "Thomas Cook European Timetable of Railroads." It's available online at **www.thomascooktimetables.com**.

Vienna has rail links to all the major cities of Europe. From Paris, a train leaves the Gare de l'Est at 7:49am, arriving in Vienna at 9:18pm. From Munich, a train leaves daily at 9:24am (arriving in Vienna at 2:18pm) and then again at 11:19pm (arriving in Vienna at 6:47am). From Zurich, you can take a 9:33pm train that arrives in Vienna at 6:45pm.

Rail travel within Austria is superb, with fast, clean trains taking you just about anywhere in the country and going through some incredibly scenic regions.

Train passengers using the **Chunnel** under the English Channel can go from London to Paris in just 3 hours and then on to Vienna (see above). Le Shuttle transports passengers along the 31-mile journey in just 35 minutes. The train also accommodates passenger cars, charter buses, taxis, and motorcycles through a tunnel from Folkestone, England, to Calais, France. Service is year-round, 24 hours a day.

Rail Passes for North American Travelers

If you plan to travel extensively in Europe, the **Eurail Global Pass** might be a good bet. It's valid for first-class rail travel in 20 European countries. With one ticket, you travel whenever and wherever you please; more than 100,000 rail miles are at your disposal. Here's how it works: The pass is sold only in North America. A Eurailpass good for 15 days costs $795; a pass for 21 days is $1,029; a 1-month pass costs $1,279; a 2-month pass is $1,809; and a 3-month pass goes for $2,235. Children under 4 travel free if they don't occupy a seat; all children under 12 who take up a seat are charged half-price. If you're under 26, you can buy a **Eurail Global Pass Youth,** which entitles you to unlimited second-class travel for 15 days ($519), 21 days ($669), 1 month ($835), 2 months ($1,179), or 3 months ($1,455). Travelers considering buying a 15-day or 1-month pass should estimate rail distance before deciding whether a pass is worthwhile. To take full advantage of the tickets for 15 days or a month, you'd have to spend a great deal of time on the train. Eurailpass holders are entitled to substantial discounts on certain buses and ferries as well. Travel agents in all towns and railway agents in such major cities as New York, Montreal, and Los Angeles sell all of these tickets. For information on Eurailpasses and other European train data, call **RailEurope** at ✆ **877/272-RAIL,** or visit it on the Web at **www.raileurope.com**.

Eurail Global Pass Saver offers a 15% discount to each person in a group of three or more people traveling together between April and September, or two people traveling together between October and March. The price of a Saverpass, valid all over Europe for first class only, is $675 for 15 days; $875 for 21 days; $1,089 for 1 month; $1,539 for 2 months; and $1,905 for 3 months. Even more freedom is offered by the **Saver Flexipass,** which is similar to the Eurail Saverpass except that you are not confined to consecutive-day travel. For travel over any 10 days within 2 months, the fare is $608; for any 15 days over 2 months, the fare is $800.

The **Eurail Select Pass** offers unlimited travel on the national rail networks of any 3, 4, or 5 bordering countries out of the 23 Eurail nations linked by train or ship. Two or more passengers can travel together for big discounts, getting 5, 6, 8, 10, or 15 days of rail travel within any 2-month period on the national rail networks of any three, four, or five adjoining Eurail countries linked by train or ship. A sample fare: for 5 days in 2 months you pay $505 for three countries. **Eurail Select Pass Youth** for travelers under 26, allow second-class travel within the same guidelines as Eurail Selectpass, with fees starting at $329. **Eurail Select Pass Saver** offers discounts for two or more people traveling together, first-class travel within the same guidelines as Eurail Selectpass, with fees starting at $429.

Rail Passes for British Travelers

If you plan to do a lot of exploring, you might prefer one of the three rail passes designed for unlimited train travel within a designated region during a predetermined number of days. These passes are sold in Britain and several other European countries and can be used only by European residents.

An **InterRail Global Pass** (www.interrail.com) allows unlimited travel through Europe, except Albania and the republics of the former Soviet Union.

Adults purchasing an InterRail global Pass can travel first or second class. In first class prices are $329 for 5 days in 10 days; $489 for 10 days in 22 days; $629 for 22 days continuous, or $809 for 1 month. In second class, the cost is $249 for 5 days in 10 days; $359 for 10 days in 22 days; $469 for 22 days continuous, and $599 for 1 month continuous.

An **InterRail Global Youth Pass** is also sold and is available only in second class. A youth is defined as those travelers ranging from age 12 through 25 years of age. The cost is $159 for 5 days in 10 days; $239 for 10 days in 22 days; $309 for 22 days continuous; and $399 for 1 month continuous.

For information on buying individual rail tickets or any of the just-mentioned passes, contact **National Rail Inquiries,**

Victoria Station, London (✆ **0845/748-4950;** www.nationalrail.co.uk). Tickets and passes are also available at any of the larger railway stations as well as selected travel agencies throughout Britain and the rest of Europe.

By Bus

Because of the excellence of rail service from all parts of the Continent into both Salzburg and Vienna, bus transit into Austria is not especially popular. But there is some limited service. **Eurolines,** part of National Express Coach Lines (✆ **0871/781-8181;** www.nationalexpress.com), operates two express buses per week between London's Victoria Coach Station and Vienna. The trip takes about 29 hours and makes 45-minute rest stops en route about every 4 hours during the transit through France, Belgium, and Germany. Buses depart from London at 8:15am every Friday and Sunday, and are equipped with reclining seats, toilets, and reading lights. The one-way London-Vienna fare is £52 to £72 ($104–$144). If you opt for a round-trip fare, priced at £80 to £104 ($160–$208), you won't need to declare your intended date of return until you actually use your ticket (although advance reservations are advisable), and the return half of your ticket will be valid for 6 months. The return to London departs from Vienna every Tuesday, Wednesday, Friday, and Saturday at 7:45pm, arriving at Victoria Coach Station about 24 hours later.

GETTING AROUND AUSTRIA

By Train

Rail travel is superb in Austria, with fast, clean trains taking you through scenic regions. Trains will take you nearly every place in Austria except to remote hamlets tucked away in almost-inaccessible mountain districts. Many other services tie in with railroad travel, among them car or bicycle rental at many stations, bus transportation links, and package tours, including boat trips and cable-car rides. Inter-City Express trains connect Vienna with all major cities in the country, including Salzburg, Klagenfurt, Graz, and Linz. A train trip from Salzburg to Vienna takes about 3 hours.

Rail Passes

See "Getting There," earlier in this chapter, for information on the **Eurailpass,** which is valid in Austria.

Adults can purchase first- or second-class passes. In first class the charge is $229 for 3 days in 1 month; $265 for 4 days in 1 month; $295 for 5 days in 1 month; $329 for 6 days in 1 month; $359 for 7 days in 1 month, and $395 for 8 days in 1 month. In second class charges are $159 for 3 days in 1 month; $179 for 4 days in 1 month; $205 for 5 days in 1 month; $229 for 6 days in 1 month; $255 for 7 days in 1 month; and $279 for 8 days in 1 month.

The **Eurail Austria Youth Pass** is available for second-class travel, and can be sold to travelers who are 25 years old or younger on their first day of travel. Charges are $105 for 3 days in 1 month; $119 for 4 days in 1 month; $135 for 5 days in 1 month; $149 for 6 days in 1 month; $165 for 7 days in 1 month; and $179 for 8 days in 1 month.

Other Railway Data

For information on short-distance round-trip tickets, cross-country passes, and passes for all lines in the individual provinces, as well as piggyback transportation for your car through the Tauern Tunnel, check with the **Austrian Federal Railways** (✆ **01/930-000;** www.oebb.at).

By Car

Driving, of course, is the best way to crisscross Austria, going up and down its scenic mountain valleys and along its vast mountain passes. It's one of the greatest countries in the world for scenery. That applies only to the summer months. Driving conditions in Austria can be difficult in winter.

Renting a car is not the most economical way to see the country; by train or bus is cheaper.

Some mountain roads require a toll. The good news is that there is almost no delay at border crossings. Motorists zip about casually—say, between Germany and Austria—but in the wake of worldwide terrorism, conditions could often change at a moment's notice for reasons you will not be aware of.

All main roads in Austria are hard-surfaced. There's a four-lane Autobahn between Salzburg and Vienna; and between Vienna and Edlitz the Autobahn has six lanes. Part of the highway system includes mountain roads; and in the alpine region drivers face gradients of 6% to 16%, or even steeper in some places. When driving in Austria, always plot your course carefully. If you have had no experience in mountain driving—much less alpine mountain driving—you might want to take a train or a bus to get to some of the loftier mountain alpine retreats.

In summer, driving conditions are good, but in winter, December through March, motorists must reckon with snow on the roads and passes at higher altitudes. Roads at altitudes of up to 1,700m (5,577 ft.) are kept open in winter, although they can be temporarily closed because of heavy snowfall or avalanche danger. If you're planning to drive in Austria in winter, you'll need snow tires or chains.

Don't take chances. Ask about road conditions before you start on a trip. This information is available in English 7 days a week from 6am to 8pm from the **Österreichischer Automobil-, Motorrad- und Touringclub (ÖAMTC),** Schubertring 1–3, A-1010 Vienna (✆ **0810/120-120;** www.oeamtc.at).

Rentals

Drivers in Austria must have been in possession of a valid driver's license for at least 1 year before renting a vehicle. They must also present a valid passport when they sign the rental agreement. Drivers not in possession of a major credit card must pay in advance a minimum deposit, plus the estimated rental cost and the estimated tax. Cars rented from most rental companies can be dropped off in major cities of Germany for no additional charge. Drop-offs in Switzerland or Italy require an extra charge, which can be quite high.

Be aware that car rentals in Austria are taxed at a whopping rate of 21.2%. This is in addition to a 15% municipal airport tax added to the cost of any car rented at an airport. Clarify in advance whether the rates you're quoted include the taxes. ***Tip:*** You might consider taking a taxi to your hotel upon arrival and then renting your vehicle from an inner-city location to avoid the 15% airport surcharge.

When you reserve a car, be sure to ask if the price includes insurance. The rental outfits offer an optional insurance policy known as a loss-damage waiver (LDW). If you accept it, you'll be charged from 25€ ($40) per day. It allows you to waive all financial responsibility for any damage to your car, even if it's eventually determined that you were the driver at fault. In some instances, certain credit card companies offer free insurance if you use their card to pay for the rental. Check directly with your credit card issuer to see if you are covered.

Budget (✆ **800/472-3325;** www.budget.com) is among the least expensive options in Austria. It maintains more than a dozen locations throughout the country, including branches at all the major airports and at downtown locations in most of the provincial capitals.

Hertz (✆ **800/654-3001;** www.hertz.com) maintains offices in about 18 cities throughout Austria. During limited periods, it sometimes publicizes price promotions worth inquiring about, depending on the season, as well as discounts to employees of some large North American corporations.

Avis (✆ **800/331-1084;** www.avis.com) operates offices in 19 Austrian cities, at airports and downtown, as well as at some of the country's larger ski resorts. Avis usually offers 10% discounts for members of such organizations as AAA and AARP. Like Budget and Hertz, it offers seasonal price promotions.

Kemwel Drive Europe (✆ **877/820-0668;** www.kemwel.com) has offices in about 10 cities throughout Asia.

AutoEurope (✆ **888/223-5555;** www.autoeurope.com) operates 12 offices in Austrian cities as well as airports.

Gasoline

Regular-grade unleaded *(blei-frei)* motor fuel is generally available in Austria. Skyrocketing gasoline prices vary from place to place but are somewhat lower at discounted or self-service gasoline stations. Austrian service stations don't accept U.S. oil company or general-purpose credit or charge cards.

Driving Rules

Traffic regulations are similar to those in other European countries where you *drive on the right.* Driving under the influence of alcohol is severely punished. The permissible blood-alcohol level is very low—two beers or 8 ounces of wine can put you over the mark. The *minimum* fine is 350€ ($560) and possible loss of a driver's license.

Use of seat belts is compulsory, and children under 12 may not sit in the front passenger seat unless a child's seat belt or a special seat has been installed. The use of hand-held cellphones is prohibited while driving, and a right turn at a red light is **not** permitted. Effective in late 2005, headlights must be on at all times day or night.

Automobile Clubs

The leading auto club of Austria is the **ÖAMTC** (Österreichischer Automobil-, Motorred- und Touringclub), Schubertring 1–3, A-1010 Vienna (✆ **0810/120-120;** www.oeamtc.at), which works in association with AAA. **ARBÖ** (✆ **050/123-123;** www.arboe.at) is another.

Breakdowns/Assistance

If your car breaks down, foreign motorists can call the two auto clubs mentioned above. Call **ARBÖ** (✆ **123**) or **ÖAMTC** (✆ **120**) anywhere in Austria. You don't need to use an area code for either number. However, if you're not a member of either of these clubs, you'll pay for emergency road service.

Motorcycles

The same requirements for operating cars in Austria hold for operating motorcycles. Both drivers and passengers of motorcycles must wear crash helmets. Lights must be kept on when the vehicle is being driven.

By Taxi

In large Austrian cities, taxis are equipped with officially sealed taximeters that show the cost of your trip in euros. If a rate change has recently been instituted, a surcharge might be added to the amount shown on the meter, pending adjustment of the taximeter. Surcharges are posted in the cab. A supplement is charged for luggage carried in the vehicle's trunk. Zone charges or set charges for standard trips are the rule in most resort areas. Tip the driver 10% of the fare.

By Plane

Austrian Airlines (✆ **800/843-0002** in the U.S. and Canada; www.austrianair.com) offers flights that link Vienna to the country's leading cities. Outgoing flights from Vienna are carefully timed to coincide with the arrivals of most of the company's transatlantic flights.

Tyrolean Airways (same telephone number and website as Austrian Airlines), an airline partially owned by Austrian Airlines, offers a very useful airborne network whose home base is the Tyrolean capital of Innsbruck. Its regular flight network consists of up to four flights per day between Vienna and Innsbruck, and four flights each between Innsbruck and both Frankfurt and Zurich. The airline also offers about five flights a week between Innsbruck and the Styrian capital of Graz. Reservations on Tyrolean Airways can be made through Austrian Airlines. Its fleet consists almost entirely of turbo-prop planes containing no more than 49 seats. The airline specializes in domestic flights and commuter runs to destinations close to the border, including Munich and Budapest.

By Bus

It's easiest to get around Austria on the country's excellent rail network, but many Austrian villages are not near rail lines. Reaching some of these areas can be best accomplished by car or bus. To facilitate travel, the Austrian government maintains two different bus networks: those maintained by the **Austrian Postal Service** (whose vehicles, in most cases, are painted a reddish-orange) and those maintained by the **Austrian Federal Railways** (which, in some, but not all, cases are painted blue and white). In recent years, efforts have been made to merge both of these systems into one overall administration identified as the **Bundesbus System,** but many Austrians continue to make a distinction between the two networks. There are also a limited number of privately owned bus companies that specialize in long-haul transits to major cities outside Austria.

Buses (some of which also carry mail) cover a network of almost 30,500km (18,952 miles) of often very remote secondary roads. One of their primary functions involves retrieving passengers at railway stations for the continuation of journeys. Bus departures are usually timed to coincide with the arrival of trains from other parts of Austria. Buses are particularly helpful at the bottom of alpine valleys, where transit is needed to carry passengers from the local railway station up toward ski resorts and hamlets at higher altitudes. Children under 6 travel free on many of these buses, and children under 15 usually receive a 50% discount.

Information about bus schedules and routings is available at most post offices, at the reception desks of most hotels whose business relies on clients arriving by bus, and at travel agencies. Specifics about routes and schedules are in the *Kursbuch* (Austrian Motor Coach Schedule), a timetable that is usually updated annually and that forms part of the basic library maintained by virtually every tourist office in Austria. Bus information is usually also merged into the thousands of railway timetables that are posted at train stations throughout the country. An especially convenient way to find out about bus schedules, if you're heading to a hotel in a remote area, is to call the hotel and ask.

By Bicycle

From April to the beginning of November, you can rent a bicycle at some 120 rail stations across Austria. Charges vary but are nominal, with a 50% discount if you present a rail ticket for the day that you're renting a bike. Photo ID must be presented at the time of rental. You can reserve a bicycle in advance, but you can almost always get a bike without making reservations. The vehicle can be returned to where it was rented or to any other Austrian railroad station during business hours.

5 MONEY & COSTS

Foreign money and euros can be brought into Austria without any restrictions. There is no restriction on taking foreign money out of the country, either.

The Euro, the U.S. & Canadian Dollar & the British Pound

Conversion ratios between the U.S. dollar and other currencies fluctuate, and their differences could affect the relative costs of your trip. The figures reflected in the currency chart below were valid at the time of this writing, but they might not be valid by the time of your departure. This chart would be useful for conversions of relatively small amounts of money, but if you're planning on any major transactions, check for updated rates prior to making any serious commitments.

For American Readers At the time of this writing, US$1 was worth approximately .625 Eurocents. Inversely stated, 1€ was worth approximately US$1.60.

For British Readers At press time, £1 equaled approximately US$2, and approximately 1.25€.

For Canadian Readers At press time, CD$1 equaled approximately US$1 and approximately 1.60€.

The chart inserted below reflects the figures in the paragraphs above, but because international currency ratios can and almost certainly will change prior to your arrival in Europe, you should confirm up-to-date currency rates shortly before you go.

Euro €	US$	UK£	CD$	Euro €	US$	UK£	CD$
1	1.60	0.80	1.60	75	120.00	60.00	120.00
2	3.20	1.60	3.20	100	160.00	80.00	160.00
3	4.80	2.40	4.80	125	200.00	100.00	200.00
4	6.40	3.20	6.40	150	240.00	120.00	240.00
5	8.00	4.00	8.00	175	280.00	140.00	280.00
6	9.60	4.80	9.60	200	320.00	160.00	320.00
7	11.20	5.60	11.20	225	360.00	180.00	360.00
8	12.80	6.40	12.80	250	400.00	200.00	400.00
9	14.40	7.20	14.40	275	440.00	220.00	440.00
10	16.00	8.00	16.00	300	480.00	240.00	480.00
15	24.00	12.00	24.00	350	560.00	280.00	560.00
20	32.00	16.00	32.00	400	640.00	320.00	640.00
25	40.00	20.00	40.00	500	800.00	400.00	800.00
50	80.00	40.00	80.00	1000	1,600.00	800.00	1,600.00

The **euro** (€) is the single European currency of Austria and other participating countries. Exchange rates of participating countries are locked into a common currency fluctuating against the dollar.

For more details on the euro, check out **www.europa.eu.int/euro**.

CREDIT CARDS

To get the best rate of exchange, use your credit cards whenever possible. They virtually always offer the best exchange rate, and there's no accompanying service charge. Credit cards are widely accepted in Austria; American Express, Visa, and

What Things Cost in Vienna	Euro€	US$	UK£
Bus from the airport to the city center	6.00	7.80	3.90
U-Bahn (subway) from St. Stephan's to Schönbrunn Palace	1.50	1.95	0.98
Double room at das Triest (expensive)	273.00	437.00	218.50
Double room at the Am Parkring (moderate)	149.00	238.00	119.00
Double room at the Pension Dr. Geissler (inexpensive)	65.00	104.00	52.00
Lunch for one, without wine, at König von Ungarn (expensive)	40.00	64.00	32.00
Lunch for one, without wine, at Griechenbeisl (moderate)	30.00	48.00	24.00
Dinner for one, without wine, at Plachutta (expensive)	40.00	64.00	32.00
Dinner for one, without wine, at Firenze Enoteca (moderate)	28.00	45.00	22.50
Dinner for one, without wine, at Café Leopold (inexpensive)	12.00	19.00	9.50
Glass of wine	3.00	4.80	2.40
Half-liter of beer in a *beisl*	4.40	7.00	3.50
Coca-Cola in cafe	3.50	5.60	2.80
Cup of coffee *(ein kleine Braun)*	3.00	4.80	2.40
Movie ticket	12.00	19.00	9.50
Admission to Schönbrunn Palace	12.90	21.00	10.50

Diners Club are the most commonly recognized. A EUROCARD or ACCESS sign displayed at an establishment means that it accepts MasterCard.

ATMS

ATMs are prevalent in all Austrian cities and even the smaller towns. ATMs are linked to a national network that most likely includes your bank at home. Both the **Cirrus** (© **800/424-7787;** www.mastercard.com) and the **PLUS** (© **800/843-7587;** www.visa.com) networks have automated ATM locators listing the banks in Austria that will accept your card. Or just search out any machine with your network's symbol emblazoned on it.

Important note: Make sure that the PINs on your bank cards and credit cards will work in Austria. You'll need a **four-digit code** (six digits won't work); if you have a six-digit code, you'll have to go into your bank and get a new PIN for your trip. If you're unsure about this, contact Cirrus or PLUS (above). Be sure to check the daily withdrawal limit at the same time.

TRAVELER'S CHECKS

You can buy traveler's checks at most banks. They are offered in denominations of $20, $50, $100, $500, and sometimes $1,000. Generally, you'll pay a service charge ranging from 1% to 4%.

Emergency Cash—The Fastest Way

If you need emergency cash over the weekend, when all banks and American Express offices are closed, you can have money wired to you from **Western Union** (✆ **800/325-6000;** www.westernunion.com). You must present valid ID to pick up the cash at the Western Union office. However, in most countries, you can pick up a money transfer even if you don't have valid identification, as long as you can answer a test question provided by the sender. Be sure to let the sender know in advance that you don't have ID. If you need to use a test question instead of ID, the sender must take cash to his or her local Western Union office rather than transfer the money over the phone or online.

The most popular traveler's checks are offered by **American Express** (✆ **800/528-4800** or 800/221-7282 for card holders; this number accepts collect calls, offers service in several foreign languages, and exempts Amex gold and platinum cardholders from the 1% fee); **Visa** (✆ **800/732-1322;** AAA members can obtain Visa checks for a $9.95 fee [for checks up to $1,500] at most AAA offices or by calling ✆ **866/339-3378**); and **MasterCard** (✆ **800/223-9920**).

American Express, Thomas Cook, Visa, and **MasterCard** offer **foreign currency traveler's checks,** which are useful if you're traveling to one country, or to the Euro zone; they're accepted at locations where dollar checks may not be.

If you carry traveler's checks, keep a record of their serial numbers separate from your checks in the event that they are stolen or lost. You'll get a refund faster if you know the numbers.

6 HEALTH

STAYING HEALTHY

You'll encounter few health problems while traveling in Austria. The tap water is generally safe to drink, the milk is pasteurized, and health services are good. Occasionally, the change in diet and water could cause some minor disturbances, so you might want to talk to your doctor.

There is no need to get any shots before visiting Austria. Just to be prepared you might pack some anti-diarrhea medications. It's not that the food or water in Austria is unhealthy; it's different and might at first cause digestive problems for those unfamiliar with it.

It's easy to get over-the-counter medicine. Fortunately, generic equivalents of common prescription drugs are available at most destinations in which you'll be traveling. It's also easy to find English-speaking doctors and to get prescriptions filled at all cities, towns, and resorts. You might experience some inconvenience, of course, if you travel in the remote hinterlands.

COMMON AILMENTS

Some concerns might arise if you're planning strenuous activities at higher altitudes. All of us, of course, are affected by a lack of oxygen at altitudes more than 2,500m (8,202 ft.). Symptoms of **altitude sickness** are often a severe headache, a feeling of nausea, dizziness, loss of appetite, and lack of sleep.

In a nutshell, high altitude sickness most often occurs when you go too high too fast. The body needs time to acclimatize itself as you climb to higher regions. This is an extremely complicated subject, and if you plan to climb the highest peaks, read the study made by Princeton University at **www.Princeton.edu/~oa/safety/altitude.html**.

In winter, higher elevations might also cause **frostbite.** Wet clothes, wind chill factor, and extreme cold can cause frostbite. Some people with poor circulation, such as those who suffer from diabetes, are particularly vulnerable. Precautions are advised—no smoking, no drinking, good food, and rest. As you proceed higher and higher, wear multiple layers of clothing, especially water-proof synthetics. Survive Outdoors Inc. has frostbite prevention advice on its website at **www.surviveoutdoors.com/reference/frostbite.asp**.

Snow blindness is caused by the exposure of your unprotected eyes to the ultraviolet rays of the sun. This often happens in conditions of great snow or ice, mostly at higher altitudes. It is usually prevented by wearing dark-lensed "glacier glasses," of the wraparound, side-shielded variety. Wear these glasses even if the sky is overcast, as ultraviolet rays can pass through masses of cloud formations.

WHAT TO DO IF YOU GET SICK AWAY FROM HOME

Nearly all doctors in Austria speak English. If you get sick, consider asking your hotel concierge to recommend a local doctor—even his or her own. You can also try the emergency room at a local hospital. Many hospitals also have walk-in clinics for emergency cases that are not life-threatening; you may not get immediate attention, but you won't pay the high price of an emergency room visit. We list hospitals and emergency numbers under the "Fast Facts" section in the various city chapters.

If you worry about getting sick away from home, consider purchasing **medical travel insurance**, and carry your ID card in your purse or wallet. In most cases, your existing health plan will provide the coverage you need. See the section on insurance, above, for more information.

If you suffer from a chronic illness, consult your doctor before you depart. For conditions such as epilepsy, diabetes, or heart problems, wear a **MedicAlert Identification Tag** (**© 888/633-4298;** www.medicalert.org), which will immediately alert doctors to your condition and give them access to your records through MedicAlert's 24-hour hot line.

Contact the **International Association for Medical Assistance to Travelers** (**IAMAT; © 716/754-4883** or 416/652-0137; www.iamat.org) for tips on travel and health concerns in the countries you're visiting and lists of local, English-speaking doctors. The U.S. **Centers for Disease Control and Prevention** (**© 800/311-3435** or 404/498-1515; www.cdc.gov) provides up-to-date information on necessary vaccines and health hazards by region or country. In Canada, check **Health Canada** at **© 613/957-2991** (www.hc.sc.gc.ca).

Travel Health Online (www.tripprep.com), sponsored by a consortium of travel medicine practitioners, may also offer helpful advice on traveling abroad. You can find listings of reliable medical clinics overseas at the **International Society of Travel Medicine** (www.istm.org).

U.K. nationals will need a **European Health Insurance Card** (**EHIC; © 0845/606-2030;** www.ehic.org.uk) to receive free or reduced-cost health benefits during a visit to a European Economic Area (EEA) country (European Union countries plus Iceland, Liechtenstein, and Norway) or Switzerland.

We list **hospitals** and **emergency numbers** under "Fast Facts: Austria," p. 481.

7 SAFETY

Never leave valuables in a car, and never travel with your car unlocked. A U.S. Department of State travel advisory warns that every car (whether parked, stopped at a traffic light, or even moving) can be a potential target for armed robbery. Report the loss or theft abroad of your passport immediately to the local police and the nearest embassy or consulate. If you are the victim of a crime while overseas, in addition to reporting to local police, contact the nearest embassy or consulate for assistance. The embassy/consulate staff, for example, can assist you in finding appropriate medical care, contacting family members or friends, and explaining how funds could be transferred. Although the investigation and prosecution of the crime is solely the responsibility of local authorities, consular officers can help you understand the local criminal justice process and find an attorney, if needed.

U.S. citizens may refer to the Department of State's pamphlet, *A Safe Trip Abroad,* for ways to promote a trouble-free journey. The pamphlet is available by mail from the Superintendent of Documents, U.S. Government Printing Office, Washington, DC 20402, or via the U.S. Department of State website at **http://travel.state.gov/travel/tips/safety/safety_1747.html**.

Austria has a low crime rate, and violent crime is rare. However, crimes involving theft of personal property have increased in recent years. Travelers can become targets of pickpockets and purse-snatchers who operate where tourists tend to gather. Some of the most frequently reported spots include Vienna's two largest train stations, the plaza around St. Stephan's Cathedral, and the nearby pedestrian shopping areas (in Vienna's 1st District).

MOUNTAIN SAFETY For information and safety tips for hikers and others planning to venture into the mountains, see "Hiking & Mountaineering," under "Special Interest Trips," below.

8 SPECIALIZED TRAVEL RESOURCES

TRAVELERS WITH DISABILITIES

Most disabilities shouldn't stop anyone from traveling. There are more options and resources out there than ever before.

Laws in Austria have compelled rail stations, airports, hotels, and most restaurants to follow a stricter set of regulations about **wheelchair accessibility** to restrooms, ticket counters, and the like. Even museums and other attractions have conformed to the regulations, which mimic many of those presently in effect in the United States. Always call ahead to check on the accessibility in hotels, restaurants, and at sights you want to visit.

Organizations that offer assistance to travelers with disabilities include **MossRehab** (✆ **800/CALL-MOSS;** www.mossresourcenet.org), which provides a library of accessible-travel resources online; **SATH** (**Society for Accessible Travel and Hospitality;** ✆ **212/447-7284;** www.sath.org), which offers a wealth of travel resources for all types of disabilities and informed recommendations on destinations, access guides, travel agents, tour operators, vehicle rentals, and companion services; and the **American Foundation for the Blind** (**AFB;** ✆ **800/232-5463** or 212/502-7600; www.afb.org), a referral resource for the blind or visually impaired that provides information on traveling with Seeing Eye dogs.

AirAmbulanceCard.com (✆ **877/424-7633**) is now partnered with SATH and allows you to preselect top-notch hospitals in case of an emergency.

Access-Able Travel Source (✆ **303/232-2979;** www.access-able.com) offers a comprehensive database on travel agents from around the world with experience in accessible travel; destination-specific access information; and links to such resources as service animals, equipment rentals, and access guides.

Many travel agencies offer customized tours and itineraries for travelers with disabilities. Among them are **Flying Wheels Travel** (✆ **507/451-5005;** www.flyingwheelstravel.com) and **Accessible Journeys** (✆ **800/846-4537** or 610/521-0339; www.disabilitytravel.com).

Flying with Disability (www.flying-with-disability.org) is a comprehensive information source on airplane travel.

Also check out the quarterly magazine ***Emerging Horizons*** (www.emerginghorizons.com), available by subscription ($17 year U.S.; $22 outside U.S).

The "Accessible Travel" link at **Mobility-Advisor.com** (www.mobility-advisor.com) offers a variety of travel resources to persons with disabilities.

British travelers should contact **Holiday Care** (✆ **0845-124-9971** in the U.K. only; www.holidaycare.org.uk) to access a wide range of travel information and resources for disabled and elderly people.

For more on organizations that offer resources to travelers with disabilities, go to Frommers.com.

GAY & LESBIAN TRAVELERS

Unlike Germany, Austria still has a prevailing antihomosexual attitude, in spite of the large number of gay people who live there. There is still much discrimination; gay liberation has a long way to go. Vienna, however, has a large gay community with many bars and restaurants catering to this demographic. For information about gay-related activities in Vienna, visit **Rainbow Online** at **www.gay.or.at**.

In Austria, the minimum age for consensual homosexual activity is 18.

The International Gay and Lesbian Travel Association (**IGLTA;** ✆ **954/776-2626**; www.iglta.org) is the trade association for the gay and lesbian travel industry, and offers an online directory of gay- and lesbian-friendly travel businesses; go to their website and click on "Members." In Canada, contact **Travel Gay Canada** (✆ **416/761-5151;** www.travelgaycanada.com).

For more gay and lesbian travel resources, visit Frommers.com.

SENIOR TRAVEL

Many Austrian hotels offer discounts for seniors. Mention the fact that you're a senior when you make your travel reservations.

Members of **AARP** (formerly known as the American Association of Retired Persons), 601 E St. NW, Washington, DC 20049 (✆ **888/687-2277;** www.aarp.org), get discounts on hotels, airfares, and car rentals. AARP offers members a wide range of benefits, including *AARP The Magazine* and a monthly newsletter. Anyone over 50 can join.

Many reliable agencies and organizations target the 50-plus market. **Elderhostel** (✆ **800/454-5768;** www.elderhostel.org) arranges study programs for those ages 55 and older (and a spouse or companion of any age) in the U.S. and in more than 80 countries around the world, including Austria. Most courses last 2 to 4 weeks and many include airfare, accommodations in university dormitories or modest inns, meals, and tuition.

Recommended publications offering travel resources and discounts for seniors include: the quarterly magazine ***Travel 50 & Beyond*** (www.travel50andbeyond.com); ***Travel Unlimited: Uncommon Adventures for the Mature Traveler*** (Avalon); and ***Unbelievably Good Deals and Great***

Adventures That You Absolutely Can't Get Unless You're Over 50 (McGraw-Hill), by Joann Rattner Heilman.

Frommers.com offers more information and resources on travel for seniors.

FAMILY TRAVEL

If you have enough trouble getting your kids out of the house in the morning, dragging them thousands of miles away may seem like an insurmountable challenge. But family travel can be immensely rewarding, giving you new ways of seeing the world through smaller pairs of eyes.

Austria is a great place to take your kids. The pleasures available for children (which most adults enjoy just as much) range from watching the magnificent Lipizzaner stallions at the Spanish Riding School in Vienna to exploring the country's many castles and dungeons.

Babysitting services are available through most hotel desks or by applying at the Tourist Information Office in the town where you're staying. Many hotels have children's game rooms and playgrounds.

Throughout the guide, look for our child-friendly "Kids" icons.

Recommended family travel Internet sites include **Family Travel Forum** (www.familytravelforum.com), a comprehensive site that offers customized trip planning; **Family Travel Network** (www.familytravelnetwork.com), an award-winning site that offers travel features, deals, and tips; **Traveling Internationally with Your Kids** (www.travelwithyourkids.com), a comprehensive site offering sound advice for long-distance and international travel with children; and **Family Travel Files** (www.thefamilytravelfiles.com), which offers an online magazine and a directory of off-the-beaten-path tours and tour operators for families.

For a list of more family-friendly travel resources, turn to the experts at Frommers.com.

9 SUSTAINABLE TOURISM

Sustainable tourism is conscientious travel. It means being careful with the environments you explore and respecting the communities you visit. Two overlapping components of sustainable travel are **ecotourism** and **ethical tourism.** The **International Ecotourism Society (TIES)** defines ecotourism as responsible travel to natural areas that conserves the environment and improves the well-being of local people. TIES suggests that ecotourists follow these principles:

- Minimize environmental impact.
- Build environmental and cultural awareness and respect.
- Provide positive experiences for visitors and hosts alike.
- Provide direct financial benefits for conservation and for local people.
- Raise sensitivity to host countries' political, environmental, and social climates.
- Support international human rights and labor agreements.

You can find some ecofriendly travel tips and statistics, as well as touring companies and associations—listed by destination under "Travel Choice"—at the **TIES** website, **www.ecotourism.org**. Also check out **Ecotravel.com**, which lets you search for sustainable touring companies in several categories (water-based, land-based, spiritually oriented, and so on).

While much of the focus of ecotourism is about reducing impacts on the natural environment, ethical tourism concentrates on ways to preserve and enhance local economies and communities, regardless of location. You can embrace ethical tourism by staying at a locally owned hotel or shopping at a store that employs local workers and sells locally produced goods.

It's Easy Being Green

Here are a few simple ways you can help conserve fuel and energy when you travel:

- Each time you take a flight or drive a car greenhouse gases release into the atmosphere. You can help neutralize this danger to the planet through "carbon offsetting"—paying someone to invest your money in programs that reduce your greenhouse gas emissions by the same amount you've added. Before buying carbon offset credits, just make sure that you're using a reputable company, one with a proven program that invests in renewable energy. Reliable carbon offset companies include **Carbonfund** (www.carbonfund.org), **TerraPass** (www.terrapass.org), and **Carbon Neutral** (www.carbonneutral.org).
- Whenever possible, choose nonstop flights; they generally require less fuel than indirect flights that stop and take off again. Try to fly during the day—some scientists estimate that nighttime flights are twice as harmful to the environment. And pack light—each 15 pounds of luggage on a 5,000-mile flight adds up to 50 pounds of carbon dioxide emitted.
- Where you stay during your travels can have a major environmental impact. To determine the green credentials of a property, ask about trash disposal and recycling, water conservation, and energy use; also question if sustainable materials were used in the construction of the property. The website **www.greenhotels.com** recommends green-rated member hotels around the world that fulfill the company's stringent environmental requirements. Also consult **www.environmentallyfriendlyhotels.com** for more green accommodation ratings.
- At hotels, request that your sheets and towels not be changed daily. (Many hotels already have programs like this in place.) Turn off the lights and air-conditioner (or heater) when you leave your room.
- Use public transport where possible—trains, buses, and even taxis are more energy-efficient forms of transport than driving. Even better is to walk or cycle; you'll produce zero emissions and stay fit and healthy on your travels.
- If renting a car is necessary, ask the rental agent for a hybrid, or rent the most fuel-efficient car available.
- Eat at locally owned and operated restaurants that use produce grown in the area. This contributes to the local economy and cuts down on greenhouse gas emissions by supporting restaurants where the food is not flown or trucked in across long distances.

Responsible Travel (www.responsibletravel.com) is a great source of sustainable travel ideas; the site is run by a spokesperson for ethical tourism in the travel industry. **Sustainable Travel International** (www.sustainabletravelinternational.org) promotes ethical tourism practices, and manages an extensive directory of sustainable properties and tour operators around the world.

In the U.K., **Tourism Concern** (www.tourismconcern.org.uk) works to reduce social and environmental problems connected to tourism. The **Association of Independent Tour Operators (AITO)** (www.aito.co.uk) is a group of specialist operators leading the field in making holidays sustainable.

Volunteer travel has become popular among those who want to venture beyond the standard group-tour experience to learn languages, interact with locals, and make a positive difference while on vacation. Volunteer travel usually doesn't require special skills—just a willingness to work hard—and programs vary in length from a few days to a number of weeks. Some programs provide free housing and food, but many require volunteers to pay for travel expenses, which can add up quickly. For general info on volunteer travel, visit **www.volunteerabroad.org** and **www.idealist.org**.

Before you commit to a volunteer program, it's important to make sure any money you're giving is truly going back to the local community, and that the work you'll be doing will be a good fit for you. **Volunteer International** (www.volunteerinternational.org) has a helpful list of questions to ask to determine the intentions and the nature of a volunteer program.

10 PACKAGES FOR THE INDEPENDENT TRAVELER

Before you start your search for the lowest airfare, you may want to consider booking your flight as part of a travel package. Package tours are not the same thing as escorted tours. Package tours are simply a way to buy the airfare, accommodations, and other elements of your trip (such as car rentals, airport transfers, and sometimes even activities) at the same time and often at discounted prices—kind of like one-stop shopping. Packages are sold in bulk to tour operators—who resell them to the public at a cost that usually undercuts standard rates.

One good source of package deals is the airlines themselves. Contact any of the airlines listed under "By Plane" under "Getting There," above.

British Airways' Holidays (✆ **800/AIRWAYS;** www.britishairways.com) offerings tend to incorporate the scenery and architecture of Austria with similar attractions across the border in Germany and Switzerland. BA can arrange a stopover in London en route for an additional fee, and allows extra time in Vienna or Zurich before or after any tour for no additional charge.

The airlines are good sources of package deals. Most major airlines offer air/land packages, but among airline packagers, **Lufthansa Airlines** (✆ **800/399-5838** or 01/805-83-84-26 in Germany; www.lufthansa.com) leads the way. You may also wish to try **American Airlines Vacations** (✆ **800/321-2121;** www.aavacations.com), **Delta Vacations** (✆ **800/654-6559;** www.deltavacations.com), **Continental Airlines Vacations** (✆ **800/301-3800;** www.covacations.com), and **United Vacations** (✆ **888/854-3899;** www.unitedvacations.com).

Several big **online travel agencies**—Expedia.com, Travelocity, Orbitz, Site59, and Lastminute.com—also do a brisk business in packages. If you're unsure about the pedigree of a smaller packager, check with the Better Business Bureau in the city where the company is based, or go online to **www.bbb.org**. If a packager won't tell you where it's based, don't fly with it.

Travel packages are also listed in the travel section of your local Sunday newspaper. Or check ads in national travel magazines such as *Arthur Frommer's Budget Travel Magazine, Travel & Leisure, National Geographic Traveler,* and *Condé Nast Traveler.*

11 ESCORTED GENERAL-INTEREST TOURS

Escorted tours are structured group tours with a group leader. The price usually includes everything from airfare to hotels, meals, admission costs, and local transportation.

Many people derive a sense of ease and security from escorted trips. Escorted tours—whether by bus, motorcoach, train, or boat—let travelers sit back and enjoy the trip without having to spend lots of time behind the wheel or worrying about details. You know your costs up front, and there are few surprises. Escorted tours can take you to the maximum number of sights in the minimum amount of time with the least amount of hassle—you don't have to sweat over the plotting and planning of a vacation schedule. Escorted tours are particularly convenient for people with limited mobility. They can also be a great way to meet people.

On the downside, an escorted tour often requires a big deposit up front, and lodging and dining choices are predetermined. You'll have few opportunities for serendipitous interactions with locals. The tours can be jam-packed with activities, leaving little room for individual sightseeing, whim, or adventure—plus they also often focus only on the heavily touristed sites, so you miss out on lesser-known gems.

American Express Vacations (✆ **800/335-3342;** www.americanexpressvacations.com) is one of the biggest tour operators in the world. Its offerings are comprehensive, and unescorted customized package tours are available, too.

Brendan Vacations (✆ **800/421-8446;** www.brendanvacations.com) has a selection of 8- to 16-day tours. Accommodations are at the better hotels, and rates include everything except airfare. **Collette Vacations** (✆ **800/340-5158;** www.collettevacations.com) has 14 tours that cover Austria and various other European cities. **Globus & Cosmos Tours** (✆ **800/338-7092;** www.globusandcosmos.com) offers 9- to 16-day escorted tours of various parts of Austria. It also has a budget branch that offers tours at lower rates. **Maupintour** (✆ **800/255-4266;** www.maupintour.com) has a selection of upscale tours, such as a 14-day Blue Danube Discovery Tour, which take in such cities as Vienna, Linz, Dürnstein, Melk, and Salzburg, and an unusual, upscale (and very expensive) tour operator, **Abercrombie and Kent** (✆ **800/554-7016;** www.abercrombiekent.com), known for its carriage-trade rail excursions through eastern Europe and the Swiss and Austrian Alps.

The oldest travel agency in Britain, **Cox & Kings,** 30 Millbank, London SW1P 4EE (✆ **020/7873-5000;** www.coxandkings.co.uk), specializes in unusual, if pricey, holidays. Offerings in Austria include organized tours through the country's many regions of natural beauty and tours of historic or aesthetic interest. Also available are opera tours to Salzburg and Vienna.

Other companies featuring offbeat adventure travel include **HF Holidays,** Catalyst House, 720 Centennial Ct., Elstree, Hertfordshire WD6-35Y (✆ **020/8732-1220;** www.hfholidays.co.uk). It offers a range of 1- to 2-week packages to Austria. **Sherpa Expeditions,** 131 A Heston Rd., Hounslow, Middlesex TW5 0RF (✆ **020/8577-2717;** www.sherpaexpeditions.com), offers treks through off-the-beaten-track regions of Europe, especially the Alps.

Travel packages are also listed in the travel section of your local Sunday newspaper. Or check ads in the national travel magazines such as *Arthur Frommer's Budget Travel Magazine, Travel & Leisure, National Geographic Traveler,* and *Condé Nast Traveler.*

Package tours can vary by leaps and bounds. Some offer a better class of hotels than others. Some offer the same hotels for lower prices. Some offer flights on scheduled airlines, while others book charters. Some limit your choice of accommodations and travel days. You are often required to make a large payment up front. On the plus side, packages can save you money, offering group prices but allowing for independent travel. Some even let you add on a few guided excursions or escorted day trips (also at prices lower than if you booked them yourself) without booking an entirely escorted tour.

Before you invest in a package tour, get some answers. Ask about the **accommodations choices** and prices for each. Then look up the hotels' reviews in a Frommer's guide, and check their rates online for your specific dates of travel. You'll also want to find out what **type of room** you get. If you need a certain type of room, ask for it; don't take whatever is thrown your way. Request a nonsmoking room, a quiet room, a room with a view, or whatever you fancy.

Finally, look for **hidden expenses.** Ask whether airport departure fees and taxes, for example, are included in the total cost.

12 SPECIAL INTEREST TRIPS

Austrians love sports and the outdoors and, although skiing is a national obsession, there are opportunities to participate in a variety of activities. Here we outline the best places to go and who can guide you there. You'll find specific information in each regional chapter.

BALLOONING

Hot-air ballooning over the dramatic landscapes of Austria, including alpine terrain, can be a real thrill ride. One of the best centers for this is Ballooning Vorarlberg in western Austria. The balloon specialist here is **Günter Schabus,** Bruderhof 12A, A-6833 (✆ **05523/51121;** www.ballooning.at), which features ballooning 7 days a week from April to September—weather permitting, of course—near the German and Swiss borders. The cost of ballooning is 220€ ($352) per person for one to five persons.

BIKING

Hindriks European Bicycle, P.O. Box 7010, citrus Heights, CA 95621 (✆ **800/852-3258;** fax 916/729-2181; www.hindrikstours.com), is the North American representative for a Dutch-based company that leads 10-day bicycle tours in Austria. You'll bike along well-laid-out paths and quiet country roads, which are thankfully flat and mostly downhill. The cost of this tour is 1,625€ ($2,600) per person based on double occupancy.

Backroads, 801 Cedar St., Berkeley, CA 94710 (✆ **800/GO-ACTIVE** in the U.S., or 510/527-1555; www.backroads.com), offers 6-day, 5-night trips that take you from Prague to Vienna going along the Danube. Lodging is either in castles or first-class country inns. The trip also includes most meals.

David Zwilling, David Zwilling, GmbH, Waldhof 64, A-5441 Abtenau (✆ **06243/30690;** fax 06243/306917; www.zwilling-resort.at), organizes Austria's best mountain-biking trips, as well as other adventure activities such as rafting, rock climbing, and paragliding.

FISHING

Austria is an angler's paradise, with many clear, unpolluted streams and deep rivers and lakes. You can try for trout, char, pike, sheatfish (monster catfish), and pikeperch in well-stocked mountain streams. In the right tributaries of the Danube, you might catch a huchen, a landlocked salmon that's an excellent fighter and a culinary delight, usually fished for in late fall. The Wörther See in Carinthia sometimes yields the North American big-mouth black bass, which once stocked the lake because of an accident by an owner of Velden Castle—intended for a pond on his estate, one barrel fell into the lake and burst, introducing the immigrants from America to a new happy home. The local tourist office in each province offers information about local fishing conditions and can advise you of the best local outfitters. Fishermen generally need two permits—a general license issued by the state and a private permit from the local owner of the land. You can also write for information from **Österreichischen Arbeiter-Fischerei-Vereine,** Lenaugasse 14, A-1080 Vienna (© **01/4032176;** www.fischerei.or.at).

GOLF

One of the country's most outstanding 18-hole courses is at the Murhof in Styria, near Frohnleiten; [illegible] near Innsbruck; Seefeld-Wildmoos in Seefeld, Dallach on the shores of the Wörther See in Carinthia; Enzesfeld and Wiener Neustadt-Foehrenwald in Lower Austria; and the oldest of them all, Vienna-Freudenau, founded in 1901. There are numerous 9-hole courses throughout the country. The season generally extends from April to October or November. For more information, contact **Österreichischer Golf-Verband,** Prinz Eugen-Strasse 12, A-1040 Vienna (© **01/505324519;** www.golf.at).

HIKING & MOUNTAINEERING

More than 70% of Austria's total area is covered by mountains of all shapes and sizes, and the rugged beauty of the Alps demands exploration. Walking, hiking, or mountain climbing across these hills and glaciers is an unforgettable experience. Paths and trails are marked and secured, guides and maps are readily available, and there's an outstanding system of huts to shelter you. Austria has more than 450 chairlifts or cable cars to open up the mountains for visitors.

Certain precautions are essential, foremost being to inform your innkeeper or host of your route. Also, suitable hiking or climbing shoes and protective clothing are imperative. Camping out overnight is strongly discouraged because of the rapidly changing mountain weather and the established system of keeping track of hikers and climbers in the mountains. More than 700 alpine huts—many of which are really full-service lodges with restaurants, rooms, and dormitories—are spaced about 4 to 5 hours apart so that you can make rest and lunch stops. Hikers are required to sign in and out of the huts and to give their destination before setting off. If you don't show up as planned, search parties go into action.

If you're advised that your chosen route is difficult, hire a mountain guide or get expert advice from some qualified local person before braving the unknown. Certified hiking and climbing guides are based in all Austrian mountain villages and can be found by looking for their signs or by asking at the local tourist office.

Above all, ***obey signs.*** Even in summer, if there's still snow on the ground, you could be in an area threatened by avalanches. There are other important rules to

Staying Healthy in the Mountains

For information on altitude sickness, frostbite, and snow blindness—conditions with which visitors unfamiliar with mountainous terrain should become familiarized—see p. 53.

follow for your own safety, and you can obtain these from the Austrian National Tourist Offices, bookstores, branches of various alpine clubs, or at local tourist offices in villages throughout the Alps.

For information about alpine trekking, contact **Österreichischer Alpenverein (Austrian Alpine Club),** Olympia-Strasse 37, A-6020 Innsbruck (✆ **0512/59547;** www.alpenverein.at). Membership costs 49€ ($78). Members receive 50% off of overnight stays in mountain refuges. One of the best trekking adventure companies in Austria is **Exodus,** 1311 63 St., Suite 200, Emeryville, CA 94608 (✆ www.exodus.co.uk). Run by avid naturalists and mountaineers, it offers hiking tours through Austria for moderately experienced hikers in good physical condition. Tours usually last 8 to 15 days.

The most cutting-edge sporting outfit in Austria, the kind of place that merges California cool with alpine adventure, is **David Zwilling,** Waldhof 64, A-5441 Abtenau (✆ **06243/30690;** fax 06243/306917; www.zwilling-resort.at). It organizes the best mountain-biking trips in Austria and is also the front-runner in mountain- and rock-climbing tours. This outfitter also arranges paragliding adventures over nerve-jangling cliffs and some incredible white-water rafting trips.

There are summer and winter mountaineering schools in at least 3 dozen resorts in all Austrian provinces except Burgenland, with regular courses, mountain tours, and camps for all ages.

SKIING

Austria is world renowned for its downhill skiing facilities. Across the country, some 3,500 lifts transport skiers and sightseers to the summits of approximately 20,113km (12,498 miles) of marked runs. Don't forget to look around on the way up; the view above is as amazing as the runs below.

Ski "circuses" allow skiers to move from mountain to mountain, and ski "swings" opening up opposite sides of the same mountain tie villages in different valleys into one big ski region.

Shuttle buses, usually free for those with a valid lift ticket, take you to valley points where you board funiculars, gondolas, aerial trains, or chairlifts. Higher up, you can leave the larger conveyance and continue by another chairlift or T-bar.

Because competition among ski resorts is so fierce, you'll probably find roughly equivalent prices at many resorts for 1-, 2-, and 3-day passes. For example, at the Arlberg in Tyrol, one of the most famous ski areas of Europe, a 1-day pass costs 40€ to 43€ ($64–$69). Discounts are granted for longer stays. A 6-day pass ranges from 192€ to 204€ ($307–$326) per person. Prices for skiing in other regions of Austria, such as the area around Lech and Zürs in the Vorarlberg, and the Ötzal region of the Tyrol, tend to be similar. And skiers who buy passes valid for more than 2 days are rewarded with a much wider diversity of skiing options.

The Austrian Ski School is noted for its fine instruction and practice techniques, available in many places: Arlberg; the posh villages of Zürs and Lech/Arlberg, where the rich and famous gather; the Silvretta mountains; and Hochgurgl, Obergurgl, Hochsölden, and Sölden in the Tyrolean Ötzal, to name a few. Year-round skiing is possible in the little villages of the Stubaital through use of a cableway on the Stubai glacier, more than 3,050m (10,007 ft.) above sea level. Kitzbühel is known to all top skiers in the world, while Seefeld lures the trendy.

Skiing is a family sport in Europe, and ski centers usually have bunny slopes and instruction for youngsters, plus babysitting services for very small children. Many of these areas offer more than just fine powder. The Valley of Gastein was known for its medicinal thermal springs long before it became a ski center. The people of Schladming, in the Dachstein Mountains, wore their local costumes and lodens well before the first cross-country skier discovered the high plateau surrounding the small, unspoiled village of Ramsau.

Among the most attractive large-scale skiing areas are the Radstädter Tauern region and Saalbach/Hinterglemm in Salzburg province. Here, as in most of the winter-sports areas, you can rest your tired legs by the crackling fire of a ski hut while enjoying hot spiced wine or a *Jägertee,* hot tea heavily laced with rum.

Snowboarding, whose popularity is spreading each year, is making inroads in Austria. The best outfitter is **Ski Europe** (✆ **800/333-5533** or 713/960-0900; www.ski-europe.com). They can arrange all sorts of vacations focused on skiing and snowboarding, as well as winter hiking.

Cross-country skiing is popular among those who want to quietly enjoy the winter beauty and get a great workout. Many miles of tracks are marked for this sport, and special instructors are available.

In the summer, you can give grass skiing a try. Ask the Austrian National Tourist Office for a list of resorts providing this sport, as well as for details about centers offering summer snow skiing.

For information about the best skiing in Austria, contact **Österreichischer Skiverband (Austrian Ski Federation),** Olympiastrasse 10, A-6020 Innsbruck (✆ **0512/33501;** www.oesv.at).

SPAS & HEALTH RESORTS

Austrians have long been aware of the therapeutic faculties of mineral water, thermal springs, and curative mud in their own country. More than 100 spas and health resorts are found here, including the Oberlaa Spa Center on the southern hills of Vienna. These institutions not only use the hidden resources of nature to prevent physical ailments, but they offer therapy and rehabilitation as well.

You can "take the waters" at *baden* (baths), with springs ranging from thermal brine to thermal sulfur water, some rich in iodine or iron and some rich with radon. (Many hot-water springs in Europe contain trace amounts of radon, which is not harmful in the doses that doctors prescribe.) Users of these facilities have found them an effective treatment for digestive troubles, rheumatism, cardiac and circulatory diseases, and gynecological and neurological ills, to name just a few.

Information about these spas and treatments is available from **Österreichischer Hellbäder-und Kuroteverband,** Josefsplatz 6, A-1010 Vienna (✆ **01/5121904**). Ask for a copy of the brochure "Nature the Healer: Spas and Health Resorts in Austria." You can also learn about "Kneipp Cures," a method developed in the 19th century as a restorative treatment and still hailed as "a magic formula in the world of natural medicine." This cure, popular among seniors with limited circulation, involves simple stretching exercises and moderate amounts of low-impact aerobics. The exercise session is then followed by immersing the feet in icy, nonsulfurous water.

WATERSPORTS

Austria has no seacoast, but from Bodensee (Lake Constance) in the west to Neusiedl See (Lake Neusiedl) in the east, the country is rich in lakes and boasts some 150 rivers and streams.

Swimming is, of course, possible year-round if you want to use an indoor pool or swim at one of the many health clubs in winter. Swimming facilities have been developed at summer resorts, especially those on the warm waters of Carinthia, where you can swim from May to October, and in the Salzkammergut lake district, between Upper Austria and Land Salzburg.

The beauty of Austria underwater is attested to by those who have tried diving in the lakes. Most outstanding are the diving and underwater exploration possibilities in the Salzkammergut lake district and in the Weissen See in Carinthia. You can receive instruction and obtain necessary equipment at both places.

If you prefer to remain on the surface, you can go sailing, windsurfing, or canoeing on the lakes and rivers.

The sailing (yachting) season lasts from May to October, with activity centered on the Attersee in the Salzkammergut lake district, on Lake Constance out of Bregenz, and on Lake Neusiedl, a large shallow lake in the east. Winds on the Austrian lakes can be treacherous, but a warning system and rescue services are alert. For information on sailing, contact **Österreichischer Segel-Verband,** Seestrasse 17b, A-7100 Neusiedl am See (✆ **02/167402430;** www.segelverband.at).

Most resorts on lakes or rivers where windsurfing can be safely enjoyed have equipment and instruction available. This sport is increasing in popularity and has been added to the curriculum of several sailing schools, especially in the area of the Wörther See in Carinthia.

If you're interested in riding the rapids of a swift mountain stream or just paddling around on a placid lake, don't miss the chance to go canoeing in Austria. You can canoe down slow-flowing lowland rivers such as the Inn or Mur, or tackle the wild waters of glacier-fed mountain streams suitable only for experts. Special schools for fast-water paddling operate May through September in the village of Klaus on the Steyr River in Upper Austria, in Opponitz in Lower Austria on the Ybbs River, and in Abtenau in Salzburg province.

13 STAYING CONNECTED

TELEPHONE

The country code for Austria is 43. To call Germany from the United States, dial the international access code 011, then 43, then the city code, then the regular phone number. ***Note:*** The phone numbers listed in this book are to be used within Austria; when calling from abroad, omit the initial 0 in the city code.

For directory assistance: Dial ✆ **1611** if you're looking for a number inside Austria, and dial ✆ **1613** for numbers to all other countries.

For operator assistance: If you need operator assistance in making a call, dial ✆ **0180/200-1033.**

Local and long-distance calls may be placed from all post offices and from most public telephone booths, about half of which operate with phone cards, the others with coins. Phone cards are sold at post offices and newsstands in denominations of 6€ to 25€ ($9.60–$40). Rates are measured in units rather than minutes. The farther the distance, the more units are consumed. Telephone calls made through hotel switchboards can double, or even quadruple, the base charges at the post office, so be alert to this before you dial. In some instances, post offices can send faxes for you; and many hotels offer Internet access, for free or for a small charge, to their guests.

Austrian phone numbers are not standard. In some places, numbers have as few as three digits. In cities, one number may have five digits, whereas the phone next door might have nine. Austrians also often hyphenate their numbers differently. But since all the area codes are the same, these various configurations should have little effect on your phone usage once you get used to the fact that numbers vary from place to place.

Be careful dialing **toll-free numbers.** Many companies maintain a service line beginning with 0180. However, these lines might appear to be toll free but really aren't, costing .12€ (19¢) per minute. Other numbers that begin with 0190 carry a surcharge of 1.85€ ($3) or more per minute. Don't be misled by calling a 1-800 number in the United States from Austria. This is not a toll-free call but costs about the same as an overseas call.

To call the U.S. or Canada from Austria, dial 01, followed by the country code (1), then the area code, and then the number. Alternatively, you can dial the various telecommunication companies in the States for cheaper rates. From Austria, the access number for **AT&T** is ✆ **0800/8880010,** for **MCI** ✆ **0800/8888000. USA Direct** can be used with all telephone cards and for collect calls. The number from Austria is ✆ **013/00010. Canada Direct** can be used with Bell Telephone Cards and for collect calls. This number from Austria is ✆ **013/00014.**

If you're calling from a public pay phone in Austria, you must deposit the basic local rate.

Toll-free numbers: Numbers beginning with 00 and followed by 00 are toll-free. But be careful. Numbers that begin with 08 followed by 36 carry a .35€ (55¢) surcharge per minute.

CELLPHONES

The three letters that define much of the world's wireless capabilities are GSM (Global System for Mobiles), a big, seamless network that makes for easy cross-border cellphone use. In general reception is good. But you'll need a SIM (Subscriber Identity Module) card. This is a small chip that gives you a local phone number and plugs you into a regional network. In the U.S., T-Mobile, AT&T Wireless, and Cingular use this quasi-universal system; in Canada, Microcell and some Rogers customers are GSM; and all Europeans and most Australians use GSM. Unfortunately, per-minute charges can be high—usually $1 to $1.50 in western Europe.

For many, **renting** a phone is a good idea. While you can rent a phone from any number of overseas sites, including kiosks at airports and at car-rental agencies, we suggest renting the phone before you leave home. North Americans can rent one before leaving home from **InTouch USA** (✆ **800/872-7626** or 703/222-7161; www.intouchglobal.com) or **RoadPost** (✆ **888/290-1616** or 905/272-5665; www.roadpost.com). InTouch will also, for free, advise you on whether your existing phone will work overseas.

Buying a phone can be economically attractive, as many nations have cheap prepaid phone systems. Once you arrive at your destination, stop by a local cellphone shop and get the cheapest package; you'll probably pay less than $100 for a phone and a starter calling card. Local calls may be as low as 10¢ per minute, and in many countries incoming calls are free.

INTERNET & E-MAIL

With Your Own Computer

More and more hotels, cafes, and retailers are offering free Wi-Fi (wireless fidelity) "hot spots." **T-Mobile Hotspot** (www.t-mobile.com/hotspot or www.t-mobile.co.uk) serves up wireless connections at coffee shops nationwide. **Boingo** (www.boingo.com) and **Wayport** (www.wayport.com) have set up networks in airports and high-class hotel lobbies. iPass providers (see below) also give you access to a few hundred wireless hotel lobby setups. To locate other hot spots that provide **free wireless networks** in cities in Austria, go to **www.jiwire.com**.

For dial-up access, most business-class hotels offer dataports for laptop modems, and a few thousand hotels in Austria now offer free high-speed Internet access. In addition, major Internet service providers (ISPs) have **local access numbers** around the world, allowing you to go online by placing a local call. The **iPass** network also has dial-up numbers around the world. You'll have to sign up with an iPass provider, who will then tell you how to set up your computer for your destination(s). For a list of iPass providers, go to www.ipass.com and click on "Individuals Buy Now." One solid provider is **i2roam** (✆ **866/811-6209** or 920/233-5863; www.i2roam.com).

Wherever you go, bring a **connection kit** of the right power and phone adapters, a spare phone cord, and a spare Ethernet network cable—or find out whether your hotel supplies them to guests.

Without Your Own Computer

To find cybercafes check **www.cybercaptive.com** and **www.cybercafe.com**. Cybercafes are found in all large Austrian cities, especially Vienna and Salzburg. They do not tend to cluster in any particular neighborhoods, but can be found on almost every business street in large cities.

Aside from formal cybercafes, most **youth hostels** and **public libraries** have Internet access. Avoid **hotel business centers** unless you're willing to pay exorbitant rates.

Most major airports now have **Internet kiosks** scattered throughout their gates. These give you basic Web access for a per-minute fee that's usually higher than cybercafe prices.

14 TIPS ON ACCOMMODATIONS

Austrian hotels, inns, and pensions (boardinghouses) are classified by the government into five different categories and are rated with stars. A five-star rating is deluxe, while one star designates a simple inn or hotel; there's a chance that not all rooms have private bathrooms. One-star hotels are most often clean and decent establishments where you get more value for your euro than anywhere else in the country.

Reservations are advised, especially if you're visiting in high season, which varies in different parts of the country. Summer is high season in Salzburg and Vienna, while Innsbruck enjoys a great deal of summer tourist business but is also the center of the bustling Tyrolean ski industry in winter. High season at ski resorts is usually from Christmas to mid-April; most resorts actually lower their prices in summer. Sometimes hotels offer a "shoulder" rate in spring and fall when business lessens; sometimes these hotels close if business is slow.

The local tourist office in any Austrian city or resort can assist you in making the necessary reservations. If a certain hotel is booked and cannot accept your reservation, the tourist office will be able to make an alternative reservation in a hotel of comparable price and character. Send your request via airmail and enclose an International Reply Coupon, obtainable at your local post office, for an airmail reply. Be sure to give the following information: hotel category (deluxe, first class, standard, or budget), desired location (center, edge of town, near a lake or ski lifts). Address your request to *Verkehrsverein* in small towns or *Tourismusverband* in large resorts and cities, adding the postal code, the town name, and *Austria.* Regional service organizations are your best bet if you want to visit several towns or resorts in one Austrian province or one of Austria's major cities. These addresses are available from the Austrian National Tourist Office abroad.

BED & BREAKFASTS

Look for the signs that say ZIMMER FREI attached to the front of a house or to a short post at the front-yard gate or driveway. This means that the proprietors rent rooms on a bed-and-breakfast basis to travelers. You'll encounter these signs along Austria's highways and along some of the most scenic byways.

Such accommodations have hot and cold running water in the bedrooms, although private bathroom and toilet facilities are rare. (There's usually a toilet on every floor and one bathroom in the house.) A continental breakfast is served.

Few homes accept advance reservations, so just stop in and inquire. When the rooms are filled, the sign is taken down or covered. The local tourist office can also help you find B&B accommodations.

You might need a few words of basic German to converse with the owner, as only a few proprietors speak English. If you're staying for only 1 night, you might be asked to pay your bill in advance, and it must be paid in euros.

FARMHOUSE ACCOMMODATIONS

Groups or whole families can stay on a farm, renting several rooms or even a wing of the house. However, a stay of at least a week is generally required, and advance reservations through a local tourist office or regional tourist board are necessary. The correct form of address for the local offices is *Verkehrsverein,* then the postal code and the name of the town near which you want to stay, and *Austria.* Regional boards should be addressed by writing to *Landesfremdenverkehrsamt,* followed by the postal code and the name of the capital of the respective Austrian province, and *Austria.* Your reservation will be confirmed upon receipt of a deposit.

SCHLOSSHOTELS (CASTLE HOTELS)

Graced with a rich and ornate imperial tradition, Austria poured funds and resources throughout its history into constructing palaces and castles. Many of these ancestral buildings have been transformed into hotels. Information on these hotels can be obtained through **Euro-Connection,** 7500 212th St. SW, Suite 103, Edmonds, WA 98026 (✆ **800/645-3876;** www.euro-connection.com), which represents castle hotels throughout Europe.

CHALETS, VILLAS & APARTMENTS

Many cottages, chalets, and condominiums are available for short-term rentals to qualified visitors. These rental properties are usually at or near sites of natural or historic beauty or in ski or lakeside resorts.

Pego Leasing Centre, Rathausgasse 11, A-6700 Bludenz (✆ **05552/65666;** www.pego.at), inventories more than 1,000 rental properties in Austria. The company arranges rentals of 1 week to a year or more for 1 to 30 occupants at a time; rentals traditionally begin and end on a Saturday. Pego usually collects most of its fee from the owners of the rental property, but the tenant usually pays an agency fee to Pego of around 10% for each booking.

PENSIONS

A pension is generally more intimate and personal than a hotel. Of course, the nature and quality of the welcome depends largely on the host or hostess, who might also be the cook and chief maid. As a general rule, a first-class pension in Austria is equal to a second-class hotel; a second-class pension is equal to a third-class hotel. Usually a continental breakfast is served; some pensions also offer dinner. Expect to be on your own for lunch.

HOME EXCHANGES

You can arrange a home exchange—swapping your home with that of an Austrian family, often with a car included—through several U.S.-based organizations. **Intervac U.S. & International,** P.O. Box 590504, San Francisco, CA 94159 (© **800/756-home;** www.intervacus.com), publishes three catalogs a year containing listings of more than 9,000 homes in more than 36 countries. Members contact each other directly. Depending on your type of membership, fees begin at 59€ ($94).

YOUTH HOSTELS

Austria has 108 youth hostels distributed throughout the provinces. Rates for a bed-and-breakfast run from 15€ ($24) per person daily. Some hostels lock their doors between 10pm and 6am to discourage late arrivals. Dormitories must be empty between 10am and 5pm. You must have an International Youth Hostel Federation membership card to use Austria's youth hostels, and advance reservations are recommended. In Austria, you can get information about hostels from any branch of the Austrian National Tourist Office. A detailed brochure is available. For information on finding a hostel worldwide, visit **www.hostels.com**.

4

Suggested Austrian Itineraries

A "lean-and-mean" schedule is called for if you want to experience the best of Austria in a relatively small amount of time. An alpine country, Austria is small, but because of its mountains and back country roads—and most definitely winter driving conditions—getting around and seeing everything can be time consuming. All the major cities are linked by express highways known as *autobahns,* but you don't see Austria from these arteries. If you're a time-pressed traveler, as many of us are, you'll find the 1- or 2-week itineraries helpful in getting you around quickly to the highlights. Use the following itinerary to make the most out of a week in Austria, but feel free to drop a place or two to save a day to relax. One week provides just barely enough time to see the highlights of Austria. There are those who will argue that the glory of Austria lies in its mountain scenery and small villages. That is true to some extent. But if you're skimming the highlights, Austria has two of the most historic attractions in Europe, the imperial cities of **Vienna** and **Salzburg,** which are treasure troves that few first-time visitors would want to miss.

As a third contender, the Tyrolean capital of alpine **Innsbruck** is a potent lure. This trip takes in all those three cities, but allows some time for drives along the **Danube** and an invasion of the **Salzkammergut,** the famous lake district around Salzburg where that classic, *The Sound of Music,* was filmed.

1 THE REGIONS IN BRIEF

The forests, mountains, and lowlands of the Austrian landscape were divided early in their history into nine distinctly different regions (see the map on the inside back cover of this guide). In addition to their topographical diversities, each region has its own history, cultural identity, and—in some cases—oddities of language and dialect.

VIENNA

Austria's capital, the former hub of a great empire, and a [illegible] in its own right, Vienna is one of Europe's most beautiful cities. Images spring to mind of imperial palaces, the angelic voices of choirboys, the Spanish Riding School, and rich cakes served in cafes. In this former seat of the once-powerful Hapsburg dynasty, you follow in the footsteps of Schubert, Strauss, Brahms, Mahler, Mozart, and Beethoven, among others. Of course, the Blue Danube (even if it's not blue) cuts through the city that controlled a great deal of Europe for more than 6 centuries until it suffered humiliating defeats in both world wars of the 20th century. After a long, dreary slumber during the postwar years, Vienna has regained its old *joie de vivre* and is now one of Europe's most vital capitals. Today, this economic power stands at the crossroads of eastern and western Europe.

LOWER AUSTRIA

Set at Austria's northeastern corner, bordering the Czech Republic and Slovakia, this is Austria's largest province. Known for its fertile plains, renowned vineyards, and prosperous bourgeoisie, it's very different from the alpine regions of western Austria. Although the region's administrative capital is the culturally ambitious city of **Sankt Pölten,** most of the region directs its focus toward Vienna, which it completely surrounds. Visitors to Lower Austria typically come on a day trip from Vienna to explore the **Wienerwald (Vienna Woods),** romanticized in operetta, literature, and the famous Strauss waltz. One of the best places to explore the Vienna Woods is **Klosterneuburg,** a major wine-producing center. Other places to explore include **Mayerling,** in the heart of the woods, and **Heiligenkreuz,** one of Austria's oldest Cistercian abbeys. The district's leading spa is **Baden bei Wien,** a lively casino town in the eastern sector of the Vienna Woods.

The other major attraction of Lower Austria is the **Wachau–Danube Valley,** rich in scenic splendor and castles. In the valley, you can visit the ancient town of **Tulln,** the early-12th-century **Herzogenburg Monastery,** the 1,000-year-old city of **Krems,** and the lovely town of **Dürnstein. Melk Abbey** is one of the world's finest baroque buildings.

BURGENLAND

The newest of the Austrian provinces was formed in 1921 from the German-speaking region of what had once been part of the Hungarian half of Austria-Hungary. Located at Austria's southeastern tip, its plains, reef-fringed lakes, and abundant bird life resemble the landscapes of Hungary. Its capital is **Eisenstadt,** the native city of composer Franz Josef Haydn. Largely agricultural, with an unusual demographic mixture of Hungarians, Croats, and German-speaking Austrians, Burgenland lacks the visual drama and grand alpine scenery of other parts of Austria. Lakes remain its primary attraction, and they are best visited in summer.

SALZBURG

A city rich with the splendors of the baroque age and the melodies of Mozart, Salzburg is one of Europe's premier architectural gems. It's also the setting for Austria's most prestigious music festival. Its natural setting is panoramic—hugging both banks of the Salzach River and "pinched" between two mountains, Mönchsberg and Kapuzinerberg.

Many travelers come here to follow in the footsteps of Julie Andrews in the fabled 1965 musical *The Sound of Music.* The von Trapps and Mozart have put Salzburg on international tourist maps.

LAND SALZBURG

The only area of Austria that can compare with Tyrol in outdoor activities and scenic grandeur alike is Land Salzburg, which lies at the doorstep of Salzburg. It's easy to spend weeks in this mountainous area. In summer, the greatest attraction is the **Grossglockner Road,** Europe's longest and most splendid highway. In winter, **Zell am See** is the most popular resort in the region, located on a lake against a mountain backdrop, but there are many other options to consider. **Golling,** in the Salzach Valley, south of Salzburg, is one of the most inviting. Visitors frequently visit the winter and summer spa resorts of **Badgastein** and **Bad Hofgastein** in the Gastein Valley. Two major ski resorts are **Saalbach** and **Hinterglemm.**

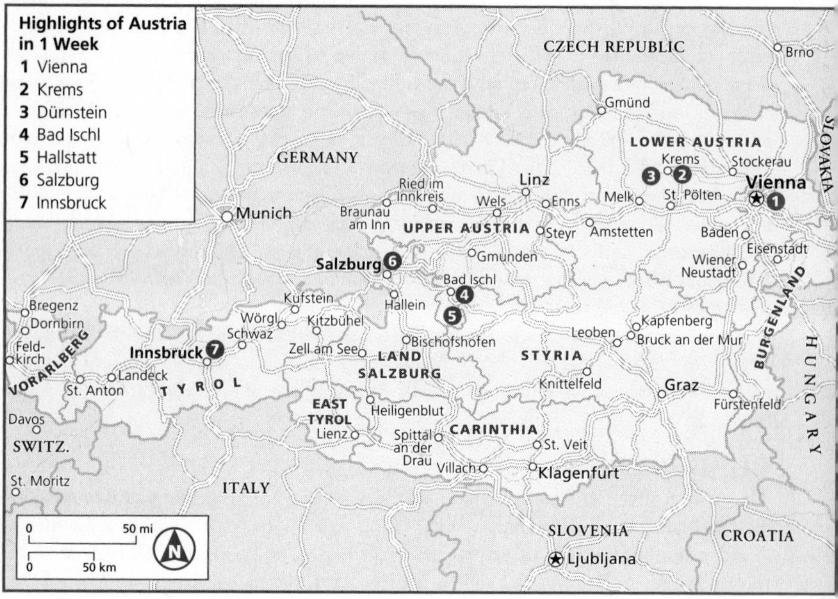
Highlights of Austria in 1 Week
1 Vienna
2 Krems
3 Dürnstein
4 Bad Ischl
5 Hallstatt
6 Salzburg
7 Innsbruck
CZECH REPUBLIC
Brno
Gmünd
LOWER AUSTRIA
SLOVAKIA
GERMANY
Krems
Stockerau
Vienna
Linz
Ried im Innkreis
Wels
Enns
Melk
St. Pölten
Munich
Braunau am Inn
UPPER AUSTRIA
Steyr
Amstetten
Baden
Eisenstadt
Salzburg
Gmunden
Wiener Neustadt
BURGENLAND
Bad Ischl
Hallein
Kufstein
Bregenz
Dornbirn
Wörgl
Kitzbühel
Kapfenberg
Schwaz
Leoben
Bruck an der Mur
Feld-kirch
Innsbruck
Zell am See
Bischofshofen
LAND SALZBURG
STYRIA
HUNGARY
VORARLBERG
Landeck
St. Anton
TYROL
Knittelfeld
Graz
Fürstenfeld
EAST TYROL
Heiligenblut
Davos
Lienz
Spittal an der Drau
CARINTHIA
St. Veit
SWITZ.
Villach
Klagenfurt
St. Moritz
ITALY
0 50 mi
0 50 km
N
SLOVENIA
CROATIA
Ljubljana

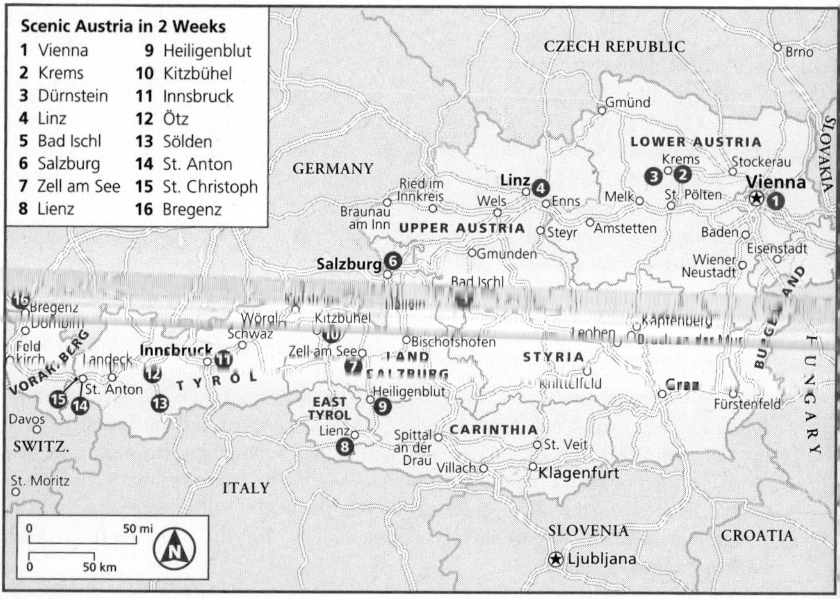
Scenic Austria in 2 Weeks
1 Vienna
2 Krems
3 Dürnstein
4 Linz
5 Bad Ischl
6 Salzburg
7 Zell am See
8 Lienz
9 Heiligenblut
10 Kitzbühel
11 Innsbruck
12 Ötz
13 Sölden
14 St. Anton
15 St. Christoph
16 Bregenz
CZECH REPUBLIC
Brno
Gmünd
LOWER AUSTRIA
SLOVAKIA
GERMANY
Krems
Stockerau
Vienna
Linz
Ried im Innkreis
Wels
Enns
Melk
St. Pölten
Braunau am Inn
UPPER AUSTRIA
Steyr
Amstetten
Baden
Eisenstadt
Salzburg
Gmunden
Wiener Neustadt
Wörgl
Kitzbühel
Schwaz
Bischofshofen
Innsbruck
Zell am See
STYRIA
St. Anton
Heiligenblut
Fürstenfeld
EAST TYROL
Davos
Lienz
Spittal an der Drau
CARINTHIA
St. Veit
SWITZ.
Villach
Klagenfurt
St. Moritz
ITALY
0 50 mi
0 50 km
N
SLOVENIA
CROATIA
Ljubljana

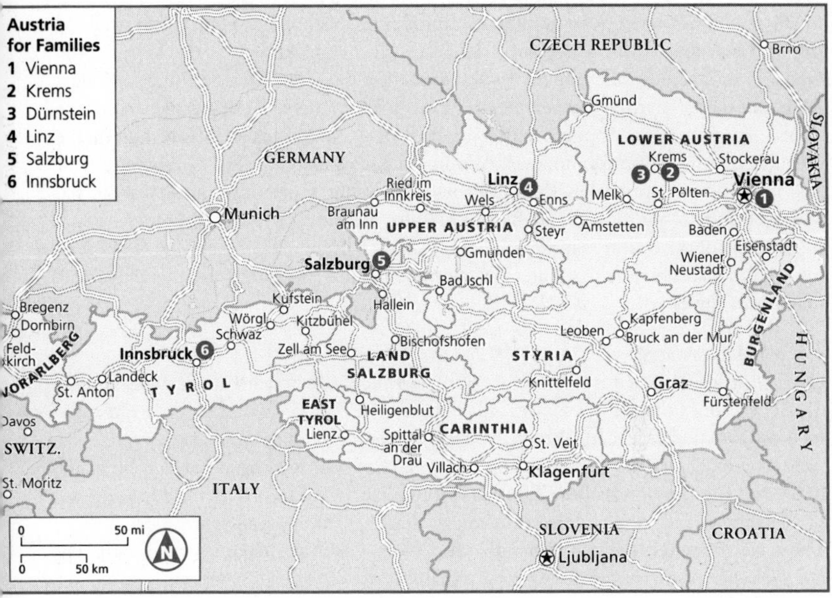
Austria
for Families
1 Vienna
2 Krems
3 Dürnstein
4 Linz
5 Salzburg
6 Innsbruck
CZECH REPUBLIC
GERMANY
LOWER AUSTRIA
UPPER AUSTRIA
SLOVAKIA
HUNGARY
BURGENLAND
STYRIA
LAND SALZBURG
TYROL
VORARLBERG
EAST TYROL
CARINTHIA
SWITZ.
ITALY
SLOVENIA
CROATIA
Brno
Gmünd
Krems
Stockerau
Vienna
Linz
Ried im Innkreis
Wels
Enns
Melk
St. Pölten
Braunau am Inn
Munich
Steyr
Amstetten
Baden
Eisenstadt
Gmunden
Salzburg
Wiener Neustadt
Bad Ischl
Kufstein
Hallein
Bregenz
Dornbirn
Wörgl
Kitzbühel
Kapfenberg
Leoben
Bruck an der Mur
Schwaz
Bischofshofen
Feld-kirch
Innsbruck
Zell am See
Landeck
St. Anton
Knittelfeld
Graz
Fürstenfeld
Heiligenblut
Davos
Lienz
Spittal an der Drau
St. Veit
Villach
Klagenfurt
St. Moritz
Ljubljana
0 50 mi
0 50 km
N

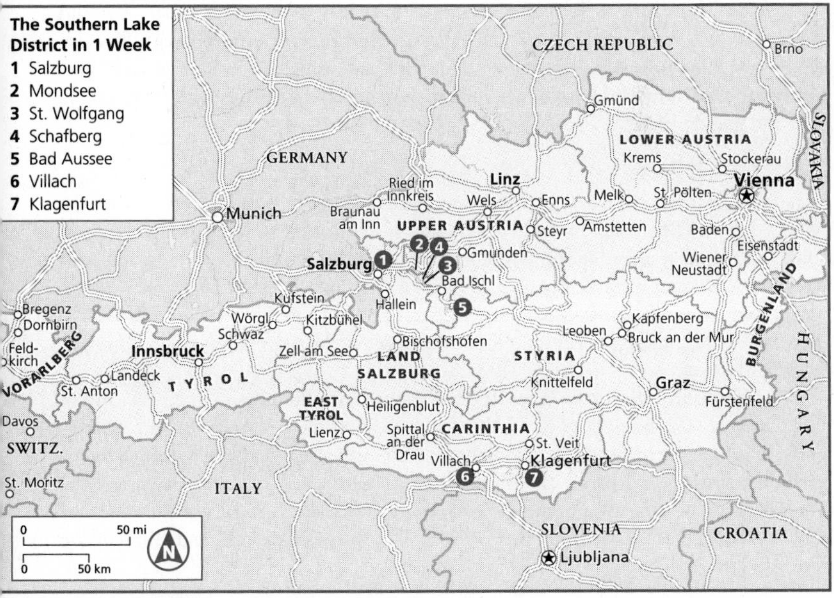
The Southern Lake
District in 1 Week
1 Salzburg
2 Mondsee
3 St. Wolfgang
4 Schafberg
5 Bad Aussee
6 Villach
7 Klagenfurt
CZECH REPUBLIC
GERMANY
LOWER AUSTRIA
UPPER AUSTRIA
SLOVAKIA
HUNGARY
BURGENLAND
STYRIA
LAND SALZBURG
TYROL
VORARLBERG
EAST TYROL
CARINTHIA
SWITZ.
ITALY
SLOVENIA
CROATIA
Brno
Gmünd
Krems
Stockerau
Vienna
Linz
Ried im Innkreis
Wels
Enns
Melk
St. Pölten
Braunau am Inn
Munich
Steyr
Amstetten
Baden
Eisenstadt
Gmunden
Salzburg
Wiener Neustadt
Bad Ischl
Kufstein
Hallein
Bregenz
Dornbirn
Wörgl
Kitzbühel
Kapfenberg
Leoben
Bruck an der Mur
Schwaz
Bischofshofen
Feld-kirch
Innsbruck
Zell am See
Landeck
St. Anton
Knittelfeld
Graz
Fürstenfeld
Heiligenblut
Davos
Lienz
Spittal an der Drau
St. Veit
Villach
Klagenfurt
St. Moritz
Ljubljana
0 50 mi
0 50 km
N

UPPER AUSTRIA

Tied to the Danube's fertile plains, which straddle that famous river, this region produces much of Austria's agricultural bounty. Its capital is the historic but heavily industrialized city of **Linz,** famous for a raspberry-chocolate concoction known as the Linzer torte. Upper Austria doesn't offer the resorts and attractions of Tyrol, Land Salzburg, or Vorarlberg, but there's charming scenery here, especially in summer at **Attersee,** the largest lake in the Austrian Alps. Another major summer resort is **Mondsee (Moon Lake),** the warmest lake in the Salzkammergut. Also in the Salzkammergut, **St. Wolfgang,** one of Austria's most romantic lakes, draws visitors to its White Horse Inn, the setting for the fabled operetta of the same name. **Bad Ischl,** once the summer retreat of Emperor Franz Josef, is one of the country's most fashionable spas. Hallstatt is the best center for exploring the province's major attractions: the salt mines of **Salt Mountain** and the spectacular **Dachstein Caves.**

TYROL

One of Austria's most historic and colorful provinces, this breathtaking mountainous district was once the medieval crossroads between the Teutonic world and Italy. Its capital is the beautiful city of **Innsbruck,** both a summer resort and a winter ski center. Filled with attractions, it's the third-most important city to visit in Austria (after Vienna and Salzburg). But the glories of the Tyrolean country hardly end in Innsbruck. The province is riddled with valleys, each filled with resorts drawing summer and winter visitors alike. These valleys include the beautiful Stubai and Wipp, where the major resorts of **Fulpmes** and **Neustift** offer vistas of glacier tops and alpine peaks.

The **Upper Inn district** is also worth a visit. The old market town of **Imst** makes a good stop along the Upper Inn. On the eastern side of the Arlberg are the resorts of **St. Anton am Arlberg,** an old village on the Arlberg Pass, and **St. Christoph,** the mountain way station of St. Anton. **Seefeld** is also a great ski resort, offering both summer and winter outdoor activities. In the Ziller Valley is another sophisticated resort, **Zell am Ziller.** The **Kitzbühel Alps** offer some of Austria's best skiing. If you have enough time, journey to **East Tyrol** to **Lienz,** a rich, folkloric town on the Isel River with romantic old inns and guesthouses.

VORARLBERG

Vorarlberg, located at the country's westernmost tip, shares most of its borders with the wild and mountainous eastern border of Switzerland; it's home to some of Austria's most sophisticated ski resorts, highest alpine peaks, and most beautiful scenery. Its capital is **Bregenz,** a pleasant town at any time of the year, although it hardly competes with the scenic grandeur of the province's resorts, such as **Lech** and **Zürs.** In winter, Lech and the even more chic and elegant Zürs, on the western side of the Arlberg, are among Europe's leading ski resorts.

The **Montafon Valley,** known for its powdery snow and sun, has been called a winter "ski stadium." The best places for skiing here are the hamlets of **Schruns** and **Tschagguns.** If you're here in summer, you might want to explore the **Bregenz Forest (Bregenzerwald),** although it's hardly the Black Forest in Germany. The northern part of the Vorarlberg alpine range is a prime place for outdoor activities. You'll want to dine and stay at **Bezau.** If you have time, the towns of **Dornbirn, Feldkirch,** and **Bludenz** are interesting to explore.

CARINTHIA

Noted for its forests, rolling hills, and hundreds of freshwater lakes, Carinthia shares most of its border with Slovenia. Although landlocked, the province has just a hint of Mediterranean flavor, which permeates its gardens, lakeside resorts, and the verdant capital city, **Klagenfurt.** Outside the capital is the striking hilltop **Hochosterwitz Castle.** The province's biggest alpine lake is **Wörther See,** where you can stay at the idyllic summer resorts of **Krumpendorf** or **Pörtschach.** The sophisticated resort of **Velden,** at the western end of Wörther See, is called the heart of the "Austrian Riviera." In the center of the lake district, **Villach,** with its nearby warm springs, is another major destination.

STYRIA

One of the most heavily forested of the Austrian provinces, Styria has landscapes that rise from lush valleys to towering alpine peaks. With a strong medieval tradition, this area originated the loden-colored jackets and felt hats with feathers that many newcomers assume are the Austrian national costume. The district's capital is **Graz,** boasting one of the best-preserved medieval cores of any Austrian city. You'll also want to visit **Bad Gleichenberg,** the province's most important summer spa, and **Mariazell,** a major pilgrimage site because of its Mariazell Basilica. Another spa, **Bad Aussee,** is in the "green heart" of the Salzkammergut, in an extremely beautiful part of Austria. You'll find the area's best skiing in the **Dachstein-Tauern,** where you can stay at the twin resorts of **Schladming** and **Rohrmoos.**

2 THE HIGHLIGHTS OF AUSTRIA IN 1 WEEK

Days 1 & 2: Vienna ★★★: Gateway to Austria

Most motor trips of Austria begin in Vienna, unless you're driving in from the west—say, after a visit to Switzerland. If so, you can use Innsbruck as your gateway and take this highlight tour in reverse.

Most visitors take a flight into Austria that puts them in Vienna on **Day 1.** Check into your hotel and enjoy an old-fashioned Austrian breakfast, including some of the fabled Viennese pastries. You might get a good enough "tuck in" that you'll skip lunch.

It would take a few weeks to see all of Vienna's major sights, but you can skim the highlights in just 2 days by concentrating on **St. Stephan's Cathedral** (p. 145) in the heart of the Inner City (Old Town). Climb its south tower for the most panoramic view. Later that morning, visit the once imperial **Schönbrunn Palace** (p. 151), summer seat of the Hapsburgs. In the afternoon call on the **Hofburg** (p. 138), visiting its major attractions such as the **Kunsthistorisches.** In the evening take your choice: an opera or a night spent in a raucous Viennese wine tavern.

On **Day 2,** take in the glories of the **MuseumsQuartier Complex** (p. 144), paying particular attention to the **Leopold Museum** and the **Kunsthalle Wien.** Attend a performance of the **Vienna Boys' Choir** (p. 139). Try for an afternoon visit to the **Belvedere Palace** (p. 150) and its fine art galleries. For a typically Viennese experience, spend your final night at one of the wine taverns on the outskirts of the city. They are called *heurigen,* and some of the best of these taverns are found in the suburb of **Grinzing.** Our *heurigen* recommendations begin on p. 180.

Day 3: The Danube River ★★★

On **Day 3,** head to Salzburg in the car you rented in Vienna. If you only have a day or two, you can hop to Salzburg on the Autobahn, but you'd miss out on so much. We suggest a 2-day leisurely journey with stops in the Danube Valley and in the lake district of Salzkammergut.

Instead of the Autobahn, take Route 3, called the "Austrian Romantic Road," west from Vienna. On the north of the river you can follow this lovely old road into **Krems** (p. 198), the most rewarding stopover in the Danube Valley, with its old churches, ancient houses, and cobblestone streets. The location is 80km (50 miles) west of Vienna. You can use Krems as a base and set out on two side trips; first to the old wine town of **Dürnstein,** 8km (5 miles) west of Krems. The town still preserves part of its once fortified walls. From Dürnstein, follow Route 33 along the south bank of the Danube to **Melk Abbey** (p. 203), the greatest baroque abbey of Austria. The distance is 31km (19 miles). You can double back along the road leading northeast into Krems for the night, or you can also select Dürnstein for an overnight stay, as it has even better and more romantic hotels than Krems.

Day ❹: Salzkammergut ★★★: Salzburg's Lake District

On the morning of **Day 4,** leave Krems and drive south to the Autobahn (E60) that runs west to Salzburg. At the junction with Route 145, head south into Bad Ischl, your best base for touring the Salzkammergut. The driving distance between Krems and Bad Ischl is [illegible]km (139 miles).

Check into a hotel in the fashionable spa of Bad Ischl and stroll its Esplanade, where former guests such as the Emperor Franz Josef used to walk. You can see the **Kaiservilla** (p. 325) where the emperor lived for 60 summers. If time remains, you can also check out **Villa Léhar** (p. 326) where Franz Léhar lived in 1912.

After lunch, drive down to **Hallstatt,** 19km (12 miles) south of Bad Ischl, where you'll discover one of the most beautiful villages in Austria. It stands on a narrow lake, the Hallstättersee, and requires about 2 hours to see. Northwest of Hallstatt you can visit the **Salzwelten/Hallstatt Salt Mines** (p. 328), one of the most distinctive geological formations in the district. Return to Bad Ischl for the night.

Day ❺ & ❻ Salzburg ★★★: Birthplace of Mozart

On the morning of **Day 5,** leave Bad Ischl following Route 158 west into Salzburg, a distance of 56km (35 miles) and our base for the next two nights. After checking into a hotel, set about exploring the second-most fascinating city (after Vienna) in Austria.

Sit at a cafe on the **Mozartplatz** for a coffee and a pastry before taking the funicular to the **Hohensalzburg Fortress** (p. 250) for a tour. After lunch, you can see **Mozart's birthplace** (p. 252) on Getreidegasse. Allow time in the afternoon for a visit to the **Residenzgalerie** (p. 251), the opulent palace and former seat of the ruling Salzburg prince-archbishops. If the **Salzburg Festival** is taking place at the time of your visit, plan to attend some cultural offerings—certainly Mozart's music—in the evening.

On **Day 6,** set out to see the sights you missed the day before, including the **Dom** or cathedral (p. 252) and **Stiftskirche St. Peter** (p. 254), as well as **Petersfriedhof** (p. 250), the cemetery of St. Peter's. Wander through the **Mirabell Gardens** (p. 257), and spend at least 2 or 3 hours in the **Altstadt** (p. 220), the Old Town, where you can shop till you drop and take in the antique buildings.

Day ❼: Innsbruck ★★★: Capital of Tyrol

On the morning of **Day 7,** leave Salzburg and drive 190km (118 miles) southwest to the "third tourist city" of Austria, Innsbruck, arriving in time for lunch. Check into a hotel for your final night. Set out on foot to explore the **Altstadt** (Old Town) for at least 2 hours, and stroll **Maria-Theresien-Strasse,** the main street. You can also see the **Golden Roof** (Goldenes Dachl), the city's major attraction (p. 346).

In the afternoon, visit **Hofkirche** (p. 347). If time remains, take in the exhibits of the **Tiroler Volkskunst Museum** (p. 348).

After Innsbruck, the glories of the Tyrol, the richest province of Austria for scenery, await you. See chapter 11 for complete coverage. When time's up, head back to Vienna (if that's your transportation hub), or head west into Switzerland for yet another adventure (see *Frommer's Switzerland* for complete coverage).

3 SCENIC AUSTRIA IN 2 WEEKS

It may seem an unlikely undertaking, but it's possible to take in "Austria in a Nutshell" in just 2 weeks with some fast moving. If you start in **Vienna** in the east and head west, via **Linz** and **Salzburg,** you can see a lot of the beauty and the attractions that sweep the entire span of the country, all the way to Vorarlberg in the west at the gateway to Switzerland.

Highlights of this vast panoramic trip include not only Vienna and Salzburg, but the other two major centers: **Linz** and **Innsbruck.** The most spectacular highlights are the lake district at **Salzkammergut** and the fabled **Grossglockner Road.**

Days ❶ & ❷: Vienna ★★★: The Launch Pad

Follow the same itinerary as outlined in the 1-week tour of Austria (see above).

Day ❸: Danube River ★★★

Explore the beautiful Danube Valley west of Vienna as described in Day 3 above.

Day ❹: Linz ★★

Instead of heading on to the Salzkammergut, as we did in Day 4 (above), we suggest you leave Krems in the morning and take the scenic Route 3, which meanders along the north of the Danube into Linz, where you can overnight. The distance from Krems to Linz is 254km (158 miles).

After checking into a hotel, set out to explore the attractions of this city, including its newest sights, the **Ars Electronica Center** (p. 306) and **Lentos Kunstmuseum Linz** (p. 308). In the afternoon, take an excursion from Linz to that baroque masterpiece, the **Abbey of St. Florian** (p. 309). Since Linz is celebrated for its Linzer torte, sample the delicacy in one of the cafes we recommend on p. 314.

Day ❺: Salzkammergut's Bad Ischl ★★★

On the morning of **Day 5,** leave Linz and head south to the Autobahn (E55), which you can follow to the junction with Route 145, leading south into the spa of **Bad Ischl,** a good overnight base before you press on to Salzburg. Take in its attractions as outlined under Day 4 in the tour above.

Days ❻ & ❼: Salzburg ★★★

Spend **Days 6** and 7 here in the birthplace of Mozart, site of the most famous musical festival in Europe. Occupy your time here as outlined under Days 5 and 6 in the 1-week tour of Austria (above).

Day ❽: South to Lienz ★: Capital of East Tyrol

Leave Salzburg on the morning of **Day 8.** Head south on Route 150 to the junction with Route 159. Follow this highway south until it merges with Route 311 going west toward Zell am See, a distance of 85km (53 miles) southwest of Salzburg.

Make this your luncheon stopover (coverage begins on p. 294). If you have time, ascend the mountain plateau of **Schmittenhöhe** (p. 296) for one of the best panoramic views of Land Salzburg.

After lunch, continue south along Route 107 into Lienz for the night, a distance of 92km (57 miles). Not to be confused with the just visited Linz (capital of Upper Austria), the Tyrolean city of Lienz lies at the junction of three valleys. You can spend the rest of the afternoon wandering its old streets and visiting Schloss Bruck (p. 401).

Day 9: Grossglockner Road ★★★: The Greatest Alpine Highway

On the morning of **Day 9,** leave Lienz and head for the most scenic drive on this tour, the legendary **Grossglockner Road.** There are several approaches to this road; for a lot more details, our coverage begins on p. 293. From our starting position in Lienz, you can drive north on Route 107 to the town of **Heiligenblut,** where you might stop for a coffee before climbing the mountain in your car. Driving distance between Lienz and Heiligenblut is 48km (30 miles).

The road will lead you to **Bruck an der Grossglocknerstrasse** in Land Salzburg, near Zell am See. From the Zell am See ski area, follow the signs to **Kitzbühel** along Routes 168 and 161, which will take you northwest into this ski resort, where you can overnight. From the Zell am See area to Kitzbühel is a distance of 55km (34 miles).

Day 10: Kitzbühel ★★★: Ski Circus

Kitzbühel has earned its fame for its winter Ski Circus, but if you're a motorist on a driving tour, chances are you'll be here in fairer weather. Visitors in warm weather can pursue a number of attractions, including the **Alpine Flower Garden** (p. 391). See More Winter & Summer Pursuits (p. 391) for a range of other activities. We suggest that you spend the good part of the day at Kitzbühel, enjoying the scenic wonders of this resort before heading out to Innsbruck for a stop of two nights (see below). To reach Innsbruck, a distance of 100km (62 miles) to the west, we recommend a cross-country scenic road, Route 170, cutting through the mountains until it links with E45/A12 going southwest into Innsbruck.

Days 11 & 12: Innsbruck ★★★: Fun in Tyrol

On the morning of **Day 11,** follow the same general plan as outlined for Day 7 in our 1-week tour of Austria (above). As **Day 12** begins, leave Innsbruck altogether to see some major Tyrolean attractions in the environs. Visits are possible to **Hungerburg** (p. 349), a plateau that's the most beautiful spot in the Tyrol, and to the renaissance palace of **Schloss Ambras** (p. 349). In 1 day, you can also work in a visit to the **Wiltener Basilica** (p. 349), which is one of the loveliest churches in Tyrol, dating from the 18th century. When you return to Innsbruck for a final overnight, hopefully there'll be an operatic presentation at the **Landestheater** (p. 364).

Day 13: West to St. Anton am Arlberg ★★★

On the morning of **Day 13,** head west out of Innsbruck along 171 to the junction with Route 186, at which point you can go south in the Ötz Valley, arguably the most scenic and panoramic in Tyrol. You'll see many waterfalls and snow-covered mountains as you dip past the glaciers and peaks of the **Ötztal Alps.** The road takes you deep into the heart of what is known as the "Tyrolean Arctic," a glacier region that is among the most beautiful in all of Austria. You can stop at **Ötz,** the main town for refueling and for lunch. It lies on a sunny slope at 822m feet (2,697 ft.). Before turning back on the main road, you might go as far as **Sölden,** climbing to 1,342m (4,403 ft.). It is a quaint old village of folkloric charm. After a stopover, head back to the main highway and continue west in the opposite direction of Innsbruck. Arrive in **St. Anton** for the night, a distance of 100km (62 miles) west of Innsbruck, and reached along Route 171. St. Anton is one of the great ski resorts of Austria. Overnight here before you begin your crossing of the Arlberg Pass in the morning.

Day ⓮: The Final Scenic Route West to Bregenz ★★

For **Day 14,** your final day in Austria, head across the **Arlberg Pass,** a scenic drive of panoramic beauty. Leave St. Anton, heading for St. Christoph at 1,784m (5,853 ft.). It's reached from St. Anton by following Route 316. The location is 8km (5 miles) distant.

Continue west into the province of Vorarlberg (westernmost in Austria) until you arrive at its capital, **Bregenz.** Follow S19 west until you hook up with the A14 Autobahn heading north. Bregenz lies 150km (90 miles) northwest of Innsbruck along the southeastern shore of the Bodensee (Lake Constance). You can spend 2 or 3 days here taking in both mountain and lakeside attractions, but you may have run out of time. If so, you are only 130km (81 miles) east of Zurich, which, of course, is one of the transportation hubs of Europe if you want to end your Austrian journey.

4 AUSTRIA FOR FAMILIES

In addition to its majestic alpine peaks and fabulous natural wonders, Austria also has many manmade attractions for kids. Your main concern with having children along is pacing yourself with enough museum time. After all, it's your vacation too. Our suggestion is to combine city attractions found in Vienna and Salzburg with some motor trips into the countryside.

Days ❶ & ❷: Vienna ★★★: Getting Started

Your kid has probably been held captive on a long jet plane ride and will be eager for exercise. Get the legs moving on **Day 1** by climbing the **Domkirche St. Stephan** (p. 145), the historic cathedral of Vienna, for a panoramic view. Later, plan on spending 2 hours at the grand Hapsburg palace, **Schönbrunn** (p. 151), where special 60-to 90-minute tours are conducted by guides through rooms that offer hands-on displays for children. If the weather is fair, get the makings of a picnic and wander into **Stadtpark** (p. 159) for a place to enjoy it. Spend the afternoon visiting the amusements, including a famous Ferris wheel, in **Praterverband** (or "The Prater" (p. 160)).

On the morning of **Day 2,** try to schedule your day around two performances—that of the concert by the **Vienna Boys' Choir** (p. 139) and a visit to see the horses at the **Spanische Reitschule** (p. 144), which kids always enjoy. Because of scheduling problems, you may not always get to hear the choir, but the whole family can see the Lipizzaners prance to the music of Johann Strauss. Spend the afternoon touring the **Hofburg Palace Complex** (p. 138), where children are generally fascinated by the Kaiserappartements, especially the splendid sections where the royal children lived. Cap the afternoon off with a stroll through the **Botanischer Garten** (p. 160).

Day ❸: The Danube Valley ★★★

After renting a car, for which arrangements should have been made in advance, take the "Austrian Romantic Road" (Route 3) west from Vienna along the more scenic northern banks of the Danube. Before leaving Vienna, pack a picnic to enjoy later at a secluded spot. Your first stopover can be at **Krems,** 80km (50 miles) west of Vienna. You don't want your child to think Austria is all about cities, and Krems is a perfect town for exploring. Kids often think it was created by Disney, with its arched gateways, narrow cobbled lanes, and ancient town walls. You can spend at least 2 hours wandering its streets. Best for exploring is a part of Krems called Stein, a villagelike section of narrow streets terraced above the river.

For your overnight stopover, we suggest you continue 8km (5 miles) west of Krems to the romantic old Danube wine town of **Dürnstein.** Richard the Lion-Hearted of England was held prisoner here in 1193. Check into one of the old inns for the night and set about to explore. The whole family can delight in wandering the town's castle fortress 159m (522 ft.) above the town. Later explore the Hauptstrasse and the many little streets that branch off from it.

Day ❹: Linz ★★: From the Baroque to the Modern

On the morning of **Day 4,** continue along Route 3 north of the Danube to the city of Linz, a distance of 158km (98 miles) from Dürnstein. Plan an overnight here. After checking into a hotel, pick up the brochure, "A Walk Through the Old Quarter" and do what it says; this attraction could take up to 2 hours of your time. For children, the most intriguing attraction is the **Ars Electronica Center** (p. 306), with its hands-on exhibits and its dancing marionettes for the digital age. Kids go on a trip "to the outer reaches of space." As reward for taking the kids here, make a visit to the **Lentos Kunstmuseum Linz** (p. 308) to see some great art. Children are often mesmerized by some of the paintings here.

Days ❺ & ❻: Salzburg ★★★: It's Not All Mozart

On the morning of **Day 5,** head south of Linz to the Autobahn (E55/E60), which will carry you directly into **Salzburg,** 130km (82 miles) to the west. Check into a hotel for 2 nights, then set about to explore the city. Head for the Mozartplatz to hear the **Glockenspiel** (p. 250) or carillon, the 35 bells that ring from the Residenz. While here, stroll through the Salzburg Dom (p. 252), or cathedral, on the south side of the Residenzplatz. In the afternoon, book tickets for the whole family for "*The Sound of Music* Tour," named after the 1965 film that still enjoys worldwide success.

On **Day 6,** take the family up to the impressive **Hohensalzburg Fortress,** which is reached by a funicular ride. Allow 1½ hours for this. After a visit, head for **Schloss Hellbrunn** (p. 265) in the environs. It's only a 20-minute drive. After a visit, call on the zoo animals at the **Salzburger Tiergarten Hellbrunn** (p. 264). Following lunch, there's still time to drive to Hallein and the **Dürrnberg Salt Mines** (p. 265). Hallein lies only 15km (10 miles) from the center of Salzburg. For many kids, a trip aboard an electric mine train going deep into the caverns will be the highlight of their visit to Salzburg.

Day ❼: Innsbruck ★★★: Center of the Tyrol

For a final look at Austria, head out from Salzburg on the morning of **Day 7** for Innsbruck, 190km (118 miles) to the southwest. Check into a hotel for your final night. Innsbruck is reached by Autobahn A8, which joins Autobahn A93 (later A12) for its final descent on the city.

In Innsbruck, spend at least 2 hours traversing the Old Town on foot. Stroll along the main street, **Maria-Theresien-Strasse,** and visit the **Goldenes Dachl,** or golden roof (p. 346). After lunch, pay a visit to the 15th-century imperial palace, **Hofburg** (p. 347), and try to budget time for the **Alpenzoo** (p. 346), on the southern slope of the Hungerburg plateau. Not only can you see mammals indigenous to the Alps, but you will also be rewarded with one of the most panoramic views in Tyrol.

5 THE SOUTHERN LAKE DISTRICT ★★★ IN 1 WEEK

Fleeing the alpine peaks, we descend on the southern lake district to wind up our final tour of Austria. Of course, this tour is recommended during the all-too-short summer months. Instead of Vienna, we use Salzburg as our gateway to the lakes, which begins in the province of Land Salzburg and ends in the summer resorts of the southeastern province of Carinthia.

Day ❶: Salzburg ★★★: Gateway to the Lakes

Salzburg, the city of Mozart, lies at the door to some of the greatest natural attractions in Europe, found in the province of Land Salzburg. After driving or flying to Salzburg, you'll have just enough time to walk the ancient streets of its Old Town (allow 2 or 3 hr.) and visit the **Residenzgalerie** (p. 251) and the **Hohensalzburg Fortress** (p. 250).

Day ❷: Mondsee ★: Austria's Moon Lake

On the morning of **Day 2,** leave Salzburg and head east on the A-1 until you see the turnoff to **Mondsee,** 27km (17 miles) to the east. Check into a hotel for the night and visit **Schloss Mondsee** (p. 321), where Maria married Captain von Trapp in *The Sound of Music.* Stroll along the lovely Marktplatz, a square filled with lively cafes. Arrangements can be made to go sailing (check with the tourist office), or you can just enjoy the lakefront beaches. "Moon Lake" (its English name) is the warmest of Land Salzburg's bodies of water.

Day ❸: St. Wolfgang ★: The Romantic Lake

For **Day 3** you can still use Mondsee as a base or transfer over to **St. Wolfgang** so you won't have to make the 40-minute drive back at night. The easiest way to get here without taking difficult roads is to head southeast along Route 154, following it around the southern rim of Wolfgangsee, then cutting back west at the signposts into St. Wolfgang, which lies on the northern tier of Wolfgangsee, arguably known as the most romantic lake in Austria. It was the setting for the popular operetta *The White Horse Inn,* written in 1896 but still performed all over Austria annually. Swimming and watersports dominate the lakefront beach life, and you can also plan visits to the Pfarrkirche St. Wolfgang (p. 323), a pilgrimage church since the 12th century. It's also possible to take an excursion to **Schafberg** (p. 324) for the most panoramic views in Upper Austria. On a clear day, you can see 13 lakes in Land Salzburg from here.

Day ❹: Bad Aussee ★: The Green Heart

On the morning of **Day 5,** head east from St. Wolfgang, retracing your steps to the main road at the junction with Bad Ischl. From here, follow Route 145 southeast to **Bad Aussee,** a distance of only 34km (22 miles). Check in for the night.

The old spa of Bad Aussee is called the "green heart" of the Salzkammergut. At Bad Aussee you'll have crossed over from the province of Land Salzburg in Syria. Its lake, **Altaussee,** is one of the most beautiful bodies of water in that province. The resort, lying 650m (2,133 ft.) above sea level, is set in a network of other lakes in the Traun Valley. Drop in at the tourist activities to hook up with any activities likely to be offered at the time of your visit. Hiking through this mini lake district is one of the joys of coming here, and it breaks up all that time at the wheel.

Day ❺: Villach ★: Heart of the Carinthian Lake District

On the morning of **Day 5,** leave Bad Aussee, heading for **Villach,** 206km (128 miles) to the southeast. Follow Route 145 southwest to the junction with the motorway A10 heading south to Spittal. Once here, continue southeast on the Autobahn (E55/E66) into Villach. After checking into a hotel for the night, explore on foot its Altstadt or Old Town, centered on the main square, Hauptplatz. After a visit to the tourist office for a map, set out for a drive into the **Villacher Alps** (p. 447 one of the most scenic drives in Carinthia, taking you for an 18km (11 mile) journey via the Villacher Alpenstrasse toll road with panoramic views in all directions.

Days ❻ & ❼: Klagenfurt ★: Carinthia's Capital

On the morning of **Day 6,** leave Villach A2 for **Klagenfurt,** 56km (35 miles) away. Anchor into Klagenfurt for 2 nights. After a tour of the Old Town and a visit to its **Domkirche** (p. 435) and **Diozesanmuseum** (p. 435), you can head for nearby Wörther See for fun in the lake water. After all this relaxation you can plan to take some nearby excursions on **Day 7,** your final day in Austria. In a period of 1 day, you can drive to **Maria Saal** (p. 442), a pilgrimage church outside Klagenfurt; **Hochosterwitz Castle,** whose origins go back to 860; and to **St. Veit an der Glan** (p. 440), the old capital of Carinthia back in 1170. After Klagenfurt, it's a 309km (192-mile) northeast drive to Vienna.

Settling into Vienna

Vienna is a city of music, cafes, waltzes, parks, and pastries. The capital of Austria has been a showplace city since the tumultuous reign of the Hapsburg dynasty, and unlike many other European capitals, it has managed to survive two world wars with most of its beautiful landmarks unscathed.

Vienna is a truly cosmopolitan city. For centuries, different tribes, races, and nationalities have fused their cultural identities into the intriguing and often cynical Viennese of today. From the time the Romans chose a Celtic settlement on the Danube for one of their most important central European forts, Vienna has played a vital role in European history. Austria grew up around this city and, in doing so, developed into one of Europe's mightiest empires. The face of the city has been altered time and again by war, siege, victory, defeat, death of an empire, birth of a republic, bombing, occupation, and the passage of time. But fortunately, the Viennese character, which includes a strict devotion to the good life, has remained intact.

1 ORIENTATION

ARRIVING

By Plane

Vienna International Airport (**VIE; ✆ 01/70070;** www.viennaairport.com) is about 19km (12 miles) southeast of the city center. Austrian Airlines and United Airlines offer nonstop service from New York (JFK), Chicago, and Washington, D.C.; Austrian Airlines and British Airways fly nonstop from London (Heathrow). Other transatlantic airlines connect to Vienna via major European hubs.

The official **Vienna Tourist Information Office,** in the arrival hall of the airport, is open daily 7am to 10pm.

There's regular bus service between the airport and the **City Air Terminal,** adjacent to the Vienna Hilton and directly across from the **Wien Mitte/Landstrasse** rail station, where you can easily connect with subway and tram lines. Buses run every 20 minutes from 6:30am to 11:30pm and hourly from midnight to 5am. The trip takes about 25 minutes and costs 6€ ($7.80) per person. Tickets are sold on the bus and must be purchased with euros. There's also bus service between the airport and two railroad stations, the Westbahnhof and the Südbahnhof, leaving every 30 minutes to an hour. A new service, the CAT bus, takes only 16 minutes. Fares are also 6€ ($7.80).

There's also local train service, Schnellbahn (S-Bahn), between the airport and the Wien Nord and Wien Mitte rail stations. Trains run hourly from 5am to 11:40pm, and leave from the basement of the airport. Trip time is 40 to 45 minutes, and the fare is 3€ ($3.90).

By Train

Vienna has four principal rail stations, with frequent connections from all Austrian cities and towns and from all major European cities. For train information for all stations, call ✆ **05/1717.**

Westbahnhof (West Railway Station), on Europaplatz, is for trains arriving from western Austria, France, Germany, Switzerland, and some eastern European countries. It has frequent links to major Austrian cities such as Salzburg, which is a 3-hour train ride from Vienna. The Westbahnhof connects with local trains, the U3 and U6 underground lines, and several tram and bus routes.

Südbahnhof (South Railway Station), on Südtirolerplatz, has train service to southern and eastern Austria, Italy, Hungary, Slovenia, and Croatia. It's linked with local rail service and tram and bus routes.

Both of these stations house useful travel agencies **(Österreichisches Verkehrsbüro)** that provide tourist information and help with hotel reservations. In the Westbahnhof, it's in the upper hall; at the Südbahnhof, it's in the lower hall.

Other stations in Vienna include **Franz-Josef Bahnhof,** on Franz-Josef-Platz, used mainly by local trains, although connections are made here to Prague and Berlin. You can take the D-tram line to the city's Ringstrasse from here. **Wien Mitte,** at Landstrasser Hauptstrasse 1, is also a terminus for local trains, plus a depot for trains to the Czech Republic and to Vienna International Airport.

By Bus

The **City Bus Terminal** is at the Wien Mitte rail station, Landstrasser Hauptstrasse 1. This is the arrival depot for Post and Bundesbuses from points all over the country, as well as the arrival point for private buses from various European cities. The terminal has lockers, currency-exchange kiosks, and a ticket counter open daily from 6:15am to 6pm. For bus information, call ✆ **01/71101** daily from 6:15am to 6pm.

By Car

Vienna can be reached from all directions via *autobahn* (major highways) or by secondary highways. The main artery from the west is Autobahn A1, coming in from Munich (468km/291 miles), Salzburg (336km/209 miles), and Linz (186km/116 miles). Autobahn A2 arrives from the south, from Graz (200km/124 miles) and Klagenfurt (308km/191 miles). Autobahn A4 comes in from the east, connecting with Route E58, which runs to Bratislava and Prague. Autobahn A22 takes traffic from the northwest, and Route E10 connects to the cities and towns of southeastern Austria and of Hungary.

VISITOR INFORMATION

Once you've arrived safely in Vienna, head for either of two information points that make it their business to have up-to-the-minute data about what to see and do in Vienna. The more centrally located of the two is the **Wien Tourist-Information** office at Albertinaplatz (✆ **01/211140;** tram: 1 or 2). Located directly behind the Vienna State Opera, on the corner of Philharmoniker Strasse, in the heart of the Innere Stadt (Inner City), it's open daily from 9am to 7pm. The staff will make free hotel reservations for anyone in need of accommodations. Larger and more administrative, but also willing to handle questions from the public, is the headquarters of the **Vienna Tourist Board,** Obere Augartenstrasse (✆ **01/21114412;** tram: 31), open Monday to Friday 8am to 4pm. Both branches stock free copies of a tourist magazine, ***Wien Monatsprogramm,*** which lists what's going on in Vienna's concert halls, theaters, and opera houses. Also worthwhile here is ***Vienna A to Z,*** a general, pocket-size guide with descriptions and locations for a slew of attractions. This booklet is also free, but don't rely on its cluttered map.

For information on Vienna and Austria, including day trips from the city, visit the **Austrian National Tourist Office,** Margaretenstrasse 1, A-1040 (✆ **01/588660**). For a rundown on the Wachau (Danube Valley) and the Wienerwald (Vienna Woods), you might want to contact **Niederösterreich Information,** Fischhof 3/3, A-1010 (✆ **01/536106200;** www.niederoesterreich.at).

CITY LAYOUT

From its origins as a Roman village on the Danubian plain, Vienna has evolved over the years into one of the largest metropolises of central Europe, with a surface area covering 414 sq. km (160 sq. miles). That area has been divided into 23 *bezirke* (districts), which are rather cumbersomely identified with a Roman numeral. Each district carries its own character or reputation; for example, the 9th District is known as Vienna's academic quarter, whereas the 10th, 11th, and 12th districts are home to blue-collar workers and are the most densely populated.

The 1st District, known as the **Innere Stadt (Inner City),** is where most foreign visitors first flock. This compact area is Vienna at its most historic, and boasts the city's astounding array of monuments, churches, palaces, and museums, in addition to its finest hotels and restaurants. Its size and shape roughly correspond to the original borders (then walls) of the medieval city; however, other than **St. Stephan's Cathedral,** very few buildings from that era remain.

The Inner City is surrounded by **Ringstrasse,** a circular boulevard about 4km (2½ miles) long. Constructed between 1859 and 1888, it's one of the most ambitious examples of urban planning and restoration in central European history. Built over the foundations of Vienna's medieval fortifications, the Ring opened new urban vistas for the dozens of monumental 19th-century buildings that line its edges today. The name of this boulevard changes as it moves around the Inner City, which can get confusing. Names that correspond with the boulevard end in *ring:* Schottenring, Dr.-Karl-Lueger-Ring, Burgring, Opernring, Kärntner Ring, Stubenring, Parkring, and Schubertring.

Ironically, the river for which Vienna is so famous, the **Danube,** doesn't really pass through the center of the city at all. Between 1868 and 1877, the river was channeled into its present muddy banks east of town, and was replaced with a small-scale substitute, the **Donaukanal (Danube Canal),** which was dug for shipping food and other supplies to the Viennese. The canal is set against Ringstrasse's eastern edge, and is traversed by five bridges in the 1st District alone.

Surrounding Ringstrasse and the Inner City, in a more or less clockwise direction, are the inner suburban districts (2–9), which contain many hotels and restaurants popular for their proximity to the city center. The villas and palaces of Vienna's 18th-century aristocrats can be found here, as well as modern apartment complexes and the homes of 19th-century middle-class entrepreneurs. These districts are profiled below under "Neighborhoods in Brief."

The outer districts (10–23) form another concentric ring of suburbs, comprising a variety of neighborhoods from industrial parks to rural villages. **Schönbrunn,** the Hapsburg's vast summer palace, is located in these outlying areas in the 13th District, **Hietzing.** Also noteworthy is the 19th District, **Döbling,** with its famous *heurigen* villages, such as Grinzing and Sievering (see "Heurigen," p. 180), and the 22nd District, **Donaustadt,** home to the verdant Donau Park and the adjoining UNO-City, an impressive modern complex of United Nations agencies.

Finding an Address

Street addresses are followed by a four-digit postal code, or sometimes a Roman numeral, that identifies the district in which the address is located. Often the code is preceded by the letter *A*. The district number is coded in the two middle digits, so if an address is in the 1st District ("01"), the postal code would read A-1010; in the 7th District, A-1070; and in the 13th District, A-1130.

A rule of thumb used by hotel concierges and taxi drivers involves the following broad-based guidelines: Odd street numbers are on one side of the street, and even numbers are on the other. The lowest numbers are usually closest to the city's geographic and spiritual center, St. Stephansplatz, and get higher as the street extends outward. Naturally, this system won't work on streets running parallel to the cathedral, so you'll have to simply test your luck.

What about the broad expanses of Vienna's Ring? Traffic always moves clockwise on the Ring, and any backtracking against the direction of the traffic must be done via side streets that radiate from the general traffic flow. Numeration on the Ring always goes from high numbers to lower numbers, as determined by the direction of the prevailing traffic (odd street numbers appear on a driver's left, and even numbers appear on the right).

Street Maps

You'll need a very good and detailed map to explore Vienna, as it has some 2,400km (1,491 miles) of streets (many of them narrow). As so many places, including restaurants and hotels, lie in these alleyways, routine overview maps that are given away at hotels or the tourist office won't do. You'll need the best city map in Vienna, which is published by **Falk** and sold at all major newsstands, bookstores, and in many upscale hotels.

NEIGHBORHOODS IN BRIEF

Many of Vienna's hotels and restaurants are conveniently located within or just outside the 1st District. In this section, we profile the Inner City, or Innere Stadt, and the adjacent districts.

Innere Stadt (1st District) This compact area, bound on all sides by the legendary Ring, is at the center of Viennese life. The Inner City has dozens of streets devoted exclusively to pedestrian traffic, including **Kärntnerstrasse,** which bypasses the Wiener Staatsoper (Vienna State Opera), and the nearby **Graben,** which backs up to Stephansplatz, home to the famous cathedral. Competing with both the cathedral and the Staatsoper as the district's most famous building is the **Hofburg,** the famous Hapsburg palace that includes the National Library, the Spanish Riding School, and six museums. Other significant landmarks include the Rathaus (City Hall), Parlament (Parliament), the Universität (University of Vienna), the Naturhistorisches (Natural History) and Kunsthistorisches (Art History) museums, and Stadtpark.

Leopoldstadt (2nd District) Once inhabited by Balkan traders, this area doesn't physically border the Ringstrasse, but it lies on the eastern side of the Danube Canal, just a short subway ride (U1) from the Inner City. Here you'll find the massive **Prater** park, which boasts an amusement park, miles of tree-lined walking paths, and numerous sports facilities, including a large stadium. Vienna's renowned trade-fair exhibition site is also in this district.

Impressions

The streets of Vienna are surfaced with culture as the streets of other cities are with asphalt.

—Karl Kraus (1874–1936)

Landstrasse (3rd District) The bucolic **Stadtpark** spreads into this district, where you'll also discover more of Vienna's imperial charm. Streets are dotted with churches, monuments, and palaces, such as the grand **Schwarzenburg Palace** and the looming **Konzerthaus (concert house).** However, the top attraction remains Prince Eugene Savoy's exquisite baroque **Belvedere Palace.** Several embassies make their home in a small section of Landstrasse known as Vienna's diplomatic quarter. The **Wien Mitte rail station** and the **City Air Terminal** are also located here.

Wieden (4th District) This small neighborhood extends south from Opernring and Kärtnerring, and it's just as fashionable as the 1st District. Most activity centers on **Karlsplatz,** a historical city square that features its domed namesake, Karlskirche. Also seated around this hub are Vienna's Technical University and the **Historical Museum of the City of Vienna.** Kärntnerstrasse, the main boulevard of the city center, turns into **Wiedner-Hauptstrasse** as it enters this district, and the **Südbahnhof,** one of the two main train stations, lies at its southern tip.

Margareten (5th District) Southwest of the 4th District, this area does not border the Ring and thus lies a bit farther from the Inner City. The historic homes of composers Franz Schubert and Christoph Gluck still stand here among modern apartment complexes and industrial centers.

Mariahilf (6th District) One of Vienna's busiest shopping streets, **Mariahilferstrasse,** runs through this bustling neighborhood. The sprawling and lively **Naschmarkt (Produce Market),** selling fresh fruits, vegetables, breads, cheeses, and more, is the ideal place for people-watching. On Saturday, the adjacent **Flea Market** adds to the lively but sometimes seedy atmosphere, as vendors sell antiques and other junk. The surrounding streets are packed with *beisls* (small eateries), theaters, cafes, and pubs. As you wander farther from the city center, however, you'll find that the landscape becomes more residential.

Neubau (7th District) Bordering the expansive Museum Quarter of the Inner City, this is an ideal place to stay, as it's easily accessible by public transportation. The picturesque and once neglected **Spittelberg quarter** lies atop a hill just beyond Vienna's most famous museums. It's a vibrant, cultural community that's popular with young and old visitors alike. The old Spittelberg houses have been renovated into boutiques, restaurants, theaters, and art galleries—a perfect backdrop for an afternoon stroll.

Josefstadt (8th District) This, the smallest of Vienna's 23 districts, is named after Hapsburg Emperor Josef II and was once home to Vienna's civil servants. Like Neubau, this quiet, friendly neighborhood sits behind the city hall and the adjacent grand museums of the Ringstrasse. You'll find everything from shady and secluded parks to elaborate

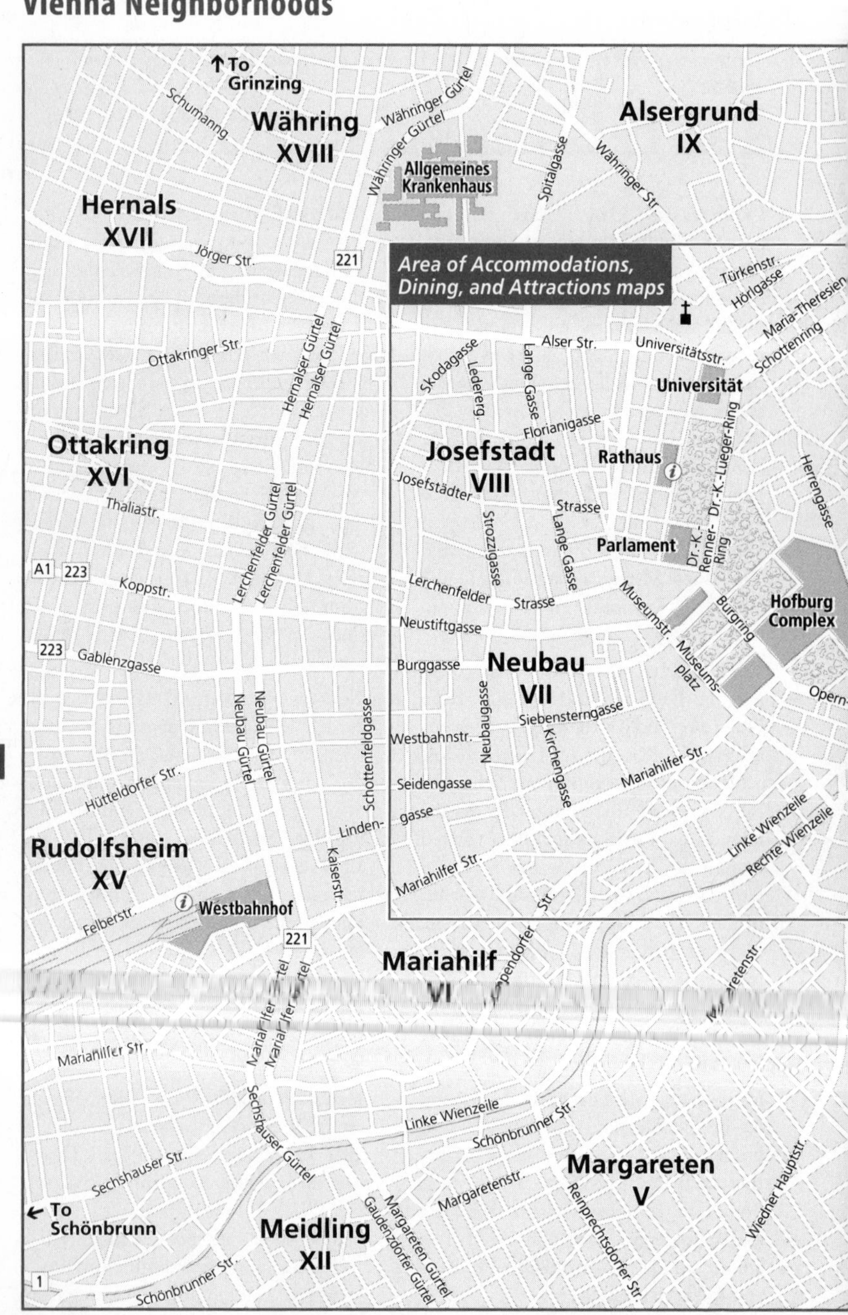
To Grinzing
Schumanng.
Währing XVIII
Währinger Gürtel
Währinger Gürtel
Allgemeines Krankenhaus
Spitalgasse
Währinger Str.
Alsergrund IX
Hernals XVII
Jörger Str.
221
Area of Accommodations, Dining, and Attractions maps
Türkenstr.
Hörlgasse
Maria-Theresien
Schottenring
Ottakringer Str.
Hernalser Gürtel
Hernalser Gürtel
Skodagasse
Ledererg.
Lange Gasse
Alser Str.
Universitätsstr.
Universität
Florianigasse
Dr.-K.-Lueger-Ring
Ottakring XVI
Josefstadt VIII
Rathaus
Josefstädter Strasse
Herrengasse
Thaliastr.
Strozzigasse
Lange Gasse
Parlament
Dr.-K.-Renner-Ring
A1
223
Koppstr.
Lerchenfelder Gürtel
Lerchenfelder Gürtel
Lerchenfelder Strasse
Museumstr.
Burgring
Hofburg Complex
Neustiftgasse
223
Gablenzgasse
Burggasse
Neubau VII
Museumsplatz
Opern-
Neubau Gürtel
Neubau Gürtel
Schottenfeldgasse
Neubaugasse
Siebensterngasse
Westbahnstr.
Kirchengasse
Hütteldorfer Str.
Seidengasse
Mariahilfer Str.
Linke Wienzeile
Rechte Wienzeile
Linden-gasse
Rudolfsheim XV
Kaiserstr.
Mariahilfer Str.
Felberstr.
Westbahnhof
221
Str.
Mariahilf VI
Mariahilfer Str.
Linke Wienzeile
Schönbrunner Str.
Sechshauser Gürtel
Sechshauser Str.
Margareten V
Wiedner Hauptstr.
Margaretenstr.
To Schönbrunn
Meidling XII
Margareten Gürtel
Gaudenzdorfer Gürtel
Reinprechtsdorfer Str.
1
Schönbrunner Str.

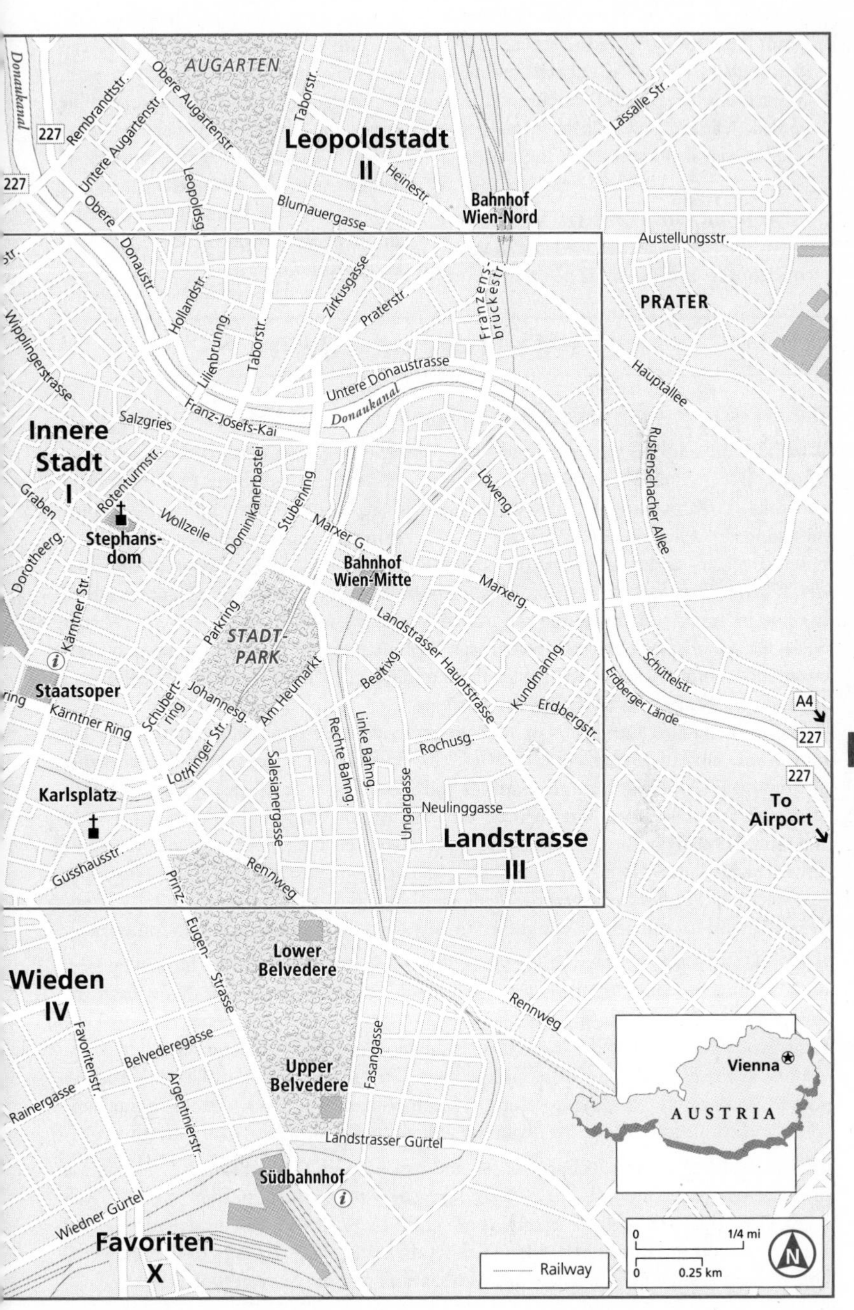
AUGARTEN
Leopoldstadt
II
Bahnhof
Wien-Nord
PRATER
Innere
Stadt
I
Stephans-
dom
Bahnhof
Wien-Mitte
STADT-
PARK
Staatsoper
Karlsplatz
Landstrasse
III
Wieden
IV
Lower
Belvedere
Upper
Belvedere
Südbahnhof
Favoriten
X
To
Airport
Vienna
AUSTRIA
Railway
0 1/4 mi
0 0.25 km

monuments and churches. Vienna's oldest and most intimate theater, **Josefstadt Theater** (Josefstadtterstrasse 26), was built in 1788. The clientele among Josefstadt's shops and restaurants is varied, featuring lawmakers from City Hall as well as students from the university.

Alsergrund (9th District) This area is often referred to as the academic quarter, not just because of its position near the University of Vienna, but also because of its many hospitals and clinics. This is Freud territory, and you can visit his home, now the Freud Museum, on Berggasse. Here you'll also stumble upon the Liechtenstein Palace, which today houses the federal Museum of Modern Art. At the northern end of Alsergrund is the **Franz-Josef Bahnhof,** an excellent depot for excursions to Lower Austria.

2 GETTING AROUND

BY PUBLIC TRANSPORTATION

Whether you want to visit the Inner City's historic buildings or the outlying Vienna Woods, *Wiener Verkehrsbetriebe* (Vienna Transport) can take you there. This vast transit network—U-Bahn (subway), streetcar, or bus—is safe, clean, and easy to use. If you plan on taking full advantage of it, pay the 1€ ($1.30) for a map that outlines the U-Bahn, buses, streetcars, and *Schnellbahn,* or S-Bahn (local trains). It's sold at ***Informationdienst der Wiener Verkehrsbetriebe*** (the Vienna Public Transport Information Center), which has five locations: Opernpassage (an underground passageway adjacent to the Wiener Staatsoper), Karlsplatz, Stephansplatz (near Vienna's cathedral), Westbahnhof, and Praterstern. For information about any of these outlets, call ✆ **01/7909100.** These offices are open Monday to Friday 6:30am to 6:30pm.

Vienna maintains a uniform fare that applies to all forms of public transport. A ticket for the bus, subway, or tram costs 1.50€ ($1.95) if you buy it in advance at a *tabac-trafiks* (a store or kiosk selling tobacco products and newspapers) or 2€ ($2.60) if you buy it on-board. Smart Viennese buy their tickets in advance, usually in blocks of at least five at a time, from any of the city's thousands of *tabac-trafiks* or at any of the public transport centers noted above. No matter what vehicle you decide to ride within Vienna, remember that once a ticket has been stamped (validated) by either a machine or a railway attendant, it's valid for one trip in one direction, anywhere in the city, including transfers.

U-BAHN (SUBWAY) Most of the top attractions in the Inner City can be seen by foot, tram, or bus, but the U-Bahn is your best bet to get across town quickly or reach the suburbs. It consists of five lines labeled as U1, U2, U3, U4, and U6 (there is no U5). Karlsplatz, in the heart of the Inner City, is the most important underground station for visitors, as the U1, U2, and U4 converge here. The U2 traces part of the Ring, the U4 goes to Schönbrunn, and the U1 stops in Stephansplatz. The U3 also stops in Stephansplatz and connects with the Westbahnhof. The U-Bahn runs daily 6am to midnight.

TRAM (STREETCAR) Riding the red-and-white trams *(Strassenbahn)* is not only a practical way to get around, but it's also a great way to see the city. Tram stops are well marked and lines are labeled as numbers or letters. Lines 1 and 2 will bring you to all the major sights on the Ringstrasse. Line D skirts the outer Ring and goes to the Südbahnhof, whereas line 18 goes between the Westbahnhof and the Südbahnhof.

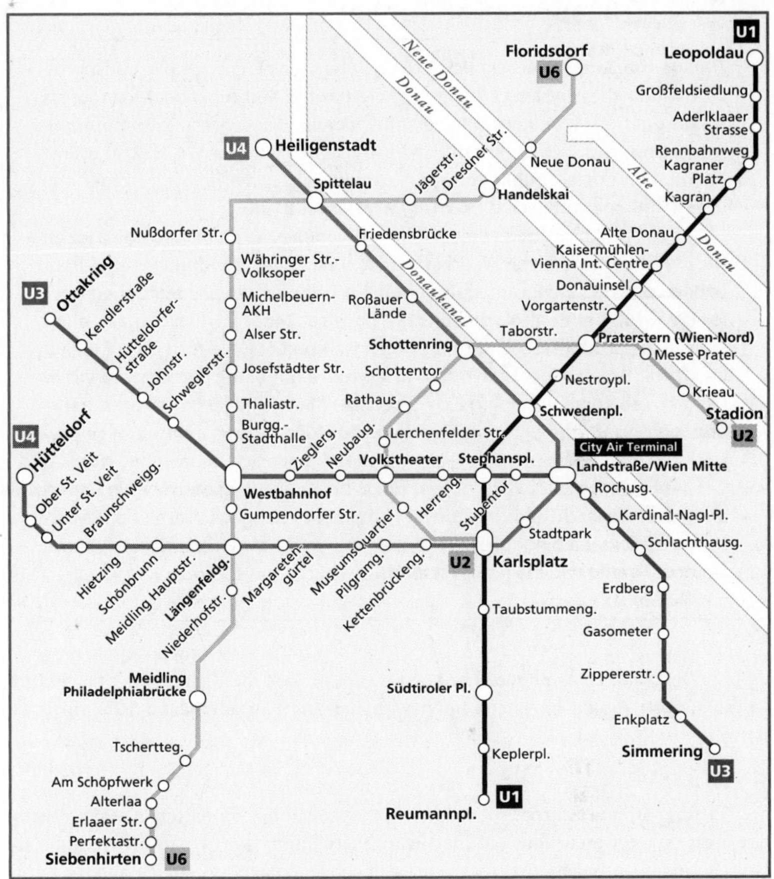

BUS Buses traverse Vienna in all directions, operating daily, including at night (but with more limited service then). Night buses leave every 10 to 30 minutes from Schwedenplatz, fanning out across the city. It is usually not necessary to change lines more than once. Normal tickets are valid aboard these late-night buses (no extra charge). On buses you can buy tickets from the driver.

BY TAXI

Taxis are easy to find within the city center, but be warned that fares can quickly add up. Taxi stands are marked by signs, or you can call ✆ **01/31300,** 60160, 81400, or 40100. The basic fare is 2.50€ ($3.25), plus 1.20€ ($1.55) per kilometer. There is an extra charge of 1€ ($1.30) for luggage in the trunk. For rides after 11pm, and for trips on Sunday and holidays, there is a surcharge of 1€ ($1.30). There is an additional charge of

Transportation for Less

The **Vienna Card** is the best ticket to use when traveling by public transportation within the city limits. It's extremely flexible and functional for tourists because it allows unlimited travel, plus various discounts at city museums, restaurants, and shops. You can purchase a Vienna Card for 17€ ($22) at tourist information offices, public transport centers, and some hotels, or order one over the phone with a credit card (✆ **01/7984400148**).

You can also buy tickets that will save you money if you plan to ride a lot on the city's transport system. A ticket valid for unlimited rides during any 24-hour period costs 5€ ($6.50); an equivalent ticket valid for any 72-hour period goes for 12€ ($16). There's also a green ticket, priced at 24€ ($31), that contains eight individual partitions. Each of these, when stamped, is good for 1 day of unlimited travel. An individual can opt to reserve all eight of the partitions for his or her own use, thereby gaining 8 days of cost-effective travel on the city's transport system. Or, the partitions can be subdivided among a group of several riders, allowing—for example—two persons 4 days each of unlimited rides.

These tickets are also available at *tabac-trafiks,* vending machines in underground stations, the airport's arrival hall (next to baggage claim), the *Reichsbrücke* (DDSG landing pier), and the *Österreichisches Verkehrsbüro* (travel agencies) of the two main train stations.

2€ ($2.60) if ordered by phone. The fare for trips outside the Vienna area (for instance, to the airport) should be agreed upon with the driver in advance; a 10% tip is the norm.

BY CAR

See "Getting around Austria," in chapter 2, for general tips on renting a car in Austria. Use a car only for excursions outside Vienna's city limits; don't try to drive around the city. Parking is a problem, the city is a maze of congested one-way streets, and the public transportation is too good to endure the hassle of driving.

If you do venture out by car, information on road conditions is available in English daily from 6am to 8pm from the **Österreichischer Automobil-, Motorrad- und Touringclub (ÖAMTC),** Schubertring 1–3, A-1010 Vienna (✆ **01/711990**). This auto club also maintains a 24-hour emergency road service number (✆ **120** or **0010/120120**).

RENTALS It's always best to reserve rental cars in advance (see chapter 2), but you can rent a car once you've arrived in Vienna. You'll need a passport and a driver's license that's at least 1 year old. Avoid renting a car at the airport, where there's an extra 15% tax, in addition to the 21% value-added tax on all rentals.

Major car-rental companies include **Avis,** Opernring 3–5 (✆ **01/5876241**); **Budget Rent-a-Car,** Hilton Air Terminal (✆ **01/7146565**); and **Hertz,** Kärntner Ring 17 (✆ **01/5128677**).

PARKING Curbside parking in Vienna's 1st District, site of most of the city's major monuments, is extremely limited—almost to the point of being nonexistent. Coin-operated parking meters are not common. When curbside parking is available at all, it's within one of the city's "blue zones," and is usually restricted to 90 minutes or less from 8am to 6pm. If you find an available spot within a blue zone, you'll need to display a *kurzpark scheine* (short-term parking voucher) on the dashboard of your car. Valid for time blocks of only 30, 60, or 90 minutes, they're sold at branch offices of Vienna Public Transport Information Center (see above) and, more conveniently, within tobacco/news shops. You'll have to write in the date and the time of your arrival before displaying the voucher on the right side of your car's dashboard. Be warned that towing of illegally parked cars is not an uncommon sight here. Frankly, it's much easier to simply pay the price that's charged by any of the city's dozens of underground parking garages and avoid the stress of looking for one of the virtually impossible-to-find curbside parking spots.

Parking garages are scattered throughout the city, and most of them charge between 3.50€ ($4.55) and 6€ ($7.80) per hour. Every hotel in Vienna is acutely aware of the location of the nearest parking garage—if you're confused, ask. Some convenient 24-hour garages within the 1st District include **Parkgarage,** Am Hof (© **01/5335571**); **Parkgarage Freyung,** Freyung (© **01/5350450**); and **APCOA,** Cobdengasse 2 (© **01/5125554**).

DRIVING & TRAFFIC REGULATIONS In general, Austria's traffic regulations do not differ much from those of other countries where you *drive on the right.* In Vienna, the speed limit is 50kmph (about 30 mph). Out of town, in such areas as the Wienerwald, the limit is 130kmph (81 mph) on motorways and 100kmph (62 mph) on all other roads. Honking car horns is forbidden in the city.

BY HORSE-DRAWN CARRIAGE

A *fiaker* (horse-drawn carriage) has been used as a form of transportation in the Inner City for some 3 centuries. You can clip-clop along in one for about 20 minutes at a cost of about 40€ ($52). Prices and the length of the ride must be negotiated in advance. In the 1st District, you'll find a *fiaker* for hire at the following sites: on the north side of St. Stephan's, on Heldenplatz near the Hofburg, and in front of the Albertina on Augustinerstrasse. There is also a 40-minute tour, and it costs 65€ ($85).

BY BIKE

Vienna has more than 250km (155 miles) of marked bicycle paths within the city limits. In the summer, many Viennese leave their cars in the garage and ride bikes. You can take bicycles on specially marked U-Bahn cars for free, but only Monday through Friday from 9am to 3pm and 6:30pm to midnight. On weekends in July and August, bicycles are carried free from 9am to midnight.

Rental stores abound at the Prater (see chapter 6) and along the banks of the Danube Canal, which is the favorite bike route for most Viennese. One of the best of the many sites specializing in bike rentals is **Pedalpower,** Ausstellungsstrasse 3 (© **01/7297234**), which is open March through October from 8am to 7pm. The Vienna Tourist Board can also supply a list of rental shops and more information about bike paths. Bike rentals begin at about 27€ ($35) per day.

Fast Facts Vienna

American Express The office at Kärntnerstrasse 21–23 (✆ **01/5124004**), near Stock-im-Eisenplatz, is open Monday to Friday 9am to 5pm and Saturday 9am to noon.

Babysitters Most hotels will provide you with names of babysitters if they do not provide their own service. Sitters charge roughly 8€ to 12€ ($10–$16) per hour, and you'll need to provide transportation home, via a cab, if they sit beyond 11pm.

Business Hours Most shops are open Monday to Friday from 9am to 6pm and Saturday from 9am to noon, 12:30pm, or 1pm, depending on the store. On the first Saturday of every month, shops customarily remain open until 4:30 or 5pm. The tradition is called *langer Samstag.*

City Code The telephone city code for Vienna is **01.** It's used only when you're calling from outside Vienna.

Dentists For dental problems, call ✆ **01/5122078,** where the staff can tell you about availability of dentists in the area.

Doctors A list of physicians can be found in the telephone directory under "Arzte." If you have a medical emergency at night, call ✆ **141** daily from 7pm to 7am.

Drug Laws Penalties are severe and could lead to either imprisonment or deportation. Selling drugs to minors is dealt with particularly harshly.

Drugstores Drugstores (chemist's shops) are open Monday to Friday from 8am to noon and 2 to 6pm, and Saturday from 8am to noon. At night and on Sunday, you'll find the names of the nearest open shops on a sign outside every drugstore.

Electricity Vienna operates on 220 volts AC (50 cycles). That means that U.S.-made appliances without a 200/110 switch will need a transformer (sometimes called a converter). Many Viennese hotels stock adapter plugs but not power transformers. Electric clocks, record players, and tape recorders, however, will not work well, even with transformers.

Emergencies Call ✆ **122** to report a fire, **133** for the police, or **144** for an ambulance.

Hospitals The major hospital is **Allgemeines Krankenhaus,** Währinger Gürtel 18–20 (✆ **01/40400**).

Internet Access **Café Stein,** Währingerstrasse 6–8 (✆ **01/3197241**), offers Internet access at the rate of 4€ ($5.20) every half hour, and is open Monday to Saturday 7am to 1pm, Sunday 9am to 1pm.

Luggage Storage & Lockers All four main train stations in Vienna have lockers available on a 24-hour basis, costing 3€ ($3.90) for 24 hours. It's also possible to store luggage at these terminals daily from 4am to midnight (1:15am at the Westbahnhof) at a cost of 2.50€ ($3.25).

Money During off-hours, you can exchange money at *bureaux de change* (exchange bureaus) throughout the Inner City (there's one at the intersection of Kohlmarkt and the Graben), as well as at travel agencies, train stations, and at the airport. There's also a 24-hour exchange service at the post office at Fleischmarkt 19.

Newspapers & Magazines Most newsstands at major hotels or news kiosks along the streets sell copies of the *International Herald Tribune* and *USA Today,* and also carry copies of the European editions of *Time* and *Newsweek.*

Police The emergency number is ✆ **133.**

Post Offices Post offices in Vienna can be found in the heart of every district. Addresses for these can be found in the telephone directory under "Post." Post offices are generally open for mail services Monday to Friday 8am to noon and 2 to 6pm. The *Hauptpostamt* (central post office), Fleischmarkt 19 (✆ **01/5138350**), and most general post offices are open 24 hours a day, 7 days a week. Postage stamps are available at all post offices and at tobacco shops, and there are stamp-vending machines outside most post offices.

Safety In recent years, Vienna has been plagued by purse-snatchers. In the area around St. Stephan's Cathedral, signs (in German only) warn about pickpockets and purse-snatchers. Small foreign children often approach sympathetic adults and ask for money. As the adult goes for his wallet or her purse, full-grown thieves rush in and grab the money, fleeing with it. Unaccompanied women should hold on to their purses tightly and never open them in public.

Taxes Vienna imposes no special city taxes, other than the national value-added tax that's tacked on to all goods and services.

Telegrams, Telexes & Faxes The central telegraph office is at Börseplatz 1.

Transit Information Information, all types of tickets, and maps of the transportation system are available at Vienna Transport's main offices on Karlsplatz or at the Stephansplatz underground station Monday to Friday 8am to 6pm and Saturday, Sunday, and holidays from 8:30am to 4pm. Alternatively, you can call ✆ **0810/222324** 24 hours a day for information in German and English about public transport anywhere within greater Vienna.

Useful Telephone Numbers Dial ✆ **05/1717** for rail information, ✆ **0810/222324** for bus schedules, and ✆ **01/211140** for tourist information daily from 9am to 7pm. For hotel reservations, call the Vienna Tourist Board's room reservations system (✆ **01/24555**) daily from 9am to 7pm.

3 WHERE TO STAY

Vienna has some of the greatest hotels in Europe and more than 300 recommendable ones. But finding a room can be a problem, especially in August and September, if you arrive without a reservation. During these peak visiting months, you might have to stay on the outskirts, in the Grinzing or the Schönbrunn district, for example, and commute to the Inner City by streetcar, bus, or U-Bahn. If you're looking to cut costs, staying outside the Inner City is not a bad option, as you can pay up to a quarter less for a hotel in the areas outside the Ringstrasse.

High season in Vienna encompasses most of the year: from May to October or early November, and during some weeks in midwinter, when the city hosts major trade fairs, conventions, and other cultural events. If you're planning a trip around Christmas and

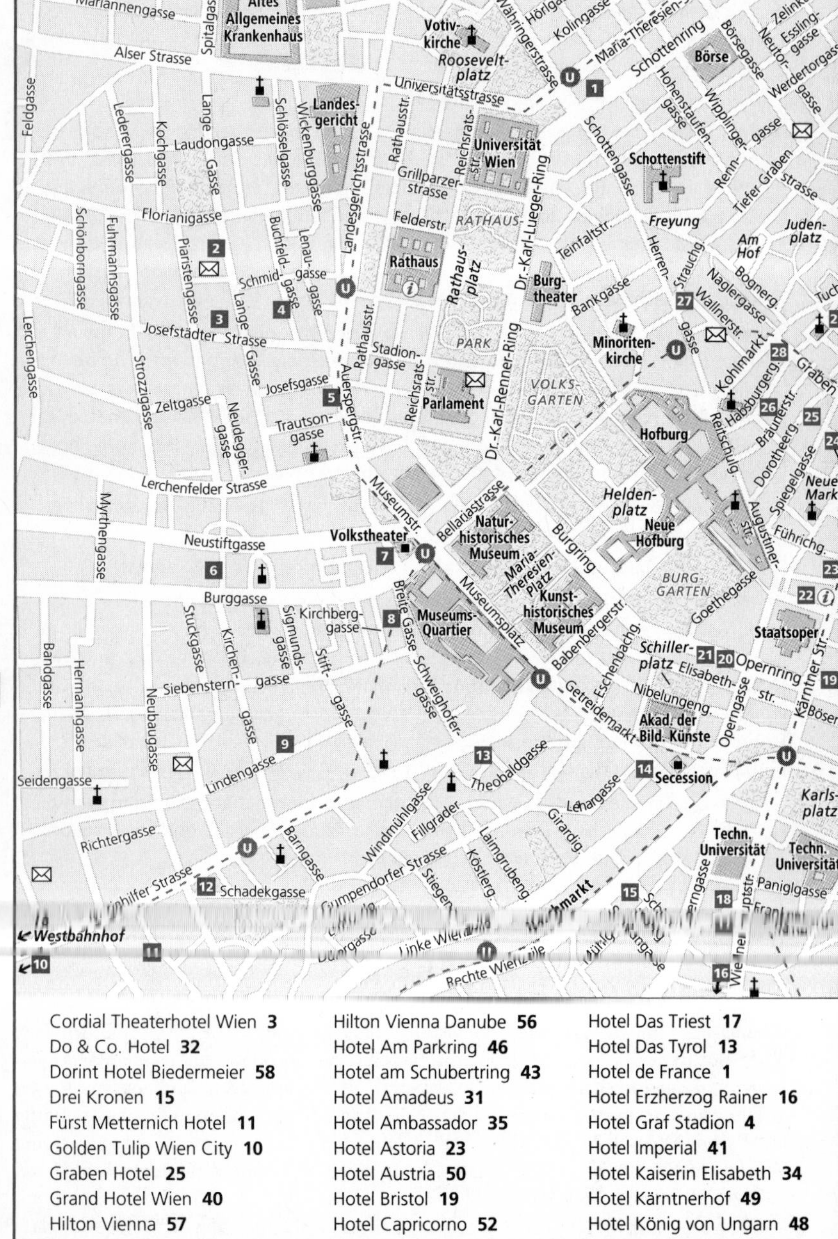

Cordial Theaterhotel Wien **3**	Hilton Vienna Danube **56**	Hotel Das Triest **17**
Do & Co. Hotel **32**	Hotel Am Parkring **46**	Hotel Das Tyrol **13**
Dorint Hotel Biedermeier **58**	Hotel am Schubertring **43**	Hotel de France **1**
Drei Kronen **15**	Hotel Amadeus **31**	Hotel Erzherzog Rainer **16**
Fürst Metternich Hotel **11**	Hotel Ambassador **35**	Hotel Graf Stadion **4**
Golden Tulip Wien City **10**	Hotel Astoria **23**	Hotel Imperial **41**
Graben Hotel **25**	Hotel Austria **50**	Hotel Kaiserin Elisabeth **34**
Grand Hotel Wien **40**	Hotel Bristol **19**	Hotel Kärntnerhof **49**
Hilton Vienna **57**	Hotel Capricorno **52**	Hotel König von Ungarn **48**

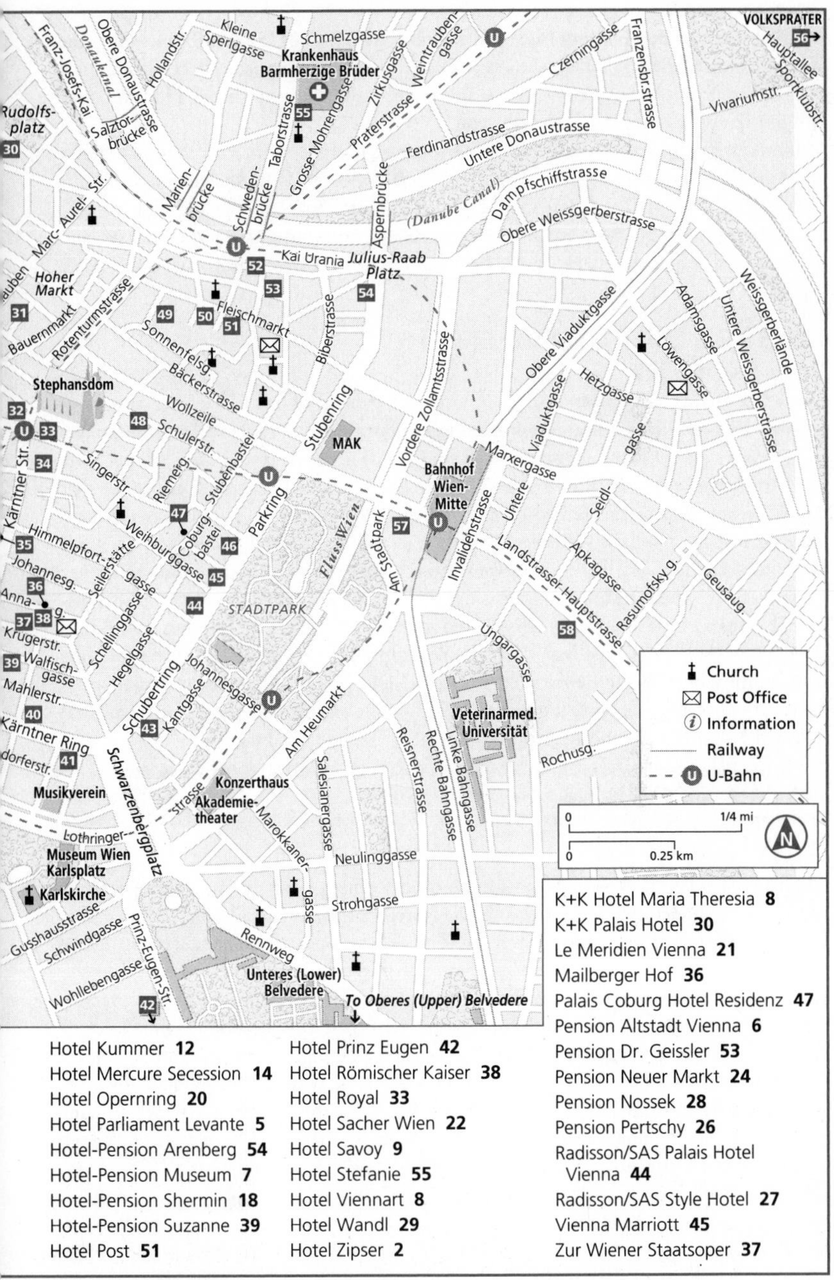

Hotel Kummer **12**
Hotel Mercure Secession **14**
Hotel Opernring **20**
Hotel Parliament Levante **5**
Hotel-Pension Arenberg **54**
Hotel-Pension Museum **7**
Hotel-Pension Shermin **18**
Hotel-Pension Suzanne **39**
Hotel Post **51**
Hotel Prinz Eugen **42**
Hotel Römischer Kaiser **38**
Hotel Royal **33**
Hotel Sacher Wien **22**
Hotel Savoy **9**
Hotel Stefanie **55**
Hotel Viennart **8**
Hotel Wandl **29**
Hotel Zipser **2**
K+K Hotel Maria Theresia **8**
K+K Palais Hotel **30**
Le Meridien Vienna **21**
Mailberger Hof **36**
Palais Coburg Hotel Residenz **47**
Pension Altstadt Vienna **6**
Pension Dr. Geissler **53**
Pension Neuer Markt **24**
Pension Nossek **28**
Pension Pertschy **26**
Radisson/SAS Palais Hotel Vienna **44**
Radisson/SAS Style Hotel **27**
Vienna Marriott **45**
Zur Wiener Staatsoper **37**

New Year's Day, room reservations should be made *at least* 1 month in advance. Some rate reductions (usually 15%–20%) are available during slower midwinter weeks—it always pays to ask.

Any branch of the **Austrian National Tourist Office** (✆ **01/588-660**), including the Vienna Tourist Board, will help you book a room. They have branch offices in the arrival halls of the airport, train stations, and major highways that access Vienna. However, they will not reserve a room in advance for you.

If you prefer to deal directly with an Austrian travel agency, three of the city's largest are **Austropa,** Friedrichsgasse 7, A-1010 (✆ **01/588-00510**); **Austrobus,** Dr.-Karl-Lueger-Ring 8, A-1010 (✆ **01/534-110**); and **Blaguss Reisen,** Wiedner Hauptstrasse 15 A-1040 (✆ **01/50180**). Any of them can reserve hotel space, sell airline tickets, and procure hard-to-get tickets for music festivals. Many of their employees speak English fluently.

INNERE STADT (INNER CITY)

Very Expensive

Do & Co. Hotel ★★ Finds In 2006, the management of one of Vienna's most consistently high-profile restaurants commandeered four floors of the Haas Haus, originally meant to be a skyscraper shopping mall, and transformed it into a stylish hotel. The result is a quirky but relentlessly upscale and obsessively design-conscious venue that almost everyone in Vienna has an opinion about. The black hulk of a building seems to grate against St. Stephan's Cathedral, which is immediately across the square. To reach the hotel reception, you'll take an elevator from a sterile-looking ground-floor entryway up to level six, where additional dramas unfold. The registration area is awkwardly positioned within a busy area that otherwise functions as a vestibule for a stylish and glossy-looking cocktail bar (Onyx Bar). Rooms are artfully minimalist and very comfortable, with yummy but hard-to-define colors of toffee and putty. Bedrooms have mahogany louvered doors, lots of polished travertine, dark-grained hardwoods, and floor plans that follow the curved walls and tucked-away balconies of the Haas Haus.

In the Haas Haus, Stephansplatz 12, 1010 Vienna. ✆ **01/24188.** Fax 01/24188444. www.doco.com. 43 units. 310€–350€ ($496–$560) double; from 740€ ($1,184) suite. AE, DC, MC, V. U-Bahn: Stephansplatz. **Amenities:** Restaurant; bar; room service; laundry service/dry cleaning. *In room:* A/C, TV, Wi-Fi, minibar, hair dryer, safe.

Grand Hotel Wien ★★ Some of the most discerning hotel guests in Europe, often music lovers, prefer this seven-story deluxe hotel to the more traditional and famous Imperial or Bristol. Only a block from the Wiener Staatsoper, it's a honey. The luxurious service begins with a doorman ushering you past the columns at the entrance into the stunning lobby and reception area. You enter a world of beveled mirrors, crystal chandeliers, marble in various hues, and brass-adorned elevators. Off the lobby is a complex of elegant shops selling expensive perfumes and pricey clothing.

The spacious soundproof accommodations are posh, with all the modern luxuries, such as heated floors, beverage makers, and phones in marble bathrooms (which contain tub/shower combinations and even antifogging mirrors). The more expensive units have more elaborate furnishings and decoration, including delicate stuccowork.

Kärntner Ring 9, 1010 Vienna. ✆ **01/515800.** Fax 01/5151310. www.grandhotelwien.com. 205 units. 400€–480€ ($640–$768) double; from 580€ ($928) junior suite; from 1,000€ ($1,600) suite. AE, DC, MC, V. Parking 28€ ($45). U-Bahn: Karlsplatz. **Amenities:** 3 restaurants; 2 bars; health club; boutiques; salon; room service; massage; babysitting; laundry service; dry cleaning; nonsmoking rooms; rooms for those w/limited mobility. *In room:* A/C, TV, Wi-Fi, minibar, coffeemaker, hair dryer, trouser press, safe.

Hotel Ambassador ★★ Until it became a hotel in 1866, the six-story Ambassador was a warehouse for wheat and flour, a far cry from its status today as one of the five most glamorous hotels in Vienna. It's no Bristol or Imperial, but it's quite posh nonetheless. The Ambassador couldn't be better located: It's between the Vienna State Opera and St. Stephan's Cathedral, on the square facing the Donner Fountain. Shop-lined Kärntnerstrasse is on the other side. Mark Twain stayed here, as have a host of diplomats and celebrities, including Theodore Roosevelt.

The sumptuous accommodations are an ideal choice for devotees of rococo *fin-de-siècle* or early-20th-century decor. Bedrooms are furnished with Biedermeier and Art Nouveau period pieces. The quieter rooms open onto Neuer Markt, although you'll miss the view of lively Kärntnerstrasse. Comfortable beds, marble bathrooms, and ample closet space add to the hotel's allure. The restaurant, Léhar, serves high-quality Austrian and international cuisine.

Kärntnerstrasse 22, A-1010 Vienna. ✆ **01/961610.** Fax 01/5132999. www.ambassador.at. 86 units. 271€–439€ ($434–$702) double; 526€ ($842) junior suite. AE, DC, MC, V. Parking 30€ ($48). U-Bahn: Stephansplatz. **Amenities:** Restaurant; bar; room service; laundry service; dry cleaning; nonsmoking rooms. *In room:* A/C, TV, Wi-Fi, minibar, hair dryer, safe.

Hotel Bristol ★★★ From the outside, this six-story landmark, a Westin hotel, looks no different from Vienna's other grand buildings, but connoisseurs of Austrian hotels maintain that this is a superb choice. Its decor evokes the height of the Hapsburg Empire—only the Hotel Imperial is grander. The hotel was constructed in 1894, next to the Vienna State Opera, and has since been updated to provide guests with black-tile bathrooms and other modern conveniences. Each bedroom includes a living-room area, and many have small balconies providing rooftop views of the Vienna State Opera and Ringstrasse.

Many of the hotel's architectural embellishments rank as *objets d'art* in their own right, including the black carved-marble fireplaces and the oil paintings in the salons. The Bristol Club Rooms in the tower offer comfortable chairs, an open fireplace, a self-service bar, library, stereo, deck, and sauna. Corkscrew columns of rare marble grace the Korso, Bristol's restaurant, which is one of the best in Vienna.

Kärntner Ring 1, 1015 Vienna. ✆ **888/625-5144** in the U.S., or 01/515160. Fax 01/51516550. www.westin.com/bristol. 146 units. 271€–439€ ($434–$702) double; from 526€ ($842) suite. Rates include breakfast. AE, DC, MC, V. Parking 30€ ($48). U-Bahn: Karlsplatz. Tram: 1 or 2. **Amenities:** 2 restaurants; bar; free access to nearby fitness center; sauna; business center; room service; babysitting; laundry service; dry cleaning; nonsmoking rooms; rooms for those w/limited mobility. *In room:* A/C, TV, Wi-Fi, minibar, hair dryer, safe.

Hotel de France ★ Hotel de France is right on the Ring and has long been a favorite. It's neighbor to the university and the Votivkirche, which makes it a centrally located choice. Its chiseled gray facade looks basically as it did when it was first erected in 1872. After World War II, the building was transformed into a hotel. Its modern elements and unobtrusively conservative decor are the result of extensive renovation. In such a subdued and appealing ambience, you often encounter businesspeople from all over the world. They appreciate the high-ceilinged public rooms and oriental carpets, the generously padded armchairs, and the full-dress portrait of Franz Josef. The bedrooms are among the finest for their price range in Vienna. The best units are on the fifth floor, although windows there are too high for you to absorb the view, unless you're very tall.

Schottenring 3, 1010 Vienna. ✆ **01/31368.** Fax 01/3195969. www.hoteldefrance.at. 212 units. 185€–330€ ($296–$528) double; from 495€ ($792) suite. Rates include buffet breakfast. AE, DC, MC, V. Parking 20€ ($32). U-Bahn: U2 or Schottentor. Tram: 1, 2, 37, or D. Bus: 1A. **Amenities:** 2 restaurants; 3 bars; sauna; room service; laundry service; dry cleaning; nonsmoking rooms. *In room:* A/C, TV, Wi-Fi, minibar, hair dryer, trouser press, safe.

Hotel Imperial ★★★ This hotel is definitely the grandest in Vienna. Luminaries from around the world use it as their headquarters, especially music stars who prefer the location—2 blocks from the Vienna State Opera and 1 block from the Musikverein. Richard Wagner stayed here with his family for a few months in 1875 (some scholars claim that he worked out key sections of both *Tannhäuser* and *Lohengrin* during that period). The hotel was built in 1869 as the private residence of the Duke of Württemberg. The Italian architect Zanotti designed the facade, which resembles a massive government building with a heroic frieze carved into the pediment below the roofline. It was converted into a private hotel in 1873. The Nazis commandeered it for their headquarters during World War II, and the Russians requisitioned it in 1945. Massive expenditures have returned it to its former glory, with special care paid to its fourth and fifth floors, which hold the most desirable rooms. Accommodations vary greatly in size, as befits a hotel of this era. Those on the mezzanine and first floors are lavishly baroque; as you go higher, appointments diminish, as do bathroom sizes.

Kärntner Ring 16, 1015 Vienna. ✆ **800/325-3589** in the U.S., or 01/501100. Fax 01/50110410. www.luxurycollection.com/imperial. 138 units. 700€ ($1,120) double; from 1,000€ ($1,600) suite. AE, DC, MC, V. Parking 32€ ($51). U-Bahn: Karlsplatz. **Amenities:** 2 restaurants; bar; health club; sauna; salon; room service; massage; babysitting; laundry service; dry cleaning; nonsmoking rooms; rooms for those w/ limited mobility. *In room:* A/C, TV, Wi-Fi, minibar, hair dryer, safe.

Hotel Sacher Wien ★★★ The Sacher was built in 1876, and despite recent improvements, partial rebuilding, and renovations, which added 40 new rooms and a deluxe spa, it still has an air of Hapsburg-era glory. Red velvet, crystal chandeliers, and brocaded curtains in the public rooms evoke Old Vienna. If you want truly grand, we think the Imperial and Bristol are superior, but the Sacher has its diehard admirers. Despite its popularity as a setting for spy novels, both the crowned heads of Europe and the deposed heads (especially those of eastern European countries) have safely dined and lived here. In addition to intrigue, the Sacher has produced culinary creations that still bear its name. Franz Sacher, the celebrated chef, left the world a fabulously caloric chocolate cake called the Sachertorte. Most rooms contain antiques or superior reproductions; those facing the Vienna State Opera have the best views. Demisuites and chambers with drawing rooms are more expensive. The reception desk is fairly flexible about making arrangements for salons or apartments, or joining two rooms together, if possible.

Philharmonikerstrasse 4, 1010 Vienna. ✆ **01/514560.** Fax 01/51256810. www.sacher.com. 152 units. 299€–464€ ($478–$742) double; from 650€ ($1,040) junior suite; from 720€ ($1,152) executive suite. AE, DC, MC, V. Parking 32€ ($51). U-Bahn: Karlsplatz. Tram: 1, 2, 62, 65, D, or J. Bus: 4A. **Amenities:** 2 restaurants; bar; spa; room service; massage; babysitting; laundry/dry cleaning. *In room:* A/C, TV, Wi-Fi, minibar, hair dryer, safe.

Palais Coburg Hotel Residenz ★★★ Originally built in 1846 as the outrageously elegant, and even more outrageously ostentatious private home of the Coburg dynasty (who managed somehow to sire most of the monarchs of western Europe), this sprawling and staggeringly historic building—except for its exterior—was gutted and rebuilt during a 6-year renovation that was completed in 2006. Much of its interior had been bashed and vandalized by the Russian army during their occupation of the site after

World War II. But all traces of the mundane have definitely been banished since its transformation into a multipurpose building, only part of which is devoted to hotel accommodations.

The full-service spa is reserved only for residents of the hotel, and then there are those suites: The smaller and less expensive are contemporary, intensely design-conscious, and very comfortable. The more expensive evoke the heyday of the Rothschilds and are posh, with many pale satin upholsteries and valuable antiques. Ironically, all this grandeur is the personal property of an (individual) Austrian investor, whose stated ambition involves the on-site compilation of the largest and most comprehensive wine collection in Europe.

Coburgbastei 4, 1010 Vienna. ✆ **01/518-180.** Fax 01/518-181. www.palais-coburg.com. 35 suites. 560€–1,900€ ($896–$3,040) suites. Rates include breakfast. Parking 40€ ($64). AE, DC, MC, V. **Amenities:** 2 restaurants; indoor pool; health club; spa; sauna; room service; laundry service/dry cleaning. *In room:* A/C, TV, Wi-Fi, full kitchen w/bar, safe.

Radisson/SAS Palais Hotel Vienna ★ This hotel is one of Vienna's grandest renovations. An unused neoclassical palace was converted into a hotel in 1985 by SAS, the Scandinavian airline; in 1994, another palace next door was added, allowing the hotel to double in size. Near Vienna's most elaborate park (the Stadtpark), the hotel boasts facades accented with cast-iron railings, reclining nymphs, and elaborate cornices. The interior is plushly outfitted with 19th-century architectural motifs, all impeccably restored and dramatically illuminated. The lobby contains arching palms, a soaring ceiling, and a bar with evening piano music. The result is an uncluttered, conservative, and well-maintained hotel that is managed in a breezy, highly efficient manner. Bedrooms are outfitted in soothing pastels or, in the new wing, summery shades of green and white. The hotel also offers several duplex suites, or *maisonettes,* conventional suites, and rooms in the Royal Club, which has upgraded luxuries and services.

Parkring 16, 1010 Vienna. ✆ **800/333-3333** in the U.S., or 01/515170. Fax 01/5122216. www.radisson.com. 247 units. 169€–284€ ($270–$454) double; from 334€ ($534) junior suite. AE, DC, MC, V. Parking 30€ ($48). U-Bahn: Stadtpark. Tram: 2. **Amenities:** Restaurant; 2 bars; fitness center; spa; Jacuzzi; sauna; room service; babysitting; laundry service; dry cleaning; nonsmoking rooms; 1 room for those w/limited mobility. *In room:* A/C, TV, Wi-Fi, minibar, hair dryer, safe.

Expensive

Hotel Amadeus ★ Cozy and convenient, this boxlike hotel is only 2 minutes away from the cathedral and within walking distance of practically everything of musical or historical note in Vienna. It was built on the site of a once-legendary tavern (Zum roten Igel) that attracted the likes of Johannes Brahms, Franz Schubert, and Moritz von Schwind. Behind a dull 1960s facade, the hotel maintains its bedrooms and carpeted public rooms in reasonable shape. Bedrooms are furnished in a comfortable, modern style, and many open onto views of the cathedral. However, ceilings are uncomfortably low. Double-glazing on the windows quiets but does not obliterate street noise. Some of the carpeting and fabrics look a little worse for wear. Tiled bathrooms are midsize, but there's not enough room to lay out your toiletries. Eight rooms have showers but no tubs. Expect a somewhat dour welcome: No one on the staff will win any Mr. or Mrs. Sunshine contests.

Wildpretmarkt 5, 1010 Vienna. ✆ **01/5338738.** Fax 01/533-87383838. www.hotel-amadeus.at. 30 units. 178€–203€ ($285–$325) double. Rates include buffet breakfast. AE, DC, MC, V. U-Bahn: Stephansplatz. **Amenities:** Breakfast room; lounge; babysitting; laundry service; dry cleaning; nonsmoking rooms; rooms for those w/limited mobility. *In room:* A/C, TV, Wi-Fi, minibar, hair dryer, safe.

Hotel Astoria ★ Hotel Astoria is for nostalgists who want to experience life as it was in the closing days of the Austro-Hungarian Empire. A first-class hotel, the Astoria has an eminently desirable location, lying on the shopping mall near St. Stephan's Cathedral and the Vienna State Opera. Decorated in a slightly frayed turn-of-the-20th-century style, the hotel offers well-appointed and traditionally decorated bedrooms. The interior rooms tend to be too dark, and singles are just too cramped. The place is, in fact, a bit on the melancholy side. Rooms contain built-in armoires and well-chosen linens and duvets on good beds, and bathrooms that, for the most part, are spacious (although the fixtures are old) and have such extras as dual basins, heated racks, and bidets. Of course, it has been renovated over the years, but the old style has been preserved, and management seems genuinely concerned about offering high-quality service.

Kärntnerstrasse 32–34, 1010 Vienna. ✆ **01/515770.** Fax 01/5157782. www.austria-trend.at. 118 units. 450€–550€ ($720–$880) double; 650€ ($1,040) suite. Rates include breakfast. AE, DC, MC, V. Parking 22€–32€ ($35–$51). U-Bahn: Stephansplatz. **Amenities:** Restaurant; bar; room service; babysitting; laundry service; dry cleaning; nonsmoking rooms. *In room:* TV, minibar, hair dryer, safe.

Hotel Das Triest ★★ Finds Sir Terence Conran, the famous English architect and designer, created the interior for this contemporary hotel in the center of Vienna, a 5-minute walk from St. Stephan's Cathedral. Conran has done for Das Triest what Philippe Starck did for New York's Paramount Hotel: created a stylish address in the heart of one of the world's most important cities. An emerging favorite with artists and musicians, this hip hotel has such grace notes as a courtyard garden. The building was originally used as a stable for horses pulling stagecoaches between Vienna and Trieste—hence its name, "City of Trieste." Its old cross-vaulted rooms, which give the structure a distinctive flair, have been transformed into lounges and suites. Bedrooms are midsize to spacious, tastefully furnished, and comfortable.

Wiedner Hauptstrasse 12, 1040 Vienna. ✆ **01/58918.** Fax 01/5891818. www.dastriest.at. 73 units. 273€ ($437) double; 338€–556€ ($541–$890) suite. Rates include buffet breakfast. AE, DC, MC, V. Parking 25€ ($40). U-Bahn: Stephansplatz. **Amenities:** Restaurant; bar; fitness center; sauna; salon; room service; massage; babysitting; laundry service; dry cleaning; nonsmoking rooms; solarium. *In room:* A/C, TV, Wi-Fi, minibar, hair dryer, trouser press, safe.

Hotel Kaiserin Elisabeth This yellow-stoned hotel is conveniently located near the cathedral. The interior is decorated with oriental rugs on well-maintained marble and wood floors. The main salon has a pale-blue skylight suspended above it, with mirrors and half-columns in natural wood. The small, quiet rooms have been considerably updated since Wolfgang Mozart, Richard Wagner, Franz Liszt, and Edvard Grieg stayed here, and their musical descendants continue to patronize the place. Polished wood, clean linens, and perhaps another oriental rug grace the rooms. Bathrooms are a bit cramped, with not enough room for your toiletries, but they are tiled and equipped with tub/shower combinations, vanity mirrors, and, in some cases, bidets.

Weihburggasse 3, 1010 Vienna. ✆ **01/515260.** Fax 01/515267. www.kaiserinelisabeth.at. 63 units. 216€–245€ ($346–$392) double. Rates include buffet breakfast. AE, DC, MC, V. Parking 30€ ($48). U-Bahn: Stephansplatz. **Amenities:** Restaurant; bar; room service; laundry service; dry cleaning. *In room:* A/C (in most units), TV, Wi-Fi, minibar, hair dryer, safe.

Hotel König Von Ungarn ★ On a narrow street near St. Stephan's, this hotel occupies a dormered building that dates back to the early 17th century. It's been receiving paying guests for more than 4 centuries and is Vienna's oldest continuously operated hotel—in all, an evocative, intimate, and cozy retreat. In 1791, Mozart reportedly resided and wrote some of his immortal music in an apartment upstairs, where you'll find a Mozart museum.

The interior abounds with old architectural details, such as marble columns supporting the arched ceiling of the King of Hungary restaurant. There's also a mirrored solarium/bar area with a glass roof over the atrium, and a live tree growing out of the pavement. Tall hinged windows overlook the Old Town, and Venetian mirrors adorn some walls. Everywhere you look, you'll find low-key luxury, tradition, and modern convenience. Try for the two rooms with balconies. Guest rooms have been newly remodeled with Biedermeier accents and traditional furnishings. Some rooms—and you should try to avoid these—lack an outside window.

Schulerstrasse 10, 1010 Vienna. ✆ **01/515840.** Fax 01/515848. www.kvu.at. 33 units. 215€ ($344) double; 295€–345€ ($472–$552) apt. Rates include breakfast. AE, DC, MC, V. U-Bahn: Stephansplatz. **Amenities:** Restaurant; bar; room service; babysitting; laundry service; dry cleaning. *In room:* A/C, TV, Wi-Fi, minibar, hair dryer, safe.

Hotel Römischer Kaiser ★ Kids A Best Western affiliate, this hotel is housed in a national trust building that has seen its share of transformations. It's located in a traffic-free zone between St. Stephan's Cathedral and the Vienna State Opera, on a side street off Kärntnerstrasse. It was constructed in 1684 as the private palace of the imperial chamberlain and later housed the Imperial School of Engineering before becoming a hostelry at the turn of the 20th century. The hotel rents romantically decorated rooms (our favorite has red satin upholstery over a chaise lounge). Double-glazed windows keep down the noise, and baroque paneling is a nice touch. Some rooms—notably nos. 12, 22, 30, and 38—can accommodate three or four beds, making this a family-friendly place.

Annagasse 16, 1010 Vienna. ✆ **800/528-1234** in the U.S., or 01/51277510. Fax 01/512775113. www.bestwestern.com. 23 units. 132€–229€ ($211–$366) double, 195€ ($312) suite. Rates include buffet breakfast. AE, DC, MC, V. Parking 21€ ($34). U-Bahn: Stephansplatz. **Amenities:** Restaurant; bar; room service; laundry service; dry cleaning; nonsmoking rooms. *In room:* A/C, TV, Wi-Fi, minibar, hair dryer, safe.

K+K Palais Hotel ★ This hotel, with its severely dignified facade, sheltered the affair of Emperor Franz Josef and his celebrated mistress, Katherina Schratt, in 1890. Occupying a desirable position near the river and a 5-minute walk from the Ring, it remained unused for 2 decades until it was renovated in 1981.

Vestiges of its imperial past remain, in spite of the contemporary but airy lobby and the lattice-covered bar. The public rooms are painted a shade of imperial Austrian yellow, and one of Ms. Schratt's antique secretaries occupies a niche near a white-sided tile stove. The bedrooms are comfortably outfitted and stylish. Rooms have a certain Far East motif, with light wood, wicker, and rattan.

Rudolfsplatz 11, 1010 Vienna. ✆ **01/5331353.** Fax 01/533135370. www.kkhotels.com. 66 units. 185€–255€ ($296–$408) double. Rates include buffet breakfast. AE, DC, MC, V. U-Bahn: Schottenring. **Amenities:** Bistro; bar; room service; babysitting; laundry service; dry cleaning; nonsmoking rooms. *In room:* A/C, TV, Wi-Fi, minibar, hair dryer, safe.

Le Meridien Vienna ★★★ Located directly on the famous Ringstrasse, this glamorous government-rated five-star property is only a short stroll from the Vienna State Opera and Hofburg Palace. This is the first hotel property in Austria for this popular French chain. A $120-million renovation converted an apartment block of turn-of-the-20th-century imperial Vienna architecture into this new city landmark. Luscious maple wood, satin-chrome steel, and glass create an aura of understated elegance in public rooms, and special illuminations and lighting effects are used dramatically. The ultramodern design certainly doesn't make this hotel a competitor for old-fashioned Viennese *luxe* hostelries such as the Imperial or the Sacher.

Opernring 13-A, A-1010 Vienna. ✆ **01/588900.** Fax 01/588909090. http://vienna.lemeridien.com. 294 units. 170€–385€ ($272–$616) double; from 655€ ($1,048) suite. AE, DC, MC, V. U-Bahn: Karlsplatz. **Amenities:** Restaurant; 2 bars; indoor heated pool; gym; sauna; room service; babysitting; laundry service; dry cleaning; nonsmoking rooms; rooms for those w/limited mobility. *In room:* A/C, TV, Wi-Fi, minibar, beverage maker, hair dryer, iron, safe.

Radisson/SAS Style Hotel ★ In the early 1900s, this building was the headquarters of an Austrian bank, but in 2005 it was converted into an elegant hotel. The result is a quirky and somewhat eccentric hotel with an enviable facade that's embellished with gilded, Secessionist-era bas reliefs, virtually no signage in front, and a style-conscious, avant-garde postmodern interior that challenged the creativity of a team of interior designers. The most appealing public area is the H-12 wine bar, a long, narrow space with hard metallic surfaces, an alabaster bar that's illuminated from within, and big-screen TVs showing either fashion *défilés* in Milan or the occasional soccer game. Bedrooms are comfortable, culturally neutral, and angular-minimalist, but with warm earth tones that make them livable and, at their best, cozy. The hotel has a central location deep in the heart of Imperial Vienna.

Herrengasse 12, 1010 Vienna. ✆ **01/227800.** Fax 01/2278077. www.style.vienna.radissonsas.com. 78 units. 199€–310€ ($318–$496) double, 555€–585€ ($888–$936) suite. AE, DC, MC, V. U-Bahn: Herrengasse. **Amenities:** Restaurant; wine bar; health club; sauna; laundry service; dry cleaning; room service. *In room:* A/C, TV, Wi-Fi, minibar, safe.

Vienna Marriott ★ The Marriott has a striking exterior and holds its own against SAS, the K+K Palais Hotel, and the Hilton, although the latter two hotels manage to evoke a more Viennese atmosphere. Opposite Stadtpark, the hotel is ideally located for visitors, as it's within walking distance of such landmarks as St. Stephan's Cathedral, the Vienna State Opera, and the Hofburg. Its Mississippi-riverboat facade displays expanses of tinted glass set in finely wrought enameled steel. About a third of the building is occupied by the American Consulate offices and a few private apartments. The hotel's lobby culminates in a stairway whose curved sides frame a splashing waterfall that's surrounded with plants. Many of the comfortably modern bedrooms are larger than those in the city's other contemporary hotels. Furnishings are a bit commercial.

Parkring 12A, A-1010 Vienna. ✆ **888/236-2427** in the U.S., or 01/515180. Fax 01/515186736. www.marriott.com. 313 units. 229€–294€ ($366–$470) double; 429€–690€ ($686–$1,104) suite. AE, DC, MC, V. [illegible] Jacuzzi; sauna; car-rental desk; salon; room service; massage; babysitting; laundry service; dry cleaning; nonsmoking rooms; rooms for those w/limited mobility; solarium. *In room:* A/C, TV, Wi-Fi, minibar, hair dryer, iron, trouser press, safe.

Moderate

Graben Hotel Back in the 18th century, this was called Zum Goldener Jägerhorn; over the years, it has attracted an array of bohemian writers and artists. The poet Franz Grillparzer was a regular guest, and during the dark days of World War II, it was a gathering place for such writers as Franz Kafka, Max Brod, and Peter Altenberg. The hotel stands on a narrow street off the Kärntnerstrasse, in the very center of the city. Guests gather around the stone fireplace in winter and look at the original postcards left by Altenberg. Rooms are high-ceilinged but rather cramped. Although there are some Art Nouveau touches, much of the furniture is a bit drab and spartan for our tastes. If there's any sunlight streaming in, it'll come from the front rooms, not the darker havens in the rear.

Dorotheergasse 3, 1010 Vienna. ✆ **01/51215310.** Fax 01/512153120. www.kremslehnerhotels.at. 41 units. 160€–195€ ($256–$312) double. Rates include buffet breakfast. AE, DC, MC, V. Parking 27€ ($43). U-Bahn: Karlsplatz. **Amenities:** Restaurant; lounge; room service; babysitting; nonsmoking rooms. *In room:* TV, Wi-Fi, minibar, hair dryer, safe.

Hotel Am Parkring This well-maintained hotel occupies the top three floors of a 13-story office building near the edge of Vienna's Stadtpark. A semiprivate elevator services only the street-level entrance and the hotel's floors. There are sweeping views of the city from all of its bedrooms, some of which overlook nearby St. Stephan's Cathedral. Bedrooms are furnished in a conservative but comfortable style, and are favored by business travelers and tourists alike, although the atmosphere is a bit sterile if you're seeking nostalgic Vienna. Rooms here are a standard, reliable choice, but don't expect fireworks. This hotel is not the kindest to the lone tourist, as single accommodations tend to be too small, and often sofa beds are used.

Parkring 12, 1015 Vienna. ✆ **01/514800.** Fax 01/5148040. www.bestwestern.com. 64 units. 149€–230€ ($238–$368) double; 360€ ($576) suite. Rates include buffet breakfast. AE, DC, MC, V. Parking 19€ ($30). U-Bahn: Stadtpark or Stubentor. Tram: 1 or 2. **Amenities:** Restaurant; bar; room service; babysitting; laundry service; dry cleaning; nonsmoking rooms. *In room:* A/C, TV, Wi-Fi, minibar, hair dryer.

Hotel Am Schubertring ★ Kids In a historic building in the very center of town, this small hotel has a certain charm and style. On the famous Ringstrasse, next to the opera, it has Viennese flair, especially in the use of Art Nouveau and Biedermeier-style furnishings in its bedrooms. Rooms are moderate in size, comfortable, and generally quiet, and eight units are suitable for three guests or more. The top-floor rooms look out over the rooftops of Vienna. At this family-friendly place, children under age 6 are housed free if sharing accommodations with a parent.

Schubertring 11, 1010 Vienna. ✆ **01/717020.** Fax 01/7139966. www.schubertring.at. 39 units. 128€–195€ ($205–$312) double; 142€–218€ ($227–$349) suite. Rates include buffet breakfast. AE, DC, MC, V. Parkring 20€ ($32). U-Bahn: Karlsplatz. **Amenities:** Snack bar; bar; room service; babysitting; laundry service; dry cleaning; nonsmoking rooms. *In room:* A/C, TV, Wi-Fi, minibar, hair dryer, safe.

Hotel Capricorno In the heart of Vienna, this government-rated four-star hotel, a short stroll from St. Stephan's and next to the Danube Canal, has more than a convenient location going for it. Outside it's a dull, cube-shape building, but inside it's rather warm and inviting, with modern Art Nouveau accents, tiles, and brass trim in the reception area. Rooms are compact—even cramped, in many cases—but are well furnished and maintained. Singles are particularly small, mainly because the beds are more spacious than most. Some units, especially those on the lower levels, suffer from noise pollution. The hotel sends its guests to its sibling, the Hotel Stefanie, across the street, for dining in a first-class restaurant, Kronprinz Rudolph, which offers Viennese and international cuisine alike.

Schwedenplatz 3–4, 1010 Vienna. ✆ **01/53331040.** Fax 01/53376714. www.schick-hotels.com. 46 units. 131€–186€ ($210–$298) double. AE, DC, MC, V. Rates include buffet breakfast. U-Bahn: Stephansplatz. **Amenities:** Breakfast room; lounge; room service; laundry service; dry cleaning; nonsmoking rooms. *In room:* A/C, TV, Wi-Fi, minibar, hair dryer.

Hotel Opernring Kids Across from the Vienna State Opera, and lying along the Ring, this government-rated four-star hotel has been much improved. Accommodations are fairly large and tastefully furnished, with such features as duvet-covered beds and spacious tiled bathrooms. Double-glazed windows cut down on the noise in the front bedrooms. Some units are reserved for nonsmokers, and some of the accommodations can sleep three to four family members comfortably. Don't judge the hotel by its rather cramped reception area or its entrance. The third-floor lounge is large and inviting; its bay window opens onto the activity of central Vienna.

Opernring 11, 1010 Vienna. ✆ **800/528-1234** in the U.S., or 01/5875518. Fax 01/587551829. www.opernring.at. 35 units. 150€–240€ ($240–$384) double; 280€–380€ ($448–$608) suite. Rates include buffet breakfast. AE, DC, MC, V. Parking 22€ ($35). U-Bahn: Karlsplatz. **Amenities:** Breakfast room; lounge; room service; babysitting; laundry service; dry cleaning; nonsmoking rooms. *In room:* TV, Wi-Fi, minibar, coffeemaker, hair dryer, safe.

Hotel-Pension Arenberg ★ This genteel but unpretentious hotel-pension, a Best Western, occupies the second and third floors of a six-story apartment house that was built around the turn of the 20th century. Set in a prestigious neighborhood on Ringstrasse, it offers small, soundproof bedrooms outfitted in old-world style with oriental carpets, conservative furniture, and intriguing artwork. The hotel remains exceptionally appealing to those with a sense of history. One enthusiastic reader described it as a small luxury hotel where the English-speaking staff couldn't be more helpful.

Stubenring 2, 1010 Vienna. ✆ **800/528-7234** in the U.S., or 01/5125291. Fax 01/5139356. www.bestwestern.com. 23 units. 158€–208€ ($253–$333) double; 293€ ($469) triple. Rates include breakfast. AE, DC, MC, V. Parking 15€ ($24). U-Bahn: Schwedenplatz. **Amenities:** Lounge; breakfast-only room service; babysitting; laundry service; dry cleaning; nonsmoking rooms; rooms for those with limited mobility. *In room:* A/C, TV, minibar, hair dryer, safe.

Hotel Royal ★★ This dignified, nine-story hotel is on one of the more prestigious streets of the old city, less than a block from St. Stephan's Cathedral. The lobby contains the piano where Wagner composed *Die Meistersinger von Nürnberg.* Each of the good-size rooms is furnished differently, with some good reproductions of antiques and even an occasional original. Opened in 1931, the hotel was rebuilt in 1982. Try for a room with a balcony and a view of the cathedral. Corner rooms with spacious foyers are also desirable, although those facing the street tend to be noisy.

Singerstrasse 3, 1010 Vienna. ✆ **01/515680.** Fax 01/513-9698. www.kremslehnerhotels.at. 81 units. 140€–200€ ($224–$320) double. Rates include breakfast. AE, DC, MC, V. U-Bahn: Stephansplatz. **Amenities:** 2 restaurants; bar; wine bar; room service; laundry service; dry cleaning; nonsmoking rooms. *In room:* TV, Wi-Fi, minibar, hair dryer.

Hotel Viennart ★ Finds More than any other hotel in Vienna, this six-story hotel, which was fully renovated, appeals to lovers of modern art. This is the most convenient place to stay for those wanting to be near the contemporary art in the newly launched MuseumsQuartier (see chapter 6). The location is at the edge of the Spittelberg, a district locals call "the Montmartre of Vienna." The decor is sock-it-to-you modern, in red, white, orange, and black. Rooms are outfitted in a functional style, with fine furnishings.

Breite Gasse 9, 1070 Vienna. ✆ **01/523-13-450.** Fax 01/523-13-45-111. www.austrotel.at. 56 units. 100€–170€ ($160–$272) double; 246€ ($394) suite. Children under 12 stay free in parent's room. Rates include buffet breakfast. AE, DC, MC, V. U-Bahn: Volkstheater. **Amenities:** Breakfast room; babysitting; laundry; dry cleaning; nonsmoking rooms. *In room:* TV, minibar, hair dryer.

Mailberger Hof This old palace was built in the 14th century as a mansion for the knights of Malta and was converted into a hotel in the 1970s. Off the main drag, Kärntnerstrasse, it lies on a typical Viennese cobblestone street. The two large wooden doors at the entrance still boast a Maltese cross. The vaulted ceiling, the leather armchairs, and maybe the marbleized walls are about all that would remind the knights of their former home. Everywhere the place has been renewed, although a cobblestone courtyard, set with tables in fair weather, remains. A family-run place with a cozy atmosphere, the hotel features moderate-size bedrooms that are often brightened with pastels. In general, though, the public rooms are more inviting than the private ones.

Annagasse 7, 1010 Vienna. ✆ **01/5120641.** Fax 01/512064110. www.mailbergerhof.at. 40 units. 180€–260€ ($288–$416) double; 210€–280€ ($336–$448) suite. Rates include buffet breakfast. AE, DC, MC, V. Parking 29€ ($46). U-Bahn: Karlsplatz. **Amenities:** Bar; room service (7am–10pm); babysitting; laundry service; dry cleaning; nonsmoking rooms. *In room:* A/C, TV, minibar, hair dryer, safe.

Inexpensive

Drei Kronen ★ Finds The celebrated architect Ignaz Drapala designed this splendid Art Nouveau building in a charming section of Vienna close to the famous Naschmarkt. The "three crowns" in the German name Drei Kronen refer to Austria, Hungary, and Bohemia from the old Austro-Hungarian Empire. A symbol of the crowns is displayed on top of the building. The hotel enjoys one of Vienna's best locations, close to such monuments as the Vienna State Opera and St. Stephan's Cathedral. Built in 1894, the five-story hotel was completely renovated in 1999. The midsize to spacious bedrooms are fresh and bright, with comfortable furnishings. Some of the rooms are large enough to contain house beds.

Schleifmuehlgasse 25, 1040 Vienna. ✆ **01/5873289.** Fax 01/587328911. www.hotel3kronen.at. 41 units. 119€ ($190) double; 139€ ($222) triple. AE, DC, MC, V. Parking 15€ ($24). U-Bahn: Karlsplatz. **Amenities:** Breakfast room; lounge; babysitting; nonsmoking rooms. *In room:* TV, safe (some).

Hotel Austria The staff here always seem willing to tell you where to go in the neighborhood for a good meal or a glass of wine, and often distribute printouts explaining the medieval origins of this section of the city center. This unpretentious, family-owned hotel sits on a small, quiet street whose name will probably be unfamiliar to many taxi drivers—a corner building on the adjoining street, Fleischmarkt 20, is the point where you'll turn onto the narrow lane. The comfortable furnishings in the lobby and in the chandeliered breakfast room are maintained in tip-top shape. Every year, one of the four floors of the hotel is completely renovated with new wallpapering, furniture, and bedding. The decor is rather functional, and the hotel is immaculately maintained and inviting.

Am Fleischmarkt 20, 1011 Vienna. ✆ **01/51523.** Fax 01/51523506. www.hotelaustria-wien.at. 46 units, 42 w/private bathroom. 69€–90€ ($110–$144) double w/shared bathroom; 115€–178€ ($184–$285) double w/private bathroom. Rates include buffet breakfast. AE, DC, MC, V. Parking 19€ ($30). U-Bahn: Schwedenplatz. Tram: 1 or 2. **Amenities:** Breakfast room; lounge; breakfast-only room service; massage; babysitting; laundry service; dry cleaning; nonsmoking rooms. *In room:* TV, minibar, hair dryer.

Hotel Kärntnerhof ★ Kids Only a 4-minute walk from the cathedral, the Kärntnerhof has been much improved, thanks to refurbishing and renovating, and is now a more desirable address than ever. The decor of the public rooms is tastefully arranged around oriental rugs, well-upholstered chairs and couches with cabriole legs, and an occasional 19th-century portrait. The midsize to spacious units are very up to date, usually with the original parquet floors and striped or patterned wallpaper set off by curtains. Many of the guest rooms are large enough to handle an extra bed or so, making this a family favorite. The owner is quite helpful, directing guests to the post office and nearby Vienna landmarks.

Grashofgasse 4, 1011 Vienna. ✆ **01/5121923.** Fax 01/513222833. www.karntnerhof.com. 44 units. 110€–162€ ($176–$259) double; 205€–252€ ($328–$403) suite. Rates include buffet breakfast. AE, DC, MC, V. Parking 17€ ($27). U-Bahn: Stephansplatz. **Amenities:** Breakfast room; lounge; room service; laundry service; dry cleaning. *In room:* TV.

Hotel-Pension Shermin The Voshmgih family welcomes you into its small, inviting, homelike boardinghouse in the city center. Bedrooms are big and comfortable, and the hotel-pension draws many repeat guests. The location is convenient for such sights as the opera house, the Imperial Palace, and the Spanish Riding School, all a 5-minute walk away. Furnishings are modern and without much flair, but are exceedingly comfortable.

Rilkeplatz 7, 1040 Vienna. ✆ **01/58661830.** Fax 01/586618310. www.hotel-pension-shermin.at. 11 units. 72€–114€ ($115–$182) double. Rates include buffet breakfast. AE, DC, MC, V. Parking 7€ ($11) Mon–Fri; free Sat–Sun. U-Bahn: Karlsplatz. **Amenities:** Breakfast room; lounge; breakfast-only room service. *In room:* TV, hair dryer.

Hotel-Pension Suzanne ★ **Kids** Only a 45-second walk from the opera house, this is a real discovery. Once you get past its post-war facade, the interior warms considerably, brightly decorated in a comfortable, traditional style with antique beds, plush chairs, and the original molded ceilings. Now into its second generation of managers, the hotel-pension is run by the welcoming Strafinger family, who like its classic Viennese turn-of-the-20th-century styling. Rooms are midsize and exceedingly well maintained, facing either the busy street or a courtyard. Families often stay here because some of the accommodations contain three beds. Some bedrooms are like small apartments, with kitchenettes.

Walfischgasse 4. ✆ **01/5132507.** Fax 01/5132500. www.pension-suzanne.at. 26 units. 100€–112€ ($160–$179) double; 135€–145€ ($216–$232) triple. Rates include buffet breakfast. AE, DC, MC, V. U-Bahn: Karlsplatz. **Amenities:** Breakfast room; lounge; breakfast-only room service; babysitting. *In room:* TV, hair dryer.

Hotel Post Hotel Post lies in the medieval slaughterhouse district, today an interesting section full of hotels and restaurants. The dignified front of this hotel is constructed of gray stone, with a facade of black marble covering the street level. The manager is quick to tell you that both Mozart and Haydn frequently stayed in a former inn at this address. Those composers would probably be amused to hear recordings of their music played in the coffeehouse, Le Café, attached to the hotel. Bedrooms, most of which are midsize, are streamlined and functionally furnished.

Fleischmarkt 24, 1010 Vienna. ✆ **01/515830.** Fax 01/51583808. www.hotel-post-wien.at. 107 units, 77 w/private bathroom. 76€ ($122) double w/shared bathroom; 125€ ($200) double w/private bathroom; 100€ ($160) triple w/shared bathroom; 152€ ($243) triple w/private bathroom. Rates include buffet breakfast. AE, DC, MC, V. Parking 18€ ($29). Tram: 1 or 2. **Amenities:** Restaurant; lounge; salon; laundry service; dry cleaning; nonsmoking rooms; 1 room for those w/limited mobility. *In room:* TV, hair dryer.

Hotel Wandl Stepping into this hotel is like stepping into a piece of a family's history—it has been under the same ownership for generations. The Wandl lies in the Inner City and offers views of the steeple of St. Stephan's Cathedral from many of its windows, which often open onto small balconies. The breakfast room is a high-ceilinged, two-toned room with hanging chandeliers and lots of ornamented plaster. The bedrooms usually offer the kind of spacious dimensions that went out of style 60 years ago. Beds are frequently renewed—all in all, this is a comfortable choice if you're not too demanding. The hotel faces St. Peter's Church.

Petersplatz 9, 1010 Vienna. ✆ **01/534550.** Fax 01/5345577. www.hotel-wandl.com. 138 units. 158€–205€ ($253–$328) double; 220€ ($352) suite. Rates include breakfast. AE, DC, MC, V. U-Bahn: Stephansplatz. **Amenities:** Breakfast room; lounge; room service; laundry service; dry cleaning; nonsmoking rooms. *In room:* TV, hair dryer, safe.

Great Summer Savings: Staying in Dorms

In Vienna, from July to September, a number of student dormitories are transformed into fully operational hotels. Three of the most viable and popular of these are the **Academia Hotel**, Pfeilgasse 3A; the **Avis Hotel**, Pfeilgasse 4; and the **Atlas Hotel**, at Lerchenfelderstrasse 1. All are within a block of one another, and each is a rather unimaginative-looking, angular, 1960s-style building. They're comfortable and reasonably priced alternatives, only a 20-minute walk west of St. Stephan's. The lodgings will definitely take you back to your college dorm days, though each room has a phone and a private bathroom. Many of them are booked well in advance by groups, but individual travelers are welcome if space is available. Depending on the hotel, doubles cost from 65€ to 85€ ($104–$136) a night, and triples run from 88€ to 105€ ($141–$168) each. Breakfast is included in the rates. Bookings at all three hotels are arranged through the Academia Hotel, which functions as the headquarters for the entire Academia chain. For reservations and information, call ✆ **01/401-76-55;** fax 01/401-76-20; or e-mail reservation@academiahotel.at. To get to the Academia and Avis hotels, take the U-Bahn to Thaliastrasse, and then transfer to tram no. 46 and get off at Strozzistrasse. For access to the Atlas Hotel, take the U-Bahn to Lerchenfelderstrasse. These hotels accept American Express, Diners Club, MasterCard, and Visa for payment.

Pension Dr. Geissler Value Unpretentious lodgings at reasonable prices are offered here, near the well-known Schwedenplatz at the edge of the Danube Canal. The bedrooms in this attractive, informal guesthouse are furnished with simple blond headboards and a few utilitarian pieces. Hallway bathrooms are generous. Most units, however, have their own private bathrooms, which are tiled and well maintained but a bit cramped.

Postgasse 14, 1010 Vienna. ✆ **01/5332803.** Fax 01/5332635. www.hotelpension.at. 35 units, 21 w/private bathroom. 65€ ($104) double w/shared bathroom; 95€ ($152) double w/private bathroom. Rates include buffet breakfast. AE, DC, MC, V. U-Bahn: Schwedenplatz. **Amenities:** Breakfast room; bar; breakfast-only room service; babysitting; laundry service; dry cleaning. *In room:* TV.

Pension Neuer Markt Near the cathedral, in the heart of Vienna, this pension is housed in a white baroque building that faces a square with an ornate fountain. The carpeted but small rooms are clean and well maintained in an updated motif of white walls and strong colors, with large windows in some. Some of the comfortable, duvet-covered beds are set into niches. Each of the units has central heating. Bathrooms with tub/shower combinations are small, seemingly added as an afterthought, but for Vienna the price is delicious. We recommend reserving 30 days in advance.

Seilergasse 9, 1010 Vienna. ✆ **01/5122316.** Fax 01/5139105. www.hotelpension.at. 37 units. 80€–135€ ($128–$216) double. Rates include buffet breakfast. AE, DC, MC, V. Parking 4.60€ ($7.40). U-Bahn: Stephansplatz. **Amenities:** Breakfast room; bar; breakfast-only room service; babysitting; laundry service; dry cleaning; nonsmoking rooms. *In room:* TV, safe.

Pension Nossek Mozart lived in this building in 1781 and 1782, when he wrote the *Haffner* symphony and *The Abduction from the Seraglio.* The pension lies on one of Vienna's best shopping streets, just blocks away from the major sights. In 1909, the building was converted into a guesthouse and has always been a good bet for clean, comfortable accommodations with decent (mostly comfortable) beds. Most of the bedrooms have been renovated, and all but a few singles contain small private bathrooms with tub/shower combinations.

Graben 17, 1010 Vienna. ✆ **01/53370410.** Fax 01/5353646. www.pension-nossek.at. 30 units. 110€–115€ ($176–$184) double; 143€ ($229) suite. Rates include breakfast. No credit cards. Free parking. U-Bahn: Stephansplatz. **Amenities:** Breakfast room; lounge; laundry service; dry cleaning. *In room:* TV, minibar, hair dryer (some).

Pension Pertschy Well-scrubbed and reputable, this simple but historic pension was originally built in the 1700s as the Palais Carviani with a restrained baroque style. Several rooms overlook a central courtyard and are scattered among six or seven private apartments, whose residents are used to foreign visitors roaming through the building. Midsize bedrooms are high-ceilinged and outfitted in old-fashioned, almost dowdy tones of cream and pink, with good beds and rather cramped shower-only bathrooms. A free Internet terminal is found in the hall. Most appealing is its prime location in the heart of Old Vienna (between Hapsburgasse and Bräunergasse, just off the Graben).

Habsburgergasse 5, 1010 Vienna. ✆ **01/534490.** Fax 01/5344949. www.pertschy.com. 50 units, 2 w/ kitchen. 141€–151€ ($226–$242) double. AE, DC, MC, V. Parking 16€ ($26). U-Bahn: Stephansplatz. **Amenities:** Breakfast room; lounge; nonsmoking rooms. *In room:* TV, minibar, hair dryer.

Zur Wiener Staatsoper ★ (Finds) This simple but well-run government-rated three-star hotel has a facade that's more lavish, more ornate, and more evocative of Vienna's late 19th-century golden age than any equivalently rated hotel in town. It was built in the neo-baroque style in 1896 as a private home, and as such, contains some of the architectural charm (and many of the architectural drawbacks) of its original layout. Don't expect grandeur: Other than some elaborate replications of the gilded stucco in the original 19th-century entryway, the decor is simple but functional, all of it the hard work of its on-site owners, the Ungersböck family. You'll register within a cubbyhole-style office near the entrance, then take an elevator to any of rooms scattered over six floors. Rooms are high-ceilinged, functional, relatively comfortable, and, other than small bathrooms (with showers only), adequate for most needs. Incidentally, literary fans appreciate the fact that in earlier days, this hotel, according to the Ungersböcks, provided the inspiration to John Irving for one of the settings (an antique, run-down hotel that had evolved into a whorehouse) within his novel, *Hotel New Hampshire.*

Krugerstrasse 11, A-1010 Wien. ✆ **01/513-12-74.** www.zurwienerstaatsoper.at. 22 units. 113€–150€ ($181–$240) double; 135€–175€ ($216–$280) triple. Rates include buffet breakfast. DC, MC, V. U-Bahn: Karlsplatz. *In room:* TV, safe.

LEOPOLDSTADT (2ND DISTRICT)

Expensive

Hilton Vienna Danube ★★ Vienna has yet a third Hilton hotel, this one lying on the Danube River next to the exhibition ground, a 10-minute ride from the city center (free shuttle service), and near Prater park. Since it's close to many international companies, business people like this one, although it's equally suitable for vacationers. The hotel has the largest guest rooms of any hotel in Vienna. Dining is a special feature here; the Symphony Donau Restaurant serves international and Austrian cuisine and has a beautiful terrace opening onto views of the river. The chef is famous for his Sunday (noon–3pm) Royal Swedish Smörgasbord, a buffet of Swedish specialties.

Handelskai 269, 1020 Vienna. ✆ **800-HILTONS** or 01/727770. Fax 01/7277782200. www.vienna-danube.hilton.com. 367 units. 125€–205€ ($200–$328) double; 250€–295€ ($400–$472) suite. AE, DC, MC, V. U-Bahn: U1 to Praterstern and then tram 21 to Meiereistrasse. **Amenities:** Restaurant; bar; outdoor pool; tennis court; gym; sauna; room service; laundry service; dry cleaning; nonsmoking rooms; rooms for those w/limited mobility. *In room:* A/C, TV, Wi-Fi, minibar, beverage maker (some), hair dryer (some), trouser press, safe.

Moderate

Hotel Stefanie This updated government-rated four-star hotel is across the Danube Canal from St. Stephan's Cathedral, but it's still easily accessible to the rest of the city. It has had a long and distinguished history, dating back to 1630. A century later, a famous inn, Weisse Rose, stood on this site. Ever since 1870, the hotel has been run by the Schick family. Over the past 20 years, all the bedrooms have had major renovations and today are well furnished in sleek Viennese styling. Some are a bit small, but they are beautifully maintained, with excellent beds and small tiled bathrooms that, for the most part, contain tub/shower combinations but not enough shelf space.

The interior is partially decorated in beautifully finished wall paneling and gilded wall sconces. Upon closer examination, much of the decor is reproductions, yet the hotel emits a hint of 19th-century rococo splendor. The bar area is filled with black leather armchairs on chrome swivel bases, and the concealed lighting throws an azure glow over the artfully displayed bottles.

Taborstrasse 12, 1020 Vienna. ✆ **800/528-1234** in the U.S., or 01/211500. Fax 01/21150160. www.schick-hotels.com. 131 units. 149€–211€ ($238–$338) double. Rates include buffet breakfast. AE, DC, MC, V. Parking 19€ ($30). U-Bahn: Schwedenplatz. Tram: 21. **Amenities:** Restaurant; bar; room service; laundry service; dry cleaning; nonsmoking rooms. *In room:* A/C, TV, minibar, hair dryer, safe.

LANDSTRASSE (3RD DISTRICT)

Very Expensive

Hilton Vienna ★★ This 15-story box overlooks the Wienfluss and offers plush accommodations and elegant public areas. Despite the hotel's modernity, it manages to provide plenty of Viennese flavor. Its soaring atrium and bustling nightlife make it a vibrant home for business travelers. The hotel offers well-appointed bedrooms in a range of styles, including Biedermeier, contemporary, baroque, and Art Nouveau. Regardless of the style, the hotel offers the highest level of comfort. Because the Hilton towers over the city skyline, it also affords great views from the top floors. Its suites and executive floors provide extra comfort for frequent travelers, but standard features in all bedrooms include tub/shower combinations. The adjacent Stadtpark is connected to the hotel and the City Air Terminal by a bridge, which walkers and joggers use during excursions into the landscaped and bird-filled park.

Am Stadtpark, 1030 Vienna. ✆ **800/445-8667** in the U.S., or 01/717000. Fax 01/7130691. www.hilton.com. 579 units. 205€–310€ ($328–$496) double; from 355€ ($568) suite. AE, DC, MC, V. Parking 27€ ($43). The Hilton is attached to the City Air Terminal, the drop-off point for buses coming in at frequent intervals from the airport. U-Bahn: Landstrasse. **Amenities:** Restaurant; bar; indoor heated pool; fitness center; Jacuzzi; sauna; car rental desk; children's playground; business center; room service; babysitting; laundry service; dry cleaning; nonsmoking rooms; rooms for those w/limited mobility. *In room:* A/C, TV, Wi-Fi, minibar, hair dryer, safe.

Expensive

Dorint Hotel Biedermeier This hotel was established in 1983 in a renovated late-19th-century apartment house. It boasts a pronounced Biedermeier style in both the public areas and the bedrooms. Although the hotel is adjacent to the Wien Mitte bus station and has roaring traffic on all sides, most bedrooms overlook a pedestrian-only walkway lined with shops and cafes. Duvets cover the firm beds, and double glazing keeps the noise level down. Bathrooms are small and tiled, with fake-marble counters and mostly tub/shower combinations. On the premises are the formal restaurant Zu den Deutschmeistern and the simpler Weissgerberstube.

Landstrasser Hauptstrasse 28, 1030 Vienna. ✆ **800/780-5734** in the U.S., or 01/716710. Fax 01/71671503. www.dorint.de. 203 units. 180€–233€ ($288–$373) double; 315€–350€ ($504–$560) suite. Rates include breakfast. AE, DC, MC, V. Parking 15€ ($24). U-Bahn: Rochusgasse. **Amenities:** 2 Restaurants; 2 bars; room service; babysitting; laundry service; dry cleaning; nonsmoking rooms; rooms for those w/limited mobility. *In room:* A/C, TV, Wi-Fi, minibar, hair dryer, trouser press, safe.

WIEDEN & MARGARETEN (4TH & 5TH DISTRICTS)

Moderate

Hotel Erzherzog Rainer Popular with groups and business travelers, this government-rated four-star, family-run hotel was built just before World War I and was gradually renovated room by room. It's only 5 minutes by foot to the Vienna State Opera and Kärntnerstrasse, with a U-Bahn stop just steps away. The bedrooms are well decorated and come in a variety of sizes; you'll find radios and good beds—but not soundproofing—in all. The singles are impossibly small; on certain days, air-conditioning is sorely missed. An informal brasserie serves Austrian specialties, and the cozy bar is modishly decorated with black and brass.

Wiedner Hauptstrasse 27–29, 1040 Vienna. ✆ **01/501110.** Fax 01/50111350. www.schick-hotels.com. 84 units. 135€–203€ ($216–$325) double. Rates include breakfast. AE, MC, V. Parking 18€ ($29). U-Bahn: Taubstummengasse. **Amenities:** Restaurant; bar; room service; babysitting; laundry service; dry cleaning; nonsmoking rooms; rooms for those w/limited mobility. *In room:* TV, minibar, hair dryer, safe (some).

Hotel Prinz Eugen ★ In a section of Vienna favored by diplomats, this hotel is immediately opposite the Belvedere Palace and the Südbahnhof rail station. Subways will carry you quickly to the center of Vienna, and there are good highway connections as well. The hotel has soundproof windows opening onto private balconies. The decor is a mixture of antiques, oriental rugs, and some glitzy touches such as glass walls with brass trim. Suites are nothing more than slightly larger double rooms with an additional bathroom. Bedrooms come in a wide range of sizes, although all are comfortable and have firm, duvet-covered beds. The single accommodations, however, are decidedly small, suitable for one traveling light. All the windows are soundproof.

Wiedner Gürtel 14, 1040 Vienna. ✆ **01/5051741.** Fax 01/505174119. www.hotelprinzeugen.at. 110 units. [illegible] double; [illegible] suite. [illegible] AE, [illegible] V. Parking 19€ ($30). U-Bahn: Südtiroler Platz or Südbahnhof. **Amenities:** Restaurant; bar; room service; babysitting; laundry service; dry cleaning; nonsmoking rooms. *In room:* TV, minibar, hair dryer, trouser press, safe.

MARIAHILF (6TH DISTRICT)

Expensive

Hotel Das Tyrol ★★ Finds It's friendly, fairly priced, and lies within a 5-minute walk of one of the densest concentrations of museums in Europe. The hotel's only drawback is that it's so good that it's often booked weeks in advance. It occupies what was originally built 175 years ago as a convent, which later functioned as a simple hotel that was the first building in its neighborhood to feature running water in each of its rooms.

In 1999, it was bought by an Austrian member of Parliament, Helena von Ramsbacher, who, at the time of her election, was one of the youngest women ever to be elected to the Austrian parliament. After pouring money into the building's restoration, she justifiably defines it as a boutique-style luxury hotel. Don't expect a scaled-down version of, say, the Imperial or the Bristol. What you get are high ceilings, comfortable and contemporary furnishings, a congenial collection of contemporary art, a sense of uncluttered spaciousness, and a winding central staircase that evokes the building's antique origins—all of this within a 5-minute walk from the Ring.

Mariahilferstrasse 15, 1060 Vienna. ✆ **01/587-54-15.** Fax 01/587-54-15-49. www.das-tyrol.at. 30 units. 185€–239€ ($296–$382) double; 259€ ($414) junior suite. Rates include breakfast. Parking 18€ ($29). U-Bahn: MuseumsQuartier, Volkstheater, or Neubaugasse. **Amenities:** Sauna; room service; laundry service/dry cleaning. *In room:* A/C, TV, minibar, safe.

Hotel Kummer Established by the Kummer family in the 19th century, this hotel was built in response to the growing power of the railways as they forged new paths of commerce and tourism through central Europe. A short walk from Vienna's Westbahnhof, the hotel sits in a busy, noisy location, but looks as ornamental as any public monument constructed during those imperial days. The facade is richly embellished with Corinthian capitals on acanthus-leaf bases, urn-shape balustrades, and representations of four heroic demigods staring down from under the building's eaves.

The bedrooms have soundproof windows and often come with stone balconies. Not all rooms are alike—some feature superior appointments and deluxe furnishings. If possible, opt for a corner room—they are better lit and more spacious.

Mariahilferstrasse 71A, 1060 Vienna. ✆ **01/588950.** Fax 01/5878133. www.hotelkummer.at. 100 units. 95€–255€ ($152–$408) double. Rates include buffet breakfast. AE, DC, MC, V. Parking 15€ ($24). U-Bahn: Neubaugasse. Bus: 13A or 14A. **Amenities:** Restaurant; bar; salon; room service; laundry service; dry cleaning; nonsmoking rooms. *In room:* TV, minibar, hair dryer, trouser press, safe.

Moderate

Fürst Metternich Hotel ★ Finds Pink-and-gray paint and ornate stone window trim identify this solidly built 19th-century hotel, formally an opulent private home. It's located between the Ring and the Westbahnhof near Mariahilferstrasse, about a 20-minute walk from the cathedral. Many of the grander architectural elements were retained, including a pair of red stone columns in the entranceway and an old-fashioned staircase guarded with griffins. The high-ceilinged bedrooms have a neutral decor, with laminated furnishings and feather pillows. They aren't generally roomy, however. Windows in the front units are soundproof in theory, but not in practice. If you want a more tranquil night's sleep, opt for a room in the rear. The Barfly's Club, a popular hangout open daily, offers 120 different exotic drinks.

Esterházygasse 33, 1060 Vienna. ✆ **01/58870.** Fax 01/5875268. www.austrotel.at. 55 units. 100€–170€ ($160–$272) double. Rates include buffet breakfast. AE, DC, MC, V. Parking 17€ ($27). U-Bahn: Zieglergasse. **Amenities:** Breakfast room; bar; babysitting; laundry service; dry cleaning. *In room:* TV, minibar.

Golden Tulip Wien City This seven-story concrete-and-glass hotel was designed in 1975 with enough angles in its facade to give each bedroom an irregular shape. Usually the units have two windows that face different skylines. Aside from the views, each of the decent-size bedrooms has comfortable furnishings and good beds. Opt for a room—really a studio with a terrace—on the seventh floor, if one is available. The hotel also has a public rooftop terrace where guests sip drinks in summer.

Wallgasse 23, A-1060 Vienna. ✆ **01/599900.** Fax 01/5967646. www.goldentulipwiencity.com. 77 units. 150€–230€ ($240–$368) double; from 270€ ($432) suite. Rates include buffet breakfast. AE, DC, MC, V. Parking 15€ ($24). U-Bahn: Gumpendorfer. Bus: 57A. **Amenities:** Breakfast room; bar; breakfast-only room service; babysitting; laundry service; dry cleaning; nonsmoking rooms. *In room:* A/C, TV, minibar, hair dryer, safe.

Hotel Mercure Secession ★ **Kids** Sitting at the corner of a well-known street, Lehárgasse, this hotel is in the center of Vienna between the Vienna State Opera and the famous Naschmarkt. It's a modern five-story building with panoramic windows on the ground floor and a red-tile roof. The interior is warmly decorated with some 19th-century antiques and comfortably upholstered chairs. Musicians, singers, actors, and other artists form part of a loyal clientele. This is one of Vienna's best small hotels; families are especially fond of the place as 35 of the accommodations contain kitchenettes.

Getreidemarkt 5, 1060 Vienna. ✆ **01/588380.** Fax 01/58838212. www.mercure.com. 68 units. 150€–175€ ($240–$280) double. Rates include buffet breakfast. AE, DC, MC, V. Parking 18€ ($29). U-Bahn: Karlsplatz. **Amenities:** Breakfast room; bar; room service; babysitting; laundry; dry cleaning; nonsmoking rooms. *In room:* A/C, TV, minibar, hair dryer, safe.

NEUBAU (7TH DISTRICT)

Expensive

K+K Hotel Maria Theresia ★ The hotel's initials are a reminder of the empire's dual monarchy (*Kaiserlich und Königlich*—"by appointment to the Emperor of Austria and King of Hungary"). Even the surrounding neighborhood, home to some major museums that lie just outside the Ring, is reminiscent of the days of Empress Maria Theresa. The hotel is in the artists' colony of Spittelberg, within walking distance of the Winter Palace gardens, the Volkstheater, and the famous shopping street Mariahilferstrasse. The hotel, built in the late 1980s, offers ample contemporary rooms. The beds (usually twins) are comfortable, and the medium-size bathrooms are attractively tiled.

Kirchberggasse 6–8, 1070 Vienna. ✆ **800/537-8483** in the U.S., or 01/52123. Fax 01/5212370. www.kkhotels.com. 123 units. 230€ ($368) double; from 280€ ($448) suite. Rates include buffet breakfast. AE, DC, MC, V. Parking 16€ ($26). U-Bahn: Volkstheater. Tram: 49. **Amenities:** Restaurant; bar; fitness center; sauna; room service; massage; babysitting; laundry service; dry cleaning; nonsmoking rooms. *In room:* A/C, TV, Wi-Fi, minibar, hair dryer, safe.

Moderate

Falkensteiner Hotel Am Schottenfeld ★ **Kids** The design of the hotel is young, modern, and chic, which sometimes characterizes many of the guests as well. The lighting seems to set the stage for every room in the hotel. From the beautiful colored lights in the lounge to the natural light in the meeting rooms, the hotel has definitely landed in the 21st century. Rooms offer not only contemporary comfort and tasteful appointments, but also bathrooms with marble floors, an image of elegance. Outside the hotel is a wide range of small bars and restaurants, along with junk shops and trendy boutiques, even antiquarian book shops.

Schottenfeldgasse 74, 1070 Vienna. ✆ **01/5265181.** Fax 01/5265181-160. www.falkensteiner.com. 95 units. 157€–249€ ($251–$398) double; 50€ ($80) extra for junior suite. AE, DC, MC, V. U-Bahn: Volkstheater. **Amenities:** Bistro; bar; sauna; solarium; Turkish bath; babysitting; kids' club; children's menus; room service; laundry service/dry cleaning; nonsmoking rooms. *In room:* A/C, TV, Wi-Fi, minibar, hair dryer, safe.

Pension Altstadt Vienna ★ **Finds** A noted connoisseur of modern art, Otto Wiesenthal, converted a century-old private home into this charming and stylish hotel in the mid-1990s. Wiesenthal comes from a long line of artists. Grandmother Greta was an opera dancer, and works by great-great-grandfather Friedrich hang in the Vienna Historic Museum as well as the hotel. Although part of the structure remains a private home, the remainder of the building contains comfortable and cozy bedrooms. Each is outfitted with a different color scheme and contains at least one work of contemporary art, usually by an Austrian painter. Many of the good-size units are a bit quirky in decor, as exemplified by a leopard print club chair set against a sponge-painted wall. Nearly all the rooms have high ceilings, antiques, parquet floors, double-glazed windows, and good beds. Out of respect to the hotel's location within the Spittelberg, Vienna's former red-light district and now a liberal and artsy residential neighborhood known for its Green-peace affiliations, the owner has dedicated one of the best and largest bedrooms in the house to Josephina Mutzenbacher. During the final days of the Hapsburgs, she was the most famous and high-profile madam in Vienna, and a hugely eccentric celebrity in her own right at the time. Naughty, a wee bit provocative, and tongue-in-cheek *(Die Liebe in Wien!/Love in Vienna!)*, it is our preferred room. About half of the accommodations contain a shower instead of a tub. The hotel added 11 rooms stylishly designed by Matteo Thun, the famous Italian architects, and these are the best appointed and most desirable.

Kirchengasse 41, 1070 Vienna. Ⓒ **01/5226666.** Fax 01/5234901. www.altstadt.at. 47 units. 129€–169€ ($206–$270) double; 169€–299€ ($270–$478) suite. AE, DC, MC, V. Parking 18€ ($29). U-Bahn: Volkstheater. **Amenities:** Breakfast room; bar; salon; room service; babysitting; laundry service; dry cleaning; nonsmoking rooms. *In room:* TV, Wi-Fi, minibar, hair dryer, safe.

Inexpensive

Hotel-Pension Museum *Value* This hotel was originally built in the 17th century as the home of an aristocratic family. Its exterior was transformed around 1890 into the elegant Art Nouveau facade it has today. It's across from the Imperial Museums, and there are plenty of palaces, museums, and monuments nearby to keep you busy for days. Bedrooms come in a wide variety of sizes; some are spacious, while others are a bit cramped. However, the rates are great for this city, and this place has its devotees for a reason.

Museumstrasse 3, 1070 Vienna. Ⓒ **01/52344260.** Fax 01/523442630. www.tiscover.com/hotel.museum. 15 units. 91€–155€ ($146–$248) double. Rates include breakfast. AE, DC, MC, V. Parking 22€ ($35) Mon–Fri; free Sat–Sun. U-Bahn: Volkstheater. **Amenities:** Breakfast room; lounge; room service; nonsmoking rooms. *In room:* TV, hair dryer.

Hotel Savoy Built in the 1960s, this well-managed hotel rises six stories above one of Vienna's busiest wholesale and retail shopping districts. Within walking distance of Ringstrasse, opposite a station for one of the city's U-Bahn lines (the U3), the hotel prides itself on tastefully decorated units with good beds. Most units offer picture-window views of the neighborhood. Although the only meal served in the hotel is breakfast, there are dozens of places to eat in the neighborhood.

Lindengasse 12, 1070 Vienna. Ⓒ **01/5234646.** Fax 01/5234640. www.hotelsavoy.at. 43 units. 83€–150€ ($133–$240) double; 121€–180€ ($194–$288) triple. Rates include buffet breakfast. AE, DC, MC, V. Parking 16€ ($26). U-Bahn: Neubaugasse. **Amenities:** Breakfast room; babysitting; laundry service; dry cleaning; nonsmoking rooms. *In room:* TV, minibar, hair dryer, safe.

JOSEFSTADT (8TH DISTRICT)

Expensive

Cordial Theaterhotel Wien This hotel was created from a 19th-century core that was radically modernized in the late 1980s. Today it's a favorite of Austrian business travelers, who profit from the hotel's proximity to the city's wholesale buying outlets.

Each simply furnished room contains its own small but efficient kitchenette, which allows guests to save on restaurant bills. The well-maintained bedrooms, available in a variety of sizes, have good beds and adequate tiled bathrooms. The on-site Theater-Restaurant is especially busy before and after performances next door at Theater in der Josefstadt.

Josefstadter Strasse 22, 1080 Vienna. ✆ **01/4053648.** Fax 01/4051406. www.cordial.at. 54 units. 199€–244€ ($318–$390) double; 270€–479€ ($432–$766) suite. Rates include buffet breakfast. AE, DC, MC, V. Parking 15€ ($24). U-Bahn: Rathaus. **Amenities:** Restaurant; bar; fitness center; sauna; massage; room service; babysitting; laundry service; dry cleaning; nonsmoking rooms. *In room:* TV, minibar, hair dryer.

Hotel Parliament Levante ★ This is a good example of the wave of new, design-conscious hotels that opened in Vienna during 2006. It sits behind a rectilinear, five-story facade of distressed concrete which, in 1908, was chiseled into a Bauhaus-inspired design that, at least for the era, was a radical departure from the neo-Gothic facade of the Rathaus (City Hall) and the cool, elegant Greek Revival style of the Austrian Parliament, both of which lie nearby, across the boulevard. It originated as a sanatorium and later evolved into a student dormitory. After a radical reconfiguration, the hotel gives the impression that every interior angle and every interior line was meticulously plotted into a postmodern, avant-garde design that includes lots of white Turkish travertine and marble, dark-grained wood, and a (sometimes excessive) use of the photos of Austrian photographer Curt Themessl and the artfully free-form glass vases and sculptures of Romanian glass-blower Ioan Nemtoi. Most of the rooms face a quiet but dull inner courtyard, and each is comfortable, decoratively neutral, and postmodern.

Auerspergstrasse 15, 1080 Vienna. ✆ **01/228-280.** Fax 01/228-2828. www.thelevante.com. 70 units. 280€ ($448) double; 355€ ($568) suite. Extra bed 45€ ($59). Rates include breakfast. Parking 22€ ($35). AE, DC, MC, V. U-Bahn: Rathaus. **Amenities:** Fitness room w/sauna; room service, laundry service/dry cleaning. *In room:* A/C, TV, minibar.

Inexpensive

Hotel Graf Stadion ★ Kids This is one of the few genuine Biedermeier-style hotels left in Vienna. It's right behind the Rathaus, a 10-minute walk from most of the central monuments. The facade evokes the building's early-19th-century elegance, with triangular or half-rounded ornamentation above many of the windows. The bedrooms have been refurbished and are comfortably old-fashioned, and many are spacious enough to accommodate an extra bed for people traveling with small children.

Buchfeldgasse 5, 1080 Vienna. ✆ **01/405-5284.** Fax 01/4050111. www.graf-stadion.com. 40 units. 105€–150€ ($168–$240) double. Rates include buffet breakfast. AE, DC, MC, V. Parking 15€ ($24). U-Bahn: Rathaus. **Amenities:** Breakfast room; bar; babysitting; laundry service; dry cleaning. *In room:* TV, hair dryer.

Hotel Zipser A 5-minute walk from the Rathaus, this pension offers rooms with wall-to-wall carpeting and central heating, many overlooking a private garden. Much of the renovated interior is tastefully adorned with wood detailing. Generous-size bedrooms are furnished in a functional, modern style, with some opening onto balconies above the garden.

Lange Gasse 49, 1080 Vienna. ✆ **01/404540.** Fax 01/4045413. www.zipser.at. 47 units. 85€–165€ ($136–$264) double. Rates include buffet breakfast. AE, DC, MC, V. Parking 14€ ($22). U-Bahn: Rathaus. Bus: 13A. **Amenities:** Breakfast room; bar; lounge. *In room:* TV, Wi-Fi, hair dryer, safe.

4 WHERE TO DINE

In Vienna, eating out is a local pastime. Befitting a historically cosmopolitan capital, Viennese restaurants serve not only Austrian and French cuisine, but also Serbian, Slovenian, Slovakian, Hungarian, and Czech, as well as Chinese, Italian, and Russian. Although meals are traditionally big and hearty, innovative chefs throughout the city are now turning out lighter versions of the classics.

Unlike those in many western European capitals, Vienna's restaurants still heed Sunday closings (marked by SONNTAG RUHETAG signs). Also, beware of those summer holiday closings, when chefs would rather rush to nearby lake resorts than cook for Vienna's visiting hordes. However, post-theater dining is fashionable in this city, and many restaurants and cafes stay open late.

INNERE STADT (INNER CITY)

Very Expensive

Kervansaray und Hummer Bar ★★ SEAFOOD Here you'll sense the historic link between the Hapsburgs and their 19th-century neighbor, the Ottoman Empire. On the restaurant's ground floor, polite waiters announce a changing array of daily specials and serve tempting salads from an hors d'oeuvre table. Upstairs, guests enjoy the bounties of the sea at the Lobster Bar. There's also a deli.

A meal often begins with a champagne cocktail, followed by one of many appetizers, including a lobster and salmon caviar cocktail. The menu has a short list of meat dishes, such as filet mignon with Roquefort sauce, but it specializes in seafood, including grilled filet of sole with fresh asparagus, Norwegian salmon with a horseradish-and-champagne sauce, and, of course, lobster. If shellfish is your weakness, be prepared to pay for your indulgence.

Mahlerstrasse 9. ✆ **01/5128843.** www.hummerbar.at. Reservations recommended. Main courses 25€–50€ ($40–$80). AE, DC, MC, V. Restaurant Mon–Sat noon–midnight. U-Bahn: Karlsplatz. Tram: 1 or 2. Bus: 3A.

König von Ungarn (King of Hungary) ★ INTERNATIONAL/VIENNESE Housed in the famous hotel of the same name, this restaurant evokes a rich atmosphere with crystal chandeliers, antiques, marble columns, and vaulted ceilings. If you're unsure of what to order, try the *tafelspitz,* elegantly dispensed from a cart. Other seasonal choices include a ragout of seafood with fresh mushrooms, tournedos of beef with a mustard-and-horseradish sauce, and appetizers such as scampi in caviar sauce. Chefs balance flavors, textures, and colors to create a cuisine that's long been favored by locals, who often bring out-of-town guests here. We have been dining here for years and have found the cuisine consistently good. However, in fairness and with warning, it should be noted that many of our discriminating readers have found the restaurant disappointing and the food unremarkable.

Schulerstrasse 10. ✆ **01/515840.** Reservations required. Main courses 16€–22€ ($26–$35); fixed-price menu 40€–49€ ($64–$78) at lunch, 30€–40€ ($48–$64) at dinner. AE, DC, MC, V. Mon–Fri noon–2:30pm and 6–11:45pm. Closed July 4–24. U-Bahn: Stephansplatz. Bus: 1A.

Korso bei der Oper ★★★ INTERNATIONAL/VIENNESE This chic and glittering choice is decorated with tasteful paneling, sparkling chandeliers, and, flanking either side of a baronial fireplace, two of the most breathtaking baroque columns in Vienna. Set

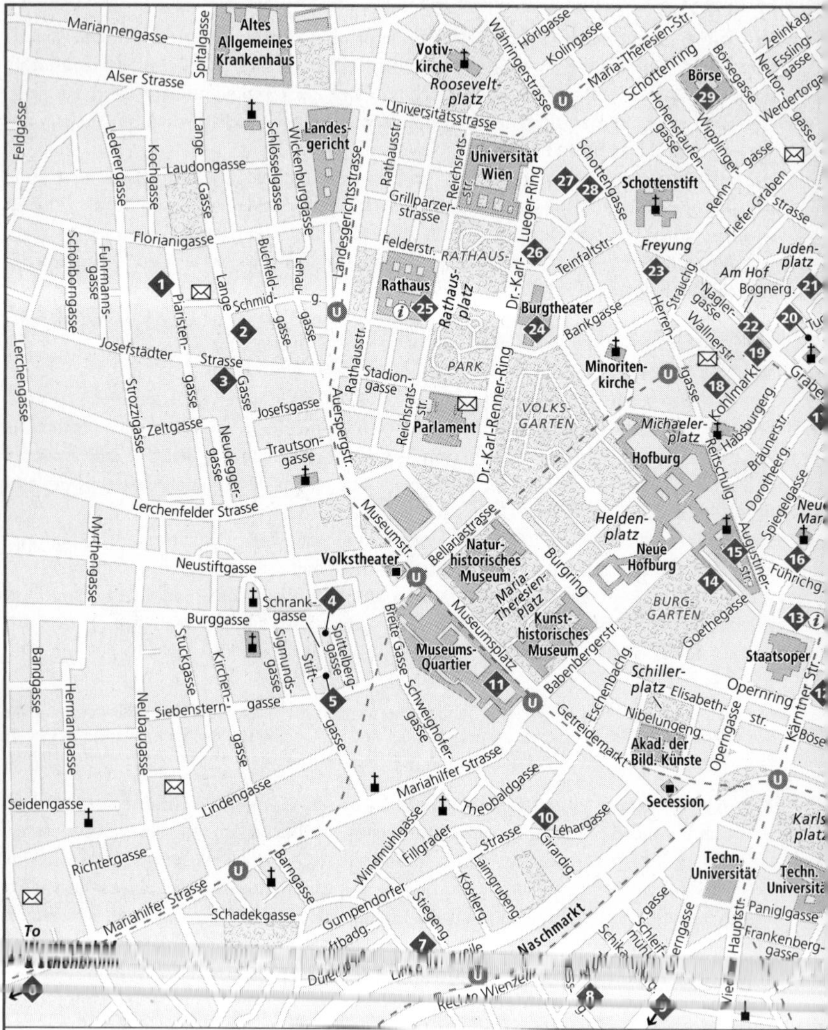

Alfi's Goldener Spiegel **7**
Alte Backstube **2**
Altes Jägerhaus **56**
Altwienerhof **6**
Augustinerkeller **15**
Bauer **52**
Bohème **4**
Buffet Trzésniewski **17**
Café Central **23**
Café Demel **18**
Café Diglas **49**
Café Dommayer **6**
Café Frauenhuber **38**
Café Imperial **40**
Café Landtmann **26**
Café Leopold **11**
Café Restaurant Halle **11**
Café-Restaurant Kunsthaus **55**
Café Sperl **10**
Café Tirolerhof **16**
Cantinetta Antinori **33**
Demmers Teehaus **27**
Die Fromme Helene **3**

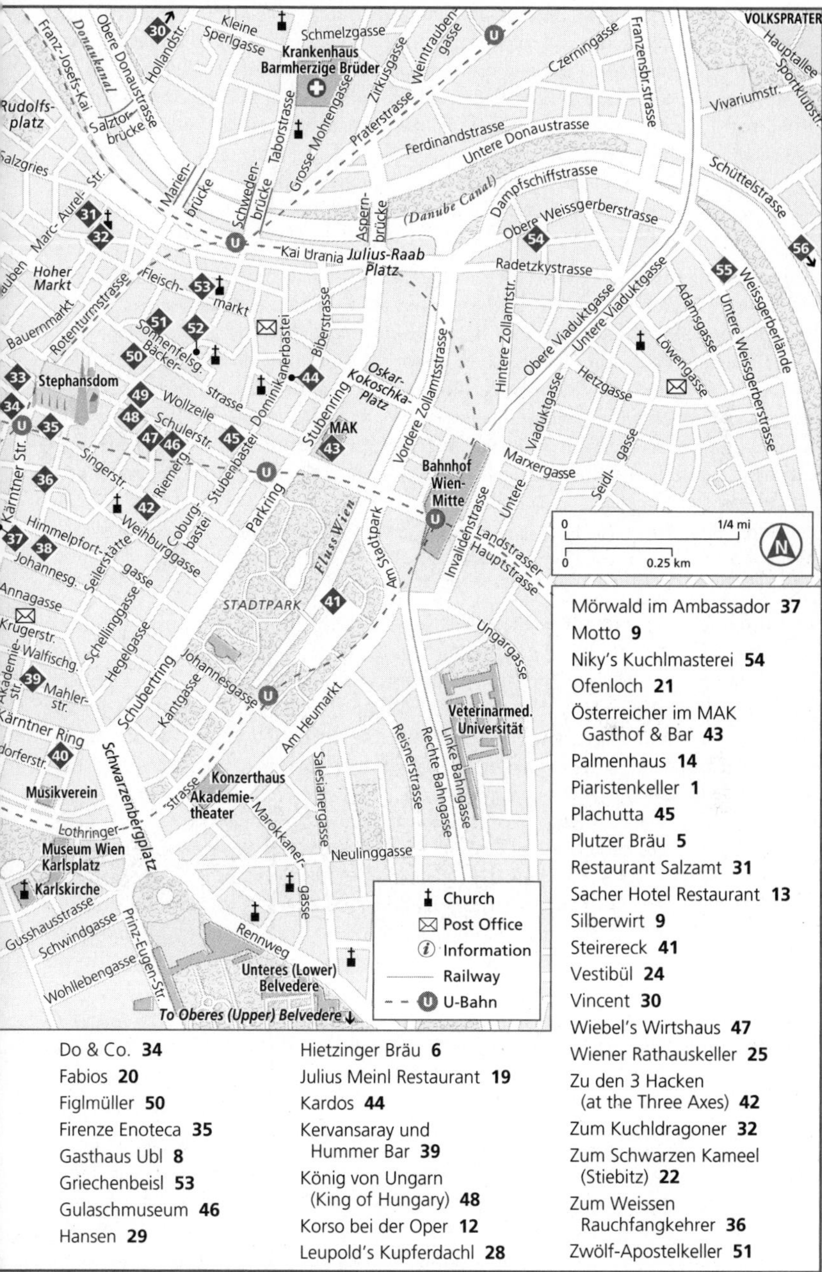

Do & Co. **34**
Fabios **20**
Figlmüller **50**
Firenze Enoteca **35**
Gasthaus Ubl **8**
Griechenbeisl **53**
Gulaschmuseum **46**
Hansen **29**
Hietzinger Bräu **6**
Julius Meinl Restaurant **19**
Kardos **44**
Kervansaray und Hummer Bar **39**
König von Ungarn (King of Hungary) **48**
Korso bei der Oper **12**
Leupold's Kupferdachl **28**
Mörwald im Ambassador **37**
Motto **9**
Niky's Kuchlmasterei **54**
Ofenloch **21**
Österreicher im MAK Gasthof & Bar **43**
Palmenhaus **14**
Piaristenkeller **1**
Plachutta **45**
Plutzer Bräu **5**
Restaurant Salzamt **31**
Sacher Hotel Restaurant **13**
Silberwirt **9**
Steirereck **41**
Vestibül **24**
Vincent **30**
Wiebel's Wirtshaus **47**
Wiener Rathauskeller **25**
Zu den 3 Hacken (at the Three Axes) **42**
Zum Kuchldragoner **32**
Zum Schwarzen Kameel (Stiebitz) **22**
Zum Weissen Rauchfangkehrer **36**
Zwölf-Apostelkeller **51**

in the elegant Hotel Bristol, the restaurant has its own entrance directly across from the Staatsoper, a position that has always attracted a legendary clientele of opera stars.

The kitchen concocts an alluring mixture of traditional and modern cuisine for discriminating palates. Your meal might feature filet of char with a sorrel sauce, saddle of veal with cèpe mushrooms and homemade noodles, or the inevitable *tafelspitz.* The rack of lamb is excellent, as are the medallions of beef with a shallot-infused butter sauce and Roquefort-flavored noodles. The wine list is extensive, and the service, as you'd expect, is impeccable.

In the Hotel Bristol, Mahlerstrasse 2. ✆ **01/51516546.** www.restaurantkorso.at. Reservations required. Main courses 28€–45€ ($45–$72); 3-course fixed-price menu 68€ ($109), 4-course fixed-price menu 90€ ($144). AE, DC, MC, V. Mon–Fri noon–3pm and Sun–Fri 7pm–1am. U-Bahn: Karlsplatz. Tram: 1 or 2.

Mörwald im Ambassador ★★★ VIENNESE Views from its greenhouse-style windows, two floors above street level, sweep out over the Neumarkt and one of Vienna's most memorable outdoor fountains. Bankers, diplomats, and what one local food critic called "Helmut Lang-clad hipsters" show up for the sophisticated twists on classic Viennese cuisine. Menu items change with the seasons, but are likely to include tartar of French-derived Limousin beef with rosemary toasts and cocktail sauce; foie gras with kumquats and a sauce made from sparkling wine; ravioli stuffed with pulverized lamb, artichoke hearts, and mint sauce; and roasted loin of veal with chanterelles and a spicy potato-based cream sauce.

On the 2nd floor of the Hotel Ambassador, Kärntner Strasse 22. ✆ **01/961610.** Reservations required. Main courses 24€–34€ ($38–$54); set price lunch 29€–39€ ($46–$62), set-price dinner 75€–110€ ($120–$176). AE, DC, MC, V. Daily noon–3pm and 6–11pm. U-Bahn: Stephansplatz.

Sacher Hotel Restaurant ★ AUSTRIAN/INTERNATIONAL/VIENNESE Most celebrities who visit Vienna are eventually spotted in this elegant dining room, most likely enjoying the restaurant's most famous dish, *tafelspitz;* the chef at Sacher prepares the boiled beef ensemble with a savory, herb-flavored sauce that is truly fit for the emperor's table. Other delectable dishes include fish terrine and veal steak with morels. For dessert, the Sachertorte enjoys world renown. It's primarily a chocolate sponge cake that's sliced in half and filled with apricot jam. This famous pastry was supposedly created in 1832 by Franz Sacher, when he served as Prince Metternich's apprentice.

Come dressed to the nines, and be sure to show up before 11pm, even though the restaurant officially closes at 1am. Despite the adherence to form and protocol here, latecomers will never go hungry, as the hotel maintains tables in the adjoining and less formal Red Bar, where the menu is available every day from noon to 11:30pm (last order). The Sacher has always been a favorite for dinner either before or after the opera.

In the Hotel Sacher Wien, Philharmonikerstrasse 4. ✆ **01/514560.** www.sacher.com/en-restaurants-vienna.htm. Reservations required. Main courses 22€–30€ ($29–$49). AE, DC, MC, V. Daily noon–3pm and 6pm–1am. U-Bahn: Karlsplatz.

Expensive

Bauer ★★ AUSTRIAN/CONTINENTAL It's upscale, it's *gemütlich,* and it's on the short list of restaurants that concierges at some of Vienna's most upscale hotels recommend to their clients. You'll find it on a narrow street a few blocks northeast of the Cathedral, beneath 500-year-old ceiling vaults, now painted a dark shade of pink, that evoke a venue that's more folksy and rustic than this sophisticated restaurant really is. The fact that there are only 30 seats enhances the coziness of a venue that was established in its present format in 1989. Expect glamorous food. The finest examples include beef carpaccio with mustard sauce; sweetbreads with vanilla sauce and braised chicory; and stuffed squid with lemon sauce and pepper-flavored cream sauce.

Sonnenfelsgasse 17. ✆ **01/512-9871.** Reservations recommended. Main courses 26€–32€ ($42–$51); 4-course set-price menu 62€ ($99). AE, DC, MC, V. Mon 6–11pm, Tues–Fri noon–2pm and 6–11pm. Closed 1 week at Easter and mid-July to mid-Aug. U-Bahn: Stephansplatz, Schwedenplatz, or Stubentor.

Do & Co. ★ INTERNATIONAL Positioned on the seventh floor of a radically angular hypermodern building that's set across from Vienna's cathedral, this restaurant is the crown jewel of an also-recommended hotel. It's difficult to overstate its fame within the complicated but steely hierarchy of fine and/or stylish Viennese dining. So great is its demand that even if there happens to be a space available during the city's key dining hours (roughly defined as between 7 and 10pm), management will simply not release that space to walk-ins who haven't pre-reserved a table, saving it instead for last-minute calls from the aides of either "celebrities of the minute" or genuinely grand Imperial dragons. At its best, it will provide a high-pressure insight into Vienna's social priorities.

Consider a predinner cocktail at the stylish and sometimes overcrowded Onyx Bar on the building's sixth floor, then climb a circular staircase through cramped hallways to the seventh-floor dining room. Here, *if you've reserved,* you'll be presented with a slightly claustrophobic table and a confusingly diverse set of menu items that the menus divide into categories that include "Tastes of the World" (Tataki of Atlantic tuna); "Catch of the Day" (potpourri of scallops with beans, comfit of tomato, and *crème fraîche*); "Beef & Co." (French breast of duck with green beans and creamy kumquat polenta); "Kebab, Wok & Curries" (dishes inspired by Asia, especially Thailand); "Austrian Classics" (deep-fried monkfish with potato salad); and many different kinds of sushi.

In the Haas Haus, Stephansplatz 12. ✆ **01/24188.** www.doco.com. Reservations required. Main courses 18€–26€ ($29–$42). AE, DC, MC, V. Daily noon–3pm and 6–11:45pm. U-Bahn: Stephansplatz.

Fabios ★★ INTERNATIONAL/MEDITERRANEAN This is the trendiest and most sought-after restaurant in Vienna, with considerable jockeying among the city's glitterati. The creation of the young and fun Fabio Giacobello, the space is bigger inside than you might think. Most of the visual distraction in this mostly black but plush and artfully lit environment comes from its fashion-conscious and usually good-looking clients, and from walls of glass that seem to bring the visual details of Vienna's historic core directly inside. The menu might include warm octopus marinated with olive oil and parsley served on a bed of cold gazpacho cream sauce, crispy sesame leaves stuffed with warm goat cheese served with Treviso radicchio and honeydew melon, and roasted rack of lamb with cold marinated eggplant and tomatoes served with deep-fried polenta gnocchetti. Incidentally, don't overlook the value of this place's wine bar as a nightlife option. There's enough drama unfolding around its rectangular surface to keep a few tabloid writers busy, and someone famous within the inner workings of Vienna's media and politics always seems to be popping up for air and a drink or two.

Tuchlauben 6. ✆ **01/532-2222.** www.fabios.at. Reservations recommended. Main courses 29€–32€ ($46–$50). AE, MC, V. Mon–Sat 10am–1am. U-Bahn: Stephansplatz.

Plachutta ★ VIENNESE Few restaurants have built such a fetish around one dish as Plachutta has done with *tafelspitz,* offering 10 variations of the boiled beef dish, which was the favorite of Emperor Franz Josef throughout his prolonged reign. The differences between the versions are a function of the cut of beef you request. We recommend *schulterscherzel* (shoulder of beef) and *beinfleisch* (shank of beef), but if you're in doubt, the waitstaff is knowledgeable about one of the oftenest-debated subjects in Viennese cuisine. Hash brown potatoes, chives, and an appealing mixture of horseradish and chopped apples accompany each order. Other Viennese staples such as goulash soup, calf's liver, and braised pork with cabbage are also available.

Wollzeile 38. ✆ **01/5121577.** www.plachutta.at. Reservations recommended. Main courses 18€–26€ ($29–$42). DC, MC, V. Daily 11:30am–midnight. U-Bahn: Stubentor.

Weibels Wirtshaus ★ Finds AUSTRIAN Don't be fooled by the unpretentious and cozy feel to this place, which at first glance might look like a simple tavern. Food is considerably better than the *wirtshaus* (tavern) appellation implies, and the clientele is a lot more upscale than the usual wurst-with-potatoes-and-beer crowd. There are only two rooms (and about 40 seats) within this wood-paneled restaurant, each on a separate floor of a building whose age is estimated to be around 400 years old. During clement weather, another 30 seats become available within a garden in back. The wine list, with more than 250 varieties of Austrian wine, looks like a patriotic, pro-Austrian statement in its own right. Menu items include pumpkinseed soup, sliced breast of duck with lentils, well-prepared schnitzels of veal and chicken, and a superb saddle of lamb with polenta and spinach.

Kumpfgasse 2. ✆ **01/5123986.** www.weibel.at. Reservations recommended. Main courses 14€–19€ ($22–$30); fixed-price menu 36€ ($58). AE, MC, V. Daily 11:30am–midnight. U-Bahn: Stephansplatz.

Wiener Rathauskeller ★★ INTERNATIONAL/VIENNESE City halls throughout the Teutonic world have traditionally maintained restaurants in their basements, and Vienna is no exception. Although Vienna's famous Rathaus was built between 1871 and 1883, its cellar-level restaurant wasn't added until 1899. Today, in half a dozen richly atmospheric dining rooms, with high vaulted ceilings and stained-glass windows, you can enjoy good and reasonably priced food. The chef's specialty is a *rathauskellerplatte* for two, consisting of various cuts of meat, including a veal schnitzel, lamb cutlets, and pork medallions. One section of the cellar is devoted every evening to a Viennese musical soiree beginning at 8pm. Live musicians ramble through the world of operetta, waltz, and *schrammel* (traditional Viennese music) as you dine.

Rathausplatz 1. ✆ **01/405-1210.** www.wiener-rathauskeller.at. Reservations required. Main courses 11€–39€ ($18–$62). AE, DC, MC, V. Mon–Sat 11:30am–3pm and 6–11pm. U-Bahn: Rathaus.

Moderate

Cantinetta Antinori ★ ITALIAN This is one of three European restaurants run by the Antinori family, who own Tuscan vineyards and whose name is nearly synonymous with Chianti. The traditions and artifacts of the original restaurant, in Florence, have been reproduced here to showcase Antinori wines and the culinary zest of Tuscany. Within a 140-year-old building overlooking the Stephansplatz and the cathedral, you'll find a high-ceilinged dining room, as well as a greenhouse-style "winter garden" that transports you straight to Tuscany. Start off with an order of *antipasti tipico,* a medley of marinated vegetables and seafood arranged by the staff. This might be followed with sumptuous ravioli stuffed with porcini mushrooms and summer truffles or perfectly grilled lamb steaks with sun-dried tomatoes and Mediterranean herbs. *Panna cotta,* a creamy flan, is a simple but flavorful way to finish a meal. A large selection of wines is served by the glass.

Jasomirgottstrasse 3–5. ✆ **01/5337722.** www.antinori.it. Reservations required. Main courses 19€–57€ ($30–$91). AE, DC, MC, V. Daily 11:30am–11pm. U-Bahn: Stephansplatz.

Firenze Enoteca ★★ ITALIAN This is one of Vienna's premier Italian restaurants. Located near St. Stephan's next to the Royal Hotel, it's furnished in Tuscan Renaissance style, with frescoes by Benozzo Gozzoli. The kitchen specializes in homemade pasta served with zesty sauces. According to the chef, the cuisine is "80% Tuscan, 20% from the rest of Italy." Start with selections from the antipasti table, and then choose among spaghetti with "fruits of the sea"; veal cutlet with ham, cheese, and sardines; or perhaps filet mignon in a tomato-garlic sauce. Be sure to complement any meal here with a classic bottle of Chianti.

Singerstrasse 3. ✆ **01/5134374.** Reservations recommended. Main courses 10€–26€ ($16–$42). AE, DC, MC, V. Daily noon–3pm and 6pm–midnight. U-Bahn: Stephansplatz.

Griechenbeisl AUSTRIAN Astonishingly, Griechenbeisl was established in 1450 and is still one of the city's leading restaurants. There's a maze of dining areas on three different floors, all with low vaulted ceilings, smoky paneling, and wrought-iron chandeliers. Watch out for the Styrian-vested waiters who scurry around with large trays of food. As you enter, look down at the grate under your feet for an illuminated view of a pirate counting his money. Inside, check out the so-called inner sanctum, with signatures of former patrons such as Mozart, Beethoven, and Mark Twain. The Pilsen beer is well chilled, and the food is hearty and ample. Menu items include fried breaded filet of chicken with cucumber-potatoes salad; and roast filet of pikeperch with almonds. As an added treat, the restaurant features nighttime accordion and zither music.

Fleischmarkt 11. ✆ **01/5331941.** www.griechenbeisl.at. Reservations required. Main courses 16€–23€ ($25–$36). AE, DC, MC, V. Daily 11am–1am (last order at 11:30pm). Tram: N, 1, 2, or 21.

Julius Meinl ★ CONTINENTAL This upscale and appealingly formal restaurant is the most sought-after of the three elements within the Julius Meinl trio, which includes, on the same premises, one of the most comprehensive delicatessens and wine shops in Austria, and a cellar-level wine bar. The restaurant occupies a site immediately upstairs from street level, with big-windowed views that sweep out over the all-pedestrian grandeur of the Graben. Although the restaurant looks as upscale as any other of the city's dining competitors, with dark paneling, touches of gilt, a voluptuous-looking service bar, and a sense of Habsburgundian charm, it's positioned within a few steps of the bustling and brightly illuminated premises of its associated delicatessen. Menu items change with the availability of fresh ingredients, but might include tuna with avocado cream and a carrot and ginger-flavored vinaigrette or marinated gratin of lobster with fennel. Our favorite is a platter containing two different preparations of quail accompanied with goose liver and marinated *boletus* mushrooms. Desserts? Consider a praline mousse with raspberries and tonka-bean ice cream, or a semolina soufflé with plums and elderberries. And then, there's the cheese trolley, a movable feast and a work of art in its own right.

Graben 19. ✆ **01/532-3334.** www.meinl.at. Reservations recommended. Main courses 24€–35€ ($38–$56). Mon–Sat 8am–midnight. U-Bahn: Stephansplatz.

Leupold's Kupferdachl ★ VIENNESE/AUSTRIAN Run by the Leopold family since the 1950s, this choice is known for "new Austrian" cuisine, although the chef does prepare traditional dishes. Recommended menu items include beef tenderloin (Old Viennese style) with dumplings boiled in a napkin, lamb loin breaded and served with potatoes, and chicken breast Kiev. The interior is both rustic and elegant, decorated with oriental rugs and cozy banquettes with intricate straight-back chairs. The restaurant operates a beer pub, with good music and better prices. The pub is open daily from 10am to midnight.

Schottengasse 7. ✆ **01/5339381.** www.leupold.at. Reservations recommended. Main courses 10€–20€ ($16–$32). AE, DC, MC, V. Mon–Fri 10am–3pm; Mon–Sat 6pm–midnight. U-Bahn: Schottentor. Tram: 2, 43, or 44.

Ofenloch VIENNESE Viennese have frequented this spot since the 1600s, when it functioned as a simple tavern. The present management dates from the mid-1970s and maintains a well-deserved reputation for its nostalgic, old-fashioned eating house. Waitresses wear classic Austrian regalia and will give you a menu that looks more like a magazine, with some amusing mock-medieval illustrations inside. The hearty soup dishes are popular, as is the schnitzel. For smaller appetites, the menu offers salads and cheese platters, plus an entire page devoted to one-dish meals. For dessert, choose from old-style Viennese specialties.

Kurrentgasse 8. ✆ **01/5338844.** www.ofenloch.at. Reservations required. Main courses 10€–19€ ($16–$30). AE, DC, MC, V. Tues–Sat 11am–midnight. U-Bahn: Stephansplatz. Bus: 1A.

Vestibül *(Finds)* AUSTRIAN For theater buffs in particular, this is a real discovery. You can not only attend performances at the Burgtheater, but enjoy good food and drink as well. The restaurant entrance originally existed for the emperor's coach. Architect Luigi Blau took the basic structure and enlarged it, creating a setting that is simultaneously antique and modern. Before or after the theater, guests gather in the elegant bar for an aperitif, digestif, or coffee. Tapas are also served here, with tables opening onto a view of the City Hall and Ringstrasse.

Beginning on the first warm spring day and lasting until the mild afternoons of autumn, tables are also placed outside in the garden. A team of skilled chefs present classic cuisine with market-fresh ingredients. An appetizer of fresh oysters might be followed by such main dishes as traditional paprika chicken (inspired by nearby Hungary) or a traditional *beuschel* (a Viennese style hash made of heart and lung). Styrian beef is also a local favorite.

Dr.-Karl-Lueger-Ring 2. ✆ **01/5324999.** www.vestibul.at. Reservations recommended. Main courses 14€–24€ ($22–$38). AE, DC, MC, V. Mon–Fri 11am–midnight; Sat 6pm–midnight (except July–Aug, when it's closed Sat). U-Bahn: Herrangosset.

Zum Schwarzen Kameel (Stiebitz) INTERNATIONAL This Jugendstil restaurant has remained in the same family since 1618. A delicatessen against one of the walls sells wine, liquor, and specialty meat items, although most of the action takes place among the chic clientele in the cafe. On Saturday mornings, the cafe is packed with locals trying to recover from a late night. Uniformed waiters will bring you a beverage here, and you can select open face sandwiches from the trays on the black countertops. The specialty is a rosy hand-carved *Beinschinken* (boiled ham with freshly grated horseradish).

Beyond the cafe is a perfectly preserved Art Deco dining room, where jeweled copper chandeliers hang from beaded strings. The walls are a combination of polished paneling, yellowed ceramic tiles, and a dusky plaster ceiling frieze of grape leaves. The restaurant has just 11 tables, and it's the perfect place for a nostalgic lunch in Vienna. The hearty and well-flavored cuisine features herring filet Oslo, potato soup, tournedos, Roman saltimbocca (veal with ham), and an array of daily fish specials.

Bognergasse 5. ✆ **01/5338125.** www.zumkameel.at. Main courses 19€–37€ ($30–$59). AE, DC, MC, V. Mon–Sat 8am–midnight. U-Bahn: Schottentor. Bus: 2A or 3A.

Zum Weissen Rauchfangkehrer VIENNESE Established in the 1860s, this dinner-only place is the former guildhall for Vienna's chimney sweeps. In fact, the restaurant's name (translated as the "white chimney sweep") comes from the story of a drunken and blackened chimney sweep who fell into a kneading trough and woke up the next day covered in flour. The dining room is rustic, with deer antlers, fanciful chandeliers, and pine banquettes that vaguely resemble church pews. A piano in one of the inner rooms provides nighttime music and adds to the comfortable ambience. Big street-level windows let in lots of light. The hearty, flavorful menu offers Viennese fried chicken, both Tyrolean and Wiener schnitzel, wild game, veal goulash, bratwurst, and several kinds of strudel. You'll certainly want to finish with the house specialty, a fabulously rich chocolate cream puff.

Weihburggasse 4. ✆ **01/5123471.** www.weissen-rauchfangkehrer.at. Reservations required. Main courses 15€–26€ ($24–$42). DC, MC, V. Tues–Sat 6pm–midnight. Closed July–Aug. U-Bahn: Stephansplatz.

Inexpensive

Akakiko (Value) ASIAN It's busy and loaded with Asians living permanently or temporarily within Vienna. And as a member of a chain with eight equivalent branches throughout Vienna, it boasts a carefully rehearsed and inexpensive formula for Asian food within an otherwise very expensive neighborhood. To reach its dining room, you'll pass by an open kitchen, where everything gives the impression of wholesomeness and a recent scrubbing. Within the brightly lit modern dining room, outfitted in tones of white and bamboo green, you'll pick from menu items that include sushi, sashimi, teppanyaki, bento boxes, and wok versions of duck, chicken, beef, fish, and vegetarian dishes inspired by the cuisines of China.

Singerstrasse 4. ✆ **057/333-140.** www.akakiko.at. Reservations not accepted. Main courses 8.95€–14€ ($14–$22). MC, V. Daily 10:30am–11:30pm. U-Bahn: Stephansplatz.

Augustinerkeller AUSTRIAN Since 1857, the Augustinerkeller has served wine, beer, and food from the basement of one of the grand Hofburg palaces. It attracts a lively and diverse crowd that gets more boisterous as the *schrammel* (traditional Viennese music) is played late into the night. The vaulted brick room, with worn pine-board floors and wooden banquettes, is an inviting place to grab a drink and a simple meal. Be aware that this long and narrow dining room is usually as packed with people as it is with character. Roaming accordion players add to the festive atmosphere. An upstairs room is quieter and less crowded. This place offers one of the best values for wine tasting in Vienna. The ground-floor lobby lists prices of vintage local wines by the glass. Tasters can sample from hundreds of bottles near the stand-up stainless-steel counter. Aside from the wine and beer, the kitchen serves simple food, including roast chicken, schnitzel, and *tafelspitz.*

Augustinerstrasse 1. ✆ **01/5331026.** Main courses 9€–17€ ($14–$27). AE, DC, MC, V. Daily 10am–midnight. U-Bahn: Stephansplatz.

Buffet Trzésniewski ★ SANDWICHES Everyone in Vienna, from the most hurried office worker to the most elite hostess, knows about this spot. Franz Kafka lived next door and used to come here for sandwiches and beer. It's unlike any buffet you've seen, with six or seven cramped tables and a rapidly moving line of people, all jostling for space next to the glass counters. Indicate to the waitress the kind of sandwich you want (if you can't read German, just point). Most people hurriedly devour the delicious finger sandwiches, which come in 18 different combinations of cream cheese, egg, onion, salami, herring, tomatoes, lobster, and many other tasty ingredients. You can also order small glasses of fruit juice, beer, or wine with your snack. If you do order a drink, the cashier will give you a rubber token, which you'll present to the person at the far end of the counter.

Dorotheergasse 1. ✆ **01/5123291.** Reservations not accepted. Sandwiches .90€ ($1.50). No credit cards. Mon–Fri 8:30am–7:30pm; Sat 9am–5pm. U-Bahn: Stephansplatz.

Café Leopold ★ Finds INTERNATIONAL This cafe and restaurant is within one of Vienna's museums. It's a postmodern version in architectural form of the Viennese expressionist paintings (including many by Egon Schiele) that are exhibited within the museum that contains it. Set one floor above street level in the Leopold Museum, and with a schedule that operates long after the museum is closed for the night, it's sheathed in the same pale pink sandstone as the museum's exterior, but enhanced with three tones (jet black, "Sahara cream," and russet) of marble. There are a minimalist-looking oak-trimmed bar, huge windows, vague and simplified references to 18th-century baroque architecture, and a chandelier that cynics say looks like a lost UFO suspended from the ceiling. During the day, the place functions as a conventional cafe and restaurant, serving a postmodern blend of *mitteleuropaïsche* (central European) and Asian food. Examples include roasted shoulder of veal with Mediterranean vegetables, Thai curries, Vietnamese spring rolls, and arugula-studded risottos. Three nights a week, however, from around 10pm till at least 2am, any hints of kitsch and coziness are banished as soon as a DJ begins cranking out dance tunes for a hard-drinking denizens-of-the-night crowd. For more on this cafe's role as a nightclub, see "Vienna After Dark," in chapter 6.

In the Leopold Museum, Museumsplatz 1. ✆ **01/5236732.** www.cafe-leopold.at. Main courses 5.90€–11€ ($9.50–$18). AE, DC, MC, V. Sun–Wed 10am–2am; Fri–Sat 10am–4pm. U-Bahn: Volkstheater or Babenbergstrasse/MuseumsQuartier.

Café Restaurant Halle INTERNATIONAL Set within the Kunsthalle, this is the direct competitor of the also-recommended Café Leopold (above). Larger and with a more sophisticated menu than the Leopold, but without any of its late-night emphasis on dance music, this is a postmodern, airy, big-windowed quartet of wood-trimmed, cream-color rooms. The menu changes every 2 weeks, and service is efficient, conscientious, and in the old-world style. The first thing you'll see when you enter is a spartan-looking cafe area, with a trio of more formal dining rooms at the top of a short flight of stairs. Despite the commitment of its staff to changing the *carte* very frequently, the menu will always contain a half-dozen meal-size salads, many garnished with strips of steak, chicken, or shrimp; two daily homemade soups; and a rotating series of platters that might include tasty braised filets of shark and roasted lamb, prepared delectably in the Greek style, with yogurt and herb dressing.

In the Kunsthalle Wien, Museumsplatz 1, in the MuseumsQuartier. ✆ **01/5237001.** Main courses 8€–17€ ($13–$27). MC, V. Daily 10am–2am. U-Bahn: MuseumsQuartier.

Dubrovnik BALKAN/CROATIAN/VIENNESE Dubrovnik's allegiance is to the culinary (and cultural) traditions of Croatia. The restaurant, founded in 1965, consists of three dining rooms on either side of a central vestibule filled with busy waiters in Croat costume. The menu lists a lengthy choice of Balkan dishes, including goose-liver pâté; stuffed cabbage; and filet of veal with boiled potatoes, sour cream, and sauerkraut. Among the fish dishes, the most exotic is *Fogosch* (a whitefish) served with potatoes and garlic. For dessert, try baklava or an assortment of Bulgarian cheeses. The restaurant schedules live piano entertainment nightly from 7:30 to 11pm. On site is an unconventional-looking cafe (the Kono-Bar) that serves drinks and many of the main courses available during the grander restaurant's daily midafternoon closing.

Am Heumarkt 5. ✆ **01/713-7102.** Reservations recommended. Main courses 8€–18€ ($13–$29). AE, DC, MC, V. Daily 11am–3pm and 6pm–midnight; cafe Mon–Fri 11am–midnight. U-Bahn: Stadtpark.

Figlmüller AUSTRIAN This is the latest branch of a wine tavern whose original home, established in 1905, lies only a few blocks away. This new branch, thanks to a location on three floors of a thick-walled 200-year-old building and lots of old-world memorabilia attached to the walls, evokes Old Vienna with style and panache. Austrian Airlines referred to its black-and-white uniformed waiters as "unflappable," and we believe that its schnitzels are the kind of plate-filling, golden-brown delicacies that people always associate with schmaltzy Vienna. Menu items include goulash soup, onion-flavored roast beef, Vienna-style fried chicken, and strudels. During mushroom season (autumn and early winter), expect many variations, perhaps most deliciously served in an herbed cream sauce over noodles. This restaurant's nearby twin, at Wollzeile 5 (✆ **01/5126177;** www.figlmueller.at), offers basically the same menu, prices, and richly nostalgic wine-tavern ambience.

Bäckerstrasse 6. ✆ **01/5121760.** Reservations recommended. Main courses 11€–15€ ($17–$23). AE, DC, MC, V. Daily 11:30am–midnight. Closed Aug. U-Bahn: Stephansplatz.

Gösser Bierklinik VIENNESE Also known as the Güldene Drache (Golden Dragon), this restaurant serves the Styrian-brewed Gösser, reportedly the finest beer in the city. The rustic institution occupies a building that, according to tradition, dates from Roman times. An inn operated here in the early 16th century, when Maximilian I ruled the empire, and the decor is strictly medieval. The harried and somewhat unresponsive waitstaff are usually carrying ample mugs of Gösser beer. When you finally get their attention, order some hearty Austrian fare, such as veal chops with dumplings.

Steindlgasse 4. ✆ **01/533-759812.** www.goesser-bierklinik.at. Reservations recommended for parties of 3 or more. Main courses 12€–18€ ($19–$29). DC, MC, V. Mon–Sat 10am–11:30pm. U-Bahn: Stephansplatz. Tram: 31 or 32.

Gulaschmuseum ★ Kids AUSTRIAN/HUNGARIAN If you thought that goulash was available in only one form, think again. This restaurant celebrates at least 15 varieties of it, each an authentic survivor of the culinary traditions of Hungary, and each redolent with the taste of the national spice, paprika. The Viennese adopted goulash from their former vassal centuries ago, and have long since added it to their culinary repertoire. You can order versions of goulash made with roast beef, veal, pork, or even fried chicken livers. Vegetarians rejoice: Versions made with potatoes, beans, or mushrooms are also available. Boiled potatoes and rough-textured brown or black bread will usually accompany your choice. An excellent starter is the Magyar national crepe, *Hortobágy Palatschinken,* stuffed with minced beef and paprika-flavored cream sauce. If you prefer an Austrian dish, there are *tafelspitz,* Wiener schnitzel, fresh fish from Austria's lakes, and such dessert specialties as homemade *apfelstrudel* and Sachertorte.

Schulerstrasse 20. ✆ **01/5121017.** www.gulasch.at. Reservations recommended. Main courses 8€–16€ ($13–$26). MC, V. Mon–Fri 9am–midnight; Sat–Sun 10am–midnight. U-Bahn: Wollzeile or Stephansplatz.

Hansen ★ Finds ASIAN/AUSTRIAN/INTERNATIONAL/MEDITERRANEAN One of the most intriguing and stylish restaurants in Vienna opened as a partnership between a time-tested culinary team and the downtown showrooms of one of Austria's most famous horticulturists and gardening stores (Lederleitner, GmbH). You'll find them cheek-by-jowl in the vaulted cellars of Vienna's stock exchange, a Beaux Arts pile designed in the 1890s by the restaurant's namesake, Theophile Hansen. Part of the charm of this place involves trekking through masses of plants and elaborate garden ornaments on your way to your dining table. Expect to be joined by the movers and shakers of corporate Vienna at lunch and at relatively early dinners, when the place is likely to be very busy. Choose from a small but savory menu that changes weekly. Examples include a spicy bean salad with strips of chicken breast served in a summer broth, risotto with cheese and sour cherries, and poached *Saibling* (something akin to trout from the cold-water streams of the Austrian Alps) with a potato and celery puree and watercress.

In the cellar of the Börsegebäude (Vienna Stock Exchange), Wipplingerstrasse 34 at the Schottenring. ✆ **01/5320542.** www.vestibuel.at. Reservations recommended. Main courses 8€–20€ ($13–$32). AE, DC, MC, V. Mon–Fri 9am–8pm (last order); Sat 9am–3:30pm (last order). U-Bahn: Schottenring.

Kardos AUSTRIAN/HUNGARIAN/SLOVENIAN This folkloric restaurant specializes in the strong flavors and potent traditions that developed in different parts of what used to be the Austro-Hungarian Empire. Similarly, the setting celebrates the idiosyncratic folklore of various regions of the Balkans and the Great Hungarian Plain. Newcomers are welcomed with piquant little rolls known as *grammel,* seasoned with minced pork and spices, and a choice of grilled meats. Other specialties include Hungarian *Fogosch* (a form of pikeperch) that's baked with vegetables and parsley potatoes, Hungarian goulash, and braised cabbage. The cellar atmosphere is Gypsy schmaltz—pine-wood accents and brightly colored Hungarian accessories. During the winter, you're likely to find a strolling violinist. To begin, try a glass of *Barack,* an aperitif made from fermented apricots.

Dominikaner Bastei 8. ✆ **01/5126949.** www.restaurantkardos.com. Reservations recommended. Main courses 8€–20€ ($13–$32). AE, DC, MC, V. Mon–Sat 11:30am–2:30pm and 6–11pm. U-Bahn: Schwedenplatz.

Kern's Beisel Value AUSTRIAN The term *beisl* implies an aggressively unpretentious tavern where food is plentiful and cheap, and the staff has minimal attitude. That's very much the case with this neighborhood favorite, although in this case, the "neighborhood" happens to be within a few steps of the city's tourist and cultural core, Stephansplatz. You'll dine in an old-fashioned wood-paneled dining room darkened by smoke throughout the ages. The tables in back, near the kitchen and separated from the front with a wooden partition, are a wee bit cozier than those near the front, which are more brightly lit. Here, you might discover groups of five or more wine-drinking friends, sometimes middle-aged ladies, celebrating their after-work rituals. Overall, it's fine, and charming in kind of a rough and mountain way. The dinner menu changes weekly and might feature a starter platter of mixed Austrian appetizers, including vegetable terrine, cooked ham, and strips of fried chicken; cream of garlic soup; and roulades of poached chicken with pumpkinseed sauce. There are also wurst with dumplings, beefsteak, goulash soup, and Wiener schnitzels of both veal and pork, and, in autumn, some well-prepared game dishes.

Kleeplattgasse 4. ✆ **01/533-9188.** www.kernbeisl.at. Reservations recommended. Main courses 7€–15€ ($11–$24) at lunch, 7€–19€ ($11–$30) at dinner. MC, V. Mon–Fri 9am–11pm. Closed Sat–Sun. U-Bahn: Stephansplatz.

Palmenhaus ★ AUSTRIAN Many architectural critics consider the Jugendstil glass canopy of this greenhouse the most beautiful in Austria. Overlooking the formal terraces of the Burggarten, it was built between 1901 and 1904 by the Habsburgs' court architect Friedrich Ohmann as a graceful architectural transition between the Albertina and the National Library. Damaged during wartime bombings, it was restored in 1998. Today, its central section functions as a chic cafe and, despite the lavishly historic setting, an appealingly informal venue. No one will mind if you drop in for just a drink and one of the voluptuous pastries displayed near the entrance. But if you want a meal, there's a sophisticated menu that changes monthly and might include fresh Austrian goat cheese with stewed peppers and zucchini salad; young herring with sour cream, horseradish, and deep-fried beignets stuffed with apples and cabbage; and squash blossoms stuffed with salmon mousse.

In the Burggarten. ✆ **01/5331033.** www.palmenhaus.at. Reservations recommended for dinner. Main courses 15€–18€ ($24–$29). AE, DC, MC. V. Daily 10am–2am. U-Bahn: Opera.

Österreicher im MAK Gasthof & Bar ★★ VIENNESE The food and beverage facilities within many of Vienna's museums are often simple, self-service snack bars, but this one, nestled within the MAK, is a deeply respected culinary destination in its own right. It occupies a pair of rooms on the museums' street level, one of them an enormous and echoing room that's capped with one of the most elaborate coffered and frescoed ceilings in town; the other a smaller, postmodern, glass-sided room with a ceiling that rolls back during clement weather for a view of the sky. There's also a garden terrace that's not immediately visible when you first enter, so if you want to dine outside (and in summer, almost everyone does), be sure to make your wishes known. Since 2006, the culinary inspiration behind all this is Helmut Österreicher, a chef who has helped to redefine the tenets of modern Viennese cuisine—a lighter interpretation of what dining with the Habsburgs really meant. The menu is divided into two categories, one featuring "classical" and the other "modern" Viennese cuisine. Favored dishes (for example, personally recommended by Herr Österreicher) among the classical choices include *zwiebelrostbraten,* roast beef with onions and sautéed potatoes; Wiener schnitzel; and *tafelspitz*—in this case, two types of prime boiled beef with fried grated potatoes, apple horseradish, and chive sauce. Recommendations from the list of modern choices include artfully presented versions of roasted chicken in a creamy paprika sauce (utterly delicious) with small creamed dumplings; salmon-trout in a muesli crust, served with potato-based noodles; and pike-perch on a bed of tomato-flavored cabbage, with parsley potatoes. Menu items change frequently with the inspiration of this gifted chef.

In the MAK *(Museum der Angewanten Kunst),* Stubenring 5. ✆ **01/714-0121.** www.oesterreicherimmak.at. Reservations recommended. Main courses 8€–18€ ($13–$29). AE, DC, MC, V. Daily 11:30am–11:30pm. U-Bahn: Stubentor or Schwedenplatz.

Restaurant Salzamt ★ AUSTRIAN This is the best restaurant in a neighborhood—the "Bermuda Triangle"—that's loaded with less desirable competitors. It evokes a turn-of-the-20th-century Viennese bistro, replete with Wiener Werkstatte–inspired chairs and lighting fixtures, cream-color walls, and dark tables and banquettes, where you're likely to see an arts-involved, sometimes surprisingly prominent clientele of loyal repeat diners, including Karl Lagerfeld and the Prince of Monaco. Sit within its vaulted interior or—if weather permits—move out to any of the tables on the square, overlooking Vienna's oldest church, St. Ruprecht. Well-prepared items include a terrine of broccoli and artichoke hearts, light-textured pastas, filets of pork with a Gorgonzola-enriched cream sauce, several kinds of goulash, and fresh fish. One of the most noteworthy of these is fried filets of *Saibling,* a fish native to the coldwater streams of western Austria, served with lemon or tartar sauce.

Ruprechtsplatz 1. ✆ **01/5335332.** www.salzamt.at. Reservations recommended. Main courses 8€–19€ ($13–$30). V. Daily 5pm–midnight. U-Bahn: Schwedenplatz.

Coffeehouses & Cafes

Café Central ★, Herrengasse 14 (✆ **01/5333764;** www.palaisevents.com; U-Bahn: Herrengasse), stands in the center of Vienna across from the Hofburg and the Spanish Riding School. This grand cafe offers a glimpse into 19th-century Viennese life–it was once the center of Austria's literati. Even Lenin is said to have met his colleagues here. The Central offers a variety of Viennese coffees, a vast selection of pastries and desserts, and Viennese and provincial dishes. It's a delightful spot for lunch. The cafe is open Monday to Saturday from 7:30am to 10pm, Sunday 10am to 10pm.

The windows of the venerated 1888 **Café Demel** ★★, Kohlmarkt 14 (✆ **01/5351717;** U-Bahn: Herrengasse; Bus: 1A or 2A), are filled with fanciful spun-sugar creations of characters from folk legends. Inside you'll find a splendidly baroque landmark where dozens of pastries are available daily, including the *Pralinen*, Senegal, truffle, *Sand*, and *Maximilian* tortes, as well as *Gugelhupfs* (cream-filled horns). Demel also serves a mammoth variety of tea sandwiches made with smoked salmon, egg salad, caviar, or shrimp. If you want to be traditional, ask for a Demel-Coffee, which is filtered coffee served with milk, cream, or whipped cream. It's open daily from 10am to 7pm.

Café Diglas, Wollzeile 10 (✆ **01/5125765;** www.diglas.at; U-Bahn: Stubentor), evokes prewar Vienna better than many of its competitors, thanks to a decor that retains some of the accessories from 1934, when it first opened. The cafe prides itself on its long association with composer Franz Léhar. It offers everything in the way of run-of-the-mill caffeine fixes, as well as more elaborate, liqueur-enriched concoctions such as a Biedermeier (with apricot schnapps and cream). If you're hungry, ask for a menu (foremost among the platters is an excellent Wiener schnitzel). The cafe is open daily from 7am to 11pm.

Café Dommayer, Auhofstrasse 2 (✆ **01/8775465;** U-Bahn: Schönbrunn), boasts a reputation for courtliness that goes back to 1787. In 1844, Johann Strauss, Jr., made his musical debut here, and beginning in 1924, the site became known as *the* place in Vienna for tea dancing. During clement weather, a garden with seats for 300 opens in back. The rest of the year, the venue is restricted to a high-ceilinged black-and-white old-world room. Every Saturday from 2 to 4pm, a pianist and violinist perform; and every third Saturday, an all-woman orchestra plays mostly Strauss. Most patrons come for coffee, tea, and pastries, but if you have a more substantial appetite, try the platters of food, including Wiener schnitzel, *Rostbraten*, and fish. It's open daily from 7am to 10pm.

Even the Viennese debate the age of **Café Frauenhuber,** Himmelpfortgasse 6 (✆ **01/5125353;** http://café-frauenhuber.at; U-Bahn: Stephansplatz). But regardless of whether its opening fell in 1788 or 1824, it has a justifiable claim to being the oldest continuously operating coffeehouse in the city. The old-time decor is a bit battered and more than a bit smoke-stained. Wiener schnitzel, served with potato salad and greens, is a good bet, as are any of the ice cream dishes and pastries. It's open daily Monday to Saturday 8am to 11pm.

Housed in the deluxe Hotel Imperial, **Café Imperial ★**, Kärntner Ring 16 (✆ **01/50110389;** www.starwoodhotels.com; U-Bahn: Karlsplatz), was a favorite of Gustav Mahler and a host of other celebrities. The "Imperial Toast" is a small meal in itself: white bread with veal, chicken, and leaf spinach topped with a gratin, baked in an oven, and served with hollandaise sauce. A daily breakfast/brunch buffet for 40€ ($64) is served Hapsburg-style daily 7am to 11am. It's said to be the only hotel buffet breakfast in Vienna that comes with champagne. The cafe is open daily from 7am to 11pm.

One of the Ring's great coffeehouses, **Café Landtmann ★**, Dr.-Karl-Lueger-Ring 4 (✆ **01/241000;** www.cafe-wien.at; tram: 1, 2, or D), has a history dating to the 1880s and has long drawn a mix of politicians, journalists, and actors. It was also Freud's favorite. The original chandeliers and the prewar chairs have been refurbished. We highly suggest spending an hour or so here, perusing the newspapers, sipping on coffee, or planning the day's itinerary. The cafe is open daily from 7:30am to midnight (lunch is served 11:30am to 3pm and dinner is served 5 to 11pm).

Part of the success of **Café Sperl,** Gumpendorferstrasse 11 (✆ **01/5864158;** www.cafesperl.at; U-Bahn: Karlsplatz), derives from the fact that the Gilded Age panels and accessories that were installed in 1880 are still in place. These details also contributed to Sperl's designation in 1998 as "Austria's best coffeehouse of the year." If you opt for a black coffee, you'll be in good company. Platters include salads; toast; baked noodles with ham, mushrooms, and cream sauce; omelets; steaks; and Wiener schnitzels. The staff evokes a bemused kind of courtliness, but in a concession to modern tastes, there's a billiard table and some dartboards on the premises. It's open Monday to Saturday 7am to 11pm and Sunday 11am to 8pm (closed Sun July–Aug).

Café Tirolerhof, Fürichgasse 8 (✆ **01/5127833;** U-Bahn: Stephansplatz or Karlsplatz), which has been under the same management for decades, makes for a convenient sightseeing break, particularly from a tour of the nearby Hofburg complex. One coffee specialty is the Maria Theresia, a large cup of mocha flavored with apricot liqueur and topped with whipped cream. If coffee sounds too hot, try the tasty milkshakes. You can also order a Viennese breakfast of coffee, tea, hot chocolate, two Viennese rolls, butter, jam, and honey. Open Monday to Saturday 7:30am to 10pm.

Thirty kinds of tea are served at **Demmers Teehaus,** Mölker Bastei 5 (✆ **01/5335995;** www.demmer.at; U-Bahn: Schottentor), along with dozens of pastries, cakes, toasts, and English sandwiches. Demmer's is managed by the previously recommended restaurant, Buffet Trzésniewski; however, the teahouse offers you a chance to sit down, relax, and enjoy your drink or snack. It's open Monday to Friday from 9am to 6pm.

Zu den 3 Hacken (at the Three Axes) ★ AUSTRIAN Cozy, small-scale, and charming, this restaurant was established 350 years ago and today bears the reputation as the oldest *gasthaus* (tavern) in Vienna. In 1827, Franz Schubert had an ongoing claim to one of the establishment's tables as a site for entertaining his cronies. Today, the establishment maintains midsummer barriers of green-painted lattices and potted ivy for tables that jut onto the sidewalk. During inclement weather, head for one of three dining rooms, each paneled and each evocative of an inn high in the Austrian Alps. Expect an old-fashioned menu replete with the kind of dishes that fueled the Austro-Hungarian Empire. Examples include *tafelspitz,* beef goulash, mixed grills piled high with chops and sausages, and desserts that include Hungarian-inspired *palatschinken* (crepes) with chocolate-hazelnut sauce. The Czech and Austrian beer here seems to taste especially good when it's dispensed from a keg.

Singerstrasse 28. ✆ **01/5125895.** www.vinum-wien.at. Reservations recommended. Main courses 7.50€–18€ ($12–$29). AE, DC, MC, V. Mon–Sat 11am–11pm. U-Bahn: Stephansplatz.

Zum Kuchldragoner AUSTRIAN Some aspects of this place will remind you of an old-fashioned Austrian tavern, perhaps one that's perched high in the mountains, far from any congested city neighborhood. The feeling is enhanced by the pine trim and the battered *gemütlichkeit* of what you'll soon discover is a bustling, irreverent, and sometimes jaded approach to feeding old-fashioned, flavorful, but far-from-cutting-edge cuisine to large numbers of urban clients, usually late into the night after everyone has had more than a drink or two. You can settle for a table inside, but our preferred venue is an outdoor table, immediately adjacent to the Romanesque foundation of Vienna's oldest church, St. Ruprechts. Come here for foaming steins of beer and such Viennese staples as Wiener schnitzel, schnitzel cordon bleu, baked eggplant layered with ham and cheese, and grilled lamb cutlets.

Seitenstettengasse 3 or Ruprechtsplatz 4–5. ✆ **015338371.** www.kuchldragoner.at. Reservations recommended. Main courses 7.80€–15€ ($13–$24). MC, V. Mon–Thurs 11am–2am; Fri–Sun 11am–4am. U-Bahn: Schwedenplatz.

Zwölf-Apostelkeller VIENNESE For those seeking a taste of old Vienna, this is the place. Sections of this wine tavern's walls predate 1561. Rows of wooden tables stand under vaulted ceilings, with lighting partially provided by streetlights set into the masonry floor. It's so deep that you feel you're entering a dungeon. Students love this place for its low prices and proximity to St. Stephan's. In addition to beer and wine, you can get hearty Austrian fare. Specialties include Hungarian goulash soup, meat dumplings, and a *schlachtplatte* (a selection of hot black pudding, liverwurst, pork, and pork sausage with a hot bacon and cabbage salad). The cooking is hardly refined, but it's very well prepared.

Sonnenfelsgasse 3. ✆ **01/5126777.** www.zwoelf-apostelkeller.at. Main courses 6.50€–12€ ($10–$19) AE, DC, MC, V. Daily 11am–midnight. Closed July. U-Bahn: Stephansplatz. Tram: 1, 2, 21, D, or N. Bus: 1A.

LEOPOLDSTADT (2ND DISTRICT)

Expensive

Vincent ★ CONTINENTAL The decor of this restaurant is smooth and cozy, and guests can opt for a seat in three different dining rooms, any of which might remind you of a richly upholstered, carefully decorated private home that's accented with flickering candles, flowers, and crystal. The set menus here change with the season and the whim of the chef. Food here is elegant, upscale, and served in convivial surroundings. The finest examples include a well-prepared rack of lamb flavored with bacon, whitefish or pikeperch in white-wine sauce, turbot with saffron sauce, filet of butterfish with tiger prawns served with a consommé of shrimp, and, in season, many different game dishes, including quail and venison.

Grosse-Pfarrgasse 7. ✆ **01/2141516.** www.restaurant.at. Reservations required. 5-course menu 50€ ($79); 7-course menu 69€ ($110); 10-course menu 95€ ($152). AE, DC, MC, V. Mon–Sat 5:30pm–1am. U-Bahn: Schwedenplatz.

Inexpensive

Altes Jägerhaus ★ AUSTRIAN/GAME Little about the decor here has changed since this place opened in 1899. Located 1.5km (1 mile) from the entrance to the Prater in a verdant park, it's a welcome escape from the more crowded restaurants of the Inner City. Grab a seat in any of the four old-fashioned dining rooms, where the beverage of choice is equally divided between beer and wine. Seasonal game, such as pheasant and venison, are the house specialty, but you'll also find an array of seafood dishes that might include freshwater and saltwater trout, zander, or salmon. The menu also features a delicious repertoire of Austrian staples such as *tafelspitz* and schnitzel.

Freudenau 255. ✆ **01/72895770.** Reservations recommended. Main courses 13€–25€ ($21–$40). AE, DC, MC, V. Daily 10am–11pm. U-Bahn: Schlachthausgasse, then bus 77A.

LANDSTRASSE (3RD DISTRICT)

Very Expensive

Steirereck ★★★ AUSTRIAN/VIENNESE *Steirereck* means "corner of Styria," which is exactly what Heinz and Birgit Reitbauer have created in this intimate and rustic restaurant. Traditional Viennese dishes and "new Austrian" selections appear on the menu. Begin with a caviar-semolina dumpling or roasted turbot with fennel (served as an appetizer), or opt for the most elegant and expensive item of all, goose-liver Steirereck. Some enticing main courses include asparagus with pigeon, saddle of lamb for two, prime Styrian roast beef, and red-pepper risotto with rabbit. The menu is wisely limited and well prepared, changing daily depending on what's fresh at the market. The restaurant is popular with after-theater diners, and the large wine cellar holds some 35,000 bottles.

Am Heumarkt 2A. ✆ **01/7133168.** http://steireck.at. Reservations required. Main courses 15€–25€ ($24–$40); 5-course fixed-price dinner 100€ ($160). AE, DC, MC, V. Mon–Fri 11:30am–2:30pm and 6:30–11pm. Closed holidays. Tram: N. Bus: 4.

Expensive

Dining Room ★★★ (Finds) INTERNATIONAL On a quiet lane outside the center of town, this little restaurant has only four tables, seating 12 guests. It's in a private home and follows a European trend of opening little hideaway restaurants for those who appreciate great food served in a very intimate and personal atmosphere. The owner and chef, Angelika Apfelthaler, prepares each meal herself, offering a set menu. Each night's menu is dedicated to a special theme, including, perhaps, white truffles in Piedmont, Moroccan nights, or cooking with spices from around the world. Top-quality products go into every menu; and not only is the bread homemade, but the jams and chutneys are as well. You might begin with a chestnut and hazelnut soup, followed by an arugula salad with sautéed porcini mushrooms. A main course might be a juicy duck breast with a creamy saffron-laced risotto.

Maygasse 31. ✆ **01/804-8586.** Reservations required. Fixed-price menu 44€ ($70). DC, MC, V. 7:30pm (but confirm exact time when you call for a reservation). U-Bahn: Hietzing, then tram 60 to riedelgasse/Orthopädisches Krankenhaus (a 5-min. walk from here).

Niky's Kuchlmasterei ★ INTERNATIONAL/VIENNESE The decor features old stonework with some modern architectural innovations, and the extensive menu boasts well-prepared food. The lively crowd of loyal habitués adds to the welcoming ambience, making Niky's a good choice for an evening meal, especially in summer when you can dine on its unforgettable terrace. After a long and pleasant meal, your bill will arrive in an elaborate box suitable for jewels, along with an amusing message in German that offers a tongue-in-cheek apology for cashing your check.

Obere Weissgerberstrasse 6. ✆ **01/7129000.** www.kuchlmasterei.at. Reservations recommended. Main courses 18€–20€ ($29–$31); 3-course fixed-price lunch 19€ ($30); 7-course fixed-price dinner 51€ ($82). AE, DC, MC, V. Mon–Sat noon–midnight. U-Bahn: Schwedenplatz.

WIEDEN & MARGARETEN (4TH & 5TH DISTRICTS)

Moderate

Motto AUSTRIAN/ITALIAN/THAI This is the premier gay-friendly restaurant of Austria, with a cavernous red-and-black interior, a busy bar, and a clientele that has included many of the glam figures (Thierry Mugler, John Galliano, and lots of theater people) of the international circuit. Even Helmut Lang worked here briefly as a waiter. It's set behind green doors and a sign that's so small and discreet as to be nearly invisible. In summer, it's enhanced with tables set up in a garden. No one will mind if you pop in just to chat, as it's a busy nightlife entity in its own right. But if you're hungry, cuisine is about as eclectic as it gets, ranging from sushi and Thai-inspired curries to *gutbürgerlich* (home and hearth) food like grandma used to make.

Schönbrunnerstrasse 30 (entrance on Rudigergasse). ✆ **01/5870672.** www.motto.at. Reservations recommended. Main courses 7€–21€ ($11–$34). MC, V. Daily 6pm–4am. U-Bahn: Pilgrimgasse.

Silberwirt VIENNESE Despite the fact that it opened a quarter of a century ago, this restaurant oozes with Old Viennese style and resembles the traditional *beisl* (bistro), with its copious portions of conservative, time-honored Viennese food. You can dine within a pair of dining rooms or move into the beer garden. Menu items include stuffed mushrooms, *tafelspitz,* schnitzels, and filets of zander, salmon, and trout. Be aware that this establishment shares the same building and address as the restaurant Schlossgasse 21 listed above.

Schlossgasse 21. ✆ **01/5444907.** www.schlossquadr.at. Reservations recommended. Main courses 9€–22€ ($14–$35). V. Daily noon–10pm. U-Bahn: Pilgrimgasse.

Inexpensive

Café Cuadro INTERNATIONAL Trendy, countercultural, and arts-oriented, this cafe and bistro is little more than a long, glassed-in corridor with vaguely Bauhaus-inspired detailing. There are clusters of industrial-looking tables, but many clients opt for a seat at the long, luncheonette-style counter above a Plexiglas floor with four-sided geometric patterns illuminated from below. In keeping with the establishment's name (Cuadro), the menu features four of everything—salads (including a very good Caesar option), juicy burgers, homemade soups, steak, and—if you're an early riser—breakfasts.

Margaretenstrasse 77. ✆ **01/544-7550.** Breakfast 4€–8€ ($6.40–$13); main courses 5€–12€ ($8–$19). V. Mon–Sat 8am–midnight; Sun 9am–11pm. U-Bahn: Pilgramgasse.

Gasthaus Ubl ★ (Finds) AUSTRIAN This is a closely guarded Viennese secret. It's where locals who want to enjoy some of the famous dishes enjoyed by their last great emperor, Franz Josef, go. This is an authentic guesthouselike atmosphere with an old

Viennese stove. Three sisters run it, and the whole place screams Old Vienna—nothing flashy or touristy here. Begin with one of the freshly made salads or soups, then follow with the classics—the best *tafelspitz* in the area or such old favorites as *schweinebraten* (a perfectly roasted pork). Desserts are old-fashioned and yummy. The staff is most welcoming.

Pressgasse 26. ✆ **01/5876437.** Reservations recommended. Main courses 10€–15€ ($16–$24). AE, DC, MC, V. Daily noon–2pm and 6–10pm. U-Bahn: Karlsplatz. Bus: 59A.

MARIAHILF (6TH DISTRICT)

Inexpensive

Alfi's Goldener Spiegel VIENNESE By everyone's account, this is the most prominent gay restaurant in Vienna, where the majority gay clientele enjoys food and ambience that might remind you of a simple Viennese *beisl* in a working-class district. (Many of the young European men you'll see here come with a price tag.) If you do decide to sit down for a meal, expect large portions of traditional Viennese specialties such as Wiener schnitzel, roulade of beef, filet steaks with pepper sauce, and *tafelspitz.* Its position near Vienna's Naschmarkt, the city's biggest food market, ensures that the food served is impeccably fresh.

Linke Wienzeile 46 (entrance on Stiegengasse). ✆ **01/5866608.** www.goldenerspiegel.com. Main courses 6.50€–15€ ($10–$24). No credit cards. Daily 7pm–2am. U-Bahn: U4 to Kettenbruckengasse.

NEUBAU (7TH DISTRICT)

Moderate

Bohème ★ INTERNATIONAL/VIENNESE This one-time bakery was originally built in 1750 in the baroque style. Today its historic street is an all-pedestrian walkway loaded with shops. Since opening in 1989, Bohème has attracted a crowd that's knowledgeable about the nuances of wine, food, and the opera music that reverberates throughout the two dining rooms. Even the decor is theatrical; it looks like a cross between a severely dignified stage set and an artsy, turn-of-the-19th-century cafe. Menu items are listed as movements in an opera, with overtures (aperitifs), prologues (appetizers), and first and second acts (soups and main courses). As you'd guess, desserts provide the finales. Some tempting items include Andalusian gazpacho, platters of mixed fish filets with tomato risotto, and *tafelspitz* with horseradish.

Spittelberggasse 19. ✆ **01/5233173.** www.boheme.at. Reservations recommended. Main courses 10€–23€ ($16–$37). AE, DC, MC, V. Mon–Sat 11am–midnight. Closed Jan 7–23. U-Bahn: Volkstheater.

Inexpensive

Amerlingbeisl AUSTRIAN The hip clientele, occasionally blasé staff, and minimalist, somewhat industrial-looking decor give Amerlingbeisl a modern sensibility. If you get nostalgic, you can opt for a table out on the cobblestones of the early-19th-century building's glassed-in courtyard, beneath a grape arbor, where horses used to be stabled. Come to this neighborhood spot for simple but good food and a glass of beer or wine. The menu ranges from simple sandwiches and salads to more elaborate fare, such as Argentinean steak with rice, turkey or pork schnitzels with potato salad, and dessert crepes stuffed with marmalade.

Stiftgasse 8. ✆ **01/526-1660.** www.amerlingbeisl.at. Main courses 7.60€–8.70€ ($12–$14). DC, MC, V. Daily 9am–2am. U-Bahn: Volkstheater.

Plutzer Bräu ★ Finds AUSTRIAN This is one of the best examples in Vienna of the explosion of hip and trendy restaurants within the city's 7th District. Maintained by the Plutzer Brewery, it occupies the cavernous cellar of an imposing 19th-century building. Any antique references are quickly lost once you're inside, thanks to an industrial-looking decor with exposed heating ducts, burnished stainless steel, and accessories that might remind you of the cafeteria in a central European factory. You can stay at the long, accommodating bar and drink fresh-brewed Plutzer beer, but if you're hungry (and this very good beer will probably encourage an appetite), head for the well-scrubbed dining room, where the menu reflects Old Viennese traditions. Food is excellent and includes veal stew in beer sauce with dumplings, "brewmaster's-style" pork steak, and pasta with herbs and feta cheese. Dessert might include curd dumplings with poppy seeds and sweet bread crumbs.

Schrankgasse 2. ✆ **01/5261215.** www.plutzerbrau.at. Reservations not necessary. Main courses 6.90€–17€ ($11–$26). MC, V. Daily 10am–midnight. U-Bahn: Volkstheater.

JOSEFSTADT (8TH DISTRICT)

Moderate

Alte Backstube HUNGARIAN/VIENNESE This spot is worth visiting just to admire the baroque sculptures that crown the top of the doorway. The building was originally designed as a private home in 1697, and 4 years later it was transformed into a bakery, complete with wood-burning stoves. For more than 2½ centuries, the establishment served the baking needs of the neighborhood. In 1963, the owners added a dining room, a dainty front room for drinking beer and tea, and a collection of baking-related artifacts. Once seated, you can order such wholesome, robust specialties as braised pork with cabbage, Viennese-style goulash, and roast venison with cranberry sauce and bread dumplings. There's an English-language menu if you need it. Try the house special dessert, cream-cheese strudel with hot vanilla sauce.

Lange Gasse 34. ✆ **01/4061101.** Reservations required. Main courses 10€–19€ ($16–$30). MC, V. Tues–Thurs and Sat–Sun noon–midnight; Fri 5pm–midnight. Closed mid-July to Aug 30. U-Bahn: Rathaus. Go east along Schmidgasse to Lange Gasse.

Die Fromme Helene ★ AUSTRIAN This is the kind of upscale tavern where the food is traditional and excellent, the crowd is animated and creative, and the staff is hip enough to recognize and recall the names of the many actors, writers, and politicians who come here regularly. Part of its theatrical allure derives from a location that's close to several of the city's theaters (including the English Theater), and to prove it, there are signed and framed photographs of many of the quasi-celebrity clients who have eaten and made merry here. Expect a wide range of traditional and well-prepared Austrian dishes, including schnitzels of veal and pork alike, pastas, and a chocolate pudding (whose name translates as "Moor in a Shirt") served with hot chocolate sauce and whipped cream. The establishment's enduring specialty is *Alt Wiener Backfleisch,* a long-marinated and spicy version of steak that's breaded, fried, and served with potato salad. There's a range of pasta and vegetarian dishes as well. The restaurant's name, incidentally, derives from the comic-book creation of a 19th-century illustrator, Wilhelm Busch, whose hard-drinking but well-meaning heroine, "pious Helen," captivated the imagination of the German-speaking world.

15 Josefstädter Strasse. ✆ **01/4069144.** www.frommehelene.at. Reservations recommended. Main courses 11€–20€ ($17–$32). AE, DC, MC, V. Mon–Sat 11am–1am. Tram: J to Theater in der Josefstadt.

Piaristenkeller AUSTRIAN Erich Emberger has successfully renovated and reassembled this wine tavern with centuries-old vaulted ceilings in a vast cellar room. The place was founded in 1697 by Piarist monks as a tavern and wine cellar. The kitchen, which once served the cloisters, still dishes out traditional Austrian specialties based on original recipes. Zither music is played beginning at 7:30pm, and in summer the garden at the church square is open from 11am to midnight. Wine and beer are available whenever the cellar is open. Advance booking is required for a guided tour of the cloister's old wine vaults.

Piaristengasse 45. ✆ **01/4059152.** Reservations recommended. Main courses 14€–22€ ($22–$35). AE, DC, MC, V. Mon–Sat 6pm–midnight. U-Bahn: Rathaus.

NEAR SCHÖNBRUNN

Very Expensive

Altwienerhof ★★★ AUSTRIAN/FRENCH A short walk from Schönbrunn Palace lies one of the premier dining spots in Vienna. The building is completely modernized, but it was originally designed as a private home in the 1870s. Mr. Günter brings sophistication and charm to the dining rooms, which retain many Biedermeier embellishments from the original construction. The chef prepares nouvelle cuisine using only the freshest and highest-quality ingredients. The menu changes frequently, and the maître d' is always willing to assist with recommendations. Each night the chef prepares a tasting menu, which is a sampling of the kitchen's best nightly dishes. The wine list consists of more than 700 selections, each of which is chosen by Mr. Günter himself. The cellar below houses about 18,000 bottles.

In the Altwienerhof Hotel, Herklotzgasse 6. ✆ **01/8926000.** www.altwienerhof.at. Reservations recommended. Main courses 12€–21€ ($19–$34). AE, DC, MC, V. Mon–Sat 5–11pm. Closed first 3 weeks in Jan. U-Bahn: Gumpendorferstrasse.

Moderate

Hietzinger Brau AUSTRIAN Established in 1743, this is the most famous and best-recommended restaurant in the vicinity of Schönbrunn Palace. Everything about it evokes a sense of bourgeois stability—wood paneling, a staff wearing folkloric costume, and platters heaped high with *gutbürgerlich* cuisine. The menu lists more than a dozen preparations of beef, including the time-tested favorite, *tafelspitz,* as well as mixed grills, all kinds of steaks, and fish that includes lobster, salmon, crab, and zander. Homage to the cuisine of Franz Josef appears in the form of very large Wiener schnitzels, a creamy goulash, and even a very old-fashioned form of braised calf's head. Wine is available, but the most popular beverage here, by far, is a foaming stein of the local brew, Hietzinger.

Auhofstrasse 1. ✆ **01/87770870.** Reservations not necessary. Main courses 16€–23€ ($26–$37). DC, MC, V. Daily 11:30am–3pm and 6–11:30pm. U-Bahn: Hietzing.

6

Exploring Vienna

In this chapter, we'll explore the many sights of this vibrant and storied city, including its palaces, museums, churches, parks, attractions for kids, and attractions for those with special sightseeing interests. Be warned that it's possible to spend a week here and only touch the surface of this multifaceted city. We'll take you through the highlights, but try to set aside some time for wandering and taking in the street life. We'll also take you shopping, and then show you the glittering world of Vienna after dark, including a look at its rich cultural life and world-class performing-arts scene.

1 THE HOFBURG PALACE COMPLEX ★★★

Once the winter palace of the Hapsburgs, the Hofburg sits in the heart of Vienna and is known for its vast, impressive courtyards. To reach it (you can hardly miss it), head up Kohlmarkt to Michaelerplatz 1, Burgring (✆ **01/5875554**), where you'll stumble upon two enormous fountains ornamented with statues. You can also take the U-Bahn to Stephansplatz, Herrengasse, or Mariahilferstrasse, or else tram no. 1, 2, D, or J to Burgring.

This complex of imperial edifices, the first of which was constructed in 1279, grew with the empire, so today the palace is virtually a city within a city. The earliest parts were built around a courtyard, the **Swiss Court,** named for the Swiss mercenaries who performed guard duty here. This oldest section of the palace is at least 700 years old.

The Hofburg's complexity of styles, which are not always harmonious, is the result of each emperor or empress opting to add to or take away some of the work done by his or her predecessors. The palace, which has withstood three major sieges and a great fire, is called simply *die Burg* (the palace) by Viennese. Of its more than 2,600 rooms, fewer than two dozen are open to the public.

Albertina ★ One of the greatest graphics collections in the world is housed within the Hofburg in a 17th-century palace. The museum, named for a son-in-law of Maria Theresia, traces the development of graphic arts since the 14th century. The most outstanding treasure is the Dürer collection. Unfortunately, what you'll usually see are copies—the originals are shown only on special occasions. Be sure to view Dürer's *Praying Hands*, which has been reproduced throughout the world. The 20,000-some drawings and more than 250,000 original etchings and prints include work by such artists as Poussin, Fragonard, Rubens, Rembrandt, Michelangelo, and da Vinci. Exhibitions of both ancient and modern drawings and prints are always changing. Visitors who remember the old Albertina are often surprised at the $110-million overhaul. Today there are three airy new galleries on four floors constructed into a former city wall. The Albertina also has enough space today to display its expanded photography collection.

Albertinaplatz. ✆ **01/534830.** www.albertina.at. Admission 9.50€ ($15) adults, 7€ ($11) students, free for children under 6. Thurs–Tues 10am–6pm; Wed 10am–9pm.

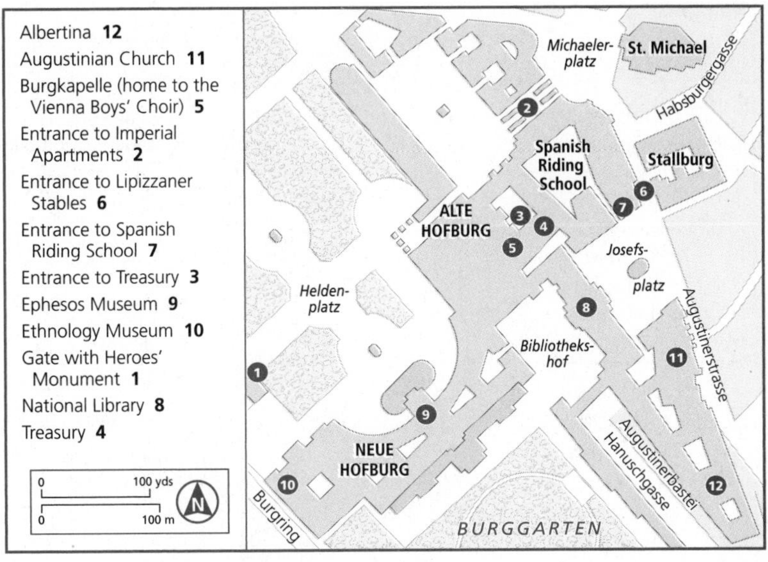

Augustinerkirche (Church of the Augustinians) ★ The 14th-century Church of the Augustinians was built within the Hofburg complex to serve as the parish church for the imperial court. In the latter part of the 18th century, it was stripped of its baroque embellishments and returned to the original Gothic features. The Chapel of St. George, dating from 1337, is entered from the right aisle. The **Tomb of Maria Christina** ★, the favorite daughter of Maria Theresia, is housed in the main nave near the rear entrance, but there's no body in it. (The princess was buried in the Imperial Crypt, described later in this section.) This richly ornamented tomb is one of Canova's masterpieces. A small room in the Loreto Chapel is filled with urns containing the hearts of the imperial Hapsburg family. They can be viewed through a window in an iron door. The Chapel of St. George and the Loreto Chapel are open to the public only by prearranged guided tour.

Not everything in the church belongs to the macabre. Maria Theresia married François of Lorraine here in 1736, and the Augustinerkirche was also the site of other royal weddings: Marie Antoinette to Louis XVI of France in 1770, Marie-Louise of Austria to Napoleon in 1810 (by proxy—he didn't show up), and Franz Josef to Elisabeth of Bavaria in 1854.

The most convenient—and most dramatic—time to visit the church is on Sunday at 11am, when a high Mass is accompanied by a choir, soloists, and an orchestra.

Augustinerstrasse 3. ✆ **01/5337099.** Free admission. Daily 6:30am–6pm. U-Bahn: Stephansplatz.

Die Burgkapelle (Home of the Vienna Boys' Choir) Construction of this Gothic chapel began in 1447 during the reign of Emperor Frederick III, but it was later massively renovated. From 1449, it was the private chapel of the royal family. Today the Burgkapelle hosts the **Hofmusikkapelle** ★★, an ensemble of the Vienna Boys' Choir and members of the Vienna State Opera chorus and orchestra, which performs works by classical and modern composers. Written applications for reserved seats should be sent at

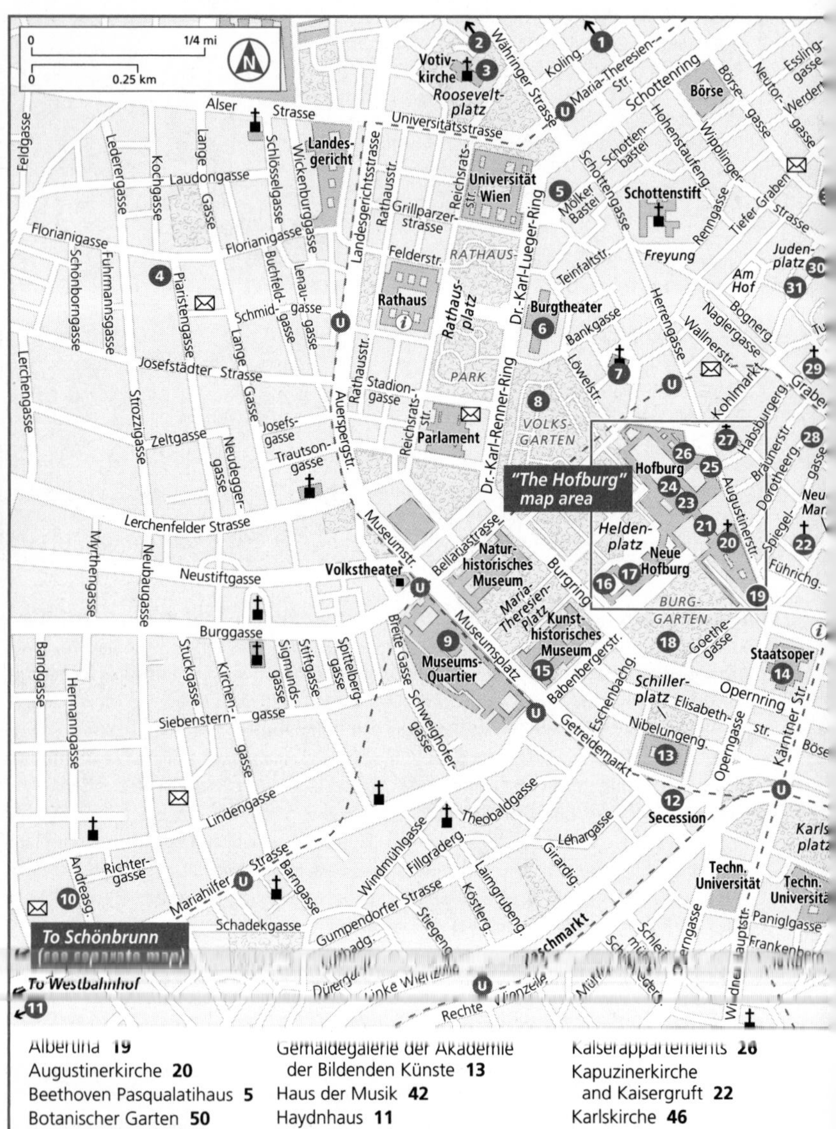

Albertina 19
Augustinerkirche 20
Beethoven Pasqualatihaus 5
Botanischer Garten 50
Burggarten 18
Burgkapelle 23
Burgtheater 6
Deutschordenskirche 38
Domkirche St. Stephan 37
Gemäldegalerie der Akademie der Bildenden Künste 13
Haus der Musik 42
Haydnhaus 11
Heeresgeschichtliches Museum 48
Hofmobiliendepot 10
Hundertwasserhaus 44
Johann Strauss Wohnung 34
Judenplatz 30
Jüdisches Museum Wien 28
Kaiserappartements 26
Kapuzinerkirche and Kaisergruft 22
Karlskirche 46
Kunsthalle Wien 9
Kunsthistorisches Museum 15
Leopold Museum 9
Liechtenstein Museum 1
Michaelerkirche 27
Minoritenkirche 7

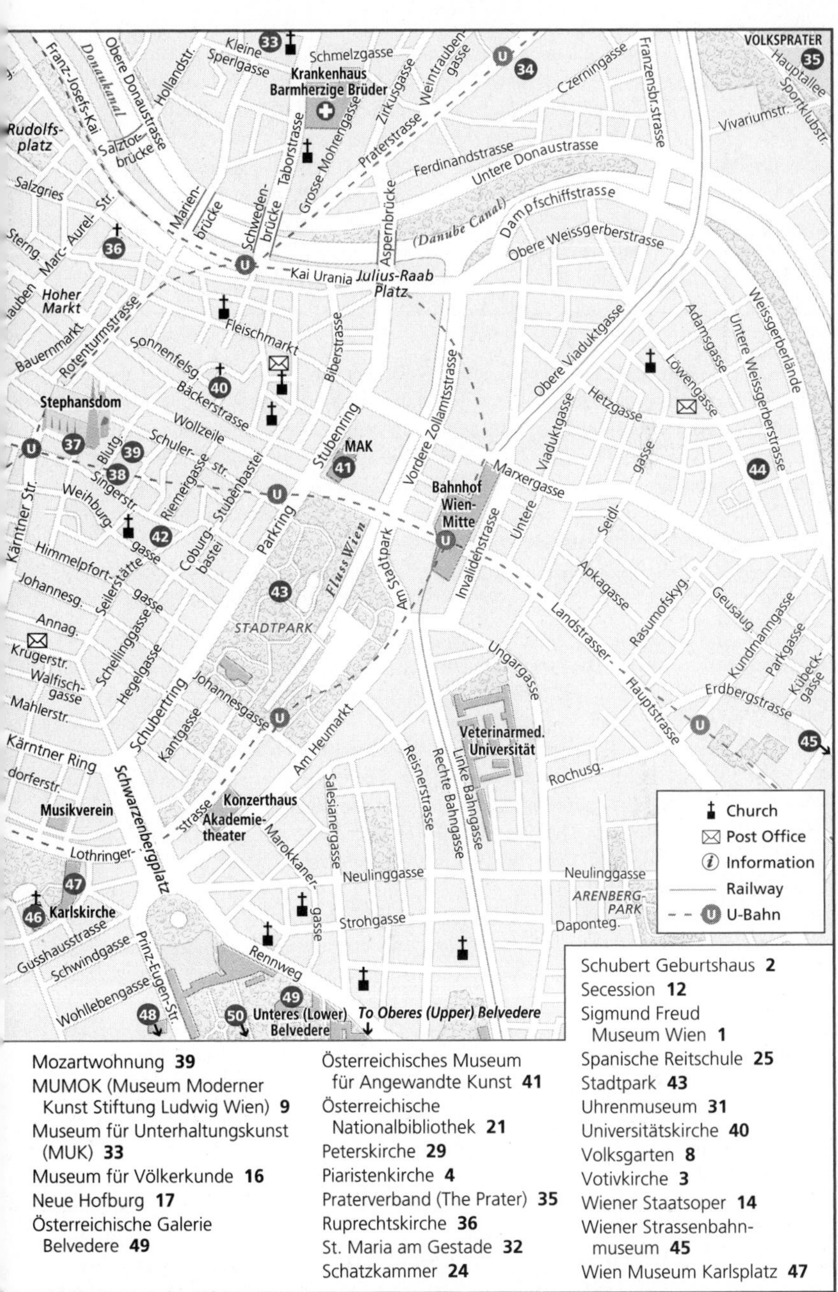
VOLKSPRATER
Hauptallee
Sportklubstr.
Vivariumstr.
Kleine Sperlgasse
Schmelzgasse
Krankenhaus Barmherzige Brüder
Weintraubengasse
Zirkusgasse
Czerningasse
Franzensbr.strasse
Franz-Josefs-Kai
Donaukanal
Obere Donaustrasse
Hollandstr.
Rudolfsplatz
Salztorbrücke
Taborstrasse
Grosse Mohrengasse
Praterstrasse
Ferdinandstrasse
Untere Donaustrasse
Salzgries
Marc-Aurel-Str.
Marienbrücke
Schwedenbrücke
Aspernbrücke
(Danube Canal)
Dampfschiffstrasse
Obere Weissgerberstrasse
Sterng.
Kai Urania
Julius-Raab Platz
Hoher Markt
Rotenturmstrasse
Bauernmarkt
Fleischmarkt
Biberstrasse
Sonnenfelsg.
Bäckerstrasse
Stephansdom
Wollzeile
Blutg.
Singerstr.
Schuler-str.
Riemergasse
Stubenbastei
Stubenring
MAK
Vordere Zollamtsstrasse
Obere Viaduktgasse
Adamsgasse
Löwengasse
Untere Weissgerberstrasse
Weissgerberlände
Hetzgasse
Viaduktgasse
Marxergasse
Bahnhof Wien-Mitte
Kärntner Str.
Weihburg-gasse
Himmelpfort-gasse
Seilerstätte
Coburg-bastei
Parkring
Fluss Wien
Am Stadtpark
Invalidenstrasse
Untere
Seidl-gasse
Apkagasse
Rasumofskyg.
Geusaug.
Kundmanngasse
Parkgasse
Kübeck-gasse
Johannesg.
Annag.
Krugerstr.
Walfisch-gasse
Mahlerstr.
Schellinggasse
Hegelgasse
STADTPARK
Landstrasser-Hauptstrasse
Ungargasse
Erdbergstrasse
Schubertring
Johannesgasse
Kantgasse
Am Heumarkt
Kärntner Ring
dorferstr.
Schwarzenbergplatz
Musikverein
Konzerthaus
Akademie-theater
Veterinarmed. Universität
Reisnerstrasse
Rechte Bahngasse
Linke Bahngasse
Salesianergasse
Rochusg.
Lothringer-strasse
Marokkanergasse
Neulinggasse
ARENBERG-PARK
Dapontegasse
Karlskirche
Strohgasse
Gusshausstrasse
Schwindgasse
Prinz-Eugen-Str.
Rennweg
Wohllebengasse
Unteres (Lower) Belvedere
To Oberes (Upper) Belvedere
Church
Post Office
Information
Railway
U-Bahn

Moments The Vienna Boys' Choir

In 1498, Emperor Maximilian I decreed that 12 boys should be included among the official court musicians. Over the next 500 years, this group evolved into the world-renowned *Wiener Sängerknaben* (Vienna Boys' Choir). They perform in Vienna at various venues, including the Staatsoper, the Volksoper, and Schönbrunn Palace. The choir also performs at Sunday and Christmas Masses with the *Hofmusikkapelle* (Court Musicians) at the Burgkapelle (see above for details). The choir's boarding school is at Augartenpalais, Obere Augartenstrasse. For more information on where they are performing and how to get tickets, go to the choir's website (www.wsk.at).

least 8 weeks in advance. Use a credit card; do not send cash or checks. For reservations, write to Verwaltung der Hofmusikkapelle, Hofburg, A-1010 Vienna. If you failed to reserve in advance, you might be lucky enough to secure tickets from a block sold at the Burgkapelle box office every Friday from 11am to 1pm or 3 to 5pm, plus Sunday from 8:15 to 8:45am. The line starts forming at least half an hour before that. If you're willing to settle for standing room, it's free. The Vienna Boys' Choir boarding school is at Palais Augarten, Obere Augartenstrasse.

Hofburg (entrance on Schweizerhof). ✆ **01/5339927.** Mass: Seats and concerts 5€–29€ ($8–$46); standing-room free. Masses held only Jan–June and mid-Sept to Dec, Sun and holidays 9:15am. Concerts May–June and Sept–Oct Fri 4pm.

Kaiserappartements (Imperial Apartments) ★★ The Kaiserappartements, on the first floor, is where the emperors and their wives and children lived. To reach the Imperial Apartments, enter through the rotunda of Michaelerplatz. The rooms are richly decorated with tapestries, many from Aubusson in France. Unfortunately, you can't visit the quarters once occupied by Empress Maria Theresia—they are now used by the president of Austria. The court tableware and silver are outrageously ornate, reflecting the splendor of a bygone era. The **Imperial Silver and Porcelain Collection,** from the Hapsburg household of the 18th and 19th centuries, provides a window into their court etiquette.

The Imperial Apartments seem to be most closely associated with the long reign of Franz Josef. A famous full-length portrait of his beautiful wife, Elisabeth (Sissi) of Bavaria, hangs in the apartments. You'll see the "iron bed" of Franz Josef, who claimed he slept like his own soldiers. Maybe that explains why his wife spent so much time traveling! **The Sissi Museum** opened in 2004 with six rooms devoted to the life and complex personality of this famous, tragic empress.

Michaelerplatz 1 (inside the Ring, about a 7-min. walk from Stephansplatz; entrance via the Kaisertor in the Inneren Burghof). ✆ **01/5337570.** www.hofburg-wien.at. Admission 9.90€ ($16) adults, 4.90€ ($7.90) students 6–15, free for children 5 and under. Daily 9am–5pm. U-Bahn: U-1 or U-3 to Stephansplatz. Tram: 1, 2, 3, or J to Burgring.

Neue Hofburg The most recent addition to the Hofburg complex is the Neue Hofburg, or New Château. Construction was started in 1881 and continued through 1913. The palace was the residence of Archduke Franz Ferdinand, the nephew and heir apparent of Franz Josef, whose assassination at Sarajevo by Serbian nationalists helped set off the chain of events that led to World War I.

The arms and armor collection, second only to that of the Metropolitan Museum of Art in New York, is in the **Hofjagd and Rüstkammer★★**, on the second floor of the Neue Hofburg. On display are crossbows, swords, pistols, and other armor, mostly the property of Hapsburg emperors and princes. Some of the exhibits, such as scimitars, were captured from the Turks as they fled their unsuccessful siege of Vienna. Of bizarre interest is the armor worn by the young (and small) Hapsburg princes.

Another section, the **Sammlung alter Musikinstrumente ★** (✆ **01/52524,** ext. 471), is devoted to old musical instruments, mainly from the 17th and 18th centuries, but some from the 16th century. Some of these instruments, especially among the pianos and harpsichords, were played by Brahms, Schubert, Mahler, Beethoven, and Austrian emperors who fancied themselves as having an ear for music.

In the **Ephesos-Museum (Museum of Ephesian Sculpture),** with an entrance behind the Prince Eugene monument, you'll see high-quality finds from Ephesus in Turkey and the Greek island of Samothrace. Here the prize exhibit is the Parthian monument, the most important relief frieze from Roman times ever found in Asia Minor. It was erected to celebrate Rome's victory in the Parthian wars (A.D. 161–65).

Visit the restored **Museum für Völkerkunde (Museum of Ethnology)** for no other reason than to see the only original Aztec feather headdress in the world. Also on display are Benin bronzes, Cook's collections of Polynesian art, and Indonesian, African, Eskimo, and pre-Columbian exhibits.

Heldenplatz. ✆ **01/52524484.** Admission for each museum 10€ ($16) adults, 3.50€ ($4.80) for children. Daily 10am–6pm.

Österreichische Nationalbibliothek (Austrian National Library) The royal library of the Hapsburgs dates from the 14th century, and the library building, developed on the premises of the court from 1723 on, is still expanding to the Neue Hofburg. The **Great Hall★★** of the present-day library was ordered by Karl VI and designed by those masters of the baroque, the von Erlachs. Its splendor is captured in the frescoes of Daniel Gran and the equestrian statue of Josef II. The complete collection of Prince Eugene of Savoy is the core of the precious holdings. With its manuscripts, rare autographs, globes, maps, and other historic memorabilia, this is among the finest libraries in the world.

Josefsplatz 1. ✆ **01/53410202.** www.onb.ac.at. Admission 7€ ($11). Tues–Wed and Fri–Sun 10am–6pm; Thurs 10am–4pm.

Schatzkammer (Imperial Treasury) ★★★ Reached by a staircase from the Swiss Court, the Schatzkammer (Imperial Treasury) is the greatest treasury in the world. It's divided into two sections: the Imperial Profane and the Sacerdotal Treasuries. The first displays the crown jewels and an assortment of imperial riches, while the other contains ecclesiastical treasures.

The most outstanding exhibit in the Schatzkammer is the imperial crown, which dates from 962. It's so big that, though padded, it probably slipped down over the ears of many a Hapsburg at his coronation. Studded with emeralds, sapphires, diamonds, and rubies, this 1,000-year-old symbol of sovereignty is a priceless treasure, a fact recognized by Adolf Hitler, who had it taken to Nürnberg in 1938 (the American army returned it to Vienna after World War II). Also on display is the imperial crown worn by the Hapsburg rulers from 1804 to the end of the empire. Be sure to have a look at the coronation robes of the imperial family, some of which date from the 12th century.

You can also view the 9th-century saber of Charlemagne and the 8th-century holy lance. The latter, a sacred emblem of imperial authority, was thought in medieval times to be the weapon that pierced the side of Christ on the cross. Among the great Schatzkammer prizes is the Burgundian Treasure. Seized in the 15th century, it's rich in vestments, oil paintings, and gems. Highlighting this collection of loot are artifacts connected with the Order of the Golden Fleece, the medieval chivalric order.

Hofburg, Schweizerhof. ✆ **01/525240.** www.khm.at. Admission 10€ ($16) adults, 3.50€ ($5.60) children, 6€ ($9.60) seniors and students, free for children under 6. Wed–Mon 10am–6pm.

Spanische Reitschule (Spanish Riding School) ★ The Spanish Riding school is a reminder that horses were an important part of everyday Vienna life for many centuries, particularly during the imperial heyday. The school is housed in a white, crystal-chandeliered ballroom in an 18th-century building. You'll marvel at the skill and beauty of the sleek Lipizzaner stallions as their adept trainers put them through their paces in a show that hasn't changed for 4 centuries. These are the world's most famous classically styled equine performers. Many North Americans have seen them in the States, but to watch the Lipizzaners prance to the music of Johann Strauss or a Chopin polonaise in their home setting is a pleasure you shouldn't miss.

Reservations for performances must be made in advance, as early as possible. Order your tickets for the Sunday and Wednesday shows by writing to Spanische Reitschule, Hofburg, A-1010 Vienna (fax 01/533903240), or through a travel agency in Vienna. Tickets for Saturday shows can be ordered only through a travel agency. Tickets for training sessions with no advance reservations can be purchased at the entrance.

Michaelerplatz 1, Hofburg. ✆ **01/5339032.** www.srs.at. Regular performances 40€–135€ ($64–$216) seats, 25€ ($40) standing-room. Classical art of riding w/music 13€–26€ ($21–$42). Regular shows Mar–June, Sept–Oct, and Dec, most Sun at 11am and some Fri at 6pm. Classical dressage w/music performances Apr–June and Sept, Tues–Sat 10am–noon.

EXPLORING THE MUSEUMSQUARTIER COMPLEX ★★★

The big cultural news of Vienna, perhaps of Europe, is the long-awaited premiere of this giant modern art complex. Art critics claimed that the assemblage of art installed in former Hapsburg stables has tipped the city's cultural center of gravity from Hapsburgian pomp into the new millennium. This massive complex, one of the largest cultural complexes in the world, is like combining the Guggenheim Museum with New York's Museum of Modern Art and tossing in the Brooklyn Academy of Music, a children's museum, an architecture-and-design center, lots of theaters, art galleries, video workshops, and much more. There's even an ecology center, architecture museum, and, yes, a tobacco museum. Take the U-Bahn to the MuseumsQuartier stop.

Kunsthalle Wien ★ Cutting-edge contemporary and classic modern art is showcased here. Exhibits focus on specific subjects and seek to establish a link between modern art and current trends. You'll find works by everyone from Picasso, Joan Miró, and Jackson Pollock to Paul Klee, Wassili Kandinsky, Andy Warhol, and, surprise, Yoko Ono. From expressionism to cubism to abstraction, exhibits reveal the major movements in contemporary art since the mid-20th century. There are five floors that can be explored in 1 to 2 hours, depending on what interests you.

Museumsplatz 1. ✆ **01/5218933.** Admission 12€ ($18) adults; 9.50€ ($15) seniors, students, and children. Daily 10am–7pm (Thurs to 10pm).

Leopold Museum ★★ This extensive collection of Austrian art includes the world's largest treasure trove of the works of Egon Schiele (1890–1918), who was once forgotten in art history but now takes his place alongside van Gogh and Modigliani in the ranks of great doomed artists. Although he died before he was 28, his collection of art at the Leopold includes more than 2,500 drawings and watercolors and 330 oil canvases. Other works by Austrian modernist masterpieces include paintings by Oskar Kokoschka, the great Gustav Klimt, Anton Romako, and Richard Gerstl. Major statements in Arts and Crafts from the late 19th and 20th centuries include works by Josef Hoffmann, Kolo Moser, Adolf Loos, and Franz Hagenauer.

Museumsplatz 1. ✆ **01/525700.** Admission 9€ ($14) adults, 5.50€ ($8.80) students and children over 7. Wed and Fri–Mon 10am–7pm; Thurs 10am–9pm.

MUMOK (Museum of Modern Art Ludwig Foundation) ★ This gallery presents one of the most outstanding collections of contemporary art in central Europe. It comprises mainly of works from American Pop Art mixed with concurrent continental movements such as Hyperrealism of the 1960s and 1970s. The museum features five exhibition levels (3 of them above ground and 2 underground). To make it easier to compare works in a single art movement, such as cubism or surrealism, paintings "in the same family" are grouped together. Expect to encounter pieces by all the fabled names, such as Robert Indiana, Jasper Johns, Roy Lichtenstein, Robert Rauschenberg, George Segal, and, of course, Andy Warhol.

Museumsplatz 1. ✆ **01/52500.** www.mumok.at. Admission 9€ ($14) adults, 6.50€ ($10) children. Fri–Wed 10am–6pm; Thurs 10am–9pm.

2 OTHER TOP ATTRACTIONS

THE INNER CITY

Domkirche St. Stephan ★★★ A basilica built on the site of a Romanesque sanctuary, the St. Stephan's Cathedral was founded in the 12th century in what was, even in the Middle Ages, the town's center.

Stephansdom was virtually destroyed in a 1258 fire that swept through Vienna, and toward the dawn of the 14th century the ruins of the basilica were replaced by a Gothic building. The cathedral suffered terribly in the Turkish siege of 1683, but then experienced peace until the Soviet bombardments of 1945. Destruction continued as the Germans bombarded the city to cover their retreat. Restored and reopened in 1948, the cathedral is today one of the greatest Gothic structures in Europe, rich in woodcarvings, altars, sculptures, and paintings. The steeple, rising some 137m (450 ft.), has come to symbolize the very spirit of Vienna.

The 107m (352-ft.) cathedral is inextricably entwined in Viennese and Austrian history. It was here that mourners attended Mozart's "pauper's funeral" in 1791, and it was on the cathedral door that Napoleon posted his farewell edict in 1805.

The **pulpit** of St. Stephan's was carved from stone by Anton Pilgrim and is his enduring masterpiece, but the chief treasure of the cathedral is the carved wooden **Wiener Neustadt altarpiece ★★** that dates from 1447. Richly painted and gilded, the altar was discovered in the Virgin's Choir. In the Apostles' Choir, look for the curious **Tomb of Emperor Frederick III ★★**. Made of a pinkish Salzburg marble, the carved 17th-century tomb depicts hideous little hobgoblins trying to enter and wake the emperor from his eternal sleep. The entrance to the catacombs or crypt is on the north side next to the Capistran pulpit. Here you'll see the funeral urns that contain the entrails of 56 members of the Hapsburg family. (As we noted earlier, the hearts are inurned in St. George's Chapel of the Augustinerkirche, and the bodies are entombed in the Imperial Crypt of the Kapuziner Church.)

You can climb the 343-step south tower, which dominates the skyline with its needlelike spire, for a view of the Vienna Woods. Called *Alter Steffl* (Old Steve), the tower was built between 1350 and 1433. The *Nordturm* (North Tower), reached by elevator, was never finished to match the South Tower, but was crowned in the Renaissance style in 1579. From here, you can get a view of the city and the Danube.

Stephansplatz 1. ✆ **01/515-523526.** www.stephanskirche.at. Cathedral free admission; tour of catacombs 4.50€ ($7.20) adults, 1.50€ ($1.95) children under 15. Guided tour of cathedral 4.50€ ($7.20) adults, 1.50€ ($2.40) children under 15. South Tower 3.50€ ($5.60) adults, 1€ ($1.60) students and children under 15. Evening tours, including tour of the roof, 10€ ($16) adults, 3.50€ ($5.60) children under 15. Cathedral daily 6am–10pm except times of service. Tour of catacombs Mon–Sat 10am–4:30pm; Sun 1:30–4:30pm. Guided tour of cathedral Mon–Sat 10:30am and 3pm; Sun at 3pm. Special evening tour Sat 7pm (June–Sept). Apr–Sept daily 9am–6pm. South Tower daily 9am–5:30pm. U-Bahn: Stephansplatz. Bus: 1A, 2A, or 3A.

Gemäldegalerie der Akademie der Bildenden Künste ★ When in Vienna, always make at least one visit to the Gallery of Painting and Fine Arts to see the ***Last Judgment*** ★★ triptych by the incomparable Hieronymus Bosch. In this masterpiece, the artist conjured up all the demons of hell for a terrifying view of the suffering and sins that humankind must endure. You'll also be able to view many Dutch and Flemish paintings, some from as far back as the 15th century, although the academy is noted for its 17th-century art. The gallery boasts works by Van Dyck, Rembrandt, and a host of other artists. There are several works by Lucas Cranach the Elder, the most outstanding being his *Lucretia,* completed in 1532. Some say it's as enigmatic as *Mona Lisa.* Rubens is represented here by more than a dozen oil sketches. You can see Rembrandt's *Portrait of a Woman* and scrutinize Guardi's scenes from 18th-century Venice.

Schillerplatz 3. ✆ **01/58816.** www.akademiegalerie.at. Admission 7€ ($11) adults, 4€ ($6.40) students and children. Tues–Sun 10am–6pm. U-Bahn: Karlsplatz.

Haus der Musik ★ Mozart is long gone, but Vienna finally got around to opening a full-scale museum devoted to music. This hands-on museum is high-tech. You can take to the podium and conduct the Vienna Philharmonic. Wandering the halls and niches of this museum, you can encounter nostalgic reminders of the great composers who have lived in Vienna—not only Mozart, but Beethoven, Schubert, Brahms, and others. In the rooms, you can listen to your favorite renditions of their works or explore memorabilia of the composers. As a sad note, a memorial, Exodus, pays tribute to the Viennese musicians driven into exile or murdered by the Nazis. At the Musicantino Restaurant on the top floor, you can enjoy a panoramic view of the city and some good food. On the ground floor is a coffeehouse.

Seilerstätte 30. ✆ **01/51648.** www.hdm.at. Admission 10€ ($16) adults, 8.50€ ($14) students and seniors, 5.50€ ($8.80) children. Daily 10am–10pm.

Hundertwasserhaus In a city filled with baroque palaces and numerous architectural adornments, this sprawling public-housing project in the rather bleak 3rd District is visited—or at least seen from the window of a tour bus—by about a million visitors annually. Completed in 1985, it was the work of self-styled "eco-architect" Friedensreich Hundertwasser. The complex, which has a facade like a gigantic black-and-white game board, is relieved with scattered splotches of red, yellow, and blue. Trees stick out at

45-degree angles from apartments designed to accommodate human tenants among the foliage.

There are 50 apartments here, and signs warn not to go inside. However, there's a tiny gift shop at the entrance where you can buy Hundertwasser posters and postcards, plus a coffee shop on the first floor. With its irregular shape, turrets, and "rolling meadows" of grass and trees, the Hundertwasserhaus is certainly the most controversial building in Vienna.

Löwengasse and Kegelgasse 3. ✆ **01/7151553.** www.hundertwasserhaus.at. U-Bahn: Landstrasse. Tram: N.

Kaiserliches Hofmobiliendepot ★ An inventory spanning 3 centuries of royal collecting, the Imperial Furniture Collection is a treasure house of the Hapsburg attics. Exhibits range from the throne of the Emperor Franz Josef to Prince Rudolf's cradle. This horde of property was inherited by the new republic at the end of World War I and the collapse of the Austro–Hungarian Empire. The empress Maria Theresia had established the collection in 1747, and it eventually totaled some 55,000 objects, an antiques-collector's dream. This Hapsburg hoard has been called "one of the world's most curious collections of household artifacts."

The furnishings and trappings are on show in a century-old warehouse complex halfway between the Hofburg Palace and the Schönbrunn Palace. Allow about 2½ hours to view this collection, which sprawls across three floors. Expect cheek-by-jowl bric-a-brac and a total of some 15,000 chairs alone used by the court.

Although much here is only of passing interest, such as fire screens and picture frames, there are prized examples of decorative and applied arts. You're brought into intimate contact with the humanity of the Hapsburgs by such items as chamber pots, spittoons, and porcelain toothbrush holders. Particularly stunning is Maria Theresia's imposing desk of palisander marquetry with a delicate bone inlay. You can even see the coffin that carried Emperor Maximilian's corpse, which was returned to Vienna from Mexico following his execution in 1867 by Benito Juárez's forces.

The collection is particularly rich in Biedermeier furnishings, which characterized the era from 1815 to 1848. The modern world also intrudes, with pieces designed by such 20th-century Viennese architects as Adolf Loos and Otto Wagner. On display is the apartment of the famous ceramist Lucie Rie, the contents of which she took with her to London in 1938 when she fled from the Nazis. The furnishings were returned to Vienna following her death in 1995.

Andreasgasse 7. ✆ **01/52433570.** Admission 6.90€ ($11) adults, 4.50€ ($6.40) students, 3.50€ ($5.60) children under 18. Tues–Sun 10am–6pm. U-Bahn: Zieglergasse.

Kunsthistorisches Museum (Museum of Fine Arts) ★★★ Across from the Hofburg Palace, this huge building houses many of the fabulous art collections gathered by the Hapsburgs as they added new territories to their empire. One highlight is the fine collection of ancient Egyptian and Greek art. The museum also has works by many of the great European masters, such as Velásquez and Titian.

On display here are Roger van der Weyden's *Crucifixion* triptych, a Memling altarpiece, and Jan van Eyck's portrait of Cardinal Albergati. But it's the work of Pieter Bruegel the Elder for which the museum is renowned. This 16th-century Flemish master is known for his sensitive yet vigorous landscapes. He did many lively studies of peasant life, and his pictures today seem almost an ethnographic study of his time. Don't leave without a glimpse of Bruegel's *Children's Games* and his *Hunters in the Snow,* one of his most celebrated pieces.

Don't miss the work of Van Dyck, especially his *Venus in the Forge of Vulcan,* or Peter Paul Rubens's *Self-Portrait* and *Woman with a Cape,* for which he is said to have used the face of his second wife, Helen Fourment. The Rembrandt collection includes two remarkable self-portraits as well as a moving portrait of his mother and one of his sons, Titus.

A highlight of any trip to Vienna is the museum's **Albrecht Dürer collection ★★**. The Renaissance German painter and engraver (1471–1528) is known for his innovative art and painstakingly detailed workmanship. *Blue Madonna* is here, as are some of his realistic landscapes, such as the *Martyrdom of 10,000 Christians.*

The glory of the French, Spanish, and Italian schools is also visible, having often come into Hapsburg hands as "gifts." Titian is represented by *A Girl with a Cloak,* Veronese by an *Adoration of the Magi,* Caravaggio by his *Virgin of the Rosary,* Raphael by *The Madonna in the Meadow,* and Tintoretto by his painting of Susanna caught off guard in her bath. One of our all-time favorite painters is Giorgione, and here visitors can gaze at his *Trio of Philosophers.*

Maria-Theresien-Platz, Burgring 5. ✆ **01/525240.** www.khn.at. Admission 10€ ($16) adults, 7.50€ ($12) students and seniors, free for children under 6. Fri–Wed 10am–6pm; Thurs until 10am–9pm. U-Bahn: Mariahilferstrasse. Tram: 1, 2, D, or J.

Liechtenstein Museum ★★★ The rare collection of art treasures from the Liechtenstein's princely collections went on display in 2004 in the royal family palace in the Rossau district. For the first time, visitors can see this fabled collection of Raphaels, Rubens, and Rembrandts, one of the world's greatest private art collections.

The palace itself is a work of art, dating from the late 17th and early 18th centuries. In 1938, as Nazi Germany was tightening its grip on Austria, the nobles of the principality, lying between Austria and Switzerland, retreated to their small capital at Vaduz.

From Valduz, in 2003, a decision was made to open the palace and its treasures to the public. This meant restoring frescoes, relandscaping the gardens, and rejuvenating the palace. Art, such as works by Frans Hals and Van Dyck, are displayed in the neoclassical Garden Palace, which became Vienna's first museum when it opened its doors in 1807. There are some 1,700 works of art in the collection, although not all of them can be displayed at once, of course.

There are usually some 200 works of art spread over eight galleries. Works range from the 13th to the 19th centuries, and include *Venus in Front of the Mirror* (ca. 1613) by Peter Paul Rubens, who is clearly the star of the museum. The galleries also present sculptures, antiques, and rare porcelain.

Of spectacular beauty is the splendid **Hercules Hall ★**, the largest secular baroque room in Vienna. Frescoes were painted between 1704 and 1708 by Andrea Pozzo. The palace also has two new restaurants: Ruben's Brasserie, serving both traditional Viennese cuisine and fare from Liechtenstein (some based on princely recipes); and Ruben's Palais, offering haute cuisine. Both restaurants have gardens in the palace's baroque courtyard.

Lichtenstein Garden Palace, Fürstengasse 1. ✆ **01/3195767252.** www.liechtensteinmuseum.at. Admission 10€ ($16) adults, 8€ ($13) seniors, 5€ ($8) students, 2€ ($3.20) children under 14; family ticket 20€ ($32). Fri–Tues 10am–5pm. U-Bahn: Rossauer Lände. Tram: D to Porzellangasse.

RINGSTRASSE ★★★

In 1857, Emperor Franz Josef ordered that all the foundations of the medieval fortifications around the Alstadt (Old Town) be removed and that a grand circular boulevard or belt of boulevards replace them.

This transformation, which virtually turned Vienna into a building site that rivaled Paris under Baron Haussmann, created the Vienna we know today. Work on this ambitious project began in 1859 and stretched to 1888 when the grand boulevard reached a distance of 4km ($2^1/_2$ miles).

You can take trams nos. 1 or 2 to circle the Ring.

This streetcar ride makes for the grandest trip in Vienna. One dozen monumental public buildings were constructed along the Ring, which changes its name as it goes along, each stretch of the boulevard ending in the word "Ring."

Extending south from the Danube Canal, the first lap of the Ring is **Schottenring** taking in the Italianate Börse or Stock Exchange and the **Votivkirche (Votive Church)** (p. 156). Running from the university, with its bookstores, bars, and cafes to Rathausplatz, the next lap of the Ring is **Karl-Lueger Ring.** The chief attraction along this stretch is the Universität Wien, dating from 1365. In the 1800s the massive new building you see today was constructed in an Italian Renaissance style.

At the end of this Ring you enter the beginning of **Darl Karl-Renner Ring** at the Rathausplatz. Here stands the Rathaus or town hall, evoking a Gothic fantasy castle, the dream work of Friedrich Schmidt. Constructed between 1872 and 1883, the town hall is the scene of summer concerts.

Across from this imposing building is the Burgtheater or the Imperial Court Theater, constructed between 1874 and 1888 in the Italian Renaissance style. Some of the world's most famous operas, including Mozart's *The Marriage of Figaro*, were premiered here. Frescoes by Gustav Klimt, and his brother, Ernest, draw visitors inside.

Next to the town hall stands Parliament with its elegant Grecian facade decked out with winged chariots.

Moving on, we next enter the **Burgring,** opposite the Hofburg Palace on either side of Maria-Theresien-Platz. Two of the city's largest and finest museums lie along this boulevard: the Kunsthistorisches Museum (Museum of Fine Arts, p. 147) and Naturhistorisches Museum (Natural History Museum).

The highlight of the next Ring, **Opernring,** begins at the Burggarten or Palace Gardens, a tranquil retreat in the heart of the city where you'll find monuments to everybody from Mozart to Emperor Franz Josef. This ring runs to Schwarzenbergstrasse with its equestrian statue, Schwarzenberg Denkmal. The architectural highlight of this Ring is the Staatsoper (State Opera; p. 150).

Finally, the **Schubertring/Stubenring** stretch of the Ring goes from Schwarzenbergstrasse to the Danube Canal. This Ring borders the Stadtpark, which was established in 1862, the first city municipal park to be laid out outside the former fortifications. The chief architectural highlight along this boulevard is the Postsparkasse or Post Office Savings Bank, near the end of the Stubenring at George-Coch-Platz 2. This Art Nouveau building was designed at the beginning of the 20th century by Otto Wagner, and it remains a bulwark of Modernist architecture.

Secession ★ Come here if for no other reason than to see Gustav Klimt's *Beethoven Frieze,* a 30m (100-ft.) visual interpretation of Beethoven's *Ninth Symphony.* Built in 1898, this dome-crowned building—itself a virtual-art manifesto—stands south of the Opernring, beside the Academy of Fine Arts. Once called "outrageous in its useless luxury," the empty dome, covered in triumphal laurel leaves, echoes that of the Karlskirche on the other side of Vienna.

The Secession building was the home of the Viennese avant-garde, which extolled the glories of Jugendstil or Art Nouveau. A young group of painters and architects launched the Secessionist movement in 1897 in rebellion against the strict confines of the Academy of Fine Arts. Klimt was a leader of the movement and defied the historicism favored by the Emperor Franz Josef. The works of Kokoschka and of the "barbarian" Gauguin were featured here. Instead of being a memorial to the great Secessionist artists of yesterday, the pavilion today displays substantial contemporary exhibits. The Belvedere Palace is still the best repository for Secessionist art.

Friedrichstrasse 12 (on the western side of Karlsplatz). ✆ **01/58753070.** www.secession.at. Admission 6€ ($9.60) adults, 3.50€ ($5.60) children 6–18. Tues–Sun 10am–6pm; Thurs 10am–8pm. U-Bahn: Karlsplatz.

Wiener Staatsoper (Vienna State Opera) ★ This is one of the most important opera houses in the world. When it was originally built in the 1860s, critics apparently upset one of the architects so much that he killed himself. In 1945, at the end of World War II, despite other pressing needs, such as public housing, Vienna started restoration work on the theater, finishing it in time to celebrate the country's independence from occupation forces in 1955. It's so important to the Austrians that they don't seem to begrudge the thousands of euros a day its operation costs taxpayers. (For information on performances held at the Staatsoper, see section 11, "Vienna after Dark.")

Opernring 2. ✆ **01/514442250.** www.staatsoper.at. Tours daily year-round, 2–5 times a day, depending on demand. Tour times are posted on a board outside the entrance. Tours 6.50€ ($10) per person. U-Bahn: Karlsplatz.

OUTSIDE THE INNER CITY

Österreichische Galerie Belvedere (Belvedere Palace) ★★ Southeast of Karlsplatz, the Belvedere sits on a slope above Vienna. You approach the palace through a long garden with a huge circular pond that reflects the sky and the looming palace buildings. Designed by Johann Lukas von Hildebrandt, who was the last major Austrian baroque architect, the Belvedere was built as a summer home for Prince Eugene of Savoy. It consists of two palatial buildings, made with a series of interlocking cubes. The interior is dominated by two great flowing staircases.

Unteres Belvedere (Lower Belvedere), with its entrance at Rennweg 6A, was completed in 1716. **Oberes Belvedere (Upper Belvedere)** was completed in 1723.

The Gold Salon in Lower Belvedere is one of the most beautiful rooms in the palace. Composer Anton Bruckner lived in one of the buildings until his death in 1896, and the palace was also the residence of Archduke Franz Ferdinand, the slain heir and a World War I spark. In May 1955, the peace treaty recognizing Austria as a sovereign state was signed in Upper Belvedere by foreign ministers of the four powers that occupied Austria at the close of World War II—France, Great Britain, the United States, and the Soviet Union.

Today visitors come to the splendid baroque palace to enjoy the panoramic view of the Wienerwald (Vienna Woods) from the terrace. A regal French-style garden lies between Upper and Lower Belvedere, both of which feature impressive art collections that are open to the public.

Lower Belvedere has a wealth of sculptural decorations and houses the **Barockmuseum (Museum of Baroque Art).** The original sculptures from the Neuermarkt fountain, the work of Georg Raphael Donner, are displayed here. During his life, Donner dominated the development of 18th-century Austrian sculpture, heavily influenced by Italian art. The four figures on the fountain represent the four major tributaries of the Danube. Works by Franz Anton Maulbertsch, an 18th-century painter, are also exhibited. Maulbertsch, strongly influenced by Tiepolo, was the most original and

Art-School Reject

One Austrian painter whose canvases will never grace any museum wall is Adolph Hitler. Aspiring to be an artist, Hitler had his traditional paintings, including one of the Auersberg Palace, rejected by the Academy of Fine Arts in Vienna. The building was accurate, but the figures were way out of proportion. Hitler did not take this failure well, denouncing the board as a "lot of old-fashioned fossilized civil servants, bureaucrats, devoid lumps of officials. The whole academy ought to be blown up!"

accomplished Austrian painter of his day. He was best known for his iridescent colors and flowing brushwork.

Museum Mittelalterlicher Kunst (Museum of Medieval Austrian Art) is located in the Orangery at Lower Belvedere. Here you'll see works from the Gothic period, as well as a Tyrolean Romanesque crucifix that dates from the 12th century. Outstanding works include seven panels by Rueland Frueauf portraying scenes from the life of the Madonna and the Passion of Christ.

Upper Belvedere houses the **Galerie des 19. and 20. Jahrhunderts (Gallery of 19th- and 20th-Century Art)** ★. In a large salon decorated in red marble, you can view the 1955 peace treaty mentioned above. A selection of Austrian and international paintings of the 19th and 20th centuries is on display, including works by Oskar Kokoschka, Vincent van Gogh, James Ensor, and C. D. Freidrich.

Most outstanding are the works of Gustav Klimt (1862–1918), one of the founders of the 1897 Secession movement. Klimt used a geometrical approach to painting, blending figures with their backgrounds in the same overall tones. Witness the extraordinary *Judith.* Other notable Klimt works on display are *The Kiss, Adam and Eve,* and five panoramic lakeside landscapes from Attersee. Sharing almost equal billing with Klimt is Egon Schiele (1890–1918), whose masterpieces include *The Wife of an Artist.* Schiele could be morbid, as exemplified by *Death and Girl,* as well as cruelly observant, as in *The Artist's Family.*

Prinz-Eugen-Strasse 27. ✆ **01/79557.** www.belvedere.at. Admission 9€ ($14) adults, free for children 11 and under. Tues–Sun 10am–6pm. Tram: D to Schloss Belvedere.

Schönbrunn Palace ★★★ A Hapsburg palace of 1,441 rooms, Schönbrunn was designed by those masters of the baroque, the von Erlachs. It was built between 1696 and 1712 at the request of Emperor Leopold I for his son, Josef I. Leopold envisioned a palace whose grandeur would surpass that of Versailles. However, Austria's treasury, drained by the cost of wars, could not support such an ambitious undertaking, and the original plans were never completed.

When Maria Theresia became empress, she had the plans altered, and Schönbrunn looks today much as she conceived it, with delicate rococo touches designed for her by Austrian Nikolaus Pacassi. Schönbrunn was the imperial summer palace during Maria Theresia's 40-year reign (1740–80), and it was the scene of great ceremonial balls, lavish banquets, and fabulous receptions held during the Congress of Vienna (1814–15). At the age of 6, Mozart performed in the Hall of Mirrors before Maria Theresia and her court, and the empress held secret meetings with her chancellor, Prince Kaunitz, in the round Chinese Room.

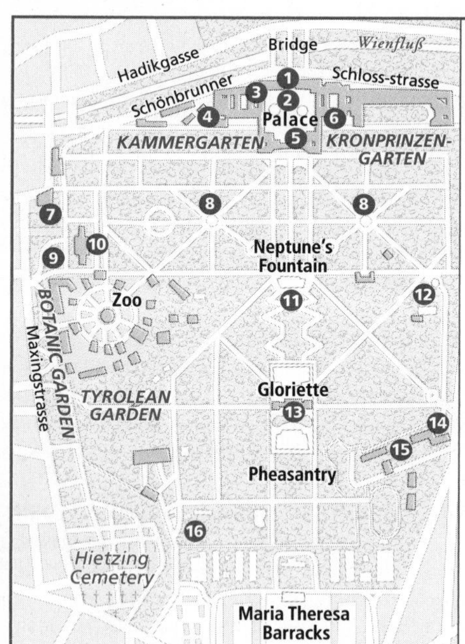

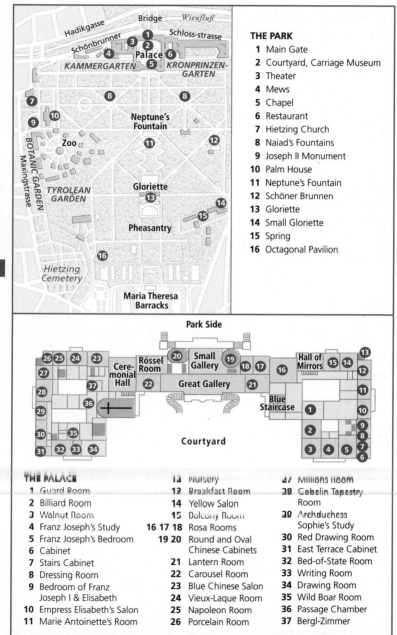

THE PARK

1 Main Gate
2 Courtyard, Carriage Museum
3 Theater
4 Mews
5 Chapel
6 Restaurant
7 Hietzing Church
8 Naiad's Fountains
9 Joseph II Monument
10 Palm House
11 Neptune's Fountain
12 Schöner Brunnen
13 Gloriette
14 Small Gloriette
15 Spring
16 Octagonal Pavilion

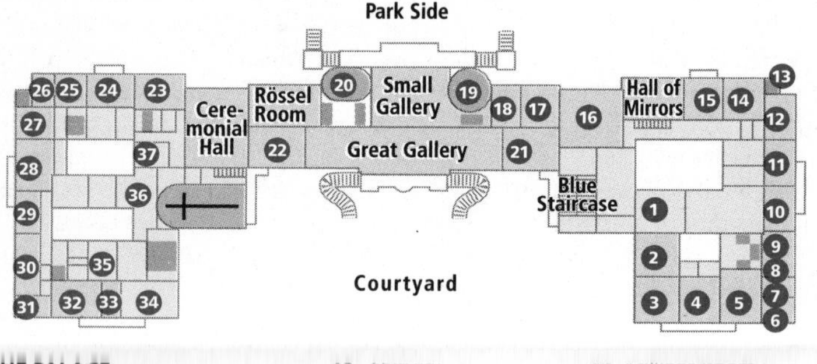

THE PALACE

1 Guard Room
2 Billiard Room
3 Walnut Room
4 Franz Joseph's Study
5 Franz Joseph's Bedroom
6 Cabinet
7 Stairs Cabinet
8 Dressing Room
9 Bedroom of Franz Joseph I & Elisabeth
10 Empress Elisabeth's Salon
11 Marie Antoinette's Room
12 Nursery
13 Breakfast Room
14 Yellow Salon
15 Balcony Room
16 17 18 Rosa Rooms
19 20 Round and Oval Chinese Cabinets
21 Lantern Room
22 Carousel Room
23 Blue Chinese Salon
24 Vieux-Laque Room
25 Napoleon Room
26 Porcelain Room
27 Millions Room
28 Gobelin Tapestry Room
29 Archduchess Sophie's Study
30 Red Drawing Room
31 East Terrace Cabinet
32 Bed-of-State Room
33 Writing Room
34 Drawing Room
35 Wild Boar Room
36 Passage Chamber
37 Bergl-Zimmer

Franz Josef was born within the palace walls, which became the setting for the lavish court life associated with his reign. He also spent the final years of his life here. The last of the Hapsburg rulers, Charles I, abdicated here on November 11, 1918.

Schönbrunn Palace was damaged in World War II by Allied bombs, but restoration has removed the scars. In complete contrast to the grim, forbidding Hofburg, Schönbrunn Palace, done in "Maria Theresia ocher," has the **Imperial Gardens ★**, embellished by the **Gloriette ★★**, a marble summerhouse topped by a stone canopy that showcases the imperial eagle. The so-called Roman Ruins are a collection of marble statues and fountains from the late 18th century, when it was fashionable to simulate the grandeur of Rome. The park, which can be visited until sunset daily, contains many fountains and statues, often depicting Greek mythological characters.

The **State Apartments ★★★** are the most stunning display in the palace. Much of the interior is decorated in the rococo style, done in red, white, and, more often than not, 23½-karat gold. Of the 40 rooms you can visit, the "Room of Millions," the grandest rococo salon in the world, decorated with Indian and Persian miniatures, is one of the more fascinating. Guided tours of the palace rooms last 50 minutes and are narrated in English every half-hour beginning at 9:30am. You should tip the guide (about 2€/$2.60).

Also on the grounds at Schönbrunn is the **Schlosstheater** (✆ **01/8764272**), which still has summer performances. Marie Antoinette appeared on its stage in pastorals during her happy youth, and Max Reinhardt, the theatrical impresario, launched an acting school here. The **Wagenburg (Carriage Museum) ★** (✆ **01/8773244**) is also worth a visit. It contains a fine display of imperial coaches from the 17th to 20th centuries. The coronation coach of Charles VI (1711–40), which was pulled by eight white stallions, is here. It was also used for several subsequent Hapsburg coronations. This intriguing museum is open from April to October daily from 9am to 6pm, and from November to March Tuesday through Sunday from 10am to 4pm. Admission is 4.15€ ($6.70) for adults and 3€ ($4.80) for seniors and children 10 and under.

Called the **Schloss Schönbrunn Experience,** 60- to 90-minute children's tours are conducted. Kids are dressed in imperial clothing and led by English-speaking guides through rooms that offer hands-on displays.

Schönbrunner Schlossstrasse. ✆ **01/811-132-39.** www.schoenbrunn.at. Admission 13€ ($21) adults, 7.90€ ($13) children 6–15, free for children under 6; Wagenburg 5€ ($8) adults, 3.50€ ($5.60) seniors and children 10 and under; Schloss Schönbrunn Experience 4.50€ ($7.20) children. Apr–June and Sept–Oct daily 8:30am–5pm; July–Aug daily 8:30am–6pm; Nov–Mar daily 8:30am–4:30pm. U-Bahn: Schönbrunn.

3 CHURCHES

For the Hofburg Palace Chapel, where the Vienna Boys' Choir performs, and the Augustinerkirche, see section 1, earlier in this chapter; for St. Stephan's Cathedral, see section 2.

THE INNER CITY

Die Deutschordenskirche The Church of the Teutonic Order and its treasury, Schatzkammer des Deutschen Ordens, will stir thoughts of the Crusades in the minds of history buffs, but the relics of vanished glory will make some visitors wish they had been among the medieval nobility. The Order of the Teutonic Knights was founded in 1190 in the Holy Land. The order came to Vienna in 1205, but the church they built dates from 1395. The building never fell prey to the baroque madness that swept the city after the Counter-Reformation. Subsequently, you see it pretty much in its original form, a Gothic church dedicated to St. Elizabeth. A choice feature is the 16th-century Flemish altarpiece on the main altar, which is richly decorated with woodcarving, gilt, and painted panel inserts. Many knights of the Teutonic Order are buried here, their heraldic shields still mounted on some of the upper walls.

In the knights' treasury, on the second floor of the church, you'll see mementos such as seals and coins illustrating the history of the order, as well as a collection of arms, vases, gold, crystal, and precious stones. Also on display are the charter given to the Teutonic Order by Henry IV of England and a collection of medieval paintings. A curious exhibit is a Viper Tongue Credenza, said to have the power to detect poison in food and render it harmless.

Singerstrasse 7. ✆ **01/5121065.** www.deutsches-order.at. Free admission to church; treasury 4€ ($6.40) adults, free children under 11. Church daily 7am–7pm; treasury Mon and Wed 3–5pm, Thurs 10am–noon, Fri 3–5pm, Sat 10am–noon and 3–5pm. U-Bahn: Stephansplatz.

Kapuzinerkirche and Kaisergruft The Kapuziner Church (just inside the Ring and behind the Staatsoper) houses the Imperial Crypt, the burial vault of the Hapsburgs for some 3 centuries. Capuchin friars guard the family's final resting place, where 12 emperors, 17 empresses, and dozens of archdukes are entombed. (Only their bodies are here. Their hearts are in urns in the Loreto Chapel of the Augustinerkirche in the Hofburg complex, while their entrails are similarly enshrined in a crypt below St. Stephan's Cathedral.)

The most outstanding imperial tomb is the double sarcophagus of Maria Theresia and her consort, Emperor Francis I (François of Lorraine), the parents of Marie Antoinette. Before her own death, the empress used to descend into the tomb often to visit the gravesite of her beloved Francis. The "King of Rome," the ill-fated son of Napoleon and Marie-Louise of Austria, was also buried here in a bronze coffin after his death at 21. (Hitler managed to anger both the Austrians and the French by having the remains of Napoleon's son transferred to Paris in 1940.) Although she was not a Hapsburg, Countess Fuchs, the governess who practically reared Maria Theresia, lies in the crypt.

Emperor Franz Josef was interred here in 1916, a frail old man who outlived his time and died just before the final collapse of his beloved empire. His wife, Empress Elisabeth, was buried in the crypt following her assassination in Geneva in 1898, as was their son, Archduke Rudolf, who allegedly committed suicide at Mayerling.

Neuer Markt. ✆ **01/5126853.** Admission 4€ ($6.40) adults, 3€ ($4.80) children. Daily 9:30am–4pm. U-Bahn: Stephansplatz.

Michaelerkirche The Church of St. Michael can trace some of its Romanesque portions to the early 1200s. The exact date of the chancel is not known, but it's probably from the mid-14th century. Over its long history, the church has felt the hand of many architects and designers, resulting in a medley of styles, not all harmonious. Perhaps only the catacombs could still be recognized as medieval.

Most of St. Michael's as it appears today dates from 1792, when the facade was redone in the neoclassical style; however, the spire is 16th century. The main altar is richly decorated in baroque style; the altarpiece, entitled *The Collapse of the Angels* (1781), is the last major baroque work completed in Vienna.

Michaelerplatz. ✆ **01/5338000.** Free admission. Mon–Sat 6:45am–8pm; Sun 8am–6:30pm. U-Bahn: Herrengasse. Bus: 1A, 2A, or 3A.

Minoritenkirche If you're tired of baroque ornamentation, visit this church of the Friar Minor Conventual, a Franciscan order also called the Minorite friars (inferior brothers). Construction began in 1250 but was not completed until the early 14th century. Its tower was damaged by the Turks in their two sieges of Vienna, and it later fell prey to baroque architects and designers in the 18th century. But in 1784, Ferdinand von Hohenberg ordered that the baroque additions be removed and the simple lines of the original Gothic church be restored, complete with Gothic cloisters. Inside you'll see a mosaic copy of da Vinci's *Last Supper.* Masses are held on Sunday at 8:30 and 11am.

Minoritenplatz 2A. ✆ **01/5334162.** Free admission. Apr–Oct Mon–Sat 8am–6pm; Nov–Mar Mon–Sat 9am–5pm. U-Bahn: Herrengasse.

St. Maria Am Gestade This church, the Church of Our Lady of the Riverbank, was once just that. With an arm of the Danube flowing by, it was a favorite place of worship for fishermen. The river was redirected, but the church still draws people with its own beauty. The original Romanesque church was rebuilt in the Gothic style between 1394 and 1427. The western facade is flamboyant, with a remarkable seven-sided Gothic tower; it's surmounted by a dome that culminates in a lacy crown.

At Passauer Platz. ✆ **01/53395940.** Free admission. Daily 7am–7pm. U-Bahn: Stephansplatz.

Universitätskirche Built during the Counter-Reformation, this church is rich in baroque embellishments. This was the university church, dedicated to the Jesuit saints Ignatius of Loyola and Francis Xavier. The high-baroque decorations—galleries, columns, and the *trompe l'oeil* painting on the ceiling, which gives the illusion of a dome—were added from 1703 to 1705. The embellishments were the work of a Jesuit lay brother, Andrea Pozzo, at the orders of Emperor Leopold I. Look for Pozzo's painting of Mary behind the main altar. Choral and orchestral services (mostly classical) are celebrated on Sunday and Holy Days at 10am.

Dr.-Ignaz-Seipel-Platz 1. ✆ **01/51213350.** Free admission to church. Daily 8am–7pm. U-Bahn: Stephansplatz or Stubentor. Tram: 1 or 2. Bus: 1A.

OUTSIDE THE INNER CITY

Karlskirche Construction on Karlskirche, dedicated to St. Charles Borromeo, was begun in 1716 by order of Emperor Charles VI. The Black Plague had swept Vienna in 1713, and the emperor made a vow to build the church if the disease would abate. The baroque master Johann Bernard Fischer von Erlach did the original work on the church from 1716 to 1722, and his son, Joseph Emanuel, completed it between 1723 and 1737. The lavishly decorated interior stands as a testament to the father-and-son duo who led the baroque movement.

The well-known ecclesiastical artist J. M. Rottmayr painted many of the frescoes inside the church from 1725 to 1730. The green copper dome of Karlskirche is 72m (236 ft.) high, a dramatic landmark on the Viennese skyline. Two columns, spin-offs from Trajan's Column in Rome, flank the front of the church, which opens onto Karlsplatz. There's also a sculpture by Henry Moore in a little pool.

Karlsplatz. ✆ **01/5046187.** www.karlskirche.at. Admission 4.50€ ($7.20) adults, free for children under 12. Mon–Fri 9am–12:30pm; Sat–Sun 1–6pm. U-Bahn: Karlsplatz.

Peterskirche St. Peter's Church is the second-oldest church in Vienna, but the spot on which it stands might well be the oldest Christian church site in the city. Many places of worship have stood here; the first is believed to date from the second half of the 4th century. Charlemagne is credited with commissioning a church on the site during the late 8th or early 9th century.

The present St. Peter's, the most lavishly decorated baroque church in Vienna, was designed in 1702 by Gabriel Montani. Von Hildebrandt, the noted architect who designed the Belvedere Palace, is believed to have finished the building in 1732. The fresco in the dome, depicting the Coronation of the Virgin, is a masterpiece by J. M. Rottmayr. The church contains many other frescoes and much gilded carved wood, plus altarpieces by many well-known artists of the period.

Petersplatz. ✆ **01/5336433.** Free admission. Daily 9am–6:30pm. U-Bahn: Stephansplatz.

Piaristenkirche Work on the Church of the Piarist Order, more popularly known as Piaristenplatz, was launched in 1716 by a Roman Catholic teaching congregation known as the Piarists (fathers of religious schools). The church, however, was not consecrated until 1771. It is believed that some of the designs submitted during that long period were drawn by von Hildebrandt, the noted architect who designed the Belvedere Palace, but many builders had a hand in its construction. This church is noteworthy for its fine classic facade as well as the frescoes by F. A. Maulbertsch, which adorn the insides of the circular cupolas.

Piaristengasse 54. ✆ **01/405-0425.** Free admission. Mon–Fri 3–6pm; Sat 10am–noon. U-Bahn: Rathaus.

Ruprechtskirche The oldest church in Vienna, St. Rupert's Church has stood here since A.D. 740, although much that you see now, such as the aisle, is from the 11th century. Beautiful new stained-glass windows—the work of Lydia Roppolt—were installed in 1993. It's believed that much of the masonry from a Roman shrine on this spot was used in the present church. The tower and nave are Romanesque; the rest of the church is Gothic. St. Rupert is the patron saint of the Danube's salt merchants.

Ruprechtsplatz, Seitenstettengasse 4–5. ✆ **01/5536003.** Free admission. Easter–Oct Mon–Fri 10am–noon. U-Bahn: Schwedenplatz.

Votivkirche After a failed assassination attempt on Emperor Franz Josef, a collection was taken for the construction of the Votive Church, which sits across from the site where the attempt was made. Heinrich von Ferstel began work on the neo-Gothic church in 1856, but it was not consecrated until 1879. The magnificent facade features awesome lacy spires and intricate sculpture. Most noteworthy is the Renaissance sarcophagus of Niklas Salm, commander of the Austrian forces during the Turkish siege in 1529.

Rooseveltplatz 8. ✆ **01/4061192.** Admission 2.90€ ($4.70). Tues–Sat 9am–1pm and 4–6pm; Sun 9am–1:30pm. U-Bahn: Schottentor.

4 MORE MUSEUMS & GALLERIES

THE INNER CITY

Judisches Museum Wien This is the main museum tracing the history of Viennese Jewry. It's not to be confused with its annex at Judenplatz (see below). This museum opened in 1993 in the former Eskeles Palace, once one of the most patrician of town houses in Vienna and a private residence. Both temporary and permanent exhibitions are on view here, the permanent exhibitions tracing the major role that Viennese Jews played in the history of Vienna until their expulsion or deaths in the Holocaust beginning in

In Memory of Vienna's Jewish Ghetto

Judenplatz (U-Bahn: Stephansplatz), lying off Wipplingerstrasse, was the heart of the Jewish Ghetto from the 13th to the 15th centuries. That memory of long ago has been brought back by the opening of a Holocaust memorial on this square.

This memorial, combined with excavations and a new museum devoted to medieval Jewish life, have re-created a center of Jewish culture on the Judenplatz. It's a place of remembrance unique in Europe.

The architect of the Holocaust memorial, Rachel Whitehead, designed it like a stylized stack of books signifying Jewish strivings toward education. The outer sides of this reinforced concrete cube are in the form of library shelves. Around the base of the monument are engraved the names of the places in which Austrian Jews were put to death during the Nazi era. Nearby is a statue of Gotthold Ephraim Lessing (1729–81), the Jewish playwright.

Museum Judenplatz, Judenplatz 8 (✆ **01/5350431**), is a new annex of the Judisches Museum Wien, Vienna's Jewish Museum. Exhibits tell the major role that Viennese Jews played in all aspects of city life, from music to medicine, until a reign of terror began against them in 1938. The main section of the museum is devoted to the exhibition on medieval Jewry in Vienna. The exhibition features a multimedia presentation of the religious, cultural, and social life of the Viennese Jews in the Middle Ages, until their expulsion and death in 1420 and 1421 during the First Viennese Gesera. The three exhibition rooms are in the basement of the Misrachi house. An underground passage connects them to the exhibitions of the medieval synagogue. The museum is open Sunday through Thursday from 10am to 6pm and Friday from 10am to 2pm; admission is 4€ ($6.40) for adults and 2.50€ ($4) for students and children under 16.

An exhibition room has been installed in the **Mittelalterliche Synagogue (Medieval Synagogue)** nearby. It's visited on the same ticket as the Jewish Museum. The late-medieval synagogue was built around the middle of the 13th century. It was one of the largest synagogues of its time. After the pogrom in 1420 and 1421, the synagogue was systematically destroyed so that only the foundations and the floor remained. These were excavated by the City of Vienna Department of Urban Archaeology from 1995 to 1998. The exhibition room shows the remnants of the central room, or "men's shul" (the room where men studied and prayed), and a smaller room annexed to it, which might have been used by women. In the middle of the central room is the foundation of the hexagonal bema (raised podium from which the Torah was read). Combined ticket (Jewish Museum, Museum Judenplatz, and Synagogue) 4€ ($6.40) adults, 2.50€ ($4) students and children.

1938. Their valuable contributions are noted in such fields as philosophy, music, and medicine. And, of course, we must mention Sigmund Freud, who escaped the Holocaust by fleeing to London. The museum defines itself as an "archive of memory" or a "place for remembering." Many objects on view were rescued from Vienna's private synagogues and prayer-houses, concealed in 1938 from the Nazis. Many other exhibits are from the old Jewish Museum that existed in Vienna until it was closed in 1938.

Dorotheergasse 11. ✆ **01/5350431.** www.jmw.at. Admission 6.50€ ($10) adults, 4€ ($6.40) students and children. Sun–Fri 10am–6pm. U-Bahn: Stephansplatz.

Österreichisches Museum für Angewandte Kunst Of special interest at the Museum of Applied Art is a rich collection of tapestries, some from the 16th century, and the most outstanding assemblage of Viennese porcelain in the world. Look for a Persian carpet depicting *The Hunt,* as well as the group of 13th-century Limoges enamels. Exhibits typically display Biedermeier furniture and other antiques, glassware, and crystal; outstanding objects of the early-20th-century crafts workshop, the Wiener Werkstätte; and large collections of lace and textiles. An entire hall is devoted to Art Nouveau.

Stubenring 5. ✆ **01/711360.** www.mak.at. Admission 9.90€ ($16) adults, 5.50€ ($8.80) children 6–18, free for children under 6. Free admission on Sat. Wed–Sun 10am–6pm; Tues 10am–midnight. U-Bahn: Stubentor. Tram: 1 or 2.

Uhrenmuseum A wide-ranging collection of timepieces—from ancient to modern—are on view at the Municipal Clock Museum. Housed in what was once the Obizzi town house, the museum dates from 1917 and displays clocks of all shapes and sizes. From all over Europe and North America, clock collectors and fans of the offbeat come here to gaze and perhaps to covet. Check out Rutschmann's astronomical clock made in the 18th century. There are several interesting cuckoo clocks and a gigantic timepiece that was once mounted in the tower of St. Stephan's.

Schulhof 2. ✆ **01/5332265.** www.museum.vienna.at. Admission 4€ ($6.40) adults, 2€ ($3.20) children. Tues–Sun 9am–4:30pm. U-Bahn: Stephansplatz.

OUTSIDE THE INNER CITY

Heeresgeschichtliches Museum The Museum of Military History is the oldest state museum in Vienna; the building was constructed from 1850 to 1856, a precursor to the Ringstrasse style. The Moorish-Byzantine and neo-Gothic designs draw attention to the museum, where the military history of the Hapsburgs, including both triumphs and defeats, is delineated.

A special display case in front of the Franz-Josef Hall contains the six orders of the House of Hapsburg that Franz Josef sported on all public occasions. The Sarajevo room is fascinating—it contains mementos of the assassination of Archduke Franz Ferdinand and his wife on June 28, 1914, the event that helped set off World War I. The archduke's bloodstained uniform is displayed, along with the bullet-scarred car in which the royal couple rode. Many exhibits concentrate on the navy of the Austro-Hungarian Empire, and frescoes depict important battles, including those fought against the Turks in and around Vienna.

Arsenal 3. ✆ **01/79561.** Admission 5.10€ ($8.20) adults, 3.30€ ($5.30) children under 14. www.hgm.or.at. Daily 9am–5pm. Closed Jan 1, Easter, May 1, Nov 1, Dec 24–25, and Dec 31. Tram: 18 or D.

Historisches Museum der Stadt Wien History buffs should seek out the fascinating but little-visited collection at the Historical Museum of Vienna. Here the full panorama of Old Vienna's history unfolds, beginning with the settlement of prehistoric tribes in the Danube basin. On display are Roman relics, artifacts from the reign of the dukes of Babenberg, and a wealth of leftovers from the Hapsburg sovereignty, as well as arms and armor from various eras. A scale model shows Vienna as it looked in the Hapsburg heyday. You'll see pottery and ceramics dating from the Roman era, 14th-century stained-glass windows, mementos of the Turkish sieges of the city in 1529 and 1683, and Biedermeier furniture. There's also a section on Vienna's Art Nouveau.

Karlsplatz 4. ✆ **01/5058747.** www.wienmuseum.at. Admission 6€ ($9.60) adults, 3€ ($4.80) children. Tues–Sun 9am–6pm. U-Bahn: Karlsplatz.

Sigmund Freud Museum Wien The museum's dark furniture (only part of it original), lace curtains, and collection of antiquities create an atmosphere into which you can imagine the doctor will walk at any moment and tell you to make yourself comfortable on the couch. His velour hat, dark walking stick with ivory handle, and other mementos are on view in the study and waiting room he used during his residence here from 1891 to 1938. The museum also has a bookshop where souvenirs are available, including a variety of postcards of the apartment, books by Freud, posters, prints, and pens.

Berggasse 19. ✆ **01/3191596.** www.freud-museum.at. Admission 7€ ($11) adults, 5.50€ ($8.80) seniors, 4.50€ ($7.20) students, 2.50€ ($4) for ages 12–18. Free 16 and under. Daily 9am–6pm. Tram: D to Schlickgasse.

5 PARKS & GARDENS

When the weather is fine, the Viennese shun city parks in favor of the **Wienerwald (Vienna Woods),** a wide arc of forested countryside that surrounds the northwestern and southwestern sides of Vienna (for more details, see chapter 7). But if you're an aficionado of parks, you'll find some magnificent ones in Vienna, where there are more than 1,600 hectares (3,954 acres) of gardens and parks and no fewer than 770 sports fields and playgrounds. Of course, you can visit **Schönbrunn Park** and **Belvedere Park** when you tour those once-royal palaces. Below, we highlight only the most popular parks of Vienna.

THE INNER CITY

The former gardens of the Hapsburg emperors, **Burggarten,** Opernring-Burgring, next to the Neue Hofburg (tram: 1, 2, 52, 58, or D), was built soon after the Volksgarten (see below). Look for the monument to Mozart, as well as an equestrian statue of Franz I, beloved husband of Maria Theresia. The only open-air statue of Franz Josef in all Vienna is also here, and there's a statue of Goethe at the park entrance.

The lovely **Stadtpark (City Park)** ★, at Parkring (tram: 1, 2, J, or T), is reached from the Ring or from Lothringer Strasse. It lies on the slope where the Danube used to overflow into the Inner City before the construction of the Danube Canal. You'll find statues of Franz Schubert and Hans Makart, a well-known artist whose work you'll see in churches and museums. But the best known is of Johann Strauss, Jr., composer of operettas and waltzes. These monuments are surrounded by verdant squares of grass, well-manicured flower gardens, and plenty of benches.

Known as the people's park, **Volksgarten** stands next to the Burgtheater (tram: 1, 2, or D). This oasis was laid out on the site of the old city wall fortifications and can be entered from Dr.-Karl-Lueger-Ring. The oldest public garden in Vienna, dating from 1820, it's dotted with monuments, including a 1907 memorial to the assassinated Empress Elisabeth. Construction of the so-called Temple of Theseus, a copy of the Theseion in Athens, was begun in 1820.

The **Praterverband (The Prater)** ★, an extensive tract of woods and meadowland in the 2nd District, has been Vienna's favorite recreation area since 1766, when Emperor Josef II opened it to the public. Previously, it had been a hunting preserve and riding ground for the aristocracy.

The Prater is the birthplace of the waltz, first introduced here in 1820 by Johann Strauss, Sr., and Josef Lanner. However, it was under Johann Strauss, Jr., who became known as "the Waltz King," that this music form reached its peak.

The best-known part of the huge park is at the end nearest the entrance from the Ring. Here you'll find the **Riesenrad** (✆ **01/7295430;** www.wienerriesenrad.com), the giant Ferris wheel, which was constructed in 1897 and reaches 67m (220 ft.) at its highest point. In 1997, the Ferris wheel celebrated its 100th anniversary, and it remains, after St. Stephan's Cathedral, the most famous landmark in Vienna. Erected at a time when European engineers were showing off their "high technology," the wheel was designed by Walter Basset, the British engineer, trying to outdo Eiffel, who had constructed his tower in Paris a decade earlier. The wheel was designed for the Universal Exhibition (1896–97), marking the golden anniversary of Franz Josef's coronation in 1848. Like the Eiffel Tower, it was supposed to be a temporary exhibition. Except for World War II damage, the Ferris wheel has been going around without interruption since 1897. It was immortalized in a famous scene from the 1949 film *The Third Man,* with Joseph Cotten and Orson Welles.

Just beside the Riesenrad is the terminus of the Lilliputian railroad, the 4km (2½-mile) narrow-gauge line that operates in summer using vintage steam locomotives. The amusement park, right behind the Ferris wheel, has all the typical attractions—roller coasters, merry-go-rounds, tunnels of love, and game arcades. Swimming pools, riding schools, and racecourses are interspersed between woodland and meadows. International soccer matches are held in the Prater stadium.

The Volare, The Flying Coaster, flies face down along a 420m (1,378-ft.) labyrinth of track at a height of 23m (76 ft.), and Starflyer where passengers are whirled along a 420m (1,378-ft.) labyrinth at around 60m (197 ft.) above the ground at speeds of up to 70kmph (44 mph).

The Prater is not a fenced-in park, but not all amusements are open throughout the year. The season lasts from March or April to October, but the Ferris wheel operates year-round. Some of the more than 150 booths and restaurants stay open in winter, including the pony merry-go-round and the gambling venues. If you drive here, don't forget to observe the no-entry and no-parking signs, which apply after 3pm daily. The place is usually jammed on Sunday afternoons in summer.

Admission to the park (✆ **01/7280516;** U-Bahn: Praterstern) is free, but you'll pay for games and rides. The Ferris wheel costs 8€ ($13) for adults and 3.20€ ($5.10) for children ages 4 to 14; it's free for children 1 to 3. The park is open May through September daily from 10am to 1am, October to November 3 daily 10am to 10pm, and November 4 to December 1 daily 10am to 8pm.

The lush **Botanischer Garten (Botanical Garden),** Rennweg 14 (✆ **01/427754100;** tram: 71 to Unteres Belvedere), contains exotic plants from all over the world, many of which are rare. Located in Landstrasse (3rd District, right next to the Belvedere Park), the Botanical Garden originated as a place where medicinal herbs were planted on orders from Maria Theresia. The gardens may be visited daily from 9am to dusk, but call ahead if the weather is inclement. Admission is free.

Tales of the Vienna Woods

Yes, dear reader, there really are Vienna Woods (*Wienerwald* in German). They weren't simply dreamed up by Johann Strauss, Jr., as the subject of musical tales in waltz time. The Wienerwald is several thousand acres of gentle paths and trees in a delightful hilly landscape that borders Vienna on its southwestern and northwestern sides. If you stroll through this area, a weekend playground for the Viennese, you'll be following in the footsteps of Strauss and Schubert. Beethoven, when his hearing was failing, claimed that the chirping birds, trees, and leafy vineyards of the Wienerwald made it easier for him to compose. Many attractions of the Wienerwald are described in chapter 7.

A round-trip through the woods takes about 3½ hours by car, a distance of some 80km (50 miles). Even if you don't have a car, the woods can be visited relatively easily. Board tram no. 1 near the Staatsoper, going to Schottentor; here, switch to tram no. 38 (the same ticket is valid) going out to **Grinzing,** home of the famous *heurigen* (wine taverns). Here you can board bus no. 38A to go through the Wienerwald to **Kahlenberg.** The whole trip takes about 1 hour each way. You might rent a bicycle nearby to make your own exploration of the woods.

Kahlenberg is located on a hill that is part of the northeasternmost spur of the Alps (483m/1,585 ft.). If the weather is clear, you can see all the way to Hungary and Slovakia. At the top of the hill is the small Church of St. Joseph, where King John Sobieski of Poland stopped to pray before leading his troops to the defense of Vienna against the Turks. For one of the best views overlooking Vienna, go to the right of the Kahlenberg restaurant. From the terrace here, you'll have a panoramic sweep, including the spires of St. Stephan's. You can also go directly to Kahlenberg from the city center in about 20 minutes by U-Bahn to Heiligenstadt; then take bus no. 38A.

A favorite pastime, especially in summer, involves fleeing the congested city and taking tram D to either Heiligenstadt (a 30-min. ride from Stephansplatz) or Nussdorf (a 45-min. ride from Stephansplatz). At either of these points you'll see a string of *heurigen* and a series of footpaths perfect for a relaxing stroll.

Located in the 22nd District, between the Danube Canal and the Old Danube, **Donaupark,** Wagramer Strasse (U-Bahn: Reichsbrücke), was converted in 1964 from a garbage dump to a park with flowers, shrubs, and walks, as well as a bird sanctuary. You'll find a bee house, an aviary with native and exotic birds, a small-animal paddock, a horse-riding course, playgrounds, and games. An outstanding feature of the park is the **Donauturm (Danube Tower),** Donauturmstrasse 4 (© **01/26335720**), a 253m (830-ft.) tower with two rotating cafe/restaurants from which you have a panoramic view of Vienna. One restaurant is at the 161m (528-ft.) level; the other is at 171m (561 ft.). International specialties and Viennese cuisine are served in both. There's also a sightseeing terrace at 151m (495 ft.). Two express elevators take people up the tower. It's open daily in summer from 10am to midnight and in winter from 10am to 10pm. The charge for the elevator is 5.50€ ($8.80) for adults and 4.10€ ($6.60) for children.

6 ESPECIALLY FOR KIDS

The greatest attraction for kids is the **Prater Amusement Park,** but there's much more in Vienna that children find amusing, especially the performances of the horses at the **Spanish Riding School.** They also love the adventure of climbing the tower of **St. Stephan's Cathedral.** Nothing quite tops a day like a picnic in the **Vienna Woods.** Below, we list other fun-filled attractions that you and your children will enjoy. (See also "Outdoor Pursuits," below.)

Schönbrunner Tiergarten, Schönbrunn Gardens (✆ **01/87792940;** U-Bahn: Hietzing), is the world's oldest zoo, founded by Franz Stephan von Lothringen, husband of Empress Maria Theresia. Maria Theresia liked to have breakfast here with her brood, favoring animal antics with her eggs. The baroque buildings in a historical park landscape provide a unique setting for modern animal keeping; the tranquillity makes for a relaxing yet interesting outing. Admission is 12€ ($19) for adults and 5€ ($8) for children. It's open March to September daily 9am to 6:30pm, October to February daily 9am to 5pm.

Other worthwhile museums for children include the **Museum für Unterhaltungskunst,** Karmelitergasse 9 (✆ **01/21106;** tram: 21 or N), a repository of the persona that clowns and circus performers have adopted throughout the centuries; and the **Wiener Straasenbahnmuseum (Streetcar Museum),** Erdbergstrasse 109 (✆ **01/790944900;** U-Bahn: Praterstern), a site commemorating the public conveyances that helped usher Vienna and the Hapsburg Empire into the Industrial Age.

7 FOR MUSIC LOVERS

If you're a fan of Mozart, Schubert, Beethoven, Strauss, or Haydn, you've landed in the right city. While in town, you can not only hear their music in the concert halls and palaces where the artists performed, but you can also visit the houses and apartments in which they lived and worked, as well as the cemeteries where they are buried.

Beethoven Pasqualatihaus Beethoven (1770–1827) lived in this building on and off from 1804 to 1814. It's likely that either the landlord was tolerant or the neighbors were deaf. Beethoven is known to have composed his *Fourth, Fifth,* and *Seventh* symphonies here, as well as *Fidelio* and other works. There isn't much to see except some family portraits and the composer's scores, but you might feel the view is worth the climb to the fourth floor (there's no elevator).

Mölker Bastei 8. ✆ **01/5358905.** Admission 2€ ($3.20) adults, 1€ ($1.60) children. Tues–Sun 10am–1pm and 2–6pm. U-Bahn: Schottentor.

Haydnhaus This is where Franz Josef Haydn (1732–1809) conceived and wrote his magnificent later oratorios *The Seasons* and *The Creation.* He lived in this house from 1797 until his death. Haydn also gave lessons to Beethoven here. There's a room in the house, which is a branch of the Historical Museum of Vienna, honoring Johannes Brahms.

Haydngasse 19. ✆ **01/5961307.** Admission 2€ ($3.20) adults, 1€ ($1.60) students and children. Wed–Thurs 10am–1pm and 2–6pm; Fri–Sun 10am–1pm. U-Bahn: Nestroyplatz.

Johann Strauss Wohnung "The King of the Waltz," Johann Strauss, Jr. (1825–99), lived at this address for a number of years, composing "The Blue Danube Waltz" here in 1867. The house is now part of the Historical Museum of Vienna.

Praterstrasse 54. ✆ **01/2140121.** Admission 2€ ($3.20) adults, 1€ ($1.60) children. Tues–Thurs 2–6pm; Fri–Sun 10am–1pm. U-Bahn: Nestroyplatz.

Mozartwohnung/Figarohaus This 17th-century house is called the House of Figaro because Mozart (1756–91) composed his opera *The Marriage of Figaro* here. The composer resided here from 1784 to 1787, a relatively happy period in what was otherwise a rather tragic life. It was here that he often played chamber-music concerts with Haydn. Over the years he lived in a dozen houses in all, which became more squalid as he aged. He died in poverty and was given a "pauper's" blessing at St. Stephan's Cathedral and then buried in St. Marx Cemetery. The Domgasse apartment has been turned into a museum.

Domgasse 5. ✆ **01/512-1791.** www.mozarthausvienna.at. Admission 10€ ($16) adults, 7.50€ ($12) students and children. Tues–Sun 10am–8pm. U-Bahn: Stephansplatz.

Schubert Geburtshaus The son of a poor schoolmaster, Franz Schubert (1797–1828) was born here in a house built earlier that century. Many Schubert mementos are on view. You can also visit the house at Kettenbrückengasse 6, where he died at age 31.

Nussdorferstrasse 54. ✆ **01/3173601.** Admission 2€ ($3.20) adults, 1€ ($1.60) students and children. Tues–Sun 10am–1pm and 2–6pm. S-Bahn: Canisiusgasse.

8 ORGANIZED TOURS

Wiener Rundfahrten (Vienna Sightseeing Tours), Starhemberggasse 25 (✆ **01/7124-6830;** www.viennasightseeingtours.com), offers the best tours, including a 1-day motorcoach excursion to Budapest, costing 99€ ($158) per person. The historical city tour costs 36€ ($58) for adults and is free for children 12 and under. It's ideal for visitors who are pressed for time and yet want to be shown the major (and most frequently photographed) monuments of Vienna. Tours leave the Staatsoper daily at 9:45 and 10:30am and 2:45pm. The tour lasts 3½ hours (U-Bahn: Karlsplatz).

"Vienna Woods—Mayerling," another popular excursion, lasting about 4 hours, leaves from the Staatsoper and takes you to the towns of Perchtoldsdorf and Modling, and to the Abbey of Heiligenkreuz, a center of Christian culture since medieval times. The tour also takes you for a short walk through Baden, the spa that was once a favorite summer resort of the aristocracy. Tours cost 43€ ($69) for adults and 15€ ($24) for children ages 10 to 16.

A **"Historical City Tour,"** which includes visits to Schönbrunn and Belvedere palaces, leaves the Staatsoper daily at 9:45 and 10:30am and 2:45pm. It lasts about 3 hours and costs 36€ ($58) for adults and 15€ ($24) for children ages 10 to 18.

A variation on the city tour includes an optional visit to the Spanish Riding School. This tour is offered Tuesday through Saturday, leaving from the Staatsoper building at 8:30am. Tickets are 61€ ($98) for adults, 30€ ($48) for children 13 and older, and free for children 3 to 12.

Information and booking for these tours can be obtained through Vienna Sightseeing Tours (see above) or through its affiliate, **Elite Tours,** Operngasse 4 (✆ **01/5132225;** www.elitetours.at).

9 OUTDOOR PURSUITS

BIKING

Vienna maintains almost 322km (200 miles) of cycling lanes and paths, many of which meander through some of the most elegant parks in Europe. Depending on their location, they're identified by a yellow image of a cyclist either stenciled directly onto the pavement or crafted from rows of red bricks set amid the cobblestones or concrete of the busy boulevards of the city center. Some of the most popular bike paths run parallel to both the Danube and the Danube Canal.

You can carry your bike onto specially marked cars of the Vienna subway system, but only during non-rush hours. Subway cars marked with a blue shield are the ones you should use for this purpose. Bicycles are *not* permitted on the system's escalators—take the stairs.

You can rent a bike for 3€ to 5€ ($4.80–$8) per hour. You'll usually be asked to leave either your passport or another form of ID as a deposit. One rental possibility is **Pedal Power,** Ausstellungsstrasse 3 (✆ **01/7297234;** www.pedalpower.at). There are rental shops at the Prater and along the banks of the Danube Canal. ***Note:*** You can also rent a bike at **Bicycle Rental Hochschaubahn,** Prater 113 (✆ **01/7295888;** www.wien.gv.at/english/leisure/bike/bikerental.htm).

One terrific bike itinerary, and quite popular as it has almost no interruptions, encompasses the long, skinny island that separates the Danube from the Neue Donau Canal. Low-lying and occasionally marshy, but with paved paths along most of its length, it provides clear views of central Europe's industrial landscape and the endless river traffic that flows by on either side.

BOATING

Wear a straw boating hat and hum a few bars of a Strauss waltz as you paddle your way around the quiet eddies of the Alte Donau. This gently curving stream bisects residential neighborhoods to the north of the Danube and is preferable to the muddy and swift-moving currents of the river itself.

At An der Obere along the Danube, you'll find some kiosks in summer, where you can negotiate for the rental of a boat or perhaps a canoe or kayak. There are, of course, organized tours of the Danube, but it's more fun to do it yourself.

HIKING

You're likely to expend plenty of shoe leather simply navigating Vienna's museums and palaces, but if you yearn for fresh air, the city tourist offices will provide information about its eight **Stadt-Wander-Wege,** carefully marked hiking paths that originate at points within the city's far-flung network of trams.

A less structured option involves heading east of town into the vast precincts of the **Lainzer Tiergarten,** where hiking trails entwine themselves amid forested hills, colonies of deer, and abundant bird life. To reach it from Vienna's center, first take the U-Bahn to the Kennedy Brücke/Heitzing station, which lies a few steps from the entrance to Schönbrunn Palace. A trek among the formal gardens of Schönbrunn might provide exercise enough, but if you're hungry for more, take tram no. 60 and then bus no. 60B into the distant but verdant confines of the Lainzer Tiergarten.

 Cruising the Danube

Its waters aren't as idyllic as the Strauss waltz would lead you to believe, and its color is usually muddy brown rather than blue, but visitors to Austria still view a day cruise along the Danube as a highlight of their trip. Until the advent of railroads and highways, the Danube played a vital role in Austria's history, helping to build the complex mercantile society that eventually became the Hapsburg Empire.

The most professional of the cruises are operated by the **DDSG Blue Danube Shipping Co.,** whose main offices are at Handelskai 265, A-1020 Vienna (✆ **01/588800;** www.ddsg-blue-danube.at). The most appealing cruise focuses on the Wachau region east of Vienna, between Vienna and Dürnstein. The cruise departs April to October every Sunday at 8:30am from the company's piers at Handelskai 265, 1020 Vienna (U-Bahn: Vorgartenstrasse), arriving in Dürnstein 6 hours later. The cost is 25€ to 38€ ($40–$61) for adults; it's half-price for children 10 to 15.

10 SHOPPING

Visitors can spend many hours shopping or browsing in Vienna's shops, where handicrafts are produced in a long-established tradition of skilled workmanship. Popular for their beauty and quality are petit point items, hand-painted Wiener Augarten porcelain, work by goldsmiths and silversmiths, handmade dolls, ceramics, enamel jewelry, leather goods, and many other items of value and interest.

The main shopping streets are in the city center (1st District). Popular destinations can be found on **Kärntnerstrasse,** between the Staatsoper and Stock-im-Eisen-Platz; the **Graben,** between Stock-im-Eisen-Platz and Kohlmarkt; **Kohlmarkt,** between the Graben and Michaelplatz; and **Rotensturmstrasse,** between Stephansplatz and Kai. There are also **Mariahilferstrasse,** between Babenbergerstrasse and Schönbrunn, one of the longest streets in Vienna; **Favoritenstrasse,** between Südtiroler Platz and Reumannplatz; and **Landstrasser Hauptstrasse.**

The **Naschmarkt,** a vegetable and fruit market, has a lively scene every day. It's at Linke and Rechte Wienzeile, south of the opera district.

Right in the heart of the city, opening onto Stephansplatz, stands the supremely modern Haas Haus, designed by the renowned Pritzker Prize-winning Hans Hollein. You can see the mirror image of the cathedral reflected in its semicircular glass facade. Today Haas Haus shelters a number of exclusive shops and boutiques, and also boasts a terrace restaurant with a panoramic view over the historic core.

ANTIQUE GLASS

Glasgalerie Kovacek Antique glass collected from estate sales and private collections throughout Austria takes up the ground floor. Most items date to the 19th and early 20th centuries, some to the 17th century. The most appealing pieces boast heraldic symbols, sometimes from branches of the Hapsburgs. Also here is a collection of cunning glass paperweights imported from Bohemia, France, Italy, and other parts of Austria.

Shopping Hours

Shops are normally open Monday through Friday from 9am to 6pm and Saturday from 9am to 1pm. Small shops close from noon to 2pm for lunch. Westbahnhof and Südbahnhof shops are open daily from 7am to 11pm, offering groceries, smokers' supplies, stationery, books, and flowers.

The upper floor holds the kind of classical paintings against which the Secessionists revolted. Look for canvases by Franz Makart, foremost of the 19th-century historic academics, as well as some Secessionist works, including two by Kokoschka. Spiegelgasse 12. ✆ **01/512-9954.** www.kovacek.at.

ANTIQUES

D&S Antiques ★ Finds Some of the greatest breakthroughs in clock-making technology occurred in Vienna between 1800 and 1840. This store, established in 1979, specializes in the acquisition, sale, and repair of antique Viennese clocks, stocking an awesome collection worthy of many world-class museums. The shop even stocks a "masterpiece" (each craftsman made only one such piece in his lifetime, to accompany his bid for entrance into the clockmakers' guild)—in this case, the work of a well-known craftsman of the early 1800s, Benedict Scheisel. Don't come here expecting a bargain—prices are astronomical—and devotees of timepieces from around the world flock to this emporium, treating it like a virtual museum of clocks. Dorotheergasse 13. ✆ **01/512-5885-0.** www.ds-antiques.com.

Dorotheum ★★ Dating from 1707, this is the oldest auction house in Europe. Emperor Joseph I established it so that impoverished aristocrats could fairly (and anonymously) get good value for their heirlooms. Today the Dorotheum holds many art auctions. If you're interested in an item, you give a small fee to a *sensal,* or licensed bidder, and he or she bids in your name. The vast array of objects for sale includes exquisite furniture and carpets, delicate objets d'art, and valuable paintings, as well as decorative jewelry. If you're unable to attend an auction, you can browse the sale rooms, selecting items you want to purchase directly to take home with you the same day. Approximately 31 auctions take place in July alone; over the course of a year, the Dorotheum handles some 250,000 pieces of art and antiques. Dorotheergasse 17. ✆ **01/51560-0.** www.dorotheum.at.

Flohmarkt ★ You might find a little of everything at this flea market near the Naschmarkt (see the box "Open-Air Markets," below) and the Kettenbrückengasse U-Bahn station. It's held every Saturday from 6:30am to 6pm, except on public holidays. The Viennese have perfected the skill of haggling, and the Flohmarkt is one of their favorite arenas. It takes a trained eye to spot the antique treasures scattered among the junk. Everything you've ever wanted is here, especially if you're seeking chunky Swiss watches from the 1970s, glassware from the Czech Republic (sold as "Venetian glassware"), and even Russian icons. Believe it or not, some of this stuff is original; other merchandise is merely knockoff. Linke Wienzeile. No phone. www.flohmarkt.at.

Galerie bei der Albertina Come here for ceramics and furniture made during the early 20th century by the iconoclastic crafts group Weiner Werkstette. Its members made good use of the machinery of the emerging industrial age in the fabrication of domestic furnishings and decor. The inventory incorporates decorative objects, sculpture, paintings from the Jugendstil (Art Nouveau) age, etchings, an occasional drawing by Egon Schiele or Gustav Klimt. Lobkowitzplatz 1. ✆ **01/513-1416.** www.galerie-albertina.at.

ART

M-ARS ★ Finds You stroll around with a shopping cart, selecting a Picasso, a Matisse, or perhaps a Gustav Klimt. We're exaggerating, of course, but this unique supermarket is stocked with works of art—not groceries. Perhaps you'll purchase for $15 the Gustav Klimt of 2050. Lying only a 5-minute walk from MuseumsQuartier, the supermarket sells more than 1,000 paintings, sculptures, and photographs, the work of some 50 artists. The artists were selected by a panel of art historians and directors from Austrian museums. 9 Westbahnstrasse. ✆ **01/890-5803.** www.m-ars.at.

Ö.W. (Österreichische Werkstatten) ★ Even if you skip every other store in Vienna, check this one out. This well-run store sells hundreds of handmade art objects. Leading artists and craftspeople throughout the country organized this cooperative to showcase their wares. The location is easy to find, only half a minute's walk from St. Stephan's Cathedral. There's an especially good selection of pewter, along with modern jewelry, glassware, brass, baskets, ceramics, and serving spoons fashioned from deer horn and bone. Take some time to wander through; you never know what treasure is hidden in a nook of this cavernous three-floor outlet. Kärntnerstrasse 6. ✆ **01/512-2418.** www.austrianarts.com.

CANDY & DESSERTS

Altmann & Kühne Many Viennese adults fondly recall the marzipan, hazelnut, or nougat their parents bought for them during strolls along the Graben. Established in 1928, this cozy shop stocks virtually nothing particularly good for your waistline or your teeth, but everything is positively and undeniably scrumptious. The visual display of all things sweet is almost as appealing. The pastries and tarts filled with fresh seasonal raspberries are, quite simply, delectable. Graben 30. ✆ **01/533-0927.**

Gerstner Gerstner competes with Café Demel (see chapter 6) as one of the city's greatest pastry makers and chocolatiers. It carries some of the most delectable-looking cakes, petits fours, and chocolates anywhere. Kärntnerstrasse 11–15. ✆ **01/512-49630.** www.feinspitz.com/ak/text/info-us.htm.

CHANDELIERS & PORCELAIN

Albin Denk ★★ Albin Denk is the oldest continuously operating porcelain store in Vienna (since 1702). Its clients have included Empress Elisabeth, and the shop you see today looks almost the same as it did when she visited. The three low-ceilinged rooms are beautifully decorated with thousands of objects from Meissen, Dresden, and other regions. Graben 13. ✆ **01/512-44390.** www.albindenk.24on.cc.

Augarten Porzellan ★★ Established in 1718, Augarten is the second-oldest (after Meissen) manufacturer of porcelain in Europe. This multitiered shop is the most visible and well-stocked outlet in the world. It can ship virtually anything anywhere. The tableware—fragile dinner plates with traditional or contemporary patterns—is elegant and much sought after. Also noteworthy are porcelain statues of the Lipizzaner horses. Stock-im-Eisenplatz 3–4. ✆ **01/512-14940.** www.augarten.at.

J. & L. Lobmeyr ★★★ If during your exploration of Vienna you admire a crystal chandelier, there's a good chance that it was made by this company. Designated purveyor to the Imperial Court of Austria in the early 19th century, it has maintained an elevated position ever since. The company is credited with designing and creating the first electric chandelier in 1883. It has also designed chandeliers for the Vienna State Opera, the Metropolitan Opera House in New York, the Assembly Hall in the Kremlin, the new concert hall in Fukuoka, Japan, and many palaces and mosques in the Near and Far East.

Behind its Art Nouveau façade, on the main shopping street of the city center, you'll see at least 50 chandeliers of all shapes and sizes. The store also sells hand-painted Hungarian porcelain, along with complete breakfast and dinner services. It will engrave your family crest on a wineglass or sell you a unique modern piece of sculptured glass from the third-floor showroom. The second floor is a museum of some of the outstanding pieces the company has made since it was established in 1823. Kärntnerstrasse 26. ✆ **01/512-0508.** www.lobmeyt.at.

CLOTHING (TRADITIONAL AUSTRIAN)

Lanz A well-known Austrian store, Lanz specializes in dirndls and other folk clothing. This rustically elegant shop's stock is mostly for women, with a limited selection of men's jackets, neckties, and hats. Clothes for toddlers begin at sizes appropriate for a 1-year-old; women's apparel begins at size 36 (American size 6). Kärntnerstrasse 10. ✆ **01/512-2456.** www.lanztrachten.at.

Loden Plankl ★★ Established in 1830 by the Plankl family, this store is the oldest and most reputable outlet in Vienna for traditional Austrian clothing. Children's sizes usually begin with items for 2-year-olds, and women's sizes range from 6 to 20 (American). Sizes for large or tall men go up to 60. Michaelerplatz 6. ✆ **01/533-8032.** http://lodenplankl.wien-twwt.com.

Mary Kindermoden Here's a store specializing in children's clothing with a regional twist. In the heart of the Old Town, near St. Stephan's Cathedral, the store has two floors that stock well-made garments, including lace swaddling clothes for christenings. Most garments are for children ages 10 months to 14 years. The staff speaks English and seems to deal well with children. Graben 14. ✆ **01/214-0213.** www.mary-kindermoden.at.

Popp & Kretschmer The staff here is usually as well dressed and elegant as the clientele, and if you appear to be a bona fide customer, the sales clerks will offer coffee, tea, or champagne as you scrutinize the carefully selected merchandise. The store carries three floors of dresses, along with shoes, handbags, belts, and a small selection of men's briefcases and travel bags. You'll find it opposite the State Opera. Kärntnerstrasse 51. ✆ **01/512-[illegible].** www.popp-kretschmer.at.

Sportalm Trachtenmoden If you're a woman looking for a coy and flattering dirndl to carry home with you, this stylish women's store stocks a staggering collection. Many are crafted as faithful replicas of designs that haven't been altered for generations; others take greater liberties and opt for brighter colors and updates that are specifically geared for modern tastes. Even if you're male and wouldn't otherwise dream of stepping into this shop, consider the possibility of procuring a lace-trimmed christening dress for a favorite niece, or a dirndl or traditional Austrian jacket that would make virtually any female child look adorable. Children's sizes fit girls ages 1 to 14. You'll find the store within the jarringly modern Haas Haus, across the plaza from St. Stephan's. Brandstätte 7–9. ✆ **01/5355289.** www.sportalm.at. U-Bahn: Stephansplatz.

Finds Vintage Threads

If you're looking for second-hand or vintage clothing, join Vienna's youth rifling through the racks at the year-round **Naschmarkt** (U-Bahn: Karlsplatz).

DEPARTMENT STORES

Steffl Kaufhaus This five-story department store is one of Vienna's most visible and well advertised. You'll find rambling racks of cosmetics, perfumes, a noteworthy section devoted to books and periodicals, housewares, and thousands of garments for men, women, and children. If you forgot to pack something for your trip, chances are very good that Steffl Kaufhaus will have it. Kärntnerstrasse 19. ✆ **01/514310.** www.kaufhaus-steffl.at.

JEWELRY

A. E. Köchert ★★★ The sixth generation of the family who served as court jewelers until the end of the Hapsburg Empire continues its tradition of fine workmanship here. The store, founded in 1814, occupies a 16th-century landmark building. The firm designed many of the crown jewels of Europe, but the staff gives equal attention to customers looking only at charms for a bracelet. Neuer Markt 15. ✆ **01/512-58280.** www.koechert.at.

Rozet & Fischmeister ★ Owned by the same family since it was established in 1770, this jewelry store specializes in gold jewelry, gemstones set in artful settings, and both antique and modern versions of silver tableware. If you opt to buy an engagement ring or a bauble for a friend, you'll be following in the footsteps of Franz Joseph I. The staff will even quietly admit that he made several discreet purchases for his legendary mistress, actress Katharina Schratt. Kohlmarkt 11. ✆ **01/533-8061.** www.rozet-fischmeister.com.

LACE & NEEDLEWORK

Zur Schwäbischen Jungfrau ★★★ This is one of the most illustrious shops in Austria, with a reputation that goes back almost 300 years. Here, Maria Theresa bought her first handkerchiefs, and thousands of debutantes have shopped for dresses. Come here for towels, bed linens, lace tablecloths, and some of the most elaborate needlepoint and embroidery anywhere. Service is courtly, cordial, and impeccable. Graben 26. ✆ **01/535-5356.** www.schwaebische-jungfrau.at.

MUSIC

Arcadia Opera Shop This respected record store is one of the best for classical music. The well-educated staff knows the music and performers (as well as the availability of recordings), and is usually eager to share that knowledge. The shop also carries books on art, music, architecture, and opera, as well as an assortment of musical memorabilia. The shop is on the street level of the Vienna State Opera, with a separate entrance on Kärntnerstrasse. Guided tours of the splendid opera house end here. Wiener Staatsoper, Kärntnerstrasse 40. ✆ **01/513-95680.** www.arcadia.at.

Da Caruso Almost adjacent to the Vienna State Opera, this store is known to music fans and musicologists worldwide. Its inventory includes rare and unusual recordings of

Moments Noshing Your Way Through Vienna's Open-Air Markets

Viennese merchants have thrived since the Middle Ages by hauling produce, dairy products, and meats in bulk from the fertile farms of Lower Austria and Burgenland into the city center. The tradition of buying the day's provisions directly from street stalls is so strong that, even today, it's tough for modern supermarkets to survive within the city center.

Odd (and inconvenient) as this might seem, you'll quickly grasp the fun of Vienna's open-air food stalls after a brief wander through one of these outdoor markets. Most of the hundreds of merchants operating within them maintain approximately the same hours: Monday through Friday from 8am to 6pm and Saturday from 8am to noon.

The largest is the **Naschmarkt,** Wienzeile, in the 6th District (U-Bahn: Karlsplatz), just south of the Ring. Because of its size, it's the most evocatively seedy and colorful of the bunch, as well as being the most firmly rooted in the life of the city.

Less comprehensive are the **Rochusmarkt,** at Landstrasser Hauptstrasse at the corner of the Erdbergstrasse, 3rd District (U-Bahn: Rochusgasse), a short distance east of the Ring, and the **Brunnenmarkt,** on the Brunnengasse, 16th District (U-Bahn: Josefstädterstrasse), a short walk north of the Westbahnhof. Even if you don't plan on stocking up on produce and foodstuff (the staff at your hotel might not be amused if you showed up with bushels of carrots or potatoes), the experience is colorful enough and, in some cases, kitschy enough, to be remembered as one of the highlights of your trip to Vienna.

historic performances by the Vienna Opera and the Vienna Philharmonic. If you're looking for a magical or particularly emotional performance by Maria Callas, Herbert von Karajan, or Bruno Walter, chances are you can get it here, digitalized on CD. There's also a collection of taped films. The staff is hip, alert, and obviously in love with music. Operngasse 4. ✆ **01/513-1326.** www.dacaruso.at.

SHOPPING CENTER

The Ringstrassen-Gallerien Rental fees for shop space in central Vienna are legendarily expensive. In response to the high rents, about 70 boutiques selling everything from hosiery to key chains to evening wear have pooled their resources and moved to labyrinthine quarters near the Staatsoper, midway between the Bristol and Anna hotels. Its prominent location guarantees a certain glamour, although the cramped dimensions of many of the stores might be a turn-off. The selection is broad, and no one can deny the gallery's easy-to-find location. Each shop is operated independently, but virtually all of them conduct business Monday to Friday 10am to 7pm and Saturday 10am to 6pm. In the Palais Corso and in the Kärntnerringhof, Kärntner Ring 5–13. ✆ **01/512518111.** U-Bahn: Karlsplatz.

TOYS

Kober ★ Kids Kober has been a household name, especially at Christmastime in Vienna, for more than 100 years. It carries old-fashioned wood toys, teddy bears straight out of a Styrian storybook, go-karts (assembly required), building sets, and car and airplane models. The occasional set of toy soldiers is more *Nutcracker Suite* than G.I. Joe. Graben 14–15. ✆ **01/533-60180.** www.kobertoys.com.

VINEGARS & OILS

Gegenbauer ★★ Finds It's true you don't have to go to Vienna to purchase more than 50 artisan vinegars and about 20 specialty oils from this unique store, as you can do so on the Internet or through such distributors as Dean & DeLuca. Running a family business—going since 1929—Erwin Gegenbauer may be the world's expert on vinegar. Ever had vinegar made from tomatoes? At this store you can purchase such, but also bottles of vinegar made from elderberry, asparagus, lemongrass, sour cherry, cucumber, and even beer. Rare oils come from fruit kernels, wine grapes, or other ingredients. Gegenbauer 14, Naschmarkt. ✆ **01/6041088.** www.gegenbauer.at.

WINE

Wein & Co. Since the colonization of Vindobona by the ancient Romans, the Viennese have always taken their wines seriously. Wein & Co. is Vienna's largest wine outlet, a sprawling cellar-level ode to the joys of the grape and the bounty of Bacchus. You'll also find wines from around the world, including South Africa and Chile. Jasomirgottstrasse 3–5. ✆ **01/535-0916.** www.weinco.at.

11 VIENNA AFTER DARK

Whatever nightlife scene turns you on, Vienna has a little bit of it. You can dance into the morning hours, hear a concert, attend an opera or festival, go to the theater, gamble, or simply sit and talk over a drink at a local tavern.

The best source of information about what's happening on the cultural scene is *Wien Monatsprogramm,* which is distributed free at tourist information offices and at many hotel reception desks. *Die Presse,* the Viennese daily, publishes a special magazine in its Thursday edition outlining the major cultural events for the coming week. It's in German but might still be helpful to you.

The Viennese are not known for discounting their cultural presentations. However, *Wien Monatsprogramm* lists outlets where you can purchase tickets in advance, thereby cutting down the surcharge imposed by travel agencies. These agencies routinely add about 22% to what might already be an expensive ticket.

If you're not a student and don't want to go bankrupt to see a performance at the Staatsoper or the Burgtheater, you can purchase standing-room tickets at a cost of about 5€ ($8).

Students under 27 with valid IDs are eligible for many discounts. For example, the Burgtheater, Akademietheater, and Staatsoper sell student tickets for just 10€ ($16) on the night of the performance. Theaters almost routinely grant students about 20% off the regular ticket price. Vienna is the home of four major symphony orchestras, including the Vienna Symphony and the Vienna Philharmonic. In addition to the ÖRF Symphony Orchestra and the Niederöster-reichische Tonkünstler, there are literally dozens of others, ranging from smaller orchestras to chamber orchestras.

THE PERFORMING ARTS

Music is at the heart of cultural life in Vienna. This has been true for a couple of centuries or so, and the city continues to lure composers, musicians, and music lovers. You can find places to enjoy everything from chamber music and waltzes to pop and jazz. There are small dance clubs and large concert halls, as well as musical theaters. If somehow you should tire of musical entertainment, Vienna's stages present classical, modern, and avant-garde dramas. Below we describe just a few of the highlights—if you're in Vienna long enough, you'll find many other diversions on your own.

Austrian State Theaters & Opera Houses

Reservations and information for the four state theaters—the Wiener Staatsoper (Vienna State Opera), Volksoper, Burgtheater (National Theater), and Akademietheater—can be obtained by contacting **Österreichische Bundestheater (Austrian Federal Theaters),** the office that coordinates reservations and information for all four theaters (✆ **01/514442959;** www.bundestheater.at). Call Monday through Friday from 8am to 5pm. ***Note:*** The number is likely to be busy; it's easier to get information and order tickets online. The major season is September through June, with more limited presentations in summer. Many tickets are issued to subscribers before the box office opens. For all four theaters, box-office sales are made only 1 month before each performance at the Bundestheaterkasse, Goethegasse 1 (✆ **01/514440**), open Monday to Friday 8am to 6pm, Saturday 9am to 2pm, and Sunday and holidays 9am to noon. Credit and charge card sales can be arranged by telephone within 6 days of a performance by calling ✆ **01/5131513** Monday through Friday from 10am to 6pm, and Saturday and Sunday from 10am to noon. Tickets for all state theater performances, including the opera, are also available by writing to the Österreichischer Bundestheaterverband, Goethegasse 1, A-1010 Vienna, from points outside Vienna. Orders must be received at least 3 weeks in advance of the performance to be booked. No one should send money through the mail. For more information on tickets, go to the websites of the venues listed below.

Note: The single most oft-repeated complaint of music lovers in Vienna is about the lack of available tickets to many highly desirable musical performances. If the suggestions above don't produce the desired tickets, you could consult a ticket broker. Their surcharge usually won't exceed 25%, except for exceptionally rare tickets, when that surcharge might be doubled or tripled. Although at least half a dozen ticket agencies maintain offices in the city, one of the most reputable agencies is **Liener Brünn** (✆ **01/5330961**), which might make tickets available months in advance or as little as a few hours before the anticipated event.

As a final [illegible] remember that the concierge of virtually every upscale hotel in Vienna long ago learned sophisticated tricks for acquiring hard-to-come-by tickets. (A gratuity of at least 10€/$16 might work wonders and will be expected anyway for the phoning this task will entail. You'll pay a hefty surcharge as well.)

Akademietheater This theater specializes in both classic and contemporary works, from Brecht to Shakespeare. The Burgtheater Company often performs here, as it's the second, smaller house of this world-famous theater (see below). Lisztstrasse 3. ✆ **01/514444740.** www.burgtheater.at. Tickets 4€–48€ ($6.40–$77) for seats, 1.50€ ($2.40) for standing room. U-Bahn: Stadtpark.

Burgtheater The Burgtheater produces classical and modern plays in German. Work started on the original structure in 1776. Mozart's *Marriage of Figaro* premiered here in

Tips A Note on Evening Dress

For concerts and theaters, dark suits and cocktail dresses are recommended. For especially festive occasions such as opera premieres, receptions, and balls, tails and dinner jackets are the preferred dress for men and evening dresses are recommended for women. You can rent men's evening wear, as well as carnival costumes, from several places in Vienna, which you'll find in the telephone directory classified section under *Kleiderleihanstalten*. It's a good idea to take a light coat when you go out in the evening, even in summer.

1786; his *Così fan Tutte* premiered in 1790. The theater was destroyed in World War II and was not reopened until 1955. It's the dream of every German-speaking actor to appear here. Dr.-Karl-Lueger-Ring 2. ✆ **01/51444140.** www.burgtheater.at. Tickets 5€–48€ ($8–$77) for seats, 1.50€ ($2.40) for standing room. Tram: 1, 2, or D to Burgtheater.

Volksoper This folk opera house presents lavish productions of Viennese operettas and other musicals September through June on a daily schedule. Tickets go on sale at the Volksoper itself 1 hour before the performance. Währingerstrasse 78. ✆ **01/514-443670.** www.volksoper.at. Tickets 7€–150€ ($11–$240) for seats, 2.50€–4€ ($4–$6.40) for standing room. U-Bahn: Volksoper.

Wiener Staatsoper ★★★ This is one of the three most important opera houses in the world. With the Vienna Philharmonic in the pit, some of the leading opera stars of the world perform here. In their day, Richard Strauss and Gustav Mahler worked as directors. Daily performances are given September through June. (For information on tours, see section 2, "Other Top Attractions.") Opernring 2. ✆ **9/51444-42960.** www.staatsoper.at. Tickets 10€–220€ ($16–$352). U-Bahn: Karlsplatz.

More Theater & Music

If your German is halfway passable, try to see a play by Arthur Schnitzler if one is being staged during your visit. This mild-mannered playwright, who died in 1931, was the most characteristically Viennese of the Austrian writers. Through his works he gave the imperial city the charm and style more often associated with Paris. Whenever possible, we attend a revival of one of his plays, such as *Einsame Weg (The Solitary Path)* or *Professor Bernhardi.* Our favorite is *Reigen,* on which the film *La Ronde* was based. Schnitzler's plays are often performed at the Theater in der Josefstadt.

Konzerthaus This major concert hall with three auditoriums was built in 1913. It's the venue for a wide cultural program, including orchestral concerts, chamber-music recitals, choir concerts, piano recitals, and opera concert stage performances. Its repertoire is classical, romantic, and folk, as well as contemporary (from recent classical music to jazz, rock, and pop). The box office is open September to June Monday to Friday 9am to 7:45pm and Saturday 9am to 1pm; in August, hours are Mon to Friday 9am to 1pm. Lothringerstrasse 20. ✆ **01/242002.** www.konzerthaus.at. Ticket prices depend on the event. U-Bahn: Stadtpark.

Musikverein Consider yourself lucky if you get to hear a concert here. The Golden Hall is regarded as one of the four acoustically best concert halls in the world. Some 600 concerts per season (Sept–June) are presented here. Only 10 to 12 of these are played by the Vienna Philharmonic, and these are subscription concerts, so they're always sold out far in advance. Standing room is available at almost any performance, but you must line up hours before the show. The box office is open August 16 to September 3 Monday to Friday 9am to noon. The rest of the year, it is open Monday to Friday 9am to 8pm and Saturday 9am to 1pm (closed July–Aug 15). Dumbastrasse 3. ✆ **01/5058190** for the box office. www.musikverein-wien.at. Tickets up to 120€ ($192) for seats, 3€ ($4.80) for standing room. U-Bahn: Karlsplatz.

Schönbrunn Palace Theater ★ A gem in a regal setting, this theater opened in 1749 for the entertainment of the court of Maria Theresia. The architecture is a medley of baroque and rococo, and there's a large, plush box where the imperial family sat to enjoy the shows. The theater belongs to Hochschule für Musik und Darstellende Kunst, and is used for performances of the Max Reinhardt Seminar (theater productions) and for opera productions throughout the year. Operettas and comic operas are performed in July and August. A wide variety of art groups, each responsible for its own ticket sales, perform here. There are various performances daily in July and August Tuesday through Saturday nights. At Schönbrunn Palace, Schönbrunner Schlossstrasse. ✆ **01/5120100.** www.musik-theater-schoenbrunn.at. Tickets 35€–85€ ($56–$136). U-Bahn: Schönbrunn.

Theater an der Wien This theater opened on June 13, 1801, and its opera and operetta presentations have been entertaining fans ever since. Beethoven's *Fidelio* premiered here in 1805; in fact, the composer once lived in this building. Johann Strauss, Jr.'s, *Die Fledermaus* premiered here in 1874, and Franz Léhar's *The Merry Widow* premiered in 1905. During the occupation after World War II, when the Staatsoper was being restored after heavy damage, the Vienna State Opera made the Theater an der Wien its home. Linke Wienzeile 6. ✆ **01/588300** for tickets. www.theateranderwien.at. Tickets 30€–140€ ($48–$224). U-Bahn: Karlsplatz.

Theater in der Josefstadt Built in 1776, this theater prides itself on presenting comedies, dramas, and tragedies, either in their original German or in German-language translations (musical performances are almost never given here). One of the most influential theaters in the Teutonic world, it reached legendary levels of excellence under the aegis of Max Reinhardt, beginning in 1924. The box office is open daily 10am to 7:30pm. Josefstädterstrasse 26. ✆ **01/42700.** www.josefstadt.org. Tickets 3€–65€ ($4.80–$104). U-Bahn: Rathaus. Tram: J. Bus: 13.

Vienna's English Theatre This is the major English-speaking theater in Vienna. It was established in 1963 and proved so popular that it has been around ever since. Many international celebrities and numerous British actors have appeared on the stage of this neo baroque theater. Works by American playwrights are occasionally presented. The box office is open Monday to Friday 10am to 7:30pm. Josefsgasse 12. ✆ **01/4021260.** www.englishtheatre.at. Tickets 20€–38€ ($31–$61). U-Bahn: Rathaus. Tram: J. Bus: 13A.

Volkstheater Built in 1889, this theater maintains a tradition of presenting plays from the classical repertoire of German-language theater, and it almost never schedules a purely musical performance. Some of the pieces produced here are videotaped for distribution and include original versions and translations of works by Nestroy, Raimund, and Strindberg. Modern plays and comedies are also presented. The theater's season runs September to May. The box office is open Monday to Saturday 10am to 7:30pm. Neustiftgasse 1. ✆ **01/521110.** www.volkstheater.at. Tickets 8€–40€ ($13–$64). U-Bahn: Volkstheater. Tram: 1, 2, 49, D, or J. Bus: 48A.

Nightclubs

Babenberger Passage This is the most futuristic club in Vienna, its patrons claiming it evokes a space ship that has landed at the point where "The Ring" joins Mariahilferstrasse. In the 1st District, the club has the most sophisticated lighting system in Vienna. Cocktails are downed in a chic bar, and there's dancing in a romantically modern bar. Cover 10€ ($16). Open Monday to Saturday 8pm to 1am. Ringstrasse at Babenbergerstrasse. ✆ **01/9618800.** www.sunshine.at. U-Bahn: MuseumsQuartier.

Café Cavina This lively club enjoys one of the most unusual settings in Vienna, as it's installed in a cavernous underground station. The club, which often presents live music, is one of the hippest places in Vienna, attracting artsy types. Every night is likely to be different—no one can predict what is going to happen. The location is outside of Ring in the 8th District. Open Monday to Thursday 6pm to 2am, Friday and Sunday 6pm to 4am. Cover can vary. Josefstadtstrasse 84/Stadtbahnbogen. ✆ **4064322.** www.cafe-carina.at. U-Bahn: Josefstadterstrasse.

Café Leopold No one ever expected that the city's homage to Viennese expressionism (the Leopold Museum) would ever rock 'n' roll with the sounds of dancing feet and high-energy music. But that's exactly what happens here 3 nights a week, when the museum's restaurant fills up with drinkers, wits, gossips, dancers, and people of all ilk on the make. There's a revolving cycle of DJs, each vying for local fame and approval, and a wide selection of party-colored cocktails, priced at around 10€ ($16) each. The cafe/restaurant section is open Sunday to Wednesday 10am to 2pm, Friday and Saturday 10am to 4pm. The disco operates only Thursday to Saturday, 9:30pm till between 2 and 3am, depending on business. In the Leopold Museum, Museumsplatz 1. ✆ **01/523-67-32.** www.cafe-leopold.at. U-Bahn: Volkstheater or Babenbergstrasse/MuseumsQuartier.

Chelsea ★ This is the city's hottest venue for underground music. From all over the continent, the best bands and DJs are imported to entertain the gyrating throngs who gather here in a sort of techno-pop atmosphere. The pulsating club lies in one of the arches of the old railway train tracks that divide the north of the city from the historic core. Open Monday to Thursday 6pm to 4am, Friday and Saturday 6pm to 5am, and Sunday 4pm to 3am. Lerchenfelder-Gürtel (Stadtbahnbögen 29-31). ✆ **01/407-93-09.** www.chelsea.co.at. Cover 6€–12€ ($7.80–$16). U-Bahn: Josefstädterstrasse/Thaliastrasse.

Club Havana ★ The Viennese versions of Jennifer Lopez or Ricky Martin show up here for "Latinpop parties." Believe it or not, at least according to the posters, Che Guevara is still a cultural icon here. "La Vida" takes the form of everything from merengue to hip-hop. The club is located a minute's walk from the Opera House on the backside of the Ringstrassengalerien. It's open nightly, 7pm to 4am. Depending on the night, you might be hit with a cover charge. Otherwise, Brazilian cocktails start at 8.90€ ($14). Mahlerstrasse 11. ✆ **01/5132075.** www.clubhavana.at. Cover varies. U-Bahn: Karlsplatz.

U-4 ★ This is one of the most famous nightclubs in Vienna, with a history going back to the '20s, and a gift for reinventing itself with each new generation of night owls. Its name has even been factored into songs by rockers throughout Europe and the world, and the roster of high-profile divas who have performed here has included, among many others, Kurt Cobain of Nirvana fame. Set on the city's western edge, not far from Schönbrunn Palace, it offers a mostly black (with mirrors) decor, two floors, each with a different sound system, and a total of three fast-moving bars. Depending on the schedule, you'll find nights focusing on different musical themes including Italian music (Mon), and "Addicted to Rock" Thursdays. Nights that are the most youth-oriented (that is, the late teens or early 20-somethings) include Tuesdays (which are packed) and Fridays (which are even more packed). A night with a somewhat more mature crowd (20s and emotionally available 30-year-olds) is Saturday. U-4 is open nightly from 10pm till around 5am, depending on demand, and closed every Sunday between June and September. Schönbrunner Strasse 222. ✆ **01/817-1192.** www.U-4.at. Cover charge 5€–11€ ($8–$18), depending on the night's venue and schedule.

Volksgarten Disco A favorite since the 1950s, this disco has stayed abreast of the times, offering everything today from hip hop to R&B. It has the best dance floor in town as well as the summer-only Volksgarten Pavillon, a garden bar. Friday and Saturday are the hottest nights, although the club is open Thursday to Sunday 10pm to 5am. Cover ranges from 7€–13€ ($11–$21). Inside the Ring at Volksgarten. ✆ **01/5330518.** U-Bahn: Volksgarten.

Rock, Salsa, Jazz & Blues

Jazzland ★ This is one of the most famous jazz pubs in Austria, noted for the quality of its U.S. and central European-based performers. It's in a deep 200-year-old cellar. Beer—which seems to be the thing to order here—costs 4.40€ ($7) for a foaming mug. Platters of Viennese food such as *tafelspitz,* Wiener schnitzel, and roulades of beef cost 5€ to 10€ ($8–$16). The place is open Monday to Saturday 7:30pm to 1:30am. Music is from 9pm to midnight, and three sets are performed. Franz-Josefs-Kai 29. ✆ **01/533-2575.** www.jazzland.at. Cover 11€–18€ ($18–$29). U-Bahn: Schwedenplatz.

Loop This bar/club/lounge boasts programs self-characterized as "queer beats," "funky dope beats," "electric soul," and even "delicious tunes." Under the U-Bahn stop, this is a sleekly contemporary nighttime rendezvous, "drawing only the coolest of the cool," the bartender assured us. Regardless of how the club's owners describe their musical offerings, the night we visited was devoted to hip-hop, jazz, and funk. Open Monday to Thursday 6pm to 2am, Friday and Saturday 6pm to 1am, and Sunday 6pm to midnight. Usually there's no cover, but drinks form an impressive *carte,* ranging from tequila to "wodka," costing from 4€ to 12€ ($6.40–$19). Lerchenfeldergürtel 26. ✆ **01/4024195.** U-Bahn: Josefstädterstrasse/Thaliastrasse.

Planet Music Planet Music is a direct competitor of the also-recommended Tunnel (see below). As such, it attracts some of the same clientele, has some of the same energy, and—with perhaps a higher percentage of folk singers, reggae, soca, and new wave artists—hosts some of the same musicians. It's also about twice as large as the Tunnel, which contributes to larger crowds and louder volumes. Planet Music rocks every Monday through Friday, with the bar drawing a heavy after-work crowd after 6pm. Live concerts can take place any day of the week, so call ahead for the live music schedule. Adalbert-Stifter-Strasse 73. ✆ **01/332-46-41.** Cover charge 9€–25€ ($14–$40). Tram: 33.

Porgy & Bess ★ Its name may suggest an all-black classical musical in the States, but this is actually the best jazz club in the city. Its array of performers from Europe and around the world is strictly first class. Established in 1993, the club became an instant hit and has since been going strong, patronized by Vienna's most avid jazz aficionados. The club opens Monday to Saturday at 7pm and Sunday at 8pm; closing times vary, often 3 or 4am. Riembergasse 11. ✆ **01/5128811.** www.porgy.at. U-Bahn: Stubentor. Tram: 1A to Riemerg.

Tunnel Experiences like the ones created in the 1960s and 1970s by Jimi Hendrix are alive and well, if in less dramatic form, at Tunnel. In a smoke-filled cellar near Town Hall, it showcases musical groups from virtually everywhere. You'll never know quite what to expect, as the only hint of what's on or off is a recorded German-language announcement of what's about to appear and occasional advertisements in local newspapers. It's open daily 9pm to 2am, with live music beginning around 10pm. Florianigasse 39. ✆ **01/405-3465.** www.tunnel-vienna-live.at. Cover 3€–15€ ($4.80–$24). U-Bahn: Rathaus.

Dance Clubs

Flex ★ No other dance club in Vienna has a history as long, as distinguished, and as "flexible" as this one. This industrial-looking venue is set uncomfortably between the edge of the canal and the subway tracks. With exterior graffiti that includes the scrawlings of street artists going back to the '70s, it's a prime venue for post-millennium fans of electronic music. Inside, you'll find a beer-soaked, congenially battered venue, where the ghosts of rock 'n' roll seem to float restlessly above a Sputnik-era linoleum floor. It's where the young and the restless (some of them teenagers) of Vienna go for access to music that's the rage, and the rave, in places such as Berlin, London, NYC, and Los Angeles. Open daily 9am to 2am. Am Donaukanal. ✆ **01/533-7525.** Cover 10€ ($16). U-Bahn: Schottenring.

Scotch Club Except for the whisky, there's not much that's Scottish about this disco and coffeehouse in Vienna's most fashionable area, a 5-minute walk from many of its premier hotels and the Parkring. It welcomes a clientele of good-looking women, whose ages begin at around 20 and travel upward into various states of careful preservation, and seemingly affluent men, whose ages range, in the words of a manager, from around 23 to "aggressive and elderly." There's a disco in the cellar (Mon–Sat 10pm–4am; free admission); a coffeehouse on the street level (Mon–Sat 10am–4am); and a "games lounge," featuring chess boards and a bar upstairs (Mon–Sat 8pm–4am). Parkring 10. ✆ **01/512-9417.** www.scotch-club.com. U-Bahn: Stadtpark or Stubentor.

Titanic A sprawling dance club that has thrived since the early 1980s, it has two different dance areas and a likable upstairs restaurant where Mexican, Italian, and international foods provide quick energy for further dancing. You'll enter a mirrored world with strobe lights, without seating areas, which encourages patrons to dance, drink, and mingle, sometimes aggressively, throughout the evening. As for the music, you're likely to find everything from soul and house to '70s-style disco and hip-hop. The restaurant serves dinner every Friday and Saturday 7pm to 3am; main courses are 10€ to 17€ ($16–$27). The dancing areas are open Friday and Saturday 10pm to around 6am, depending on business. Beer costs 3€ to 4€ ($4.80–$6.40). Theobaldgasse 11. ✆ **01/587-4758.** www.titanic.at. U-Bahn: Mariahilferstrasse.

THE BAR SCENE

Viennese bars range from time-honored upscale haunts to loud, trendy establishments that stay open until dawn. The most popular area (among locals and visitors) for experiencing Vienna's blossoming bar scene is the **Bermuda Triangle** (U-Bahn: Schwedenplatz). It's roughly bordered by Judengasse, Seitenstättengasse Rabensteig, and Franz-Josefs-Kai. You'll find everything from intimate watering holes to large bars with live music. Below is a sampling of bars that will appeal to a broad spectrum of tastes.

Barfly's Club ★ Finds This is the most urbane and sophisticated cocktail bar in town, frequented by journalists, actors, and politicians. It's got a laissez-faire ambience that combines aspects of Vienna's *grande bourgeoisie* with its discreet avant-garde. A menu lists about 370 cocktails that include every kind of mixed drink imaginable, priced at 7€ to 11€ ($11–$18). The only food served is "toast" (warm sandwiches), priced at 5€ ($8). It's open daily, 6pm to between 2 and 4am, depending on the night of the week. In the Hotel Fürst Metternich, Esterházygasse 33. ✆ **01/586-0825.** http://barflys.at. U-Bahn: Kirchengasse. Tram: 5.

Esterházykeller The ancient bricks and scarred wooden tables of this drinking spot, famous since 1683, are permeated with the aroma of endless pints of spilled beer. An outing here isn't recommended for everyone, but if you decide to chance it, choose the left entrance (facing from the street), grip the railing firmly, and begin your descent. Wine, a specialty, starts at 1.45€ ($2.30). The place is open Monday to Friday 11am to 11pm, and Saturday and Sunday 4 to 11pm. Haarhof 1. ✆ **01/533-3482.** www.esterhazykeller.at. U-Bahn: Stephansplatz.

Krah Krah This place is the most animated and well-known singles bar in the area. An attractive, and sometimes available, after-work crowd fills this woodsy, somewhat battered space. Beer is the drink of choice here, with more than 60 kinds available, from 3.40€ to 4.90€ ($5.50–$7.90) each. Sandwiches, snacks, and simple platters of food, including hefty portions of Weiner schnitzel, start at 8.50€ ($14). It's open daily 11am to 2am. Rabensteig 8. ✆ **01/533-8193.** www.krah-krah.at. U-Bahn: Schwedenplatz.

La Divina ★★ Artful, artsy, and immediately adjacent to the side entrance of the Albertina, this is a cocktail bar that would be a lot of fun anywhere, but thanks to its links to the Vienna State Opera, it sometimes rises to "divine" levels of operatic camp. Its name derives from the moniker any opera lover associates with über-diva Maria Callas (1923–1977). The sinuous line of the bartop was inspired by the neck of a violin, and the old-fashioned red velour cubbyhole—ideal for an intimate drink—evokes one of the boxes at the Vienna State Opera. And then there's that Bösendorfer grand piano, where every Wednesday to Saturday, from 9:30 to 11:30pm, some operatic wannabe will be crashing out arias. The menu is light on food (snacks only) but rich (more than 100) in cocktails, 15 of which feature some variation of champagne. Glasses of wine and cocktails cost 7.50€ to 18€ ($12–$29) each, and the bar is open daily 4pm to 2am. Hanuschgasse 3. ✆ **01/513-43-19.** www.ladivina.at. U-Bahn: Karlsplatz.

Loos American Bar ★ **Finds** One of the most unusual and interesting bars in the center of Vienna, this very dark, sometimes mysterious bar was designed by the noteworthy architect Adolf Loos in 1908. At the time, it functioned as the drinking room of a private men's club, but today it's more democratic, and welcomes a mostly bilingual crowd of very hip singles from Vienna's arts-and-media scene. Walls, floors, and ceilings sport layers of dark marble and black onyx, making this one of the most expensive small-scale decors in the city. No food is served, but the mixologist's specialties include six kinds of martinis, plus five kinds of Manhattans, each 10€ ($16). Beer costs from 2.60€ ($4.20). It's open daily noon to 4am. Kärntnerdurchgang 10. ✆ **01/512-3283.** U-Bahn: Stephansplatz.

Mocca Club This hip, trendy coffeehouse/cafe/bar may have been born on the ruins of a failed Starbucks, but caffeine and alcohol drinkers alike agree that the combination here is successful. You'll select from a jumble of sofas, deep armchairs, and conventional tables and chairs, and then order the drug of your choice from a vast menu of more than 93 kinds of tea, 52 kinds of coffee, and 200 creatively defined cocktails. If you want a cocktail, try a mojito. Tea lovers should consider a delicate *Bai Mei* from China, and the

Indian Monsoon Malabar coffee is soft, genteel—even heavenly. Cocktails range from 8€ to 10€ ($13–$16); coffees from 1.80€ to 2.50€ ($2.90–$4). Open Sunday to Thursday 10am to midnight, Friday to Saturday 10am to 2am. Linke Wienzeile 4. ✆ **01/587-0087.** www.moccaclub.com. U-Bahn: Karlsplatz.

Onyx Bar One of the most visible and best known, though crowded, bars near the Stephansplatz is on the sixth (next-to-uppermost) floor of one of Vienna's most controversial buildings—Haas Haus. Lunch is served from noon to 3pm daily; dinner is served from 6pm to midnight. The staff serves a long and varied cocktail menu from 6pm to 2am, including strawberry margaritas and caipirinhas, each priced from 10€ to 15€ ($16–$24). Live and recorded music is presented, usually beginning after 8:30pm. In the Haas Haus, Stephansplatz 12. ✆ **01/53539690.** U-Bahn: Stephansplatz.

Rhiz Bar Modern Hip, multicultural, and electronically sophisticated, with no trace at all of Hapsburg nostalgia, this bar is nested into the vaulted, century-old niches created by the trusses of the U6 subway line, a few blocks west of the Ring. A Web cam constantly broadcasts images of the hipster clientele over the Internet every night from 10pm to 3am. Drinks include Austrian wine, Scottish whisky, and beer from everywhere in Europe. A large beer costs 3.40€ ($5.50). It's open Monday to Saturday 6pm to 4am and Sunday 6pm to 2am. Llerchenfeldergürtel 37–38, Stadtbahnbögen. ✆ **01/409-2505.** www.rhiz.org. U-Bahn: Josefstädterstrasse.

Sacher Eck Even the venerable Sacher has shown that it keeps up with the times, in the form of its street-level cafe, the Sacher-Ecke, a new "Sacher Light" that's a deliberately toned down, more youthful version of the Hapsburgundian dragon represented by the hotel itself. The Sacher-Ecke (literally, "Sacher-Corner") occupies the corner of the Sacher that faces the mobs of pedestrian traffic along the Kärntnerstrasse. Rock music plays softly, and there's wine by the glass, cocktails, and Sachertorte by the slice. Accompanied with a swirl of whipped cream, it's priced at 6€ ($9.60). A Bellini costs 9.50€ ($15); champagne, champagne cocktails, and Sekt go from 7€ to 17€ ($11–$27). A buffet breakfast goes for 25€ ($40) and includes ham, cheese, yogurt, breads, jam, butter, and coffee. It's open daily 9am to 1am. Kärntnerstrasse 38 (corner of Philharmonikerstrasse). ✆ **01/51-456-699.** www.sacher.com/en-sacher-eck.htm. U-Bahn: Karlsplatz.

Schikaneder If you're young and hot, and want to meet locals who share those same traits, come here. There's plenty of conversation, good drinks, and sympathetic company. The bar starts filling up by 9:30pm and by midnight it's packed, often with university students. Don't dare tell anyone in this hip crowd that you're a tourist. Open daily 6pm to 4am. You can also order various wines by the glass. Margaretenstrasse 22–24. ✆ **01/5855888.** www.schikaneder.at. U-Bahn: Margaretengürtel.

Sky Bar ★ Local hipsters ridicule this place as a posh see-and-be-seen venue for Vienna's social striving *nouveaux riches.* We think the place is well designed and, under the right circumstances, can be a lot of fun, particularly when we remind ourselves that the Steffl building was erected on the site of the (long-ago demolished) house where Mozart died. Take an elevator to the top floor of the building for a sweeping view over the city. Open Monday to Saturday 6pm to 2am. Kärntnerstrasse 19. ✆ **01/513-1712.** www.skybar.at. U-Bahn: Karlsplatz.

The Wine Bar at Julius Meinl Part of its allure derives from its role as a showcase for the wine-buying savvy of Vienna's most comprehensive delicatessen (Julius Meinl) and wine shop. It's small and cozy, set in the cellar of a food shop that leaves most gastronomes salivating, and accessible through a separate entrance that's open long after the delicatessen has closed. Within a decor that evokes the interior of a farmhouse on, say, the Austro-Italian border, it features a changing array of wines from around the world, and platters of flavorful but uncomplicated food that's deliberately selected as a foil for (what else?) the wines. You'll be amply satisfied with the dozens of wines listed on the blackboard or on the menu, but if there's a particular bottle you're hankering for in the stacks of wine within the street-level deli, a staff member will sell it to you and uncork it at a surcharge of only 10% more than what you'd have paid for it retail. Glasses of wine cost 3.80€ to 25€ ($6.10–$40); platters of food 9€ to 15€ ($14–$24) each. Open Monday to Saturday 11am to midnight. Graben 19. ✆ **01/532-3334-6100.** www.meinlamgraben.at. U-Bahn: Stephansplatz.

GAY & LESBIAN BARS

Alfi's Goldener Spiegel The most enduring gay restaurant in Vienna (p. 135) is also its most popular gay bar, attracting mostly male clients to its position near Vienna's Naschmarkt. You don't need to come here to dine, but you can patronize the bar, where almost any gay male from abroad drops in for a look-see. The place is very cruisy, and the bar is open Wednesday to Monday 7pm to 2am. Linke Wienzeile 46. ✆ **01/586-6608.** U-Bahn: Kettenbruckengasse.

Café Savoy Soaring frescoed ceilings and a smoke-stained beaux-arts decor that evokes the grand Imperial days of the Hapsburgs make this cruisy cafe/bar an appealing setting. Open Monday to Friday 5pm to 2am, Saturday 9am to 2am. Linke Wienzeile 36. ✆ **01/586-7348.** U-Bahn: Kettenbruckengasse.

Eagle Bar This is one of the premier leather and denim bars for gay men in Vienna. There's no dancing, and the bar even offers a back room where free condoms are distributed. It's open daily 9pm to 4am. Large beers begin at 3€ ($4.80). Blümelgasse 1. ✆ **01/587-26-61.** www.eagle-vienna.com. U-Bahn: Neubaugasse.

Felixx ★ It's the classiest gay bar and cafe in town, thanks to a refurbishment. The decor emphasizes turn-of-the-20th-century cove moldings, a crystal chandelier that could proudly grace any Opera Ball, and a huge late-19th-century portrait of the female cabaret entertainer, Mela Mars, who introduced *lieder* (live singing) for the first time to a generation of wine- and coffee-drinkers. Ironically, the venue is less kitschy than you'd think, managing to pull off a lasting impression of elegance and good taste. On Saturday and Sunday, breakfast is served here from 10am to 4pm. Open daily 7pm to 3am. Gumpendorferstrasse 5. ✆ **01/920-4714.** U-Bahn: Babenbergerstrasse or MuseumsQuartier.

Frauencafé Frauencafé is exactly what a translation of its name would imply: a politically conscious café for lesbian and (to a lesser degree) heterosexual women who appreciate the company of other women. Established in 1977 in the cramped quarters of a century-old building, it's filled with magazines, newspapers, modern paintings, and a clientele of Austrian and foreign women. Next door is a feminist bookstore loosely affiliated with the cafe. Frauencafé is open Tuesday to Saturday 6:30pm to 2am. Glasses of wine begin at 2.50€ ($4). Langegasse 11. ✆ **01/4063754.** www.frauencafe.com. U-Bahn: Lerchenfelderstrasse.

HEURIGEN

These wine taverns on the outskirts of Vienna have long been celebrated in operetta, film, and song. Grinzing is the most visited district, but other *heurigen* neighborhoods include Sievering, Neustift, Nussdorf, or Heiligenstadt.

Grinzing lies at the edge of the Vienna Woods, a short distance northwest of the center. Once it was a separate village, now overtaken by the ever-increasing city boundaries of Vienna. Much of Grinzing remains unchanged and looks the same as it did in the days when Beethoven lived nearby. It's a district of crooked old streets and houses, their thick walls built around inner courtyards where grape arbors shelter Viennese wine drinkers on a summer night. The sound of zithers and accordions lasts long into the night.

Which brings up another point. If you're a motorist, don't drive out to the *heurigen.* Police patrols are very strict, and you're not allowed to drive with more than .08% alcohol in your bloodstream. It's much better to take public transportation. Most *heurigen* are reached in 30 to 40 minutes. Take tram no. 1 from Schottentor, and change there for tram no. 38 to Grinzing or Sievering, or no. 41 to Neustift am Wald. Sievering is also reached by bus no. 39A. Heiligenstadt is reached by U-Bahn no. 4.

We'll start you off with some of our favorites.

Alter Klosterkeller im Passauerhof One of Vienna's well-known wine taverns, this spot maintains an old-fashioned ambience little changed since the turn of the 20th century. Specialties include such familiar fare as *tafelspitz,* an array of roasts, and plenty of strudel. Main courses range from 15€ to 25€ ($24–$40). Drinks begin at 3€ ($4.80). It's open daily 5pm until midnight. Live music is played from 6 to midnight. It's closed January to mid-March. Cobenzigasse 9, Grinzing. ✆ **01/320-6345.**

Der Rudolfshof ★ One of the most appealing wine restaurants in Grinzing dates back to 1848, when it was little more than a shack within a garden. Its real fame came around the turn of the 20th century, when Crown Prince Rudolf, son of Emperor Franz Josef, adopted it as his favorite watering hole. A verdant garden, scattered with tables, is favored by Viennese apartment dwellers on warm summer evenings. Inside, portraits of Rudolf decorate a setting that evokes an old-fashioned hunting lodge. Come here for pitchers of the fruity white wine *grüner Veltliner* and a light red, *roter Bok.* Glasses of wine cost 3€ to 5€ ($4.80–$8). The menu lists schnitzels, roasts, and soups, but the house specialty is shish kabob. The salad bar is very fresh. Main courses cost 10€ to 13€ ($16–$21). Open daily 3 to 11pm. Cobenzlgasse 8, Grinzing. ✆ **01/32021-08.** www.rudolfshof.at.

Heurige Mayer ★ This historic house was some 130 years old when Beethoven composed sections of his *Ninth Symphony* while living here in 1817. The same kind of fruity dry wine is still sold to guests in the shady courtyard of the rose garden. The menu includes grilled chicken, savory pork, and a buffet of well-prepared country food. Reservations are suggested. It's open Monday to Friday 4pm to midnight, and on Sunday and holidays 4pm to midnight. Live music is played every Sunday and Friday 7pm to midnight. Closed Saturday. Wine sells for 1.40€ ($2.30) a glass, with meals beginning at 13€ ($21). It's closed December 21 to January 15. Am Pfarrplatz 2, Heiligenstadt. ✆ **01/3703361,** or 01/370-1287 after 4pm.

Weingut Wolff Although aficionados claim that the best *heurigen* are "deep in the countryside" of lower Austria, this one comes closest to offering an authentic experience just 20 minutes from the center of Vienna. In summer, you're welcomed into a flower-decked garden set against a backdrop of ancient vineyards. You can fill up your platter with some of the best wursts and roast meats (especially the delectable pork), along with freshly made salads. Save room for one of the luscious and velvety-smooth Austrian cakes. Find a table under a cluster of grapes and sample the fruity young wines, especially the chardonnay, Sylvaner, or *gruner Veltliner.* The tavern is open daily 11am to 1am, with main courses ranging from 8€ to 15€ ($13–$24). Rathstrasse 50, Neustift. ✆ **01/440-3727.** www.wienerheuriger.at.

Zum Figlmüller One of the city's most popular wine restaurants is this suburban branch of Vienna's Figlmüller. Although there's a set of indoor dining rooms, most visitors prefer the flowering terrace with its romantic garden. The restaurant prides itself on serving wines produced only under its own supervision, beginning at 3€ ($4.80) per glass. Meals include a wide array of light salads, as well as more substantial food. Prices range from 7€ to 15€ ($11–$24). Open daily 11:30am to midnight. Grinzinger Strasse 55, Grinzing. ✆ **01/320-4257.** www.figlmueller.at.

12 MORE ENTERTAINMENT

CASINO

Casino Wien You'll need to show your passport to get into this casino, opened in 1968. There are gaming tables for French and American roulette, blackjack, and chemin de fer, as well as the ever-present slot machines. The casino is open daily 11am to 3am, with the tables closing at 3pm. Esterházy Palace, Kärntnerstrasse 41. ✆ **01/512-4836.** www.casinos.at.

FILMS

Filmmuseum This cinema shows films in their original languages and presents retrospectives of such directors as Fritz Lang. The museum presents avant-garde, experimental, and classic films. A monthly program is available free inside the Albertina, and a copy is posted outside. The film library inside the government-funded museum includes more than 11,000 book titles, and the still collection numbers more than 100,000. Admission costs 9.50€ ($15) for nonmembers. Membership for 24 hours costs 5.50€ ($8.80). In the Albertina, Augustinerstrasse 1. ✆ **01/533-7054.** www.filmmuseum.at. U-Bahn: Karlsplatz.

13 ONLY IN VIENNA

We've recommended a variety of nightspots, but none seems to capture the true Viennese spirit quite like the establishments below. Each has its own atmosphere and decor, and each continues to retain uniquely Viennese.

Alt Wien Set on one of the oldest, narrowest streets of medieval Vienna, a short walk north of the cathedral, this is the kind of smoky, mysterious, and shadowy cafe that evokes subversive plots, doomed romances, and revolutionary movements being hatched and plotted. During the day, it's a busy workaday restaurant patronized by virtually everybody. But as the night progresses, you're likely to rub elbows with denizens of late-night Wien who get more sentimental and schmaltzy with each beer. Foaming mugs sell for 3€ ($4.80) each and can be accompanied by heaping platters of goulash and schnitzels. Main courses range from 6€ to 10€ ($9.60–$16). It's open daily 10am to 2am. Bäckerstrasse 9 (1). ✆ **01/512-5222.** U-Bahn: Stephansplatz.

Karl Kolarik's Schweizerhaus References to this old-fashioned eating house are about as old as the Prater itself. Awash with beer and central European kitsch, it sprawls across a *biergarten* landscape that might remind you of the Hapsburg Empire at its most indulgent. Indulgence is indeed the word—the vastly proportioned main dishes could feed an entire 19th-century army. The menu stresses old-fashioned schnitzels and its house specialty, roasted pork hocks *(Hintere Schweinsstelze)* served with dollops of mustard and horseradish. Wash it all down with mugs of Czech Budweiser. A half-liter of beer costs 3.70€ ($5.90); main courses range from 5€ to 12€ ($8–$19). It's open from March 15 to October 31 daily 11am to 11pm. In the Prater, Strasse des Ersten Mai 116. ✆ **01/728-01-52.** U-Bahn: Praterstern.

Möbel Locals perch along the long stainless-steel countertop for a glass of wine, a coffee, and light platters of food. But what makes this cafe-cum-art-gallery unusual is the hypermodern furniture that's for sale, ranging from coffee tables and reclining chairs to bookshelves and even a ceramic-sided wood-burning stove priced at 1,300€ ($2,080). Baguettes cost 4.90€ ($7.90), and glasses of wine range from 1.80€ to 3€ ($2.90–$4.80). It's open daily 10am to 1am. Burggasse 10. ✆ **01/524-9497.** www.dasmoebel.at. U-Bahn: Volkstheater.

Pavillion Even the Viennese stumble when trying to describe this civic monument from the Sputnik-era of the 1950s. During the day, it's a cozy cafe with a multigenerational clientele and a sweeping garden overlooking the Heldenplatz (forecourt to the Hofburg). Come here to peruse the newspapers, chat with locals, and drink coffee, wine, beer, or schnapps. The place grows much more animated after the music (funk, soul, blues, and jazz) begins around 8pm. Platters of Viennese food are priced from 6.50€ to 12€ ($10–$19). It's open daily 9am to 2am between April and October. Burgring 2. ✆ **01/532-0907.** U-Bahn: Volkstheater.

Schnitzelwirt Schmidt The waitresses wear dirndls, the portions are huge, and the cuisine—only pork and some chicken—celebrates the culinary folklore of central Europe. The setting is rustic, a kind of tongue-in-cheek bucolic homage to the Old Vienna Woods, and schnitzels are almost guaranteed to hang over the sides of the plates. Regardless of what you order, it will be accompanied by french fries, salad, and copious quantities of beer and wine. Go for the good value, unmistakably Viennese ambience, and great people-watching. Main courses cost 6€ to 10€ ($9.60–$16). It's open Monday to Saturday 11am to 10pm. Neubaugasse 52 (7). ✆ **01/523-3771.** U-Bahn: Mariahilferstrasse. Tram: 49.

Wiener Stamperl (The Viennese Dram) Named after a medieval unit of liquid measurement, this is about as beer-soaked and as rowdy a nighttime venue as we're willing to recommend. It occupies a battered, woodsy-looking room reeking of spilled beer, stale smoke, and the unmistakable scent of hundreds of boisterous drinkers. At the horseshoe-shape bar, order foaming steins of Ottakinger beer or glasses of new wine from nearby vineyards, served from an old-fashioned barrel. The menu consists entirely of an array of coarse bread slathered with spicy, high-cholesterol ingredients, such as various wursts and cheeses and, for anyone devoted to authentic old-time cuisine, lard specked with bits of bacon. It's open Monday to Thursday 11am to 2am, and Friday and Saturday 11pm to 4am. Sterngasse 1. ✆ **01/533-6230.** U-Bahn: Schwedenplatz.

7

Lower Austria

Lower Austria (Niederösterreich), known as "the cradle of Austria's history," is the largest of the nine federal states that make up the country today. Although the province is located to the east of *Upper* Austria, it's named *Lower* Austria because it sits lower on the Danube, which flows through it from west to east. The 19,171 sq. km (7,402 sq. miles) of the state are bordered on the north by the Czech Republic, on the east by Slovakia, on the south by the province of Styria, and on the west by Upper Austria. It lies on Vienna's doorstep and can easily be visited from there.

This historic area was once heavily fortified, as some 550 fortresses and castles testify—many are still standing, but often in ruins. The medieval Kuenringer and Babenberger dynasties had their hereditary estates here. At the foothills of the Alps is Wiener Neustadt, the former imperial city. Along the Danube, Dürnstein, with terraced vineyards, was where Richard the Lion-Hearted was held prisoner. Many monasteries and churches, from Romanesque and Gothic structures to the much later baroque abbeys, are also found in Lower Austria. Klosterneuburg Abbey dates from 1114, and Heiligenkreuz, founded in 1133, is the country's most ancient Cistercian abbey. The province is filled with vineyards, and in summer it booms with music festivals and classical and contemporary theater.

It's relatively inexpensive to travel in Lower Austria—prices here are about 30% lower than those in Vienna, Salzburg, and Innsbruck. This price differential explains why many travelers stay in one of the neighboring towns of Lower Austria when they come to explore Vienna.

One of Lower Austria's most celebrated districts is the Waldviertel-Weinviertel (a *Viertel* is a traditional division of Lower Austria). In this case, the Viertels are the woods *(Wald)* and wine *(Wein)* areas. They contain thousands of miles of marked hiking paths and many mellow old wine cellars.

Some 60% of Austria's grape harvest is produced in Lower Austria, from the rolling hillsides of the Wienerwald to the terraces of the Wachau. Many visitors like to take a "wine route" through the province, stopping often at cozy taverns to sample the local vintages of Krems, Klosterneuburg, Dürnstein, Langenlois, Retz, Gumpoldskirchen, Poysdorf, and other towns.

Lower Austria is also home to more than a dozen spa resorts, including Baden, the most frequented. Innkeepers welcome families with children at these resorts, which can be an inviting retreat from the city. Most hotels accommodate children up to 6 years old for free; children ages 7 to 12 stay for half price. Many towns and villages have attractions designed especially for kids. Some hotels have only a postal code for an address, as they do not lie on a street plan. (If you're writing to them, this postal code is their complete address.) When you reach one of these small towns, finding a hotel isn't a problem because they're signposted at the various approaches to the resort or village. Parking is rarely a problem in these places, and, unless otherwise noted, you park for free.

1 THE WIENERWALD (VIENNA WOODS) ★

The **Vienna Woods**—romanticized in operetta, literature, and the famous Strauss waltz—stretch all the way from Vienna's city limits to the foothills of the Alps to the south. You can hike through the woods along marked paths or take a leisurely drive, stopping off at country towns to sample the wine and the local cuisine, which is usually hearty, filling, and reasonably priced. The Viennese and a horde of foreign tourists, principally German, usually descend on the local wine taverns and cellars on weekends—we advise you to make any summer visit on a weekday. The best time of year to go is in September and October, when the grapes are harvested from the terraced hills.

ESSENTIALS

GETTING THERE You can visit the expansive and pastoral Vienna Woods by car or by public transportation. We recommend renting a car so you can stop and explore some of the villages and vineyards along the way. Public transportation will get you around, but it will take much more time. Either way, you can easily reach all of the destinations listed below within a day's trip from Vienna. If you have more time, spend the night in one or more of the quintessential Austrian towns along the way.

VISITOR INFORMATION Before you go, visit the tourist office for **Klosterneuburg** at Niedermarkt 4, A-3400 (✆ **02243/32038;** www.klosterneuburg.com). It's the best source of information for the Vienna Woods, and is open daily 10am to 7pm.

ORGANIZED TOURS **Vienna Sightseeing Tours,** Starhemberggasse 25 (✆ **01/712-468-30;** fax 01/714-11-41; www.viennasightseeingtours.com), runs a popular 4-hour tour called "Vienna Woods–Mayerling." It goes through the Vienna Woods, past the Castle of Liechtenstein and the old Roman city of Baden. There's an excursion to Mayerling. You'll also go to the Cistercian abbey of Heiligenkreuz-Höldrichsmühle-Seegrotte and take a boat ride on Seegrotte, the largest subterranean lake in Europe. The office is open for tours April to October daily 6:30am to 7:30pm, and November to March daily 6:30am to 5pm. It costs 43€ ($69) for adults and 15€ ($24) for children, including admission fees and a guide.

KLOSTERNEUBURG

On the northwestern outskirts of Vienna, Klosterneuburg is an old market town in the major wine-producing center of Austria. The Babenbergs founded the town in the eastern foothills of the Vienna Woods, making it an ideal spot to enjoy the countryside within easy reach of Vienna, 11km (7 miles) southeast.

Austrians and tourists gather in Klosterneuburg annually to celebrate St. Leopold's Day on November 15, with music, banquets, and a parade.

Essentials

GETTING THERE If you're driving from Vienna, take Route 14 northwest, following the south bank of the Danube to Klosterneuburg. By public transportation, take the U-Bahn to Heiligenstadt, where you can then board bus no. 239 or 341 to Klosterneuburg, or catch the S-Bahn from Franz-Josef Bahnhof to Klosterneuburg-Kierling.

Klosterneuburg Abbey

Stift Klosterneuburg (Klosterneuburg Abbey) ★, Stiftsplatz 1 (✆ **02243/41212**), is the most significant abbey in Austria. It was founded in 1114 by the Babenberg margrave Leopold III and was once the residence of the famous Hapsburg emperor Charles VI.

The abbey is visited not only for its history, but also for its art treasures. The most valuable piece is the world-famous enamel altar of Nikolaus of Verdun, created in 1181. The monastery also boasts the largest private library in Austria, with more than 1,250 handwritten books and many antique paintings. Guided tours of the monastery are given daily year-round. On the tour, you visit the Cathedral of the Monastery (unless Masses are underway), the cloister, St. Leopold's Chapel (with the Verdun altar), the former well house, and the residential apartments of the emperors.

The monastery itself remains open year-round, but the museum of the monastery is closed from mid-November to April. The museum can be visited without a guide from May to mid-November Tuesday to Sunday 10am to 5pm. Visits to the monastery itself, however, require participation in a guided tour. These are available at hourly intervals year-round daily from 9am to noon and 1:30 to 4:30pm. Except for a specially designated English-language tour conducted every Sunday at 2pm, most tours are conducted in German, with occasional snippets of English if the guide is able. The price is 8€ ($13) for adults and 5€ ($8) for children. Additional English-language tours can be arranged in advance. You can purchase a cost-effective combination ticket to the monastery and museum for 12€ ($18) for adults and 7€ ($11) for children 6 to 14.

Where to Stay & Dine

Hotel Josef Buschenretter Built in 1970, 1.6km (a mile) south of the town center, this hotel is white-walled with a mansard roof rising above the balcony on the fourth floor. A roof terrace and a cozy bar provide diversion for hotel guests. The well-kept medium-size bedrooms are comfortably furnished and have bathrooms equipped with shower units.

Wienerstrasse 188, A-3400 Klosterneuburg. ✆ **02243/32385.** Fax 02243/3238-5160. www.hotel-buschenretter.at. 30 units. 78€ ($125) double. Rates include buffet breakfast. AE, DC, MC, V. Free parking. Closed Dec 15–Jan 15. **Amenities:** Breakfast-only restaurant; bar; indoor heated pool. *In room:* TV.

Hotel Schrannenhof Originally dating from the Middle Ages, this hotel has been completely renovated and modernized. The owners rent guest rooms with large living and sleeping rooms and small kitchens, as well as quiet and comfortable double rooms with showers. International and Austrian specialties are served in Veit, the hotel's cafe-restaurant next door. The hotel also runs the Pension Alte Mühle (see below).

Niedermarkt 17–19, A-3400 Klosterneuburg. ✆ **02243/32072.** Fax 02243/320-7213. www.schrannenhof.at. 14 units. 92€–108€ ($147–$173) double; 128€ ($205) suite. Rates include buffet breakfast. AE, DC, MC. Free parking. **Amenities:** Breakfast room; lounge. *In room:* A/C (in some), TV, kitchenette (in some), minibar, hair dryer, safe.

Pension Alte Mühle Housed in a simple two-story building from the 1930s, this hotel is gracious and hospitable. The breakfast room offers a bountiful morning buffet; the comfortable restaurant-cafe, Veit, is only 800m (2,624 ft.) away. Bedrooms are furnished in a cozy, traditional style, with well-maintained, if small, private bathrooms with shower units. The Veit family owns the place, and in summer their pleasant garden lures guests.

Mühlengasse 36, A-3400 Klosterneuburg. ✆ **02243/37788.** Fax 02243/377-8822. www.hotel-altemuehle.at. 13 units. 80€ ($128) double. Rates include breakfast. AE, DC, MC. Free parking. **Amenities:** Breakfast room; laundry service. *In room:* TV, minibar, hair dryer, safe.

PERCHTOLDSDORF: A STOP ON THE WINE TOUR

This old market town with colorful buildings, referred to locally as Petersdorf, is one of the most visited spots in Lower Austria when the Viennese go on a wine tour. You'll find many *heurigen* here, where you can sample local wines and enjoy good, hearty cuisine. Perchtoldsdorf is not as well known as Grinzing, which is actually within the city limits of Vienna, but many visitors find it less touristy. It has a Gothic church, and part of its defense tower dates from the early 16th century. A vintners' festival, held annually in early November, attracts many Viennese. Local growers make a "goat" from grapes for this festive occasion.

Essentials

GETTING THERE Perchtoldsdorf lies 18km (11 miles) from the center of Vienna (it's actually at the southwestern city limits) and 14km (9 miles) north of Baden. From Vienna's Westbahnhof, you can take the S-Bahn to Liesing. From here, Perchtoldsdorf is just a short taxi ride away (cabs are found at the train station).

VISITOR INFORMATION The **tourist information office,** in the center of Perchtoldsdorf (✆ **01/536100;** www.noe.co.at), is open Monday to Friday 8:30am to 4pm.

Restaurant Jahreszeiten ★ AUSTRIAN/FRENCH/INTERNATIONAL Set within what was a private villa in the 1800s, this restaurant, the best in town, provides a haven for escapist Viennese looking for hints of the country life. In a pair of elegantly rustic dining rooms illuminated at night with flickering candles, you can enjoy such well-crafted dishes as rare poached salmon served with herbs and truffled noodles, Chinese-style prawns in an Asiatic sauce prepared by the kitchen's Japanese cooks, and filet of turbot with morels and asparagus-studded risotto. Try a soufflé for dessert. A tremendous effort is made to secure the freshest produce. Service is polite, hardworking, and discreet.

Hochstrasse 17. ✆ **01/8656080.** www.jahreszeiten.at. Reservations recommended. Main courses 14€–20€ ($22–$32). Set menus 30€ ($48). AE, DC, MC, V. Daily 11:30am–11pm. Closed 3 weeks in Aug.

HINTERBRÜHL

You'll find good accommodations and good food in this hamlet that is really no more than a cluster of bucolic homes, much favored by Viennese who like to escape the city for a long weekend. Hinterbrühl holds memories of Franz Schubert, who wrote *Der Lindenbaum* here. This tiny area is also home to Europe's largest subterranean lake (see below).

Essentials

GETTING THERE The village is 26km (16 miles) south of Vienna and 3km (2 miles) south of Mölding, the nearest large town. To reach Hinterbrühl from Vienna, take the S-Bahn from the Südbahnhof to Mölding (trip time: 15 min.) and then catch a connecting bus to Hinterbrühl, the last stop (12 min.). By car, drive southwest along the A21, exiting at the signs to Gisshubel. From there, follow the signs to Hinterbrühl and Mölding.

VISITOR INFORMATION The **tourist information office,** in Kaiserin-Elisabeth 2, Mölding (✆ **02236/26727**), is open Monday to Friday 9am to 5pm.

An Underground Lake

Seegrotte Hinterbrühl ★ Finds Some of the village of Hinterbrühl was built directly above the stalactite-covered waters of Europe's largest underground lake. From the entrance a few hundred yards from the edge of town, you'll descend a steep flight of stairs before facing the extensively illuminated waters of a shallow, very still, and very cold underground lake. The famous natural marvel was the site of the construction of the world's first jet plane and other aircraft during World War II. Expect a running commentary in German and broken English during the 20-minute boat ride.

Grutschgasse 2A, Hinterbrühl. ✆ **02235/26364.** www.seagrotte.at. Admission and boat ride 9€ ($14) adult, 6€ ($9.60) children under 14 and students. Apr–Oct daily 9am–5pm; Nov–Mar Mon–Fri 9am–noon and 1–3pm, Sat–Sun 9am–3:30pm.

Where to Stay

Hotel Beethoven This hotel in the heart of the hamlet boasts one of the village's oldest buildings, a private house originally constructed around 1785. In 1992, the hotel renovated most of the interior and built a new wing. It was again renovated in 2002. The average-size bedrooms are cozy, traditional, and well maintained, with good beds and adequate bathrooms equipped mostly with tub/shower combinations. There's no formal restaurant on the premises, but management maintains an all-day cafe where coffee, drinks, pastries, ice cream, salads, and platters of regional food are served daily.

Beethovengasse 8, A-2371 Hinterbrühl. ✆ **02236/26252.** Fax 02236/277017. www.hotel-beethoven.cc. 25 units. 84€–92€ ($134–$147) double. Rates include buffet breakfast. AE, DC, MC, V. Free parking. **Amenities:** Cafe; bar. *In room:* TV, minibar, hair dryer, safe (in some).

Where to Dine

Restaurant Hexensitz ★ AUSTRIAN/INTERNATIONAL Featuring impeccable service, this restaurant celebrates the subtleties of Austrian country cooking. Its upscale setting is a century-old building whose trio of dining rooms are outfitted "in the Lower Austrian style," with wood paneling and country antiques. In summer, the restaurant expands outward into a well-kept garden. It offers daily changing dishes such as Styrian venison with kohlrabi, wine sauce, and homemade noodles; medallions of pork with spinach and herbs; and sea bass with forest mushrooms. The traditional desserts are luscious. The kitchen personnel are devoted and professional, and the food is savory and nearly always delightful.

Johannesstrasse 35. ✆ **02236/22937.** www.hexensitz.at. Reservations recommended. Main courses 12€–22€ ($19–$35); fixed-price lunch 25€ ($40) available on Sun; fixed-price dinner 40€ ($64). MC, V. Tues 6–10pm; Wed–Sat 11:30am–2pm and 6–10pm; Sun 11:30am–2pm.

MAYERLING

This beautiful spot, 29km (18 miles) west of Vienna in the heart of the Wienerwald, is best known for the unresolved deaths of Archduke Rudolf, son of Emperor Franz Joseph, and his mistress in 1889. The event, which took place in a hunting lodge (now a Carmelite convent), altered the line of Austro-Hungarian succession. The heir apparent became Franz Joseph's nephew, Archduke Ferdinand, whose murder in Sarajevo sparked World War I. Mayerling, incidentally, is only a small hamlet, not even a village.

Essentials

GETTING THERE By **car,** head southwest on A-21 to Alland and take 210 to Mayerling. Or take **bus** no. 1123, 1124, or 1127, marked ALLAND, from Vienna's Südtirolerplatz (trip time: 90 min.). From Baden, hop on bus no. 1140 or 1141.

VISITOR INFORMATION Contact the local authorities at the **Rathaus,** in nearby Heiligenkreuz (✆ **02258/8720;** www.heiligenkreuz.at). It's open Monday to Friday 8am to noon and 2 to 5pm.

Seeing the Sights

Abbey Heiligenkreuz (Abbey of the Holy Cross) Margrave Leopold III founded this abbey. It was built in the 12th century and subsequently gained an overlay of Gothic and baroque additions, with some 13th- and 14th-century stained glass still in place. The Romanesque and Gothic cloisters, with some 300 pillars of red marble, date from 1240. Some of the dukes of Babenberg were buried in the chapter house, including Duke Friedrich II, the last of his line. Heiligenkreuz has more relics of the Holy Cross than any other site in Europe except Rome.

Today a vital community of 50 Cistercian monks lives in Heiligenkreuz. In summer, at noon and 6pm daily, visitors can attend the solemn choir prayers.

Heiligenkreuz. ✆ **02258/8703.** Admission 6.60€ ($11) adults, 3.30€ ($5.30) children. Daily 9–11:30am and 1:30–5pm (until 4pm Nov–Feb). Tours daily 10 and 11am and 2 and 3pm, plus 4pm Easter–Sept. From Mayerling, take Heiliqenkreuzstrasse 4.8km (3 miles) to Heiligenkreuz.

Jagdschloss A Carmelite abbey, Karmeliten Kloster Mayerling, stands on the site of the infamous hunting lodge where Archduke Rudolf and his mistress supposedly committed suicide (see "Twilight of the Hapsburgs," below). If it hadn't been torn down, the

Twilight of the Hapsburgs

On January 30, 1889, a hunting lodge in Mayerling was the setting of a grim tragedy that altered the line of succession of the Austro-Hungarian Empire and shocked the world. On a snowy night, Archduke Rudolf, the only son of Emperor Franz Joseph and Empress Elisabeth, and his 18-year-old mistress, Maria Vetsera, were found dead. It was announced that they had shot themselves, although no weapon ever surfaced for examination. All doors and windows to the room had been locked when the bodies were discovered. All evidence that might have shed light on the deaths was subsequently destroyed. Had it been a double suicide or an assassination?

Rudolf, a sensitive eccentric, was locked in an unhappy marriage, and neither his father nor Pope Leo XIII would allow an annulment. He had fallen in love with Maria at a German embassy ball when she was only 17. Maria's public snubbing of Archduchess Stephanie of Belgium, Rudolf's wife, at a reception given by the German ambassador to Vienna led to a heated argument between Rudolf and his father. Because of the young archduke's liberal leanings and sympathy for certain Hungarian partisans, he was not popular with his country's aristocracy, which gave rise to lurid speculation about a cleverly designed plot. Supporters of the assassination theory included Empress Zita von Hapsburg, the last Hapsburg heir, who in 1982 told the Vienna daily *Kronen Zeitung* that she believed their deaths were the culmination of a conspiracy against the family. Franz Joseph, grief-stricken at the loss of his only son, ordered the hunting lodge torn down and a Carmelite nunnery built in its place.

Maria Vetsera was buried in a village cemetery in Heiligenkreuz. The inscription over her tomb reads, *Wie eine Blume sprosst der mensch auf und wird gebrochen* ("Human beings, like flowers, bloom and are crushed"). In a curious incident in 1988, her coffin was exhumed and stolen by a Linz executive, who was distraught at the death of his wife and obsessed with the Mayerling affair. It took police 4 years to recover the coffin.

hunting lodge would be a much more fascinating—if macabre—attraction. Although nothing remains of the lodge, history buffs enjoy visiting the abbey.

Mayerling. ✆ **02258/2275.** Admission 3€ ($4.80) adults, 1.50€ ($2.40) children under 14. Mon–Sat 9am–6pm (5pm Oct–Mar); Sun 10am–6pm (5pm Oct–Mar).

Where to Stay & Dine

Hotel Hanner The best hotel in town rises three stories, in a conservative but very modern format of respectability and charm. Bedrooms are streamlined, comfortable, and modern, with a color scheme that varies slightly, each from its neighbor, in its use of pastels. Guests appreciate the calm, the quiet, and the proximity to the acres of natural beauty in the surrounding region.

Mayerling #1, A-2534 Mayerling. ✆ **02258/2378.** www.hanner.cc. Fax 02258/237841. 27 units. 142€–208€ ($227–$333) double. Rates include breakfast. AE, DC, MC, V. Free parking. **Amenities:** Restaurant; bar; fitness center; sauna; room service; laundry; dry cleaning; nonsmoking rooms. *In room:* TV, minibar, hair dryer, safe.

Restaurant Hanner AUSTRIAN Dignified, conservatively modern, and well managed, this is the best restaurant in a town not noted for lots of competition. Large windows take in a panoramic view over the surrounding forests, and dishes change with the seasons and according to the whim of the chef. Examples include fresh fish, goulash, breast of chicken with paprika-flavored noodles, and filets of venison in port-wine sauce.

In the Hotel Hanner, Mayerling #1. ✆ **02258/2378.** Reservations not necessary. Main courses 15€–40€ ($24–$64); 5-course tasting menu 98€ ($157); 7-course tasting menu 118€ ($189). AE, DC, MC, V. Daily noon–2pm and 6–10pm.

2 THE SPA TOWN OF BADEN BEI WIEN ★

24km (15 miles) SW of Vienna; 299km (186 miles) E of Salzburg

Around A.D. 100, the Romans were drawn to Aquae, the name they gave to Baden, by its 15 thermal springs whose temperatures reach 95°F (35°C). You can still see the **Römerquelle (Roman Spring)** in the Kurpark, which is the center of **Baden bei Wien** ★ today. The resort is officially named Baden bei Wien to differentiate it from other Badens not near Vienna.

Czar Peter the Great of Russia ushered in Baden's golden age by establishing a spa there at the beginning of the 18th century. The Soviet army used the resort city as its occupation headquarters from the end of World War II to 1955, but the Russians left little mark on "the dowager empress of European health spas."

Although the spa was at its most fashionable in the early 18th century, it continued to lure royalty and their entourages, musicians, and intellectuals for much of the 19th century. This lively casino town and spa in the eastern sector of the Vienna Woods was for years the summer residence of the Hapsburg court. In 1803, Franz I began annual summer visits to Baden.

During the mid- to late 19th century, Baden became known for its Schönbrunn yellow (Maria Theresia ocher) Biedermeier buildings, which still contribute to the city's charm. The Kurpark, Baden's center, is handsomely laid out and beautifully maintained. Public concerts performed here pay tribute to great Austrian composers.

The bathing complex was constructed over more than a dozen sulfur springs. Visitors today flock to the half-dozen bath establishments, as well as the four outdoor thermal springs. These springs reach temperatures ranging from 75° to 95°F (24°–35°C). The thermal complex also has a "sandy beach" and a restaurant. It lies west of the center in the Doblhoffpark, a natural park featuring a lake where you can rent sailboats. There's also a rose garden restaurant in the park.

ESSENTIALS

GETTING THERE If you're driving from Vienna, head south on Autobahn A2, cutting west at the junction of Route 210, which leads to Baden. By train, Baden is a local rather than an express stop. Trains depart daily from 4:40am to midnight from Vienna's Südbahnhof (trip time: 20 min.). For schedules, call ✆ **05/1717** in Vienna, or check **www.oebb.at**. By bus, the Badner Bahn leaves every 15 minutes from the Staatsoper (trip time: 1 hr.).

VISITOR INFORMATION The **tourist information office,** at Brusattiplatz 3 (✆ **02252/22-600-600;** www.baden.at), is open Monday to Friday 9am to 6pm, Saturday 9am to 2pm. From October to April, the office is closed on Saturday and Sunday.

In the Hauptplatz (Main Square) is the **Trinity Column,** built in 1714, which commemorates the lifting of the plague that swept over Vienna and the Wienerwald in the Middle Ages. Also here are the **Rathaus** (✆ **02252/86800**) and, at no. 17, the **Kaiserhaus,** Franz II's summer residence from 1813 to 1834.

Every summer between 1821 and 1823, Beethoven rented the upper floor of a modest house, above what used to be a shop on the Rathausgasse, in Baden, for about 2 weeks, hoping to find a cure for his increasing deafness. The site has been reconfigured by the city of Baden into a small museum commemorating the time he spent here, at **Beethovenhaus,** Rathausgasse 10 (✆ **02252/868-00230**). Inside you'll find a trio of small, relatively modest rooms, furnished with one of Beethoven's pianos, his bed, several pieces of porcelain, photographs of others of his residences around the German-speaking world, some mementos, and copies of the musical folios he completed (or at least worked on) during his time in Baden. The museum is open year-round Tuesday to Friday 4 to 6pm, and Saturday and Sunday 10am to noon and 4 to 6pm. Admission is 3€ ($4.80) for adults, 1.50€ ($2.40) for students and children under 18, free for children under 6.

Among the other sights in Baden, there's a celebrated death mask collection at the **Stadtisches Rolletmuseum,** Weikersdorfer-Platz 1 (✆ **02252/48255**). The museum possesses many items of historic and artistic interest. Furniture and the art of the Biedermeier period are especially represented. It's open Monday to Wednesday and Friday to Sunday 3 to 6pm. Admission is 3€ ($4.80) for adults and 1.50€ ($2.40) for children. To reach the museum from Hauptplatz, go south to Josefs Platz and then continue south along Vöslauer Strasse, cutting right when you come to Elisabeth Strasse, which leads directly to the square on which the museum sits.

Northeast of Hauptplatz on the Franz-Kaiser Ring is the **Stadttheater** (✆ **02252/48338**), built in 1909, and on nearby Pfarrgasse, the 15th-century parish church of **St. Stephan's** (✆ **02252/48426**). Inside there's a commemorative plaque to Mozart, who allegedly composed his *Ave Verum* here for the parish choirmaster.

The real reason to come to Baden is the sprawling and beautiful **Kurpark** ★. Here you can attend concerts, plays, and operas at an open-air theater, or try your luck at the casino (see "Baden After Dark," below). The Römerquelle (Roman Springs) can be seen gurgling from an intricate rock basin, which is surrounded by monuments to Beethoven, Mozart, and the great playwright Grillparzer. From the park's numerous paths you can view Baden and the surrounding hills.

Taking a Bath

As you might expect from waters which have attracted health-seekers for thousands of years, there are several different ways you can experience the local mineral baths. The **Kurhaus** (also known sometimes as the **Kurzentrum**), at Brussatiplatz 4 (✆ **02252/44531**), in the heart of town, is a strictly medical facility, which requires doctors' appointments in advance. The less structured enterprise immediately next door (also at Brussatiplatz 4; same phone), is the *Römertherme,* a complex of hot mineral baths, which are open, with no reservations needed, to anyone who shows up. The *Römertherme* charges according to how long you spend inside. Two hours (the minimum charge) costs 9.10€ ($15), with each additional hour priced at 1.60€ ($2.60). A full day is 13€ ($21) per person, unless you opt to enter after 8pm, in which event you'll pay 4.60€ ($7.40). Access to any of the saunas inside costs an additional 3.80€ ($6.10), and access to the exercise and fitness area is 12€ ($19) per person.

WHERE TO STAY

Expensive

Grand Hotel Sauerhof zu Rauhenstein ★ Although this estate dates to 1583, it became famous in 1757, when a sulfur-enriched spring bubbled up after a cataclysmic earthquake in faraway Portugal. The present building was constructed in 1810 on the site of that spring, which continues to supply water to its spa facilities today. In the past, the property served as an army rehabilitation center, a sanatorium during the two world wars, and headquarters for the Russian army. In 1978, after extravagant renovations, the Sauerhof reopened as one of the region's most upscale spa hotels.

The neoclassical building, with a steep slate roof, rambles across a wide lawn. Few of the original furnishings remain, and the management has collected a handful of vintage Biedermeier sofas and chairs to fill the elegant but somewhat underfurnished public rooms. A covered courtyard, styled on ancient Rome, has a vaulted ceiling supported by chiseled stone columns. The generous-size guest rooms are decorated in contemporary style.

Weilburgstrasse 11–13, A-2500 Baden bei Wien. ✆ **02252/412510.** Fax 02252/43626. www.sauerhof.at. 88 units. 215€ ($344) double; from 650€ ($1,040) suite. Rates include buffet breakfast; half-board 27€ ($43) per person extra. AE, DC, MC, V. Free parking. **Amenities:** Restaurant; bar; indoor heated pool; 2 tennis courts; fitness center; spa; sauna; salon; room service; laundry service; dry cleaning; nonsmoking rooms; solarium. *In room:* TV, minibar, hair dryer, safe.

Moderate

Krainerhütte (Kids) Run by Josef Dietmann and his family, this hotel stands on tree-filled grounds 8km (5 miles) west of Baden at Helenental. It's a large A-frame chalet with rows of wooden balconies. The interior has more detailing than you might expect in such a modern hotel. There are separate children's rooms and play areas. The medium-size rooms and small bathrooms with tub/shower combinations are well maintained. In the cozy restaurant or on the terrace, you can dine on international and Austrian cuisine; the fish and deer come from the hotel grounds. Hiking in the owner's forests, hunting, and fishing are possible. *Postbus* (mail bus) service to Baden is available all day.

Helenental, A-2500 Baden bei Wien. ✆ **02252/44511.** Fax 02252/44514. www.krainerhuette.at. 62 units. 65€–130€ ($104–$208) double; from 160€ ($256) suite. Rates include breakfast; half-board 25€ ($40) per person extra. AE, MC, V. Free parking. **Amenities:** Restaurant; bar; indoor heated pool; tennis court; fitness center; sauna; room service; babysitting; laundry service; dry cleaning; nonsmoking rooms. *In room:* TV, Wi-Fi, minibar, hair dryer.

Parkhotel Baden This contemporary hotel sits in the middle of an inner-city park dotted with trees and statuary. The high-ceilinged lobby has a marble floor padded with thick oriental carpets and ringed with richly grained paneling. Most of the good-size, sunny guest rooms have their own loggia overlooking century-old trees; each contains a good bathroom with tub/shower combination and plenty of shelf space.

Kaiser-Franz-Ring 5, A-2500 Baden bei Wien. ✆ **02252/443860.** Fax 02252/80578. www.niederoesterreich.at/parkhotel-baden. 87 units. 170€ ($272) double; 280€ ($448) suite. Rates include breakfast. AE, DC, MC, V. Free parking. **Amenities:** 2 restaurants; bar; indoor heated pool; health club; sauna; massage; room service; babysitting; laundry service; dry cleaning. *In room:* TV, Wi-Fi, minibar, hair dryer.

Schloss Weikersdorf The oldest part of the hotel has massive beams, arched and vaulted ceilings, an Italianate loggia stretching toward the manicured gardens, and an inner courtyard with stone arcades. Accommodations, which include 77 bedrooms in the main house plus 27 in the annex, are handsomely furnished and most comfortable. The rooms in the newer section repeat the older section's arches and high ceilings, and sport ornate chandeliers and antique or reproduction furniture.

Schlossgasse 9–11, A-2500 Baden bei Wien. ✆ **02252/48301.** Fax 02252/4830-1150. www.hotelschlossweikersdorf.at. 104 units. 124€–150€ ($198–$240) double; 250€ ($400) suite. Rates include breakfast. AE, DC, MC, V. Free parking. **Amenities:** Restaurant; bar; indoor heated pool; 2 tennis courts; sauna; room service; massage; laundry service; dry cleaning; nonsmoking rooms; bowling alley; rooms for those w/ limited mobility. *In room:* TV, minibar, hair dryer, safe.

WHERE TO DINE

Kupferdachl AUSTRIAN A local cornerstone since 1966, this family favorite serves rib-sticking fare that the locals adore, everything from cabbage soup to *apfelstrudel* for dessert. For a main dish, the chefs make the spa's best Wiener schnitzel, served with a freshly made salad and rice. Veal cutlet also appears cordon bleu. Expect good, old-fashioned Austrian cookery that was known before WWII.

Heiligenkreuzegasse 2. ✆ **02252/41617.** Reservations recommended. Main courses 10€–14€ ($16–$22). No credit cards. Mon–Fri 8am–6:30pm; Sat–Sun 9:30am–4pm.

BADEN AFTER DARK

Casino Baden The town's major evening attraction is the casino, where you can play roulette, blackjack, baccarat, poker (seven-card stud), money wheel, and slot machines. Many visitors from Vienna come down to Baden for a night of gambling, eating, and drinking; there are two bars and a restaurant. Guests are often fashionably dressed, and you'll feel more comfortable if you are, too (men should wear jackets and ties). It's open daily 3pm to 3am. A less formal casino on the premises, the Casino Leger, is open daily noon to midnight. In the Kurpark. ✆ **02252/444960.** www.casinos.at. Free admission; 25€ ($40) worth of chips for 21€ ($34).

3 WIENER NEUSTADT

45km (28 miles) S of Vienna; 309km (192 miles) E of Salzburg

Heading south from Vienna on the Südautobahn, the former imperial city of Wiener Neustadt is a good first stop. It was once the official residence of Emperor Friedrich III. Called *Allzeit Getreue* (forever loyal) because of its loyalty to the throne, this thriving city between the foothills of the Alps and the edge of the Pannonian lowland is steeped in history.

Unfortunately, Wiener Neustadt was a target for Allied bombs during World War II, as it was the point where the routes from Vienna diverge, one toward the Semmering Pass and the other to Hungary. The 200-year-old military academy that developed officers for the Austrian army might have been an added attraction to bombers. German Gen. Erwin Rommel, "the Desert Fox," was the academy's first commandant during the Nazi era. At any rate, the Allies dropped more bombs on the city than on any other town in Austria. It's estimated that some 60% of its buildings were leveled.

The town was founded in 1192, when its castle was built by Duke Leopold V of the ruling house of Babenberg as a bulwark against Magyar attacks from the east. From 1440 to 1493, Austrian emperors lived in this fortress in the southeastern corner of the old town. Maximilian I, called "the last of the knights," was born here in 1459 and lies buried in the Church of St. George in the castle. In 1752, Maria Theresia ordered that the structures comprising the castle be turned into a military academy.

ESSENTIALS

GETTING THERE If you're driving from Vienna, head south along Autobahn A2 until you reach the junction with Route 21, at which point you head east to Wiener Neustadt.

To reach Wiener Neustadt by train, take the S-Bahn from Landstrasse-Stadt Mitte in Vienna, a fast and efficient electronic train. There are no buses from Landstrasse-Stadt Mitte.

VISITOR INFORMATION The Wiener Neustadt **tourist information office,** at Hauptplatz in Rathaus (✆ **02622/29551**), is open Monday to Friday 8am to 5pm, Saturday 8am to noon.

WALKING AROUND WIENER NEUSTADT

You can visit the **St. Georgenkirche (Church of St. George),** Burgplatz 1 (✆ **02622/3810**), daily from 8am to 6pm. The gable of the church is adorned with more than 100 heraldic shields of the Hapsburgs. It's noted for its handsome interior, decorated in the late-Gothic style.

Neukloster, Neuklostergasse 1 (✆ **02622/23102**), a Cistercian abbey, was founded in 1250 and reconstructed in the 18th century. The Neuklosterkirche (New Abbey Church), near the Hauptplatz, is Gothic and has a beautiful choir. It contains the tomb of Empress Eleanor of Portugal, wife of Friedrich III and mother of Maximilian I. Mozart's *Requiem* was first presented here in 1793. Admission is free, and it's open Monday to Friday from 9am to noon and 2 to 5pm.

Liebfrauenkirche, Domplatz (✆ **02622/23202**), was once the headquarters of an Episcopal see. It's graced by a 13th-century Romanesque nave, but the choir is Gothic. The west towers have been rebuilt. Admission is free, and the church is open daily from 8am to noon and 2 to 6pm.

In the town is a **Recturm,** Babenberger Ring (✆ **02622/27924**), a Gothic tower said to have been built with the ransom money paid for Richard the Lion-Hearted. It's open from March to October Tuesday to Thursday from 10am to noon and 2 to 4pm, and Saturday and Sunday from 10am to noon only. Admission is free.

WHERE TO STAY

Hotel Corvinus ★ The best hotel in town, built in the 1970s, sits in a quiet neighborhood near the city park, a 2-minute walk south of the main rail station. The good-size rooms have modern comforts, such as firm beds and well-maintained bathrooms equipped with tub/shower combinations. There's also an inviting bar area, a parasol-covered sun terrace, and a lightheartedly elegant restaurant serving Austrian and international dishes.

Bahngasse 29–33, A-2700 Wiener Neustadt. ✆ **02622/24134.** Fax 02622/24139. www.hotel-corvinus.at. 68 units. 120€ ($192) double. Rates include buffet breakfast. AE, DC, MC, V. Free parking. **Amenities:** Restaurant; bar; Jacuzzi; sauna; room service; laundry service; dry cleaning; nonsmoking rooms; solarium. *In room:* TV, Wi-Fi, minibar, hair dryer.

WHERE TO DINE

Gaststube Stachl ★ CONTINENTAL Set within the city's all-pedestrian zone, in the heart of town, this is one of the most popular and well-respected restaurants in the region, with a thriving catering business on the side. Food items are well presented and flavorful, served within an environment that includes a busy bar area independent of the restaurant. Begin a meal here with a carpaccio of Styrian beef with wild mushrooms and arugula; strips of marinated salmon with pesto sauce; then continue perhaps with a truffled version of mushroom risotto; Wiener schnitzel with salad; *tafelspitz* with chive sauce and horseradish; or perhaps a filet of local lakefish *(zander)* with herbed noodles. For dessert, consider a platter containing light and dark versions of chocolate mousse topped with berry sauce.

Lange Gasse 20. ✆ **02622/25221.** www.stachl.at. Reservations recommended. Main courses 12€–20€ ($19–$32). MC, V. Mon–Fri 5pm–12:30am; Sat 5pm–midnight.

4 THE DANUBE VALLEY ★★★

The Danube, of course, is one of the most legendary rivers in Europe, and the surrounding area is rich in scenic splendor, historic wealth, and architectural grandeur. With rolling hills and fertile soil, the Wachau, a section of the Danube Valley northwest of Vienna, is one of the most beautiful and historic parts of Austria. Throughout this part of the Danube Valley, you'll find castles, celebrated vineyards, some of the most famous medieval monasteries in central Europe, and ruins from the Stone Age, the Celts, the Romans, and the Hapsburgs. This prosperous district has won many awards for the authenticity of its historic renovations.

A great way to see the area is by paddleboat steamer, most of which operate only from April to October. You can travel by armchair, lounging on the deck along the longest river in central Europe.

If you're really "doing the Danube," you can begin your trip at Passau, Germany, and go all the way to the Black Sea and across to the Crimean Peninsula in the Ukraine. However, the Vienna-Yalta portion of the trip alone takes nearly a week. Most visitors limit themselves to a more restricted look at the Danube, taking one of the many popular trips from Vienna. If you go westward on the river, your first stop might be Klosterneuburg (see section 1, "The Wienerwald [Vienna Woods]," earlier in this chapter).

ESSENTIALS

GETTING THERE If you have only 1 day to explore the Danube Valley, we highly recommend one of the tours listed below. If you have more time, however, rent a car and explore this district yourself, driving inland from the river now and then to visit the towns and sights listed below. You can also take public transportation to the towns we've highlighted (see individual listings).

VISITOR INFORMATION Before you venture into the Danube Valley, pick up maps and other helpful information at the **tourist office for Lower Austria,** Postfach 10.000, A-1010 Vienna (✆ **01/536106200;** fax 01/536106060; www.niederoesterreich.at).

TIPS ON EXPLORING THE DANUBE VALLEY If you have only a day to see the Danube Valley, we highly recommend the tours listed below. If you have more time, rent a car and explore this district yourself, driving inland from the river now and then to visit the towns and sights listed below. You can also take public transportation to the towns we've highlighted (see individual listings).

The Wachau and the rest of the Danube Valley contain some of the most impressive monuments in Austria, but because of their far-flung locations, many prefer to participate in an organized tour. The best of these are conducted by **Vienna Sightseeing Tours,**

Starhemberggasse 25 (✆ **01/7124-6830;** fax 01/714-1141; www.viennasightseeing tours.com), which offers guided tours by motorcoach in winter and by both motorcoach and boat in summer. Stops on this 8-hour trip include Krems, Dürnstein, and Melk Abbey. Prices are 61€ ($98) for adults and 30€ ($48) for children under 12, and do not include lunch. Prices include lunch in winter. Advance reservations are required.

TULLN: THE FLOWER TOWN

Originally a naval base, Comagena, and later a center for the Babenberg dynasty, Tulln is one of the most ancient towns in Austria. Located on the right bank of the Danube, it is called "the flower town" because of the masses of blossoms you'll see in spring and summer. It's the place, according to the saga of the Nibelungen, where Kriemhild, the Burgundian princess of Worms, met Etzel, king of the Huns. A well-known "son of Tulln" was Kurt Waldheim, former secretary-general of the United Nations and president of Austria, who was plagued by his past Nazi affiliations.

Essentials

GETTING THERE Tulln lies 42km (26 miles) west of Vienna, on the south bank of the Danube, and 13km (8 miles) southwest of Stockerau, the next big town, on the north bank of the Danube. If you're driving from Vienna, head west along Route 14.

S-Bahn trains depart from the Wien Nord Station and, more frequently, from the Wien Franz-Josefs Bahnhof daily from 4:30am to 8:30pm (trip time: 27–45 min.). Tulln lies on the busy main rail lines linking Vienna with Prague, and most local timetables list Gmund, an Austrian city on the border of the Czech Republic, as the final destination. For more information, call ✆ **05/1717,** or check **www.oebb.at**. We don't recommend taking the bus from Vienna, as it would require multiple transfers.

VISITOR INFORMATION The **tourist office** in Tulln, Minoritenplatz 2 (✆ **02272/67566;** www.tulln.at), is open from November to April, Monday to Friday 8am to 3pm; May to October Monday to Friday 9am to 7pm, Saturday and Sunday 10am to 7pm.

EXPLORING TULLN The twin-towered **Pfarrkirche (Parish Church)** of St. Stephan on Wiener Strasse grew out of a 12th-century Romanesque basilica dedicated to St. Stephan. Its west portal was built in the 13th century. A Gothic overlay added in its early centuries fell victim to the 18th-century baroque craze that swept the country. A 1786 altarpiece commemorates the martyrdom of St. Stephan.

Adjoining the church is the **Karner (Charnel)** ★★. This funereal chapel is the major sight of Tulln, the finest of its kind in the entire country. Built in the mid-13th century in the shape of a polygon, it's richly decorated with capitals and arches. The Romanesque dome is adorned with frescoes.

In a restored former prison, Tulln has opened the **Egon Schiele Museum** ★★, Donaulände 28 (✆ **02272/64570**), devoted to its other famous son, born here in 1890. Schiele is one of the greatest Austrian artists of the early 1900s. The prison setting might be appropriate, as the expressionist painter spent 24 days in jail in 1912 in the town of Neulengbach for possession of what back then was regarded as pornography. While awaiting trial, he produced 13 watercolors, most of which are now in the Albertina in Vienna. The Tulln museum has more than 90 of his oil paintings, watercolors, and designs, along with much memorabilia. It's open daily from 10am to 6pm. Admission is 3.50€ ($5.60) adults and 2€ ($3.20) children. The museum is closed in December and January.

Where to Stay & Dine

Gasthaus zur Sonne (Gasthaus Sodoma) ★ AUSTRIAN This is Tulln's finest and most famous restaurant. The 1940s building, on the main street a short walk from the railway station, looks like a cross between a chalet and a villa. Under the direction of the Sodoma family since 1968, it consists of two cozy dining rooms lined with oil paintings. Customers, including the mayor of Vienna and other Austrian celebrities, have enjoyed dishes that change with the season. The menu invariably includes well-prepared versions of dumplings stuffed with minced meat, pumpkin soup, a marvelous Weiner schnitzel, onion-studded roast beef, *tafelspitz,* and perfectly cooked zander (freshwater lake fish) served with potatoes and butter sauce.

Bahnhofstrasse 48. ✆ **02272/64616.** Reservations recommended. Main courses 9€–27€ ($14–$43). No credit cards. Tues–Sat 11:30am–1:30pm and 6–9pm.

Hotel Römerhof Built in 1972, this hotel near the train station has a simple modern facade of white walls and unadorned windows. The interior is warmly outfitted with earth tones, a macramé wall hanging, and pendant lighting fixtures. The bedrooms are comfortable but utterly functional, with duvet-covered beds. Bathrooms have well-kept showers but limited storage space.

Langenlebarnerstrasse 66, A-3430 Tulln an der Donau. ✆ **02272/62954.** www.hotel-roemerhof.at. 51 units. 76€–90€ ($122–$144) double. Rates include buffet breakfast. MC, V. Free parking. **Amenities:** Breakfast room; bar; sauna; beer garden. *In room:* TV, minibar, hair dryer, safe.

HERZOGENBURG MONASTERY

Founded in the early 12th century by a German bishop from Passau, the Augustinian **Herzogenburg Monastery,** A-3130 Herzogenburg (✆ **02782/83113**), 11km (7 miles) south of Traismauer, has a long history. The present complex of buildings comprising the church and the abbey was reconstructed in the baroque style. Fischer von Erlach, a master of the style, designed some of the complex. The art painted on the high altar of the church is by Daniel Gran, and the most outstanding works owned by the abbey are a series of 16th-century paintings on wood, displayed in a room devoted to Gothic art. The monastery is well known for a library containing more than 80,000 works.

Entrance is 7€ ($11) for adults, 5€ ($8) for seniors and students. You can wander around alone or participate in a guided tour, departing daily at 9:30, 11am, and at 1:30, 2:30, and 3pm. The monastery is open only April to October daily from 9am to 6pm. There's a wine tavern in the complex where you can grab some Austrian fare while sampling the local grapes.

Essentials

GETTING THERE Located 16km (10 miles) south of the Danube, the monastery is reached by taking Wiener Strasse (Rte. 1) out of St. Pölten. Head east for 13km (8 miles) toward Kapelln, and turn left at the sign along a minor road to Herzogenburg.

KREMS ★

In the eastern part of the Wachau on the left bank of the Danube lies the 1,000-year-old city of Krems. The city today encompasses Stein and Mautern, once separate towns. Krems is a mellow town of courtyards, old churches, and ancient houses in the heart of vineyard country, with some partially preserved town walls. Just as the Viennese flock to Grinzing and other suburbs to sample new wine in the *heurigen,* so the people of the

Wachau come here to taste the fruit of the vine, which appears in Krems earlier in the year.

Essentials

GETTING THERE Krems is located 80km (50 miles) west of Vienna and 29km (18 miles) north of St. Pölten. If you're driving from Vienna, drive north along the A22 until it splits into three roads near the town of Stockerau. Here, drive due west along Route 3, following the signs to Krems.

Trains depart from both the Wien Nord Station and the Wien Franz-Josefs Bahnhof for Krems daily every hour or so from 2:30am to 11:30pm (trip time: 60–95 min.). Many are direct, although some require a transfer at Absdorf-Hippersdorf or St. Pölten. For schedules, call ✆ **05/1717** in Vienna, or check **www.oebb.at**. Traveling by bus from Vienna to Krems is not recommended because of the many transfers required. Krems, however, is well connected by local bus lines to surrounding villages.

Between mid-May and late September, the Linz-based **Worm & Koeck Donau Schiffahrt GmbH** (✆ **0732/783607;** www.donauschiffahrt.de) runs river cruises which depart from Vienna every Sunday morning at 7:30am, arriving in Kems around 12:20pm. After a tour through the abbey at Krems, most passengers take any of the frequent trains back to Vienna.

VISITOR INFORMATION The Krems **tourist office,** at Undstrasse 6 (✆ **02732/82676;** www.krems.at), is open Monday to Friday 9am to 6pm, Saturday 11am to 5pm, Sunday 11am to 4pm.

Exploring Krems

The most scenic part of Krems today is what used to be the little village of **Stein.** Narrow streets are terraced above the river, and the single main street, **Steinlanderstrasse,** is flanked with houses, many from the 16th century. The **Grosser Passauerhof,** Steinlanderstrasse 76 (✆ **02732/82188**), is a Gothic structure decorated with an oriel. Another house, at Steinlanderstrasse 84, combines Byzantine and Venetian elements among other architectural influences; it was once the imperial tollhouse. In days of yore, the aristocrats of Krems barricaded the Danube and extracted heavy tolls from the river traffic. Sometimes the tolls were more than the hapless victims could pay, so the townspeople just confiscated the cargo. In the Altstadt, the **Steiner Tor,** a 1480 gate, is a landmark.

Pfarrkirche St. Viet (✆ **02732/857100**), the parish church of Krems, stands in the center of town at the Rathaus, reached by going along either Untere Landstrasse or Obere Landstrasse. The overly ornate church is rich with gilt and statuary. Construction on this, one of the oldest baroque churches in the province, began in 1616. In the 18th century, Martin Johann Schmidt, better known as Kremser Schmidt, painted many of the frescoes inside the church.

You'll find the **Weinstadt Museum Krems (Museum of Krems),** Körnermarkt 14 (✆ **02732/801567**), in a restored Dominican monastery. The Gothic abbey is from the 13th and 14th centuries. Its gallery displays the paintings of Martin Johann Schmidt, mentioned above. One of the more intriguing displays is a copy of a 32,000-year-old statuette, the country's most ancient work of art. Of further interest are the cellar tunnels from the 1500s that were excavated underneath the cloister. The complex also has an interesting **Weinbaumuseum (Wine Museum),** exhibiting artifacts, many quite old, gathered from the vineyards along the Danube. Admission to both areas of the museum is 4€ ($6.40). It's open only March to November Tuesday to Sunday 10am to 6pm.

Nearby Attractions

Twenty-nine kilometers (18 miles) north of Krems at St. Pölten is the Museum of Lower Austria, formerly located in Vienna. Now called **Landes Museum,** it's at Franz-Schubert-Platz (✆ **2742/908-090-999**). This museum exhibits the geology, flora, and fauna of the area surrounding Vienna. It also exhibits a collection of arts and crafts, including baroque and Biedermeier; temporary shows featuring 20th-century works are presented as well. Admission is 8€ ($13) for adults and 7€ ($11) for children. It's open Tuesday to Sunday 9am to 5pm.

Where to Stay

Donauhotel Krems This large, glass-walled hotel built in the 1970s has a wooden canopy stretched over the front entrance. The bedrooms are comfortably furnished and well maintained. They are a little small for long stays but are suitable for an overnight, as the beds are fluffy and the bathrooms (most with tub/shower combinations) are spotless. Austrian fare is available in the airy cafe, on the terrace, or in the more formal restaurant.

Edmund-Hofbauer-Strasse 19, A-3500 Krems. ✆ **02732/87565.** Fax 02732/875-6552. donauhotel-krems@aon.at. 60 units. 84€ ($134) double. Rates include buffet breakfast; half-board 14€ ($22) per person extra. AE, DC, MC, V. Free parking. **Amenities:** Restaurant; bar; fitness center; sauna; solarium (latter 3 for women only). *In room:* TV, hair dryer, safe.

Gourmethotel am Förthof ★ Finds In the Stein sector of the city, this big-windowed hotel has white-stucco walls and flower-covered balconies. A rose garden surrounds the base of an alfresco cafe; inside are oriental rugs and a scattering of antiques amid newer furniture. Each of the high-ceilinged bedrooms has a foyer and a shared balcony. Most bedrooms are fairly spacious. Bathrooms, though small, have well-kept tub/shower combinations. The hotel is entirely nonsmoking.

Donauländе 8, A-3500 Krems. ✆ **02732/83345.** Fax 02732/833-4540. www.niederoesterreich.at/gourmethotel. 20 units. 90€–140€ ($144–$224) double. Rates include breakfast; half-board 25€ ($33) per person extra. AE, DC, MC, V. Free parking. **Amenities:** Restaurant; bar; outdoor pool; sauna; room service (7am–10pm); babysitting; laundry service; dry cleaning. *In room:* TV, minibar, hair dryer, safe.

Where to Dine

Restaurant Bacher ★ AUSTRIAN/INTERNATIONAL Lisl and Klaus Wagner-Bacher operate this excellent restaurant-hotel, with an elegant dining room and a well-kept garden. Specialties include crabmeat salad dressed with nut oil, and zucchini stuffed with fish and accompanied by two kinds of sauces. Dessert might be beigners with apricot sauce and vanilla ice cream. Lisl has won awards for her cuisine, as her enthusiastic clientele will tell you. The wine list has more than 600 selections.

Eight double and three single rooms are offered. Rooms contain TVs, minibars, phones, and radios, and each is attractively furnished with good beds and well-maintained bathrooms. Rates are 120€ to 170€ ($192–$272) for a double with buffet breakfast. The establishment is 4km (2½ miles) from Krems.

Südtiroler Platz 208, A-2352 Mautern. ✆ **02732/82937.** Fax 02732/74337. Reservations required. Main courses 24€–39€ ($38–$62); fixed-price menus 72€–99€ ($115–$158). DC, V. Wed–Sat 11:30am–1:30pm and 6:30–9pm; Sun 11:30am–9pm. Closed mid-Jan to mid-Feb.

DÜRNSTEIN ★★

Less than 8km (5 miles) west of Krems, Dürnstein is the loveliest town along the Danube and, accordingly, draws throngs of tour groups in summer. Terraced vineyards mark this as a Danube wine town, and the town's fortified walls are partially preserved.

Essentials

GETTING THERE The town is 80km (50 miles) west of Vienna. If you're driving, take Route 3 west. From Krems, continue driving west along Route 3 for 8km (5 miles). Train travel to Dürnstein from Vienna requires a transfer in Krems (see above). In Krems, trains depart approximately every 2 hours on river-running routes; it's a 6km (4-mile) trip to Dürnstein. For schedules, call ✆ **05/1717** in Vienna, or check **www.oebb.at**. There's also bus service between Krems and Dürnstein (trip time: 20 min.).

VISITOR INFORMATION A little **tourist office,** housed in a tiny shed in the east parking lot called Parkplatz Ost (✆ **02711/200**), is open April to October 19 only. Hours are daily 11am to 1pm and 2 to 6:30pm.

Where Richard the Lion-Hearted Was Held Prisoner

The ruins of a **castle fortress,** 159m (522 ft.) above the town, are inextricably linked to the Crusades. Here Leopold V, the Babenberg duke ruling the country at that time, held Richard the Lion-Hearted of England prisoner in 1193. For quite some time, nobody knew exactly where in Austria Richard was incarcerated, but his loyal minstrel companion, Blondel, had a clever idea. He went from castle to castle, playing his lute and singing Richard's favorite songs. The tactic paid off, the legend says, for at Dürnstein, Richard heard Blondel's singing and sang the lyrics in reply. The discovery forced Leopold to transfer Richard to a castle in the Rhineland Palatinate, but by then everybody knew where he was. So Leopold set a high ransom on the king's head, which was eventually met, and Richard was set free. The castle was virtually demolished by the Swedes in 1645, but you can visit the ruins if you don't mind a vigorous climb (allow 1 hr.). The castle isn't much, but the view of Dürnstein and the Wachau is more than worth the effort.

Back in town, take in the principal artery, **Hauptstrasse ★**, which is flanked by richly adorned old residences. Many of these date from the 1500s and have been well maintained through the centuries.

The 15th-century **Pfarrkirche (parish church)** also merits a visit. The building was originally an Augustinian monastery and was reconstructed when the baroque style swept Austria. The church tower is the finest baroque example in the whole country and a prominent landmark in the Danube Valley. Kremser Schmidt, the noted baroque painter, did some of the altar paintings.

Where to Stay & Dine

Gartenhotel Weinhof Pfeffel (Value) This black-roofed, white-walled hotel is partially concealed by well-landscaped shrubbery. One of the best bargains in town, the hotel takes its name from its garden courtyard with flowering trees, where tasty (but not fancy) meals are served. The public rooms are furnished with traditional pieces. The bedrooms are handsomely furnished in a traditional Austrian motif, with comfortable armchairs and good beds. Leopold Pfeffel, your host, serves wine from his own terraced vineyard.

A-3601 Dürnstein. ✆ **02711/206.** Fax 02711/12068. www.pfeffel.at. 40 units. 112€–132€ ($179–$211) double; from 136€ ($218) suite. Rates include breakfast. MC, V. Free parking. Closed Dec–Feb. **Amenities:** Restaurant; bar; outdoor pool; sauna; room service; laundry service; dry cleaning; nonsmoking rooms. *In room:* TV, Wi-Fi, minibar, hair dryer, safe.

Hotel-Restaurant Sänger Blondel ★ (Finds) Lemon-colored and charmingly old-fashioned, with green shutters and clusters of flowers at the windows, this hotel is named after the faithful minstrel who searched the countryside for Richard the Lion-Hearted. Bedrooms are furnished in a rustic style and are quite comfortable, containing small bathrooms equipped with shower units. All have good beds with fresh linens. Each Thursday, an evening of zither music is presented. If the weather is good, the music is played outside in the flowery chestnut garden near the baroque church tower. There's a good and reasonably priced restaurant serving regional cuisine.

A-3601 Dürnstein. ✆ **02711/253.** Fax 02711/2537. www.saengerblondel.at. 15 units. 92€–110€ ($147–$176) double; 130€ ($208) suite. Rates include breakfast. MC, V. Parking 7€ ($11). Closed Dec–Feb. **Amenities:** Restaurant; lounge; laundry service; dry cleaning. *In room:* TV, hair dryer.

Hotel Schloss Dürnstein ★★ The baroque tower of this Renaissance castle rises above the scenic Danube. It's one of the best-decorated hotels in Austria, with white ceramic stoves, vaulted ceilings, parquet floors, oriental rugs, and gilt mirrors. A beautiful shady terrace is only a stone's throw from the river. Elegantly furnished bedrooms come in a wide variety of styles, ranging from those that are large and palatial to others that are rather small and modern. Modern bathrooms with tub/shower combinations are in all the bedrooms, though sometimes in cramped conditions. The restaurant serves well-prepared dishes from the kitchen of an experienced chef.

A-3601 Dürnstein. ✆ **02711/212.** Fax 02711/212-30. www.schloss.at. 41 units. 235€–253€ ($376–$405) double; from 338€–365€ ($541–$584) suite. Rates include breakfast. AE, DC, MC, V. Free parking. Closed Nov 1–Easter. A pickup can be arranged at the Dürnstein rail station. **Amenities:** Restaurant; bar; 2 pools (1 heated indoor); fitness center; gymnastics center; sauna; room service; massage; babysitting; laundry service; dry cleaning. *In room:* TV, Wi-Fi, minibar, hair dryer, safe.

Romantik Hotel Richard Löwenherz ★★ This hotel was founded in the 1950s on the site of a 700-year-old nunnery, originally dedicated to the sisters of Santa Clara in 1289. Its richly historical interior is filled with antiques, Renaissance sculpture, elegant chandeliers, stone vaulting, and paneling that's been polished over the years to a mellow patina. An arbor-covered sun terrace with restaurant tables extends toward the Danube. The spacious bedrooms, especially those in the balconied modern section, are filled with cheerful furniture. The duvet-covered beds are the finest in the area. Each unit also has a beautifully kept bathroom with a tub/shower combination. The restaurant offers a fine selection of local wines among its many regional specialties.

A-3601 Dürnstein. ✆ **02711/222.** Fax 02711/22218. www.richardloewenherz.at. 38 units. 166€–191€ ($266–$306) double; 310€ ($496) suite. Rates include buffet breakfast. AE, MC, V. Free parking. Closed Nov to mid-Apr. **Amenities:** Restaurant; lounge; outdoor heated pool; room service; laundry service; non-smoking rooms. *In room:* TV, Wi-Fi, hair dryer.

MELK

The words of Empress Maria Theresa speak volumes about Melk: "If I had never come here I would have regretted it." The main attraction is the Melk Abbey, a sprawling baroque building overlooking the Danube basin. Melk marks the western terminus of the Wachau and lies upstream from Krems.

Essentials

GETTING THERE Melk is 89km (55 miles) west of Vienna. **Motorists** can take Autobahn A-1, exiting at the signs for Melk. If you prefer a more romantic and scenic road, try Route 3, which parallels the Danube but takes 30 to 45 minutes longer. **Trains** leave frequently from Vienna's Westbahnhof to Melk, with two brief stops en route (trip time: about 1 hr.).

VISITOR INFORMATION The **Melk tourist office** at Babenbergerstrasse 1 (✆ **02752/52307410;** www.tiscover.com/melk), in the center of town, is open April and

October Monday to Friday 9am to noon and 2 to 6pm, Sunday 10am to 2pm; May, June, and September Monday to Friday 9am to noon and 2 to 6pm, Saturday and Sunday 10am to 2pm; July and August Monday to Saturday 9am to 7pm, Sunday 10am to 2pm.

Seeing the Sights

Melk Abbey ★★ One of the finest baroque buildings in the world, Melk Abbey and the **Stiftskirche (abbey church) ★★★** are the major attractions today. However, Melk has been an important place in the Danube Basin ever since the Romans built a fortress on a promontory looking out onto a tiny "arm" of the Danube. Melk also figures in the *Nibelungenlied* (the German epic poem), in which it is called *Medelike.*

The rock-strewn bluff where the abbey now stands overlooking the river was the seat of the Babenbergs, who ruled Austria from 976 until the Hapsburgs took over. In the 11th century, Leopold II of the House of Babenberg presented Melk to the Benedictine monks, who turned it into a fortified abbey. Its influence and reputation as a center of learning and culture spread all over Austria, a fact that is familiar to readers of Umberto Eco's *The Name of the Rose.* The Reformation and the 1683 Turkish invasion took a toll on the abbey, although it was spared from direct attack when the Ottoman armies were repelled outside Vienna. The construction of the new building began in 1702, just in time to be given the full baroque treatment.

Most of the design of the present abbey was by the architect Jakob Prandtauer. Its marble hall, called the Marmorsaal, contains pilasters coated in red marble. A richly painted allegorical picture on the ceiling is the work of Paul Troger. The library, rising two floors, again with a Troger ceiling, contains some 80,000 volumes. The Kaisergang, or emperors' gallery, 198m (650 ft.) long, is decorated with portraits of Austrian rulers.

Despite all the adornment in the abbey, it is still surpassed in lavish glory by the Stiftskirche, the golden abbey church. Damaged by fire in 1947, the church has been fully restored, including the regilding statues and altars with gold bouillon. The church has an astonishing number of windows, and it's richly embellished with marble and frescoes. Many of the paintings are by Johann Michael Rottmayr, but Troger also contributed.

Melk is still a working abbey, and you might see black-robed Benedictine monks going about their business or students rushing out of the gates. Visitors head for the terrace for a view of the river. Napoleon probably used it for a lookout when he made Melk his headquarters during the campaign against Austria.

Throughout the year, the abbey is open every day. From May to September, tours depart at intervals of 15 to 20 minutes. The first tour begins at 9am and the last is at 5pm; guides make efforts to translate into English a running commentary that is otherwise German.

Dietmayerstrasse 1, A-3390 Melk. ✆ **02752/555-225** for tour information. www.stiftmelk.at. Guided tours 9.30€ ($15) adults, 5.90€ ($9.50) children, unguided tours 7.50€ ($12) adults, 4.10€ ($6.60) children;daily 9am–4:30pm (until 5:30pm May–Sept), last entry 30 min. before closing.

Where to Stay

Hotel Stadt Melk ★ Value Just below the town's palace, this four-story hotel, with a gabled roof and stucco walls, was originally built a century ago as a private home. It was eventually converted into this cozy, family-run hotel, and now has simply furnished bedrooms that are clean and comfortable, with sturdy beds and well-maintained bathrooms that, though small, are adequate and equipped with tub/shower combinations.

Rooms in the rear open onto views of the abbey. The pleasant restaurant has leaded-glass windows in round bull's-eye patterns of greenish glass. Meals, beginning at 40€ ($64), are also served on a balcony at the front of the hotel. The food is quite good.

Hauptplatz 1, A-3390 Melk. ✆ **02752/52475.** Fax 02752/524-7519. www.tiscover.at/hotel-stadt-melk. 14 units. 93€ ($149) double; 180€ ($288) suite. Rates include breakfast. AE, DC, MC, V. Free parking. **Amenities:** 2 restaurants; bar; sauna; laundry service; dry cleaning service. *In room:* TV, minibar, hair dryer, safe.

Where to Dine

Stiftsrestaurant Melk BURGENLANDER If you're visiting Melk, this place is required dining, lying right at the entrance to the abbey. Don't let its cafeterialike dimensions sway you from its fine cuisine. This modernly decorated restaurant is well equipped to handle large groups—some 3,000 visitors a day frequent the establishment during peak season. From the reasonable fixed-price menu you might opt for the asparagus-and-ham soup with crispy dumplings; hunter's roast with mushrooms, potato croquettes, and cranberry sauce; and the famed Sachertorte for dessert.

Abt-Berthold-Dietmayrstrasse 3. ✆ **02752/52555.** www.stiftmelk.at. Main courses 10€–14€ ($16–$22). AE, MC, V. Mid-Mar to Dec daily 8am–7pm. Closed otherwise.

8

Burgenland

Austria's easternmost and newest province, Burgenland is a little border region created in 1921 from German-speaking areas of what was formerly Hungary. It marks the beginning of a large, flat *puszta* (steppe) that almost reaches Budapest, yet also lies practically on Vienna's doorstep. The province shares a western border with Styria and Lower Austria, and its long eastern boundary separates it from Hungary.

Called "the vegetable garden of Vienna," Burgenland is mostly an agricultural province. It's noted for its vineyards, producing more than one-third of all the wine made in Austria. The province is situated where the Hungarian *puszta* gradually modulates into the foothills of the eastern Alps; forests cover 29% of its area, and vineyards compose 7% of its agricultural lands. Its wonderful climate consists of hot summers with little rainfall and moderate winters. For the most part, you can enjoy sunny days from early spring until late autumn.

Burgenland's population represents a middle-Europe melting pot. Around 2% of the population is Hungarian, while some 10% consists of Croats who settled here in the 16th century after fleeing their southern Slav homes before the advance of Turkish armies. For hundreds of years, the Croats, Hungarians, and German-speaking people have lived together in this area. Many Burgenlanders still wear their traditional garb on Sunday.

This ethnic diversity has resulted in a regional cuisine that's among the best in Europe. Its eastern neighbors, especially Hungary, provide strong influences that you'll appreciate when you savor goulashes and strudels, as well as goose dishes. Much wild game lives in the wooded areas of Burgenland and is often featured on menus.

Eisenstadt, the small provincial capital of Burgenland since 1924, was for many years the home of Franz Josef Haydn, and the composer is buried here. Near Eisenstadt is another composer's shrine: Franz Liszt's birthplace. Each summer there's an International Operetta Festival at Mörbisch am See, using Neusiedler See (Lake Neusiedl) as a theatrical backdrop. Neusiedl is the only steppe lake in central Europe. If you're here in summer, we suggest exploring it by motorboat. Seewinkel, a marshy haven for birds and rare flora, surrounds Illmitz, an old village near Lake Neusiedl. Many Viennese come to Burgenland on weekends for sailing, bird-watching, and other outdoor activities. The summer resort of Rust is famous for its stork nests and its town walls built in 1614.

Like Lower Austria, Burgenland contains numerous fortresses and castles, many in ruins. You'll see several affiliated with the Esterházy family, a great Hungarian family descended from Attila the Hun. These include Schloss Esterházy and the Eisenstadt château, as well as Forchtenstein Castle, dating from the 13th century.

Accommodations in this province are extremely limited, but they're among the least expensive in the country. You'll find a few romantic castle hotels, as well as small guesthouses. Parking is rarely a problem in these places, and, unless otherwise noted, you park for free. The touring season in Burgenland lasts April through October.

1 EISENSTADT: HAYDN'S HOME

50km (31 miles) SE of Vienna

When Burgenland joined Austria in the 1920s, it was a province without a capital—its former seat of government, Ödenburg (now the far-western Hungarian city of Sopron), voted to remain a part of Hungary. In 1924, Burgenlanders bestowed the honor on Eisenstadt. This small town lies at the foot of the Leitha Mountains, at the beginning of the steppe extending into Hungary. Surrounded by vineyards, forests, and fruit trees, it's a convenient stop for exploring Lake Neusiedl, 10km (6 miles) east.

ESSENTIALS

GETTING THERE Board one of the many trains heading toward Budapest from the Südbahnhof (South Railway Station) in Vienna, and change trains in the railway junction of Neusiedl am See. Connections are timed to link up with the 16 or so trains that continue on to Eisenstadt (trip time: 90 min.). For schedules, call ✆ **05/1717** in Vienna, or check **www.oebb.at**.

Many visitors prefer to go by bus leaving Vienna from Südtirol Platz (site of a U-Bahn) Station. Suburban buses begin their runs at this huge depot. From lane no. 24, a bus leaves during the day for Eisenstadt on an hourly basis, the trip taking anywhere from 47 to 70 minutes.

If you're driving from Vienna, take Route 10 east to Parndorf Ort, and then head southwest along Route 50 to Eisenstadt.

VISITOR INFORMATION The **Eisenstadt tourist office,** Schloss Esterházy (✆ **02682/67390**), will make hotel reservations for you at no charge and distributes information (in English).

WHERE JOSEF HAYDN LIVED & WORKED

Even before assuming its new role as capital, Eisenstadt was renowned as the place where the great composer Franz Josef Haydn lived and worked while under the patronage of the Esterházys. For a good part of his life (1732–1809), Haydn divided his time between Eisenstadt and Esterházy Castle in Hungary. Prince Esterházy eventually gave the composer his own orchestra and a concert hall in which to perform.

In September, the **Haydn Days** festival presents an ongoing roster of the composer's works at various venues throughout town—the castle, local churches, parks—when the weather is good.

Bergkirche (Church of the Calvary) If you want to pay your final respects to Haydn, follow Hauptstrasse to Esterházystrasse, which leads to this church containing Haydn's white marble tomb. Until 1954, only the composer's headless body was here. His skull was in the Vienna's Sammlung alter Musikinstrumente (p. 143), where curious spectators were actually allowed to touch it. It was stolen a few days after his death and wasn't reunited with his body for 145 years. In a long and complicated journey, the head traveled from one owner to another before finally, we hope, coming to rest with the other part of Haydn's remains at Eisenstadt.

Josef-Haydn-Platz 1. ✆ **02682/62638.** Church free admission; Haydn's tomb 2.50€ ($4) adults, 2€ ($3.20) seniors, 1€ ($1.60) students. Daily 9am–noon and 1–5pm. Closed Nov–Mar. From Esterházy Platz at the castle, head directly west along Esterházystrasse, a slightly uphill walk.

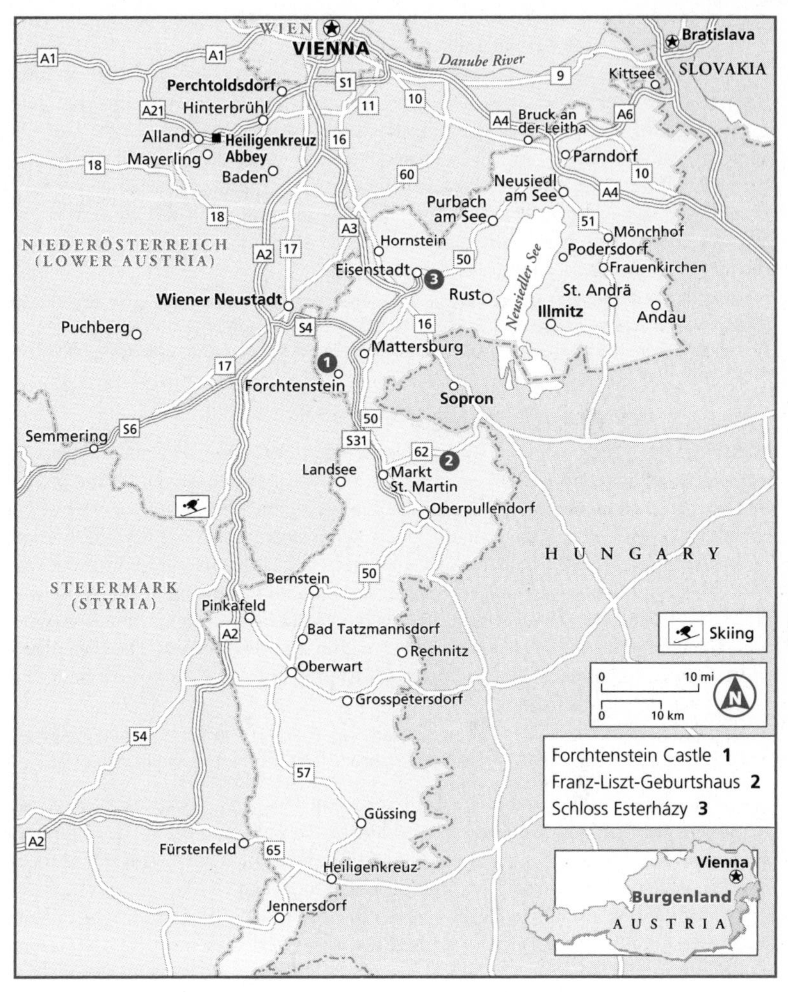

Haydn Museum The little home of the composer from 1766 to 1778 is now a museum. Although he appeared in court nearly every night, Haydn actually lived very modestly when he was at home. A little flower-filled courtyard is one of the few luxuries. The museum has collected mementos of Haydn's life and work.

Haydn-Gasse 21. ✆ **02682/7193900.** Admission 3.50€ ($5.60) adults; 3€ ($4.80) children, seniors, and students. Daily 9am–5pm. Closed Nov–Mar. Pass Schloss Esterházy and turn left onto Haydn-Gasse.

Schloss Esterházy ★ Haydn worked in this château built on the site of a medieval castle and owned by the Esterházy princes. The Esterházy clan was a great Hungarian family with vast estates that ruled over Eisenstadt and its surrounding area. They claimed descent from Attila the Hun. The Esterházys helped the Hapsburgs gain control in Hungary; so great was their loyalty to Austria, in fact, that when Napoleon offered the crown of Hungary to Nic Esterházy in 1809, he refused it.

The castle, built around an inner courtyard, was designed by the Italian architect Carlo Antonio Carlone, who began work on it in 1663. Subsequently, many other architects remodeled it, resulting in sweeping alterations to its appearance. In the late 17th and early 18th centuries, it was given a baroque pastel facade. On the first floor, the great baronial hall was made into the Haydnsaal, where the composer conducted the orchestra Prince Esterházy had provided for him. The walls and ceilings of this concert hall are elaborately decorated, but the floor is of bare wood, which, it is claimed, is the reason for the room's acoustic perfection.

Esterházy Platz. ✆ **2682/7193000.** www.schloss-esterhazy.at. Admission 6.50€ ($10) adults; 5.50€ ($8.80) children, seniors, and students; 15€ ($24) family ticket. Mar 16–Nov 11 daily 8:30am–6pm; Nov 12–March 15 Mon–Thurs 9am–6pm, Fri 9am–3pm. From the bus station at Domplatz, follow the sign to the castle (a 10-min. walk).

WHERE TO STAY & DINE

Gasthof Öhr Although the rooms of this pleasant inn are clean and comfortable, with exposed paneling, comfortable beds, and a sense of old-fashioned charm, the place is more famous and more consistently popular as a restaurant, where main courses cost 10€ to 20€ ($16–$32) each, and where the kitchen consistently turns out flavorful portions of *tafelspitz,* Wiener schnitzel, and such freshwater fish dishes as zander in white wine with capers, and pan-fried trout, sometimes with almonds, sometimes with white wine and butter. These are served within any of four old-fashioned dining rooms accented with wood trim, or during clement weather, within a garden in back. The restaurant is open Tuesday to Sunday 11am to 10pm. This inn is just across from Eisenstadt's bus station, behind a white facade.

Ruster Strasse 51, A-7000 Eisenstadt. ✆ **02682/62460.** www.hotelohr.at. 30 units. 95€–145€ ($152–$232) double. DC, MC, V. Parking 7€ ($11). **Amenities:** Restaurant; room service; babysitting. *In room:* TV.

Hotel Burgenland Hotel Burgenland opened in 1982 and quickly established itself as the best in Eisenstadt. A mansard roof, white stucco walls, and big windows form the exterior of this hotel located directly northeast of the bus station at Domplatz. The rooms have lots of light, comfortable beds and functional furniture.

One of the best restaurants in Burgenland is the hotel's Bienenkorb. Bright and airy, it serves traditional dishes such as cabbage soup and veal steak with fresh vegetables along with some Hungarian specialties.

Schubertplatz 1, A-7000 Eisenstadt. ✆ **02682/6960.** Fax 02682/65531. www.hotelburgenland.at. 88 units. 145€ ($232) double; from 250€ ($400) suite. Rates include buffet breakfast. AE, DC, MC, V. Parking 10€ ($16). **Amenities:** 2 restaurants; bar; indoor heated pool; fitness center; sauna; room service; babysitting; laundry service; dry cleaning; nonsmoking rooms. *In room:* TV w/pay movies, Wi-Fi, minibar, hair dryer, trouser press, safe.

SHOPPING

With a little effort, you can find some tempting shops in Eisenstadt's old town. Most appealing to visitors in our opinion is **Trachten Tack,** Hauptstrasse 8 (✆ **02682/62428**), where you'll find folkloric Burgenland-derived clothing, as well as the widest selection of handicrafts in town.

Carrying an impressive inventory of wine, **Schloss Weingut Esterházy,** Schloss Esterházy (✆ **02682/63345**), is set on the street level of Eisenstadt's most famous building. Most of the wine is produced on the 60 hectares (148 acres) of vineyards associated with the castle. One part of the store is devoted to native son Josef Haydn and sells souvenirs related to his accomplishments.

EISENSTADT AFTER DARK

Don't expect a lot, as there simply isn't much nightlife within small and sleepy Eisenstadt. You might have a quiet drink or two at such popular spots as the **Café Alex Nöhrer,** Ignaz-Semmelweisse-Gasse 1 (✆ **02682/65593**), or at any of the hidden bars whose clientele and flavor changes depending on what time of day you happen to arrive and on whoever happens to be there when you show up. Currently enjoying popularity are the **Mango Bar,** Domplatz 4 (✆ **06649/793160**), and **Bodega La Ina,** Hauptstrasse 48 (✆ **02682/62305**). And if you want to go dancing, head for the town's only dance club, the **James Dean,** Mattesburgerstrasse 26 (✆ **2682/62449**), an interesting combination of *Mitteleuropa* and 1950s America.

A SIDE TRIP TO FRANZ LISZT'S BIRTHPLACE

In Raiding, a small nearby village 55km south of Eisenstadt, the **Franz-Liszt-Geburtshaus** contains many mementos of the composer's life, including an old church organ he used to play.

To get to the museum (✆ **02619/51057**), take Route S31 south of Eisenstadt; then cut east onto a minor unmarked road at Lackenbach (follow the signs to Raiding from there). It's open only from Easter to October (daily 9am–noon and 1–5pm). Admission is 3.50€ ($5.60) for adults and 2€ ($3.20) for seniors, children, and students; a family ticket sells for 7€ ($11).

2 LAKE NEUSIEDL ★

The Lake Neusiedl region is a famous getaway for the Viennese, and North Americans will find it just as desirable. The lake offers countless diversions, making it an ideal destination for families or active travelers. You can play in and around the lake all day, and then relax over a fine meal of Burgenland cuisine. The geological anomaly of the Neusiedler (see "The Capricious Lake," below) and the steppe landscape make for intriguing hikes and strolls. The towns tend to be small, sleepy hamlets offering little more than lakeside relaxation, but they are ideal bases for exploring the surrounding countryside.

NEUSIEDL AM SEE

On the northern shore of Lake Neusiedl lies this popular summer weekend spot, where watersports prevail. You can rent sailboats here and spend the day drifting around the lake. The town's Gothic parish church is noted for its "ship pulpit." A watchtower from the Middle Ages still stands guard over the town, although it's no longer occupied. Many vineyards cover the nearby fields. If you plan to be here on a summer weekend, make advance reservations.

The Capricious Lake

Neusiedler See (Lake Neusiedl) is a popular steppe lake lying in the northern part of Burgenland. But this strange lake should never be taken for granted—in fact, from 1868 to 1872, it completely dried up, as it has done periodically throughout its known history. Such behavior has led to some confusing real-estate disputes among bordering landowners. The lake was once part of a body of water that blanketed all of the Pannonian Plain. Today its greatest depth is about 1.8m (6 ft.), and the wind can shift the water dramatically, even causing parts of the lake to dry up. The lake is between 7 and 15km ($4\frac{1}{4}$–$9\frac{1}{4}$ miles) wide and about 35km (22 miles) long.

A broad belt of reeds encircles the huge expanse. This thicket is an ideal habitat for many varieties of waterfowl. In all, some 250 different species of birds inhabit the lake, including the usual collection of storks, geese, duck, and herons. The plant and animal life in the lake is unique in Europe. Within its slightly salty waters, alpine, Baltic, and Pannonian flora and fauna meet.

Viennese flock to the lake throughout the year, in summer to fish, sail, and windsurf, and in winter to skate. Nearly every lakeside village has a beach (although on any given day it might be swallowed up by the lake or be miles from the shore, depending on which way the wind blows). The temperate climate and fertile soil surrounding the west bank are ideal for vineyards. Washed in sun, the orchards in Rust produce famous award-winning vintages.

Essentials

GETTING THERE Neusiedl am See lies 45km (28 miles) southeast of Vienna, 359km (223 miles) east of Salzburg, and 34km (21 miles) northeast of Eisenstadt. This town is your gateway to the lake, as it's less than an hour by express **train** from Vienna (© **05/1717;** www.oebb.at). If you're **driving** from Vienna, take the A-4 or Route 10 east. If you're in Eisenstadt, head northeast along Route 50, cutting east along Route 51 for a short distance. It's better to have a car if you're exploring Lake Neusiedl, although there are **bus** connections that depart several times daily from the Domplatz bus station at Eisenstadt.

VISITOR INFORMATION The **Neusiedl am See tourist office**, in the Rathaus (town hall), Hauptplatz 1 (© **02167/2229**), distributes information about accommodations and boat rentals. Open July and August Monday to Friday 8am to 6pm, Saturday 10am to noon and 2 to 6pm; September to June Monday to Thursday 8am to noon and 1 to 4:30pm, Friday 8am to 1pm.

Where to Stay & Dine

Gasthof zur Traube This small hotel stands on the town's bustling main street. The pleasant ground-floor restaurant is filled with country trim and wrought-iron table dividers. You can stop in for a meal from 11am to 10pm, or book one of the cozy upstairs rooms. Both the rooms and shower-only bathrooms are a bit on the small size. In summer, guests can relax in the garden. Franz Rittsteuer and his family are the owners.

Hauptplatz 9, A-7100 Neusiedl am See. ✆ **02167/2423.** Fax 02167/24236. www.zur-traube.at. 7 units. 66€ ($106) double. Rates include breakfast. MC, V. Free parking. **Amenities:** Restaurant; bar. *In room:* TV.

Hotel Wende ★ This place is actually a complex of three sprawling buildings interconnected by rambling corridors. Set at the edge of town on the road leading to the water, the hotel is almost a village unto itself. The bedrooms are well furnished, with well-maintained bathrooms containing tub/shower combinations.

The best food and best service, as well as the most formal setting, are found in the hotel's restaurant. Under a wood-beamed ceiling, the rich and bountiful table of Burgenland is set to perfection. In summer, tables are placed outside overlooking the grounds. Because Burgenland is a border state, the menu reflects the cuisines of Hungary and Austria. The menu includes a savory soup made with fresh carp from nearby lakes; pork cutlets with homemade noodles, bacon-flavored *rösti* (fried potatoes), baby carrots, and fresh herbs; Hungarian crepes stuffed with minced veal and covered with paprika-cream sauce; and, for dessert, a strudel studded with fresh dates and topped with marzipan-flavored whipped cream.

Seestrasse 40–50, A-7100 Neusiedl am See. ✆ **02167/8111.** Fax 02167/811-1649. www.hotel-wende.at. 106 units. 134€–164€ ($214–$262) double; 290€–310€ ($464–$496) suite. Rates include half-board. AE, DC, MC, V. Parking garage 10€ ($16). Closed last week in Jan and first 2 weeks in Feb. Free pickup at the train station. **Amenities:** Restaurant; bar; indoor heated pool; 3 tennis courts; fitness center; Jacuzzi; sauna; salon; room service; massage; babysitting; laundry service; dry cleaning; nonsmoking rooms. *In room:* TV, Wi-Fi, minibar, hair dryer.

PURBACH AM SEE

If you take Route 50 south from the northern tip of Lake Neusiedl, your first stop might be in this little resort village, which has some decent accommodations. Purbach is also a market town, and you can buy Burgenland wine in the shops. Some of the town walls, built against invading Turks, still stand.

Essentials

GETTING THERE Purbach is 50km (31 miles) southeast of Vienna and 18km (11 miles) northeast of Eisenstadt. From Eisenstadt, you can take a daily bus that leaves from the station at Domplatz. If you're driving from Eisenstadt, head northeast along Route 50; if you're coming from Vienna, cut southeast along Route 10.

VISITOR INFORMATION Contact the **Neusiedler See tourist office** in Neusiedl am See, Hauptplatz 1 (✆ **02167/2229**). It's open July and August, Monday to Friday from 8am to 7pm, Saturday 10am to noon and 2 to 6pm, Sunday from 4 to 7pm; September to June, Monday to Thursday from 8am to noon and 1 to 4:30pm, Friday 8am to 1pm.

Where to Stay

Am Spitz The main building of this hotel has a gable trimmed with baroque embellishments, lying 2km (1¼ miles) from the center. The Holzl-Schwarz family is your host here, where a hotel has stood for more than 600 years. The current incarnation includes accommodations with wonderful views of the lake. The hotel staff takes care and pride in the maintenance of its average-size rooms and small but quite serviceable shower-only bathrooms. The hotel is well directed, conservative, and deserving of its three-star government rating. The adjoining restaurant is one of the best places in the region for Burgenland cuisine.

Waldsiedlung 2, A-7083 Purbach am See. ✆ **02683/5519.** Fax 02683/551920. www.klosteramspitz.at. 15 units. 100€–120€ ($160–$192) double. Rates include buffet breakfast. MC, V. Free parking. Closed Jan 1–Mar 5. The hotel will pick up guests at the bus station. **Amenities:** Restaurant; lounge; room service; coin-operated laundry. *In room:* TV, Wi-Fi, minibar, hair dryer.

Where to Dine

Am Spitz Restaurant BURGENLAND/PANNONIAN The regional artifacts that adorn the space and the excellent waitstaff make this restaurant a warm and inviting place. Chefs borrow heavily from the recipes of Burgenland and the neighboring province of Pannonia. The setting, in a former 17th-century abbey with a flower garden extending in summer to the lake itself, is beautiful.

The menu changes daily but always features the catch of the day (from the nearby lake) that can be prepared to your desires. Meat and poultry are other main dishes, and we're especially fond of their pan-fried chicken schnitzel or their perfectly grilled tender beef. Roast veal steak is another menu highlight. Most diners prefer to begin with a bowl of the spicy Hungarian-inspired fish soup. All the luscious desserts are made fresh daily. The wine cellar stocks hundreds of bottles—in fact, the hotel owns around 14 hectares (35 acres) of vineyards and produces its own wines.

Waldsiedlung 2. ✆ **02683/5519.** Reservations recommended. Main courses 13€–22€ ($21–$35); fixed-price menus 52€–60€ ($83–$96). Mid-Mar to mid-Dec Thurs–Sun noon–2pm and 6–9pm.

RUST

Leaving Purbach, head south toward Rust, a small resort village with limited accommodations. It's famous for its stork nests, which are perched on chimneys throughout the town. Its antiquated but charming town center is well preserved and clean, and its walls were built in 1614 for protection against the Turks.

Rust is the capital of the Burgenland lake district, lying in a rich setting of vineyards famed for the Burgenlander grape. If available, try the *Blaufränkisch,* a red wine mostly consumed by the locals and visiting Viennese who flock to the area. Sometimes you can go right up to the door of a vintner's farmhouse, especially if a green bough is displayed, to sample and buy wine on the spot.

The little lakeshore resort has a friendly atmosphere. Summers are often hot, and the lake water is surprisingly tepid. Sailboats and windsurfers can be rented on the banks of the shallow Neusiedler See.

Essentials

GETTING THERE The village is 18km (11 miles) northeast of Eisenstadt, 71km (44 miles) southeast of Vienna, and 349km (217 miles) east of Salzburg. There's no train station, but buses connect Eisenstadt with Rust. For bus information, call (✆ **01/5266048**). From Eisenstadt by car, head east on Route 52. From Purbach, take Route 50 south toward Eisenstadt. At Seehof, take a left fork to Oggau and Rust.

VISITOR INFORMATION The **Rust tourist office,** in the Rathaus (town hall) in the center of the village (✆ **02685/502**), can arrange inexpensive stays with English-speaking families. It's open Monday to Friday 9am to noon and 1 to 6pm, Saturday 1 to 4pm, and Sunday 9am to noon.

Where to Stay & Dine

Hotel-Restaurant Sifkovitz ★ Attracting summer visitors from Vienna and Hungary, this hotel consists of an older building with a new wing. Rooms get a lot of sun and are functional but comfortably furnished. There's no great style here, but the beds are firm and the bathrooms, although not large, are well maintained and equipped with tub/shower combinations. There is access to tennis courts, but they're on the grounds of another hotel nearby (the staff will make arrangements). Food, both Austrian and Hungarian, is served daily.

Am Seekanal 8, A-7071 Rust. ✆ **02685/276.** Fax 02685/36012. www.sifkovits.at. 35 units. 96€–122€ ($154–$195) per person double. Rates include buffet breakfast. AE, DC, MC, V. Closed Dec–Mar. **Amenities:** Restaurant; bar; fitness center; sauna; room service; laundry service; dry cleaning; nonsmoking rooms. *In room:* TV, Wi-Fi, minibar, hair dryer, safe.

Mooslechner's Burgerhaus ★ AUSTRIAN/CONTINENTAL Rust has several other restaurants fixated on innovative and more expensive cuisine, but we prefer this *gemütlich,* middle-bracket tavern in the heart of town. Within a venue that dates from the 1530s, it provides plenty of old-fashioned charm. The food, focused on traditional preparations of zander, goose, and, in season, game dishes, evokes traditional Austria at its best. The cook here is particularly proud of the terrines of goose liver that emerge from the kitchen. The venue is cozy and rather charming (seating only 60–80 diners).

Hauptstrasse 1. ✆ **02685/6416.** Reservations recommended only in midsummer. Set-price menus 39€–76€ ($62–$122). DC, MC, V. Daily noon–2pm and 6pm–midnight. Closed Jan–Feb.

Seehotel Rust ★ Seehotel Rust is one of the most attractive hotels in the lake district, set on a grassy lawn at the edge of the lake. This well-designed hotel remains open year-round, and offers pleasantly furnished bedrooms and clean bathrooms equipped with a shower unit. The rooms are a little too "peas-in-the-pod" for most tastes; however, an overnight stopover can be just fine. Offerings in the restaurant include *tafelspitz* with chive sauce, calves' brains with a honey vinegar, watercress soup, and sole meunière. A Gypsy band provides entertainment.

Am Seekanal 2–4, A-7071 Rust. ✆ **02685/3810.** Fax 02685/381419. www.seehotel-rust.at. 110 units. 95€ ($152) per person double; 165€ ($264) per person suite. Rates include half-board. AE, DC, MC, V. Free parking. **Amenities:** Restaurant; bar; indoor heated pool; 4 tennis courts (2 indoor); squash court; sauna; boat rental; room service; babysitting; laundry service; dry cleaning; nonsmoking rooms. *In room:* TV, Wi-Fi, minibar, hair dryer.

ILLMITZ: A STEPPE VILLAGE

This old *puszta* (steppe) village on the east side of the lake has grown into a town with a moderate tourist business in summer. From Eisenstadt, take Route 50 northeast, through Purbach, cutting southeast on Route 51, via Podersdorf, to Illmitz. It's a 61km (38-mile) drive, which seems long because traffic must swing around the lake's northern perimeter before heading south to Illmitz.

Nearby Offbeat Attractions

Leaving Illmitz, head east on the main route and then cut north at the junction with Route 51. From Route 51, the little villages of St. Andrä bei Frauenkirchen and Andau are both signposted.

Near the Hungarian border, the tiny village of **St. Andrä bei Frauenkirchen** is filled with thatch houses. The town is known for its basket weaving, so you might want to drive here for a shopping expedition.

A short drive farther will take you to **Andau,** which became the focus of world attention in 1956 during the Hungarian uprising. It was through this point that hundreds of Hungarians dashed to freedom in the west, fleeing the grim Soviet invasion of Budapest.

Starting in the late 1940s, the border with Hungary was closely guarded, and people who tried to escape into Austria were shot from the Communist-controlled watchtowers. But now all that has changed. In 1989, the fortifications were rendered obsolete, and before the year was out, the once fortified border was completely opened.

The surrounding marshy area of this remote sector of Austria, called **Seewinkel,** is a large natural wildlife sanctuary. The area, dotted with windmills and reed thickets, is a haven for birds, many small animals, and some rare flora.

Seewinkel is very different from Austria's celebrated Alps and thick forests, and is little known to North Americans or even to most Europeans. In other words, it's a great place to get off the beaten track and add a little adventure to your travels.

Where to Stay & Dine

Weingut-Weingasthof Rosenhof ★ This charming baroque hotel stands in a gardenlike setting. Through the arched gateway, framed by a gold-and-white facade, is a rose-laden courtyard filled with arbors. The tile-roofed building, capped with platforms for storks' nests, contains cozy, perfectly maintained bedrooms and bathrooms with shower units.

In an older section, you'll find a wine restaurant whose star attraction is the recent vintage produced by the Haider family's wine presses. The restaurant serves Hungarian and Burgenland specialties to its guests and much of the neighborhood. Dishes might be as exotic as wild boar cooked in a marinade and thickened with regional walnuts. Local fish, such as carp and the meaty zander from the Danube, are available. In autumn, the inn serves *traubensaft*—delectable juice made from freshly harvested grapes that is consumed before it becomes alcoholic. In the evening, musicians fill the air with Gypsy music.

Florianigasse 1, A-7142 Illmitz. ✆ **02175/2232.** Fax 02175/22324. www.rosenhof.cc. 15 units. 86€–94€ ($138–$150) per person double. Rates include half-board. MC, V. Closed Nov–Easter. **Amenities:** Restaurant; bar; laundry service; dry cleaning. *In room:* TV, hair dryer.

PODERSDORF: BEST IN SWIMMING

Podersdorf am See is one of the best places to go swimming in the lake, as the shoreline here is relatively free of reeds. Over the years, the little town has become a modest summer resort. The parish church in the village dates from the late 18th century. Check out the thatched roof cottages where you might see storks nesting in the chimneys. The Viennese like to drive out here during the summer to go for a swim and to purchase wine from the local vintners

Essentials

GETTING THERE Podersdorf lies 14km (9 miles) south of the major center along the lake, Neusiedl am See (see above). It's easiest to drive here, although buses run throughout the day from Eisenstadt, going via Neusiedl am See. If you're driving from Eisenstadt, head northeast along Route 50, via Purbach, cutting southeast at the junction with Route 51; you'll go via Neusiedl am See before cutting south along the lake to Podersdorf.

VISITOR INFORMATION In summer, a little **tourist office** at Hauptstrasse 2 (✆ **02177/2227**) dispenses information daily 8am to 5pm.

Where to Stay

Gasthof Seewirt This hotel sits at the edge of the lake, within a short walk of a great swath of marshland. Rooms are clean, comfortable, and utilitarian, but only medium in size. Duvets cover the comfortable beds, and the shower-only bathrooms are a bit cramped but spotlessly kept. Public areas bear the owners' personal touch and include one of the best restaurants in town (see below).

Strandplatz 1, A-7141 Podersdorf. ✆ **02177/2415.** Fax 02177/246530. 35 units. 95€–170€ ($152–$272) double. Rates include half-board. AE, MC, V. Closed Nov–Mar. **Amenities:** Restaurant; lounge; indoor heated pool; Jacuzzi; sauna; room service; nonsmoking rooms; rooms for those w/limited mobility. *In room:* TV, hair dryer, safe.

Haus Attila This hotel was enlarged in 2004, with its best rooms overlooking the lake. The light-grained balconies are partially shielded by a row of trees, and many overlook the lake. Rooms are clean and comfortable, and the tiny shower-only bathrooms are well maintained. Many visitors who check in for a couple of days of lakeside relaxation never move too far, consuming their meals in the dining room of the Seewirt, less than 91m (298 ft.) away. In the basement of a nearby annex is a well-stocked wine cellar, where a member of the Karner family can take you for a wine tasting. Some of the vintages are produced from their own vineyards.

Strandplatz 8, A-7141 Podersdorf. ✆ **02177/2415.** Fax 02177/246530. www.seewirtkarner.at. 38 units. 101€–165€ ($162–$264) double. Rates include breakfast. AE, DC, MC, V. Closed Nov 1–Mar 30. **Amenities:** Lounge; indoor heated pool; sauna; room service; nonsmoking rooms; rooms for those w/limited mobility. *In room:* TV, hair dryer, safe.

Seehotel Herlinde An excellent government-rated two-star choice, this vacation spot is on the beach of Lake Neusiedl away from the main highway. All the functionally furnished rooms have their own balconies; the best have views of the lake. Room size is only adequate; the beds are nothing special, though the mattresses are firm. The food and wine are plentiful, the latter often enjoyed on a 200-seat terrace. The hotel is entirely nonsmoking.

Strandplatz 17, A-7141 Podersdorf. ✆ **02177/2273.** Fax 02177/2430. 40 units. 106€ ($170) double. Rates include breakfast and lunch. MC, V. **Amenities:** Restaurant; bar; sauna; laundry service. *In room:* TV, minibar, hair dryer.

Where to Dine

Gasthof Seewirt Café Restaurant ★ BURGENLANDER/INTERNATIONAL The preferred place for dining at the resort is this likable and unpretentious hotel restaurant that prepares bountiful dishes served by formally dressed waiters who are eager to describe the local cuisine. The Karner family—well-known vintners whose excellent Rieslings, red and white pinots, and Weisburgunders are available for consumption—are proud of their long-established traditions and a local cuisine that in some ways resembles that of neighboring Hungary. A house specialty is *Palatschinken Marmaladen,* consisting of tender roast beef glazed with apricot jam, and a dessert called *Somloer Nockerl,* made of vanilla pudding, whipped cream, raisins, and nuts in a biscuit shell.

Strandplatz 1. ✆ **02177/2415.** Main courses 8€–14€ ($13–$22). AE, MC, V. Daily 11:30am–2:30pm and 6–9:30pm. Closed Nov–Mar.

3 FORCHTENSTEIN

This town resembles so many others along the way that you could easily pass through it without taking much notice. However, Forchtenstein is home to one of the most famous of the Esterházy castles, which is reason enough make it a stop on your trip.

ESSENTIALS

GETTING THERE From Eisenstadt, take Route S-31 southwest to Mattersburg, and from there follow the signs along a very minor road southwest to Forchtenstein. Three buses per day (only one on Sun) run from Vienna to Forchtenstein. There are no direct trains; the nearest railway station is 10km (6¼ miles) away, in Mattersburg. From here, take a taxi or one of the three daily buses that go to Forchtenstein.

VISITOR INFORMATION In lieu of a tourist office, the **town council,** in the mayor's office at Hauptstrasse 52 (✆ **02685/7744**), provides information Monday to Friday 9am to noon and 1 to 6pm, Saturday and Sunday 9am to noon.

SEEING THE SIGHTS

The castle **Burg Forchtenstein,** Burgplatz 1 (✆ **02626/81212**), 14km (8¾ miles) southeast of Wiener Neustadt in Lower Austria, was constructed on a rocky base by order of the counts of Mattersdorf in the 13th century. The Esterházy family had it greatly expanded around 1636. From its belvedere, you can see as far as the Great Hungarian Plain.

The castle saw action in the Turkish sieges of Austria in 1529 and 1683. A museum since 1815, it holds the Prince Esterházy collections, which consist of family memorabilia, a portrait gallery, large battle paintings, historical banners, and Turkish war booty and hunting arms. It's the largest private collection of historical arms in Austria. Legend has it that Turkish prisoners carved the castle cistern out of the rock, more than 137m (449 ft.) deep.

Admission is 8€ ($13) for adults, 7€ ($11) for students and children 6 to 15, free for children under 6. The castle is open April to October daily 9am to 5pm; November to March, tours are offered only when requested in advance. A guide shows you through.

WHERE TO STAY

Gasthof Sauerzapf This hotel has two stories of weathered stucco, renovated windows, and a roofline that's red on one side and black on the other. The updated interior is cozy and attractive, albeit simple, and is kept immaculate. Anna Daskalakis-Sauerzapf, the owner, rents modestly furnished rooms that are reasonably comfortable for the price. Their style is reminiscent of your great-aunt's house—comfortable beds and just-adequate shower-only bathrooms, inviting nonetheless. The restaurant serves good food and an array of local wines.

Rosalienstrasse 39, A-7212 Forchtenstein. ✆/fax **02626/81217.** 12 units. 48€ ($77) double. Rates include breakfast. No credit cards. Free parking. **Amenities:** Restaurant (closed Wed); lounge. *In room:* No phone.

WHERE TO DINE

Reisner (Value) AUSTRIAN The area's best restaurant has expanded over the years from its original century-old core. Here you'll find good food, particularly the regional specialties and Burgenland wines. Our favorite area is the cozy, rustic, smaller room, which the locals prefer as well. Besides the especially good steaks, you might enjoy trout filet served with a savory ragout of tomatoes, zucchini, potatoes, and basil. In winter, the menu lists many different preparations of venison. The five-course fixed-price meal is gargantuan.

Hauptstrasse 141. ✆ **02626/63139.** Reservations recommended. Main courses 8€–22€ ($13–$35); fixed-price dinner menus 22€–44€ ($35–$70). No credit cards. Wed–Sun 9am–2:30pm and 6–10pm.

9

Salzburg: City of Mozart

A baroque city on the banks of the Salzach River, Salzburg is the beautiful capital of Land Salzburg. This former site of the Roman town of Juvavum is set against a pristine mountain backdrop. The city and the river were named after the early residents who earned their living in the region's salt mines.

This "heart of the heart of Europe" is the city of Mozart, who was born here in 1756. The composer's association with the city continues to draw loads of tourist revenue and tourists, who come to visit this favorite son's birthplace, the Geburtshaus, an old burgher's house.

The Old Town lies on the left bank of the river, where a monastery and bishopric were founded in A.D. 700. From that simple start, Salzburg grew in power and prestige, becoming an archbishopric see in 798. At the height of the prince-archbishop's power, the city was known as the "German Rome." On medieval maps, the little province of Land Salzburg was titled "church lands." Long a part of the Holy Roman Empire, Land Salzburg was joined to Austria in 1816 following the Congress of Vienna.

Salzburg, a city of 17th- and 18th-century houses, is internationally known for its architectural grandeur. Much of the work was done by the masters of the baroque, Fischer von Erlach and Johann Lukas von Hildebrandt. The Salzburg Cathedral is the first deliberately Italian-style church to be built north of the Alps. Several beautiful castles and palaces dot the city: Hohensalzburg Fortress, the former stronghold of the prince-archbishops of Salzburg; Residenz, an opulent palace and seat of the Salzburg prince-archbishops after they abandoned the gloomy Hohensalzburg; and Schloss Hellbrunn, 5km (3 miles) south of the city, summer residence of the prince-archbishops. The beautifully baroque Mirabell Gardens were laid out by the famous Fischer von Erlach.

The city is the setting for the Salzburg Festival, a world-renowned annual event that attracts music lovers, especially Mozart fans, from all over the globe. Salzburg was also the setting for *The Sound of Music;* yes, the hills are alive with music—and reachable by tour.

Ever since the end of World War II, Salzburg has had a strong American connection. While the Soviets occupied a section of Vienna and Lower Austria, Salzburg was a part of the American zone. The real postwar economy didn't develop in Eastern Austria until 1955 when the Russians pulled out. However, economic development began in Salzburg right at the end of the war, giving the city a 10-year head start and cementing its friendship with the United States.

1 ORIENTATION

Salzburg is only a short distance from the Austrian-German frontier, so it's convenient for exploring many of the nearby attractions in Bavaria (see *Frommer's Germany* or *Frommer's Munich & the Bavarian Alps*). On the northern slopes of the Alps, the city is at the intersection of traditional European trade routes and is well served today by air, Autobahn, and rail.

GETTING THERE

By Plane

The **Salzburg Airport–W. A. Mozart,** Innsbrucker Bundesstrasse 95 (✆ **0662/8580;** www.salzburg-airport.com), lies 3km (2 miles) southwest of the city center. It has regularly scheduled air service to all Austrian airports, as well as to Frankfurt, Amsterdam, Brussels, Berlin, Dresden, Düsseldorf, Hamburg, London, Paris, and Zurich. Major airlines serving the Salzburg airport are Austrian Airlines (✆ **0662/854511**), Air France (✆ **01/502222400**), Lufthansa (✆ **081010/258080**), and Tyrolean (✆ **0662/854533**).

Bus no. 2 runs between the airport and Salzburg's main rail station. Departures are every 10 to 20 minutes (Sun and public holidays every 30 min.), and the 20-minute trip costs 2€ ($3.20) one-way. By taxi it's only about 15 minutes, but you'll pay at least 12€ to 18€ ($19–$29).

By Train

Salzburg's main rail station, the **Salzburg Hauptbahnhof,** Südtirolerplatz (✆ **05/1717;** www.oebb.at), is on the major rail lines of Europe, with frequent arrivals not only from all the main cities of Austria, but also from other European cities such as Munich. Between 5:30am and 11:40pm, trains arrive every 30 minutes from Vienna (trip time: 2½–3½ hr.). A one-way fare costs 44€ ($71). There are 19 daily trains from Innsbruck (trip time: 2 hr.). A one-way fare costs 34€ ($54). Trains also arrive every 30 minutes from Munich (trip time: 90 min.–2 hr.), with a one-way ticket costing 29€ ($46).

From the train station, buses depart to various parts of the city, including the Altstadt (Old Town), or you can walk from the rail station to the Old Town in about 20 minutes. The rail station sells tickets and has a currency exchange and storage lockers.

By Car

Salzburg is 336km (209 miles) southwest of Vienna and 153km (95 miles) east of Munich. It's reached from all directions by good roads, including Autobahn A8 from the west (Munich), A1 from the east (Vienna), and A10 from the south. Route 20 comes into Salzburg from points north and west, and Route 159 serves towns and cities from the southeast.

VISITOR INFORMATION

There are two separate branches of the **Salzburg Tourist Information Office** that accept visits and calls from the general public. They include a branch on Platform 2A of the Hauptbahnhof, Südtirolerplatz (✆ **0662/88987-340**), and another in the heart of the city's historic core, at Mozartplatz 5 (✆ **0662/88987-330;** www.salzburginfo). Either of these offices can book tour guides for you and dispense information about attractions and where to stay. They'll also book hotel reservation for you through their Web facilities, **www.salzburg.info**. Hours of the office at the railway station are July to September 9am to 7pm and October to June 9am to 6pm. Hours of the office on the Mozartplatz are October to May daily 9am to 6pm and June to September 9am to 7pm.

CITY LAYOUT

Most of what visitors come to see lies on the left bank of the Salzach River in the **Altstadt (Old Town).** If you're driving, you must leave your car in the modern part of town—the right bank of the Salzach—and enter the Old Town on foot, as most of it is for pedestrians only.

NEIGHBORHOODS IN BRIEF

ALTSTADT Most visitors head for the Altstadt, or Old Town, on the left bank of the Salzach, that part stretching from the river to Mönchsberg. This is a section of narrow streets (many from the Middle Ages) and slender houses, in complete contrast to the town constructed by the prince-archbishops across the river. The Old Town contains many of Salzburg's top attractions, including the cathedral, Mozart's birthplace, and St. Peter's Cemetery.

NONNBERG The eastern hill occupied by the Hohensalzburg Fortress, Nonnberg, rises to 455m (1,493 ft.). Some of the scenes from *The Sound of Music* were shot here. Nonnberg stands to the south of Kajetanerplatz. Stift Nonnberg is a Benedictine nunnery founded about A.D. 700 by St. Rupert. Dominating the entire district, however, is the towering Hohensalzburg Fortress, lying south of the Old Town on the southwestern summit of Mönchsberg.

MÖNCHSBERG To the west of the Hohensalzburg, this area is a mountain ridge slightly less than 3km (2 miles) long. It rises over the Old Town to a height of 542m (1,778 ft.). Fortifications atop it are from the 15th through the 17th centuries.

RIGHT BANK The newer part of town is on the right bank of the Salzach, below Kapuzinerberg, the right-bank counterpart of Mönchsberg. This peak rises 637m (2,090 ft.) and is a lovely woodland area.

The heart of the inner city is **Residenzplatz,** which has the largest and finest baroque fountain this side of the Alps. On the western side of the square stands the **Residenz,** palace of the prince-archbishops; and, on the southern side, is the **Salzburg Dom (Salzburg Cathedral).** To the west of the Dom lies **Domplatz,** linked by archways dating from 1658. Squares to the north and south appear totally enclosed.

On the southern side of Max-Reinhardt-Platz and Hofstallgasse, edging toward **Mönchsberg,** stands the **Festspielhaus (Festival Theater),** built on the foundations of the 17th-century court stables.

STREET MAPS You'll find handy pocket-size maps, with street indexes, all over the city at bookstores, newsstands, and hotels.

2 GETTING AROUND

BY PUBLIC TRANSPORTATION

Information about local public transportation is available at the local tourist office.

The city buses and trams provide quick, comfortable service through the city center from the Nonntal parking lot to Sigsmundsplatz, the city-center parking lot. The one-ride fare is 2€ ($3.20) for adults and 1€ ($1.60) for children 6 to 15; those 5 and under travel free. Buses stop running at either 11pm or 11:20pm, depending on what part of Salzburg you're in.

DISCOUNT PASSES The Salzburg Card not only lets you use unlimited public transportation, but it also acts as an admission ticket to the city's most important cultural sights. With the card you can visit Mozart's birthplace, the Hohensalzburg Fortress, the Residenz gallery, the world-famous water fountain gardens at Hellbrunn, the Baroque Museum in the Mirabell Gardens, and the gala rooms in the Archbishop's Residence. The card is also good for sights outside of town, including the Hellbrunn Zoo, the open-air museum in Grossingmain, the salt mines of the Dürrnberg, and the gondola trip at Unterberg. The card, approximately the size of a credit card, comes with a brochure with maps and sightseeing hints. Cards are valid for 24, 48, and 72 hours and cost 21€ ($34), 29€ ($46), and 34€ ($54), respectively. Children up to 15 years of age receive a 50% discount. You can buy the pass from Salzburg travel agencies, hotels, tobacconists, and municipal offices.

BY CAR

Driving a car in Salzburg is definitely *not* recommended. In most places it's impossible, since the monumental landmark center is for pedestrians only. Public parking lots—designated with a large P—are conveniently located throughout the city. If you're driving into Salzburg, leave your car on the left bank of the Salzach River. You'll find convenient underground parking lots like the one at Mönchsberg, from which it's an easy walk to the center and Domplatz.

However, we do recommend a car for touring around Land Salzburg (see chapter 10); relying on public transportation means a lot of travel time.

RENTALS Car rentals are best made in advance (see chapter 3). If not, try **Avis** (**✆ 0662/877278**) or **Hertz** (**✆ 0662/876674**), both located at Ferdinand-Porsche-Strasse 7. Avis is open Monday to Friday 7:30am to 6pm and Saturday 8am to noon; Hertz is open Monday to Friday 8am to 6pm, Saturday 8am to 1pm.

REPAIRS Try **ÖAMTC (Austrian Automobile Service),** Alpenstrasse 102 (**✆ 0662/639990**), or **ARBÖ (Austrian Motorists Association),** Münchner Bundesstrasse 9 (**✆ 0662/433601**), day or night. The emergency number, in case of automobile breakdowns, is **✆ 120** for ÖAMTC and **✆ 123** for ARBÖ.

BY TAXI & HORSE-DRAWN CAB

You'll find taxi stands scattered at key points all over the city center and in the suburbs. The Salzburg Funktaxi–Vereinigung (radio taxis) office is at Rainerstrasse 27 (**✆ 0662/8111** to order a taxi in advance). Fares start at 3€ ($4.80).

A "traditional taxi"—a *fiaker* (horse-drawn cab)—will not only provide you with a ride, but also a bit of history of the region as well. You can also rent a *fiaker* at Residenzplatz. Four people usually pay 36€ ($58) for 20 minutes and 72€ ($115) for 50 minutes, but all fares are subject to negotiation.

BY BICYCLE

In an effort to keep cars out of the center, Salzburg officials have developed a network of bicycle paths, which are indicated on city maps. One bike path goes along the Salzach River for 14km (9 miles) or so to Hallein, the second-largest town in Land Salzburg (see "Side Trips from Salzburg," later in this chapter).

May to September, you can rent bicycles at **Topbike,** Heringstrasse 8 (**✆ 06272/4656**), daily from 9am to 7pm. Rentals cost about 15€ ($24) per day, with a 20% discount for Salzburg Card holders.

Fast Facts Salzburg

American Express The office, located at Mozartplatz 5–7 (✆ **0662/8080**), adjacent to Residenzplatz, is open Monday to Friday 9am to 5:30pm and Saturday 9am to noon.

Babysitters Arrangements can be made through **Hilfswerk Salzburg,** Klessheimer Allée 45 (✆ **0662/1799**), at a cost of 10€ to 15€ ($16–$24) per hour.

Business Hours Most shops and stores are open Monday to Friday 9am to 6pm. Some smaller shops shut down at noon for a lunch break, which can last 1 or 2 hours. Saturday hours in general are 9am to noon. Salzburg observes *langer Samstag,* which means that on the first Saturday of every month, most stores stay open 9am to 5pm. Banks are open Monday to Friday 8am to noon and 2 to 4:30pm.

Currency Exchange You can exchange money at the Hauptbahnhof, on Südtirolerplatz, daily from 7am to 10pm, and at the airport daily from 9am to 4pm.

Dentists For information on how to find an English-speaking dentist, call Dentistenkammer, Faberstrasse 2 (✆ **0662/873466**).

Doctors If you suddenly fall ill, your best source of information for finding a doctor is the reception desk of your hotel. If you want a comprehensive list of doctors and their respective specialties, which you can acquire in Salzburg or even before your arrival, contact **Ärztekammer für Salzburg,** Bergstrasse 14, A-5020 Salzburg (✆ **0662/871327**). And if your troubles flare up over a weekend, the **Medical Emergency Center of the Austrian Red Cross** maintains a hotline (✆ **141**), which you can use to describe your problem. A staff member here will either ask you to visit their headquarters at Karl Renner Strasse 7 or send a medical expert to wherever you're staying. This service is available from 5pm on Friday to 8am on Monday and on public holidays. For more information on medical emergencies, refer to "Hospitals," below.

Drugstores Larger pharmacies, especially those in the city center, tend to remain open, without a break, Monday to Friday 8am to 6pm and Saturday 8am to noon. Pharmacies in small towns near Salzburg and in the suburbs have similar hours but close for lunch, usually from 12:30 to 2:30pm Monday to Friday. For night service, and service on Saturday afternoon and Sunday, pharmacies display a sign giving the address of the nearest pharmacy that has agreed to remain open over the weekend or throughout the night. A pharmacy that's particularly convenient to Salzburg's commercial center is **Elisabeth-Apotheke,** Elisabethstrasse 1A (✆ **0662/871484**), north of Rainerstrasse, toward the train station.

Embassies & Consulates The **Consulate of Great Britain,** Alter Markt 4 (✆ **0662/848133**), is open Monday to Friday 9am to noon. **U.S. citizens** needing business with their consulate should go to Vienna.

Emergencies For emergencies, call the following numbers: police ✆ **133,** fire ✆ **122,** and ambulance ✆ **144.**

Hospitals Salzburg is well equipped with medical facilities, including **Unfahl Hospital,** on Dr.-Franz-Rehrl-Platz 5 (✆ **0662/65800**); and **Krankenhaus und Konvent der Barmherzigen Brüder,** Kajetanerplatz 1 (✆ **0662/80880**).

Internet Access The most convenient cafe with Internet capability is the **Internet Café,** Mozartplatz 5 (✆ **0662/844822**), across from the tourist office. It's open daily 9am to 11pm and charges 9€ ($14) per hour of Internet access.

Luggage Storage & Lockers Lockers are available at the Hauptbahnhof, Südtirolerplatz (✆ **0043/51717**), open 24 hours daily. For 2 days, you can rent a large locker for 3.50€ ($5.60) or a small locker for 2€ ($4). The luggage storage counter, with an attendant, is open 4am to midnight daily.

Police For the police, call ✆ **133.**

Post Offices The main post office is at Residenzplatz 9 (✆ **0662/8441210**). The post office at the main railway station is open daily from 7am to 10pm. The postal code for Salzburg is A-5020; for Anif, A-5081; and for Bergheim, A-5101.

Safety Salzburg has a low crime rate compared with most European cities, but there is crime here. Take the usual precautions here as you would elsewhere. Use discretion, of course, and common sense.

Taxes The government value-added tax (VAT) and the service charge are included in restaurant and hotel bills presented to you. For a VAT refund, see "Fast Facts: Austria," in the appendix. Other than this blanket tax mentioned above, Salzburg imposes no special city taxes.

Toilets These are identified by the WC sign and are found throughout the city in museums and at sightseeing attractions, the rail station, and the airport. You can stop at a cafe, but these establishments prefer you to be a customer, even if it's only a small purchase.

Transit Information **Stadtbus Salzburg** is the organization that's equipped to give information about the bus lines which crisscross the city. For information on where they're headed and other related details, visit the city transport office at Alpenstrasse 91, call ✆ **0662/44801500,** or click on **www.stadtbus.at**.

Useful Telephone Numbers For the airport, call ✆ **0662/8580;** for train information, call ✆ **05/1717.**

3 WHERE TO STAY

Some of the best places to stay, particularly the castle hotels, converted farmhouse pensions, and boardinghouses, lie on the outskirts of Salzburg, within an easy drive of the city. But if you don't have a car, you'll probably want to stay right in the city, within walking distance of all the major sightseeing attractions.

If you have access to a car, check chapter 10 before selecting a hotel. Because Salzburg hotels are often very crowded in summer (and are impossibly booked during the Salzburg Festival in Aug), you might want to reserve less-expensive accommodations in Land Salzburg and drive into Salzburg.

A pension or guesthouse in Salzburg does not necessarily mean a less-expensive rate. These places can be luxurious, with a five-star rating, or of a more modest class, comparable to (but often better than) a third-class hotel.

ACCOMMODATIONS ■
Altstadt SAS Radisson **34**
Altstadthotel Weisse Taube **31**
Altstadt Hotel Wolf-Dietrich **66**
Bayerischer Hof **51**
Bergland Hotel **71**
Cordial Theater Hotel **74**
Goldener Hirsch **12**
Haus Arenberg **76**
Hotel Amadeus **64**
Hotel Auersberg **69**
Hotel Blaue Gans **8**
Hotel Bristol **48**
Hotel Drei Kreuz **73**
Hotel Elefant **40**
Hotel Goldene Krone **62**
Hotel Jedermann **72**
Hotel Kasererbräu **20**
Hotel Mozart **68**
Hotel NH Salzburg **67**
Hotel Gablerbräu **59**
Hotel Sacher Salzburg Hof **46**
Hotel Schloss Mönchstein **4**
Hotel Stein **44**
Hotel Stieglbräu **51**
Hotel Trumer Stube **57**
Neutor **15**
Pension Adlerhof **51**
Pension Wolf **30**
Rosenvilla **77**
Salzburg Sheraton Hotel **53**

ATTRACTIONS ●
Festspielhaus **14**
Friedhof St. Sebastian **63**
Glockenspiel (Carillon) **28**
Historische Musikinstrumente **11**
Hohensalzburg Fortress **17**
Kollegienkirche **38**
Mozart Audio & Film Museum **47**
Mozart Geburtshaus **42**
Mozart Wohnhaus **47**
Mozarteum **49**
Museum der Moderne Salzburg **5**
Panorama Museum **29**
Petersfriedhof **22**
Residenz State Rooms **26**
Rupertinum Museum (Museum of Modern Art Salzburg) **25**
Salzburger Barockmuseum **56**
Salzburger Dom **27**
Salzburg Museum/Neue Residenz **29**
Schloss Mirabell **55**
Spielzeug Museum **11**
Stift Nonnberg **19**
Stiftskirche St. Peter **23**

DINING ◆
Alter Fuchs **65**
Alt-Salzburg **11**
BIO Wirtshaus Hirschenwirt **52**
Café Bazar **45**
Café-Konditorei Fürst **10**
Café Tomaselli **36**
Carpe Diem Finest Fingerfood **9**
Culinarium **50**
Die Weisse **70**
Esszimmer **1**
Fasties **32**
Festungsrestaurant **17**
Goldener Hirsch **12**
Hagenauer Stub'n **39**
Herzl Tavern **13**
Hotel Stadtkrug Restaurant **61**
Konditorei Ratzka **75**
Krimpelstätter **2**
Magazin **3**
Mundenhamer Bräu **54**
Polo Lounge **48**
Purzelbaum **18**
Restaurant K & K **33**
Restaurant M32 **5**
Restaurant Symphonie **34**
Restaurant Wasserfall **60**
Ristorante/Pizzeria Il Sole **6**
Schatz-Konditorei **41**
Stadtgasthof Blaue Gans **8**
Sternbräu **7**
Stiftskeller St. Peter (Peterskeller) **24**
Strasserwirt **16**
Weisses Kreuz Balkan Restaurant **21**
Zipfer Bierhaus **37**
Zum Eulenspiegel **43**
Zum Fidelen Affen **58**
Zum Mohren **35**

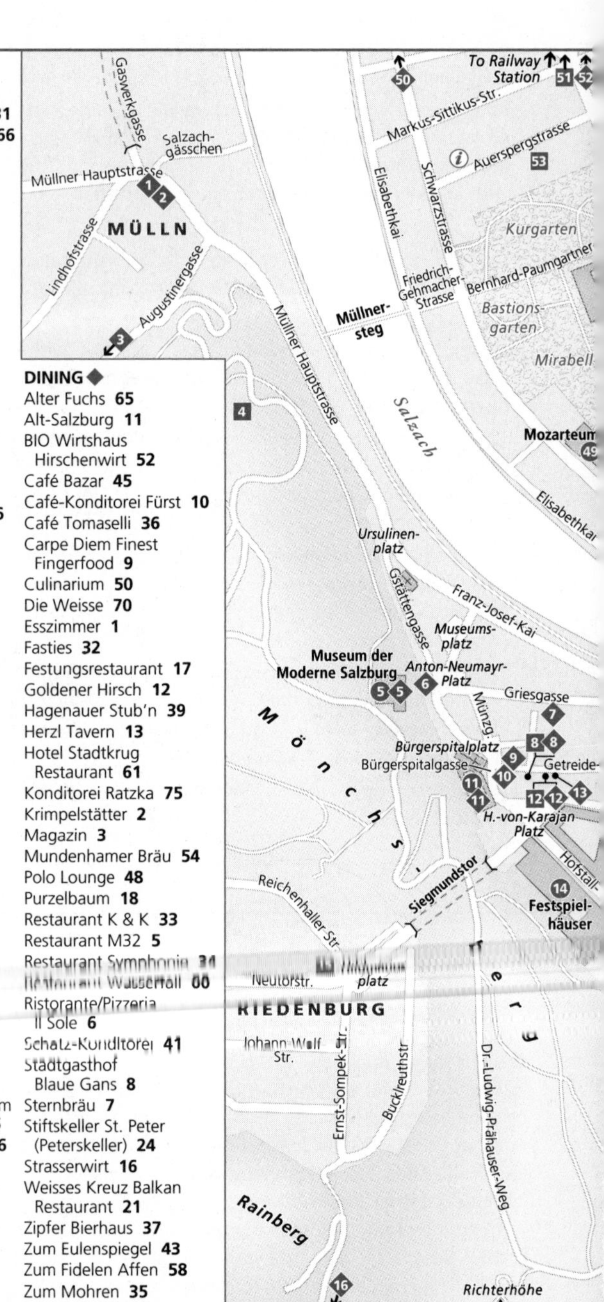

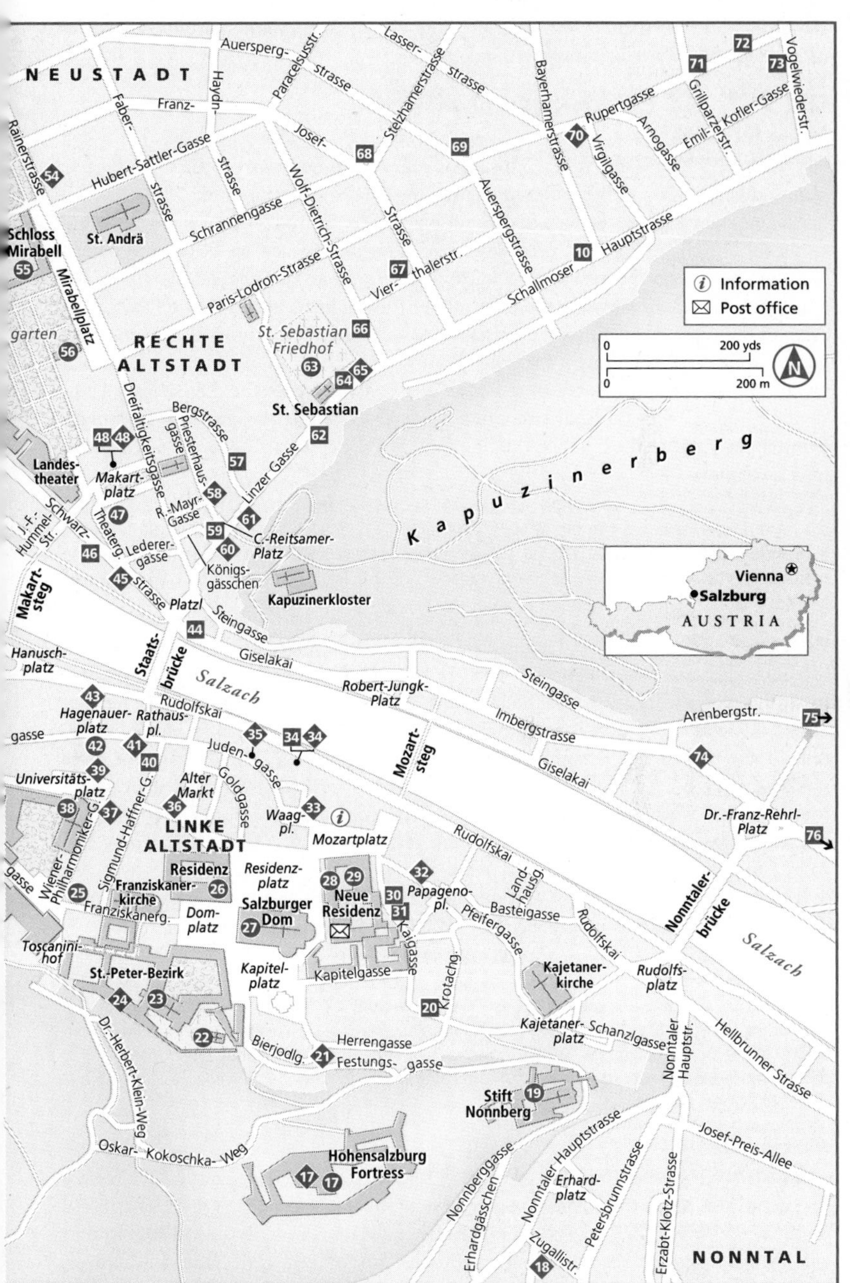
NEUSTADT
RECHTE ALTSTADT
LINKE ALTSTADT
NONNTAL
Kapuzinerberg
Salzach
Information
Post office
200 yds
200 m
Vienna
Salzburg
AUSTRIA
Schloss Mirabell
St. Andrä
St. Sebastian
Kapuzinerkloster
Residenz
Salzburger Dom
Neue Residenz
Franziskanerkirche
St.-Peter-Bezirk
Kajetanerkirche
Stift Nonnberg
Hohensalzburg Fortress
Landestheater
Makartplatz
Mozartplatz
Residenzplatz
Domplatz
Kapitelplatz
Alter Markt
Universitätsplatz
Hanuschplatz
Rathauspl.
Waagpl.
Papagenopl.
Robert-Jungk-Platz
Dr.-Franz-Rehrl-Platz
Rudolfsplatz
Kajetanerplatz
Erhardplatz
C.-Reitsamer-Platz
Makartsteg
Staatsbrücke
Mozartsteg
Nonntalerbrücke
Rainerstrasse
Mirabellplatz
Auersperg-strasse
Lasser-strasse
Paracelsusstr.
Franz-Josef-Strasse
Haydnstrasse
Faberstrasse
Hubert-Sattler-Gasse
Schrannengasse
Wolf-Dietrich-Strasse
Stelzhamerstrasse
Bayerhamerstrasse
Rupertgasse
Virgilgasse
Arnogasse
Grillparzerstr.
Emil-Kofler-Gasse
Vogelweiderstr.
Auerspergstrasse
Schallmoser Hauptstrasse
Paris-Lodron-Strasse
Vierthalerstr.
St. Sebastian Friedhof
Dreifaltigkeitsgasse
Bergstrasse
Priesterhausgasse
Linzer Gasse
R.-Mayr-Gasse
Theaterg.
Schwarzstrasse
J.-F.-Hummel-Str.
Lederergasse
Königsgässchen
Platzl
Steingasse
Giselakai
Rudolfskai
Imbergstrasse
Arenbergstr.
Hagenauerplatz
Judengasse
Goldgasse
Sigmund-Haffner-G.
Wiener-Philharmoniker-G.
Franziskanerg.
Toscaninihof
Kaigasse
Kapitelgasse
Krotachg.
Landhausg.
Basteigasse
Pfeifergasse
Schanzlgasse
Nonntaler Hauptstr.
Hellbrunner Strasse
Herrengasse
Bierjodlg.
Festungsgasse
Dr.-Herbert-Klein-Weg
Oskar-Kokoschka-Weg
Nonnberggasse
Erhardgässchen
Nonntaler Hauptstrasse
Petersbrunnstrasse
Erzabt-Klotz-Strasse
Josef-Preis-Allee
Zugallistr.
Mirabellgarten

Many hotels in the Old City must be reached on foot because of the pedestrian-only streets. However, taxis are allowed to take passengers from the airport or the rail and bus stations and deliver them to the door of a hotel. Many hotels away from the city center can be reached by public transportation.

ON THE LEFT BANK (OLD TOWN)

Very Expensive

Altstadt SAS Radisson ★★ This is not your typical Radisson property—in fact, its style and charm are a rather radical departure for the chain. Dating from 1377, this is a luxuriously and elegantly converted Altstadt inn. Its closest rival in town is the old-world Goldener Hirsch, to which it comes in second. The old and new are blended in perfect harmony here, with the historic facade concealing top-rate comforts and luxuries. The cozy, antiques-filled lobby sets the tone, while a flower-lined, sky-lit atrium adds cheer even on the darkest of days. Stone arches from the medieval structure still remain. Most guests are housed in the main building. Rooms vary greatly in size but have a certain charm and sparkle, with some of the city's best beds, complemented by elegant bathrooms equipped with tub/shower combinations. Overlooking the river, the Restaurant Symphonie is one of the best hotel dining rooms in the city (see "Where to Dine," later in this chapter).

Rudolfskai 28/Judengasse 15, A-5020 Salzburg. ✆ **800/333-3333** in the U.S., or 0662/848571. Fax 0662/8485716. www.austria-trend.at. 62 units. 310€–345€ ($496–$552) double; from 650€ ($1,040) suite. Rates include buffet breakfast. AE, DC, MC, V. Parking 28€ ($45). Bus: 3, 5, or 6. **Amenities:** Restaurant; bar; room service; babysitting; laundry service; dry cleaning; nonsmoking rooms. *In room:* TV, Wi-Fi, minibar, hair dryer, safe.

Goldener Hirsch ★★★ Goldener Hirsch wins the award for the finest hotel in Salzburg; this establishment is so steeped in legend and history that any Austrian will instantly recognize its name. The hotel is built on a small scale, yet it absolutely reeks of aristocratic elegance, which is enhanced by the superb staff. Sitting in an enviable position in the Old Town, a few doors from Mozart's birthplace, it's composed of three medieval town houses joined together in a labyrinth of rustic hallways and staircases. A fourth, called "The Coppersmith's House," is across the street and has 17 charming and elegant rooms. Street-side units have double-glazed windows. All are beautifully furnished and maintained.

The formal Goldener Hirsch and the more casual Herzl Tavern are two of the more distinguished restaurants in Salzburg (see "Where to Dine," later in this chapter).

Getreidegasse 37, A-5020 Salzburg. ✆ **800/325-3535** in the U.S., or 0662/8084. Fax 0662/8084288. www.starwoodhotels.com. 69 units. 500€–660€ ($800–$1,056) double; from 1,000€ ($1,726) suite. Higher rates at festival time (the first week of Apr and mid-July to Aug). AE, DC, MC, V. You can double park in front of the Getreidegasse entrance or at the Karajanplatz entrance, and a staff member will take your vehicle to the hotel's garage for 33€ ($53). Bus: 1 or 2. **Amenities:** 2 restaurants; bar; room service; babysitting; laundry service; dry cleaning; nonsmoking rooms. *In room:* A/C, TV, Wi-Fi, minibar, coffeemaker, hair dryer, safe.

Moderate

Altstadthotel Weisse Taube The hotel is in the pedestrian area of the Old Town a few steps from Mozartplatz, but you can drive up to it to unload baggage. Constructed in 1365, the Weisse Taube has been owned by the Haubner family since 1904. Rooms are, for the most part, renovated and comfortably streamlined, with traditional furnishings, and frequently renewed beds.

Kaigasse 9, A-5020 Salzburg. ✆ **0662/842404.** Fax 0662/841783. www.weissetaube.at. 31 units. 98€–185€ ($157–$296) double. Rates include breakfast. AE, DC, MC, V. Garage 9€ ($12). Bus: 3, 5, or 6. **Amenities:** Breakfast room; bar; lounge. *In room:* TV, Wi-Fi, minibar, hair dryer, safe.

Cordial Theater Hotel Set within a short walk of Salzburg's medieval core, this establishment contains time-share units and some conventional hotel accommodations. Most of the theatrical-looking design you'll see today derives from a radical renovation that occurred in the late 1980s, when a 19th-century shell was gutted and reconfigured into the vaguely Jugendstil-style setting you see today. Accommodations are scattered over three floors; each is painted a pale yellow and named after a composer or a writer. All rooms are comfortable, neatly maintained, and equipped with well-kept shower-only bathrooms. As a result of its artistic theme, the hotel's clientele includes lots of singers and composers. The Barcarole restaurant serves dinner only.

Schallmooser Hauptstrasse 13, A-5020 Salzburg. ✆ **0662/8816810.** Fax 0662/88168692. www.tiscover.at/chsalzburg. 68 units. 115€–180€ ($184–$288) double. Rates include buffet breakfast. AE, DC, MC, V. Bus: 4. **Amenities:** Restaurant; bar; sauna; room service; massage; babysitting; laundry service; dry cleaning; nonsmoking rooms; solarium. *In room:* TV, minibar, hair dryer.

Hotel Blaue Gans "The Blue Goose" lies in the historic core of Salzburg, near the underground garages of the Mönchsberg, a few doors away from hotels that charge almost twice as much. The building that contains it is probably 700 years old, but the rooms are renovated. Each has modern furniture and generous space. Rooms opening onto the courtyard are quieter than those facing the street; nos. 332 and 336 are probably the biggest. You'll register in an understated lobby, one that's so discreetly tucked away that it might be hard to identify. Within the same building is a historic restaurant and beer hall, Stadtgasthof Blaue Gans (see "Where to Dine," later in this chapter).

Getreidegasse 43, A-5020 Salzburg. ✆ **0662/8424910.** Fax 0662/8413179. www.blauegans.at. 38 units. 125€–235€ ($200–$376) double; from 410€ ($656) suite. Rates include buffet breakfast. AE, DC, MC, V. Parking 14€ ($22). Bus: 1 or 2. **Amenities:** Restaurant; bar; babysitting; laundry service; dry cleaning. *In room:* TV, minibar, hair dryer, safe.

Hotel Elefant Near the Old Town Rathaus, in a quiet alley off Getreidegasse, is this well-established, family-run hotel. It, too, is in one of Salzburg's most ancient buildings—it's more than 700 years old. The well-furnished and high-ceilinged rooms have small bathrooms. Within the hotel are two restaurants serving Austrian and international cuisine. One of our favorites is the vaulted Bürgerstüberl, where high wooden banquettes separate the tables. You can also dine in the historic Ratsherrnkeller, which was known as the wine cellar of Salzburg in the 17th century.

Sigmund-Haffner-Gasse 4, A-5020 Salzburg. ✆ **0662/8433970.** Fax 0662/84010928. www.elefant.at. 31 units. 109€–195€ ($174–$312) double. Rates include buffet breakfast. AE, DC, MC, V. Parking 11€ ($18). Bus: 1 or 2. **Amenities:** 2 restaurants; bar; room service; babysitting; laundry service; dry cleaning; nonsmoking rooms. *In room:* TV, Wi-Fi, minibar, hair dryer, safe.

Hotel Kasererbräu In one of the Old Town's most colorful neighborhoods, a few blocks from the cathedral, the Kasererbräu has baroque and Biedermeier furniture that goes well with the oriental rugs and embellished plaster ceilings. Most double rooms are spacious and all are cozy. Rooms are equipped with double beds or paired twins. Many bathrooms are squeezed into small spaces, but even so, doubles have bidets, along with tub/shower combinations. The small singles have half-tubs or shower stalls. In the hotel there is an area called Sanitarium, a recreation section with a waterfall, sauna, steam bath, and solarium. There is also an Indian restaurant called Siddhartha next door.

Kaigasse 33, A-5020 Salzburg. ✆ **0662/842445.** Fax 0662/84244551. www.kasererbraeu.at. 43 units. 130€–218€ ($208–$349) double; 210€–358€ ($336–$573) apt accommodating up to 4 persons. Rates include buffet breakfast. AE, DC, MC, V. Parking 12€ ($19). Bus: 2. **Amenities:** Restaurant; cafe; lounge; sauna; steam room; massage; laundry service; dry cleaning; solarium. *In room:* TV, minibar.

Neutor ★ (Finds This hotel has long been known as a meeting place for artists because of its central location, only a 3-minute walk from the famous Getreidegasse. It is close to many art events, and a frequent stopover for visiting orchestral groups, choirs, and musicians in general. It is especially popular during the Salzburg Festival. The location, at the gateway to Altstadt, next to the tunnel that was dug through Mönchsberg, is divided between two structures on opposite sides of the street. Accommodations in either building are on par with each other, as all the rooms are comfortably and beautifully furnished. Because many performing artists are up late at night, the hotel offers "sleep-late floors," which don't have to be vacated until 1pm. On site is the Artist's Café, decorated with local artwork.

Neutorstrasse 8, A-5020. ✆ **0662/844154-0.** Fax 0662/84415416. www.schwaerzler-hotels.com. 89 units. 108€–186€ ($173–$298) double; 122€–198€ ($195–$317) penthouse units. AE, DC, MC, V. Free parking. **Amenities:** Restaurant; bar; room service; laundry service. *In room:* TV, safe.

Pension Wolf (Value Ideally located near Mozartplatz, this place dates from 1429. A stucco exterior with big shutters hides the rustic and inviting interior that is decorated with a few baroque touches and often sunny rooms. Many new bathrooms have been installed, making this a more inviting choice than ever. The rooms are a bit cramped, as are the shower-only bathrooms. Still, this pension represents very good value for high-priced Salzburg. Since the hotel is usually full, reservations are imperative.

Kaigasse 7, A-5020 Salzburg. ✆ **0662/8434530.** Fax 0662/8424234. www.hotelwolf.com. 15 units. 108€–214€ ($173–$342) double; 188€–249€ ($301–$398) suite. Rates include buffet breakfast. AE, MC, V. Tram: 3, 5, or 6. **Amenities:** Breakfast room; lounge. *In room:* TV.

ON THE RIGHT BANK

Expensive

Hotel Bristol ★ Built in 1890, this traditional government-rated five-star hotel lies near the Mirabell Gardens and opposite Mozart's former home, encompassing a view of the Hohensalzburg Fortress. Compared with the noble courtliness of the Goldener Hirsch, this hotel appears a bit frumpy, although improvements have been made, and it was recently renovated. And despite its rather blatant commercialism, the hotel is often fully booked. Rooms range from upper class functional to opulently baroque, with decorated ceilings and crystal chandeliers. Most have been redecorated with antiques, chandeliers, oriental rugs, often half-canopied beds, and spacious closets. Try for a front room with a view of Mirabell Palace.

Restaurants include the Polo Lounge, seating 40, and the Crystal Room, seating 80. High-standard Austrian and international cuisine is served. The piano bar has terrazzo floors, oriental rugs, and discreet music.

Makartplatz 4, A-5020 Salzburg. ✆ **0662/873557.** Fax 0662/8735576. www.bristol-salzburg.at. 61 units. 183€–470€ ($293–$752) double; 390€–670€ ($624–$1,072) suite. Rates include buffet breakfast. AE, DC, MC, V. Self-parking 13€ ($21); valet parking 26€ ($42). Closed Feb 1–Mar 26. Bus: 1, 2, or 51. **Amenities:** 2 restaurants; bar; room service; massage; babysitting; laundry service; dry cleaning; nonsmoking rooms. *In room:* A/C, TV, Wi-Fi, minibar, hair dryer, safe.

Hotel Sacher Salzburg Hof ★★★ Built originally as the Hotel d'Autriche in 1866, this popular hotel was soon attracting guests from all over the world. It has survived the ravages of war, always keeping up with the times through renovations and expansions. A new era began when the Gürtler family, owners of the Hotel Sacher in Vienna, took over. After a year of renovating, the Café Sacher, as its guests fondly call it, has become a jewel of the riverbank. However, it still lacks the charm and personal service of the Goldener Hirsch. Inside are big windows with panoramic views of the Old Town. The cheerful and comfortable rooms are well furnished, with excellent beds. Try to reserve a room overlooking the river. Most doubles are large; singles tend to be small.

A host of drinking and dining facilities is available, including the Wintergarden, a cozy bar with piano music in the evening; the Roter Salon, an elegant dining room facing the river; the Zirbelzimmer, an award-winning restaurant; the Salzachgrill, offering everything from a snack to a steak, with a riverside terrace; the Café Sacher, a traditional Austrian cafe, also with a riverside terrace; and a pastry shop that sells the famous Sachertorte.

Schwarzstrasse 5–7, A-5020 Salzburg. ✆ **800/223-6800** in the U.S. and Canada, or 0662/88977. Fax 0662/88977551. www.sacher.com. 116 units. 245€–320€ ($392–$512) double; 480€ ($768) suite. AE, DC, MC, V. Parking 29€ ($46). Bus: 1 or 5. **Amenities:** 3 restaurants; 2 bars; cafe; lounge; health club; sauna; steam room; room service; massage; babysitting; laundry service; dry cleaning; nonsmoking rooms; rooms for those w/limited mobility. *In room:* A/C, TV, Wi-Fi, minibar, hair dryer, safe.

Hotel Stein ★★ This revitalized designer-styled and government-rated hotel lies directly on the water with a panoramic view of the historic Old Town of Salzburg. The hotel is in the new part of town (across the Staatsbrücke from the Old Town), within an 18th-century, six-story building that was radically modernized and upgraded. The Stein, which had grown stodgy, was refitted with a contemporary look from its animal prints to its flatscreen TV, and the rooftop cafe has accurately been called "divine." The bedrooms, ranging from beautifully furnished doubles to luxurious suites, are well appointed, with state-of-the-art private marble bathrooms. Suites have leather bedspreads, leather upholsteries, and zebra-skin patterns on others of the in-room fabrics; other rooms are outfitted in either a "Mozart" motif (that is, vaguely rococo patterns) or the "Stein" design (conservatively modern) style. After a restful night's sleep, you're served a breakfast buffet in an atmospheric dining salon. The location is about a 10-minute walk from the main train station.

Giselakai 3–5, A-5020 Salzburg. ✆ **0662/8743460.** Fax 0662/8743469. www.hotelstein.at. 54 units. 140€–165€ ($224–$264) double; 205€–255€ ($328–$408) junior suite; 220€–275€ ($352–$440) suite. Rates include breakfast. AE, DC, MC, V. Parking: 13€ ($21). Bus: 3, 5, or 6. **Amenities:** Cafe bar on top floor; room service; babysitting; laundry service; dry cleaning. *In room:* TV, Wi-Fi, safe, hair dryer.

Rosenvilla ★ Finds The setting is a gracefully proportioned 100-year-old villa, located in a residential suburb within a 20-minute walk southwest of Salzburg's historic core, across the Salzach River from the city's center. Sheathed with ocher-colored stucco and flanked with roses that climb over wrought-iron supports and a small garden, it's small-scale, personalized, conservative, and a bit sleepy. Bedrooms are more lavish than you'd expect, with wooden floors, theatrical draperies, deep upholsteries, and a decor that you might have expected in a conservative and well-mannered private home. Some have four-poster beds draped with fabric, and in some cases, the bathrooms are unusually plush. Regardless of the category of the room you opt for, all bathrooms have tub/shower combinations. Other than breakfast, no meals are served here. The hotel is entirely nonsmoking.

Höfelgasse 4, A-5020 Salzburg. ✆ **0662/621765.** Fax 0662/6252308. www.rosenvilla.com. 14 units. 128€–159€ ($205–$255) double; 158€–255€ ($253–$408) junior suite. Rates include breakfast. Children under 12 stay free in parent's room. AE, DC, MC, V. Bus: 7. **Amenities:** Laundry service; dry cleaning. *In room:* TV, Wi-Fi, safe.

Salzburg Sheraton Hotel ★★ One of the crown jewels of the Sheraton chain, this government-rated five-star, seven-story hotel opened in 1984 in a desirable location about a 10-minute walk from Mozartplatz. The Austrian architect who designed this place took great pains to incorporate it into its 19th-century neighborhood. The exterior is capped with a mansard roof, and the casement windows are ringed with elaborate trim. As you enter, the lobby opens to reveal sun-flooded views of the garden. Rooms have thick wall-to-wall carpeting and contain beds with built-in headboards. The exclusive junior, queen, and president suites are filled with elegant Biedermeier furniture. Half the rooms look out over Mirabell Park.

The cream-and-crystal Restaurant Mirabell serves a good-value luncheon buffet Monday through Friday and a dressed-up version on Saturday and Sunday. A less formal dining area, the Bistro, offers daily specials, wine, and beer. A piano bar is outfitted with burnished brass, richly grained wood, and an Art Nouveau decor.

Auerspergstrasse 4, A-5020 Salzburg. ✆ **800/325-3535** in the U.S., or 0662/889990. Fax 0662/881776. www.sheraton.at. 161 units. 120€–255€ ($192–$408) double; 300€–600€ ($480–$960) suite. AE, DC, MC, V. Parking 15€ ($24). Bus: 1 or 2. **Amenities:** 2 restaurants; bar; indoor heated pool; sauna; room service; babysitting; laundry service; dry cleaning; nonsmoking rooms; 1 room for those w/limited mobility. *In room:* TV, Wi-Fi, minibar, coffeemaker, hair dryer, safe.

Moderate

Bayerischer Hof A 2-block walk from the railway station, close to the Mirabell Gardens, this streamlined hotel often hosts groups of central Europeans. The attractive, modern lobby is paneled with light-grained oak and is carpeted. Rooms are well-insulated refuges from the surrounding commercial neighborhood. The beds are comfortable and the bathrooms are moderate in size with tub/shower combinations. Housekeeping is a definite plus here. The hotel's thriving trio of dining rooms features Austrian, Italian, and Indian specialties.

Kaiserschützenstrasse 1, A-5020 Salzburg. ✆ **0662/46970.** Fax 0662/4697025. www.bayrischerhof.com. 32 units. 98€–195€ ($157–$312) double; from 205€ ($328) suite. Rates include breakfast. AE, DC, MC, V. Free parking outdoors. **Amenities:** Restaurant; bar; room service; babysitting; laundry service; dry cleaning; nonsmoking rooms. *In room:* TV, minibar, hair dryer.

Hotel Auersperg ★ A traditional family-run hotel near the right bank of the Salzach, this hotel lies only a 5-minute walk from the Altstadt, former stamping ground of Mozart. With its own sunny gardens, it consists of two buildings: a main structure and a less expensive annex. The inviting rooms are warm, large, and cozy with big windows, excellent beds, and well-equipped bathrooms, moderate in size. There's an old-fashioned charm to the place, from the reception hall with its 19th-century molded ceilings to the antiques-filled drawing room. The library bar is not only convivial and informal, but also one of our favorite spots for drinking and conversation in Salzburg. The hotel also has a good restaurant. On the top floor, you'll find a roof terrace offering nice views of Salzburg.

Auerspergstrasse 61, A-5020 Salzburg. ✆ **0662/889440.** Fax 0662/8894455. www.auersperg.at. 51 units. 125€–210€ ($200–$336) double; 180€–240€ ($288–$384) suite. Rates include buffet breakfast. AE, DC, MC, V. Free parking. Bus: 1, 4, or 15 from the train station. **Amenities:** Breakfast room; bar; fitness center; sauna; steam room; laundry service; dry cleaning; nonsmoking rooms. *In room:* TV, Wi-Fi, minibar, coffeemaker (some), hair dryer, safe.

Hotel Mozart Kids Value The six-story Hotel Mozart, known for its unpretentious charm and welcoming hospitality, is a comfortable family-run hotel located in the city center. Everything is homey and traditional, with oriental rugs, local paintings, and an attractive TV lounge. It's a 10-minute walk from the train station and only 5 minutes from the pedestrian area of Linzergasse and the famous Mirabell Gardens. Rooms are often sunny and come with all the standard extras. Most are quite spacious, with built-in furniture and twin beds. The accommodations facing the street are soundproof. Some of the guest rooms are big enough to sleep four comfortably. The courteously attentive staff provides careful service and thoughtful touches.

Franz-Josef-Strasse 27, A-5020 Salzburg. ✆ **0662/872274.** Fax 0662/870079. www.hotel-mozart.at. 33 units. 90€–155€ ($144–$248) double; 110€–175€ ($176–$280) triple. AE, MC, V. Parking 10€ ($16). Closed Nov 9–26. **Amenities:** Breakfast room; room service; babysitting; laundry service; dry cleaning; nonsmoking rooms. *In room:* TV, minibar, hair dryer, safe.

Hotel NH Salzburg Kids This welcome addition brings a successful chain format to Salzburg, although it lacks the style of the Sheraton. Unlike most Novotels (which tend to be on the outskirts of cities), this one is centrally located, within walking distance of many major sights. Rooms, although no style-setters, are well maintained, with good beds and medium-size bathrooms with tub/shower combinations. Nevertheless, for families, this is a favorite; and by Salzburg standards, its prices are reasonable. Geared to early or late arrivals, the mediocre restaurant, bar, and cafe are open daily from 6am to midnight.

Franz-Josef-Strasse 26, A-5020 Salzburg. ✆ **800/232-9860** in the U.S., or 0662/8820410. Fax 0662/874240. www.nh-hotels.com. 140 units. 131€–186€ ($210–$298) double. AE, DC, MC, V. Parking 15€ ($24). Bus: 1 or 4. **Amenities:** Restaurant; bar; cafe; exercise room; sauna; room service; laundry service; dry cleaning; rooms for those w/limited mobility. *In room:* TV, Wi-Fi, minibar, hair dryer, safe.

Hotel Stieglbräu Located in the Mirabell district, this hotel provides comfortable and contemporary accommodations within a 10-minute walk of Salzburg's historic core and a 5-minute walk from the railway station. The clean rooms have big windows and simple furniture, including comfortable beds. Bathrooms are spotless and equipped with tub/shower combinations. Two pleasant restaurants, serving international cuisine, offer at least half a dozen cozy dining rooms and a spacious outdoor garden-style terrace for warm-weather drinking and dining.

Rainerstrasse 14, A-5020 Salzburg. ✆ **0662/88992.** Fax 0662/8899271. www.imlauer.com. 50 units. 163€–192€ ($261–$307) double; 180€–215€ ($288–$344) suite. Rates include buffet breakfast. AE, DC, MC, V. Free parking. Bus: 1. **Amenities:** Restaurant; bar; room service; massage; laundry service; dry cleaning; nonsmoking rooms. *In room:* A/C, TV, Wi-Fi, minibar, hair dryer.

Inexpensive

Altstadt-Hotel Wolf-Dietrich ★ Kids Two 19th-century town houses were joined together to make this select little hotel. The lobby and ground floor reception area have a friendly and elegant atmosphere and bright, classical furnishings. The smallish rooms are comfortably furnished, appealing, and cozy, with excellent beds. The ground-floor cafe, Wiener Kaffeehaus, is reminiscent of the large extravagant coffeehouses built in the former century in Vienna, Budapest, and Prague. Alpine carvings and graceful pine detailing adorn one of the two restaurants. Decorating the indoor swimming pool are mirrors and unusual murals of Neptune chasing a sea nymph.

Wolf-Dietrich-Strasse 7, A-5020 Salzburg. ✆ **0662/871275.** Fax 0662/8712759. www.salzburg-hotel.at. 27 units. 114€–194€ ($182–$310) double; 164€–224€ ($262–$358) suite. Children under 12 stay free in parent's room. Rates include buffet breakfast. AE, DC, MC, V. Parking 13€ ($21). **Amenities:** Restaurant;

bar; cafe; indoor heated pool; spa; massage; room service; babysitting; laundry service; dry cleaning; solarium. *In room:* TV, Wi-Fi, minibar, hair dryer.

Bergland Hotel ★ Finds Cozy, personalized, and substantial, this guesthouse sits within a quiet residential neighborhood. It was bought by the grandfather of the present owner in 1912 and rebuilt after its destruction during World War II. Today it welcomes visitors in a "music room," where there's a beer, wine, and coffee bar and a collection of guitars and lutes displayed on the walls. There's an on-site computer, with an Internet connection so guests can check their e-mail; a green *Kachelofen* (tiled stove); and decor that might remind you of a ski lodge high in the Alps. Rooms are comfortable and modern-looking with pieces of furniture often hand-made by members of the Kuhn family, your hosts. The pension will rent you a bike and dispense information about where to ride. The hotel is entirely nonsmoking.

Rupertsgasse 15, A-5020 Salzburg. ✆ **0662/872318.** Fax 0662/8723188. www.berglandhotel.at. 18 units. 90€ ($144) double; 140€ ($224) suite. Rates include buffet breakfast. AE, DC, MC, V. Free parking. Closed Dec 20–Jan 31. Bus: 1 or 4. **Amenities:** Breakfast room; lounge. *In room:* TV, hair dryer.

Haus Arenberg Staying in a place like this gives you the chance to enjoy the best of the Austrian countryside while being only a short bus ride from the Old Town. On a fieldstone foundation, on a slope of the Kapuzinerberg, the two balconied stories feature white stucco and wood detailing. Parts of the interior are completely covered in blond paneling, while the scenic breakfast room is accented with hunting trophies and oriental rugs. Rooms are rather small, but the staff works hard to ensure comfort by providing well-managed bathrooms with tub/shower combinations and spotless housekeeping. Views usually encompass the nearby city. Don't expect a lot of style, but count on a tranquil retreat. Breakfast is the only meal served.

Blumensteinstrasse 8, A-5020 Salzburg. ✆ **0662/640097.** Fax 0662/6400973. www.arenberg-salzburg.at. 13 units. 159€ ($254) double; 176€ ($282) triple. Rates include buffet breakfast. AE, MC, V. Free parking. Bus: 6. **Amenities:** Breakfast room; lounge. *In room:* TV, coffeemaker.

Hotel Amadeus The walls and foundations of this government-rated three-star, four-story hotel date from the 15th century, but much of what you'll experience today is a post-millennium improvement. The quietest rooms are those overlooking the rear, with views of the graveyard where Mozart's wife is buried. Rooms are pleasant and decorated with reproductions of country-Austrian furniture. Breakfasts are generous; the staff is helpful. The building's ground-floor cafe, the Amadeus, serves drinks and bistro-style food throughout the day and evening.

Linzer Gasse [illegible], A-5020 Salzburg. ✆ **0662/871401.** Fax 0662/8714017. www.hotelamadeus.at. 30 units. 140€–170€ ($224–$272) double; 180€–210€ ($288–$336) triple. Rates include buffet breakfast. AE, DC, MC, V. Parking 15€ ($24). Bus: 1 or 2 to Makartplatz. **Amenities:** Breakfast room; cafe. *In room:* TV, hair dryer, safe.

Hotel Drei Kreuz The name *Drei Kreuz* refers to the three crosses of the nearby Kapuzinerberg, which was the site of public executions centuries ago. Once you get past the dreary bunkerlike facade, you'll find a warmly decorated and inviting interior. The restaurant has some of the most massive beams we've ever seen in Austria, and a cozy bar with rustic decor. The often small rooms are tasteful and well furnished. It's about a 10-minute walk from the historic center.

Vogelweiderstrasse 9, A-5020 Salzburg. ✆ **0662/8727900.** Fax 0662/8727906. www.hoteldreikreuz.at. 24 units. 78€–169€ ($125–$270) double; 99€–189€ ($158–$302) triple. Rates include breakfast. AE, DC,

MC, V. Free parking. Bus: 4. **Amenities:** Restaurant; bar; laundry service; dry cleaning; nonsmoking rooms. *In room:* TV, hair dryer.

Hotel Goldene Krone Our favorite part of this family-run guesthouse is the big sun terrace with ivy-covered walls, where a family member will serve you coffee after a tiring day in the city. The hotel is only a few minutes from the Staatsbrücke. Rooms range from small to medium, but furnishings, including the beds, are comfortable. A breakfast buffet is the only meal served.

Linzer Gasse 48, A-5020 Salzburg. ✆ **0662/872300.** Fax 0662/87230066. www.hotel-goldenekrone.com. 25 units. 99€–130€ ($158–$208) double. Rates include breakfast. AE, DC, MC, V. Parking 13€ ($21). Bus: 1, 3, 5, or 6. **Amenities:** Breakfast room; lounge. *In room:* TV.

Hotel Jedermann Set within a quiet, tree-lined residential neighborhood less than 1km (1/2 mile) north of Salzburg's medieval core, this is a respectable and decent pension that has received favorable recommendations from Frommer's readers. The building was constructed as a spacious private home in the 1930s, and today it remains home to the Gmachl family, its owners and managers. Public areas contain soothingly old or old-fashioned furnishings that create a comfortable atmosphere. Rooms, last renovated in 2002, have modern furniture and good beds. Breakfast is the only meal served.

Rupertgasse 25, A-5020 Salzburg. ✆ **0662/8732410.** Fax 0662/8732419. www.hotel-jedermann.com. 16 units. 95€–160€ ($152–$256) double; 160€–220€ ($256–$352) apt. Rates include buffet breakfast. AE, DC, MC, V. Bus: 4 or 27. **Amenities:** Breakfast room; lounge; nonsmoking rooms. *In room:* TV, minibar.

Hotel Restaurant Gablerbräu This inviting hotel is near the Makartplatz. Rooms are furnished in a simple, modern style—an utter functionalism that deters lingering or long stays. Nonetheless, beds are frequently renewed, housekeeping is good, and the tiny shower-only bathrooms are well kept. Inside are three restaurants: one with vaulted ceilings and murals, another covered with wrought-iron detailing, and the third—the least formal—a beer hall.

Linzergasse 9, A-5020 Salzburg. ✆ **0662/88965.** Fax 0662/8896555. www.gablerbrau.com. 52 units. 104€–168€ ($166–$269) double; 144€–210€ ($230–$336) junior suite. Rates include buffet breakfast. AE, DC, MC, V. Parking 13€ ($21). Bus: 1. **Amenities:** Restaurant; bar; room service; nonsmoking rooms; rooms for those w/limited mobility. *In room:* TV, hair dryer, safe.

Hotel Trumer Stube Originally built in 1869 as a private home, this pink-fronted town house rises six floors above a desirable location that's midway between the Mirabellplatz and the Staatsbrücke, about a 6-minute stroll from Mozart's birthplace, and across the river from the Altstadt. For years, it thrived as a restaurant, but when meals were discontinued in the 1970s, it retained its original name (Trumer Stube), a fact that sometimes causes confusion as visitors assume that it's still a restaurant. The ground floor, presided over by the kindly manager, Silvia Rettenbacher, is devoted to the reception and breakfast rooms. Upstairs, an elevator carries you to a collection of cozily rustic, country-baroque rooms, each with smallish but well-designed bathrooms.

Bergstrasse 6, A-5020 Salzburg. ✆ **0662/874776** or 0662/875168. Fax 0662/874326. www.trumer-stube.at. 22 units. 105€ ($168) double; 154€ ($246) triple; 164€ ($262) quad. Rates include buffet breakfast. AE, DC, MC, V. Parking 11€ ($18). Closed Feb 1–Mar 16. Bus: 1, 3, 5, 6, 25, or 26 to Mirabellplatz. **Amenities:** Breakfast room; lounge; nonsmoking rooms. *In room:* TV.

Pension Adlerhof Only the second and third floors of this guesthouse near the train station retain their original baroque embellishments. The high-ceilinged but cozy interior has wooden furniture with occasional painted designs, plus many folksy touches. Rooms, frequently renovated, are *very* snug and cozy, suitable for an overnight stay—not a long vacation. Bathrooms with shower units are a bit cramped, but housekeeping is exemplary. The Pregartbauer family owns the hotel.

Elisabethstrasse 25, A-5020 Salzburg. ✆ **0662/875236.** Fax 0662/873663. www.gosalzburg.com. 35 units, 28 with bathroom. 72€ ($115) double without bathroom; 108€ ($173) double with bathroom. Rates include continental breakfast. No credit cards. **Amenities:** Breakfast room; lounge. *In room:* TV.

AT MÖNCHSTEIN

Very Expensive

Hotel Schloss Mönchstein ★★ This Teutonic-style manor house, really a small castle, stands on top of a hill above the center of Salzburg. Be warned in advance that the hotel is glacially snobby, attracting a so-called "exclusive" clientele that is socially secure, many of whom return year after year. From its elegant salons, guests can enjoy panoramic views of the city. The site was constructed as a fortified tower in 1350 and wasn't transformed into a hotel until 1950. It is easy to see why the hotel has claimed the motto "urban sanctuary of the world." On the premises are a wedding chapel and a garden terrace overlooking a statue of Apollo in the private park. Rooms come in varying sizes and styles, but are all uniformly comfortable, with roomy closets. Some are rather elegant, with oriental rugs resting on parquet floors, king-size beds, and CD players. The suites are some of the most spectacularly decorated rooms in Salzburg. The restaurant and bar, Paris Lodron, serves first-rate Austrian and international dishes at elegant, candlelit tables. Harp concerts are regularly featured. The hotel also has a garden terrace, Apollo, and a cocktail bar, P. L. There is also a restaurant called "The Smallest Restaurant in the World" for up to four people, located in the castle tower with a panoramic view.

Mönchsberg Park 26, A-5020 Salzburg. ✆ **800/44-UTELL** in the U.S., or 0662/8485550. Fax 0662/848559. www.monchstein.at. 24 units. 350€–550€ ($560–$880) double; from 575€ ($920) suite. Rates include buffet breakfast. AE, DC, MC, V. Free parking. **Amenities:** Restaurant; bar; cafe; access to nearby health club; tour desk; secretarial services; room service; in-room massage; babysitting; laundry service; dry cleaning; nonsmoking rooms. *In room:* TV, Wi-Fi, minibar, hair dryer, safe.

AT ROTT

Inexpensive

Pension Helmhof (Value) On the western outskirts, Pension Helmhof is an appealingly rustic stucco chalet with flower-bedecked balconies and a stone-trimmed sun terrace. Rooms are comfortably furnished and well kept, with small bathrooms equipped with tub/shower combinations. There is old-fashioned chalet-style comfort to this snug nest.

Lieferinger Hauptstrasse (Kirchengasse 30), A-5020 Salzburg-Liefering. ✆ **0662/433079.** Fax 0662/433079. www.helmhof.at. 16 units. 68€–74€ ($109–$118) double; 90€–96€ ($144–$154) triple. Rates include breakfast. AE, MC, V. Free parking. Bus 1 or 2. Adjacent to the Salzburg-Mitte exit off A1 Autobahn. **Amenities:** Breakfast room; lounge; outdoor pool. *In room:* TV.

IN ANIF

Moderate

Hotel Friesacher ★ This elegant chalet has a hipped roof, a long expanse of gables, and natural-grained wooden balconies covered with flowers. An older building a few steps away across the flowering lawn serves as a well-furnished annex. Rooms are generally spacious and well furnished, with good beds and ample bathrooms equipped with tub/shower combinations. Service is provided by the Friesacher family. There's a country-style dining room, one of the finest in the area. In summer, guests can eat on the open-air terrace. Food is served Thursday to Tuesday noon to 2:30pm and 6 to 9:30pm, so you might want to drive out for an evening here even if you aren't staying in Anif. Specialties are typically Austrian, including *tafelspitz* and dumpling soups, along with such classic sweets as *topfenstrudel* (made with cottage cheese) and *palatschinken* (dessert crepes).

Hellbrunnerstrasse 17, A-5081 Anif. ✆ **06246/8977.** Fax 06246/897749. www.hotelfriesacher.com. 90 units. 160€–205€ ($256–$328) double. Rates include breakfast. AE, DC, MC, V. Free parking. Bus: 25. Take Westautobahn toward Graz and exit at Salzburg-Süd. Follow signs to Salzburg and then Anif. In Anif, make a left at 1st traffic light. **Amenities:** Restaurant; 2 bars; exercise room; sauna; outdoor heated pool; nonsmoking rooms; rooms for those w/limited mobility. *In room:* TV, minibar, hair dryer, safe.

Romantik Hotel Schlosswirt ★ This country inn on the outskirts of Anif, 6km (4 miles) south of the center of Salzburg, was founded in 1607; with its flagstone floors and collection of local artifacts and hunting trophies, it's done a thriving business ever since. It's so well known that Austrians sometimes drive all the way from Innsbruck to dine here. Rooms have Biedermeier furniture and good beds. If you're a late riser, be warned that beginning at 7am, traffic might disturb you if you're housed in the annex, which is right on the highway. There's a generous breakfast buffet of wurst, cheese, and poached eggs. Dinner is an elegant experience. Menu items include matjes herring with dill, wild game (in season), and duckling in rosemary sauce. A kind English-speaking hostess in regional dress will help you with translations.

Salwachtalvumess 7, A-5081 Anif. ✆ **06246/72175.** Fax 06246/721758. www.schlosswirt-anif.com. 28 units. 130€–158€ ($208–$253) double; 220€–258€ ($352–$413) suite. Rates include buffet breakfast. AE, DC, MC, V. Free parking. Closed Feb. Take the Salzburg-Süd exit from Autobahn A10 and drive less than 1km (½ mile). Bus: 25. **Amenities:** Restaurant; bar; room service; laundry service; dry cleaning. *In room:* TV, minibar, hair dryer.

IN AIGEN

Inexpensive

Hotel-Gasthof Doktorwirt (Kids) On the southern edge of Salzburg, 10 minutes by bus from the Old Town, this chalet has prominent gables, a red-tile roof, and white stucco walls. The adjoining restaurant produces many of the sausages it serves, as well as a collection of tempting pastries. The decor is rustic, sunny, and pleasant, with wood detailing. The cozy rooms come in sizes ranging from singles to junior suites. The triple rooms and the family units are extremely popular, as the Schnöll clan prides itself on running a family hotel. The best rooms are the two tower units.

Glaserstrasse 9, A-5026 Salzburg-Aigen. ✆ **0662/622973.** Fax 0662/62297325. www.doktorwirt.co.at. 41 units. 110€–170€ ($176–$272) double. Rates include breakfast. AE, DC, MC, V. Parking 8€ ($13). Bus: 7 from Salzburg. Exit from Autobahn A10 at Salzburg-Süd. **Amenities:** Restaurant; bar; 2 pools (1 heated indoor); fitness center; sauna; room service; babysitting; laundry service; dry cleaning. *In room:* TV, Wi-Fi, hair dryer, safe.

AT GERSBERG

Expensive

Romantic Hotel Die Gersberg Alm ★★ (Finds) The former farmstead traces its origins back to the 16th century, and in Mozart's time it was a popular dining excursion from Salzburg. The estate overlooks the city from its mountain perch on the Gersberg, with panoramic views in all directions, yet the location is only about a 15-minute drive from the center. Today, following a restoration, modern comforts have been installed in the once-rustic precincts, yet much of the 1832 alpine architectural features were left intact. The individually decorated bedrooms are comfortably furnished and filled with much charm. From a summer garden to a blazing fireplace in winter, there is much here to lure you away from Salzburg itself.

Gersberg 37, A-5020. ✆ **0662/641257.** Fax 0662/644248. www.gersbergalm.at. 43 units. 137€–295€ ($219–$472) double; 287€–349€ ($459–$558) suite. AE, DC, MC, V. **Amenities:** Restaurant; bar; outdoor pool; sauna. *In room:* TV, minibar, hair dryer.

A CASTLE HOTEL IN OBERALM

The main reason for visiting Oberalm, directly north of Hallein and also north of Golling, is to stay at the castle hotel recommended below, which lies 16km (10 miles) south of Salzburg. From Salzburg, take the A10 south; from Golling, take the A10 north. However, if you're nearby, you might want to stop to see the Romanesque **Pfarrkirche (Parish Church),** with Gothic extensions. It has a magnificent high altar from 1707 by J. G. Mohr. The church is embellished with baroque furnishings and heraldic tombstones. Be sure to see the funereal shield from 1671.

Schloss Haunsperg ★ (Finds) Signposted at the approach to town, this early-14th-century castle is decorated with towers and interior ornamentation. A small but ornate baroque chapel adjoins the hotel. The public areas include a series of vaulted corridors furnished with antiques and rustic chandeliers, several salons with parquet or flagstone floors, and a collection of antiques. Our favorite is the second-floor music salon. Many of the accommodations, which contain period furniture, are divided into suites of two or three rooms, along with some doubles. The von Gernerth-Mautner Markhof family owns the castle.

A-5411 Oberalm bei Hallein. ✆ **06245/80662.** Fax 06245/85680. www.schlosshaunsperg.com. 8 units. 135€–170€ ($216–$272) double; 170€–210€ ($272–$336) suite. Rates include buffet breakfast. AE, DC, MC, V. Free parking. **Amenities:** Breakfast room; lounge; tennis court. *In room:* TV, hair dryer.

4 WHERE TO DINE

Two special desserts you'll want to sample while in Salzburg are the famous *Salzburger Nockerln,* a light mixture of stiff egg whites, and *Mozart-Kugeln,* with bittersweet chocolate, hazelnut nougat, and marzipan. You should also try a beer in one of the numerous Salzburg breweries.

If you want to picnic, the city has a number of delis where you can stock up on supplies. The best place to eat your picnic goodies is Mirabell Gardens, on the right bank (see section 5, "Seeing the Sights," later in this chapter).

While Salzburg is not a late-night dining town in the way that New York and some European cities are, many restaurants stay open late, often to accommodate concert- or theatergoers. But "late" in this sense rarely means beyond 11pm.

ON THE LEFT BANK (OLD TOWN)

Very Expensive

Esszimmer ★★ FRENCH/AUSTRIAN A star on the Salzburg's hip culinary scene, this restaurant is operated by one of the town's most inventive chefs, Andreas Kaiblinger. The interior is a funky modern designer affair, and the restaurant serves classic French cuisine with an Austrian twist. The well-chosen menu changes every week and features the best produce at the market. Two flatscreens show videos, and another highlight is a glass-floor installation, allowing guests to look down on the Almkanal that virtually flows right through the restaurant. Windows also offer a view of the kitchen so that diners can see the creative chefs at work. The best menu items include marinated trout with pumpkin rösti and pumpkin-flavored vinegar; cold filet of veal with goose liver in aspic; sautéed breast of pigeon with braised leeks, cepes, and a sweet potato purée; saddle of venison with red cabbage and polenta; and white chocolate gateau with peaches and poppyseeds.

Müllner Hauptstrasse 3. ✆ **0662/870899.** www.esszimmer.com. Reservations required. Main courses 26€–29€ ($42–$46); 5-course vegetarian menu 49€ ($78); 5-course fish menu 61€ ($98); 3-course lunch menu 26€ ($42); 7-course chef's menu 78€ ($125). AE, DC, MC, V. Tues–Sat noon–2pm and 6:30–9:30pm. Open Mon during 2-week Christmas holiday and Mon during Salzburg Festival.

Goldener Hirsch ★★★ AUSTRIAN/VIENNESE Fans of this place are willing to travel long distances just to enjoy the authentic ambience of this renovated inn, established in 1407. Don't be fooled by the relatively simple decor of this place, a kind of well-scrubbed and decent simplicity that's emulated by dozens of other restaurants in resorts throughout Austria. Cuisine is superb, and the wine list is virtually unsurpassed. The venue is chic, top-notch, impeccable, and charming, richly sought after during peak season. The restaurant is staffed with a superb team of chefs and waiters. The food is so tasty and beautifully served that the kitchen ranks among the top three in Salzburg. Specialties include saddle of farm-raised venison with red cabbage, king prawns in an okra-curry ragout served with perfumed Thai rice, and tenderloin of beef and veal on morel cream sauce with cream potatoes. In season, expect a dish devoted to game, such as venison or roast duckling.

Getreidegasse 37. ✆ **0662/80840.** Reservations required. Main courses 20€–28€ ($32–$45). AE, DC, MC, V. Daily noon–2:30pm and 6:30–9:30pm. Bus: 1 or 2.

Expensive

Alt-Salzburg ★ AUSTRIAN/INTERNATIONAL A retreat into old-world elegance, Alt-Salzburg is one of the most venerated restaurants in the city, a bastion of formal service, snobbism, and refined cuisine. The restaurant, which often gives you an icy reception unless they know you, occupies a building constructed into the side of the steep and rocky cliffs of Mönchsberg. The wood-ceiling room is crafted to reveal part of the chiseled rock of the Mönchsberg. The menu features main dishes such as filet of river char sautéed with tomatoes, mushrooms and capers, leaf spinach, and potatoes; and lamb chops sautéed in an herb crust and thyme sauce with zucchini and potato cakes. In August, the restaurant is also open on Sunday and Monday for lunch.

Bürgerspitalgasse 2. ✆ **0662/841476.** www.altsalzburg.at. Reservations required. Main courses 12€–24€ ($19–$38); fixed-price menu 41€–49€ ($66–$78). AE, DC, MC, V. Mon 6–10:30pm; Tues–Sat 11:30am–2pm and 6–10:30pm (to midnight in Aug). Closed last week in Feb. Bus: 1.

Magazin ★★ INTERNATIONAL This is the trendiest dining post in all of Salzburg. Somewhat hidden away, it's worth the search. Once you get here, you discover the town's most stylish wine bar, and that's not all. There's also a wine shop, a floral decoration store, and a restaurant in a mountainous gallery set in an architectural complex of avant-garde buildings on top of and next to each other. At this multipurpose hub for the epicurean set, you're treated to Marcus Radauer's market-fresh cuisine. The food is often as unusual as it is delicious. And with every plate, you're assured of some of the best wines in the area, with an emphasis on those of Austria. You're also courteously welcomed into the bright dining room, where efficient servers see to your comfort and desires. The culinary creations are sometimes simple, sometimes complex, rarely mannered, and never pointless. The chef does wonders with Styrian beef. The fish dishes are handled to near perfection. You're never certain what's on the menu but expect a surprise—a pleasant one that is.

Augustinergasse 13. ✆ **0662/841584.** www.magazin.co.at. Reservations required. 4-course fixed-price menu 45€–55€ ($72–$88). AE, DC, MC, V. Tues–Sat 10am–midnight. Bus: 2.

Purzelbaum ★ AUSTRIAN/VIENNESE During the Salzburg Festival, you're likely to see the most dedicated music lovers in Europe congregating around the tables of this sophisticated bistro. Located in a residential neighborhood not often frequented by tourists, it's near a duck pond at the bottom of a steep incline leading up to Salzburg Castle. A cramped corner of the bar is reserved for visitors who want to drop in for only a drink.

Cafes

Café Bazar ★, Schwarzstrasse 3 (✆ **0662/874278;** www.cafe-bazar.at; bus: 1 or 5), is deeply entrenched in Salzburg's social life and has been since 1906. Its regular clientele comes from all walks of life. Housed in a palatial pink-stucco building with many baroque features, it's located across the river from the main section of the Old Town. The interior is high-ceilinged and vaguely Art Deco. You'll still occasionally see someone with a Franz Josef mustache wearing a gray flannel Styrian suit with loden trim, but a growing number of the patrons are young and stylish. You can order salads, sandwiches, and omelets. It's open Monday to Saturday 7:30am to 11pm, Sunday 9 to 6pm.

At the **Café-Konditorei Fürst,** Brodgasse 13, at the corner of Getreidegasse (✆ **0662/843759**), *Mozart-Kugeln* (traditional marzipan-pistachio chocolate-dipped cookies) are sold. The owner invented this sweet in 1890 but forgot to patent the recipe. The treat is often duplicated, but here you can sample it from the authentic and original recipe. Norbert Fürst, a descendant of the original founder, still makes these fine chocolates with a recipe handed down to him by his great-grandfather. In addition to the *Mozart-Kugeln,* there's a wide range of other chocolates and truffle specialties, including such Austrian favorites as the Sachertorte, the Dobosch torte, and the inevitable *apfelstrudel.* Open Monday to Saturday 8am to 9pm, Sunday 9am to 9pm

Established in 1705, **Café Tomaselli** ★, Alter Markt 9 (✆ **0662/844488;** www.tomaselli.at; bus: 2 or 5), opens onto one of the most charming cobblestone squares of the Altstadt. Aside from the chairs placed outdoors during summer, you'll find a room with a high ceiling and many tables (it's a great place to sit and talk), and another more formal room to the right of the entrance that houses oil portraits of well-known 19th-century Salzburgers and attracts a haute bourgeois crowd. Choose from 40 different kinds of cakes or other menu items, including omelets, wursts, ice cream, and a wide range of

Most guests, however, reserve a table in one of the trio of rooms containing an Art Nouveau ceiling and marble buffets from an antique bistro in France. Menu items change according to the whim of the chef and include well-prepared dishes such as turbot-and-olive casserole, a selection of wild game (in season), lamb in white-wine sauce with beans and polenta, and the house specialty, scampi Grüstl, composed of fresh shrimp with sliced potatoes baked with herbs in a casserole. During the Salzburg Festival, the restaurant is also open on Sunday.

Zugallistrasse 7. ✆ **0662/848843.** www.purzelbaun.at. Reservations required. Main courses 20€–26€ ($32–$42); 4-course fixed-price menu 48€ ($77). AE, DC, MC, V. Mon–Sat noon–2pm and 6–11pm. Closed July 1–14. Bus: 5 or 55.

Restaurant M32 ★★ INTERNATIONAL All day long, Chef Sepp Schellhorn, an award-winning chef, cookbook author, and president of the Austrian Hotelier Association, feeds visitors to the Museum der Moderne Art (p. 255), but in the evening the restaurant feeds even more refined palates. The setting alone, with the grandest panorama

drinks. Of course, the pastries and ice cream are all homemade. The cafe is open Monday to Saturday 7am to 9pm; Sunday 8am to 9pm.

A melody by Mozart, who was born next door, might accompany your before-dinner drink at **Hagenauerstuben,** Universitätsplatz 14 (✆ **0662/842657;** tram: 2, 49, or 95). Many visitors never get beyond the street-level bar, where snacks (such as salads and goulash) and drinks are served in a 14th-century room with stone floors and a vaulted ceiling, highlighted by a changing exhibition of modern lithographs and watercolors. At the top of a narrow flight of stone steps, you'll discover an austere trio of thick-walled rooms decorated with a ceramic stove and wooden armoires. A central serving table holds an array of salads and hors d'oeuvres. The cafe is open daily 9am to 1am.

The small **Konditorei Ratzka,** Imbergstrasse 45 (✆ **0662/640024;** bus: 2 or 5), 10 minutes from the center of town, is owned by its pastry chef, Herwig Ratzka. A master at his craft, he uses the freshest ingredients to produce about 30 different pastries. Because the cakes are made fresh every day, much of the selection is gone by late afternoon, so go early. It's open Tuesday through Friday 8am to 5pm and Saturday 8am to 12:30pm and 1:30 to 6pm. Closed 2 weeks in January, June, and September. Mr. Ratzka requests that patrons don't smoke in the shop.

Almost every item sold at the old-time Austrian confectionery **Schatz-Konditorei,** Getreidegasse 3 (✆ **0662/842792;** bus: 2 or 5), is made from traditional recipes. Our favorite treat is the well-known *Mozart-Kugeln,* a cookie of pistachio, marzipan, and hazelnut nougat, all dipped in chocolate. You can enjoy the pastries and coffees at a table inside the cafe or take them away. Some varieties of pastry, including the *Mozart-Kugeln,* can be shipped around the world. It's open Monday to Friday 8:30am to 6:30pm and Saturday 8am to 5pm, with extended hours during the summer Salzburg Festival.

of any restaurant in Salzburg, makes it a worthy choice. But it offers so much more in the way of a cuisine that bursts with freshness and originality. But, first, you absorb the ambience, including a tremendous light installation of 500 deer antlers by architect Matteo Thun.

Among some of the better dishes here are *tafelspitz* with egg noodles. We're particularly fond of the braised beefsteak with quail eggs or the sautéed morels with potato-based noodles and a tapenade of olives and Styrian tomatoes. How about finishing off with a cheese plate with red pepper strips, a white chocolate mousse, and a salad of bitter oranges with fresh berries and a vanilla-flavored cream sauce?

Mönchsberg 32. ✆ **0662/841000.** Reservations required for dinner. Main courses 13€–25€ ($21–$40); set-lunch menu 14€ ($22). AE, MC, V. Sept–July Tues–Sat noon–2:30pm and 6–10pm, Sun 9am–6pm; Aug daily 9am–1am. Take the Mönchsberg elevator to the top.

Restaurant Symphonie ★ INTERNATIONAL Set within a riverfront building whose origins go back to the 15th century, this restaurant evokes the kind of 18th-century country-baroque setting where a young Mozart might have given a concert. Most menu items focus on traditional Austrian specialties, including marinated fried chicken, Viennese-style *tafelspitz,* and a vegetarian specialty consisting of creamed mushrooms with rosemary and herbs. Fish dishes include filet of sole with a zucchini crust and olive puree, and crispy-roasted filet of char with parsley potatoes and salad. For dessert, consider buttermilk dumplings with marinated cherries.

In the Hotel Altstadt SAS Radisson, Rudolfskai 28. ✆ **0662/84857155.** Reservations recommended. Main courses 19€–25€ ($31–$40); 3-course fixed-price menu 39€ ($62); 4-course fixed-price menu 46€ ($74); 5-course fixed-price menu 52€ ($83). AE, DC, MC, V. Mon–Sat noon–2pm and 6:30–10:30pm. Bus: 3, 5, or 6.

Moderate

Carpe Diem Finest Fingerfood ★★ (Finds) INTERNATIONAL This is a new concept in Salzburg dining, a huge, exclusively styled pub on two floors, with lounges, a cafe area, and bar. It's the creation of Dietrich Mateschitz, who became famous for inventing the energy drink Red Bull. He is equally passionate about sports and cuisine, and has hired the noted star chef, Jörg Wörther, to oversee the delights that emerge from the kitchen here. The chef's creations are intensely flavored, often combining different temperatures. For example, you might be served a warm scallop resting atop cool whipped alpine cream. Food is packed into waffle shells or cones. Some of the dishes we sampled—and left raving about—included hot smoked catfish with endive salad in a Dijon mustard marinade, yellowfin tuna in salad with avocado and ginger in a pumpkin cone, and, finally, prime beef with cream spinach and horseradish in a potato cone. Breakfast, lunch, and dinner, all with different dishes, can be savored here, and the cafe and bar are the perfect places for a gourmet snack.

Getreidegasse 50. ✆ **0662/848800.** www.finestfingerfood.com. Reservations required. Breakfast 10€–16€ ($16–$26). Cones 4.90€–12€ ($7.90–$18) depending on the filling. Fixed-price menus: 18€ ($28) 3 courses; 23€ ($36) 4 courses; 28€ ($44) 5 courses; 33€ ($52) 6 courses; 38€ ($60) 7 courses. AE, DC, MC, V. Daily 8:30am–midnight. Bus: 1 or 2.

Herzl Tavern ★★ (Value) AUSTRIAN/VIENNESE With an entrance on the landmark Karajanplatz, Herzl Tavern lies next door to the glamorous Goldener Hirsch, of which it's a part. Good value attracts visitors and locals alike to its pair of cozy rooms, one paneled and timbered. You'll see photos of musicians who have dined here while performing at the Salzburg Festival, including Leonard Bernstein, Herbert von Karajan,

Helmut Luhner, and actor Curt Jurgens. Waitresses in dirndls serve appetizing entrees, which are likely to include roast pork with dumplings, various grills, game stew (in season), and, for the heartiest eaters, a farmer's plate of boiled pork, roast pork, grilled sausages, dumplings, and sauerkraut.

Karajanplatz 7. ✆ **0662/8084889.** Reservations recommended. Main courses 7€–23€ ($11–$37); fixed-price menu 13€–20€ ($21–$32). AE, DC, MC, V. Daily 11:30am–10pm. Bus: 1.

Restaurant K & K AUSTRIAN/INTERNATIONAL Separated into about half a dozen intimate dining rooms on four floors, the K & K is decorated with wood paneling, slabs of salmon-colored marble, flickering candles, antique accessories, and a well-dressed clientele. An elaborate wrought-iron and gilt bracket holds a sign marking the location above a giant plaza near the cathedral. The menu contains a medley of well-crafted dishes, ranging from the traditional to the innovative, including roast filet of beef in a cognac-cream sauce with fresh mushrooms and green peppercorns, *tafelspitz,* breast of chicken in a curry-cream sauce, and several kinds of shellfish. If you'd like to check out a cool informal hangout and witness a marvel of masonry, head down the massive stone staircase to reach the *Bierkeller,* a beer cellar that serves drinks and snack food to a sometimes rowdy crowd.

Waagplatz 2. ✆ **0662/842157.** Reservations required. Main courses 13€–20€ ($21–$32); fixed-price menu 22€–44€ ($35–$70). AE, DC, MC, V. Daily 11:30am–2:30pm and 6–11:30pm; drinks and snacks daily 11:30am–midnight. Bus: 1.

Stiftskeller St. Peter (Peterskeller) ★ AUSTRIAN/VIENNESE Legend has it that Mephistopheles met with Faust in this tavern, which was established by Benedictine monks in A.D. 803. In fact, it's the oldest restaurant in Europe, housed in the abbey of the church that supposedly brought Christianity to Austria. Aside from a collection of baroque banquet rooms, there's an inner courtyard with vaults cut from the living rock, a handful of dignified wood-paneled rooms, and a brick-vaulted cellar with a tile floor and rustic chandeliers. In addition to wine from the abbey's own vineyards, the tavern serves good home-style Austrian cooking, including roast pork in gravy with sauerkraut and bread dumplings, braised oxtail with mushrooms and fried polenta, and loin of lamb with asparagus. Vegetarian dishes, such as semolina dumplings on noodles in a parsley sauce, are also featured. They are especially known here for their desserts. Try the apple strudel or sweet curd strudel with vanilla sauce or ice cream, and, most definitely, the famed *Salzburger Nockerln.*

St.-Peter-Bezirk 1–4. ✆ **0662/8412680.** Reservations recommended. Main courses 12€–22€ ($19–$35); fixed-price menus 16€–45€ ($26–$72). AE, DC, MC, V. Daily 11:30am–2:30pm and 6–10pm. Closed Dec 24. Bus: 29.

Weisses Kreuz Balkan Restaurant BALKAN Just south of the cathedral, this restaurant's stone facade is almost hidden on a small villagelike street. A grape arbor shelters the front terrace, where in summer tables are set out for relaxed eating and drinking. The cuisine includes Balkan bean soup, boiled beef, mutton chops, and roast beef in a cream-and-onion sauce. More exotic specialties include moussaka, fried mincemeat loaf with pickled peppers, and Dalmatian steak with rice and stuffed cabbage. Stuffed eggplant and venison steak are also popular dishes, along with a catchall specialty called the Balkan platter. The staff speaks very little English.

In the Hotel Weisses Kreuz, Bierjodlgasse 6. ✆ **0662/845641.** Reservations recommended. Main courses 12€–20€ ($19–$32); 3-course fixed-price menu 12€ ($19). AE, DC, MC, V. Daily 11:30am–2:45pm and 5–11pm. Bus: 2, 5, or 6.

Zum Eulenspiegel ★ AUSTRIAN/VIENNESE Housed in a white-and-peach building opposite Mozart's birthplace, Zum Eulenspiegel sits at one end of a quiet cobblestone square in the Old Town. Inside, guests have a choice of five rooms on three different levels, all rustically but elegantly decorated. You really can pick where you want to sit, so feel free to look around if all the tables aren't full. A small and rustic bar area on the ground floor is a pleasant place for predinner drinks. Traditional Austrian cuisine is meticulously adhered to here. The menu features such classic dishes as *tafelspitz,* Wiener schnitzel, braised trout with dill-flavored potatoes, filet of pork with warm cabbage salad and bacon, and, for dessert, *Salzburger Nockerln* or peaches with hot fudge and vanilla ice cream.

Hagenauerplatz 2. ✆ **0662/843180.** www.zum-eulenspiegel.at. Reservations required. Main courses 13€–23€ ($21–$36). AE, MC, V. Mon–Sat 11am–2pm and 6–10:30pm. Closed Feb 1–Mar 15. Tram: 2. Bus: 2.

Inexpensive

Fasties INTERNATIONAL This is an inexpensive, unpretentious restaurant that doesn't take itself too seriously. It specializes in "fasties," but, unlike most fast food, the fasties actually contain flavor and nutrients. Set at the corner of the Papagenoplatz, in one of the most historic neighborhoods of Salzburg, the restaurant has a stand-up counter where you place your order and three large communal wooden tables where a staff member will serve you. When the weather cooperates, additional tables are set up on the square outside. The menu, written on a blackboard, changes daily, but invariably includes at least two soups, salads, and sandwiches. Platters are more substantial, consisting of assorted pâtés and cheeses, goulashes, roasts, and at least one vegetarian special. A second branch of this restaurant that's even more cramped is in an inconvenient location across the river from the historic core, less than 1km (1/2 mile) north of the center at Lasserstrasse 19 (✆ **0662/873876;** bus: 2, 3, or 5).

Pfeifergasse 3. ✆ **0662/844774.** Reservations not accepted. Main courses 5€–8€ ($8–$13). MC, V. Mon–Fri 7:30am–9pm; Sat 8am–5pm. Bus: 1.

Festungsrestaurant ★ (Kids) SALZBURG/AUSTRIAN The venue of this well-known restaurant is modern, warmly decorated, and airy, with the enviable bonus of being perched atop the former stronghold of the prince-archbishops of Salzburg, atop a huge rocky spur about 122m (400 ft.) above the Old Town and the Salzach River. From its evenly spaced windows, you'll have a sweeping view over the city and the surrounding countryside. The kitchen offers fish, well-prepared beef, pork, lamb, and such old-fashioned and traditional dishes as a *Salzburger bauernschmaus* (a bubbling stewpot of veal, pork, sausage, and dumplings), *Salzburger schnitzel, Salzburger Gröstl* (a form of beef hash with potatoes and onions), and *käse Spätzle* (*spätzle* with cheese). There's also wild game dishes served in season. One of the rooms within this restaurant complex, the Fürstenzimmer, offers occasional concerts, often featuring the works of Mozart. For ticket information, call ✆ **0662/825858.**

Hohensalzburg, Mönchsberg 34. ✆ **0662/841780.** www.festungsrestaurant.at. Reservations required July–Aug. Main courses 10€–21€ ($16–$34). AE, DC, MC, V. Mar–Jan 7 daily 10am–9pm. Closed Jan 8–Feb 28. Funicular from the Old Town.

Krimpelstätter SALZBURGIAN/AUSTRIAN This restaurant has been an enduring favorite in Salzburg, with a history dating from 1548. Originally designed and constructed as an inn, it retains chiseled stone columns that support the vaulted ceilings and heavy timbers. In summer, the beer garden, full of roses and trellises, attracts up to 300 visitors at a time. If you want a snack, a beer, or a glass of wine, head for the paneled door marked GASTZIMMER in the entry corridor. If you're looking for a more formal, less visited area, a trio of cozy antique dining rooms sits atop a flight of narrow stone steps. Each room serves the same menu, tasty and high-quality Land Salzburg regional cuisine featuring wild game dishes. Start with the cream of goose soup or else homemade chamois sausage. Traditional main courses include roast pork with dumplings, and fried sausages with sauerkraut and potatoes. Spinach dumplings are topped with a cheese sauce, and marinated beef stew comes with noodles in butter. From its blood sausages to its pork lights (lungs) with dumplings, this is definitely not the place to watch the calories or the cholesterol.

Müllner Hauptstrasse 31. ✆ **0662/432274.** Reservations recommended. Main courses 8€–16€ ($13–$26). MC, V. Tues–Sat 11am–midnight; Sun 10am–3pm (also Mon in Aug). Closed 3 weeks in Jan. Bus: 2 or 4.

Ristorante/Pizzeria Il Sole ITALIAN The venue is charming and convivial, and the prices are relatively modest at this well-managed Italian restaurant that sits immediately adjacent to the lower stage of the Mönchsberg elevator. The Austrian-born owners, the Rauzenberger brothers, are "Italian by adoption," thanks to the dozens of business and holiday trips they've made south of the border during the acquisition of the Italy-derived foodstuffs and decorative objects that are showcased within this restaurant. The street level is less formal and more animated than the dining room upstairs, but regardless of where you opt to sit, the menu is the same. We recently enjoyed a tantalizing fettuccine with shrimp as well as vegetable tortellini stuffed with blue cheese and spinach. Equally vibrant was a platter of chicken Il Sole, with fresh parmesan, a zesty tomato sauce, and pesto. The lemon-flavored chicken with fresh tagliatelle was a delight, as was a selection of grilled or sautéed fresh fish. Pizzas come in 15 different flavors, with the house brand (Il Sole, made with ham, salami, artichoke hearts, and mozzarella) being the most consistently popular.

Gstättengasse 15. ✆ **0662/843284.** Reservations not necessary. Pizzas and pastas 6€–9€ ($9.60–$14); main courses 11€–15€ ($18–$24). AE, DC, MC, V. Daily 11:30am–2:30pm and 5:30pm–midnight. Closed Tues Mar–June and Sept–Nov. Bus: 1.

Stadtgasthof Blaue Gans AUSTRIAN This restaurant consistently attracts local residents, some of whom plan their week around a meal here, and is an old-fashioned testimonial to *gutbürgerlich* (home-style) cooking. Within a timeless setting that includes vaulted ceilings that were originally designed in 1432 and a scattering of antique oil paintings, you can order such dishes as Wiener schnitzel, one of the best in town; *tafelspitz;* and *osso buco* of lamb with polenta. Pink-roasted lamb is an enduring favorite. Don't overlook this establishment's newest addition, a stone-built cellar, 500 years old, some of which is visible from above via a tempered glass plate set directly into the floor of the upstairs bar.

In the Arthotel Blaue Gans, Getreidegasse 43. ✆ **0662/842491.** Reservations recommended. Main courses 10€–25€ ($16–$40). AE, DC, MC, V. Wed–Mon 10am–10pm (last order 10pm).

Sternbräu AUSTRIAN The entrance to this establishment is through an arched cobblestone passageway leading off a street in the Old Town. The place seems big enough to have fed half the Austro-Hungarian army, with a series of eight rooms in varying degrees of formality. The Hofbräustübl is a rustic fantasy combining masonry columns with hand-hewn beams and wood paneling. Other rooms have such accessories as sea-green tile stoves, marble columns, and oil paintings. You can also eat in the chestnut tree-shaded beer garden, which is usually packed on summer nights, or under the weathered arcades of an inner courtyard. Drinks are served in the restaurant's bar, Grünstern. Daily specials include typically Austrian dishes such as Wiener and chicken schnitzels, trout, cold marinated herring, Hungarian goulash, hearty regional soups, and many other solid selections. Come here for the filling portions—not for refined cuisine.

Griesgasse 23. ✆ **0662/842140.** www.sternbraeu.com. Reservations not accepted. Main courses 11€–16€ ($17–$25). AE, MC, V. Daily 9am–11pm (until midnight July–Aug). Bus: 5.

Zipfer Bierhaus AUSTRIAN This longtime favorite is especially popular with the after-concert crowd. In a building dating from the 1400s, the establishment, in spite of its name, is more of a restaurant than a beer hall, although the decor is definitely in the beer-house tradition. The good food is familiar if you've been in Austria for a while: noodle casserole with ham in a cream sauce, breaded and fried filet of plaice or trout, veal goulash, and a spicy paprika salad with wurst and cheese. The food is well prepared and the portions are generous.

Sigmund-Haffner-Gasse 12. ✆ **0662/840745.** Reservations recommended. Main courses 7.60€–16€ ($12–$26). AE, DC, MC, V. Mon–Sat 10am–midnight (kitchen closes at 10pm). Bus: 3, 5, or 25.

Zum Mohren ★ AUSTRIAN A statue of an exotic-looking Moor sits atop the wrought-iron sign at the entrance to this restaurant, in a house built in 1423. You'll have to descend a flight of stone steps to reach the three distinctly different eating areas, the best of which is on the right of the entrance. Replicas of Moors, gold earrings and all, in either bas-relief or full-rounded sculpture, provide an offbeat decor. A third area, on the left as you enter, is more cavelike, with an orange ceramic stove and a low ceiling. Meals might include entrecote, Parisian style; sirloin steak with herb butter; grilled lamb chops; a good selection of cheeses; and many rich desserts. It's great to eat here in autumn and midwinter, when the restaurant emphasizes game, usually from the mountains near Salzburg, including fresh venison from the Unterberg (a mountain visible from the center of town); fresh local mushrooms known as *Eier Schwammel* in herb sauce, a dish favored by regional gourmets; and breast of duckling with apple and red-cabbage dressing and homemade dumplings.

Judengasse 9. ✆ **0662/840680.** Reservations recommended. Main courses 12€–21€ ($19–$34). MC, V. Mon–Sat 11am–11pm. Bus: 5.

ON THE RIGHT BANK

Expensive

Polo Lounge (aka The Restaurant in the Bristol Hotel) AUSTRIAN/ITALIAN/INTERNATIONAL This is the dining counterpart of the upscale restaurant within Salzburg's other top-notch hotel, the Goldener Hirsch. In this case, the venue is a stately, baronial-looking area outfitted in tones of pale orange and accented with large-scale oil paintings. A well-trained staff organizes meals which might feature freshwater crab salad with mango, tuna carpaccio with horseradish cream sauce, goose-liver parfait with apple chutney, grilled filet of beef with pinot noir sauce, roast loin of lamb with a pumpkin-flavored risotto, or perhaps grilled loin of veal with morel-flavored cream sauce. And for dessert, consider the warm chocolate mousse served with hot and sour cherries. Expect the kind of pomp and circumstance that comes almost automatically with a hotel of this stature, and some extremely well-prepared food. Immediately adjacent to the restaurant is a club-style bar with the requisite leather upholsteries and well-oiled paneling.

In the Hotel Bristol, Makartplatz 4. ✆ **0662/873557.** Reservations recommended. Main courses 18€–26€ ($29–$42). AE, DC, MC, V. Sept–June Mon–Sat noon–2:30pm and 6–10pm; July–Aug daily noon–2:30pm and 6–10pm. Bus: 1, 2, or 51.

Moderate

Alter Fuchs (Kids) TYROLEAN/AUSTRIAN Traditional Tyrolean dishes are served along with mugs of the local brew, Weiniger, in a vaulted stone cellar tavern. The restaurant is comfortable, the food is uncomplicated but made with high quality ingredients, and the service is friendly and efficient. Kids are also welcome; if they're toddlers, high seats are provided for them. When the chef is asked about his specialties, he says, "All my dishes are special." An array of fresh fish and such classics as Wiener schnitzel are served along with an array of food that Tyroleans have been eating for years. You can drop in for a snack or a full meal. Portions, such as sausages, roast pork, baked ham, and dumplings, are large and will satisfy the trencherman in women and men alike. The bread is often exceptionally good, including honest-to-God pretzels.

Linzer Gasse 47–49. ✆ **0662/882022.** Reservations recommended. Main courses 10€–21€ ($16–$34). MC, V. Mon–Sat 11:30am–midnight.

BIO Wirtshaus Hirschenwirt ★ (Finds) AUSTRIAN This is a hotel dining room, but a hotel dining room with a difference: All of the ingredients used in its cuisine derive from organically grown ingredients, raised in Austria without chemical fertilizers or insecticides. The setting is a quartet of cozy and traditional-looking dining rooms, each with a name that evokes a chalet high in the mountains. There's the *Stüberl,* strictly reserved for nonsmokers; the *Schank* (a bar area with a handful of dining tables); the *Spiesesaal* (the richly paneled main dining room); and *Hirsch Saal* (Deer Room, with lots of memorabilia related to hunting). Menu items change with the season but might include a creamy pumpkin soup, carpaccio of Austrian beef, *tafelspitz,* several versions of Wiener schnitzel, and about five different vegetarian dishes, the best example of which is small *Spätzle* in a cheese-flavored onion sauce.

In the Hotel zum Hirschen, St. Julien Strasse 23. ✆ **0662/881335.** www.biowirtshaus.at. Reservations recommended. Main courses 9€–14€ ($14–$22). AE, DC, MC, V. Daily 4pm–midnight. Bus: 1 or 2.

Die Weisse AUSTRIAN This is one of the best restaurant-cum-breweries in Salzburg. It's old-fashioned and traditional, serving food that went over big in 1890. Carry a big appetite if you dine here, as portions are huge. Instead of butter, cold lard and cracklings are spread over dark rye bread. This is followed with the biggest Wiener schnitzel we've ever encountered in Salzburg. The platter is accompanied by a freshly made salad, potatoes, and cranberry sauce for added flavor. Other rib-sticking fare includes a platter of mixed sausages and perfectly roasted ham. Dumplings accompany main dishes. Some diehard Austrian diners make a meal out of the dumplings themselves, especially the small Pinzgauer cheese dumplings, which come in their own sauté pan, bubbling with a very tangy cheese. Naturally there's plenty of beer to wash everything down, along with a bakery full of pretzels and freshly baked breads. For dessert, finish off with an *apfelstrudel.*

Rupertgasse 10. ✆ **0662/872246.** www.dieweisse.at. Reservations not required. Main courses 8€–16€ ($13–$26). AE, MC, V. Mon–Sat 10am–midnight. Closed Dec 24–31. Bus: 29.

Hotel Stadtkrug Restaurant AUSTRIAN/INTERNATIONAL Across the river from the Old Town, on the site of what used to be a 14th-century farm, this restaurant occupies a structure that was rebuilt from an older core in 1458. In the 1960s, a hotel was added in back of the old-fashioned dining rooms, which now serve as one of the neighborhood's most popular restaurants. In an artfully rustic setting, illuminated by gilded wooden chandeliers, you can enjoy conservative and flavorful Austrian cuisine. Good, hearty dishes include cream of potato soup "Old Vienna" style; braised beef with burgundy sauce; grilled trout or catfish; and glazed cutlet of pork with caraway seeds, deep-fried potatoes, and French beans with bacon. A dessert specialty is a honey parfait with raspberry sauce.

Linzer Gasse 20. ✆ **0662/873545.** www.stadtkrug.at/gastronomie.php. Reservations recommended. Main courses 15€–25€ ($24–$40). AE, DC, MC, V. Sept–June Wed–Mon noon–2pm and 6–11pm; July–Aug daily noon–2pm and 6–11pm. Bus: 1 or 2.

Mundenhamer Bräu SALZBURGIAN/INTERNATIONAL This warm-hued restaurant near the main train station has been serving copious portions of food to Salzburgers since the 1930s. There are several different seating areas—our favorite is the big-windowed section with a view of a city park. In season, game is a specialty; otherwise, menu items might include Salzburger cream schnitzel, paprika cutlets, mushroom ragout, and a house specialty called Mundenhamer potpourri, a mixed grill for two. The menu is in English and the portions are large.

Rainerstrasse 2. ✆ **0662/8756930.** Reservations recommended. Main courses 7.20€–16€ ($12–$26); fixed-price menus 10€–12€ ($16–$19). AE, DC, MC, V. Mon–Sat 11:30am–2pm and 5:30–11:30pm. Bus: 3 or 5.

Restaurant Wasserfall ★ Finds ITALIAN This discovery serves some of the best Northern Italian fare in Salzburg to the sounds of quiet jazz and gurgling water from a waterfall. Nestled into the rocks of the Kapuzinerberg, in a rather romantic setting, it's an ideal dining choice for very friendly couples. The Kapuzinerberg (p. 256) is the forested area on the right bank of the Salzach River, rising over the cityscape of Salzburg. Excellent local produce and some fine imported ingredients from Italy go into the creation of this fresh-tasting and well-prepared cuisine. The cookery is basically simple, nothing to interfere with the natural flavor of the food. We prefer the fresh fish dishes, preferably grilled to our request, with some lemon and fresh herbs adding flavor. The succulent pasta dishes come with a number of flavorful and tangy sauces. The atmosphere, although casual, doesn't mean you can show up in shorts.

Linzergasse 10. ✆ **0662/873331.** Reservations required. Main courses 7€–22€ ($11–$35). AE, DC, MC, V. Mon–Sat 6–10:30pm. Closed mid-July to mid-Aug. Bus: 2, 5, 6, 15, 27, 29, 51, or 55.

Strassewirt ★ AUSTRIAN Set within a 10-minute walk south of Salzburg's historic core, this restaurant occupies three indoor dining rooms and also, during clement weather, one of the most charming gardens in town. The much-renovated building that contains it was constructed 200 years ago, and now houses the culinary intelligence of Chef Christian Sussetz and his wife, Alexandra, who oversees the service of the dining room staff. Menu items celebrate the cuisine and the agrarian bounty of Austria. Main courses include roasted mountain lamb from nearby high-altitude meadows, served with polenta and zucchini; venison that exerts a strong appeal, served with a celery-flavored cream sauce; and fresh Atlantic char that's simply grilled and served with cucumber salad and roasted potatoes. Wiener schnitzels and goulash are delightful, albeit not particularly exotic.

Leopoldskronestrasse 39. ✆ **0662/826391.** www.zumstrassewirt.com. Reservations recommended. Main courses 9.50€–25€ ($15–$40); 4-course set-price menu 39€ ($62) without wine, 50€ ($80) with wine. DC, MC, V. Tues–Sat 11:30am–2pm and 6–10pm. Closed for 2 weeks in Oct and 2 weeks in Feb. Bus: 21.

Zum Fidelen Affen AUSTRIAN Set on the eastern edge of the river near the Staatsbrücke, this restaurant is the closest thing in Salzburg to a loud, animated, and jovial pub with food service. Its circular bar is great for those who just stop in for a drink, although many patrons eventually wander into dinner, too. Management allows only three tables on any particular evening to be reserved; the remainder are given to whomever happens to show up. It's best to give your name to the maître d' and then wait at the bar.

Menu items are simple, inexpensive, and based on regional culinary traditions. A house specialty is a gratin of green (spinach-flavored) noodles in cream sauce with strips of ham. Also popular are Wiener schnitzels, ham goulash with dumplings, and at least three different kinds of main-course dumplings flavored with meats, cheeses, herbs, and various sauces. Dessert might be a cheese dumpling or one of several kinds of pastries. True to the establishment's name, translated as "The Funny Monkey," its interior depicts painted and sculpted simians cavorting across the walls.

Priesterhausgasse 8. ✆ **0662/877361.** Reservations recommended. Main courses 9€–16€ ($14–$26). DC, MC, V. Mon–Sat 5pm–1am (the kitchen closes at 10:45pm).

ON THE OUTSKIRTS

Very Expensive

Ikarus in Hangar 7 ★★ *Finds* INTERNATIONAL In no other major city of Europe do we recommend that you go to the airport for fine dining. The unique Ikarus is installed in Hangar 7, in a glass-and-steel ellipsoid near the airport, and managed by star chef Eckard Weizigmann. He employs a different award-winning, international chef each month to create his specialties. This giant ellipsoid houses a collection of historic aircrafts, two bars, and Ikarus itself, which features formal dining from a highly inventive menu. Believe it or not, some rich Austrian foodies fly in for dinner in their private planes. "Parking spaces" are available right in front of Hangar 7. Despite the changing chefs, the food is consistently of high quality. Each chef puts together three different menus, so you can never be sure what you're going to get. Finely crafted dishes might include rabbit with cabbage, barley, and blood orange; an oxtail ragout; red mullet with eggplant confit in a basil sauce; halibut on a chorizo couscous and bell pepper foam; leg of lamb with Mediterranean vegetables; a delice of pear, Cassis, and chocolate; and an ice cream of tonka beans, followed by an international selection of cheese. Cuisine can be combined with technology; guided tours of the on-site Flight Museum are offered at various times at Hangar 7.

7A Wilhelm-Spazier Strasse (5km west of Salzburg). ✆ **0662/219-777.** www.hangar-7.com. Reservations required. Main courses 32€–50€ ($51–$80); set-price menus 95€–135€ ($152–$216). AE, DC, MC, V. Daily noon–2pm and 6:30–10pm. Bus: 2.

Pfefferschiff ★ *Finds* CONTINENTAL Its setting is a country-baroque rectory, originally built about 300 years ago as a home for the village priest, immediately adjacent to a church and a domed 17th-century chapel in the suburb of Hallwang, 3.2km (2 miles) northeast of Salzburg's center. Inside, a trio of high-ceilinged, rather stiffly formal dining rooms, each evoking a sense of solidly upper-class bourgeois values, showcases the cuisine of owner and chef Klaus Fleishhaker. His wife, Petra, oversees the dining rooms, where fine china, silver, and crystal contribute to the hushed and somewhat restrained sense of propriety. The menu changes frequently, with an emphasis on whatever is fresh within the region at the time. The finest dishes include monkfish in an olive-based crust with pesto-laced polenta, pan-fried foie gras with gingerbread and spinach salad, and a ragout of scallops and seafood in a saffron-flavored cream sauce. Desserts are sublime—especially the rhubarb tart served with buttermilk-flavored ice cream. Take a cab, or else drive along the north edge of the Kapuzinerberg in the direction to Hallwang, and then follow the signposts into Söllheim.

Söllheim 3, in the suburb of Hallwang. ✆ **0662/661242.** Reservations required. Main courses 16€–32€ ($26–$51); fixed-price menus 52€–80€ ($83–$128). DC, MC, V. Tues–Fri 6–10pm, Sat noon–1:30pm and 6–10pm; Aug only Sun noon–1:30pm and 6–10pm.

Restaurant Paris Lodron ★★★ INTERNATIONAL This is the most glamorous and prestigious restaurant in Salzburg, thanks to a historic pedigree and cuisine that defines it as one of the most appealing Relais & Châteaux members in Austria. Named after the medieval archbishop of Salzburg who commissioned the construction of the Schloss Mönchstein in which it's housed, the establishment is composed of two separate dining rooms, both elegantly outfitted. There's also an outdoor terrace open in good weather. Menu items change with the seasons and the whims of the chefs, but might include delectable king prawns with sesame oil and fresh ginger, butter-fried filets of pikeperch nestled on a puree of celery, filet of sole in an herb-enriched crust with a mild mustard sauce, or a roasted loin of lamb dredged in pumpkin seeds and served with sage sauce. In autumn and early winter, savory game dishes include medallions of venison with rosemary sauce.

In the Hotel Schloss Mönchstein, Mönchsberg Park 26. ✆ **0662/8485550.** www.monchstein.at. Reservations recommended. Main courses 25€–50€ ($40–$80). AE, DC, MC, V. Daily noon–2pm and 6–10pm. Limited menu available daily 2–6pm.

Expensive

Brandstätter ★ AUSTRIAN One of the best restaurants in Salzburg is actually right outside the city limits in Liefering, lying just off the Autobahn-Mitte. It's northwest of the city, about 30 minutes by bus, or 20 minutes if you prefer to take a taxi. Brandstätter is an intimate, cozy choice for a special meal. Diners like this friendly place so much that they often linger long after their meal is finished.

The daily menus are seasonal so that the best and freshest produce, game, and meat are used. We recommend beginning with the terrine of goose liver with an apple-and-celery salad and proceeding to the salmon trout with white-wine sauce. Some dishes might be only for the adventurous—for example, veal lungs with dumplings—but others are quite elegant, including a perfectly cooked roast pheasant breast with a bacon-and-cranberry sauce. Finish your meal with one of the homemade desserts, such as a hazelnut parfait.

Münchner Bundesstrasse 69, Liefering. ✆ **0662/434535.** Reservations required. Main courses 8€–27€ ($13–$43). AE, MC, V. Mon–Sat 11:30am–2pm and 6–11pm. Closed 1 week in Jan. Bus: 4 from the center of Salzburg to the Fischergasse stop.

Obauer ★★ Finds AUSTRIAN/ITALIAN It's worth the 45-minute train ride from Salzburg to sample the cuisine of Karl and Rudolph Obauer, who worked for some of the greatest chefs of Europe before opening their own little hotel and restaurant. You might arrive early to explore the hilltop village of Werfen itself, with its pretty shops and old houses. The windows of the restaurant look out upon mountain vistas and the town's ancient fortress, and there's a lovely garden in back. Beamed ceilings and stone walls are an old-fashioned touch, though the color scheme of lavender and terra cotta is very modern.

You're greeted with pots of butter and chicken-liver mousse. Perhaps you'll begin with a terrine of venison and pickled quail's eggs. Great care goes into the selection of the produce, including young salmon and trout from nearby streams, "farmer's chicken," and even Pongau lamb and veal from nearby mountain pastures. Sole with green beans, peaches, and nutmeg is a signature dish. One of our favorites is tender Werfen lamb in its pan juices with a side order of buttery Swiss chard and an onion stuffed with white polenta. For dessert, we'd recommend the Banyuls-soaked prunes topped with ganache. The village of Werfen lies near the A10 (the Tauern Autobahn), 35km (22 miles) from Salzburg. The Werfen train station is only a 5-minute walk from the hotel.

Markt 46, Werfen. ✆ **0646/852120.** www.obauer.com. Reservations required. Main courses 22€–45€ ($35–$72); 3-course menu 35€ ($56); 4-course menu 65€ ($104); 5-course menu 75€ ($120); 6-course menu 90€ ($144). AE, MC, V. Wed–Sun noon–2pm and 7–9:30pm.

Moderate

Gasthof Riedenburg ★ CONTINENTAL One of the best restaurants in and around Salzburg occupies a substantial-looking white-sided villa in the suburb of Riedenburg, about 3km (2 miles) south of the city's historic core. Elegant and well-respected by virtually everyone in town, it attracts well-groomed and well-heeled members of the local bourgeoisie. Enter a trio of paneled dining rooms, each with an elegantly rustic motif of Land Salzburgundian charm. Menu items are urbane, sophisticated, and delicious—some of the best in town. Examples include lamb cutlets with couscous and chives; marinated brook trout with sweet-and-sour vegetables and fresh herbs; cream of crabmeat soup with aged port; turbot with lobster mousse, spinach, and fennel; and filet of venison with white pepper sauce, noodles, and artichokes. Dessert might be a white chocolate mousse with mandarin oranges. Let the house pick a glass of whatever the wine steward thinks will be appropriate with each course of your meal—the results can be surprisingly delectable.

Neutorstrasse 31. ✆ **0662/830815.** www.riedenburg.at. Reservations recommended. Main courses 28€–33€ ($45–$53); fixed-price menus 59€–79€ ($94–$126). AE, DC, MC, V. Sept–July Tue–Sat noon–2pm and 6–10pm; Aug daily noon–2pm and 6–10pm. Bus: 1 or 2.

5 SEEING THE SIGHTS

The Old Town lies between the left bank of the Salzach River and the ridge known as the Mönchsberg, which rises to a height of 503m (1,650 ft.) and is the site of Salzburg's casino. The main street of the Old Town is Getreidegasse, a narrow thoroughfare lined with five- and six-story burghers' buildings. Most of the houses along the street date from the 17th and 18th centuries. Mozart was born at no. 9 (see below). Many of the houses display lacy-looking wrought-iron signs over carved windows.

You might begin your explorations at **Mozartplatz,** with its outdoor cafes. From here you can walk to the even more expansive **Residenzplatz,** where torchlight dancing is staged every year, along with outdoor performances.

THE TOP ATTRACTIONS

Festspielhaus Designed by Wolf Dietrich and built in 1607, this festival hall was once the court stables. Today it's the center for the major musical events of Salzburg, its cultural activity peaking during the August festival. The modern hall seats 2,300 spectators, and most major concerts and big operas are performed here. Many outstanding Austrian artists contributed to the decoration of the modern Festival Hall. Call and make reservations if you plan on stopping by. *Note:* Tours are canceled if there is a rehearsal or performance of virtually anything, so this is no longer a major stop on the Salzburg tourist scene, but a grace note fitted in for music buffs when more pressing musical or theatrical events don't override it.

Hofstallgasse 1. ✆ **0662/8045-500.** Admission to tours 5€ ($8). Jan 7–May 30 and Oct 1–Dec 20 daily at 2pm; June and Sept daily at 2pm and 3:30pm, July–Aug daily at 9:30am, 2 and 3:30pm. Bus: 1.

Glockenspiel (Carillon) ★ Kids The celebrated glockenspiel with its 35 bells stands across from the Residenz. You can hear this 18th-century carillon at 7 and 11am, and 6pm. Currently, access to the interior is prohibited. The ideal way to hear the chimes is from one of the cafes lining the edges of the Mozartplatz while sipping your favorite coffee or drink.

Mozartplatz 1. ✆ **0662/80422784.** Bus: 1.

Hohensalzburg Fortress ★★ Kids The stronghold of the ruling prince-archbishops before they moved "downtown" to the Residenz, this fortress towers 122m (400 ft.) above the Salzach River on a rocky dolomite ledge. The massive fortress crowns the Festungsberg and literally dominates Salzburg. To get here, you can hike up one of the paths or lanes leading to the fortress, or you can walk from Kapitelplatz by way of Festungsgasse or from the Mönchsberg via the Schartentor. You can also take the funicular from Festungsgasse (✆ **0662/842682**) at the station behind the cathedral. You can purchase an advance ticket to the museum, which includes admission and the funicular ride. Call the museum or the Festungsgasse telephone number in advance for ticket availability.

Work on Hohensalzburg began in 1077 and was not finished until 1681, during which time many builders of widely different tastes and purposes had a hand in the construction. This is the largest completely preserved castle left in central Europe. Functions of defense and state were combined in this fortress for 6 centuries.

The elegant state apartments, once the dwellings of the prince-archbishops and their courts, are on display. Note the coffered ceilings and intricate ironwork, and check out the early-16th-century porcelain stove in the Golden Room.

The **Burgmuseum** is distinguished mainly by its collection of medieval art. Plans and prints tracing the growth of Salzburg are on display, as are instruments of torture and many Gothic artifacts. The Salzburger Stier (Salzburg Bull), an open-air barrel organ built in 1502, plays melodies by Mozart and his friend Haydn in daily concerts following the glockenspiel chimes. The **Rainermuseum** has arms and armor exhibits. The beautiful late-Gothic St. George's Chapel, dating from 1501, has marble reliefs of the Apostles.

Visit Hohensalzburg, even if you're not interested in the fortress, for the view from the terrace. From the Reck watchtower, you get a panoramic sweep of the Alps. The Kuenberg bastion has a fine view of Salzburg's domes and towers.

Mönchsberg 34. ✆ **0662/84243011.** www.salzburg-burgen.at/en/hohensalzburg. Admission 10€ ($16) adults, 5.70€ ($9.10) children 6–19, free for children 5 and under; family ticket 23€ ($37). Fortress and museums Oct–Mar daily 9:30am–5pm; Apr–Sept daily 9am–6pm.

Petersfriedhof ★★ St. Peter's Cemetery lies at the stone wall that merges into the bottom of the rock called the Mönchsberg. Many of the aristocratic families of Salzburg lie buried here alongside many other noted persons, including Nannerl Mozart, sister of Wolfgang Amadeus (4 years older than her better-known brother, Nannerl was also an exceptionally gifted musician). You can also see the Romanesque Chapel of the Holy

Cross and St. Margaret's Chapel, dating from the 15th century. The cemetery and its chapels are rich in blue-blooded history; monuments to a way of life long vanished. You can also take a self-guided tour through the early Christian catacombs in the rock above the church cemetery.

St.-Peter-Bezirk. ✆ **0662/8445760.** Free admission to cemetery. Catacombs 1€ ($1.60) adults, .60€ ($1) children ages 6–15. May–Sept daily 10:30am–5pm; Oct–Apr daily 10:30am–3:30pm. Bus: 1.

Residenz State Rooms/Residenzgalerie Salzburg ★★ This opulent palace, just north of Domplatz in the pedestrian zone, was the seat of the Salzburg prince-archbishops after they no longer needed the protection of the gloomy Hohensalzburg Fortress of Mönchsberg. The Residenz dates from 1120, but work on a series of palaces, which comprised the ecclesiastical complex of the ruling church princes, began in the late 1500s and continued until about 1796. The lavish rebuilding was originally ordered by Archbishop Wolfgang (usually called "Wolf") Dietrich. The Residenz fountain, from the 17th century, is one of the largest and most impressive baroque fountains north of the Alps.

The child prodigy Mozart often played here in the Conference Room for guests. In 1867, Emperor Franz Josef received Napoleon III here. More than a dozen state rooms, each richly decorated, are open to the public via guided tour.

On the second floor, you can visit the **Residenzgalerie Salzburg** (✆ **0662/840451**), an art gallery founded in 1923, which now contains European paintings from the 16th to the 19th century, displayed in 15 historic rooms. Paintings from the Dutch, Flemish, French, Italian, Austrian baroque, and Austrian 19th-century schools are exhibited. Self-guided audio tours are included in the admission.

Residenzplatz 1. ✆ **0662/80422690.** Admission to Residenz state rooms 5.70€ ($9.10) adults, 2.10€ ($3.40) children 6–15, free for children 5 and under; combined ticket to state rooms and gallery 8.20€ ($13) adults, 2.60€ ($4.20) children 6–15, free for children 5 and under, family ticket 19€ ($30); Residenz Gallery 5.70€ ($9.10) adults, 2.70€ ($4.30) children 6–16. Daily 9am–5pm. Bus: 5 or 6.

Salzburg Museum/Neue Residenz ★★ A series of attractions are sheltered in the "New Residence" complex, which isn't new at all. It actually dates from the 1600s, when it was Prince-Archbishop Wolf-Dietrich's "overflow palace." The main part of the new Residence is a series of state reception rooms that marked the beginning of the Renaissance in Salzburg.

One of the highlights of the museum is the exhibitions once housed in the Museum Carolino Augusteum. Rare archaeological treasures are found here, including Hallstatt Age relics, plus fragments of ruins from the town's Roman occupation. A Celtic bronze flagon is one of the chief treasures.

The museum is noted for its collection of Old Masters, with a rich trove of Gothic panel paintings and much art work from the Romantic period. The Gothic altarpieces show fine craftsmanship, and you may want to seek out works by Hans Makart, an artist born in Salzburg in 1840.

In the basement of the Neue Residenz is the **Kunsthalle,** a multifunctional circular hall where special exhibitions are staged every year, many devoted to artists who had a special relationship with Salzburg.

Mozartplatz 1. ✆ **0662/620808-700.** www.salzburgmuseum.at. Admission 7€ ($11) adults, 4€ ($6.40) students, 3€ ($4.80) ages 6–15. Tues–Wed and Fri–Sat 9am–5pm, Thurs 9am–8pm; July–Sept also Mon 9am–5pm.

Salzburger Dom ★ Located where Residenzplatz flows into Domplatz (where you'll see a 1771 statue of the Virgin), this cathedral is world-renowned for its 4,000-pipe organ. The original building from A.D. 774 was superseded by a late-Romanesque structure erected from 1181 to 1200. When this edifice was destroyed by fire in 1598, Prince-Archbishop Wolf Dietrich commissioned construction of a new cathedral, but his overthrow prevented the completion of this project. His successor, Archbishop Markus Sittikus Count Hohenems, commissioned the Italian architect Santino Solari to build the present cathedral, which was consecrated in 1628 by Archbishop Paris Count Lodron.

Hailed by some critics as the "most perfect" Renaissance building in the Germanic countries, the cathedral has a marble facade and twin symmetrical towers. The mighty

In Mozart's Footsteps

Wolfgang Amadeus Mozart was born in Salzburg on January 27, 1756, son of an overly managerial father, Leopold Mozart, whose controlling power he eventually fled. Amadeus was a child prodigy, writing musical notes at the age of 4, before he could even shape the letters of the alphabet. By the time he'd reached the ripe old age of 6, he was performing at the Schönbrunn Palace in Vienna before assembled royalty and aristocrats.

For a time he pleased the audiences of Vienna, but he once complained that the audiences in his hometown of Salzburg were rather wooden and no more responsive than "tables and chairs." Ironically, while Salzburg today pays great tribute to Mozart—many merchants live solely off his reputation—he was not appreciated here in his lifetime and often struggled to make ends meet. In spite of the success of *The Magic Flute* in 1791, his career ended in obscurity.

Mozart's image is everywhere in Salzburg. In the heart of town, **Mozartplatz** bears his name, with a statue of the composer erected in 1842, the first recognition of his birth he'd received in the town since his death.

A music academy in Salzburg is named after Mozart, and, of course, his music dominates the Salzburg Festival. Too bad he couldn't have been more honored during his lifetime. He died in Vienna on December 5, 1791, and the body of the 35-year-old musical genius was carried in a pauper's hearse to a common grave in the cemetery of Vienna's St. Marx. Today, if his grave site had been better marked, it would be a world-class memorial.

You can visit **Mozart Geburtshaus (Birthplace)** ★, Getreidegasse 9 (✆ **0662/844313**, www.gasthofschorn.at). He lived here until he was 17—that is, when he was in Salzburg at all and wasn't touring such cities as Prague or Vienna. There are three floors of exhibition rooms, which include the Mozart family apartment. The main treasures are the valuable paintings (such as the well-known oil painting *Mozart and the Piano,* left unfinished by Joseph Lange) and the original instruments: the violin Mozart used as a child, his concert violin, and his viola, fortepiano, and clavichord. It's open daily from 9am to 6pm. Admission is 5.50€ ($8.80) for adults and 1.50€ ($2.40) for children.

You can also visit the restored **Mozart Wohnhaus** ★, Makartplatz 8 (✆ **0662/87422740**), where the composer lived from 1773 to 1780. Damaged bronze doors were created in 1959. The themes are Faith, Hope, and Love. The interior has a rich baroque style with elaborate frescoes, the most important of which, along with the altarpieces, were designed by Mascagni of Florence. In the cathedral, you can see the Romanesque font at which Mozart was baptized. The dome was damaged during World War II but was restored by 1959. In the crypt, traces of the old Romanesque cathedral that once stood on this spot have been unearthed.

The treasure of the cathedral, and the "arts and wonders" the archbishops collected in the 17th century, are displayed in the **Dom Museum** (✆ **0662/8047-1860**), entered through the cathedral.

in World War II air raids, the house reopened in 1996, honoring the year of Mozart's 240th birthday. In 1773, the Mozart family vacated the cramped quarters of Mozart's birthplace for this haunt on Makartplatz. In the rooms of these former apartments, a museum documents the history of the house, life, and work of Wolfgang Amadeus Mozart. There's a mechanized audio tour in six languages with musical samples. The museum is open June to September daily 9am to 5pm and October to May daily 9am to 6pm. Admission is 6.50€ ($10) for adults, 5.50€ ($8.80) for students, and 1.50€ ($2.40) for children.

Mozart aficionados will want to stop by the International Mozarteum Foundation's **Mozart Audio & Film Museum,** Makartplatz 8 (✆ **0662/883454**). Here is a collection of 11,000 audio and 1,000 video titles, all concerned with Mozart's compositions. There are also sections devoted to the work of contemporary Salzburg composers. You can watch and listen to eight video and 10 audio stations, and there's a large-scale screen for groups. The museum, which is free, is open Monday, Tuesday, and Friday 9am to 1pm and Wednesday and Thursday 1 to 5pm.

You have to make an appointment to visit the **Mozarteum,** Schwarzstrasse 26 (✆ **0662/8894030**). This is the center of the International Mozarteum Foundation, an edifice in Munich Jugendstil architecture, built from 1910 to 1914. The jewel on the second floor is the library—a *Bibliotheca Mozartiana*—with approximately 12,000 titles devoted to Mozart. The Viennese Hall seats 200 people and provides an intimate atmosphere for concerts and conferences. The wing at Schwarzstrasse 28 houses the larger concert hall, where up to 800 guests enjoy concerts held throughout the year. The highlight is the celebratory festival *Mozartwoche,* which commemorates Mozart's birthday (Jan 27) with 10 days of concerts and operas. It's open Monday to Friday from 9am to 5pm.

In the garden stands the **Magic Flute House,** a little wood structure in which Mozart composed *The Magic Flute* in 1791. It was shipped here from the Naschmarkt in Vienna. In 1971, the Mozarteum was designated as the College of Music and the Performing Arts.

The **cathedral excavations** (✆ **0662/845295**) are entered around the corner (left of the Dom entrance). This exhibition of excavation work shows ruins of the original foundation.

The allegorical play *Everyman,* adapted by Hugo von Hofmannsthal, is performed near the cathedral in Domplatz during the Salzburg Festival.

South side of Residenzplatz. ✆ **0662/844189.** Free admission to cathedral; excavations 5€ ($8) adults, 1.50€ ($2.40) children 6–18, free for children 5 and under; museum 5€ ($8) adults, 1.50€ ($2.40) children. Cathedral daily 8am–7pm (to 5pm in winter); excavations Easter–Sept Tues–Sun 10:30am–5pm; Oct–Apr Wed–Thurs 10:30am–3:30pm, Fri–Sun 10:30am–4pm; museum Wed–Sun 9am–5pm, Sun 1–6pm. Closed Nov 6–24 and Jan 8–Apr 7. Bus: 1.

Schloss Mirabell ★ This palace and its gardens (see "Parks & Gardens," below) were originally built as a luxurious private residence called Altenau. Prince-Archbishop Wolf Dietrich had it constructed in 1606 for his mistress and the mother of his children, Salome Alt. Unfortunately, not much remains of the original grand structure. Johann Lukas von Hildebrandt rebuilt the Schloss in the first quarter of the 18th century, and it was modified after a great fire in 1818. The official residence of the mayor of Salzburg is now in the palace, which is like a smaller rendition of the Tuileries in Paris. The ceremonial marble *Barockstiege-Englesstiege* (angel staircase), with sculptured cherubs, carved by Raphael Donner in 1726, leads to the Marmorsaal, a marble-and-gold hall used for private concerts and weddings.

Rainerstrasse. ✆ **0662/80722334.** Free admission. Mon–Thurs 8am–4pm, Fri 8am–2:30pm; closed on other days.

Stiftskirche St. Peter ★★ Founded in A.D. 696 by St. Rupert, whose tomb is here, this is the church of St. Peter's Abbey and Benedictine Monastery. Once a Romanesque basilica with three aisles, the church was completely overhauled in the 17th and 18th centuries in an elegant baroque style. The west door dates from 1240. The church is richly adorned with art treasures, including some altar paintings by Kremser Schmidt. The Salzburg Madonna, in the left chancel, is from the early 15th century.

St.-Peter-Bezirk 1. ✆ **0662/844578.** Free admission. Daily 9am–noon. Bus: 5.

MORE ATTRACTIONS

For the many sites and attractions focusing on Salzburg's favorite son, Mozart, see the box "In Mozart's Footsteps," above.

Churches

Friedhof St. Sebastian Prince-Archbishop Wolf Dietrich commissioned this cemetery in 1595 to be laid out like an Italian *campo santo.* The tombs of Mozart's wife and

Mozart Cycle Path

A new cycle path, named for hometown boy Wolfgang Amadeus Mozart, now runs from the city of Salzburg through the Salzburg Lake District and on to Bavaria and its lakes, such as Ciemsee, before ending at Berchtesgaden, near Hitler's former vacation retreat. The route stretches more than 410km (255 miles) and is primarily flat, with just a few hills along the way. It's ideal for families. Salzburg tourist offices will provide trail maps.

his father, Leopold, are here. In the middle of the cemetery is St. Gabriel's Chapel, containing the mausoleum of Dietrich. The mausoleum's interior is lined with multicolored porcelain.

To reach the cemetery, walk down the Italian-style steps from St. Sebastian's Church. The original late-Gothic edifice dated from the early 16th century. It was rebuilt and enlarged in 1749, in the rococo style. Destroyed by fire in 1818, it was later reconstructed. Only the 1752 rococo doorway remains from the old church building. Paracelsus, the Renaissance doctor and philosopher who died in 1541, is entombed here. According to ancient Roman Catholic tradition, ceremonies here are carried out entirely in Latin.

Linzergasse. ✆ **0662/875208.** Free admission. Daily 9am–7pm (until dusk in winter). Bus: 1.

Kollegienkirche Opening onto an open-air marketplace, Collegiate Church was built between 1694 and 1707 for the Benedictine university founded in 1622 and designed by the great baroque architect Fischer von Erlach. The university, disbanded in 1810, was reopened in 1962 as part of the University of Salzburg (the main campus is in the suburb of Nonntal). There are a few other old university buildings in the area, including a fine library and reading room. This, von Erlach's greatest and largest Salzburg church, is one of the most celebrated baroque churches in all of Austria (and that's saying a lot). Altar paintings are by Rottmayr.

Universitätsplatz. ✆ **0662/84132772.** Free admission. Daily 9am–6pm. Bus: 2.

Museums

Historische Musikinstrumente (Historic Musical Instruments) Part of the Salzburg Museum, this museum is designed for music lovers, housing rare instruments such as musical instruments of the 16th and 17th centuries. The collection includes antique keyboard, wind, string, plucked, and percussion instruments. The collection is especially impressive in its baroque string instruments or its wind instruments of the late baroque and classic eras. An admission ticket is also valid for the Toy Museum.

Bürgerspitalgasse 2. ✆ **0662/620808-300.** Admission 3€ ($4.80) adults, 2€ ($3.20) students, 1€ ($1.60) ages 6–15. Tues–Sun 9am–5pm; July–Aug and Dec Mon also 9am–5pm.

Museum der Moderne Art ★ It's not the Pompidou in Paris, but this Salzburg museum is devoted to some of the best of contemporary art and is built on the side of Mönchsberg mountain, overlooking the city. The director, Toni Stoos, told us that Salzburg is "taking its task as a contemporary art center most seriously. Perhaps we're not as avant-garde as Vienna, but modern art has been around here for many years, and it's time we showcased it." An urban landscape and a natural setting of beauty are dovetailed here in the exhibitions, which also highlight the Austrian Gallery of Photography. The design alone makes this one of the most beautiful museums of Austria. Large rotating exhibitions of international modern art are displayed in the spacious and beautifully lit exhibition salons. If you get bored with the artwork itself (highly unlikely), you can take in the views of the mountains in the distance.

Mönchsberg 32. ✆ **0662/842220403.** Admission 8€ ($13) adults; 6€ ($9.60) seniors, students, and children. Tues–Sun 10am–6pm (Wed until 9pm); summer Mon also 10am–6pm. Take the Mönchsberg elevator to the top.

Panorama Museum This museum is devoted to displaying one of the few remaining 360-degree panoramic paintings in the world. It shows Salzburg as it looked in the early

 1800s. It was created by Johann Michael Sattler (1786–1847), covering 125 square meters. Telescopes on the visitors' platform allow a closer view of the details of domestic architecture as it existed at the time. Around the Panorama, large format paintings of motifs from all over the world are by Johann Michael Sattler's son, Hubert.

Residenzplatz 9. ✆ **0662/620808-730.** Admission 2€ ($3.20) adults, 1.50€ ($2.40) students, 1€ ($1.60) ages 6–15. Daily 9am–5pm (until 8pm Thurs); reduced hours Dec 24, 31, Jan 1; closed Nov 1 and Dec 25.

Rupertinum (Museum of Modern Art Salzburg) This gallery, housed in a 17th-century building, is known for its wide variety of temporary exhibits, plus a permanent collection of works by Klimt, Kokoschka, and lesser-known artists. There is also a display of photography and graphic arts. Although it's a fairly minor attraction, it's a nice stop for those interested in 20th-century art.

Wiener Philharmonikergasse 9. ✆ **0662/80422541.** Admission 6€ ($9.60) adults, 4€ ($6.40) students, free for children 15 and under. Tues–Fri 10am–6pm (Wed to 9pm). Bus: 29.

Salzburger Barockmuseum The museum in the orangery of the Mirabell Gardens (see "Parks & Gardens," below) displays 17th- and 18th-century European art, with works by Giordano, Rottmayr, Bernini, Straub, and others.

Mirabellgarten 3. ✆ **0662/877432.** Admission 4.50€ ($7.20) adults, 3.70€ ($5.90) students 15–18 and seniors, free for children 14 and under. Sept–June Tues–Sat 9am–noon and 2–5pm, Sun and holidays 10am–1pm; July–Aug Mon–Sat 10am–5pm, Sun 10am–1pm. Bus: 1.

Spielzeug Museum (Toy Museum) (Kids) Founded in 1978 and part of the Salzburg Museum, this museum shares an entrance with the Museum of Historic Musical Instruments. In fact, a ticket for that museum also entitles you to admission to the Toy Museum—or vice versa. The Toy Museum possesses the largest collection in Austria of historical European toys. Feast upon an array of antique dolls and doll houses, paper theaters, metal and wooden toys, and soft and furry toys, especially the collection of teddy bears.

There is also a selection of optical toys, tin and pewter figures, and railway sets. A Punch and Judy show is scheduled every Tuesday and Wednesday at 3pm except in summer. An on-site shop sells a wide array of toys in the Bürgerspital or civilian hospital, which was constructed around the most beautiful Renaissance courtyard in Salzburg.

Bürgerspitalgasse 2. ✆ **0662/620808300.** www.smca.at. Admission 3€ ($4.80) adults, 2€ ($3.20) students, 1€ ($1.60) ages 6–15. Tues–Sun 9am–5pm; July–Aug and Dec also Mon 9am–5pm.

PANORAMIC VIEWS

Kapuzinerberg

This forested area on the right bank of the Salzach River rises more than 610m (2,001 ft.) above the city and is today a landscaped park. To get here, cross the Staatsbrücke spanning the Salzach to the right bank, continue walking for 2 minutes until you come to Steingasse, and cut right; after exploring Steingasse, walk through the Steintor, then climb an adjoining stone stairway, and follow the signs to Kapuzinerberg. You can also take bus no. 2, 5, 6, 15, 27, 29, 51, or 55.

A Capuchin friary was built here at the very end of the 16th century, constructed inside an old medieval fortification. On the south side of the hill are Steingasse, a pretty street from medieval times, and the Steintor, which was once a gate in the walls of Salzburg. From vantage points on the Kapuzinerberg, you can see into Bavaria, in Germany.

Mönchsberg

West of the Hohensalzburg Fortress, this heavily forested ridge extends for some 2km (1½ miles) above the Old Town and has fortifications dating from the 15th century. From several vantage points, including the Mönchsberg Terrace just in front of the Grand Café Winkler, you can see Salzburg.

You can get up here by taking the express elevators leaving from Gstättengasse 13 (✆ **0662/44806285**). The elevators leave daily from 9am to 1am. Round-trip fare is 2.90€ ($4.70) for adults and 1.60€ ($2.60) for children 6 to 15; it's free for children 5 and under.

PARKS & GARDENS

On the right bank of the river, laid out by Fischer von Erlach, the baroque **Mirabell Gardens** ★, off Makartplatz, are the finest in Salzburg. Now a public park, they're studded with statues and reflecting pools. Von Erlach also designed some of the marble balustrades and urns. There's a natural theater as well. For the best view of the gardens and also of Salzburg, pause at the top of the steps where Julie Andrews and her seven charges showed off their singing voices in *The Sound of Music.* As you wander in the gardens, be sure to visit Zwerglgarten, the bastion with fantastic marble baroque dwarfs and other figures. It's located by the Pegasus Fountains in the lavish garden west of Schloss Mirabell. From the garden, you have an excellent view of the Hohensalzburg Fortress. The marble statues make Mirabell Gardens virtually an open-air museum. The gardens are open daily from 7am to 8pm. In summer, free brass band concerts are held Wednesday at 8:30pm and Sunday at 10:30am.

ESPECIALLY FOR KIDS

Of the attractions already reviewed, those that children will most like include the **Glockenspiel, Hohensalzburg Fortress, Mönchsberg,** and, on the outskirts, the **Hellbrunn Zoo** (see "Side Trips from Salzburg," later in this chapter). Kids will also enjoy the **Salzburger Marionetten Theater** (see section 8, "Salzburg after Dark," below).

Spielzeugmuseum (Kids) In what used to be the Salzburg City Hospital, this museum is a toy wonderland—from the toys that kids played with in the 1500s to those that are popular today. The vintage model trains, the early carousels, the old musical instruments, and the large collection of arts and crafts delight children and adults alike.

Bürgerspitalgasse 2. ✆ **0662/0808300.** Admission (including entrance to the Punch and Judy shows) 3€ ($4.80) adults, 1€ ($1.60) children 6–15, free for children 5 and under. Daily 9am–5pm; Punch and Judy shows Tues–Wed at 3pm. Bus: 1.

6 ORGANIZED TOURS

The best organized tours are offered by **Salzburg Panorama Tours,** Mirabellplatz (✆ **0662/8832110;** www.panoramatours.at), which is the Gray Line company for Salzburg.

The original **"*Sound of Music* Tour"** combines the Salzburg city tour with an excursion to the lake district and other places where the 1965 film with Julie Andrews was shot. The English-speaking guide shows you not only the highlights from the film, but also historical and architectural landmarks in Salzburg and parts of the Salzkammergut countryside. The 4½-hour tour departs daily at 9:30am and 2pm and costs 37€ ($59).

You must take your passport along for any of the three trips into Bavaria in Germany. One of these—the "Eagle's Nest Tour"—takes visitors to Berchtesgaden and on to Obersalzburg, where Hitler and his inner circle had a vacation retreat. The 4½-hour tour departs daily at 9am from May 15 to October 31 and costs 50€ ($80).

"The City & Country Highlights" tour takes in historic castles and the surrounding Land Salzburg landscape. This 5-hour tour departs daily at 1pm and costs 50€ ($80). Coffee and pastry at the Castle Fuschl are an added treat.

You can book these tours at the bus terminal at Mirabellplatz/St. Andrä Kirche (✆ **0662/874029**). Tour prices are the same for all ages.

7 SHOPPING

While Salzburg doesn't have Vienna's wide range of merchandise, there's still plenty of shopping here. Good buys in Salzburg include souvenirs of Land Salzburg (dirndls, lederhosen, and petit point) and all types of sports gear. **Getreidegasse** is a main shopping thoroughfare, but you'll also find some intriguing little shops on **Residenzplatz.**

Most stores are open Monday through Friday from 9am to 6pm, but note that many stores, especially smaller shops, take a 1- or 2-hour break for lunch. On weekends, stores are generally open only Saturday mornings.

SHOPPING A TO Z

Books & Prints

Eduard Höllrigl This is the oldest bookstore in the country, dating from 1594. In addition to books, you'll find an array of maps, sheet music, and the best postcards in town. Sigmund-Haffner-Gasse 10. ✆ **0662/841146.** Bus: 3, 5, or 6.

China & Crystal

Lobmeyr Lobmeyr is the Salzburg branch of the famous store in Vienna's Kärntnerstrasse. Lobmeyr offers a wide range of crystal drinking sets and elegant Herendchina, as well as some of the prettiest breakfast services one can find, many made in Hungary. Schwarzstrasse 20. ✆ **0662/873181.** www.lobmeyr.at. Bus: 3, 5, or 6.

Crafts

Lackner Gertraud If you like wood crafts, there's no better place in Salzburg. It offers both antique and modern country furniture, especially chairs. Among the newly made items are chests, chessboards, angels, cupboards, crèches, and candlesticks. Radergasse 2. ✆ **0662/842385.** Bus: 3, 5, or 6.

Salzburger Heimatwerk In a dignified stone building in the least-crowded section of Residenzplatz, with a discreet sign announcing its location, this is one of the best places in town to buy local Austrian handicrafts and original *tracht,* or costumes. Items include Austrian silver and garnet jewelry, painted boxes, candles, woodcarvings, copper and brass ceramics, tablecloths, and alpine designs for cross-stitched samplers. A special section sells dressmaking materials such as cotton and silk, with dressmaker patterns. Another section sells Austrian *tracht* such as dirndls, capes, and the rest of the regalia that's still worn during commemorative ceremonies and festivals. Wherever you go in this curious store, you're bound to find little treasures, so keep exploring. Am Residenzplatz 9. ✆ **0662/844119.** Bus: 3, 5, or 6.

Wiener Porzellanmanufaktur Augarten Gesellschaft This is the premier shop in Salzburg for Austrian porcelain, specializing in Augarten porcelain. Such patterns as Viennese Rose and Maria Theresia are still very popular, but its most famous item is the black-and-white coffee set created by architect/designer Josef Hoffmann. Alter Markt 11. ✆ **0662/840714.** www.augarten.at. Bus: 3, 5, or 6.

Fashion

Brigitte Kinder-Trachten Children up to age 14 are dressed here in plain or embroidered knit jackets, dirndls, and folk dresses that are the longtime favorite apparel of Land Salzburg. Lederhosen for boys come in full or short lengths with all the appropriate accompaniments. Although American kids often prefer their jeans, Austrian and German children (or at least their parents) sometimes like these looks. Universitätsplatz 7. ✆ **0662/841193.** Bus: 3, 5, or 6.

Jahn-Markl This small and elegant clothing store in Old Town has been in the same family for four generations, although its origins date from 1408. It carries lederhosen, leather skirts, and traditional Austrian coats and blazers. Leather for both women and men is also sold, including jackets, pants, and gloves. Some children's clothing is available. Less expensive items can be bought off the racks, but more expensive pieces are usually made to order in 4 weeks and can be mailed anywhere in the world for an additional charge. Residenzplatz 3. ✆ **0662/842610.** www.jahn-markl.at. Bus: 3, 5, or 6.

Lanz At this well-stocked store across the river from the Old Town, you'll find one of the widest collections of long-skirted dirndls in town, in dozens of different fabrics and colors. Men's clothing includes loden-colored overcoats. The store also sells dirndls for little girls and hand-knit sweaters. There's another branch along the main shopping street of Salzburg, at Kranzlmarkt 1, Getreidegasse (✆ **0662/840300**). Schwarzstrasse 4. ✆ **0662/874272.** Bus: 3, 5, or 6.

Music

Musikhaus Pühringer Established in 1910, this store sells all kinds of classical musical instruments, as well as a large selection of electronics (including synthesizers and amplifiers). You'll find classical and folk-music CDs and tapes. The store is only a few buildings away from Mozart's birthplace. Getreidegasse 13. ✆ **0662/843267.** www.musikinstrumente.at. Bus: 3, 5, or 6.

Pastries

Schatz-Konditorei (Kids) This excellent pastry shop (reviewed above in the "Cafes" box in "Where to Dine") is one of the few in Salzburg that will mail cakes around the world. The store's specialty is the highly acclaimed *Mozart Kugeln,* a cookie of pistachio, marzipan, and hazelnut nougat dipped in chocolate. Packages of this gourmet delight can be airmailed to North America. Getreidegasse 3. ✆ **0662/842792.** Bus: 3, 5, or 6.

Sporting Goods

Sporting Goods Dschulnigg Queen Elizabeth II and Prince Philip have been photographed on a shopping expedition at this upper-crust emporium for clothes and sporting goods. Among the items sold are many kinds of sporting goods, including guns, as well as children's outfits, overcoats for men and women both, intricately patterned sweaters, and fur-lined hats. You can get hunting rifles (but not pistols or revolvers) in Austria without a license, although the Customs officers back home might present a problem. Griesgasse 8. ✆ **0662/8423760.** Bus: 3, 5, or 6.

Toys & Souvenirs

Neumüller Spielwaren In winter, this store sells children's toys. In summer, the stock changes with the tourist influx, and the shelves fill up with handcrafted souvenirs such as mugs, cowbells, and rustic art objects. Rathausplatz 3. ✆ **0662/841429.** www.neumueller.vedes.at. Bus: 3, 5, or 6.

8 SALZBURG AFTER DARK

The annual cultural events, which reach their peak at the Salzburg Festival, overshadow any after-dark amusements such as dance clubs and beer halls. Clubs come and go in Salzburg fairly rapidly.

It's said that there's a musical event—often a Mozart concert—staged virtually every night in Salzburg. To find out what's playing, visit the **Salzburg tourist office,** Mozartplatz 5 (✆ **0662/889870;** www.2.salzburg.info), or get a free copy of ***Offizieller Wochenspiegel,*** a monthly pamphlet listing all major and many minor local cultural events; it's available in most hotels. The annual Mozart Week is in January.

FREE CONCERTS & SPECIAL EVENTS

Free concerts are frequently presented by students in the **Mozarteum,** Schwarzstrasse 26 (✆ **0662/8894030;** bus: 1 or 5). In summer, free brass-band concerts are performed in the **Mirabell Gardens** on Wednesday at 8:30pm and, depending on the venue, either Saturday or Sunday at 10:30am; Sunday chamber-music concerts are held throughout the city at major landmarks such as the **Residenz.**

The second-most famous music festival in Salzburg is the **Osterfestspiele (Easter Festival),** which features high-quality operas and concerts performed in the Festspielhaus. Some, but not all, of the music focuses on works associated with the resurrection of Christ as interpreted by the great 18th- and 19th-century composers. Established by Herbert von Karajan in the 1960s, the festival requires that spectators purchase tickets to the opera and each of the three concerts associated with the event. Prices for the series are anything but cheap: They range, per person, from 90€ to 720€ ($144–$1,152). For information and ticket purchases, contact the **Osterfestspiele,** Herbert von Karajan Platz 9, A-5020 Salzburg (✆ **0662/8045361;** www.osterfestspiele-salzburg.at; bus: 1).

Christmas Eve in Salzburg is unforgettable. Traditionally, in the little chapel of Oberndorf, north of Salzburg, "Silent Night" is performed. Franz Gruber wrote the melody to that song here when he was an organist in the early 19th century.

BUYING TICKETS

If you don't want to pay a ticket agent's commission, you can go directly to the box office of a theater or concert hall. However, many of the best seats might have already been sold, especially those at the Salzburg Festival. Despite the availability of ticket outlets in any of the below-mentioned theaters, many visitors head for the larger umbrella ticket agency, **Salzburger Ticket Office,** Mozartplatz 5 (✆ **0662/840310**), which is affiliated with the city of Salzburg and adjacent to Salzburg's main tourist office. Open Monday to Saturday 9am to 6pm (to 7pm in midsummer) and Sunday 10am to 6pm, it's the single best source for cultural information and ticket sales in town, usually with tickets to virtually every musical event in the city on sale—except, of course, to those events that are sold out long in advance.

The Salzburg Festival

One of the premier music attractions of Europe, the Salzburg Festival celebrates its 87th season in 2007. Composer Richard Strauss founded the festival, aided by director Max Reinhardt and writer Hugo von Hofmannsthal.

An annual event is Hofmannsthal's adaptation of the morality play *Jedermann (Everyman),* performed in German and staged outside the cathedral in Domplatz. Concerts are usually conducted in the Rittersaal of the Residenz Palace (Mozart conducted here) and in the marble salon of Mirabell Palace (Mozart's father, Leopold, conducted here). The Salzburger Marionetten Theater (see below) also presents performances. Ballet performances are usually given by the Vienna State Opera Ballet with the Vienna State Opera Chorus and the Vienna Philharmonic. International soloists are invited annually, and the London Symphony or the Berlin Philharmonic is also likely to be invited.

Festival tickets, however, are in great demand, and there never are enough of them. Don't arrive expecting to get into any of the major events unless you've already purchased tickets. Travel agents can often get tickets for you, and you can also go to branches of the Austrian National Tourist Office at home or abroad. Hotel concierges, particularly at the deluxe and first-class hotels of Salzburg, always have some tickets on hand, but expect to pay outrageous prices for them, depending on the particular performance you want to attend. At first-night performances of the major productions, remember that evening dress is de rigueur.

Subject to many exceptions and variations, and without agent commissions, drama tickets generally run 30€ to 200€ ($48–$320). Opera tickets can begin as low as 45€ ($72), ranging upward to 300€ ($480).

For festival details, contact the Salzburg Festival box office, Hofstallgasse 1, A-5020 Salzburg, Austria (✆ **0662/8045;** www.salzburgfestival.at).

Curiously, though Salzburg is known as a city of music and culture, it has no famed local troupes. However, it does attract visiting guest artists with blue-chip credentials in the world of performing arts.

THE PERFORMING ARTS

Opera, Dance & Music

Festspielhaus All the premier ballet, opera, and musical concerts are performed at this world-famous citadel of Salzburg culture. The *Grosses Haus* (Big House), the larger venue, seats 2,170. The *Kleines Haus* (Small House) seats 1,323. Most performances begin at 7:30 or 8pm, although there are matinees from time to time at 11am and 3pm. Hofstallgasse 1. ✆ **0662/8045.** Tickets 8€–200€ ($13–$320) (the higher cost is for the best seats at the Salzburg Festival); average but good seats run 35€–80€ ($56–$128). Bus: 1 or 5.

Festung Hohensalzburg If your visit to Salzburg doesn't happen to coincide with any of the city's annual music festivals, you can always attend the concerts that are presented within the Hohensalzburg Fortress. Here, in historic and dramatic settings, you're likely to hear heavy doses of Mozart and, to a lesser degree, works by Schubert, Brahms, and Beethoven. From mid-May to mid-October, performances are likely to be held at 8 or 8:30pm every night of the week. The rest of the year, they're presented most (but not all) nights, with occasional weeklong breaks, usually at 7:30pm. The box office for the events is at Adlgasser Weg 22 (✆ **0662/825858;** www.salzburg-burgen-at/en/hohensalzburg). Mönchsberg 34. ✆ **0662/84243011.** Tickets cost 10€ ($16) adults, 5.70€ ($9.10) ages 6–14, and 23€ ($37) family ticket. To reach the fortress, take the funicular from Festungsgasse.

Mozarteum On the right bank of the Salzach River, near Mirabell Gardens, is the Mozarteum, Salzburg's major music and concert hall. All the big orchestra concerts, as well as organ recitals and chamber-music evenings, are presented here. In the old building at Schwarzstrasse, there are two concert halls, the Grosser Saal and the Wiener Saal. In the newer building on Mirabellplatz, concert halls include the Grosses Studio, the Leopold-Mozart Saal, and the Paumgartner Studio. Make sure to find out which hall your musical event is in. It's also a music school, and you can ask about free events staged by the students. The box office is open Monday through Thursday from 9am to 2pm and Friday from 9am to 4pm. Performances are at 11am or 7:30pm. Schwarzstrasse 26 and Mirabellplatz 1. ✆ **0662/8894030.** www.mozarteum.at. Tickets 10€–55€ ($16–$88). Bus: 1 or 5.

Salzburger Schlosskonzerte The Salzburger Schlosskonzerte (Palace Concerts) are privately owned by Salzburg violinist Luz Leskowitz, who carries on the 44-year-old tradition of presenting the best ensembles. The carefully chosen programs combine with the beautiful, historic venue (the Marmorsaal, where Mozart himself played) to create an atmosphere of perfect harmony. Mozart's music is heavily featured, but the famed music of classical Austria and Italy are also included in the repertoire. Beethoven, Mendelssohn, Schubert, Bach, Brahms, Vivaldi, Haydn—the list is endless. Unchanged since the days of Mozart, concerts are staged in the richly decorated baroque chambers. The box office is open Monday to Friday 9am to 5:30pm. Schloss Mirabell, Mirabellplatz. Booking office, Theatergasse 2. ✆ **0662/848586.** www.salzburger-schlosskonzerte.at. Tickets 29€–35€ ($46–$56) adults, 16€ ($26) students. Bus: 3, 5, or 6.

Theater

Although the **Salzburger Landestheater,** Schwarzstrasse 22 (✆ **0662/8715120;** www.theater.co.at; bus: 3, 5, or 6), doesn't always play for summer visitors, you can see its regular repertoire of operas (not just Mozart) and operettas if you're in Salzburg from September to mid-June. You might see a thrilling performance of Verdi's *Traviata.* Opera tickets usually range from 25€ to 64€ ($40–$102). In July and August, Salzburg Festival performances are held here.

Salzburger Marionetten Theater, Schwarzstrasse 24 (✆ **0662/8724060;** www.marionetten.at; bus: 3, 5, or 6), presents shows from Easter to September, as well as special shows at Christmas and during Mozart Week, the last week of January. The puppets perform both opera (usually Mozart) and ballet, to the delight of adults and children alike. Founded in 1913, the theater continues to be one of the most unusual and enjoyable theatrical experiences in Salzburg. You might forget that marionettes are onstage—it's that realistic. Tickets are 20€ to 40€ ($32–$64).

THE CLUB & MUSIC SCENE

The best alternative music spot is **Rockhouse,** Schallmooser Hauptstrasse 46 (✆ **0662/884914;** www.rockhouse.at; bus: 1 or 4), which also has a cafe. Local and European bands are booked to play this tunnel-like venue, which offers everything from blues and funk to jazz and techno pop. Sometimes groups from the United States or even Africa appear here. The structure itself is from the 1840s, having once been a wine cellar and ice-storage depot. Cover is 9€ to 30€ ($14–$48), depending on the act. Call to see what's happening at the time of your visit.

There's something disheveled and disorganized about the **Republic Cafe,** Anton Neumayr Platz 2 (✆ **0664/841613;** www.republic-cafe.at; bus: 2), but it's a hotbed of countercultural activities in Salzburg. It defines itself as a cross between a bar and a cafe, with a "radical performance space." Its nerve center is a battered street-level bar and cafe, open Sunday to Thursday from 8am to 1am, Friday and Saturday from 8am to 4pm. You can hang out at the bar, chatting with hard-rock music fans, rave participants, and all kinds of grunge musicians, and ordering mugs of beer costing 3€ to 4€ ($4.80–$6.40). Radiating from the cafe are several performance spaces which might or might not be booked by local jazz ensembles, avant-garde theater groups, performance artists, or nihilist poets, depending on the week's schedule. Frankly, there's a lot that's slipshod and disorganized about this place, but part of its charm derives from a haphazard schedule and its own sense that it's a cauldron for artistic-statements-in-the-making.

THE BEST BARS

Bar Saitensprung This very hip bar spins the most recent music in a cave that's partially natural and partly dug by hand several centuries ago into the rock of the Kapuzinerberg. The bar serves a full menu of cocktails, including American-style martinis at 4.30€ ($6.90) each, and the even more popular roster of Austrian wine by the glass, priced at 4€ ($6.40). There's a limited food menu, in case you get hungry. Prosciutto with cheese and pâté platters are priced at around 8.70€ ($14) each. The crowd tends to be young, 20 to 25. It's open nightly from 9pm to at least 4am. Steingasse 11. ✆ **0662/881377.** Bus: 3, 5, or 6.

Chez Roland Roland Kübler has maintained this stylish, unusual cocktail bar since the mid-1970s. In the process, he's entertained some of the biggest names of the Salzburg Festival and nurtured an arts-conscious crowd ranging in age from 25 to 75. The bar is set within an old salt storage cellar with a vaulted ceiling that allows natural illumination. You can always order a martini, but the large majority of drinkers here opt for glasses of Austrian wine. Priced at 3€ to 5€ ($4.80–$8), they include many vintages of Styrian chardonnays and sauvignons. There's also Beck's beer selling for 2.80€ ($4.50) and a limited menu of "toasts" (warm sandwiches). It's open daily 7pm to at least 4am and usually later, depending on business. Giselakai 24. ✆ **0662/874335.** www.chez-roland.com. Bus: 1.

O'Malley's With a name like O'Malley's, this could only be an Irish pub. Opened in 1998, this pub opts for authenticity by importing wooden bars created by Irish tradesmen in Belfast from the timbers of a disused 3-centuries-old church. The pub is decorated with some of the architectural details of the church, even musical instruments from the Emerald Isle. This bar, featuring live music, attracts a young crowd and has one of the most jovial atmospheres of any place in town. Beer costs from 3€ ($4.80). Hours are Sunday to Thursday 6pm to 2am, Friday and Saturday 6pm to 4am. Rudolfskai 16. ✆ **0662/849263.** www.omalleyssalzburg.com. Bus: 5, 6, or 55.

Segabar A fun-loving crowd of young people, especially on Friday and Saturday nights, packs this joint, one of the busiest bars in town. Blaring music and TV broadcasts add to the raucous fun. Beer is consumed at a rate to suggest that the supply might dry up. Drinks cost 3€ to 5€ ($4.80–$8); there is no cover. Open daily 8pm to 4am. Rudolfskai 18. ✆ **0662/846898.** www.segabar.at. Bus: 5, 6, or 55.

Stieglkeller To reach this place, you'll have to negotiate a steep cobblestone street that drops off on one side to reveal a panoramic view of Salzburg. Part of the establishment is carved into the rocks of Mönchsberg Mountain, so all that's visible from the outside is a gilded iron gate and a short stone stairway. The cavernous interior is open only in summer, when you can join hundreds of others in drinking beer and eating sausages, schnitzels, and other *Bierkeller* food. Menus cost 16€ to 21€ ($26–$33).

On the first Sunday of the month, a *Fruhschoppen*—a traditional Salzburger music fest—is presented from 10:30pm to midnight. No ticket is necessary—you pay for what you eat and drink. Likewise, no ticket is necessary to attend another musical evening, a *Happing,* staged from May to September, every Thursday from 6 to 8pm. Festungsgasse 10. ✆ **0662/842681.** www.imlauer.com. Bus: 5.

Zwelstein This is the leading club for Salzburg's gay and lesbian community. Sometimes there's entertainment, but don't count on it. The contemporary art on the walls changes monthly. The international gay crowd, mostly under 35, likes the friendly, welcoming environment. On weekends, the place becomes almost overcrowded. Cocktails range from 5.80€ to 6.80€ ($9.30–$11). Open Sunday to Wednesday 6pm to 4am, Thursday to Saturday 6pm to 5am. Giselakai 9. ✆ **0662/877179.** Bus: 51.

A CASINO

Casino Salzburg Schloss Klessheim The only year-round casino in Land Salzburg occupies the soaring Schloss Klessheim, a baroque palace designed by one of the most influential architects of Austria's baroque age, Fischer von Erlach. Monday night is poker night. To enter the casino, you must present some form of identification, either a driver's license or a passport. There's also a dress code: Except during the hottest months of summer, men are encouraged to wear jackets and ties. The complex is open daily from 3pm to 3am.

To get here, drive west along highway A1, exiting at the SCHLOSS KLESSHEIM exit, about 1.5km (1 mile) west of the center of Salzburg. The casino also runs a shuttle taxi that departs, without charge, from the rocky base of the Mönchsberg every hour on the half-hour daily from 5pm to midnight. A-5071 Walzsezenheim. ✆ **0662/854455.** www.casinos.at. Cover 23€ ($37); includes 25€ ($40) worth of casino chips.

9 SIDE TRIPS FROM SALZBURG

The environs of Salzburg are incredibly scenic; to explore them fully, refer to chapter 9, "Land Salzburg." The area is a setting of old castles, charming villages, glacial lakes, salt mines, ice caves, and some of the most panoramic alpine scenery in Europe. But before heading to Land Salzburg, here are a few attractions right on the city's doorstep.

A PALACE, ZOO & MUSEUM IN HELLBRUNN

Volkskundemuseum Overlooking Hellbrunn Park, 5km (3 miles) south of Salzburg, the Volkskunde Museum offers a folk collection assembled by Prince-Archbishop Markus Sittikus in 1615. The displays, spread over three floors, reflect a cross-section of local folk art and depict popular religious beliefs, folk medicine, and the traditional costumes of Land Salzburg.

Monatsschlösschen, Hellbrunn. ✆ **0662/620808500.** Admission 2.50€ ($4) adults, 2€ ($3.20) students, 1€ ($1.60) ages 6–15. Apr–Oct 10am–5:30pm. Bus: 25.

Salzburger Tiergarten Hellbrunn Kids The beautiful landscape provides a wonderful setting for viewing the diverse animals of the Zoo Hellbrunn, located just south of Salzburg. Chamois, otter, white rhinoceros, and antelope share large outdoor enclosures. You can also see cheetahs and free-flying griffin vultures. There's a children's zoo as well.

Schloss Hellbrunn, Morzgerstrasse. ✆ **0662/820176.** Admission 9€ ($14) adults, 7€ ($11) students, 4€ ($6.40) youths 4–14, free for children 3 and under. Oct–Mar daily 8:30am–4pm; Apr–Sept Mon–Thurs and Sun 8:30am–7:30pm, Fri–Sat 8:30am–10:30pm. Bus: 25.

Schloss Hellbrunn ★ A popular spot for outings from Salzburg, this palace dates from the early 17th century and was built as a hunting lodge and summer residence for Prince-Archbishop Markus Sittikus. The Hellbrunn Zoo, also here, was formerly the palace deer park. It's a 20-minute drive from Salzburg; turn off Alpenstrasse at the Mobil gas station.

The palace **gardens,** one of the oldest baroque formal gardens in all Europe, are known for their trick fountains. As you walk through, take care—you might be showered from a surprise source, such as a set of antlers. Set to organ music, some 265 figures in a mechanical theater are set in motion hydraulically.

The rooms of the palace are furnished and decorated in 18th-century style. See, in particular, the banquet hall with its *trompe l'oeil* painting. There's also a domed octagonal room that was used as a music and reception hall.

On the grounds, a natural gorge forms the **Stone Theater,** where the first opera in the German-speaking world was presented in 1617. This attraction (signposted) is reached on foot, about a 20-minute walk from the castle. A Hellbrunn Festival is held in the gardens, palace, and theater in August.

Fürstenweg 37, Hellbrunn. ✆ **0662/8203720.** www.hellbrunn.at. Admission 8.50€ ($14) adults, 6.50€ ($10) students, 3.80€ ($6.10) children. Tours given July–Aug daily 9am–10pm; May–June and Sept daily 9am–5:30pm; Apr and Oct daily 9am–4:30pm. Bus: 25.

HALLEIN & THE DÜRRNBERG SALT MINES

The second-largest town in Land Salzburg, Hallein, once a center for processing the salt from the mines of Dürrnberg, was a prize possession of the prince-archbishops of Salzburg. Today you pass through this industrial town on the Salzach River on the way to the Dürrnberg mines. The **tourist office,** Mauttorpromenade 6, A-5400 Hallein (✆ **0662/88987330**), is open Monday to Saturday 9am to 6pm (until 7pm July–Aug).

On the north side of the Hallein parish church are the former home and tomb of the man who composed the music for Mohr's "Silent Night," Franz-Xaver Gruber, a schoolteacher who died in 1863.

The **Dürrnberg salt mines (Salzbergwerk Hallein;** ✆ **06245/835110;** www.salzwelten.at) are the big draw. This popular attraction is easily visited on a day trip from Salzburg. On guided tours, visitors walk downhill from the ticket office to the mine entrance, and then board an electric mine train that goes deep into the caverns. From here, tourists go on foot through galleries, changing levels by sliding down polished wooden slides before exiting the mine on the train that brought them in. An underground museum traces the history of salt mining back to ancient times.

To get to the mines, you can either drive to Hallein from Salzburg or take a train there from Salzburg's main railway station (they depart throughout the day at 20-minute intervals). From a point just in front of the railway station at Hallein, you'll then board a bus for the ongoing 12-minute ride to Dürnnberg. (Be warned in advance that the buses are less frequent than the trains—they depart every hour, 55 min. past the hour, throughout the day.)

Tours of the salt mines and the lectures that precede them last about 90 minutes each and are conducted from April to October daily 9am to 5pm, November to March daily 11am to 3pm. Admission to the mines costs 17€ ($27) for adults, 10€ ($16) for students and children 7 to 15, and 8€ ($13) for children 4 to 6. Children under 4 are not admitted.

If you embark upon this adventure from Salzburg's main railway station, you can buy from any ticket counter a combined ticket for round-trip transport on the train and the subsequent bus to Dürrnberg, with admission to the salt mines included, for 26€ ($42) per adult.

THE ICE CAVES OF EISRIESENWELT ★★

Some 48km (30 miles) south of Salzburg by train is the "World of the Ice Giants," the largest known **ice caves** in the world. The caves, opening at some 1,678m (5,505 ft.), stretch for about 42km (26 miles), although only a portion of that length is open to the public. Fantastic ice formations at the entrance extend for half a mile. This underground wonderland is lined with amazing ice figures and frozen waterfalls. The climax of this chill underworld tour is the spectacular "Ice Palace."

Please keep in mind that a visit to this spelunking oddity is recommended only for those who are quite fit and hardy, and is not suggested for elderly travelers or small children. You'll be walking down narrow, slippery passages.

To reach the **Eisriesenwelt,** begin by heading for the hamlet of Werfen, which is located approximately 24 miles (40km) south of Salzburg. The village of Werfen is also the home of **Castle (Schloss) Hohenwerfen** (✆ **06468/7603**), which was founded in the 11th century and frequently reconstructed. One of the most important castles in Land Salzburg, it's visible for miles around. You can get to Werfen by driving along the main A10 highway (the Tauern motorway), or by taking a train from Salzburg's Hauptbahnhof to Werfen station.

From the village of Werfen, you'll drive up a steep and narrow 6km (3½-mile) access road, following the signs to Eisriesenwelt, which leads to a high-altitude parking lot. If you don't have a car, there's a local bus service (the Eisriesenwelt Line; ✆ **06468/5293** for information). For a fee of 3.50€ ($5.60) per person, it will haul you along the above-described 6km (3½-mile) road. Service is provided only between May and October at 8:20 and 10:20am, and 12:20 and 2:20pm. It's often more convenient to pay around 11€ ($18) to hire any of the local taxis in lieu of waiting for the bus, and hardy hikers sometimes opt to walk the steep incline to the above-mentioned parking lot. If you opt to hike, know in advance that the altitude from the debut to the end of your climb will rise from 488 to 915m (from 1,601 to 3,002 ft.)—it is very steep indeed.

Once you reach the parking lot, expect an additional, relatively easy 20-minute mostly shaded uphill hike to reach the cable car which hauls you vertiginously upward to the entrance to the caves. If you opt to avoid the cable car in favor of walking, expect to spend 90 sweaty minutes with sweeping views. Even if you do opt for the cable car, you'll face an additional 20-minute climb from the top of the cable car to the entrance to the ice caves.

There's a cafe and restaurant en route within a woodsy-looking building, the Dr.-Friedrich-Oedl-Haus, located at 1,568m (5,144 ft) above sea level. Supervised tours of the inside of the caves generally last 70 to 80 minutes, and cost 8.50€ ($14) for adults, 7.50€ ($12) for students, and 4.50€ ($7.20) for ages 4 to 14. The caves are open only from May to October, with tours beginning each hour on the half-hour between 9:30am and 3:30pm (until 4:30pm July–Aug). A combined ticket for round-trip access on the cable car, with a tour of the caves included, costs 19€ ($30) for adults, 17€ ($27) for students, and 9.50€ ($15) for children ages 4 to 14.

From Werfen, allow about 6 hours for the entire trip. Dress warmly and wear shoes appropriate for hiking. Even if you don't want to go underground, consider the trek from Salzburg to the mouth of the cave for the scenery.

Eisriesenwelt Werfen is entered at Wimmstrasse 24 (✆ **06468/5248** or 0662/842690; www.eisriesenwelt.at).

10

Land Salzburg

The geographic borders of this lofty province in the high Alps might appear to be the work of a mapmaker gone haywire, but actually they follow the dictates of nature over those of man. Craggy mountains, deep valleys, winding rivers, lakes, and rolling foothills, plus a little political expediency, all affected the cartographer's pen. Within this *bundesland* (state or province) of some 7,154 sq. km (2,762 sq. miles) are some of the most beautiful waterfalls in Austria. The spectacular Krimml Falls are the highest in Europe.

Land Salzburg is an outdoor playground, perfect for those seeking Austria's clear alpine air and blue mountain lakes, the country made famous in *The Sound of Music.* You can begin by exploring the Salzkammergut lake country, a narrow corridor in Land Salzburg between Bavaria and Upper Austria. Many parts of Salzkammergut, which means "domain of the salt office," grew rich from mining salt—and also gold.

Although there are often Land Salzburg excursions leaving from Salzburg, we think it's much more fun and less expensive to do it on your own. Most people involved in tourist services speak English, and you can travel in relative security and comfort.

This is a land of summer and winter sports, with such celebrated spas as Badgastein and renowned ski resorts such as Zell am See, Kaprun, Saalbach, and Hinterglemm. Relax at a lakeside resort, such as St. Gilgen, or stay at a mountain hotel where the air is crisp.

Of course, Land Salzburg is a skier's paradise. The season begins about 10 days before Christmas and usually lasts until Easter or beyond, depending on snow conditions. Skiing on some of the lofty plateaus is possible year-round. Kaprun, Saalbach, and Zell am See are long-established *and* expensive resorts. However, in the true spirit of the Frommer's guides, we've sought less familiar and even undiscovered places—many known only to the Austrians and an occasional German tourist.

The terrain directly around Salzburg is flat, but most of Land Salzburg is mountainous. Always inquire about local weather conditions before embarking on a day's sightseeing, particularly if you're going to be traversing one of those lofty alpine highways. The highest mountain range in Austria, the Hohe Tauern, lies on the southern fringe of Land Salzburg. The Hohe Tauern national park encompasses one of the most beautiful areas of the eastern Alps and remains mainly undeveloped. The park's core is formed of mighty mountains, steep rock faces, glaciers, and glacial streams, one of which feeds the Krimml Falls. Mountain meadows, alpine pastures, and protective woods comprise the park's periphery. Other natural attractions are Liechtensteinklamm, south of St. Johann in Pongau, the most dramatic gorge in the eastern Alps; Gollinger Wasserfälle (the Golling Waterfall), between the Valley of Kaprun and its powerful dams; and an ascent to the Kitzsteinhorn at 2,931m (9,616 ft.).

The Tauern Highway is one of the most important north-south roads over the Alps. Vehicles pass through two tunnels while traversing the highway. The Tauerntunnel is 6km (4 miles) long, and the Katschbergtunnel is 5km (3¼ miles) long. Because many of the alpine highways require extensive upkeep, tolls are charged, but they're not excessive. The Grossglockner Road, with hairpin turns and bends, is Europe's longest and prettiest alpine highway.

Unlike regions of Austria more devoted to serious skiing, Land Salzburg derives a good percentage of its income from midwinter vacationers who appreciate the region's accessibility from the major (snow-free) highways and rail routes of Austria. Prices in August tend to be roughly equivalent to prices in January and February, and cheaper in off-season months, such as June and October. (Resort hotels in Land Salzburg often close completely during the gray meltdown days of early spring and the rainy days of late autumn.)

Instead of staying in Salzburg, especially crowded during the Salzburg Festival months, reserve a room at a resort described below and commute to the province's capital city. You'll find the prices often lower and the atmosphere more laid-back.

Accommodations are wide-ranging, from deluxe resorts to a mountain hut. There are a few castle hotels in Land Salzburg to suit those who have traditional tastes and don't always demand the latest in plumbing fixtures.

Most hotels in the district automatically price your accommodations with half-board included. Although you can always request a bed-and-breakfast rate and take your meals elsewhere, the supplement for half-board usually represents a good value, sometimes allowing you to eat your main meal of the day for between 12€ to 20€ ($16–$26) per person. You could try out the local restaurants at lunch. Hotels here almost always have the best restaurants anyway, so we suggest selecting a hotel dining room for dinner. Parking is rarely a problem in these places, and, unless otherwise noted, you park for free.

Long cut off from the rest of the world but now accessible because of modern engineering achievements, some sections of Land Salzburg still cling tenaciously to their traditions. Old costumes and folklore still flourish in the province.

For information on Land Salzburg, contact the **Salzburg State Tourist Board,** P.O. Box 1, Wiener Bundesstrasse 23, A-5300 Hallwang (✆ **0662/66880;** fax 0662/668866; www.salzburgerland.com).

TIPS FOR ACTIVE TRAVELERS

The district of Land Salzburg seems like one vast outdoor playland—from skiing in winter to canoeing, fishing, golfing, hiking, and much more in summer.

CANOEING & RAFTING In summer, many visitors head for either the Salzkammergut or the Pinzgau, regions of Land Salzburg known for their beautiful lakes and roaring white-water streams. Lakes here are ideal for canoeing, rafting, or kayaking because the waters aren't polluted and the government limits powerboats, making the waters safer.

One of the best outfitters is **Club Zwilling,** Waldhof 64, Abtenau (✆ **06243/3069**), and well recommended is **Motion Center,** Andreas Voglastätter, Lofer (✆ **06588/7524**), located at the edge of Lake Sallachsee.

Other centers for watersports include **Rafting Center Taxenbach,** Marktstrasse 38 (✆ **06543/5352**), at the edge of the Salzach River. You can also call **Adventure Service,** Steinergrasse 9, in Zell am See (✆ **06542/73525**), a cheerful and well-managed outfit that offers guided excursions with instruction in rafting, white-water kayaking, sailing, canoeing, paragliding, hiking, and mountain climbing.

CROSS-COUNTRY SKIING & DOWNHILL SKIING We've previewed in this chapter the most important ski resorts. For more options, contact one of the 120 local tourist offices for details on the dozens of ski schools in the province that provide instruction to novice and experienced skiers. For complete skiing data, write or call the Salzburg State Tourist Board (see above).

FISHING You'll find some wonderful places to fish, but you'll need a license, which you can obtain at the local tourist office where you're staying. For more information about where to fish in the province, call the Salzburg State Tourist Board (see above).

GOLF If you'd like to play a round of alpine golf, you can get a complete listing of the provincial courses from the Salzburg State Tourist Board (see above).

HIKING This is a great place to hike. The Salzburg State Tourist Board (above) stocks a very helpful brochure called "Walking and Trekking," which surveys the many trails in the province.

1 THE TENNENGAU

The Tennengau, named for the Tennen massif, is a division of the Salzach Valley, south of Salzburg, characterized by rolling hills and woodlands. Waterfalls dot the landscape—those outside the town of Golling are the most visited. Much of the Tennengau area, especially the houses with their gables and window boxes full of geraniums, will remind visitors of neighboring Bavaria.

As you leave Salzburg, going south on the left bank of the Salzach River, you'll pass through Anif, on the outskirts of Salzburg. You'll find some excellent old romantic accommodations in Anif (reviewed in chapter 8) if you'd like to stay near the provincial capital.

If you don't want to stay in the Tennengau region, you might consider a day trip from Salzburg. Its chief sight is the Dürrnberg Salt Mines outside Hallein (see "Side Trips from Salzburg," in chapter 8). However, if you'd like to stay in the district, you'll find good accommodations in Golling.

GOLLING

Golling was first mentioned in historical sources as a farm hamlet in the 9th century. Today residents of this quietly stylish outlying burg tend to commute to work in Salzburg. Many visitors use Golling as a base for various outdoor activities in the nearby mountains.

Essentials

GETTING THERE It's on the rail lines for local **trains** that head south to Villach and Klagenfurt in Carinthia. Trains depart from Salzburg for the 31km (19-mile) journey at 1- to 2-hour intervals; the trip takes 20 minutes. Railway officials refer to the village station as Golling-Abtenau. For rail information in Salzburg, call ✆ **05/1717,** or visit **www.oebb.at**.

Buses depart approximately every hour throughout the day from Salzburg's main railway station (with a subsequent stop at Mirabellplatz). The trip to Golling takes about

65 minutes. For information about buses from Salzburg to the outlying regions, call the local tourist office (see below).

VISITOR INFORMATION For **tourist information,** go to Verkehrsverein, Am Marktplatz 51 (just follow the signs), in the center of town. The office (✆ **06244/4356**) is open in winter Monday to Friday 9am to noon and 3 to 6pm, and in summer Monday to Friday 9am to noon and 1:30 to 6pm. It's open on Saturday only in August, 9am to noon and 1:30 to 6pm.

The Golling Waterfall ★★ & Salzach Gorge

What draws visitors to Golling, 12km (7½ miles) south of Hallein via the A10, is the **Gollinger Wasserfall (Golling Waterfall).** It's 2km (1½ miles) west of the little resort along an unnumbered local road (look for signs saying GOLLINGER WASSERFALL), followed by a 20-minute walk from the parking lot to the falls. The waterfall—between Golling and Kuchl, 27km (17 miles) south of Salzburg—tumbles down more than 153m (502 ft.) over a rock wall.

You can also visit the **Salzach Gorge** near Golling. It's an hour's walk from Golling up to Pass Lueg. It lies 3km (2 miles) south of Golling and is accessible by following Highway B159. The entrance is not strictly regulated. You might arrive before the park attendants do (as local climbers are known to). Admission is 3€ ($3.90) per person. In winter, snow and ice block access, and the gorge is unsafe except for experienced rock and ice climbers. Visits both to the falls and the gorge are possible from May to October daily from 9am to 6pm; or if you're a bit adventurous, you can visit year-round at your own risk. It's best to go while attendants are on hand.

Heimatmuseum Burg Golling, Markt 1 (✆ **06244/4356-0**) has a chapel and an interesting folklore collection. You'll see remains of cave bears, fossils, and copies of rock drawings, plus old pictures of the village. There's also a hunting room, exhibits of regional costumes, and a chamber of torture. It's open from June to mid-September Tuesday through Sunday from 10am to noon. Admission is 4€ ($6.40) for adults, 1.50€ ($2.40) for children.

Where to Stay & Dine

Goldener Stern Built in the 12th century but given its present antique look in 1925, Goldener Stern sits amid a row of picture-book houses in the center of the village. Rustic yet modern furniture fills the interior. Rooms are cozy and comfortable, with spotless bathrooms. The hotel even has a sauna and a solarium.

Many of the region's gourmets frequent the in-house restaurant, the Döllerer, serving Austrian, French, and Italian food. Its specialties include dried alpine beef, sliced waferthin and served with pearl onions and pickles; beef Stroganoff; an Austrian version of the Italian saltimbocca (veal with ham); and a number of seafood dishes. The distinguished wine list includes mainly Austrian and Italian vintages. The dining room is open Tuesday to Sunday 8am to midnight; reservations are suggested. On the premises are a deli and a wine store.

Am Marktplatz 56, A-5440 Golling. ✆ **06244/42200.** Fax 06244/691242. www.doellerer.at. 20 units. 110€–160€ ($176–$256) double; 150€–180€ ($240–$288) suite. Half-board 19€ ($30) per person. Rates include breakfast. DC, MC, V. **Amenities:** 2 restaurants; bar; sauna; room service; babysitting; laundry service; dry cleaning; nonsmoking rooms; solarium. *In room:* TV, Wi-Fi, minibar, hair dryer, safe.

2 THE PONGAU

Badgastein and Bad Hofgastein, covered in greater detail later in this chapter, are part of an area of Land Salzburg known as the Pongau—one of several sections of an alpine valley called Salzach. The Pinzgau section (also later in this chapter) of the Salzach Valley is to the southwest.

Visitors to the Pongau most frequently go through the **Gastein Valley,** of which Badgastein and Bad Hofgastein are a part. For many centuries, the Gastein Valley has been known for its hot springs, but since World War II it has also become a winter-sports center. As a consequence, many old spas such as Badgastein suddenly find themselves overrun with skiers in winter.

The **Radstädter Tauern** region is the second-most popular section of the Pongau. It sprawls across five mountains and four valleys, with a mammoth expanse of terrain from St. Johann to Obertauern. In between, you'll find that Wagrain, Flachau, Altenmarkt, and Radstadt have many places to stay. It's helpful to have a car here, although most of Radstädter Tauern can be reached by lifts and runs.

GOLDEGG

Goldegg lies on a small lake dominated by a 14th-century castle. This winter- and summer-sports resort is reached by going through Schwarzach–St. Veit at the western end of the Pongau. A 9-hole golf course is nearby.

Don't expect crystal-clear waters from the shallow lake, Goldeggersee, whose waters abut the town center: Years of percolating through the surrounding moors have infused the waters with organic matter, mostly peat, and transformed them into a greenish-brown brew, resembling weak tea. Locals claim that the waters are healthy and beneficial, but only one hotel, the Hotel Gesinger Zur Post (see below), pipes the water into its in-house spa. Incidentally, the brown color of the water absorbs sunlight faster than clear water, so in summer, the water actually becomes tepid.

Essentials

GETTING THERE Goldegg is 71km (44 miles) south of Salzburg and 389km (242 miles) southwest of Vienna. No rail lines go directly to Goldegg. **Trains** run from Salzburg to the nearby railway station at Schwarzach–St. Veit; call © **05/1717,** or visit **www.oebb.at** for schedules. From here, **buses** make the 15-minute run at intervals of between 45 minutes and 2 hours throughout the day.

If you're **driving** from Salzburg, take the A10 south to the junction with Route 311. Continue west until you see the signposted turnoff to Goldegg. Then head northwest along an unmarked road.

VISITOR INFORMATION Goldegg's **tourist information office** is at Hofmarkt 18 (© **06415/8131;** www.goldeggamsee.at), in the town center. It's open in winter Monday to Friday 8:15am to noon, and in summer Monday to Friday from 8:15am to noon and 1:30 to 6pm.

The Old Castle of Goldegg

Count Christoph of Schernberg bought the old castle of Goldegg in the 16th century and added the Rittersaal, a big hall now decorated with paintings of the Roman–German Empire, Renaissance ornaments, Christian images, and depictions of ancient myths. In 1973, the local municipality bought the building and began renovating it. The Count of Galen still lives in the village.

In the castle is the **Pongau Folk Museum,** Hofmarkt 1 (© **06415/8131** for the tourist office). It displays old tools used in the everyday lives of those who once lived here, as well as local sports equipment from the past 300 years. Guided tours in German are conducted in May, June, and September on Thursday and Sunday at 3 and 4pm; July and August Tuesday, Thursday, and Sunday at 3 and 4pm; and October to April Thursday at 2pm. Hours are Monday, Tuesday, and Thursday to Saturday from 10am to noon and 3 to 5pm, Sunday 3 to 5pm. Closed Wednesday. Adults pay 3.50€ ($5.60), children 1€ ($1.60).

Where to Stay & Dine

Hotel Gesinger Zur Post ★ This lakeside hotel with a mountain view consists of two interconnected country-style buildings, both with flowered balconies and window boxes. The oldest part of the building was erected in 1890. The interior is outfitted with painted regional furniture, polished pine paneling, and homelike details. The congenial hosts, Raimund and Hertha Gesinger, do everything they can to make guests comfortable. The cozy rooms are equipped with spacious private bathrooms, and usually have enclosed sleeping compartments behind full-length curtains.

The Most Spectacular Gorge in the Eastern Alps

Just 3km (2 miles) south of St. Johann in Pongau is the most spectacular gorge of the eastern Alps, the **Liechtensteinklamm** ★, which attracts more visitors than any other such site. A path has been blasted through to the 1km-long (3/4-mile) gorge, and during a 25-minute trek you can climb up the mammoth gorge with rock walls some 305m (1,001 ft.) high. At its tiny waist, the gorge is only 4m (13 ft.) wide. A tunnel leads to the waterfall, with a drop of about 61m (200 ft.) at the gorge's end.

The wooden bridges and the footpath that runs along the bottom of the gorge were paid for by the prince of Liechtenstein, who supposedly lent his name to the site. In some areas the ravine is so narrow that the sky is barely visible from the bottom. Roaring waterfalls and swiftly flowing waters add to the site's allure.

To reach the Liechtensteinklamm, go approximately 1.5km (1 mile) by road to Grossarl. The road to the gorge is marked. From here, count on about an hour by foot. The gorge can be visited May to September daily from 8am to 6pm, October daily 9am to 4pm. Admission is 3.50€ ($5.60) for adults and 2.20€ ($3.50) for children 6 to 18.

Under the rafters of what was a barn, the hotel has installed a pub complete with hanging lanterns and intimate corners. The Hotel Zur Post Restaurant serves Austrian and international cuisine. You might want to dine here even if you're not a guest of the hotel. The owners have a private beach on the nearby lake, available only in the summer, of course.

Hofmarkt 9, A-5622 Goldegg. ✆ **06415/81030.** Fax 06415/8104. www.hotelpost-goldegg.at. 38 units. 110€–169€ ($176–$270) double; 172€–198€ ($275–$317) suite. Rates include breakfast. Half-board 11€ ($18) per person. MC, V. Free parking outside, 10€ ($16) in the garage. Closed Apr and Nov. **Amenities:** 3 restaurants; bar; spa; sauna; bike rentals; game room; room service; massage; babysitting; laundry service; dry cleaning; nonsmoking rooms. *In room:* TV, Wi-Fi, hair dryer, safe.

Hotel Seehof ★ Hotel Seehof is filled with the kind of rustic artifacts and local painted furniture that many of us spend weeks looking for in antiques shops. This hotel dates from 1449 and sits on the lake, which reflects the chalet's forest-green shutters and the flowerpots on the hotel's balconies. An outdoor terrace sports sun umbrellas. In summer, guests can enjoy the private lakeside beach, and in winter the hotel rents ski equipment for the nearby slopes. Rooms are contemporary and warm, with good beds and modern private bathrooms. Units often have private balconies and sloped, paneled ceilings.

The owner, Mr. Schellhorn, is director of the cross-country ski school of Goldegg, where you can find 58km (36 miles) of the best groomed cross-country ski trails in Land Salzburg. He's also the director of the resort's golf course and offers hotel residents discounts on greens fees.

Hofmarkt 8, A-5622 Goldegg. ✆ **06415/8137-0.** Fax 06415/8276. www.seehof-goldegg.com. 30 units. 220€–330€ ($352–$528) double; 390€ ($624) suite. Rates include half-board. AE, DC, MC, V. Closed Apr and Nov. **Amenities:** Restaurant; bar; 18-hole golf course; sauna; room service; babysitting; laundry service; dry cleaning; nonsmoking rooms. *In room:* TV, Wi-Fi, hair dryer, safe.

ST. JOHANN IM PONGAU

St. Johann im Pongau (there's a larger St. Johann in Tyrol) is 61km (38 miles) south of Salzburg on a sun-drenched terrace on the right bank of the river.

The winter-sports season here lasts December through April, and there are more than 52 lifts and cable cars in the tri-resort area, plus some 97km (60 miles) of prepared runs. This well-known ski-lift network in the Salzburg Mountains is called Drei-Taler-Skischaukel (Three-Valley Ski Swing).

If you're a nature lover, St. Johann is a good base for visiting the **Grossarilbach Valley** to the south of the town and the mouth of **Wagrainer Tal** to the north.

The town's twin-towered **Pfarrkirche (Parish Church)** was built in 1855, but a house of worship has stood on this site since A.D. 924.

Essentials

GETTING THERE St. Johann lies directly on the main rail line connecting Munich and Salzburg with Klagenfurt, Venice, and Trieste. Between 4:50am and 10:20pm, these **trains** depart from Salzburg's Hauptbahnhof no more than 2 hours apart (trip time: 1 hr. and 8 min., when no train changes en route). If the delay between trains poses an inconvenience, consider taking one of the more frequent trains between Salzburg and the important railway junction of Schwarzach–St. Veit, and then backtrack, taking a taxi or bus the 5km (3 miles) to St. Johann. For rail information in Salzburg, call ✆ **05/1717** (www.oebb.at).

Unless you're coming in from one of the neighboring villages, arriving by **bus** in St. Johann isn't practical because of the multiple transfers required from such cities as Salzburg and Innsbruck.

If you're **driving,** head south from Salzburg on the A10, and then cut southwest at the junction with Route 311.

VISITOR INFORMATION St. Johann's **tourist office** is at Hauptstrasse 16 (✆ **06412/6036;** www.ifyouski.com). It's open in winter Monday to Friday 8am to 6pm, Saturday 9am to noon and 2 to 5pm, Sunday 9 to 11am; in summer Monday to Friday 8am to 6pm, Saturday 9am to noon.

Where to Stay & Dine

Alpenland ★ Set in the heart of the village, this is the largest hotel in St. Johann and one of the largest time-sharing resorts in Land Salzburg. Built in the 1980s and designed like a big interconnected series of alpine chalets, it contains an excellent set of facilities and comfortable accommodations that are among the best in town. Each is furnished with vaguely chalet-style decor, a bit [illegible] with excellent beds and good-size bathrooms. On the premises are two restaurants (Italian and Austrian) with an attentive and helpful staff. Throughout, you'll find burnished pine and regional accessories. Meals in the most formal of the restaurants begin at 26€ ($42), although many less expensive options are available on-site. The hotel rents bicycles to anyone interested in exploring the nearby region for 12€ ($19) per day.

Hans-Kappacher-Strasse 7, A-5600 St. Johann im Pongau. ✆ **06412/70210.** Fax 06412/702151. www.alpenland.at. 144 units. Winter 152€–220€ ($243–$352) double, 318€ ($509) junior suite; off-season 186€–264€ ($298–$422) double, 384€ ($614) junior suite. Half-board 18€ ($29) per person. AE, DC, MC, V. Free parking. **Amenities:** 2 restaurants; 2 bars; nightclub; lounge; indoor heated pool; 2 tennis courts; fitness center; Jacuzzi; sauna; room service; massage; babysitting; laundry service; dry cleaning; boutiques. *In room:* TV, Wi-Fi, minibar, hair dryer.

3 BAD HOFGASTEIN ★

88km (55 miles) S of Salzburg; 8km (5 miles) NW of Badgastein; 42km (26 miles) SE of Zell am See

The old, established spa of **Bad Hofgastein** (elevation 869m/2,851 ft.) has long been a rival of Badgastein for the tourist euro. It's smaller than Badgastein but almost as charming. The little resort is actually almost a satellite of the larger spa, as the radioactive waters of Badgastein are pumped to its neighbor. Some hardy visitors like to follow a marked footpath on the 2½-hour walk between the two towns. The two resorts welcome almost as many visitors as Salzburg.

ESSENTIALS

GETTING THERE Bad Hofgastein is a major stop on the main rail lines connecting Munich and Salzburg with Klagenfurt and Venice. Most efficient are the express **trains** from Salzburg, which depart about once an hour throughout the day (trip time: 1¼ hr). Night trains might require a transfer at Schwarzach–St. Veit, 68km (42 miles) south of Salzburg. Dozens of trains traveling from Innsbruck also stop in Schwarzach–St. Veit. Call ✆ **05/1717,** or visit **www.oebb.at** for more information.

One daily **bus** runs in both directions between Salzburg's Mirabellplatz and the railway station in Bad Hofgastein. This bus continues on to Badgastein.

If you're **driving,** take the A10 south of Salzburg, cut right onto Route 311, and continue west to the junction with Route 167, where you head south to Badgastein.

VISITOR INFORMATION The **tourist information office** in the town center (✆ **06432/3393260;** www.gastein.com) is open Monday to Saturday 8am to 6pm.

SPA FACILITIES

The thermally heated waters of Bad Hofgastein originate in the same high-altitude springs that feed the spa facilities of Badgastein, 8km (5 miles) away. Bad Hofgastein is the newer of the two, and a bit more upscale and glamorous as well. The waters are rich in radon, a controversial element that doctors once dismissed as harmful but now say is beneficial in small doses of no more than 20 minutes of immersion per day.

There are no public facilities here as in Badgastein; instead, three local hotels have built full spa facilities on their premises. You won't have to move between buildings for treatments, a bonus during cold or snowy weather.

The most complete Bad Hofgastein spa lies within the Grand Park Hotel (see below). The spa treatments are great for the foot-sore (and leg, and back, and more) traveler. You can get all types of massages, electrotherapy, aromatherapy, saunas, steam baths, and mud packs, or take part in aerobic classes or gymnastics. Less scientific "cures" include lying prone on plastic bags filled with dried flowers, or being partially buried in tubs of wet straw that have been soaked in the hot thermal waters.

SEEING THE SIGHTS

The **Pfarrkirche (Parish Church)** of this tiny village is late Gothic, dating from the late 15th century, although it has a baroque altar. Some sights, such as old houses with turrets, are reminders of the gold-mining days of the Gastein Valley. In the 16th century, the nearby gold mines made Bad Hofgastein rival even Salzburg in wealth. A rich mining family lived at the 15th-century Weitmoserchlössl, which has now been turned into a cafe.

The Gastein Valley and Bad Hofgastein are attracting more and more winter-sports fans. Some 50 gondolas and ski lifts provide access to more than 241km (150 miles) of well-marked and well-groomed ski runs. Thanks to the high capacity of an updated funicular, a mono-cable rotation gondola lift with cabins for six passengers, two quadruple chairlifts, and a triple chairlift, skiers don't have to wait in long lines. The Dorfgastein-Grossarl connection and the lift network from Schlossalm via the Angertal and Jungeralm ski center up to the Stubnerkogel (the largest lift interconnection in Land Salzburg) provide some of the most enjoyable ski runs in the valley.

Also available are cross-country skiing on well-maintained tracks, tobogganing, skating, and riding in horse-drawn sleighs.

WHERE TO STAY & DINE

Very Expensive

Grand Park Hotel ★★ Originally constructed in the 1920s, this government-rated five-star hotel was completely rebuilt in the early 1990s and reopened in 1994. It's a majestic, classically styled building set in its own birch-filled park, with a swimming pool and lawn chairs on the grassy lawns around it. The elegant interior is filled with stone and polished wood, plush carpets, and shining brass. Rooms are handsomely furnished and beautifully maintained, with excellent beds and ample bathrooms. The hotel restaurant, open to nonguests, is one of the area's finest, serving Austrian and international cuisine. A pianist entertains every evening.

Kurgartenstrasse 26, A-5630 Bad Hofgastein. ✆ **06432/63560.** Fax 06432/8454. www.grandparkhotel.at. 89 units. Summer 250€–360€ ($400–$576) double, 380€ ($608) suite; off-season 204€–324€ ($326–$518) double, 344€ ($550) suite. Rates include half-board. MC, V. **Amenities:** Restaurant; bar; indoor thermal pool; fitness center; spa; Jacuzzi; sauna; bike rentals; room service; massage; babysitting; laundry service; dry cleaning; nonsmoking rooms; 1 room for those w/limited mobility. *In room:* TV, Wi-Fi, minibar, hair dryer, safe.

Expensive

Kurhotel Palace ★ Finds Situated in a quiet, sunny spot, this first-class hotel is a few minutes' walk from the resort center. This is a surprisingly snug and cozy retreat in spite of its large size. The well-furnished rooms all have radios and balconies. Beds are about the finest in the resort, so comfortable that you might not want to get out of them; bathrooms are generous in size and well maintained. A daily program of entertainment and activities includes a lively nightclub, a Vienna coffeehouse, and bars. The Salzburger Stüberl serves Austrian, international, and vegetarian cuisine, and the Wiener Café offers homemade cakes and tarts

Alexander-Moser-Allee 13, A-5630 Bad Hofgastein. ✆ **06432/67150.** Fax 06432/6715567. www.kurhotelpalace.at. 90 units. 166€–184€ ($266–$294) double. Rates include half-board. AE, DC, MC, V. Parking 8€ ($13). **Amenities:** Restaurant; 2 bars; nightclub; cafe; Indoor thermal pool; 2 tennis courts; fitness center; spa; sauna; salon; babysitting; laundry service; dry cleaning; solarium. *In room:* TV, Wi-Fi, minibar, hair dryer, safe, radio.

Moderate

Hotel Sendlhof ★ The six floors here are surrounded by balconies and potted flowers, and an outdoor heated swimming pool lies across the lawn. The interior has large windows, inviting fireplaces, and extra touches such as ceramic stoves. Management sometimes provides live zither music in the evening. The elegant, cozy rooms have exposed wood, and most have private balconies. Bathrooms, although neatly kept, might be a bit cramped.

Pyrkerstrasse 34, A-5630 Bad Hofgastein. ✆ **06432/38380.** Fax 06432/3838-60. www.sendlhof.co.at. 60 units. Winter 150€–246€ ($240–$394) double; summer 118€–186€ ($189–$298) double. Rates include half-board. No credit cards. Parking 5€ ($8). Closed Apr 20–May 22 and Oct 15–Dec 18. **Amenities:** Restaurant; bar; outdoor heated pool; fitness center; sauna; room service; babysitting; laundry service; dry cleaning. *In room:* TV, Wi-Fi, hair dryer, safe.

Hotel St. Georg ★ An elegant country-house atmosphere prevails at this hotel offering attractive and well-furnished rooms and family suites designed for discerning guests. The manager and hotel staff make sure rooms, with medium-size bathrooms, are well maintained. Half-board includes a buffet breakfast and a five-course dinner. Tempting Austrian cuisine is served in the country-style restaurant, and special diets can be accommodated. Although it's not as well known as the previously recommended hotel, it has its devotees.

Dr. Zimmermann-Strasse 7, A-5630 Bad Hofgastein. ✆ **06432/6100.** Fax 06432/610061. www.stgeorg.com. 50 units. Winter 196€–218€ ($314–$349) per person double, 226€–274€ ($362–$438) suite for 2; summer 140€–166€ ($224–$266) per person double, 200€ ($320) suite. Rates include half-board. MC, V. Parking 3€ ($4.80) in summer, 6€ ($9.60) in winter. Closed Nov 10–Dec 19. **Amenities:** Restaurant; bar; indoor heated pool; fitness center; sauna; room service; massage; babysitting; laundry service; dry cleaning; solarium. *In room:* TV, Wi-Fi, hair dryer, safe.

Kurhotel Germania ★ Beautiful Victorian antiques (including an exquisite collection of armchairs) fill some of the big-windowed public areas of this four-star hotel, which dates from around 1900. If your guest room has a balcony—and many of the pleasant and sunny rooms do—you'll have a view of the houses and barns of the valley below. Traditional alpine furnishings are somewhat functional but retain a bit of charm.

Kurpromenade 4, A-5630 Bad Hofgastein. ✆ **06432/6232.** Fax 06432/623265. www.hotelgermania.at. 70 units. Winter 158€–238€ ($253–$381) double; summer 146€–154€ ($234–$247) double. Rates include half-board. MC, V. Parking 10€ ($16). Closed Nov–Dec 16 and Apr 16–May 13. **Amenities:** Restaurant; lounge; indoor heated pool; fitness center; massage; health spa; sauna; room service; laundry service; dry cleaning. *In room:* TV, Wi-Fi.

Kur-Sport-Hotel Astoria ★ This government-rated four-star hotel, built in the 1950s, is a generously proportioned five-story building with a simple wood-balconied facade. The interior has been renovated in a contemporary design of streamlined furniture and warm, inviting colors. Rooms are only standard in size, but each is quite comfortable, with good beds and small bathrooms. Austrian regional specialties are served, and a country buffet is offered once a week.

Salzburger Strasse 24, A-5630 Bad Hofgastein. ✆ **06432/62770.** Fax 06432/627777. www.kur-sporthotel-astoria.com. 73 units. Winter 150€–304€ ($240–$486) double; 84€–170€ ($134–$272) double. Rates include half-board. AE, DC, MC, V. Closed June and Oct 10–Dec 20. **Amenities:** Restaurant; bar; indoor heated pool; fitness center; spa; sauna; room service; babysitting; laundry service; dry cleaning; nonsmoking rooms. *In room:* TV, Wi-Fi, minibar, hair dryer, safe.

Inexpensive

Hotel Carinthia ★ This large, solid-looking chalet has flower-filled balconies on all sides. The interior has elegant and unusual touches, such as the tucked-away corner bar and modern chandeliers in the high-ceilinged dining room. The spacious rooms have a contemporary decor; each is well equipped, with excellent beds and a medium-size bathroom.

Dr. Zimmermann-Strasse 2, A-5630 Bad Hofgastein. ✆ **06432/83740.** Fax 06432/837475. www.hotel-carinthia.com. 35 units. Winter 134€–198€ ($214–$317) double; summer 124€–138€ ($198–$221) double. Rates include half-board. No credit cards. Closed Easter–May 10 and Oct 20–Dec 20. **Amenities:** Dining room; bar; indoor heated pool; thermal pools; tennis and squash court; fitness center; Jacuzzi; sauna; massage; babysitting; laundry service; dry cleaning; nonsmoking rooms. *In room:* TV, Wi-Fi, minibar, hair dryer, safe.

Kurhotel Völserhof Built in the 1960s, this hotel rises five balconied stories above a flowering garden near the edge of town. In summer, masses of red flowers bloom above the windows of the second-floor restaurant. Rooms are rather small and don't have much charm, but each is comfortably equipped with good beds. The city's recreation center is within a 5-minute walk, and the terminus of the funicular, Schlossalm Bahn, is 10 minutes away. The Lang family, your host, is very helpful in providing information about the area. One of the best times to book here is during the last 3 weeks of January and the last 2 weeks in March, when rates are even lower than they are in the discounted summer season.

Pyrkerstrasse 28, A-5630 Bad Hofgastein. ✆ **06432/8288.** Fax 06432/828810. www.voelserhof.com. 30 units. 116€–164€ ($186–$262) double. Rates include half-board. No credit cards. Closed Oct 25–Dec 7 and the first 2 weeks of May. **Amenities:** Dining room; bar; sauna; babysitting; laundry service; dry cleaning. *In room:* TV, minibar, hair dryer.

Kur- und Sporthotel Moser ★ Value On the main town square, this hotel has sections dating from the 12th century. You'd never know it from the facade, which is pleasantly balconied above the street-level awnings. The interior, however, is vaulted and cozy, with old exposed wood, heavy beams, and oriental rugs. The furnishings are rustic and regional, with homey touches such as racks of pewter in the dining room. When the weather is good, the rooms are often flooded with sunlight. Although the hotel dates from the Middle Ages, the emphasis is on comfort, as reflected by the traditional furniture and duvet-covered beds. There's an intimate lounge and terrace dining, as well as a cozy cellar for dining and dancing in winter.

Kaiser-Franz-Platz 2, A-5630 Bad Hofgastein. ✆ **06432/6209.** Fax 06432/620988. www.dasmoser.com. 54 units. 120€–160€ ($192–$256) double. Rates include half-board. AE, DC, MC, V. Parking 6.50€ ($10). Closed Apr and Nov 1–Dec 15. **Amenities:** Restaurant; bar; spa; fitness center; indoor heated thermal pool; bike rentals; sauna; room service; massage; babysitting; nonsmoking rooms. *In room:* TV, Wi-Fi, hair dryer, safe.

BAD HOFGASTEIN AFTER DARK

For your big night on the town, take a taxi from Bad Hofgastein to Badgastein to gamble at the casino (see below). In Bad Hofgastein, you can go clubbing, sit in a tavern beside an open fire, or dance to the music of a live band at one of the hotels in the winter season. The tourist office will give you the latest information on which hotels or clubs are likely to have nightlife at any given time.

One of Bad Hofgastein's busiest nightspots is the **Norica Bar,** just off the lobby of the Hotel Norica, Kaiser-Franz-Platz 3 (✆ **06432/8391-0**). Open every day from 5pm until 2am, it offers some kind of music act, from evergreen oompah to rock 'n' roll, in both winter and summer. There's no cover charge, and beer costs 3€ to 5€ ($4.80–$8). Closing time varies, depending on business.

4 BADGASTEIN ★★: AUSTRIA'S PREMIER SPA

100km (62 miles) S of Salzburg; 410km (255 miles) SW of Vienna

Badgastein is not only Austria's premier spa, it's also one of the great spa towns of Europe. The local tourist industry began when Frederick, Duke of Styria, came here in the 15th century for treatment of a gangrenous wound. The duke was healed, and word spread. Badgastein had made its way onto the medieval tourist map. Royalty and aristocrats flocked here around the turn of the 19th century to "take the waters." And good waters they are—radioactive springs with healing properties.

Badgastein lies on the north slope of the Tauern massif in one of the most scenic spots in Austria. The spa town is spread across steep hillsides split by the waters of the tumbling Gasteiner Ache. Hotels, many with water piped in directly from the Ache, adorn the steep slopes formed by the cascading waterfall. The spa's indoor swimming pool is carved into a rock filled with the radon waters.

Although Badgastein was first a summer retreat, it's now also a center for winter sports. With its pristine alpine air, skiing equal to that of St. Moritz in Switzerland, the finest hotels in Land Salzburg, 18 hot springs for thermal hydrotherapy, and a mountain tunnel that has been called "the world's only natural giant sauna," Badgastein is the pinnacle of mountain spa resorts.

ESSENTIALS

GETTING THERE Badgastein is a major stop on the main rail line connecting Munich and Salzburg with Klagenfurt and Venice. Express **trains** from Salzburg depart every hour throughout the day (trip time: 1½ hr). Certain trains, especially night trains from Salzburg, might require a transfer in the railway junction of Schwarzach–St. Veit, 68km (42 miles) south of Salzburg. Dozens of trains traveling from Innsbruck also stop in Schwarzach–St. Veit. Call ✆ **05/1717** (www.oebb.at) in Salzburg for schedules.

One daily **bus** makes a 2-hour run in both directions between Salzburg's Mirabellplatz and the railway station in Badgastein. Buses from Badgastein make frequent runs into the surrounding villages.

If you're **driving,** take the A10 south of Salzburg and cut west at the junction with Route 311. At the junction with Route 167, head south.

VISITOR INFORMATION The **tourist office** (✆ **06434/25310**) in the center of town is open year-round Monday to Friday 8am to 6pm. In winter, it's also open Saturday 10am to 6pm and Sunday 10am to 2pm.

SEEING THE SIGHTS

Along with the natural scenery of the town and the surrounding area, you can see the **Nikolauskirche,** a 15th-century church with well-preserved Gothic frescoes, a late-Gothic stone pulpit, and baroque altars and tombs.

In summer, besides swimming in thermal baths, the spa offers a host of saunas, massages, and solariums. There's also an 18-hole golf course, tennis courts, horseback riding, hiking, and a variety of excursions, perhaps in a *fiaker* (horse-drawn carriage). Cable cars and chairlifts are not only for winter-sports crowds; in summer, take one up to the top and get a panoramic view of the Hohe Tauern.

In winter, most visitors are drawn to this region for the great skiing. In 1958, Graukogel, one of the main ski areas, was the site of the world championships.

NEARBY ATTRACTIONS

One of the region's most quirky attractions is the **Gasteiner Heilstollen,** A-5645 Bergstein (✆ **06434/3753;** www.gasteiner-heilstollen.com), a labyrinth of underground tunnels carved out of the **Böckstein** during the 18th and 19th centuries as a gold mine. It has been transformed into a small-scale health spa, where tiny cars carrying six patients are shuttled through the tunnels on a narrow-gauge railway. The 15-minute trip through the heated and mildly radioactive air (local doctors claim the effects are dispersed from the body within an hour) is cited as a cure for arthritis.

Between mid-January and October, you can ride through the tunnels Monday to Saturday 8am to 4pm for 52€ ($83). The tunnels are 3km (2 miles) from Badgastein. Follow the signs from Bergsteinerstrasse, or take one of the hourly blue-and-gray Lackner buses.

Graukogel (2,508m/8,228 ft.), to the east of the valley, is reached by bus from Badgastein. Expert European skiers crowd these slopes in the afternoon. A chairlift takes skiers to the halfway station, and a double chairlift or surface lift takes them to the top. A round-trip ticket costs around 15€ ($24). A mountain restaurant stands at the halfway station. This is also a favorite starting point for alpine walking tours. Call © **06434/2005** for ticket information. Service is daily 9am to 4pm.

On the west side of the valley rises **Stubnerkogel** (2,230m/7,316 ft.). A six-seat gondola takes you most of the way; however, it takes a chairlift and a couple of surface lifts to reach the top. There's also a mountain restaurant with a panoramic view. The gondola and the chairlift (© **06434/2322**) are in service from late May to mid-October daily from 8:30am to 4pm; a round-trip ticket costs 16.50€ ($26).

Kreuzkogel (2,684m/8,806 ft.) is at **Sportgastein,** 8km (5 miles) up the valley to the south of the village of Böckstein, site of the tunnel sauna mentioned above. This is a great place to come for high-altitude bowl skiing. It's about a 20-minute bus ride from Badgastein. A chairlift will take you to the halfway station, with a surface lift pulling you to Kreuzkogel's top station. Besides the well-equipped skiing facilities here, including cross-country trails, you can enjoy hiking, indoor horseback riding, indoor tennis, curling, and ice-skating.

You can drive from Badgastein to Sportgastein along Gasteiner Alpenstrasse at elevations ranging from 900m to 1,454m (2,953 ft.–4,770 ft.). The toll charge is 3€ ($4.80) per person; it's free for children 4 and under. In winter, the ski-season ticket includes the road toll.

WHERE TO STAY & DINE

Expensive

Elisabethpark ★★ This is Badgastein's premier address. The vastly improved four-star government-rated hotel has a ceiling covered with heavily textured knotty pine and rooms crowned with Moorish patterns of geometric greens and reds. The public areas stretch on and on—not surprising, since the hotel is a vast, sprawling collection of buildings with a white exterior, many balconies, and a series of hallways that are decorated with unusual paintings, hunting trophies, and regional antiques. Available in a wide variety of sizes, the rooms are traditionally furnished, often with antiques. The hotel's a la carte restaurant is one of the best at the spa, offering Austrian and international dishes alike.

Franz-Josef-Strasse 5, A-5640 Badgastein. © **06434/25510.** Fax 06434/255110. www.elisabeth.park.at. 119 units. Winter 208€–262€ ($333–$419) double, 248€–282€ ($397–$451) junior suite, from 322€ ($515) suite; off-season 136€–196€ ($218–$314) double, 176€–216€ ($282–$346) junior suite, from 236€ ($378) suite. Rates include half-board. AE, DC, MC, V. Parking 11€ ($18). **Amenities:** 2 restaurants; coffee house; bar; indoor heated pool; fitness center; sauna; room service; massage; babysitting; laundry service; dry cleaning; nonsmoking rooms. *In room:* TV, Wi-Fi, minibar, hair dryer.

Hotel Grüner-Baum ★★ This hotel is a complex of five chalets surrounding a grassy area in the Kötschach Valley on the outskirts of Badgastein. During its long history, the establishment has offered hospitality to Kaiser Wilhelm, the shah of Iran, conductor Arturo Toscanini, and actor Charles Laughton. The oldest parts of the building are exquisitely crafted of local woods, sometimes with elaborate regional carvings, and decorated with hunting trophies beneath the beamed ceilings. Rooms are cozy and rustic, with wood paneling and a recessed sleeping alcove in some of the singles. The beds and mattresses ensure a good night's sleep.

Organized weekly activities and a bar with dancing provide the entertainment. The hotel's restaurants, Gunghoferstüberl, Rösslstube, and Hochzeitsstube, are open from 6pm to midnight in winter and from 6 to 11pm in summer, serving excellently prepared Austrian and international specialties. There's also a garden restaurant in summer.

Kötschachtalstrasse 25, A-5640 Badgastein. ✆ **06434/25160.** Fax 06434/251625. www.hoteldorf.com. 100 units. 208€–296€ ($333–$474) double; 298€–336€ ($477–$538) suite. Rates include half-board. AE, DC, MC, V. Parking 8€–10€ ($13–$16). Closed Oct 26–Dec 6. **Amenities:** 3 restaurants; bar; lounge; outdoor heated pool; indoor heated thermal pool; 2 tennis courts; fitness center; sauna; room service; massage; babysitting; laundry service; dry cleaning; nonsmoking rooms; bowling alley. *In room:* TV, Wi-Fi, minibar, hair dryer, safe.

Hotel Weismayr ★ Situated prominently in the town center between the congress hall and the casino, the Hotel Weismayr has been one of the leading hotels in the Gastein Valley since 1832. Surrounded by the soaring Alps, the hotel makes an ideal starting point for outdoor activities in the valley: golfing, horseback riding, skiing, swimming, hiking, climbing, relaxing, and more. At this cozy abode, rooms are well furnished with especially good beds. Parasols and plants dot the terrace cafe, and the elegant, high-ceilinged dining room is beautifully decorated. Austrian and international dishes are prepared with the freshest ingredients.

Franz-Josef-Strasse 6, A-5640 Badgastein. ✆ **06434/2594.** Fax 06434/259414. www.weismayr.com. 89 units. Winter 210€–280€ ($336–$448) double, 225€–300€ ($360–$480) suite for 2; summer 110€–142€ ($176–$227) double, 121€–145€ ($194–$232) suite for 2. Rates include half-board. AE, DC, MC, V. Parking 10€ ($16). **Amenities:** Restaurant; bar; cafe; indoor heated pool; fitness center; sauna; beauty treatments; room service; massage; babysitting; laundry service; dry cleaning. *In room:* TV, Wi-Fi, minibar, hair dryer, safe.

Moderate

Hotel and Spa Haus Hirt ★ Originally built in 1930 and completely renovated in 1997, this hotel retains touches of folkloric and old-fashioned charm that some newer hotels have a hard time matching. It's a 20-minute walk downhill from the center of town. All rooms have comfortable furnishings and neatly maintained bathrooms with tub/shower combinations. There's a bar, sweeping views over the Gastein Valley, and a sense of family-run thrift and virtue, thanks to the on-site presence of the owners. The hotel's cozily paneled dining room serves Austrian specialties that taste particularly good after a day in the great outdoors. There's even a sunny, wind-sheltered terrace that attracts many sunbathers.

An der Kaiserpromenade, A-5640 Badgastein. ✆ **06434/2797.** Fax 06434/279748. www.haus-hirt.com. 30 units. Winter 184€–272€ ($294–$435) double, 234€–290€ ($374–$464) suite; summer 138€–260€ ($221–$416) double, 230€–284€ ($368–$454) suite. Rates include half-board. AE, MC, V. Closed mid-Oct to Nov and mid-Apr to May. Parking 7€ ($11). **Amenities:** Restaurant; bar; indoor heated pool; fitness center; sauna; game room; room service; massage; babysitting; laundry service; dry cleaning; nonsmoking rooms; sun beds. *In room:* TV, Wi-Fi, minibar, hair dryer, safe.

Hotel Wildbad (Value) With its dark-yellow facade, big windows, and prominent balconies, Hotel Wildbad, in the center of the village near the indoor thermal pools and the ski lifts, stands out from the buildings around it. The medium-size rooms have much comfort. Most offer panoramic valley views; some have a sitting area. There's also a terrace sun deck with chaise lounges and cafe tables. Gerhard Hörtnagl, owner and manager, sees to it that excellent food is provided, with a superb salad bar and a buffet breakfast.

K. H. Waggerlstrasse 20, A-5640 Badgastein. ✆ **06434/3761.** Fax 06434/376170. www.hotel-wildbad.com. 40 units. Winter 238€–272€ ($381–$435) double; summer 144€–186€ ($230–$298) double. Rates include half-board. MC, V. Closed Apr 15–May 15 and Oct 15–Dec 15. **Amenities:** Restaurant; bar; lounge; 18-hole golf course; fitness center; spa; sauna; room service; massage; babysitting; laundry service; dry cleaning; nonsmoking rooms; rooms for those w/limited mobility. *In room:* TV, Wi-Fi, minibar, hair dryer, safe.

Kurhotel Miramonte On the landscaped side of an alpine hill, the Miramonte offers a panoramic view of the valley. A big terrace with sun umbrellas provides a nice spot to sit and relax. The comfortable and traditionally furnished rooms make for a snug retreat. Although the hotel dates from the 1950s, its accommodations have been renovated many times. The public areas are elegant yet simple.

Reitelpromenade 3, A-5640 Badgastein. ✆ **06434/2577.** Fax 06434/25789. www.hotelmiramonte.com. 36 units. 68€–75€ ($109–$120) per person. Rates include half-board. AE, DC, MC, V. Parking 4€ ($6.40). Closed Sept 25–Dec 7. **Amenities:** Restaurant; bar; fitness room; Jacuzzi; sauna; breakfast-only room service; massage; babysitting; laundry service; dry cleaning. *In room:* TV, Wi-Fi, minibar, hair dryer, safe.

Inexpensive

Alpenblick (Kids) This is a well-managed hotel whose charms are especially obvious in summer, when a garden with a small *kneipe* (pub) and lots of flowing water and flowering shrubs make it an alpine idyll. And, in winter, guests can ski almost to the building's front door. Its core, built around 1900, continued to grow, just like Topsy, with enlargements and renovations. This chalet has a side wing containing comfortable rooms with balconies and big windows offering mountain views. Beds are good, and the bathrooms, although tiny, are tidily kept. Well-prepared and rather hearty meals are served in the timbered and beamed dining room. In summer, a children's playground with a trampoline is featured.

Kötschachtalerstrasse 17, A-5640 Badgastein. ✆ **06434/2062-0.** Fax 06434/206258. www.alpenblick-gastein.at. 38 units. Winter 53€–70€ ($85–$112) per person; summer 44€–67€ ($70–$107) per person. Rates include half-board. AE, MC, V. Closed Nov 6–Dec 7. **Amenities:** Restaurant; bar; outdoor pool; fitness center; sauna; room service; babysitting; laundry service; dry-cleaning. *In room:* TV, Wi-Fi, hair dryer.

Hotel Mozart (Value) This unusual hotel, designed in the 19th century, has a long veranda on the ground floor and a gabled mansard roof. Inside, beautifully patterned oriental rugs cover the floor of the wood-paneled lobby area, and crystal chandeliers hang from the detailed plaster ceiling. All the comfortably furnished rooms have private, immaculate bathrooms, in addition to the thermally heated baths on each floor. Rooms aren't large, but the beds are comfortable and housekeeping is first-rate. Both traditional and innovative cuisine is served in the hotel's restaurant, the Mozartstuben.

Kaiser-Franz-Josef-Strasse 25, A-5640 Badgastein. ✆ **06434/26860.** Fax 06434/268662. www.hotelmozart.at. 70 units. Winter 82€–108€ ($131–$173) double; off-season 76€–84€ ($122–$134) double. Rates include breakfast. DC, MC, V. **Amenities:** Restaurant; bar; fitness center; sauna; Jacuzzi; nonsmoking rooms; rooms for those w/limited mobility. *In room:* TV, Wi-Fi.

Villa Hubertus (Value) Unpretentious and evocative of the final days of the Hapsburgs, this government-rated two-star hotel, a 5-minute walk from the center of town, was built as a Jugendstil-inspired villa in 1908. Two rooms have private balconies; the others are simple but comfortably outfitted. The on-site restaurant is open only to residents. The room used for breakfast and resident dinners is especially noteworthy, as it is pure Jugendstil in design with an authentic turn-of-the-20th-century decor. The venue is small scale, family oriented, and kindly.

Kaiser-Franz-Josef-Strasse 24, A-5640 Badgastein. ✆/fax **06434/2607.** 6 units. Winter 92€–128€ ($147–$205) double with half-board; summer 60€–69€ ($96–$110) double. Rates include breakfast. No credit cards. **Amenities:** Winter restaurant; breakfast room; lounge. *In room:* No phone.

AFTER DARK IN BADGASTEIN

There's actually a lot to do at night in Badgastein, with cabaret, theater, folk events, and other activities. The center of nightlife—and the place to be seen—is the **Casino Badgastein** (✆ **06434/2465**). Here you can play roulette, baccarat, poker, and blackjack, but you'll need a passport to get in. The entrance fee is 21€ ($34), which entitles you to 25€ ($40) worth of chips. The casino is open Christmas through April 30 and July 1 through September 3 daily from 7pm to 2am.

At **Tanzlokal Schialm,** Böcksteiner Bundesstrasse 27 (✆ **06434/2055**), by the light of a blazing open fireplace, young and old enjoy dance music and the romantic and very rustic looking alpine atmosphere of this popular beer and dance hall. Nightly themes range from a cheese-and-knockwurst evening (Mon) to a re-creation of a *heurige,* complete with Austrian wines and music (Wed), to a candlelit dance (Sat). Drinks begin at 5.50€ ($8.80), and full meals are served daily from 6 to 9pm.

If you want more conventional dancing, head for the **Elisabethpark** (see "Where to Stay & Dine," above). This elegant nightspot is the place to go if you want to get all dolled up.

5 THE PINZGAU

The Pinzgau section of Land Salzburg stretches east from the Gerlos Pass to the Gastein Valley, with the Salzach River flowing through. To the south lies Hohe Tauern, and to the north is the Kitzbühel alpine region.

For visitors, skiing is the reason to come. The twin villages of **Saalbach** and **Hinterglemm** lie at the end of a valley ringed by a horseshoe of mountains laced with more than 40 ski lifts. The chief resort of the Pinzgau is **Zell am See** (see section 7, later in this chapter). Another outstanding ski resort in the Upper Pinzgau region is **Kaprun.** The **Grossglockner Road** also begins in Pinzgau (see section 6, later in this chapter).

LOFER ★

Ideally situated among forests, valleys, and mountain rivers is the old market town of Lofer. This is a good base for exploring much of Land Salzburg, including Salzburg itself, the Grossglockner alpine road, Krimml Falls, the dams at Kaprun, Kitzbühel, and Innsbruck, as well as Lake Chiemsee and Berchtesgaden in Germany. Within an hour's drive are three 18-hole golf courses.

Essentials

GETTING THERE The nearest railway stations are at St. Johann in Tyrol and at Saalfelden. From Saalfelden, nine **buses** depart every day for the 39km (24-mile) trek to the northwest. From St. Johann, 10 buses depart daily for the 43km (27-mile) ride northeast to Lofer. Note that some bus routes, traversing the strip of Germany that juts into Austria at this point, travel directly from Salzburg's railway station about five times a day; the trip takes about an hour. If you choose this route, you might be asked to show your passport.

Motorists can take Route 305 southwest of Salzburg through Germany, and then continue southwest at the junction with Route 312.

Exploring Lofer

Lofer has a **Bauerntheater (Peasant Theater)** and a Gothic-style **Pfarrkirche (Parish Church),** whose tower dominates the town with its two onion-shape domes. Many houses are decorated with oriels, an architectural style inspired by nearby Bavaria.

Lofer doubles as a health resort and a ski center, offering hospitality, tradition, and rural charm. It's known for its peat-water and mud baths, as well as its Kneipp cures. The area around Lofer is nice for walking or hiking in both summer and winter. Sports facilities include a tennis court, skating rink, miniature golf course, and enclosed swimming pool.

A ski school operates here, and there are nine T-bar lifts. A chairlift will deliver you to the Sonnegg-Loderbühel at 1,003m (3,291 ft.) and the upper station of the Loferer Alm at 1,403m (4,603 ft.). Rising in the background of the town are the Loferer Steinberge and the Reiter Steinberge.

You can visit **Lamprechtshöhle** (© **06582/8343**), Austria's deepest water-bearing cave, on the road from Lofer to Weissbach (Rte. 311), about 60km (37 miles) from Salzburg by bus. A guided tour takes about 40 minutes. The cavern is open daily 8:30am to 6pm; admission is 3.60€ ($5.80) for adults and 1.80€ ($2.90) for children. It's closed March to April 15 and October 20 to December 15.

Where to Stay & Dine

Hotel St. Hubertus ★★ This hotel, the largest and best in Lofer, was built in the mid-1960s. The chalet windows provide great views over the Saalach River and the Loferer Steinberge mountain ranges. Rooms are well furnished, and most have balconies. The doubles are large enough to be rented as triples, and the suites (without kitchen) are big enough to house two to four guests. In summer, guests enjoy the garden with its sunny terrace. About a 5-minute walk from the village center and the cableways, it's near several walking paths and promenades. For cross-country skiers, tracks begin only 2 minutes from the hotel. Half-board includes a buffet breakfast followed that evening by a four-course meal with a large choice of desserts and cheeses. The hotel bar provides a cozy retreat.

Grisseman, A-5090 Lofer 180. © **06588/8266.** Fax 06588/7465. www.hubertus-lofer.net. 56 units. Winter 104€ ($166) double; off season 98€ ($157) double. Rates include half-board. AE, DC, MC, V. Closed late Apr to mid May and Nov 1–Dec 15. **Amenities:** Dining room; bar; indoor heated pool; sauna; breakfast-only room service, massage, laundry service; dry cleaning; nonsmoking rooms. *In room:* TV, hair dryer, safe.

ST. MARTIN BEI LOFER

This tiny, quaint village, about 2km (1½ miles) south of Lofer, is visited for its pilgrimage church, a large baroque edifice called **Maria Kirchenthal.** The building was designed by the renowned baroque master J. B. Fischer von Erlach. The church's museum displays votive pictures from the 17th to the 19th centuries. About 1.5km (1 mile) west of the village, the church is reached by a toll road open only in summer, or by an hour's walk from Lofer.

Vorderkaser Gorge (© **06588/8527,** the tourist office in St. Martin bei Lofer) can be visited from St. Martin. A 2.5km (1½-mile) road connects the gorge with the Mittelpinzgau road near the Vorderkaser bus stop. It's open to the public from the second weekend in May to October 20 daily from 9am to 5pm. Admission is 2.50€ ($4) for adults and 1.20€ ($1.90) for children.

A restaurant at Prommer Rudolf, open daily in summer from 9am to 8pm (but closed in winter), provides a good place to eat and drink.

Essentials

GETTING THERE Getting to St. Martin is similar to getting to Lofer. The **buses** that originate in Saalfelden and Salzburg also stop in St. Martin. If you take a bus in St. Johann, however, you'll have to transfer to another bus in Lofer or call a taxi for the short continuation to St. Martin. If you're **driving,** continue south of Lofer along Route 311.

SAALBACH & HINTERGLEMM ★

This internationally known tourist resort, at an elevation of 1,003m (3,291 ft.), emphasizes relaxation, recreation, and sports—both summer and winter. It's located 64km (40 miles) southwest of Salzburg, 399km (248 miles) southwest of Vienna, and 185km (115 miles) southwest of Linz.

Saalbach has seen rapid growth as a winter-sports resort in recent years. Hinterglemm, its twin, is about an 8-minute drive west on an unclassified road that's signposted at the head of the valley. Often the region is spoken of as a unit—the Saalbach-Hinterglemm ski area. The resorts are linked by a lift system and ski bus.

Saalbach has numerous lifts near the center of town. There's one cable car big enough to carry 100 passengers, along with 40 tows and chairlifts that provide access to a variety of well-groomed slopes and deep-powder runs. The major lift, the Schattberg cableway, leaves from the heart of Saalbach, taking skiers to the top station (2,001m/6,565 ft.), where an excellent restaurant boasts a sunny terrace with a panoramic view. Of course, summer visitors can also take the cableway to enjoy the scenery.

The Glenntal Ski Pass, valid for the 60 lifts and the 193km (120 miles) of downhill runs of the Obertauern region (Saalbach, Hinterglemm, and Leogang), costs 41€ ($65) for 1 day, 112€ ($179) for 3 days, and 196€ ($313) for 6 days. It's sold at the bottom of the biggest ski lift as well as the **Schi-Pass Kasenbureau** on Dorfstrasse (✆ **06541/6271**).

The Saalbach-Hinterglemm visitors' racing course is open Tuesday through Sunday from 10am to noon and 2 to 4pm, with slaloms, giant slaloms, and parallel slaloms being held. Both resorts have ski schools and provide ski-circus runs. In the winter, tobogganing is also popular, as are ski-bobbing, sleigh rides, and curling. Many cross-country ski tracks start from here.

From spring until late in the autumn, you can take quiet walks or extended hikes along some 257km (160 miles) of well-laid-out footpaths, as well as go mountain climbing, horseback riding, or bowling, or play minigolf and tennis. A nearby lake is great for swimming and sailing. A kindergarten caters exclusively to vacationers' children.

Saalbach can be a good base for exploring the neighboring resorts of Kaprun and Zell am See (see below).

Essentials

GETTING THERE The nearest **railway** line is at Zell am See (see section 7). Here, you'll have to transfer to one of the many **buses** that travel up the winding valley road. Buses depart from the railway station at Zell am See about every hour throughout the day, stopping first at Saalbach (trip time: 30 min.) and then continuing on to Hinterglemm (40 min.).

 If you're **driving,** take Route 312 southwest from Salzburg to Lofer, and then cut south at the junction with Route 311.

VISITOR INFORMATION The **tourist office** (✆ **06541/680068**) is in the center of Saalbach but also provides information for Hinterglemm. It's open in winter Monday to Saturday 9am to 6pm, and Sunday 9am to noon; in summer Monday to Friday 8:15am to noon and 1:30 to 6pm, Saturday 8:15am to noon and 3 to 6pm, Sunday 9am to noon.

Where to Stay & Dine

Most visitors dine at their hotels.

Expensive

Alpenhotel Saalbach ★ Built in 1968, this fairly large chalet-style hotel is renovated in part every 2 years. Its convenient location in the center of Saalbach is near the cable car, chairlifts, and tennis courts. The cozy, well-furnished interior includes a collection of country artifacts and several fireplaces. Your host, the Thomas family, rents comfortable rooms plus a series of suites or apartments sleeping two to six guests, suitable for extended stays. Those opening onto private balconies are the most requested.

Part of the hotel's draw is that it's a major gathering spot for the whole resort. It has a trio of restaurants, including the Pipamex, the Vitrine, and La Trattoria. La Trattoria, for example, is both an Italian pizzeria and a Spanish bodega. Pipamex is also a pizzeria but offers Mexican tacos, nachos, and fajitas. The most popular after-dark diversion is the Arena, which is also a nightclub.

Dorfstrasse 212, A-5753 Saalbach. ✆ **06541/6666.** Fax 06541/6666888. www.alpenhotel.at. 96 units. Winter 140€–320€ ($224–$512) double, 240€–570€ ($384–$912) suite; summer 98€–200€ ($157–$320) double, 198€–276€ ($317–$442) suite. Rates include half-board. AE, DC, MC, V. Parking 11€ ($18). Closed Apr 15–May 20 and Oct 15–Dec 19. **Amenities:** 3 restaurants; 3 bars; indoor heated pool; health club; Jacuzzi; sauna; bike rentals; room service; babysitting; laundry service; dry cleaning. *In room:* TV, Wi-Fi, minibar, hair dryer, safe.

Eva Village Hotel ★★ The Unterkofler family has taken over this popular hotel—once called the Ingonda—and have improved it considerably, pampering guests as never before. This hotel restaurant exudes an aura of well-established, even antique, prosperity. The hotel enjoys a status as the finest of the government-rated four-star hotels in town. In the center of Saalbach in a traffic-free zone, it is first class all the way. The hotel contains well-furnished rooms, each with a balcony, armchairs, and desk space.

Skiers appreciate the hotel's proximity to the village's three ski lifts, a 1-minute trek from the entrance on skis. In the well-recommended restaurant, guests enjoy such specialties as scampi flambeed in gin, filet of beef jambalaya, tender cuts of well-seasoned beef, and homemade strudels. If you're dropping in to dine in season, reserve a table. Aside from Eva's five-star restaurant, the social center is a rambling pine-covered bar with an intricately crafted wood ceiling and comfortable leather chairs.

Dorfstrasse 218, A-5753 Saalbach. ✆ **06541/6262-0.** Fax 06541/626262. www.evahotels.at. 73 units. Winter 226€–448€ ($362–$717) double, 294€–450€ ($470–$720) suite; off-season 106€–158€ ($170–$253) double, 136€–234€ ($218–$374) suite. Rates include half-board. AE, DC, MC, V. Parking 9€ ($14) in winter, free in summer. Closed Oct to mid-Dec. **Amenities:** Restaurant; bar; indoor heated pool; fitness center; Jacuzzi; sauna; room service; massage; babysitting; rooms for those w/limited mobility; solarium. *In room:* TV, Wi-Fi, minibar, hair dryer, safe.

Hotel Glemmtalerhof This chalet-style hotel rises six stories above the village's central street. Built in 1951, it was partially rebuilt in 1992. The street level contains a few small shops. Inside, the hotel offers cozy public areas, some with fireplaces. There are public tennis courts only a few buildings away. Rooms, covered with mellow pine and invitingly lit, are medium-size and exceedingly comfortable, with fine beds and ample bathrooms. A *tagesmenu* (daily menu) is offered at lunch and dinner. The hotel staff can also organize mountain or biking excursions for you.

Glemmtalerlaudstrasse 150, A-5754 Hinterglemm. © **06541/7135.** Fax 06541/713563. www.glemmtalerhof.at. 85 units. Winter 168€–258€ ($269–$413) double; summer 118€–156€ ($189–$250) double. Rates include half-board. AE, DC, MC, V. Parking 8€ ($13). Closed Apr 15–May 15 and Nov 1–Dec 15. **Amenities:** Restaurant; 3 bars; cafe; nightclub; indoor heated pool; 3 tennis courts (nearby); fitness center; sauna; room service; massage; babysitting; laundry service; dry cleaning. *In room:* TV, Wi-Fi, hair dryer, safe.

Moderate

Gasthof Unterwirt Built in 1973 as a modern interpretation of a traditional chalet, this pleasant and relaxed establishment, with its rustic decor of ceiling beams and ceramic tile stoves, is owned by the Kroll family. Rooms range from small to medium and have traditional alpine furnishings. Bathrooms are equipped mostly with tub/shower combinations and are beautifully maintained. The international and regional cuisine is hearty and plentiful.

Unterdorf 31, A-5753 Saalbach. © **06541/6274.** Fax 06541/627455. www.saalbach-unterwirt.at. 53 units. Winter 160€–210€ ($256–$336) double; summer 102€–110€ ($163–$176) double. Rates include half-board. MC, V. Closed Mar 30–May 15 and Nov 1–Dec 10. **Amenities:** Restaurant; bar; sauna; steam bath; laundry service; dry cleaning. *In room:* TV, Wi-Fi, hair dryer.

Hotel Haus Wolf If you're interested in ski lessons, this might be an ideal place to stay, since the local ski school is headquartered here. The hotel, right beside the Reiterkogel cable car, has wooden balconies and a first-floor sun terrace. In winter, fires burn beneath copper-sheathed chimneys, and guests often congregate in one of the several bars or restaurants. A smaller annex provides comfortable but less-inspired accommodations. The alpine-style rooms have good, firm beds, and small but efficient bathrooms.

Reiterkogelweg 169, A-5754 Hinterglemm. © **06541/6346.** Fax 06541/634669. www.wolf-hotels.at. 45 units. 188€ ($301) double; 228€ ($365) suite. Rates include half-board. MC, V. Closed Apr 15–May 15 and Oct 15–Dec 20. **Amenities:** Restaurant; bar; indoor heated pool; sauna; babysitting; laundry service; dry cleaning. *In room:* TV, minibar, hair dryer, safe.

Hotel Kristiana ★ (Value) A local favorite since it was built in 1979, this well-managed hotel lies a short walk uphill from the village center. Balconies adorn its facade, and in one corner, just above the sun terrace, an artist has executed a series of etched panels depicting the seasons. The interior is a rustic fantasy of carved beams and well-polished paneling, open fireplaces, and comfortable, well-planned rooms. Most rooms have fine views and individual character, and all are equipped with good beds and spotless bathrooms. Owner Johann Breitfuss and his family serve tasty meals to hotel guests only and maintain a pleasant bar.

Oberdorf 40, A-5753 Saalbach. © **06541/6253.** Fax 06541/625399. www.kristiana.at. 34 units. Winter 152€–270€ ($243–$432) double; summer 120€–256€ ($192–$410) double. Rates include half-board. MC, V. Closed Apr–May 15 and Oct–Dec 10. **Amenities:** Restaurant; bar; sauna; room service; babysitting. *In room:* TV, Wi-Fi, hair dryer, safe.

The Resorts After Dark

Saalbach is one of the liveliest centers in Land Salzburg for nightlife. The after-skiing crowd shuttles back and forth between Saalbach and Hinterglemm, and after a few drinks, the resorts seem to merge into one.

Hexenhäusl, Zwolferkogelbahnweg 122 (© **06541/6334**), is one of the busiest and most consistently popular après-ski venues in Hinterglemm. Positioned at the bottom of the Zwolferkogelbahn gondola, it combines the functions of a bar, pub, and cafe into a rowdy, sudsy, beery, schnapps-permeated mountain hut. Cozy, dark, candlelit, and moderately claustrophobic, it's a place where English and French skiers mingle with locals, some of whom aren't particularly interested in skiing at all. Beer sells for 2.50€ to 6€ ($4–$9.60); snacks such as strudels, pizzas, and baguettes sell for 1.75€ to 5.50€ ($2.80–$8.80). You'll recognize the place by the carved effigies of *hexen* (witches) that decorate the outside and inside of this folkloric but very hip place. From May to October, it's open Tuesday to Saturday 3pm to 6am; November to April it's open daily 3pm to 6am—so late that anyone who actually remains on-site till closing will probably not venture onto the ski slopes the following day.

Since its opening in the 1950s, **Hotel Glemmtalerhof,** Glemmtalerlaudstrasse 150, Hinterglemm (✆ **06541/7135**), has always maintained an active nightlife for both vacationers and local residents. The folksy Glemmerkeller Nightclub hosts a series of live bands performing everything from Bavarian oompah music to more modern (and highly danceable) tunes. It's open every night 9pm to 3am, although during ski season it's also open every afternoon for post-slopes revelry from 4 to 6pm. A small but energetic dance club, the **Almbar** plays high-volume sounds from New York, London, and Los Angeles. There's no cover to get into either bar, and beer costs 3€ ($4.80) in summer and 4€ ($6.40) in winter.

In winter, live dance music is usually featured at **Knappenhof Knappenkeller,** Knappenhof Tirolerhof, Hauptstrasse 222, Hinterglemm (✆ **06541/6497**), while the adjacent dance club plays recorded tunes. Sometimes Tyrolean music is interspersed with more modern sounds. Grilled specialties are offered as well as Wiener schnitzel, pizza, and Italian food, with meals beginning at 10€ ($16). The cover charge of 8€ ($13) includes your first drink. Open daily from 9pm to 4am; closed in October.

The cellar at **Saalbacher Hof,** Dorfstrasse 27, Saalbach (✆ **06541/7111**), is devoted every Wednesday to drinking, dancing, and alpine folk music. On other nights of the week, the theme is more modern. The music begins around 8:30pm in summer and winter. There's no cover; beer costs 4.50€ ($7.20).

Club Discoteque Club, in Berger's Sporthotel, Dorfstrasse 33, Saalbach (✆ **06541/6577**), offers good bands and good drinks (often many good drinks) to a young crowd energized by a day on the slopes. A beer starts at 4€ ($6.40). It's open December to March daily from 9pm to 3am.

SAALFELDEN ★

An old market town lying in a broad valley formed by the Saalbach River, Saalfelden is set against a background of towering mountains in the Middle Pinzgau. This is a good center for exploring the **Steinernes Meer,** or Sea of Stone, a limestone plateau with underground rivers and caverns that the Austrian government has turned into a nature reserve. Saalfelden lies 64km (40 miles) south of Salzburg and 399km (248 miles) southwest of Vienna.

Although Saalfelden is primarily a summer resort, winter-sports areas in the mountains are within easy reach. The town has a **Pfarrkirche (Parish Church)** with a gothic crypt beneath the choir and a late-Gothic triptych in the presbytery.

At **Ritzen Castle** (✆ **06582/72759**), which dates from 1563, the Heimatmuseum is devoted to life in the Pinzgau region. Here you'll see a rich collection of Christmas cribs by artist Xandl Schläffer. Another hall displays pictures and ecclesiastic art along with exhibits tracing the geology of Saalfelden, a peasant's room from the 1700s, an open-hearth kitchen, native handicrafts, and various documents on the history of the area. Admission is 3.30€ ($5.30) for adults and 1€ ($1.60) for children. It's open from June 16 to September 15 Tuesday to Friday from 10am to noon and 2 to 5pm, and Saturday and Sunday from 2 to 5pm; off-season, it's open Wednesday, Saturday, and Sunday from 2 to 4pm and is closed in March, April, and November.

Essentials

GETTING THERE Saalfelden is a major stop on express and local trains from both Innsbruck and Salzburg. **Trains** from Innsbruck are usually direct, while trains from Salzburg sometimes require a change in Schwarzach–St. Veit. With transfers included, the trip from both cities to Saalfelden takes about 1 2/3 hours. Trains arrive there about once an hour throughout the day. For train information, call ✆ **05/1717,** or visit **www.oebb.at**.

Although Saalfelden is the transfer point for many **bus** routes heading into the surrounding mountains, few visitors would consider reaching Saalfelden by bus from any large Austrian city, with the possible exception of Salzburg. These buses depart from Salzburg's main railway station about six times a day, making many stops en route (trip time: about 95 min.).

If you're **driving** from Zell am See, head north along Route 311. From Salzburg, head southwest on Route 312. At Lofer, continue south on Route 311.

VISITOR INFORMATION The **tourist office** is at Bahnhofstrasse 10 (✆ **06582/70660;** www.leogang-saalfelden.at). It's open in winter Monday to Friday 8am to 5pm, and Saturday from 9am to noon; in summer Monday to Friday from 8am to 6pm, Saturday from 9am to noon.

Where to Stay

Hotel Gasthof Hindenburg ★★ Set in the heart of Saalfelden, this hotel is one of the oldest in the region, with foundations and a reputation for hospitality that date back more than 500 years, and an alpine design that looks a lot older than the 1992 renovation that transformed it into the hip-roofed, many-gabled design you'll see today. Rooms are cozily outfitted with mostly contemporary furniture. There's a trio of restaurants, the most formal of which is the richly paneled Gastestube. Overall, it's a worthy government-rated four-star choice with as many luxuries and conveniences as any of its competitors in Saalfelden.

Bahnhofstrasse 6, A-5760 Saalfelden. ✆ **06582/7930.** Fax 06582/79378. www.hotel-hindenburg.at. 45 units. 178€–208€ ($285–$333) double. Rates include half-board. AE, DC, MC, V. **Amenities:** 3 restaurants; bar; sauna; room service; babysitting; laundry service; dry cleaning; solarium. *In room:* TV, Wi-Fi, minibar, hair dryer, safe.

Where to Dine

Restaurant Schatzbichl AUSTRIAN At this alpine country house, waitresses wearing regional garb serve time-honored recipes. Specialties are often brought to your table in a copper pan for members of your party to dig into with forks and spoons. You might enjoy *Kasfarfeln* (thick consommé with cheese, onions, chives, and dumplings) or our favorite, *Erdäpfelgröstl* (a big pot with potatoes, broth, sausages, onions, and chives).

Ramseiden 82. ✆ **06582/73281.** www.schatzbichl.at. Reservations recommended. Main courses 9.80€–15€ ($16–$24). AE, DC, MC, V. Fri–Wed noon–2pm and 6–10pm.

KAPRUN & ITS DAMS

A summer resort and a winter ski center, Kaprun is known for its high glacier skiing. The town is hardly the most attractive or the most atmospheric in Land Salzburg, but serious skiers don't seem to mind.

Essentials

GETTING THERE The nearest railway station is in Zell am See, 8km (5 miles) north. From here, about 14 **buses** a day depart for the 15-minute uphill run to Kaprun. (***Note:*** Don't confuse the village of Kaprun with the more southerly and much more isolated ski hamlet of Kaprun Heidnische Kirche, which requires an additional transfer.) **Motorists** in Zell am See should head west on Route 168 to Fürth, at which point they can cut south on an unclassified road to Kaprun.

VISITOR INFORMATION The **tourist office** (✆ **06547/8643**) is in the town center. Open Monday to Friday 9am to 6pm, Saturday 9am to noon, and Sunday 2 to 6pm.

Exploring the Valley of Kaprun

The area takes in the Valley of Kaprun and its powerful dams, as well as the surrounding heights. An ascent to the **Kitzsteinhorn** (2,931m/9,616 ft.) can be quite complicated, involving postal buses, funiculars, and cableways, but it's equally rewarding. Always have your routes outlined at the tourist office with a detailed area map before you set forth. An English-speaking staff member will supply the best possible routes and provide you with the most up-to-date information on hours, costs, types of services likely to be available at the time of your visit, and weather conditions. For example, after mid-October, tours to the valley of the dams might not be possible. However, a visit to the Kitzsteinhorn is an attraction in both summer and winter.

To reach the Kitzsteinhorn, you can take either a cable car, transferring to the *langweidbahn* (a chairlift), or the glacier railway, an underground funicular, to the Restaurant Alpincenter (2,446m/8,025 ft.), where you can enjoy lunch with a view halfway up Kitzsteinhorn. At Alpincenter, change to a cable car, which swings west, coming to a stop near the summit of the Kitzsteinhorn.

A little below the summit, you'll find the 305m (1,001-ft.) **Panoramatunnel** (✆ **06547/86210**) cut through the mountain and opening onto an incredible view of Nationalpark Hohe Tauern. On clear days, you'll be able to see Grossglockner, the highest peak in Austria, at 3,764m (12,349 ft.). You can also eat at the Aussichtsrestaurant (talk about dining with a view!), or if you want to feel snow in summer, you can take a short cable car down to the glacier.

It's best to purchase a day ticket—round-trip, naturally—for both the cable railway and the glacier lift; it costs 35€ ($56) for adults and 17€ ($27) for children under 15. It's open daily from 8am to 4pm.

The Dams

The **Kapruner Tal** ★, or the Valley of Kaprun, is visited in summer for its dams, one of the more dramatic alpine sights. Constructed in tiers, the dams were originally built as part of the U.S.-financed Marshall Plan. Experts from all over the world come here to study these hydroelectric constructions, which are brilliant feats of engineering.

Visit the hydroelectric plant, Turbinenhaus, inside the **Tauernkraftwerke** (✆ **06547/7 151527**). Its shafts, tunnels, turbines, and bulwarks are an interesting change of pace for most visitors. A small museum, filled with technical drawings and photographs, conveys the magnitude of the project.

If you want to explore the region and see how the dams manage to hold back up to 19 billion gallons of alpine water, the staff at Kaprun's tourist information office offers a self-guided full-day tour for 18€ ($23) that encompasses overviews of the three lakes formed by the dams and transportation. The ascent up to the dams, including the **Limsbergsperre,** the **Moosersperre ★★**, and the **Drossensperre,** is via yellow post buses and a funicular. You can visit daily from 8am to 4pm from mid-May to mid-October, depending on weather conditions.

Where to Stay & Dine

Hotel Orgler (Kids) This cream-colored house is in the middle of the village. Slightly isolated from its neighbors, it offers peace, quiet, and a rustic interior of high ceilings, heavy beams, and chalet furniture. Each room has a balcony and a medium-size bathroom. Apartments with three or four beds are available for families. The hotel's dining room and restaurant are furnished in traditional Austrian style, as are the cozy lounges and the bar with an open fireplace.

Schlossstrasse 22, A-5710 Kaprun. ✆ **06547/8205.** Fax 06547/7567. www.hotel-orgler.at. 37 units. Winter 146€–260€ ($234–$416) double, 230€–357€ ($368–$571) suite; summer 139€–145€ ($222–$232) double, 250€ ($400) per person apt. Rates include half-board. DC, MC, V. Parking 10€ ($16). **Amenities:** Restaurant; bar; 36-hole golf course; tennis court; fitness center; Jacuzzi; sauna; room service; babysitting; laundry service; dry cleaning; nonsmoking rooms; solarium. *In room:* TV, Wi-Fi, minibar, hair dryer, safe.

Sporthotel Kaprun On the village's outskirts, this large chalet has a sloping roof and flowered balconies. Built in 1977, it has paneled ceilings, big windows, and spacious public areas. The good-size rooms are modern and comfortable, and most have a balcony. Bathrooms are carefully maintained and equipped mostly with tub/shower combinations. There's a restaurant for half-board diners, plus a pizzeria.

A-5710 Kaprun. ✆ **06547/86250.** Fax 06547/862519. www.sporthotel-kaprun.at. 60 units. 128€–194€ ($205–$310) double. Rates include half-board. AE, MC, V. Take the cable lift to the stations at the southern exit of Kaprun. **Amenities:** Restaurant; bar; fitness center; game room; sauna; room service; babysitting; laundry service; dry cleaning; nonsmoking rooms; solarium. *In room:* TV, Wi-Fi, minibar, hair dryer, safe.

Kaprun After Dark

Kaprun has its own relatively modest nightlife, but should you ever get bored, take the shuttle bus over to Zell am See for much more excitement. Nightlife reaches its modest peak in Kaprun on Friday and Saturday nights. On other nights you might like to turn in with a good book or sit and drink around an open fire. Nearly all hotels and pensions welcome outside guests.

One of the most popular spots in town is the coffee shop, **Morokutti,** Nikolaus-Gassner-Strasse 572 (✆ **06547/8424**). It's open daily from 9:30am to 11pm but is closed Tuesday in April and June. A glass of wine costs 3€ ($4.80), and hot coffee starts at 2.80€ ($4.50).

Café Baum Bar (✆ **06547/8216**) is less than 1.5km (1 mile) north of Kaprun's center, far enough from all the hotels that the noisy crowd won't disturb anyone's sleep. This is the largest, most crowded, and most sociable watering hole in town. Although a part of it is devoted to serving pizzas, Wiener schnitzels, pastas, salads, and sandwiches, it's best known as a dance club that thumps every night of the week, summer and winter, from 9pm to 3am. Kitchen hours vary according to demand but usually last to midnight. Management runs minivans between Kaprun's center and the Baum at frequent intervals, although some visitors opt for a midnight walk (or crawl) to and from the site. The place was built, incidentally, as an outbuilding for a local cattle farm in the 1930s. Pizzas cost

6€ to 10€ ($9.60–$16). The dance club's cover charge is 2€ to 7€ ($3.20–$11), depending on the live act; it's free when there's recorded music. Beer begins at 2€ ($3.20) in the early afternoon but increases in price to 3€ ($4.80) after 9pm.

There's also dancing at the **Nindl Café,** Nikolaus-Gassner-Strasse 380 (✆ **06547/8259**). In winter, folk shows are presented along with live and recorded music. There's no cover. Call to find out what's happening at the time of your visit. It's open daily from 11am to 1am in winter (5pm–1am in summer), but is closed 2 weeks in June and September. Beer costs 3€ ($4.80). Snacks, such as salads, pizzas, and hamburgers, are served at Nindl's cafe daily from 4pm to 2am.

KRIMML

Krimml is the best base for exploring the Krimml Falls. The village is in a heavily forested valley called Krimmler Ache, between the Kitzbühel Alps and the Hohe Tauern. Although it's mostly a summer resort, there's also good skiing at **Gerlosplatte** (1,708m/5,604 ft.), 11km (7 miles) away.

Essentials

GETTING THERE A slow local **train,** making more than 50 stops en route, travels from Zell am See to Krimml. Trains depart every 2 to 3 hours (trip time: about 90 min.). Contact ✆ **05/1717** (www.oebb.at) for rail information. About a dozen buses depart every day from the railway station at Zell am See for Krimml (trip time: about 75 min.). If you're **driving** from Zell am See, take Route 168 west to Mittersill, and continue west along Route 165.

VISITOR INFORMATION The **tourist office** (✆ **06564/7239-0;** www.krimml.at) in the town center is open Monday to Friday 8:30am to noon and 2:30 to 5:30pm, Sunday 8:30 to 10:30am and 4:30 to 6pm. Krimml lies 153km (95 miles) southwest of Salzburg.

Krimml Falls ★★★

This village in the far-western extremity of Land Salzburg is visited mainly for the iridescent **Krimmler Wasserfälle (Krimml Falls)** (✆ **06564/7212**). The highest in Europe, these spectacular falls drop 381m (1,250 ft.) in three stages. They lie to the south of the Gerlos Pass, which connects the Salzach Valley in Land Salzburg to the Siller Valley in the Tyrol.

If you drive here, you can either leave your car at the parking lot at the south of the village and walk 30 minutes to the lower falls, or take the Gerlos Pass toll road, open from June 1 to September 30. If you don't have a car, you can take one of the frequent buses marked [illegible] from the center of town. Get off at Maustelle Ort, where the path to the falls begins. The falls are open from the end of April to the end of October daily from 8am to 6pm; it costs 1.80€ ($2.90) for adults and .50€ (80¢) for children.

Visitors should allow about 3½ hours to explore the entire falls area. On a sunny day, try to visit around noon when the falls are at their most dramatic. In summer, the waterfalls are likely to be floodlit on Wednesday nights, depending on weather conditions. Wear good, sturdy shoes and, if you don't want to get sprayed, a raincoat.

After you've checked out the lower falls, if you want to see the second stage, count on another 12-minute walk. From here it's only another 5 minutes to the third and final stage for viewing the cataracts. There are paths leading to two more viewing points. The middle part of the falls can be seen at the sixth and seventh lookouts. At the Bergerblick, you'll have your greatest view of the waterfalls, reached by continuing another 20 minutes from the seventh viewing point. If you want, you can go on to the Schettbrücke (1,464m/4,803 ft.) for a look at the upper cascades. The waterfalls lie under a deep ice layer during the winter.

Where to Stay & Dine

Hotel Klockerhaus (Value) This peaceful two-story chalet has wooden balconies from which you can view the Krimml Falls. Located on the border of the Hohe Tauern National Park, the family hotel has well-furnished lounges. Rooms range from small to medium, each tastefully decorated and immaculately kept with good beds, ample bathrooms with mostly tub/shower combinations, and balconies. The kitchen serves Austrian and international specialties. The proprietor, Mr. Ingo Czerny, sees to the well-being of his customers.

Wasserfallstrasse 10, A-5743 Krimml. ✆ **06564/7208.** Fax 06564/720846. www.klockerhaus.com. 43 units. Winter 90€–172€ ($144–$275) double; summer 72€–92€ ($115–$147) double. Rates include breakfast. MC, V. Closed Nov. **Amenities:** Restaurant; lounge; fitness center; sauna; Jacuzzi; massage; rooms for those w/limited mobility. *In room:* TV, hair dryer.

Hotel Krimmlerfälle (Kids) Sea-green shutters and wood siding cover the third and fourth floors of this pretty four-story house, built a century ago but renovated many times since. The congenial hosts, the Schöppl family, rent tasteful and comfortable rooms with balconies covered in pink and red flowers in summer. Some rooms are in a less desirable annex nearby. These are rather bland and only functionally furnished, but they're still comfortable. Rooms in the main building tend to be more spacious, but all are equipped with comfortable beds and small but spotless bathrooms.

Wasserfallstrasse 42, A-5743 Krimml. ✆ **06564/7203.** Fax 06564/7473. www.krimmlerfaelle.at. 58 units. Winter 130€–238€ ($208–$381) double; summer 100€–154€ ($160–$246) double. Rates include half-board. AE, DC, MC, V. Closed Oct 19–Dec 12. **Amenities:** Restaurant; bar; lounge; 2 heated pools (1 indoor, 1 outdoor); spa; sauna; children's playrooms; room service; massage; babysitting. *In room:* TV, hair dryer.

6 THE GROSSGLOCKNER ROAD ★★★

The longest and most splendid alpine highway in Europe, and one of the biggest tourist attractions on the continent, **Grossglocknerstrasse** (Rte. 107) will afford you one of the greatest drives of your life.

The hairpin turns and bends would challenge even Grand Prix drivers. It's believed that this was the same route through the Alps used by the Romans, although this was forgotten until 1930, when engineers building the highway discovered remains of the work their road-building predecessors did some 19 centuries earlier. This engineering feat was finished in 1935. Switzerland and France copied it years later when they built their own alpine highways.

The highway runs for nearly 48km (30 miles), beginning at Bruck an der Grossglocknerstrasse at 757m (2,484 ft.), via Fusch/Grossglocknerstrasse; heading toward Ferleiten, Hochmais, and Fuschtörl through the Hochtortunnel, where the highest point is 2,507m (8,225 ft.); and then to Guttal and Heiligenblut (1,301m/4,268 ft.) in Carinthia. The actual mountain part of the road stretches for some 22km (14 miles), usually at about 1,983m (6,506 ft.). It has a maximum gradient of 12%.

Many visitors opt to drive this spectacular stretch, but because of the high altitudes, the road is passable only from mid-May to mid-November, depending on weather conditions. Always check with some authority about the road conditions before considering such a drive, especially in spring and autumn. The passenger car toll for a round-trip is 28€ ($45) for an 8-day ticket or 8€ ($13) for a 1-day ticket, and is collected at either Ferleiten or Heiligenblut.

You can also take a yellow-sided Austrian Postal Bus from Zell am See. From May to October, the buses depart from in front of the main railway station twice daily at 8:50 and 9:50am. Stopping at about a dozen small villages en route, the buses meander up Grossglockner to its most panoramic point, the Franz-Josefs-Höhe, where passengers can get out and explore for about 2½ hours before boarding the same buses (at 2:45 and 3:45pm, respectively) and returning to Zell am See. A round-trip ticket costs 18€ ($29). For information, call either the tourist office in Zell am See (✆ **06542/7700**) or the local bus station (✆ **06542/544412**).

Going south from Bruck, you enter the Foscher Valley, where the road winds through beautiful alpine scenery. Six kilometers (4 miles) from the Hochtortunnel on the north side, you can branch off onto Edelweiss-Strasse, going along for about 2km (1½ miles) to the parking lot at the Edelweiss-Spitze (2,572m/8,438 ft.). The stunning view from here encompasses mountains rising 3,048m (10,000-ft.). This is the best vantage point to take in the tremendous mountain and alpine lakes of the **Hohe Tauern National Park.** Really a massive mountain range, the Hohe Tauern covers 29 towns, 304 separate mountains, and nearly 250 glaciers. At Edelweiss-Spitze is an observation tower, going up to more than 2,577m (8,455 ft.).

One of the interesting detours along the road is to the stone terrace of the **Franz-Josefs-Höhe ★★★**. It's named for the emperor who once had a mansion constructed here in the foothills of the Pasterze Glacier. The stretch from Gletscherstrasse to Franz-Josefs-Höhe (2,370m/7,776 ft.) is some 8km (5 miles) long, branching off near Guttal. This road lies above the Pasterze Glacier, opposite the Grossglockner (3,791m/12,438 ft.). The Pasterze, incidentally, is the largest glacier in the eastern Alps, 9km (5½ miles) long.

If you're traveling in spring and autumn, it might not be possible to take detours to the Edelweiss-Spitze or the Franz-Josefs-Höhe if heavy snow falls. If you do take the side trip to the latter site, avoid arriving there around midday. On a bright, sunny day in summer, the place is literally mobbed. It has an outstanding view of the majestic Grossglockner.

From May to September it's possible to descend from Freiwandeck to Pasterze Glacier by funicular. Service is available every hour daily 8am to 4pm.

7 ZELL AM SEE ★

389km (242 miles) SW of Vienna; 85km (53 miles) SW of Salzburg

Founded by monks around the middle of the 8th century, the old part of Zell am See lies on the shore of the Zeller See (Lake Zell), under a backdrop of mountains. The Zeller See is a deep glacial lake filled with clear blue alpine water. The town today is the most popular resort in the Middle Pinzgau, a district that has already been previewed in section 5, "The Pinzgau." Zell is crowded and fashionable in both summer and winter. It's also a center for those who'd like to get an early start and travel the Grossglockner alpine highway, described above.

ESSENTIALS

GETTING THERE Zell am See is one of the most important stops astride the rail lines carrying passengers between Salzburg and Innsbruck. Consequently, express **trains** arrive from Innsbruck about once an hour, after the under-2-hour trip. Trains from Salzburg take about 90 minutes and depart about once an hour as well. Frequent connections are also possible to and from Klagenfurt, although a transfer is required at the nearby railway junction of Schwarzach–St. Veit, about 34km (21 miles) to the east. Contact ✆ **05/1717** (www.oebb.at) for rail information.

Zell am See is the junction for several **bus** routes heading upward into the surrounding mountains. Because of the many transfers required for passengers coming from outside the immediate region, however, most visitors arrive by train.

If you're **driving** from Salzburg, cut south on the A10 to the junction with Route 311, at which point you head west.

VISITOR INFORMATION The **tourist office** on Bruckner Bundesstrasse (✆ **06542/7700;** www.zellamsee-kaprun.com) is open Monday to Friday 9am to 6pm, Saturday 9am to noon, and Sunday 10am to noon.

SEEING THE SIGHTS

Unlike most resorts in Land Salzburg, Zell am See has some old buildings worth exploring. These include the **Kastnerturm,** or Constable's Tower, the oldest building in town, dating from the 12th century. It was once used as a grain silo. The town's **Pfarrkirche (Parish Church)** is an 11th-century Romanesque structure. Inside is a late-gothic choir from the 16th century. **Castle Rosenberg,** also from the 16th century, was once an elegant residence of the free state of Salzburg, built in the southern Bavarian style. Today it houses the Rathaus (town hall) with a gallery.

The **folklore museum** is in the old tower, the Vogtturm, near the town square. The tower is about 1,200 years old. In the museum, old costumes are displayed, and exhibited artifacts show the traditional way of life in old Land Salzburg. From May to October, the museum is open Monday, Wednesday, and Friday 1:30 to 5:30pm. Admission is 2.80€ ($4.50) for adults and 1.50€ ($2.40) children ages 6 to 15; family ticket 4.50€ ($7.20).

WINTER & SUMMER SPORTS

For winter visitors, snow conditions in the Zell area are usually ideal from December to the end of April. Zell am See attracts beginner and intermediate skiers, plus many nonskiers—people who like the bustling life of the winter resort even if they never take to the slopes. Even if skiing isn't your thing, take the chairlift (shoes are fine) for the alpine scenery. Skiing is possible at elevations ranging from 915 to 2,745m (3,002 to 9,006 ft.).

There is a Zell/Kaprun Ski Pass that covers both Zell am See and Kaprun. A 2-day pass costs 65€ ($104) and is sold at the tourist office in Zell am See and often at the lifts. A free shuttle bus runs between the two resorts during the day from December 20 to April 13 every 15 minutes. If you're coming to Land Salzburg to ski, we recommend purchasing a ski package from your travel agent. A package will include the cost of all lifts and ski passes, and will be more economical than paying for each activity separately.

Sports fans gravitate to the **Kur-und-Sportzentrum,** an arena northwest of the resort housing a mammoth indoor swimming pool as well as saunas and an ice rink (sometimes in cold weather the lake is frozen over).

Zell am See also attracts visitors in the peak summer months. **Lake Zell,** which has been called the cleanest lake in Europe, is warm, maintaining an average temperature of some 70°F (21°C) in summer. The lake is 4km (2$^1/_2$ miles) long and 2km (1 mile) wide. Motorboats can be rented. You can go along a footpath from the town to the bathing station at Seespitz, a half-hour walk.

GOING UP THE SCHMITTENHÖHE ★★

Schmittenhöhe, at 1,967m (6,453 ft.), towers to the west of Zell am See. There are four different ways to ascend the mountain, with even more options for getting down. In summer, the hardy have been known to climb it in 4 hours. We suggest, however, that you take the cableway. The view from here is one of the finest in the Kitzbühel Alps, the majestic glacial peaks of the Grossglockner range. You can have lunch at the Berghotel at the upper station. From the west side of Zell am See, you can also take a four-seat cableway to the middle station. From here you can connect with several lifts that will take you to the upper platform. A sun terrace at the upper station is popular in both summer and winter. Don't be surprised to see bare breasts, even in February. It's about 1.5km (1 mile) up Schmittenhöhe. Figure on at least 1$^3/_4$ hours for your round-trip, plus another 18 minutes by cable car. In summer, service is every half-hour.

You can also take the Sonnalm cableway (entrance near the Schmittenhöhe terminus) to Sonnalm at 1,385m (4,544 ft.). Another restaurant is perched here. From Sonnalm, it's possible to go by chairlift to Sonnkogel (1,836m/6,024 ft.) and by surface lift to Hochmais (1,728m/5,669 ft.). From the eastern part of Lake Zell, you can take the chairlift up to Ronachkopf (1,487m/4,879 ft.).

From Zell am See, you can also take a funicular to Kaprun (see section 5, earlier in this chapter), at the foot of the Kitzsteinhorn, for glacier and year-round skiing. In fact, some of the most spectacular excursions possible from Kaprun can be made easily from Zell am See (refer to the Kaprun section for more details).

WHERE TO STAY & DINE

Expensive

Hotel Salzburgerhof ★★ Just a glimpse of the handcrafted interior of this government-rated five-star chalet-style hotel near the lake, and you know you're in for a treat. Inside, a fire blazes in an unusual stucco fireplace in the salon. The Holleis family maintains the pleasant outdoor garden with its sun terrace for summer barbecues. Evening programs include dancing, playing the zither, and telling folk tales. Accommodations include suites with private saunas and open fireplaces. Rooms are carpeted and well maintained, if lacking in style, they have generous storage space and balconies with a nice view.

The hotel's restaurant serves some of the area's finest regional specialties. A 6-course fixed-price menu might include such classic dishes as cream of sauerkraut with smoked meat dumplings, cream of black salsify (oyster plant) with truffled dumplings, and filet of jack salmon in a potato crust. Many of the chef's best dishes are fish from either the lake or the sea.

Auerspergstrasse 11, A-5700 Zell am See. ✆ **06542/765.** Fax 06542/76566. www.salzburgerhof.at. 70 units. Winter 300€–570€ ($480–$912) double, 330€–900€ ($528–$1,440) suite for 2; summer 250€–320€ ($400–$512) double, 280€–610€ ($448–$976) suite for 2. Rates include half-board. AE, DC, MC, V. Free parking outside. Closed Nov. **Amenities:** Restaurant; bar; indoor heated pool; 36-hole golf course; fitness center; spa; Jacuzzi; sauna; salon; room service; massage; babysitting; laundry service; dry cleaning; nonsmoking rooms. *In room:* TV, Wi-Fi, minibar, hair dryer, safe.

Moderate

Grand Hotel ★ This is the third "grand hotel" that has stood on this site over the years, with the present structure dating from 1986. Based on a late-Victorian model, it's a wedding cake of mansard roofs and cream-colored stonework whose elaborate cornices and moldings are reflected in the cold waters of the lake. Centrally located on its own peninsula, it has a private beach and sun terrace. Although there are other four-star hotels in town of comparable range, this one enjoys the most desirable location, jutting into the lake. Most of the suites are in the main (Grand Hotel) building; the single and double rooms are in a more lackluster annex. Accommodations come in a wide range of sizes and designs, and some have kitchenettes. Sofa beds are comfortable, and the bathrooms are superb. Recreation instructors offer special programs on such sports as parasailing, river rafting, and glacier skiing. The indoor pool has a panoramic view overlooking the lake.

The restaurant offers fresh fish daily; equally appealing is the Imperial, a cozy bar.

Esplanade 4, A-5700 Zell am See. ✆ **06542/788-0.** Fax 06542/788305. www.grandhotel-zellamsee.at. 115 units. Winter 95€–180€ ($152–$288) per person double, 140€–242€ ($224–$387) per person suite; summer 75€–145€ ($120–$232) per person double, 130€–198€ ($208–$317) per person suite. Rates include half-board. AE, DC, MC, V. Parking 7€ ($11). Closed mid-Oct to mid-Nov and 2 weeks around Easter. **Amenities:** Restaurant; bar; indoor heated pool; fitness room; Jacuzzi; sauna; room service; massage; babysitting; laundry service; dry cleaning. *In room:* TV, Wi-Fi, dataport (some), minibar, hair dryer, safe.

Hotel St. Georg ★ Finds Hotel St. Georg, the stylish country hotel of Zell am See, is graced with flowery balconies and curved awnings. The interior has beamed ceilings, antique wrought iron, and old painted chests. Rooms are medium-size, well kept, and nicely decorated, with bathrooms equipped with tub/shower combinations. The hotel also rents five two-bedroom apartments, a favorite with families. Depending on the season, these apartments rent for 85€ to 160€ ($136–$256) per person. Apartments are suitable for up to five guests.

The restaurant has vaulted ceilings and a circular open fireplace. The Austrian cuisine is highly recommended. Try the marinated slices of ox with corn salad and tomato vinaigrette, or perhaps smoked salmon tartar. Main dishes might include medallions of deer in a juniper-cream sauce flavored with cinnamon, or filet of lamb in a thyme sauce with spinach.

Schillerstrasse 32, A-5700 Zell am See. ✆ **06542/768.** Fax 06542/768300. st.georg@zell-am-see.at. 36 units. Winter 152€–246€ ($243–$394) double, 314€ ($502) suite; off-season 122€–144€ ($195–$230) double, 264€ ($422) suite. Rates include half-board. AE, DC, MC, V. Free parking. Closed Apr. **Amenities:** Restaurant; bar; indoor heated pool; fitness center; sauna; room service; babysitting; laundry service; dry cleaning. *In room:* TV, Wi-Fi, minibar, hair dryer, safe.

Hotel St. Hubertushof ★ Value This large, sprawling hotel is designed like a collection of balconied chalets clustered into a single unit. The sober, elegant decor attracts many repeat visitors, and the flat-roofed dance bar ranks as one of the area's top nightspots. Run by owner Josef Hollaus, the hotel is located in one of the resort's sunniest spots. The large, comfortable, and rustic rooms are a bit cramped if you have a lot of ski equipment, but they contain fine beds. The menu in the adjoining restaurant includes international specialties as well as a few regional recipes. Meals are well prepared and beautifully served.

Seeuferstrasse 7, Thumersbach, A-5700 Zell am See. ✆ **06542/767.** Fax 06542/76771. www.zellamsee.at/hubertushof. 110 units. Winter 80€–134€ ($128–$214) double; summer 78€–116€ ($125–$186) double. Rates include half-board. AE, DC, MC, V. Closed mid-Oct to Nov. **Amenities:** Restaurant; bar; sauna. *In room:* TV, Wi-Fi.

Hotel Zum Hirschen Members of the Pacalt family are the congenial, hardworking owners of this balconied hotel with a central location across from the post office. The snug and comfortable rooms are traditionally furnished and bathrooms are moderate in size with spotless housekeeping. Guests can use the golf course for reduced fees.

Restaurant Zum Hirschen has a rustic setting of light-grained paneling. Specialties include fresh white fish from the nearby lake, mountain game, and homemade pâté. There's also creamed chipped veal or entrecote Café de Paris.

Dreifaltigkeitsstrasse 1, A-5700 Zell am See. ✆ **06542/774.** Fax 06542/7740. 45 units. Winiter 166€–196€ ($266–$314) double, 196€–286€ ($314–$458) suite; off-season 124€–140€ ($198–$224) double, 144€–184€ ($230–$294) suite. Rates include half-board. MC, V. Parking 8€ ($13). Closed mid-Apr to mid-May and mid-Oct to Dec 1. **Amenities:** Restaurant; bar; indoor heated pool; fitness center; sauna; room service; massage; babysitting; laundry service; dry cleaning; solarium; nonsmoking rooms. *In room:* TV, Wi-Fi, minibar, hair dryer, safe.

Schloss Prielau Hotel ★★ *Finds* This fairy-tale castle has been restored with its turreted towers intact, and now provides the most elegant accommodations on Lake Zell. Set in a park and completely isolated, the Schloss was built in 1425 and, since then, has been modified and improved over the years. It's not so much of a castle as a country house, and is painted white with red shutters. The bedrooms are furnished beautifully and comfortably, with authentic country pieces and antiques. Fabrics are elegant and tasteful, and some of the rooms are a bit dark because the windows are small. Opposite in a country house is an award-winning restaurant, serving classic Austrian cuisine. The service is top rate, and the welcome is one of the more inviting in the area.

Hofmannsthalstrasse 10, A-5700 Zell am See. ✆ **06542/729110.** Fax 06542/7260955. www.schlosshotels.co.at. 7 units. 180€–220€ ($288–$352) double; 620€ ($992) suite. Rates include breakfast. Half-board 25€ ($40) extra. AE, DC, MC, V. Closed mid-Apr to mid-May and Nov to early Dec. **Amenities:** Restaurant; bar; sauna; bike rentals; children's playground; babysitting; laundry service; dry cleaning; solarium. *In room:* TV, Wi-Fi, minibar, hair dryer.

ZELL AM SEE AFTER DARK

Zell am See has one of the liveliest after-ski scenes in Land Salzburg. All the clubs and taverns are very informal and, unlike some other resorts, are unpretentious. In addition to the establishments below, there are countless taverns where you can sit around an open fire and enjoy a cold pint of beer or warm wine.

Bacchuskeller, in the Hotel Waldhof, Schmittenstrasse 47 (✆ **06542/775**), is a rustic alpine tavern that often has a local musician, attired in lederhosen and red stockings, play for skiers, who like to dance on the small floor. A beer costs 2.95€ ($4.70), and a four-course supper goes for 15€ to 32€ ($24–$51). It's open daily from 7 to 10:30pm; closed April 15 through April 30 and October 15 through December 15.

Gasthof Alpenblick, Alte Landersstrasse 6 (✆ **06542/5433**), is a typical Austrian Bierstüberl in the satellite hamlet of Schüttdorf on the road to Kaprun. Zither music is usually played every evening in winter. There's a restaurant on the premises, popular with hikers in summer and skiers in winter. It serves food daily from noon to 9pm in summer and from noon to 10:30pm in winter. Meals here cost 11€ to 27€ ($18–$42), and beer goes for 3.50€ ($5.60). The Gasthof is closed April 5 to May 5 and November 28 to December 28.

8 THE FLACHGAU

So far, we've been exploring sections of Land Salzburg south and southwest of Salzburg; now we'll introduce you to resorts northeast of Salzburg, on our way to Linz in Upper Austria (see chapter 11). One of the chief attractions of the Flachgau district is **Wolfgangsee (Lake Wolfgang),** which lies mainly in Land Salzburg, although its major center, St. Wolfgang, is in Upper Austria. The best-known lake in the Salzkammergut, the Wolfgangsee is 10km (6 miles) long and 2km (1¹/₄ miles) wide. The northwestern shores are fairly inaccessible. The major Land Salzburg resort on the lake is St. Gilgen. Many people visit Lake Wolfgang on day trips from Salzburg, as it's within easy commuting distance.

The Flachgau is a relatively flat area, dividing the Austrian province of Styria from Bavaria in Germany. Unlike the other areas of Land Salzburg discussed above, the Flachgau is primarily a summer resort area for those who enjoy lakeside retreats.

HOF BEI SALZBURG

About 15 minutes from Salzburg on Lake Fuschl is this resort, once popular with Salzburg aristocrats who came for its private hunting and fishing preserves set among mountains, woods, and alpine waters.

There's a 9-hole golf course here, and you can lazily spend the day fishing for trout on the lake. From here it's easy to explore not only the Fuschlsee, but also the Wolfgangsee and the Mondsee.

Like the suburb of Anif (see chapter 9), Hof bei Salzburg is an ideal spot for traditional accommodations, especially come festival time in August, when hotel rooms are virtually impossible to obtain in Salzburg.

Essentials

GETTING THERE There are no railway lines running into Hof bei Salzburg, but **buses** run frequently to and from the nearest railway junctions, at Salzburg and at Bad Ischl. From the railway station at Bad Ischl, about a dozen buses depart every day, each of which stops in Fuschl (trip time: 1 hr.). An equal number of buses depart from the railway station at Salzburg (trip time: 30 min.). If you're **driving,** take Route 158 east of Salzburg for 18km (11 miles). Hof bei Salzburg lies 299km (186 miles) southwest of Vienna.

VISITOR INFORMATION The **tourist office** at Postplattenstr 1 (© **06229/2249**) is open in winter Monday to Friday 8am to noon and 2 to 5pm; in summer Monday to Friday 8am to noon and 2 to 6pm.

Where to Stay & Dine

Gasthof Nussbaumer INTERNATIONAL The decor of this old-fashioned restaurant is woodsy and folkloric, reflecting the village atmosphere of the surrounding region. But the clientele (thanks to the dormitory-style bedrooms upstairs that house workers for many of the surrounding hotels) is young, energetic, and sometimes after work—a bit raucous. Because of the youthful emphasis of this place, it's likely to be a bit more hip and a bit more "modern" than you'd have expected from a conventional dining room. Menu items include both chicken and pork schnitzels, *tafelspitz* (boiled beef), fondues, salads, soups, and the kind of rib-sticking fare that hard-working people appreciate in the great outdoors. On the premises is something akin to a singles bar, with rustic-looking accessories and a lot of off-duty, sometimes good-looking, and sometimes hard drinking waitstaff and maintenance staffs from other nearby hotels.

Gitzen 13, A-5322 Hof bei Salzburg. ✆ **06229/2275.** Reservations not required. Fixed-price lunch 8€ ($13); main courses 8€–15€ ($13–$24). MC, V. Kitchen daily 10am–11pm; bar daily 8pm–2am.

Hotel Jagdhof ★★ This well-managed government-rated four-star hotel is owned and operated by the same group that manages the nearby (and recommended, below) Hotel Schloss Fuschl. Providing less expensive accommodations than those at its grander (five-star) neighbor, it was originally built in the 1500s as a farmhouse and has an authentic style that many Austrian hotels have tried to emulate. Rooms, renovated in 2002, vary in size and design, but each is cozily furnished and inviting with excellent beds. The hotel is well maintained and tasteful, with an accommodating staff and an excellent restaurant. A la carte meals begin at around 14€ to 18€ ($22–$29) each. Specialties include pike terrine with green sauce, and a wide choice of fish and game dishes.

A-5322 Hof bei Salzburg. ✆ **06229/23720.** Fax 06229/2553-1531. www.hoteljagdhof-fuschlsee.at. 143 units. 175€–215€ ($280–$344) double; from 265€–485€ ($424–$776) suite. Rates include breakfast. AE, DC, MC, V. Free parking. **Amenities:** 2 restaurants; bar; indoor heated pool; 9-hole golf course; tennis court; fitness center; spa; Jacuzzi; sauna; game room; concierge; room service; massage; babysitting; laundry service; dry cleaning; nonsmoking rooms; rooms for those w/limited mobility. *In room:* TV, Wi-Fi, minibar, coffeemaker, hair dryer, iron, safe.

Hotel Schloss Fuschl ★★★ The main section of this castle built in 1450 has a simple facade of unadorned windows. Its former guests have included Jawaharlal Nehru, Eleanor Roosevelt, and Nikita Khrushchev. In World War II, von Ribbentrop selected the Schloss as his headquarters; later, Mussolini came here to meet with Nazi leaders. It was the former hunting lodge of the prince-archbishops of Salzburg, who cultivated the peninsula garden jutting into Lake Fuschl. The interior is decorated with elegant fireplaces, timbered ceilings, stone columns, and handcrafted stonework. The swimming pool is dedicated to the Roman goddess Diana. You can rent either a modern, well-furnished room inside the hotel or a luxurious suite fit for a prince and studded with valuable antiques. From the ample bathrooms to the luxurious beds, each room is inviting and warmly and individually decorated.

The wonderful food at Schloss Restaurant makes it one of the most popular restaurants in Land Salzburg. Patrons may dine in the winter garden or, in summer, on the terrace overlooking the lake. Inside are several elegant rooms, all decorated with antiques and paintings. The view encompasses much of the lake and sometimes a peek of Salzburg. On the menu are lobster terrine with caviar, summer truffles, and a host of seasonal specialties. Reservations are needed. The dining room is open daily from 12:15 to 2pm and 7 to 9pm.

A-5322 Hof bei Salzburg. ✆ **06229/22530.** Fax 06229/22531531. www.schlossfuschlresort.at. 110 units. 450€ ($720) double; from 650€ ($1,040) suite. Rates include breakfast. Half-board 25€ ($40) per person extra. AE, DC, MC, V. Free parking. **Amenities:** 2 restaurants; 2 bars; indoor heated pool; 9-hole golf course; tennis court; fitness center; spa; Jacuzzi; sauna; massage; room service; babysitting; laundry service; dry cleaning; nonsmoking rooms; rooms for those w/limited mobility. *In room:* TV, Wi-Fi, minibar, hair dryer, safe.

FUSCHL AM SEE

Fuschlsee, the Land Salzburg lake closest to Salzburg, lies 31km (19 miles) east of the festival city, reached by Route 158. The fact that there isn't much to do in Fuschl is the very reason it's so crowded with Salzburgers on weekends, who come to relax by the beautiful lake, and eat and drink in the taverns. Lake Fuschl is ringed by woodland, some of which comprises a nature reserve. The lake, lying to the northwest of the larger Lake Wolfgang, is only 4km (2½ miles) long and less than 1.5km (1 mile) wide. Fuschl, strictly a summer resort, is on the eastern strip of the lake, across from Hof Bei Salzburg.

You might choose to stay in Fuschl am See as an alternative to Salzburg at any time of the year, but it is especially worth considering during the festival season. From here you can also explore Wolfgangsee.

Essentials

GETTING THERE There are no railway lines running into Fuschl, but **buses** run frequently to and from the nearest railway junctions, at Salzburg and at Bad Ischl. From the railway station at Bad Ischl, about a dozen buses depart every day, each of which stops in Fuschl (trip time: 1 hr.). An equal number of buses depart from the railway station at Salzburg (trip time: 35 min.).

VISITOR INFORMATION The **tourist office** in the town center (✆ **06226/8250**) is open in winter Monday to Friday from 9am to noon and 3 to 5pm; in summer Monday to Friday from 8am to noon and 2 to 6pm, Saturday 8am to noon, Sunday 10am to noon.

Where to Stay

Ebner's Waldhof, Silencehotel ★ Opened in the late 1950s as a small inn, this first-class chalet hotel has expanded to become the largest and one of the most prestigious in the village. The interior has a crackling open fireplace. Opening onto geranium-lined balconies, each of the individually decorated and comfortable rooms is warm and inviting. Guests can sign up for guided nature walks, which often end up at the local tavern.

Seepromenade, A-5330 Fuschl am See. ✆ **06226/8264.** Fax 06226/8644. www.ebners-waldhof.at. 75 units. 220€–268€ ($352–$429) double; 272€–446€ ($435–$714) suite. Rates include half-board. DC, MC, V. Closed mid-Mar to Apr and Nov–Dec 15. **Amenities:** Restaurant; bar; 2 heated pools (indoor and outdoor); fitness center; sauna; salon; room service; massage; babysitting; laundry service; dry cleaning; nonsmoking rooms; shooting gallery. *In room:* TV, Wi-Fi, minibar, hair dryer, safe.

Where to Dine

Brunnwirt ★ Finds AUSTRIAN Brunnwirt is one of the region's leading restaurants, serving light and well-prepared meals to vacationing gourmets from as far away as Vienna. Housed in a 15th-century building thick with atmosphere, the restaurant serves cuisine inspired by regional recipes. The kitchen staff is directed by Frau Brandstätter, who insists on strictly fresh ingredients. Specialties include game dishes, veal, and lamb. The menu changes frequently, and portions are generous. Main dishes include roast venison with an herb-flavored cream sauce, mushrooms, and dumplings; marinated char with asparagus mousse; and breast of duckling with orange sauce. Herr Brandstätter will help you select a wine.

Wolfgangseestrasse 11, A-5330 Fuschl am See. ✆ **0664/2807192.** www.brunnwirt.at. Reservations recommended. Main courses 17€–33€ ($26–$53). AE, DC, MC, V. Feb–June and Sept–Dec Tues–Sat 6–11pm, Sun noon–1:30pm and 6–11pm; July–Aug daily noon–2pm and 6–11pm. Closed Jan.

ST. GILGEN

This leading lakeside resort lies at the western edge of the Wolfgangsee. It's easily accessible from Salzburg, just 29km (18 miles) away. Once a stronghold of the prince-archbishops of Salzburg, St. Gilgen today is the playground for the city's new aristocracy: the fashionable and wealthy who maintain mountain villas here. Parties at festival time tend to be lavish, and you're lucky if you get an invitation. In summer the resort attracts mainly Austrians and Germans to the indoor swimming pool and bathing beach.

The town has many Mozart connections. In the vicinity of the Rathaus (Town Hall) is the house in which Mozart's mother, Anna Maria Pertl, was born in 1720. After the composer's sister, Nannerl, married Baron Berchtold zu Sonnenberg, she also settled in St. Gilgen. The Mozart Fountain, built in 1927, stands on the main square in front of the Rathaus.

Essentials

GETTING THERE There are no railway lines running into St. Gilgen, but **buses** (the same line serving Fuschl am See and Hof bei Salzburg) run frequently to and from the nearest railway junctions, stopping in St. Gilgen after a ride from Salzburg (trip time: 50 min.) or Bad Ischl (trip time: 40 min.). **Motorists** should head east of Salzburg for 34km (21 miles) on Route 158.

VISITOR INFORMATION The **tourist office** (✆ **06227/23480;** http://euroalps.eu) in the town center is open in summer daily 9am to 7pm. Winter hours are only on Saturday from 9am to noon and 2 to 6pm.

Where to Stay & Dine

Parkhotel Billroth ★ Finds About 1.5km (1 mile) from the resort, this hotel, standing on its own spacious grounds, was built in the 1890s and vastly revamped and enlarged in the 1960s. One wing was designed in a white-walled villa style, while the main section looks more like an overblown chalet. The view from the rooms and from the parasol-dotted sun terrace takes in the lake and the mountains beyond. Most rooms are well furnished, with oriental carpets and often several windows. The hotel has its own lakeside beach, with a floating raft ideal for sunbathing. It also allows easy access to the ski lifts.

Billrothstrasse 2, A-5340 St. Gilgen. ✆ **06227/2217.** Fax 06227/221825. www.billroth.at. 52 units. Summer 124€–224€ ($198–$358) double; winter 98€–130€ ($157–$208) double. Rates include breakfast. MC, V. Closed mid-Dec to mid-Jan. **Amenities:** Restaurant; bar; tennis court; sauna; massage; babysitting; nonsmoking rooms. *In room:* TV, Wi-Fi, safe.

11

Upper Austria

Too often neglected by North Americans unaware of its charms, Upper Austria contains some of the country's most beautiful scenery. It's a land of mountains, lakes, and picturesque valleys, with Styria and Land Salzburg to its south and Bavaria to the west. To the north it borders the Bohemian forest in the Czech Republic. Its eastern neighbor is Lower Austria. The Austrian name of this province is Bundesland–Ober Österreiche—*ober,* or upper, because it's closer to the source of the Danube than its twin, Lower Austria.

Upper Austria has three different landscapes. In the north are granite- and gneiss-laden hills, separated in the center of the province by the Valley of the Danube. There are also the limestone Alps and the Salzkammergut lake district, about a 30-minute drive from Linz, which crosses into Upper Austria. Here you'll find the area's most idyllic settings. You can center your activities at the Mondsee or Attersee, Austria's largest lake. Other possible bases are the Traunsee, one of the biggest lakes in the Salzkammergut, or the Wolfgangsee, Austria's most romantic lake.

These *seen* (lakes) are all great for boating, but if you like to swim, know that the *see* water here is not as warm as you'll find in Carinthia (see chapter 14). The lake district is dotted with farms and fruit trees, from which an excellent cider is produced that actually competes with wine for popularity among the locals.

Upper Austria is a choice location for nature lovers. Most of its towns are small, and although there's a lot of industry, it doesn't blight the province with grime. Industrial installations are often discreetly hidden away, much as they are in Switzerland. Linz, the provincial capital, harbors many historic treasures. Near Linz, the former Nazi concentration camp at Mauthausen is a tragic reminder of the horrors of World War II. Bad Ischl, once a retreat of the imperial court, is the area's most fashionable spa. Emperor Franz Josef summered here for 60 years. From the beautiful village of Hallstatt, you can tour still-active salt mines at Salt Mountain.

Historic abbeys abound in the province: Abbey of St. Florian, outside Linz, the province's largest abbey and an outstanding example of baroque architecture; Lambach Abbey, outside Wels, a Benedictine abbey founded in 1056; and Kremsmünster Abbey, near Bad Hall, a Benedictine abbey from 777, noted for its famed fish pond and Hall of the Emperors.

You'll find most hotels in the Salzkammergut region, but in every town and village are one or two moderately priced to inexpensive inns. There are few deluxe accommodations here, although several old castles have been turned into romantic lodges. Most hotels around the lakes are open only in the summer. Parking is rarely a problem in these places, and, unless otherwise noted, you park for free.

May is an ideal time to visit. These areas tend to be overrun with visitors, especially Germans, in the peak months of July and August.

Many North Americans aren't familiar with the ski areas of Upper Austria, as they lie for the most part in the southeastern corner. The **Dachstein** is a major ski area—and the **Dachstein Caves** are a spectacular natural attraction. If you like to ski and don't demand massive facilities and a big night scene, you'll find Upper Austria's emerging ski resorts far less expensive than the more popular and frequented resorts in Tyrol and Land Salzburg.

1 LINZ: THE PROVINCIAL CAPITAL ★★

187km (116 miles) NW of Vienna; 130km (81 miles) NE of Salzburg; 269km (167 miles) E of Munich

Linz, the provincial capital of Upper Austria, is the third-largest city in the country after Vienna and Graz. It's the biggest port on the Danube, which widens out considerably here to become a majestic thoroughfare. Three bridges connect Linz with the suburb of Urfahr, on the left bank of the river. If you enter the country from Passau, Germany, Linz will be your gateway to Austria.

Linz was the site of a Roman castle and settlement, Lentia, in the 1st century A.D. By the Middle Ages it had become a thriving center of trade because of its position on the river. Emperor Friedrich III lived here from 1489 to 1493. Now the city sits on a direct rail route linking the Adriatic and Baltic seas. It was here that Austria's first railroad terminated. Because of these factors, Linz became an industrial and manufacturing center, with blast furnaces and steel factories. Its industrial capacity was rapidly built up after Hitler seized Austria in 1938, and the Nazis later established chemical plants here. Unfortunately, Linz's industrial boom made it a frequent target of Allied bombing; it took years to repair the destruction rained upon the city.

Linz today is one of the leading cultural centers of Austria, although it doesn't rival Vienna or Salzburg. The city's name appears in numerous Germanic songs, and many notable figures have been connected with Linz, including native son and composer Anton Bruckner. Mozart dedicated a symphony to the city, and Beethoven wrote his *Eighth Symphony* here. Franz Schubert described with pleasure his holidays in Linz. Goethe, who had a romance with a Linz *Fräulein,* dedicated one of his most lyrical works "to the beautiful girls of Linz."

ESSENTIALS

Getting There

BY PLANE Austrian Airlines and its subsidiary, Tyrolean Airways, are the major connections into Linz, especially if you're flying in from another Austrian city. Foreign airlines serving Linz include Lufthansa and Swissair; connections are possible from Düsseldorf, Frankfurt, London, Paris, and Zurich. **Flughafen Linz,** or Blue Danube Airport (✆ **07221/6000;** www.flughafen-linz.at), is 12km ($7\frac{1}{2}$ miles) southwest of the city, near the hamlet of Hörsching. There's no bus that runs all the way into Linz, although the airport maintains a 24-hour shuttle bus from the airport to the railway station at Hörsching; from here, you can take one of the commuter trains into Linz—there's one about every hour from early morning to midnight. It's more convenient to take a taxi, which will cost about 30€ ($48) one-way to virtually anywhere in Linz.

BY TRAIN Linz sits directly astride the rail lines that connect Salzburg with Vienna, and on those that connect Prague to Graz and the major cities of Slovenia and Croatia. Trains, many of them express, depart at hourly intervals throughout the day and night from Vienna's Westbahnhof (trip time: 2 hr.) and from Salzburg's main station ($1\frac{1}{4}$ hr.). One train every 2 hours throughout the day departs from Graz for Linz ($3\frac{1}{2}$ hr.). For rail information, call ✆ **05/1717,** or visit **www.oebb.at**. The train station is located south of the city center at Bahnhofplatz.

BY BUS Linz is the center of an extensive network of bus lines carrying passengers from its busy railway station to the outlying villages and hamlets of Upper Austria. However, because of its frequent rail connections to Vienna, Salzburg, and the major cities of Europe, few passengers would consider traveling long distances to Linz by bus rather than by train.

BY CAR If you're driving from Salzburg, head northeast along the Autobahn A-1; from Vienna, take the A-1 Autobahn west.

Getting Around

Most visitors limit their exposure in Linz to the city's historic core, most of which is a pedestrian zone centered on the Hauptplatz. Expect lots of shopping possibilities, lots of cafes serving the city's best-known confection (the Linzer torte), and access via tram nos. 1 and 3 and bus nos. 19 and 19A, any of which make access to the center from the periphery easy. Buses and trams operate daily from 5am to midnight and cost 1.60€ ($2.60) per ride, for access between any points in Greater Linz. For more information, contact the city tourist office. There is also a 1-day ticket valid for 24 hours, costing 3€ ($4.80).

The **Linz tourist office** is at Hauptplatz 1 (✆ **0732/70701777;** www.linz.at), and is open Monday to Friday 8am to 7pm (6pm in winter), Saturday and Sunday 10am to 7pm (6pm in winter).

American Express, Bürgerstrasse 14 (✆ **0732/669013**), is open Monday to Friday 9am to 5:30pm and Saturday from 9am to noon.

EXPLORING LINZ'S CHURCHES & HISTORICAL BUILDINGS

Among the four major cities of Austria, Linz is the least publicized and the least visited by foreign tourists, but its charms are many and its history as a Danube port is long and illustrious. The best way to explore the town is to hire one of the officially sanctioned English-speaking guides provided by the **Linz tourist office,** Hauptplatz 1 (✆ **0732/70701777;** www.linz.at). Do-it-yourselfers can request the brochure "A Walk through the Old Quarter," which highlights the city's main attractions.

The most popular shopping district in the city is **Landstrasse,** which is filled with a variety of boutiques.

Hauptplatz was the original marketplace and is now one of Europe's biggest and most beautiful squares, with baroque and rococo facades surrounding it. On the east side is the **Rathaus (Town Hall).** In the heart of the square stands the **Dreifaltigkeitssäule (Trinity Column),** built in 1723 to mark the city's deliverance from plague, fire, and Turkish invasions. This marble column rises 26m (85 ft.).

The **Brucknerhaus** concert hall was named in honor of Anton Bruckner, the Linz-born composer, and has an elliptical facade of glass and steel with a wooden interior. Concerts presented in this acoustically perfect hall have been transmitted throughout the world. The building was constructed from 1969 to 1973 as a cultural and conference center.

Alter Dom The largest baroque church in the city and formerly the cathedral of Linz, the Alter Dom was constructed by the Jesuits at the end of the 17th century. You mustn't judge this church by its relatively simple exterior. The inside warms up considerably with pink marble columns, an intricately carved pulpit, and lots of statues. The high altar is bedecked with marble images. Native son Anton Bruckner was the church organist for 12 years, and the annual Bruckner Festival is centered here. Two other composers are honored at the same time—Mozart, who composed his *Linz Symphony* (no. 36) at the building now designated as the city tourist office (Hauptplatz 1), and Beethoven, who composed part of his *Eighth Symphony* in Linz.

Domgasse. ✆ **0732/7700660.** Free admission. Daily 7am–noon and 3–7pm. Bus 11.

Ars Electronica Center ★ This museum accurately calls itself "the museum of the future." The place will certainly give you a thrill; a full body flight simulator takes you on a whirlwind "tour" over Upper Austria without leaving the building. The on-site "Airacuda" glides through the water like a fish. This is most definitely a hands-on museum, and you're entertained with marionettes for the digital age (that is, with no strings attached). Several levels allow you to enjoy a hands-on experience. In the interactive 3-D room on the ground level, you can explore "the outer reaches of space," or so it will seem. The location of the new museum is over the bridge from Hauptplatz.

Hauptstrasse 2. ✆ **0732/72720.** www.aec.at. Admission 6€ ($9.60) adults; 3€ ($4.80) students, children, and seniors. Wed–Fri 9am–5pm, Sat–Sun 10am–6pm.

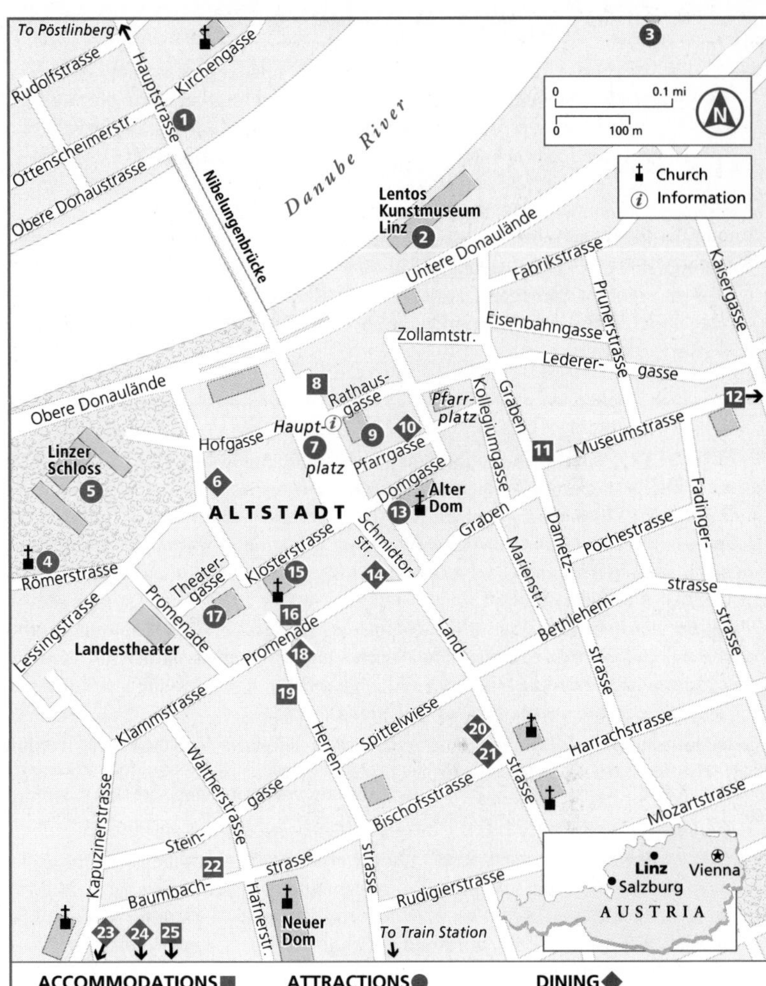

ACCOMMODATIONS

Austria Trend Hotel Schillerpark **25**
Drei Mohren **16**
Dom Hotel **22**
Hotel Mühlviertlerhof **11**
Hotel Prielmayerhof **12**
Hotel-Restaurant Zur Lokomotive **25**
Hotel Wolfinger **8**
Zum Schwarzen Bären **19**

ATTRACTIONS

Alter Dom **13**
Ars Electronica Center **1**
Brucknerhaus **3**
Dreifaltigkeitssäule **7**
Landhaus **17**
Lentos Kunstmuseum Linz **2**
Linzer Schloss **5**
Martinskirche **4**
Minoritenkirche (Landhauskirche) **15**
Rathaus **9**

DINING

Café am Park **24**
Café Traxlmayr **18**
Herberstein **6**
Papa Joe's **20**
Promenadenhof **14**
Restaurant Verdi and Restaurant Einkeher **23**
Stieglbräu Klosterhof **21**
Wachauer Weinstube **10**

The Silicon Valley of Mitteleuropa

Linz is not as preoccupied with its baroque and imperial past as many visitors believe. It's also home to a new generation of computer-industry whiz kids, who are transforming prosperous but staid Upper Austria into the Silicon Valley of Mitteleuropa (central Europe). Their ambitions are celebrated at Linz's **Ars Electronica** festival, held annually over a 5- or 6-day period during early September. Originating in 1979, it awards the coveted Golden Nika Prize to whichever entrepreneur or developer has created the previous year's most memorable electronic product. The festival has been called "The Oscar Awards Ceremony of the European Computer World." Previous awards have gone to the developer of the best international website and the developers of the most realistic computer game.

Landhaus One of the most important historic buildings in Linz, the Landhaus today serves as the headquarters for Upper Austria's government. The original structure was built around 1570 with a gracefully arcaded courtyard surrounding a fountain. The complex served as the city's university during the 1600s and is still celebrated as the site where Johannes Kepler, the noted astronomer and mathematician, taught and developed his theories of planetary motion.

Within the Landhaus's labyrinthine confines are the Church of the Minorite Brothers (see below) and the richly furnished apartments used by Empress Elisabeth ("Sissi") on the night she spent en route from her childhood home in Bavaria to the Hapsburg court in Vienna just before her marriage to Franz Josef in 1854.

Klosterstrasse 7. ✆ **0732/77200.** Free admission for views of the courtyard and the Minorite church; for more extensive visits, join one of the tourist office's organized tours. Mon–Tues and Thurs 7:30am–1pm and 2–6pm; Wed 7:30am–1:30pm; Fri 7:30am–1pm. (Hours extended for tourist office's organized tours.) Bus: 33.

Lentos Kunstmuseum Linz ★★ On the border of the Danube River, this gallery is one of the most important repositories of contemporary painting in Linz. Many art lovers drive all the way from Vienna to feast on the array of paintings—some 1,500 works in all that include pieces from Andy Warhol, Picasso, Chagall, Matisse, and more. Even more enthralling to us is the collection of the paintings and graphic works by Klimt and Schiele. The gallery also owns 850 rare photographs, including the work of Man Ray. The earliest paintings are from the first half of the 19th century, but most of the collection is after 1945 at the end of the war. The museum plans an active program of acquisition, and, of course, there are those bequests that inevitably come in, usually upon the death of a collector. One of the greatest gifts came from a Berlin art dealer, Wolfgang Gurlitt (1888–1965), who managed to amass a stunning collection of 120 important art works. The building itself is one of the finest examples of modern architecture in Linz, a glass-and-concrete structure designed to present art in the best possible light.

Ernst-Koref-promenade 1. ✆ **0732/70703600.** www.lentos.at. Admission 6.50€ ($10) adults, 4.50€ ($7.20) seniors and students under 26. Fri–Tues 10am–6pm; Thurs 10am–10pm. Tram: 1, 2, or 3.

A Baroque Masterpiece: The Abbey of St. Florian

Abbey of St. Florian ★★, the largest in Upper Austria, is an outstanding example of baroque architecture. Augustinians have occupied this site since the 11th century, although the baroque structures you see today were built between 1686 and 1751. St. Florian was a Christian martyr who was drowned in the Enns River around A.D. 304. He is often called upon by the faithful to protect their homes against flood and fire. The abbey was constructed over his grave.

The greatest composer of church music in 19th-century Austria, Anton Bruckner (1824–96) became the organist at St. Florian as a young man and composed many of his masterpieces here. Although he went on to greater fame in Vienna, he was granted his wish and buried at the abbey church underneath the organ he loved so dearly. You can visit the crypt as well as the room where the composer lived for about a decade.

The western exterior of the abbey is crowned with a trio of towers. The doorway is especially striking. As you enter the inner court, you'll see the **Fountain of the Eagle.** In the library, which contains some 140,000 books and manuscripts, are allegorical ceiling frescoes by Bartolomeo Altomonte. The marble salon honors Prince Eugene of Savoy for his heroic defense of Vienna against a major siege by the Turks. The ceiling paintings here depict the Austrian victory over the "infidels."

Altdorfer Gallery is the most outstanding part of the abbey, surpassing even the Imperial Apartments. Well-known works by Albrecht Altdorfer, a 16th-century master of the Danube school of painting, are displayed. Altdorfer was a warm, romantic contemporary of Dürer, to whom he is often compared. He painted more than a dozen panels for the abbey's Gothic church, depicting, among other scenes, the martyrdom of St. Sebastian.

The **Imperial Apartments,** the Kaiserzimmer, are reached by climbing a splendid staircase. Pope Pius VI once stayed here, and a whole host of royalty has occupied these richly decorated quarters. You're allowed to visit the bedrooms of the emperors and empresses.

The **abbey church** has twin towers reaching 79m (259 ft.). The church is distinguished by columns of pink marble, quarried near Salzburg. Lavish stucco decoration was used in the interior, and the pulpit is in black marble. The choir stalls are heavily gilded and adorned with ornamentation and carving. You should allow about an hour for a tour.

Visitors can enter the church free, but guided tours of the monastery are 5.30€ ($8.50) for adults and 2€ ($3.20) for children. Tours are conducted April through October daily at 10 and 11am and at 2, 3, and 4pm. Otherwise, you must write to the abbey for permission to visit.

The abbey, Stiftstrasse 1, St. Florian (✆ **07224/890230**), lies 19km (12 miles) southeast of Linz. It has its own exit (St. Florian) from the Autobahn linking Linz and Vienna. In addition, bus nos. 2040 and 2042 run throughout the day from Linz to St. Florian.

European Capital of Culture in 2009

Linz will be in the spotlight in 2009 when a series of cultural programs will be featured here when it is elevated to "European Capital of Culture," at least for the year 2009. Linz was selected to be the center of this media attention because of its position at the crossroads of the East-West axis from Paris to the Black Sea and the North-South axis of the Rhine-Main-Danube River route. It wasn't just geography that put Linz in this lofty role, but its performance both as a cultural center and a city of industry. Information about what's coming up will be posted on **www.linz09.at**.

Linzer Schloss ★ High above the river and a 5-minute walk west of Hauptplatz stands the castle used by Emperor Friedrich III when he and his court resided in Linz (1486–89). At the turn of the 17th century, Rudolf II erected a new building. A catastrophic fire destroyed the south wing in the early 19th century. Today the castle houses the **Provincial Museum of Upper Austria.** Its exhibits range from medieval art to works by the great moderns. There's an extensive arts-and-crafts department and a folklore collection. During the last few years, the permanent exhibitions have been expanded to include special exhibitions on cultural history.

Tummelplatz 10. ✆ **0732/774419-0.** www.schlossmuseum.at. Admission 3€ ($4.80) adults, 1.70€ ($2.70) students and seniors. Tues–Fri 9am–6pm; Sat–Sun and holidays 10am–5pm. Bus: 27.

Martinskirche The finest example of Carolingian architecture in the region, St. Martin's Church is the most ancient church in Austria still (more or less) in its original form. Constructed by Charlemagne during the 700s, it used the ruins of an ancient Roman wall for parts of its foundation. Its interior is decorated with frescoes, several fine examples of baroque art, and a 15th-century Gothic choir. Restored in 1948, the church stands a 10-minute walk west of Hauptplatz, in a neighborhood filled with commercial buildings. A covered passageway connects it directly to the Linzer Schloss (see above). Although it's not open to the public, the church is almost always included as part of the official tours sponsored by the Linz tourist office (✆ **0732/70701777**).

Römerstrasse. Free admission as part of tourist office's official guided tours. Bus: 33.

Minoritenkirche (Landhauskirche) Originally built during the 1200s in the early Gothic style, the Church of the Minorite Brothers was for some time the seat of the city's municipal government until the larger Landhaus was built around it in the late 1500s. The interior was given a baroque overlay in 1758. The building's masterpiece is the high altar by Bartolomeo Altomonte, depicting the Annunciation. The church also contains three red-marble side altars.

Klosterstrasse. ✆ **0732/772011364.** Free admission. Summer daily 8am–4pm; off-season daily 8–11am; hours extended for tourist office's organized tours. Bus: 33.

WHERE TO STAY

Expensive

Austria Trend Hotel Schillerpark ★★ The finest and most prestigious hotel in town, this mirror-covered structure was built around 1980 at the edge of the city's pedestrian zone, a 5-minute walk north of the railway station. A center of nightlife in Linz, the government-rated five-star hotel contains three comfortable restaurants, two bars, and a casino, open daily from 3pm to 3am. Rooms are airy, sunny, and filled with tastefully streamlined furniture. The beds are very comfortable, and the bathrooms are well equipped with robes and tub/shower combinations. Two rooms are furnished with waterbeds, which must be specially requested when reservations are made.

Of the three restaurants within the hotel, the Rouge et Noir, serving French and Austrian cuisine, is the best; the Primo Piano offers upscale dining, serving regional cuisine; and the Café am Pair serves small meals plus snacks, pastries, and coffees.

Rainerstrasse 2–4, A-4020 Linz. ✆ **0732/6950.** Fax 0732/69509. www.austria-trend.at. 111 units. 125€–322€ ($200–$515) suite. AE, DC, MC, V. Parking 13€ ($21). Tram: 3. **Amenities:** 2 restaurants; 3 bars; fitness center; sauna; room service; babysitting; laundry service; dry cleaning; nonsmoking rooms; casino; solarium. *In room:* A/C, TV, Wi-Fi, minibar, hair dryer, safe.

Drei Mohren ★★ This is the smallest government-rated four-star hotel in Linz, and also one of the best for those desiring an intimate atmosphere and top-notch service. Renovations and improvements have been so drastic that the hotel was granted another star. It takes its name from the "Three Moors" (English translation). It is told that these gents from the Far East were stranded in 1770 in a violent snowstorm in Linz and liked the place so much they decided to live here. Opposite the Landhaus Park, the inn lies in the center of town, taking over a trio of buildings from the 1500s which have been considerably modernized and upgraded over the ages. Most of the rooms are spacious doubles with regal furnishings; there are also less desirable accommodations with less lavish adornments.

Promenade 17, A-4020 Linz. ✆ **0732/772626-0.** Fax 0732/772626-6. www.drei-mohren.at. 25 units. 142€ ($227) double; 220€–350€ ($352–$560) suite. AE, DC, MC, V. **Amenities:** Bar; room service; laundry service/dry cleaning. *In room:* A/C, TV, Wi-Fi, minibar, hair dryer, safe.

Moderate

Dom Hotel ★ Ideally located in a quiet area in the center of town, this hotel is only a few minutes' walk from the main rail station. It was built in the 1970s and renovated in the late 1990s, and today it provides five floors of subdued decor a few steps from the cathedral. The owners maintain the hotel as a cozy stopping place. The comfortably furnished rooms have private (though small) bathrooms, with adequate shelf space and mostly tub/shower combinations. On the ground floor is a cocktail bar, and the hotel restaurant serves international specialties and Austrian dishes.

Baumbachstrasse 17, A-4020 Linz. ✆ **0732/778441.** Fax 0732/775432. www.domhotel.at. 44 units. 140€ ($224) double. Rates include breakfast. AE, DC, MC, V. Tram: 1 or 3. **Amenities:** Restaurant; bar; fitness center; sauna; babysitting; laundry service; dry cleaning; nonsmoking rooms; solarium. *In room:* TV, Wi-Fi, minibar, hair dryer.

Hotel Prielmayerhof ★ This government-rated four-star hotel is housed in a distinguished-looking five-story structure, one of the few privately owned buildings constructed in Linz during World War II (in 1942); a new wing was added in 1994. Between 1945 and 1955, the hotel housed American occupation troops, who faced their Soviet counterparts across the Danube during the early days of the Cold War. Today the hotel is owned by Franz Zihitner, the English-speaking son of the original builders. It contains efficiently modern and comfortable rooms, with well-maintained bathrooms. In the restaurant, Prielmayerhof, a *tagesmenu* (daily menu) depends on the chef's whims and market availability.

Weissenwolfstrasse 33, A-4020 Linz. ✆ **0732/774131-0.** Fax 0732/771569. www.prielmayerhof.at. 64 units. 127€ ($203) double. Rates include buffet breakfast. AE, DC, MC, V. Less than 1km (½ mile) east of Hauptplatz. Bus: 21. **Amenities:** Restaurant, lounge; sauna; laundry service; dry cleaning; nonsmoking rooms; rooms for those w/limited mobility. *In room:* TV, Wi-Fi, minibar, hair dryer, safe.

Hotel Wolfinger Hotel Wolfinger is housed in a 500-year-old building on what is the largest and best preserved baroque square in Europe. The entrance is through an arcade, a short distance from the Danube, in the middle of a pedestrian zone. A new wing was added to the hotel in 1992. Since 1975, the Dangl family, with the help of an enthusiastic staff, has run the hotel. With a respect for tradition, they have added modern comforts. Rooms are furnished with antiques. The beds are comfortable, and the small, well-maintained bathrooms.

Hauptplatz 19, A-4020 Linz. ✆ **0732/773291.** Fax 0732/77329155. www.hotelwolfinger.at. 46 units. 176€–252€ ($282–$403) double; from 188€ ($301) suite. Rates include buffet breakfast. AE, DC, MC, V. Bus: 26 or 27. **Amenities:** Restaurant; bar; lounge; babysitting; nonsmoking rooms. *In room:* TV, Wi-Fi.

Inexpensive

Hotel Mühlviertlerhof (Value) This three-story town house, originally built in the 1740s, is maintained by the Lumpi family. Cozy and comfortable, with a convenient location about 90m (295 ft.) from Hauptplatz, the hotel offers well-scrubbed accommodations designed with both charm and efficiency in mind. The small rooms have good beds and well-organized bathrooms. About half the rooms offer views of a small garden in back. The Klosterhof Restaurant, under different management, occupies part of the building's street level. Parking is usually available free after 6pm on nearby streets.

Graben 24–25, A-4020 Linz. ✆ **0732/772268.** Fax 0732/77226834. www.activehotels.com. 23 units. 97€–111€ ($155–$178) double. Rates include breakfast. AE, DC, MC, V. Tram: 3. Parking: 12€ ($19). **Amenities:** Restaurant; bar. *In room:* TV, Wi-Fi.

Hotel-Restaurant Zur Lokomotive This simple, unpretentious, and comfortable place is a family-operated hostelry in a five-story building erected just before World War I. Its interior was efficiently renovated in 2003. Rooms are a bit small, as are the bathrooms, which have tub/shower combinations. A restaurant on the premises serves traditional Austrian food to many business workers throughout the day, as well as passengers departing from or arriving at the railway station, which is about a minute's walk away.

Weingartshofstrasse 40, A-4020 Linz. ✆ **0732/654555.** Fax 0732/658337. www.hotel-lokomotive.at. 46 units. 88€–98€ ($141–$157) double; 108€ ($173) triple. Rates include buffet breakfast. AE, DC, MC, V. Tram: 3. **Amenities:** Restaurant; bar; room service. *In room:* TV, Wi-Fi.

Zum Schwarzen Bären (Value) Set within a block of the main, all-pedestrian shopping street of Linz, this is a substantial stucco-covered building that offers a traditional-looking restaurant and *weinstube* (wine tavern); a sense of solid, somewhat unimaginative tradition; and well-scrubbed but not overly large bedrooms. Each of them has touches of wooden paneling, or at least varnished wooden trim, a mixture of alpine and blandly contemporary furniture, and a tile-sheathed bathroom with a shower (in rare instances, there's a tub/shower combination). A plaque in front identifies the building as the birthplace of one of Linz's most renowned native sons, Richard Tauber (1891–1948), an opera singer who was born here long before the many architectural alterations enlarged and revised the original design of the house.

Herrenstrasse 9–11, A-4020 Linz. ✆ **0732/772477.** Fax 0732/77247747. www.linz-hotel.at. 30 units. 96€–128€ ($154–$205) double. Rates include breakfast. AE, DC, MC, V. Parking 7€ ($11). Bus: 33. **Amenities:** Restaurant; wine tavern; laundry service; nonsmoking rooms. *In room:* TV, Wi-Fi in lobby.

WHERE TO DINE

Expensive

Herberstein ★ AUSTRIAN/ASIAN In the center of the old city, in a historic building, Kremsmünsterhaus, this restaurant has been modernized and draws sophisticated foodies to its stylish precincts. Many locals patronize its lively bar. In summer you can sit outside in the inviting courtyard, perusing a limited but well-chosen menu. Count on an enticing daily special. There is always a freshly made soup of the day, plus a selection of appetizers including such delights as smoked salmon in a gazpacho jelly. Pastas such as penne are served in a fresh tomato sauce. You can follow with fish dishes such as dorado in a bouillabaisse sauce or filet of pork served with gnocchi. Some of the dishes are prepared in a wok, and a delicate fish tempura is a local favorite.

Altstadt 10. ✆ **0732/786161.** Reservations required. Fixed-price menu 89€ ($142). Main courses 18€–22€ ($28–$35). AE, DC, MC, V. Tues–Fri 11:30am–2:30pm and daily 6–10:30pm.

Restaurant Verdi and Restaurant Einkeher ★★ MODERN CONTINENTAL/AUSTRIAN The core of this house, whose panoramic view sweeps out over and above Linz, was built about a century ago, but because of frequent alterations, very little of it is still recognizable. Many Linzers come here for the view, the fresh high-altitude air, and a cuisine that includes both conservative time-tested folkloric dishes (in Einkeher) and more experimental modern cuisine (in Verdi). Frankly, the main allure that attracts residents as a destination in its own right is Verdi, where rich-looking earth tones and leather-covered chairs create the kind of place where you can hang out for a prolonged evening meal. Menu items reflect the changing seasons and a willingness to experiment on the part of the kitchen staff. The best examples include cannelloni stuffed with a purée of celeriac, served with king prawns and lobster sauce; roasted rack of lamb with gnocchi, thyme, and antipasti-style roasted peppers; and—in season—filet of venison with apple-studded cabbage, two different sauces, and bread dumplings. Previous diners have included the captains and coaches of some of Austria's most venerated soccer teams, politicians, and discreetly rich local residents.

Pachmayrstrasse 137, in Lichtenberg, A-4040 Linz. ✆ **0732/733005.** www.verdi.at. Reservations recommended for Verdi, not necessary at Einkeher. Verdi main courses 18€–21€ ($29–$34); Einkeher main courses 7€–13€ ($11–$21). DC, MC, V. Tues–Sat 5:30pm–midnight. There's no public bus to this place. Either take a taxi or drive north from Linz, following the Leonfelder Strasse for 3km (2 miles). On the outskirts of the village of Lichtenberg, you'll see a sign pointing to the Restaurant Verdi.

Inexpensive

Papa Joe's ★ Finds CAJUN/CREOLE/CARIBBEAN Between the mid-1400s and 1975, this dignified-looking building was an Ursuline convent. In 1999, one of the town's hippest restaurants opened within its historic premises. Today you'll find a busy American-style bar area near the entrance, with margaritas selling for 6.50€ ($10) each and a trio of New Orleans–inspired dining rooms filled with chattering diners and the smell of spicy Cajun and Creole cuisine. Come here for a reminder of some of the restaurant themes you left behind in the U.S. and for the possibility of meeting a local at the bar. Savory menu items include jambalaya, gumbos and stews, jerk chicken and pork, and, when it's available, spicy preparations of fish that include catfish. There's live music virtually every night—pianos, guitars, and jazz trios—beginning between 7 and 10pm, depending on the night's schedule.

Landstrasse 31, A-4040 Linz. ✆ **0732/774686.** www.papa-joe.at. Reservations not necessary. Main courses 8.20€–20€ ($13–$31). MC, V. Daily 10am–2am. Tram: 1 or 5.

Promenadenhof ★ AUSTRIAN/MEDITERRANEAN Dining here in summer is a special delight, as you can ask for a table on the roofed garden which is like a fabulous flower garden. Another feature is the wine cellar where you will be escorted to select your own bottle for the night from among one of the best selections of vintages in town. You can also request the waiter to bring you wine by the glass. Some of the town's best regional cuisine is served here, with *tafelspitz* (boiled beef) being the chef's specialty. Daily specials are also featured based on the shopping at the market on any given day. We have found the desserts to be among the best in Linz, especially a special baked apple dumpling accompanied by a wine sauce.

Promenade 39. ✆ **0732/777661.** Reservations recommended. Main courses 8€–16€ ($13–$26). AE, DC, MC, V. Mon–Sat 10am–1am.

Stieglbräu Klosterhof AUSTRIAN In some rooms of this large homelike restaurant, formally dressed waiters serve food under high ceilings, with 18th-century paintings by local artists on the walls; in others, youths in jeans and leather jackets, along with a scattering of older people fill the air with smoke and loud talk. A quick tour of the variety of rooms might help you decide where you feel most comfortable. (The most sedate areas tend to be one floor above street level.)

Centuries ago, this building served as one of the outposts of Kremsmünster Abbey, several days' horseback ride away. Today, from a position on the edge of Linz, it functions as the town's most likable beer garden, with a sprawling outdoor terrace and a cavernous interior. An old-fashioned, overworked staff serves copious portions of traditional Austrian food throughout. Menu items include Wiener schnitzels, pork schnitzels, paprika goulash, salads, and braised beef served with mushrooms. Desserts include a Linzer torte covered with apricot jam. Many people come for just a drink.

Landstrasse 30. ✆ **0732/773373.** www.klosterhof-linz.at. Reservations recommended. Main courses 8.90€–22€ ($14–$34). DC, MC, V. Daily 9am–midnight. Tram: 1 or 3.

Cafes

Linz is world famous for the Linzer torte, which looks like an open jam pie. The torte is filled mainly with raspberry jam or preserves, while the batter, made in part from ground unblanched almonds, is flavored with cinnamon, cloves, and cocoa. The treat is cut in thin wedges and sprinkled with confectioners' sugar. You shouldn't leave Linz without trying a piece.

Café am Park, in the Hotel Schillerpark, Rainerstrasse 2–4 (✆ **0732/6950;** tram: 1 or 3), is the hottest and most popular place to go on a Sunday afternoon in Linz. It's a big L-shape room redecorated in 1994 in a streamlined modern style. You can get all the beverages and light snacks you'd expect, as well as wholesome meals priced from 8.50€ to 15€ ($14–$24). It's open daily 6:30am to 11pm.

Café Traxlmayr, Promenade 16 (✆ **0732/773353**; www.traxlmayr.at; bus: 26 or 27), has an amazing pre–World War I mystique. This 150-year-old coffeehouse is next to a baroque palace on a wide ornamental boulevard, in a beige-and-brown building. Its outdoor sun terrace is lined with thick privets and geraniums. It even has a fountain in front, designed to resemble a little boy playing with two gurgling fish. Inside, the formally dressed staff scurry around with trays of coffee and cakes. The decor includes 1890s-style round marble tables, big mirrors, and crystal-and-gilt chandeliers. A rack of Austrian and foreign-language newspapers gives this place all the trappings of a Viennese coffeehouse. During cold weather, hot dishes, such as goulash, are served. Elaborate pastries are priced from 3.50€ ($5.60); coffee starts at 3€ ($4.80). It's open Monday to Saturday 10am to 8pm, Sunday 10am to 6pm.

Wachauer Weinstube AUSTRIAN A baroque bas-relief of an ecstatic saint adorns the corner of this historic building on a cobblestone sidewalk near the old cathedral. The smallest portion of any wine sold here is a quarter liter, about two full glasses. Wines from the Wachau region are featured, including five whites, four reds, and one rosé. There is a limited array of conventional platters served here, including wursts, salads, and the occasional schnitzel.

Pfarrgasse 20. ✆ **0732/774618.** Reservations recommended. Main courses 4.50€–11€ ($7.20–$18). AE, MC, V. Mon–Sat 11am–1am. Bus: 33.

SHOPPING

Quietly prosperous, Linz is the regional center of the antiques trade, so if you're interested in adding a piece or two to your collection, consider dropping into **Richard Kirchmayr Antiquitäten,** Bethlehemstrasse 5 (✆ **0732/770117**), or any of the shops listed below.

Linz is home to a branch of the Vienna-based **Dorotheum,** Fabrikstrasse 26 (✆ **0732/7731320**), an auction house that has allowed many socially prominent but impoverished families to keep their bills paid during hard times by means of discreet auctions of the family heirlooms. Auctions take place every Wednesday at 1:30pm, but there's plenty of time for viewing the objects during normal business hours in the week preceding the sale.

Less desirable objects are scattered randomly among the display tables at the **Linzer Flohmarkt (Linz Flea Market),** which takes place on the Hauptplatz every Saturday from March to mid-November from 7am to around 2pm, or until the inventories are depleted. Amid lots of junk and debris from estate sales throughout the region, it's still possible to find something charming and handcrafted.

At **O. Ö. Heimatwerk,** Landstrasse 31 (✆ **0732/7733770**), you can buy local handicrafts such as pewter, intricately patterned silver, rustic ceramic pots, slippers, dresses, and dressmaking fabrics in regional patterns (lots of polka dots). The entrance to the airy, sunny store is under an arcade, although the shop windows face the busy pedestrian walkway of Linz's main shopping district.

LINZ AFTER DARK

Although the nightlife here isn't as trendy or as edgy as what you'll find in Vienna, Linz offers reputable theater and music venues, and enough nocturnal diversions to keep you amused during your stay.

Cultural Linz

The city's most prestigious and visible theater is the historic **Landestheater,** Promenade 39 (✆ **0732/76110;** www.landestheater-linz.at; bus: 26 or 27). Originally built in 1670 and home to the local opera company, it's the city's all-purpose venue for theater, dance, and music of all kinds. Part of its interior is devoted to the smaller **Kammerspiele** (same address and phone), which tends to put on more contemporary and, in many cases, more experimental theater. A more modern concert venue is the one within the **Brucknerhaus,** Untere Donaulände 7 (✆ **0732/76120;** www.brucknerhaus.at; bus: 19 or 19A). Originally built in the 1970s, it presents concerts every year from mid-September to early October as part of the city's annual Bruckner Festival. Although most of the performances are devoted to the symphonies of Linz's native son, Anton Bruckner, works by Beethoven and Mozart are also included.

Tickets to performances within any of the theaters mentioned above can be obtained directly at their box offices (Mon–Fri 9am–6pm) or by contacting the ticket agency that represents virtually everything in Upper Austria, **Kartenbüro,** Herrenstrasse 4

(✆ **0732/778800;** tram: 1 or 3). For a rundown on what's going on in Upper Austria, ask for a copy of the monthly pamphlet "Was Ist Los in Linz und Oberösterreich" ("What's Happening in Linz and Upper Austria"). The tourist office will usually give you a copy for free; it will cost you 3€ ($4.80) if you buy it at a local newsstand.

The Bar & Club Scene

At night, Linz becomes a little more active than you might expect, judging from its daytime pace. At **Stonewall**, Rainerstrasse 22 (✆ **0732/600438**), you can expect a gay and lesbian crowd, although many straights come here as well. Dancing begins Friday and Saturday at 10pm. During the week it attracts devotees to its bar.

Looking to linger over a glass of wine in Old Austria? Head for the **Alte Welt Weinkeller,** Hauptplatz 4 (✆ **0732/770053;** www.altewelt.at; tram: 1 or 3), where a choice of mostly Austrian and Hungarian wines are sold by the glass or the bottle in a very old, very traditional setting that, judging by the state of the wood, has been here virtually forever. At least once a week, based on an iffy schedule, live bands perform or poets and writers read from their works, usually in German.

Dancing

If you want to go dancing, or at least see where Linzers go to boogie and flirt, consider a visit to the town's biggest dance club, **Mausefalle,** Wegscheider Strasse 3 (✆ **0650/8613740**; www.mausefalle-linz.at; tram: 1 or 3), where one large dance floor is serviced by several different bars, some with independent sound systems. There is a cover charge of 5€ ($8), which gives you free, unrestricted access to all areas of this dance and drinking complex. It's open every Monday and Wednesday to Saturday from 8pm till at least 3am, and sometimes as late as 6am the following morning.

Casino Action

Yes, there's a **casino** in Linz, within the Austria Trend Hotel Schillerpark (see earlier in this chapter), Rainerstrasse 2–4 (✆ **0732/6544870;** tram: 1 or 3), but nothing so scintillating that it will tempt you to mortgage your house or spend the children's college fund. The casino contains two separate sections of different degrees of formality. The **Casino Léger,** open daily noon to midnight, has no dress code and houses most of the establishment's slot machines. A step away, the **Linzer Casino,** open daily 3pm to 4am, is more formal and grand. A ticket that grants admission to both sections costs 23€ ($37), but it is accompanied by gaming tokens worth 25€ ($40). You must be over 18 and present a valid passport to enter either area.

SIDE TRIPS FROM LINZ

Pöstlingberg

The most popular day trip from Linz is to Pöstlingberg, 5km (3 miles) northwest of the city on the north bank of the Danube. You can drive here via Rudolfstrasse on the left bank of the river, taking a right turn onto Hagenstrasse; or, you can take the electric railway.

Pöstlingberg has a **botanical garden** with exotic tropical plants, and the summit terrace is a riot of blooming flowers in summer. A defensive tower now houses a grotto with a miniature railway, a favorite with children. The **pilgrimage church** is worth a visit for its 18th-century carved wood Pietà, but most tourists make the ascent mainly to take in the view over the Danube Valley, with Linz spread out below. The panorama stretches all the way to the foothills of the Alps and to the Bohemian Forest in the Czech Republic.

Mauthausen: The Concentration Camp

You can make a sobering outing from Linz to Mauthausen, 29km (18 miles) down the Danube (southeast) from the provincial capital. The village is very beautiful in its own right and is often visited for its medieval architecture. Overshadowing its attractiveness is the fact that during World War II, the Nazis operated a concentration camp and extermination center about 3km (2 miles) northwest of the village. Austria's Jews were slaughtered in great numbers, and the camp remains a horrifying testament to the evils of Nazism. Thousands of other so-called undesirables were also annihilated here, including homosexuals and Gypsies.

The Austrian government doesn't try to hide the site of so many atrocities. The camp was declared a national monument in 1949, and often schoolchildren are brought here and taught what went on in this notorious camp. Various countries that lost citizens here have erected memorials outside the camp to honor their dead. It's believed that the Nazis killed some 200,000 victims here, although exact figures are not known.

You can visit the huts where the condemned, most of whom almost surely knew their fate, were kept. You are also led down the infamous "Stairway of Death," which the prisoners took on their last walk. To visit the ghastly site is a shattering experience, but still people come here to be painfully reminded of a cruel and savage era.

To reach Mauthausen from Linz, take one of the dozen or so local buses departing from Linz's main railway station for Mauthausen (trip time: 1 hr.).

It takes about 1½ hours to take a tour of the camp. The camp is open February to April and October to December 15 daily 9am to 4pm, and May to October daily 9am to 6pm; it's closed November to January. For more information, call ✆ **07238/2269.** Admission is 3€ ($4.80) for adults and 1€ ($1.60) for children.

2 LAKES ATTERSEE & MONDSEE

ATTERSEE ★★

The largest lake in the Austrian Alps, Attersee comes alive in summer when a sports-loving crowd flocks to the resort town that bears the lake's name. In our opinion, the lake is too cold for swimming almost all the time (although Polar Bear Club members might disagree), but it's a great draw for boaters in summer. Attersee is 50km (31 miles) east of Salzburg and 69km (43 miles) west of Linz.

Those interested in fishing will appreciate the lake's clear alpine waters, with trout, char, and, in little tributaries, brook trout just beneath the surface. At many guesthouses along the shore you can have the fish you caught for dinner.

The blue-green *see* (lake) is 20km (13 miles) long and about 2km (1½ miles) wide, with many orchards growing on its uplands. There's a road around the entire body of water. From the southern part of the lake to the west of Burgau, you can take a 12-minute walk to a beautiful gorge, the **Burggrabenklamm,** with a waterfall, one of the most scenic sights along the Attersee.

Essentials

GETTING THERE Attersee lies at the terminus of a small railway running from the junction of Vöcklamarkt, just less than 14km (9 miles) to the north (about a dozen trains make the short run from Vöcklamarkt to Attersee every day). Reaching Vöcklamarkt is

The Great Outdoors in the Salzkammergut

The **Salzkammergut** is one of Europe's summer playgrounds, centered on the towns of **Bad Ischl, St. Wolfgang,** and **Hallstatt.** Soaring mountains with needlelike peaks and shimmering lakes along forested valleys are the backdrop for any number of outdoor activities, including boating, fishing, swimming, and hiking. The best known of all the Salzkammergut's 27 lakes lie to the west of Bad Ischl: the **Mondsee,** the **Attersee,** and the **Wolfgangsee.**

BIKING While most of the province's terrain is too hilly for biking, you'll find great places to bike in the districts around the lakes, particularly around the Attersee or the Traunsee. The best cycling path is the 14km (9 miles) from Bad Ischl to St. Wolfgang; of course, biking on the back roads is more scenic. Tourist offices in either town will help you plan routes. You can rent bikes from the most visible gas station in Attersee, **Petrol Schweiger** (© **07666/7821**), for around 10€ ($16) per day. If you'd like to join a local bicycle tour through and around the region, consider **Eurobike Eurofun Touristik,** Mühlstrasse 20, Obertraun am See (© **06219/7444**).

BOATING Most of the lakes scattered amid the forests of Upper Austria are deep, cold, and clear, and as such, boaters love them. If you want to rent a boat, the local tourist offices of every lakefront resort covered within this chapter can recommend local outfitters, one of the most visible of which is **Wolfgangsee-schiffahrt,** A-5360 St. Wolfgang (© **06138/22320**).

If you're interested in exploring one of the lakes while someone else worries about navigation and maintenance of the equipment, consider one of the Attersee tours offered by **Stern Schiffahrt,** A-4863 Attersee (© **07666/7806**). From June to mid-September, a 2-hour cruise along the south shore of the Attersee is 12€ ($19); cruises depart every 2 hours from 9am to 5pm. During the same time period, a 1-hour tour along the lake's north shore costs 10€ ($16) and departs at hourly intervals every day from 10am to 5pm.

CANOEING/KAYAKING/SAILING Some of Upper Austria's best white water lies along the swift-flowing Traun River. The region's best recommended canoe, kayak, and sailboat rental company lies in the neighboring hamlet of Nussdorf: **Yachtschule Kolloer,** A-4865 Nussdorf (© **0676/3305253**), where a 4-hour rental of a watercraft costs between 20€ to 25€ ($32–$40), depending on its pedigree. They also offer sailing lessons.

easy, as rapid trains stop there every 2 hours or less from both Salzburg and Linz. For rail information, contact © **05/1717** (www.oebb.at). Attersee is not served by bus lines. If you're driving from Linz, head west along the A-1; from Salzburg, go east on the A-1.

VISITOR INFORMATION The **tourist office,** A-4864 Attersee (© **07666/62324070;** www.attersee.at), is in the town center. It's open in winter Monday to Friday 9am to noon and 2 to 5pm; in summer daily 9am to 6pm.

FISHING The Salzkammergut is one of the best places to fish in all of Austria—or Europe, for that matter. The easiest way, in terms of legalities, involves buying a fishing license, valid for 1 week's fishing on the Attersee (but not in any of the swift-flowing rivers) for a one-time fee of 21€ ($34), available through any branch of the local tourist offices. Acquiring a permit for fishing in the streams of the region is much more complicated, involving permission from at least one local bureaucracy. For information, contact any local tourist office.

GOLF The best course is the **Salzkammergut Golfclub** at Bad Ischl (✆ **06132/26340;** www.salzammergut-golf.at). This 18-hole, par-71 course charges greens fees of 50€ to 60€ ($80–$96) daily.

HIKING The Salzkammergut is great hiking country, and local tourist offices not only suggest hikes, but also provide route maps. The Bad Ischl area, for example, has more than 100km (62 miles) of trails. In the Attersee area, one 35km (22-mile) hike takes 8 hours to finish. One of the best hiking trips involves circumnavigating Austria's largest lake (Attersee), which can take anywhere from 3 to 5 days, depending on your fitness level and how extensive an itinerary you want to pursue. Depending on your route, you can hike between 50 and 97km (31–60 miles), and choose paths of varying degrees of difficulty. For more details about possible outings, the tourist office in Attersee (✆ **07666/7719**) will send you a booklet indicating the hiking possibilities and their estimated times.

TENNIS Your best bet is the **Tennisclub Bad Ischl** in the heart of the resort (✆ **06132/23926**). The club offers both indoor and outdoor courts along with ball-throwing machines. You can also rent rackets.

WATERSPORTS Because of their proximity to such cities as Linz and Salzburg, the lakes of Upper Austria are popular spots for water-skiing and scuba diving. If you want to go water-skiing, the reception desk at lakeside hotels can provide names and addresses of suitable establishments. A well-recommended company on the Attersee, however, is **Häuplhof,** which operates out of the hamlet of Muhlbach, near Attersee (✆ **07666/7788**). And if you want to scuba-dive in waters that originated high in the Alps, head for **Reiter,** in the town of Unterach (✆ **07665/8524**), which specializes in year-round dives into the cold, dark waters of lakes whose depths sometimes exceed 168m (551 ft.).

Where to Stay & Dine

In Town

Hotel Seegasthof Oberndorfer This well-established, traditional family-owned hotel sits on the shores of the Attersee. The sunny, carpeted, and comfortable medium-size rooms have balconies. From the rooms there's a good view over the lake to the Höllengebirge. Gertrude Oberndorfer serves excellent Austrian cuisine, and in warm weather, meals are served on a terrace next to the lake, which is shaded by old chestnut trees.

Hauptstrasse 18, A-4864 Attersee. ✆ **07666/78640.** Fax 07666/786491. www.oberoesterreich.at/oberndorfer. 25 units. 100€–202€ ($160–$323) double; 226€ ($362) suite. Rates include buffet breakfast. Notify desk at reservations if you intend to use a credit card. AE, MC, V. Free parking in a lot next to the hotel, 8€ ($13) in the garage. Closed Nov. **Amenities:** Restaurant; bar; swimming lake; sauna; room service; massage; babysitting; laundry service; dry cleaning; nonsmoking rooms. *In room:* TV, Wi-Fi, minibar, hair dryer.

Around the Lake

At the northern extremity of the Attersee is the small village and holiday resort of **Seewachen am Attersee,** which offers sailing and other watersports. However, the main reason we recommend it is the Residenz Häupl (see below).

You could also base yourself at the lakeside hamlet of **Unterach am Attersee.** It's so small it doesn't appear on most maps, but it occupies one of the loveliest positions on the lake—on the right bank, across from Weissenbach—from where you can explore either the Attersee or Mondsee.

Hotel Georgshof (Value) Built in the early 1980s of well-preserved wood and cream-colored stucco, this cozy chalet (one of the town's two hotels) is set on a hillside about a 5-minute uphill walk from the center; it's 183m (600 ft.) higher than the town itself. Windows are embellished with regional designs and look out onto a backyard with a sun terrace. Inside is a timber-and-stucco bar area. The Hollerweger family offers spacious and tastefully furnished bedrooms. Beds are comfortable, with well-kept bathrooms.

Atterseestrasse 86, A-4866 Unterach am Attersee. ✆ **07665/8501.** Fax 07665/85018. www.oberoesterreich.at/georgshof. 25 units. 60€–96€ ($96–$154) double. Rates include half-board. Children under 11 stay free in parent's room. AE, DC, MC, V. Closed the last week of Nov–Dec 20. **Amenities:** Dining room; lounge; indoor heated pool; sauna; laundry service; dry cleaning. *In room:* TV, Wi-Fi.

Residenz Häupl ★★ One of the region's most elegant hotels, with some of the finest food, too, this establishment began its life as a simple inn during the 1600s. Today, it stays open year-round, unusual for these parts. It sits in the center of the village, across the street from the lakeshore. From the street side, it has a pleasant facade and a steeply sloped series of interconnected gables. From the lakeside, masses of flowers hang from boxes on handcrafted balconies. The interior looks like a tastefully opulent private house. Rooms are well furnished, beautifully maintained, and often quite large.

In the rustic dining room, one of the region's best, the chef prepares such delicacies as grilled char from the lake with baby vegetables in a savory sauce, perhaps followed by a dessert of curd-paste dumplings with stewed plums. Frau Häupl, whose family has run this place for the past seven generations, inspires the culinary techniques of an able group of chefs. Except for December 24, the restaurant is open daily from 11:30am to 2pm and 6 to 9:45pm.

Hauptstrasse 20, A-4863 Seewachen am Attersee. ✆ **07662/6363.** Fax 07662/636363. www.residenz-haeupl.at. 33 units. 90€–164€ ($144–$262) double; 180€–250€ ($288–$400) suite. Rates include buffet breakfast. AE, DC, MC, V. **Amenities:** Restaurant; bar; health club; sauna; steam room; bike rental; room service; babysitting; laundry service; dry cleaning; nonsmoking rooms. *In room:* TV, Wi-Fi, minibar, safe.

MONDSEE ★

Mondsee (Moon Lake) is one of the warmest lakes in the Salzkammergut. Since Roman times, this crescent-shape lake has been named for the celestial body it resembles. The Salzburg–Vienna Autobahn runs along the south shores of this, the third-largest lake in the Salzkammergut district. In the background you can see the **Drachenwand** and the **Schafberg** mountains.

The lake is sparsely settled, so if you want to find accommodations, you should head to the northwest corner for the village of Mondsee. A popular summer resort, with sailing schools and beaches, Mondsee is 270km (168 miles) southwest of Vienna, 27km (17 miles) east of Salzburg, and 100km (62 miles) southwest of Linz.

Essentials

GETTING THERE No rail lines extend to Mondsee. Most visitors travel by train to either Salzburg or Strasswalchen, a town conveniently on the main line between Salzburg and Vienna. For rail information, contact © **05/1717** (www.oebb.at). Buses depart from the railway station in Salzburg every hour throughout the day (trip time: 50 min.). From Strasswalchen, about half a dozen buses head south every day for Mondsee (trip time: 35 min.). From Salzburg, drivers head east on the A-1; from Linz, they go west on the A-1.

VISITOR INFORMATION The **tourist office** (© **06232/4070**) is in the town center at Dr. Franz Müllerstrasse 3. It's open year-round Monday to Saturday 8am to noon and 1 to 6pm. It's also open Sunday 8am to 7pm in July and August.

Exploring Mondsee

A Benedictine abbey was once situated in Mondsee, dating from A.D. 748. However, when Emperor Josef II ordered the abbey dissolved in 1791, the abbey church became the **Pfarrkirche (Parish Church),** still a point of interest in the village. It's a 15th-century structure with an added baroque exterior, but its crypt dates from the 11th century. The church was richly decorated by Meinrad Guggenbichler, a sculptor born in 1649. He designed seven of the more than dozen altars.

Part of the abbey is now the **Schloss Mondsee.** The castle, where the wedding scene in *The Sound of Music* was filmed, is adjacent to the church.

Heimatmuseum und Pfahlbaumuseum This museum is in the former cloisters of the abbey. Local artifacts related to the province's earlier eras are displayed in the Heimatmuseum. The Pfahlbaumuseum is dedicated to prehistoric archaeology; its exhibits trace local habitation from the time Neolithic humans constructed dwellings on pilings in the lake. Discoveries from as far back as 3000 B.C., up to the disappearance of prehistoric people in 1800 B.C., include Mondsee-Keramik pottery.

Hilfbergstrasse. © **06223/2270.** Admission 3€ ($4.80) adults, 1.50€ ($2.40) children. May to mid-Sept Tues–Sun 10am–6pm; mid-Sept to mid-Oct Tues–Sun 10am–5pm; mid-Oct to Oct 31 Sat–Sun only, 10am–5pm. Closed Nov–Apr.

Mondseer Rauchhaus This rustic wood chalet flanked by outbuildings was once a smokehouse used by farmers from the district. There's no chimney above the vaulted hearth.

Hilfbergstrasse. © 06232/2270; www.austria-info. Admission 2.20€ ($3.50) adults, 1.10€ ($1.80) children. May–Sept daily 10am–6pm; Apr and Oct 15–31 Sat–Sun 10am–5pm. Closed Oct 1–14 and Nov–Apr.

Where to Stay

Austria Classic Hotel Leitnerbräu ★ Dating back to the 17th century, this site was a popular brewery, which closed in 1904. Since then, the place has functioned as a hotel, run by many generations of the Marschallinger family. Their house stands in the center of Mondsee opposite the famous Pfarrkirche. Rooms are usually generous in size. Some have sitting areas and private balconies. Bikes are available free of charge. Guests enjoy good, hearty Austrian cuisine.

Steinerbachstrasse 6, A-5310 Mondsee. © **06232/6500.** Fax 06232/650022. www.leitnerbraeu.at. 30 units. 120€–145€ ($192–$232) double. AE, DC, MC, V. **Amenities:** Restaurant; bar; fitness center; Jacuzzi; sauna; steam room; bike rental; room service; massage; babysitting; laundry service; dry cleaning. *In room:* TV, Wi-Fi, minibar, hair dryer, safe.

Café Frauenschuh ★ PASTRIES/SNACKS This famous establishment, which has flourished since the 1950s, is known by sweet tooths throughout the region for its delectable pastries and chocolates. Set in the middle of the village, it offers racks of fruited and chocolate-covered confections, which you can eat on the spot or buy by the dozen. In midsummer, rows of tables are set up amid flowerpots outdoors. One of the most popular items, a piece of strudel with ice cream or whipped cream, costs 5.10€ ($8.20). Other pastries begin at 2.50€ ($4), with a coffee going for 2.75€ ($4.40). The cafe also offers sandwiches and salads.

Marktplatz. ✆ **06232/2312.** Daily 7am–7pm (until 11pm July–Aug). Closed Wed off-season.

La Farandole FRENCH An outdoor terrace, used during good weather, provides a view of the nearby forest. Specialties change with the seasons and include a delectable tartare of lake fish from the Mondsee, duck confit salad with fresh seasonal greens, roast rack of lamb with garlic, roebuck with chanterelle sauce, and marinated filets of salmon. Dessert might be a heavenly symphony of black- and white-chocolate mousses or artfully arranged truffles.

Schlössl 150. ✆ **06232/3475.** Reservations recommended. Main courses 12€–22€ ($19–$35). MC, V. July–Aug Tues–Sat noon–2pm and 7–9:30pm, Sun noon–2pm; Sept–Feb and May–June Tues–Sat noon–2pm and 7–9:30pm, Sun noon–2pm. Closed Mar. Many guests walk the 1/2 mile north from the center, but the bus marked MONDSEE–ZELL AM MOOS passes nearby as well.

3 ST. WOLFGANG & BAD ISCHL

These two resorts, though only a short distance apart in the Salzkammergut, are quite different in character.

St. Wolfgang lies on the Wolfgangsee (see section 8, "The Flachgau," in chapter 9). The boundary between Land Salzburg and Upper Austria crosses the lake. St. Wolfgang is 50km (31 miles) east of Salzburg, 114km (71 miles) southwest of Linz, and 13km (8 miles) west of Bad Ischl.

ST. WOLFGANG ★

In the mountains of the Salzkammergut, the **Wolfgangsee** is one of the most romantic lakes in Austria. St. Wolfgang, a little holiday resort on the northeastern side of the lake below the Schafberg (see below), is set among all this natural beauty. In summer, the resort is overrun with visitors.

If you drive here, there are two parking lots at the entrance to the town. You can park your car and then explore the town on foot. Late spring to early fall, it's better to go to St. Wolfgang by boat, leaving from the landing stage at Gschwendt, on the southern rim of the lake. Departures from mid-May to mid-October are usually hourly.

Other than a cog railway, which extends from St. Wolfgang to the top of the Schafbergspitz, St. Wolfgang is not serviced by any rail lines. Its only access is by bus, taxi, or car.

Essentials

GETTING THERE Buses depart from the railway station of Bad Ischl about a dozen times a day, making stops at both the marketplace (St. Wolfgang Marktplatz) and the base of the Schafbergbahn (St. Wolfgang Schafberg Rack Railway). Trip time to either is about 40 minutes.

If you're driving from Salzburg, take Route 158 east. From Linz, head southwest on the A-1; then cut southwest at the junction with Route 145 to Bad Ischl. From Bad Ischl, continue west on Route 158.

VISITOR INFORMATION The St. Wolfgang **tourist office** (✆ **06138/2239;** www.wolfgangsee.at) is in the town center. It's open in winter Monday to Friday 9am to noon and 2 to 5pm, Saturday 9am to noon; in summer Monday to Friday from 9am to 8pm, Saturday 9am to noon and 2 to 6pm, Sunday 1 to 6pm.

Swimming, Hiking, Skiing & More

In summer, swimming, watersports, and just sitting at a beach cafe are all highly regarded activities at this resort. Hiking is also possible in almost any direction.

There's skiing in the hills, usually December to mid-March, and you'll also find facilities here for skating, curling, and horse-drawn sleigh rides.

St. Wolfgang is the site of the celebrated **White Horse Inn** (see below); the landscape provided the perfect setting for Ralph Benatzky's operetta *White Horse Inn,* which brought glory to the town.

Pfarrkirche St. Wolfgang Since the 12th century, long before it was a vacation resort, St. Wolfgang was a renowned pilgrimage center. This church is said to stand on the same rocky spur of land above the lake where St. Wolfgang built a hermitage (signs from the center point the way). The church contains a magnificent Michael Pacher altarpiece (1481), pictured in many Gothic art books. Pacher's altarpiece is luxuriantly adorned with panel paintings and masterfully carved figures. The main panel depicts the *Coronation of the Virgin.* A new museum recently opened within the tower of the church; however, at press time, visitation at the museum was restricted to summer only, by appointment, Tuesday to Saturday from 2 to 4pm.

A-5360, St. Wolfgang im Salzkammergut. ✆ **06138/2321.** Free admission. Church May–Sept daily 9am–6pm; Oct–Apr Mon–Sat 10am–4pm, Sun 11am–4pm. Museum July–Aug by request Tues–Sun 2–4pm.

Where to Stay & Dine

Gasthof/Pension Zimmerbräu Value This 400-year-old house was once a local beer brewery, and for more than a century it's been a guesthouse run by the Scharf family. Set in the center of town, it doesn't open onto the lake; however, it has its own private beach cabin with a sun terrace on the lake. The traditionally furnished rooms have balconies, good beds, and ample bathrooms. Consider dining here, as the food is reasonably priced and the chef is known for his Austrian specialties, including homemade beef goulash, braised beef in red wine, deer stew, and a selection of fish. One section of the menu, called "healthy and light," has vegetarian dishes. The inn is entirely nonsmoking.

Markt 89, A-5360 St. Wolfgang. ✆ **06138/2204.** Fax 06138/220445. www.zimmerbraeu.com. 26 units. 80€–96€ ($128–$154) double. Rates include buffet breakfast. MC, V. Free parking at hotel; 7€ ($11) garage parking. Closed Nov. **Amenities:** Restaurant; bar; lounge. *In room:* TV, Wi-Fi, coffeemaker, hair dryer, safe.

Hotel Landhaus zu Appesbach ★ Set within a 5-minute walk downhill from the center of St. Wolfgang, this gracefully proportioned lakefront inn was originally built as a private home in the late 19th century. Sometime during its tenure as a private home, the Duke of Windsor spent several weeks here, a visit that added immeasurably to the building's social gloss. Today it's a socially correct address with a scattering of antique and contemporary furnishings and frequent but vague references to the building's illustrious past. Rooms are well furnished, in a wide range of sizes, as befits a former private home.

 Staff is polite and charming. There's a bar and a restaurant on the premises, but both are open only to residents of the hotel and their guests.

Au Promenade 18, A-5360 Wolfgang. ✆ **06138/22090.** Fax 06138/220914. www.appesbach.com. 25 units. 155€–295€ ($248–$472) double; 225€–322€ ($360–$515) suite. Rates include buffet breakfast. AE, DC, MC, V. **Amenities:** Restaurant; bar; tennis court; exercise room; sauna; room service; massage; laundry service; dry cleaning; nonsmoking rooms; solarium. *In room:* TV, Wi-Fi, minibar, hair dryer, safe.

Im Weissen Rössl (White Horse Inn) ★★ This hotel was the setting used for a popular play *(Im Weissen Rössl am Wolfgangsee)* written in 1896 and adapted for the Berlin stage by a group of actors and directors who returned here to rewrite it in 1930. Actually, there has been an inn on this site since 1474, with continuous ownership by the Peter family since 1912. Much of the hotel you see today dates from 1955, when the historic core was enlarged and expanded in a style true to the original design.

This scene of the famous operetta absolutely exudes a romantic atmosphere. Its stippled yellow facade conceals a collection of carved antiques. The public areas are large and sunny, usually wood-paneled and upholstered in cheerful colors. Rooms come in a variety of sizes, but all have fine beds. There is a wide lakeside sun terrace within view of the village church and sailing, water-skiing, and windsurfing facilities along their private beach. In the evening the management usually provides live piano or zither music. The inn's two restaurants serve both Austrian and international specialties, and are among the finest in the area—but overly touristy.

Markt 74, A-5360 St. Wolfgang. ✆ **06138/23060.** Fax 06138/230641. www.weissesroessl.at. 72 units. 130€–236€ ($208–$378) double; 200€–356€ ($320–$570) suite. Rates include buffet breakfast. Half-board (3-day minimum) 26€ ($42) per person supplement. AE, DC, MC, V. Parking 10€ ($16). Closed Nov. **Amenities:** 2 restaurants; bar; 2 heated pools (1 indoor); 2 tennis courts; fitness center; Jacuzzi; sauna; room service; massage; babysitting; laundry service; dry cleaning; nonsmoking rooms; solarium. *In room:* TV, Wi-Fi, minibar, hair dryer, safe.

A Side Trip to Schafberg

The most popular excursion from St. Wolfgang is to **Schafberg ★★**, which offers the most stunning view in Upper Austria. Legend has it that you can see 13 lakes of the Salzkammergut from here, but we've never been able to do so. However, you're almost sure to have a good view of the Mondsee and the Attersee, and, of course, the entire Wolfgangsee. On a clear day, you can see as far as the Berchtesgaden Alps. You can also gaze at the wonderful backdrop to the lakes, the peaks of the Höllengebirge, and the glacier-capped Dachstein.

The whole trip to Schafberg takes about 4½ hours, nearly half by rack rail called **Schafbergbahn**, which operates from early May to late October. Once you're here, allow for about 30 minutes of walking. Departures are hourly: from mid-May to mid-June daily from 8:30am to 4:30pm; from mid-June to mid-September daily from 8:05am to 6:40pm; and from mid September to mid October daily from 8:30am to 6:20pm. Round-trip fare is 27€ ($43) for adults and 14€ ($22) for children. For more information, call ✆ **06138/2232;** www.schafbergbahn.at. There's a hotel on the summit of the mountain, which rises to 1,784m (5,853 ft.).

THE SPA OF BAD ISCHL ★

Bad Ischl is one of the country's most fashionable spas and was the summer seat of Emperor Franz Josef for more than 60 years. The town, constructed on a peninsula between the Traun River and its tributary, the Ischl, still reflects a certain imperial conceit in its architecture, much of it left over from the heyday of the Austro–Hungarian Empire.

The spa establishments provide relaxing brine-sulfur mud baths, which might not be the most aromatic of experiences but supposedly are beneficial for a variety of ailments.

Essentials

GETTING THERE Bad Ischl sits astride a secondary rail line that runs north to the major rail junction of Attnang-Puchheim and south to the equally important junction of Stainach-Irdning. At these junctions, trains connect frequently with those traveling from Salzburg, Vienna, Linz, and Graz. The trip from Vienna, with connections, takes 3¾ hours; from Graz, it's around 4½ hours. For rail information, contact ✆ **05/1717** (www.oebb.at).

Many travelers opt for one of the buses that depart every hour from Salzburg's main railway station for Bad Ischl. The trip takes about 90 minutes, and transfers are usually not required. By car, Bad Ischl can be reached from Salzburg or Munich by taking Route 158 east from Salzburg.

VISITOR INFORMATION The **tourist office,** at Bahnhofstrasse 6 (✆ **06132/2775-07;** www.badischl.com), will give you complete directions and information about all the sights in the immediate vicinity if you'd like to make some day trips from the spa. It's open Monday to Friday 8am to 6pm, Saturday 9am to 3pm, Sunday 9am to 1pm.

Exploring Bad Ischl

Bad Ischl has chic shopping, as you'll note if you go along **Pfarrgasse.** This street comes to an end at the **Esplanade,** a shaded promenade where the most famous figures in Europe once strolled. Wealthy salt merchants lived along this promenade, and Maximilian, ill-fated emperor of Mexico, was born in a royal dwelling here in 1832.

The former pump room, **Trinkhalle,** where the fashionable have eaten and drunk since 1831, is in the middle of town on Ferdinand-Auböck-Platz. Many of the buildings on the square are in Biedermeier style. The 1753 **Pfarrkirche (Parish Church)** was rebuilt when Maria Theresia was empress.

Kaiservilla ★★ The most important attraction in town is this imperial villa close to the center. Emperor Franz Josef used this Biedermeier palace for 60 summers as a residence and recreation center. Highlights include the Gray Salon, where Empress Elisabeth lived and from which she left on July 16, 1898 for Switzerland, a trip that ended with her assassination. In the emperor's study, Franz Josef signed the Manifest, a declaration of war that led to World War I.

In the Kaiserpark. ✆ **06132/23241.** www.kaiservilla.at. Admission 11€ ($18) adults, 7€ ($11) children. May to mid-Oct daily 9:30am–5pm. Closed off-season.

Marmorschlössl Surrounded by the Kaiserpark, this structure, dating from the mid-1800s, houses a photo-historic collection (Sammlung Frank) documenting the history of the spa. The tiny place was once used by Empress Elisabeth as a tea pavilion.

In the Kaiserpark. ✆ **06132/24422.** Admission to museum 2€ ($3.20) adults, 1€ ($1.60) children. Apr–Oct daily 9:30am–5pm. Closed Nov–Mar.

Museum der Stadt Bad Ischl This is the house where Emperor Franz Josef announced his engagement to the Bavarian princess Elisabeth von Wittelsbach, nicknamed "Sissi." Today it's a city museum devoted to the spa's history and culture, with memorabilia not only about the emperor, but also from famous composers who vacationed or lived here.

Esplanade 10. ✆ **06132/25476.** www.museum-badischl.at. Admission 4.70€ ($7.50) adults, 2.30€ ($3.70) children. Apr–Oct and Dec Tues and Thurs–Sun 10am–5pm, Wed 2–7pm; Jan–Mar Fri–Sun 10am–5pm. Closed Nov.

Villa Léhar This lovely villa, now a museum, stands on the opposite bank of the Traun River. Franz Léhar (1870–1948), the composer best known for his operetta *The Merry Widow,* lived here from 1912 until his death.

Traunkai. ✆ **06132/26992.** Admission 4.80€ ($7.70) adults, 2.20€ ($3.50) children. May–Sept daily 10am–noon and 2–5pm. Closed Oct–Apr.

Where to Stay

Austria Classic Hotel Goldenes Schiff ★ This hotel has a great location—central but quiet—plus a garden overlooking the Traun River and the Villa Léhar. Rooms are generally spacious and offer tiny but well-kept bathrooms equipped mostly with tub/shower combinations. The riverfront rooms contain balconies and anterooms, and all are well furnished with radios and wall safes. Mr. Edwin and family try to satisfy all guests in this snug retreat. In the cozy dining rooms, you'll enjoy excellent cuisine. There is a personal computer with Internet access in the lobby for hotel guests.

Stifterkai 3, A-4820 Bad Ischl. ✆ **06132/24241.** Fax 06132/2424158. www.goldenes-schiff.at. 53 units. 108€–152€ ($173–$243) double; 152€–166€ ($243–$266) junior suite. Rates include buffet breakfast. AE, DC, MC, V. **Amenities:** Restaurant; bar; fitness center; sauna; room service; massage; laundry service; nonsmoking rooms; solarium. *In room:* TV, Wi-Fi, minibar, hair dryer, safe.

Where to Dine

Villa Schratt ★★ AUSTRIAN During the heyday of Bad Ischl, when the aristocracy of the Hapsburg Empire descended on the town every summer with Emperor Franz Josef, one of the town's brightest inhabitants was the actress Katharina Schratt. Famous throughout the German-speaking world, she rose to a discreet kind of stardom as the mistress of the emperor, a relationship that lasted many years with the tacit approval of Franz Josef's estranged wife, the Empress Elisabeth ("Sissi").

Today the villa that Katharina occupied is a touristy but rather upscale restaurant. Set about 4km (2½ miles) west of town, beside the highway leading to Salzburg, the house was originally built in 1610 and was acquired by Ms. Schratt in 1889. She occupied it every summer until the death of Franz Josef in 1916.

In the restaurant's dining rooms, where all the references to Ms. Schratt seem vague and ever-so-polite, you can order such menu items as a terrine of duck *en gelée,* carpaccio of salmon-trout with salad, neck of lamb with garlic sauce, filet of venison with elderberry sauce, and, for dessert, cheese dumplings with cinnamon and fruit sauce. The extensive wine list contains selections from Austrian, Italian, and French vineyards.

Steinbrüch 43. ✆ **06132/27647.** www.villaschratt.at. Reservations required. Main courses 18€–35€ ($28–$55). AE, MC. Thurs–Mon 11:30am–[illegible] and [illegible]. Closed [illegible].

Weinhaus Attwenger ★ AUSTRIAN This is one of the region's best-known restaurants, with strong connections to musical prodigies Bruckner, who dined here frequently, and Léhar, who lived next door and shared a garden and many glasses of fine wine with the owners. The restaurant's central section was originally built in 1540, and its old-style decor is much imitated. In summer, you can dine or just savor a glass of wine or coffee on the sun terrace over the Traun River. If you want a full meal, the delicious menu includes medallions of veal chef's style, paprika schnitzel or pork schnitzel, *tafelspitz,* and several kinds of fresh lake fish.

Léharkai 12. ✆ **06132/23327.** www.weinhaus-attwenger.com. Reservations recommended. Main courses 8.75€–22€ ($14–$34); 4-course fixed-price menu 29€ ($46). MC, V. Tues–Sun 11:30am–2pm and 6–9:30pm. Closed 1 month around Christmas.

A Cafe: The Oldest In Austria

After viewing the summer playgrounds of the Hapsburg monarchs, anyone with a love of history should head to **Konditorei Zauner,** Pfarrgasse 7 (✆ **06132/2331020;** www.zauner.at), the oldest pastry shop and coffeehouse in Austria. The imperial court used to order pastries here, and it was said that the easiest way to tap into the pulse of the empire was to eavesdrop on a nearby table during July and August. The cafe's guest book shows a clientele as rich and diverse as the pastry offerings.

You can buy the exquisite pastries from the gold-and-white rococo showroom (which has been renovated to handle the flood of summer tourists) or eat at the small tables in a series of elegant inner rooms. Many items can be mailed as gifts. Sandwiches and salads are also on the menu. Coffee costs 2.95€ ($4.70), with pastries starting at 4€ ($6.40). It's open daily 8:30am to 6pm.

Bad Ischl After Dark

Most of the year, Bad Ischl seems trapped in its imperial past, a nostalgia that can be relaxing at best and soporific at worst. During July and August, however, the spa livens up a bit and presents a well-rehearsed operetta in whichever public building can accommodate it. In the past, *The Merry Widow* or Johann Strauss's *Der Tzigeunerbaron* have been presented 3 nights a week, usually at 8pm. Tickets cost 28€ to 68€ ($45–$109). For reservations and information, call ✆ **06132/23839**.

4 HALLSTATT

88km (55 miles) SE of Salzburg; 19km (12 miles) S of Bad Ischl

Hallstatt, a small market town south of Bad Ischl, is a beautiful Austrian village. It stands on the left bank of the dark, brooding Hallstättersee in the Salzkammergut, at the province's southernmost tip, bordering Land Salzburg (see chapter 9) and Styria (see chapter 14). Many people drive to the lake through Styria, via Bad Aussee.

The Hallstättersee is a narrow lake, about 8km (5 miles) long and 2km (1½ miles) at its widest, almost completely surrounded by mountains. Its waters are so dark they're often called black.

Now a modern town, Hallstatt is the oldest still-inhabited village in Europe, owing its longevity to the local deposits of salt. Its perch against a mountain on a rocky terrace overlooking the Hallstättersee seems like a curious place to build a town, but this was the site of an early Iron Age culture dating from 800 to 400 B.C. Many Iron Age relics have been unearthed in the area. The mining of salt from the mountain behind Hallstatt was known among pre-Celtic tribes of 1000 B.C. It died out in medieval times but was revived by the Hapsburgs and continues to flourish today.

ESSENTIALS

GETTING THERE Hallstatt is serviced by the same rail lines that go to Bad Ischl, which lies two stops to the north. (For more information, see "St. Wolfgang & Bad Ischl," earlier in this chapter.) Hallstatt is 43km (27 miles) north of the rail junction at Stainach-Irdning and 64km (40 miles) south of the rail junction at Attnang-Puchheim. The trip to Hallstatt from Linz, with connections, takes 2 hours; from Vienna, it takes 4 hours. For rail information, contact ✆ **05/1717** (www.oebb.at).

Around eight buses per day depart from the railway station at Bad Ischl, through Bad Goisern, and continue on to Hallstatt (trip time: about 35 min.).

If you're driving, go to Bad Ischl, continue south along Route 145 until you reach Route 166, and then head south via Steeg to Hallstatt.

VISITOR INFORMATION The **tourist office** is in the Kultur- und Kongresshaus, Seestrasse 169 (✆ **06134/8208;** www.hallstaat.net). It's open Monday to Friday 9am to 5pm, Saturday 10am to 5pm.

WHAT TO SEE & DO

Exploring the Village

The village of Hallstatt, with its narrow and often steep streets, gave its name to one of the most important eras of prehistory. Some 2,000 graves of prehistoric people, half of them cremated, have been excavated in the area, which Austrians refer to as a "cradle of civilization." Many of the artifacts excavated here dating from Neolithic times are displayed in the **Prähistorisches Museum,** Seestrasse 56 (✆ **06134/828015**). The cremation graves have revealed artifacts that indicated the existence of a ruling class. Apparently the burials continued to about 350 B.C., the late Iron Age. The museum is open May to September daily 10am to 6pm, October and April daily 10am to 4pm, and November to March Monday and Tuesday 11am to 3pm. Admission is 8€ ($13) for adults and 4€ ($6.40) for children.

The center of this beautifully situated village, with views of the Dachstein mountain massif, is the **Marktplatz (Market Square),** which contains some 16th-century buildings.

You can visit the **Pfarrkirche (Parish Church),** which is situated within a churchyard bordering the dark waters of the lake. The house of worship is a large structure from the latter part of the 15th century. Visitors can also go to the **Chapel of St. Michael,** a Gothic church next to the parish church. The cemetery was so small that this *karner* (charnel house or bone house) had to be used as a burial site starting in the 17th century.

Outdoor Activities

Numerous cable cars and lifts are available in town and the surrounding area to take you up the mountains, where you can take in panoramic views. If you'd like a little exercise, there are many walking paths or hiking trails as well. Mountain climbing is also possible on the nearby **Dachstein** massif (2,995m/9,826 ft.), and you can explore the **Dachstein Giant Ice Caves,** although the mountain is more easily reached from nearby Obertraun than from Hallstatt. For a great way to spend a morning, fish in the Hallstättersee and the Traun River, or try sailing, rowing, motorboating, swimming, or scuba. In winter, Hallstatt is also a sports center, with snow from November to April. You can go skiing, sledding, curling, and ice-skating, or hike along pleasant winter footpaths. The tourist office (above) will provide complete details about which of these activities will be available at the time of your visit.

The Salt Mines in Salzburg

Northwest of Hallstatt is one of the most distinctive geological formations in the region, **Salzwelten/Hallstatt** ★ (✆ **06134/8251;** www.salzwelten.at), which is not to be confused with Salzburg, the city. Miners have been hauling vast quantities of salt out of the mountain for centuries; the mines are still active and visitors can tour them to get insight into the amount of work needed to create and run a modern mine. Teams of archaeologists have accumulated many rare objects from the debris left by former miners.

To reach Salt Mountain from Hallstatt, take an uphill ride on the cable car that departs from the western suburb of Lahn, a 5-minute walk from Hallstatt's railway station. In May and from mid-September to mid-October, the funicular runs daily from 9am to 4:30pm; from June to mid-September, it runs daily from 9am to 6pm. The only way you can visit the mines is as part of a guided tour, which is 22€ ($35) for adults, 13€ ($21) for children ages 7 to 15, and 11€ ($18) for children ages 4 to 6; children under 4 are not admitted. The price includes round-trip transfers on the funicular. From May 1 to May 24 and from mid-September to late October, tours are conducted daily at frequent intervals, from 9:30am to 3pm. From May 25 to September 13, tours are conducted daily from 9:30am to 4:30pm. The mines are closed from late October to April 13. Although tours of the mines take only 50 minutes, you should allow 2½ hours for the full experience.

There's a restaurant and snack bar with a terrace and a belvedere for taking in the view. Hikers can go all the way from here to the **Iron Age cemetery,** an approximately 1½-hour trip. If you ask, the tourist office will outline a series of hikes in the area. One that goes along the Echerntal to **Waldbachstrub,** at the top of the valley, has lovely waterfalls along the way. You can also climb to the **Tiergartenhütte,** which has a small inn, and on to the **Wiesberghaus,** 1,885m (6,184 ft.). After that, only the hardy continue to the **Simony-Hüttee** at 2,205m (7,235 ft.), where there's another small inn lying at the foot of the Hallstatt Glacier. From Simony-Hüttee, mountain climbers can summit the **Hoher Dachstein,** the loftiest peak in the massif (2,995m/9,826 ft.); the climb takes 3½ hours.

Dachstein Caves ★

The Dachstein Ice Caves, Dachstein Bahn, A-4831 Obertraun, are among the most spectacular natural sights of Upper Austria. To reach them, drive to Obertraun, 6km (3¾ miles) east of Hallstatt, where a sign in the vicinity will direct you to the lower station of the cableway that takes you to the caves. The cableway deposits you at the intermediate platform (1,351m/4,432 ft.) on the Schönbergalm. From here, it's about a 20-minute walk to the entrance to the caves. A round-trip ticket costs 14€ ($22) for adults and 7.70€ ($12) for children.

Among the many attractions is the **Rieseneishöhle (Giant Ice Cave),** where even in summer the temperature is about 30°F (–1°C). Be sure to dress for the cold. Among the ice cave's breathtaking features are the frozen waterfalls. You'll also see the so-called King Arthur's Cave and the Great Ice Chapel. The ice cave is open from the first of May until mid- to late October daily from 9am to 4pm; a guided tour is 8.80€ ($14) for adults and 5.20€ ($8.30) for children. If you also want to visit Mammoth Cave, a combined ticket is 14€ ($22) for adults and 7.60€ ($12) for children. Mammoth Cave has large galleries (subterranean passageways) cut through the rock by ancient underground torrents. It takes about 1½ hours to go on a guided tour of these caves. You're allowed to visit only a small part of the cave network, which totals 37km (23 miles) in length, with a drop of 1,180m (3,871 ft.). For information, call ✆ **06134/8400.**

From the Schönbergalm station, you can go by cableway to the upper platform at a height of 2,111m (6,926 ft.). This is the **Hoher Krippenstein** ★★, which offers a panoramic view of the Dachstein massif. A chapel erected in the 1950s commemorates the accidental deaths of 13 teachers and students that took place here. The cableway operates every 15 minutes daily from 9am to 4pm. In summer, don't be surprised if there's a line. From Krippenstein you can take a cable car down to **Gjaidalm** (1,793m/5,883 ft.).

Other Natural Attractions

The region around Hallstatt is riddled with geological oddities, including caves, caverns, and glaciers whose ice never melts. A local cavern that's particularly easy to visit is **Koppenbrüllerhöhle (Koppenbrüller Cave).** Within its bowels, there's a raging underground stream whose activity causes continual erosion (and enlargement) of the cavern. The local municipality views it as a natural wonder and, as such, maintains a series of underground catwalks and galleries that you can walk along.

The easiest way to reach the cave is by car or taxi, but it's also accessible via trains, about three a day, that pull into the local station, Koppenbrüllerhöhle, after a 15-minute ride from Hallstatt or a 5-minute ride from Obertraun. There's a hotel, the Gasthaus Koppenrast, nearly adjacent to the railway station, which serves as an additional landmark for motorists. From here, you have to walk for about 15 minutes across well-marked trails to reach the cave. One-hour guided tours are conducted from early May to late September daily from 9am to 4pm for 7.50€ ($12) for adults and 4.40€ ($7) for children.

A final option for natural sightseeing is to check out the view over the steep and foreboding south wall of the Dachstein. For the best outlook, take the **Gletscherbahn** cable car uphill to an alpine plateau known as **Hunerkogel,** site of a hotel with its own cafe and restaurant. To reach the base of the Gletscherbahn cable car, drive for 16km (10 miles) along Route 166, following the signs to Ramsau (which you'll pass through) and Schladming, which lies across the border from Upper Austria, in Styria. The 12-minute cable car ride operates year-round daily from 8am to 5pm, with the exception of annual closings between November and Christmas and from early April to mid-May. At the upper belvedere (the above-mentioned Hunerkogel, 2,696m/8,845 ft. above sea level), you'll enjoy a panoramic view that includes the Grossglockner Pass and the Salzkammergut Alps, and a sweep of the Schladminger Gletscher, where some hardy locals sometimes ski on rock-strewn, granular snow even in midsummer.

WHERE TO STAY & DINE

Gasthof Zauner ★ Value In the center of the town's historic market square stands this century-old inn where you are welcomed by its mountaineering owner bedecked in traditional lederhosen. A long-enduring family-run hotel, the guesthouse is often visited by nonresidents who know that it serves the freshest fish specialties direct from Hallstatt Lake. The wine cellar also enjoys local renown. The wooden chalet is a cliché of Austrian folkloric charm, with balconies overlooking the village and a lake where a delectable white fish, the mild *Reinanke,* is caught and made ready for the grill. The pine-paneled rooms are rustically but comfortably furnished with carved [illegible]

Marktplatz, A-4830 Hallstatt. ✆ **06134/8246.** Fax 06134/82468. www.zauner.hallstatt.net. 12 units. 86€–106€ ($138–$170) double. Rates include breakfast. DC, MC, V. Closed mid-Nov to mid-Dec. **Amenities:** Restaurant. *In room:* TV, hair dryer.

Seehotel Grüner Baum This historic and rustically elegant hotel was originally established around 200 years ago as a lakeside inn and was amply enlarged around 1900. Capped with a hipped roof of hammered copper, it has an ocher-colored facade with white, heavily bordered windows. Prices for the comfortable rooms are determined almost exclusively by the views, of either Marktplatz (the town's main square), the lake, or the street. Rooms come in a variety of sizes and all are equipped with comfortable beds. The hotel's sun terrace extends out over the water on a pier, where you can go swimming or simply relax with a drink on a chaise lounge. The hotel contains a restaurant that specializes in fish from the nearby lake, when available. The hotel maintains an apartment for larger parties.

Marktplatz 104, A-4830 Hallstatt. ✆ **06134/826344.** Fax 06134/8263-44. www.gruenerbaum.cc. 19 units. 110€–165€ ($176–$264) double; 180€–200€ ($288–$320) apt. Rates include breakfast. AE, DC, MC, V. Closed Oct 17–May 1. **Amenities:** Restaurant; bar, lounge; exercise room; sauna; babysitting; laundry service; dry cleaning; solarium. *In room:* TV, dataport.

5 THE TRAUNSEE ★★

One of the biggest lakes in the Salzkammergut, the Traunsee is about 12km (7½ miles) long and some 3km (2 miles) wide at its broadest. It lies east of the two major lakes already explored: the Attersee and the Mondsee. Three mountain peaks—Traunstein, Hochkogel, and Eriakogel—form a silhouette that Austrians call Schlafende Griechin (Sleeping Greek Girl). Some sections of the Salzkammergut road (Rte. 145) run along the western edge of the lake.

The most dramatic part of this road is from the Ebensee, at the lake's southwestern tip, to Trauenkirchen. A feat of engineering, this corniche had to be hewn out of rock. The Traunsee is ringed with a number of resorts, the chief town being Gmunden. There's a lake steamer service in summer. To reach this lake from Bad Ischl (see section 3, earlier in this chapter), drive northeast along the Traun River (Rte. 145) and follow the signs.

GMUNDEN ★

This is one of the most popular summer resorts in the Salzkammergut, perched on the northern rim of the Traunsee with pine-green mountains forming the backdrop. Gmunden is located 169km (105 miles) southwest of Vienna, 40km (25 miles) southwest of Linz, and 76km (47 miles) northeast of Salzburg.

Essentials

GETTING THERE All train passengers to Gmunden must transfer in the railway junction of either Attnang-Puchheim (the more convenient) or Lambach. Both sit directly on the main rail line between Linz and Salzburg, handling many express trains throughout the day.

From Attnang-Puchheim, about 64km (40 miles) to the north, about a dozen trains continue on to Gmunden's Hauptbahnhof (main railway station). From Lambach, only around three trains per day run to Gmunden's Seebahnhof (lakeside railway station). Taxis are readily available for the short trip between these two stations, although the Hauptbahnhof is more convenient to most hotels. Gmunden is the starting point for many buses heading out into the surrounding valleys. For rail information, contact ✆ **05/1717** (www.oebb.at).

To reach Gmunden from Linz by car, take the A-1 southwest to the junction with Route 144, at which point you head south.

VISITOR INFORMATION The **tourist office,** Toscanapark 1 (✆ **07612/64305;** www.traunsee.at), is open in winter Monday to Friday 9am to 5pm, Saturday and Sunday 9am to 1pm; in summer Monday to Friday 8am to 8pm, Saturday and Sunday 10am to 7pm.

Walking Around Gmunden

Chestnut trees line the mile-long, traffic-free **Esplanade** ★, the town's chief attraction. You can walk from **Rathausplatz (Town Hall Square)** to the **Strandbad (Lakeside Beach),** watching the many majestic swans glide serenely along the lake. In days of yore, emperors, kings, and members of the aristocracy strolled along the Esplanade and in the town's park, just as you can do today. The Welfen from Hannover, Württembergs, Bourbons, and archdukes of Austria favored Gmunden as a pleasure ground, as did Franz Schubert, Friedrich Hebbel, and Johannes Brahms, among others.

The lake beaches are some of the best in the whole area, and in summer you can enjoy a wide variety of lakeside activities, from swimming and sailing to windsurfing and water-skiing, as well as tennis and horseback riding. For the experienced, it's also possible to do a little mountain climbing. For those in the mood for less strenuous activity, there are folkloric performances and dance clubs, or you can just relax in a wine tavern or an outdoor cafe. The tourist office will supply details.

Gmunden, former center of the salt trade, has long produced Gmundner ceramics, and you'll see artistic work in faience (opaque-colored glazes) and green-flamed pottery.

One of the more evocative curiosities of Gmunden is the **Schloss Ort (Ort Castle)** ★, now a ruined jumble of stones built on ancient Roman foundations that's set on a small island a few yards offshore from Gmunden's town center, at the far end of the Esplanade. Visitors are free to wander among the ruins or stop at a nearby restaurant, the Orther Stuben (✆ **07612/62499**), a short distance from the ruins. Guided tours can be arranged with several days' advance notice through the tourist office (above), although most visitors to Gmunden opt to wander around on their own.

The region around Gmunden is rich with sweeping panoramas. From a well-marked spot close to the town center, you can take a cable car, the **Grünberg Seilbahn** (✆ **07612/6601445;** www.greunberg-gmunden.net), to the top of the town's nearest mountain, the Grünberg, where you'll be able to see out over the Traunsee and the Dachstein. The cable car, hauling four persons up and downhill within each of its *cabines,* operates only May through October; it charges 12€ ($18) for adults and 6.80€ ($11) for children round-trip from Gmunden to the top, a 12-minute ride each way. May, June, September, and October, it operates daily 9am to 5pm; July and August, daily 9am to 6pm.

In winter, ski lifts, runs, and slopes on the Grünberg are easily reached from Gmunden. Other winter activities in Gmunden are curling, ice-skating, and walking along the lake.

Where to Stay & Dine

Pension Haus Magerl These premises were originally built in the 1600s and converted to a farmhouse around 1900. In the 1950s, members of the Magerl family transformed it into a pleasant hotel, with an annex added in 1991. The establishment you see today sits in a grassy meadow less than a kilometer (1/2 mile) east of Gmunden, with a view overlooking the nearby lake. Each floor contains a residents' lounge, and rooms are simple yet comfortable. Beds are adequate, not spectacular, and the bathrooms are a bit small but equipped with tub/shower combinations. Housekeeping, however, is excellent.

Ackerweg 18, A-4810 Gmunden. ✆ **07612/63675.** Fax 07612/63675220. 70 units. 90€ ($144) double. Rate includes breakfast. DC, MC, V. **Amenities:** Breakfast room; lounge; indoor heated pool; fitness center; sauna; nonsmoking rooms; rooms for those w/limited mobility. *In room:* TV, Wi-Fi, hair dryer, safe.

Schlosshotel Freisitz Roith ★★ On foundations dating from the 15th century, this castle was built as a summer house by the Hapsburg emperor Rudolf II in 1597. After centuries of private ownership, it was transformed into a hotel in 1965. One mile east of the town center, it's set amid a garden on a forested hillside, overlooking the lake. It looks like a combination baroque private house and a Victorian-style hotel. Dozens of architectural oddities include a crenellated tower with tall arched windows, wrought-iron window bars, jutting parapets over many of the balconied windows, and a stone terrace—site of a well-recommended restaurant—built into the slope of the grass-covered hill. On the grounds, a private footpath leads downhill to a beach at the edge of the lake.

The interior incorporates modern building materials with the older stone-accented design of vaulted ceilings. Rooms range from old-fashioned and dignified to contemporary yet conservatively furnished. As befits such an old castle, rooms come in a variety of sizes, and all have comfortable beds. Bathrooms have been equipped with spotlessly maintained tub/shower combinations.

Traunsteinstrasse 87, A-4810 Gmunden. ✆ **07612/64905.** Fax 07612/490517. www.freisitzroith.at. 24 units. 150€–230€ ($240–$368) double; 230€–320€ ($368–$512) suite. Rates include breakfast. AE, DC, MC, V. **Amenities:** Restaurant; bar; fitness center; Jacuzzi; sauna; room service; babysitting; laundry service; dry cleaning; nonsmoking rooms. *In room:* TV, Wi-Fi, minibar, hair dryer, safe.

6 WELS ★

200km (124 miles) W of Vienna; 32km (20 miles) SW of Linz; 105km (65 miles) NE of Salzburg

A flourishing town in Roman times, **Wels** lies on the left bank of the Traun River in the center of a large farm belt known today for its agricultural fairs. Wels is most often used as a base for exploring the hinterlands, although it has some attractions of its own. In about 1½ hours, you can walk through the town and see all the major sights.

ESSENTIALS

GETTING THERE Wels sits astride the main rail line connecting Salzburg with Linz and Vienna's Westbahnhof (West Railway Station). From both directions, at least three trains per hour pull into Wels, many of them express. The trip from Vienna takes about 2 hours; from Salzburg, about 1 hour; and from Linz, only 15 minutes. For rail information, contact ✆ **05/1717** (www.oebb.at).

Because of the frequency of trains, few local residents would consider taking the bus from most other large cities in Austria. Wels is, however, the point of origin of many bus lines heading into the surrounding hills and valleys. There's also bus service from Linz's main railway station to Wels around four times a day. Compared to the train, the trip is slow, taking about 50 minutes.

If you're driving from Linz, head southwest on Autobahn A-1 and cut west onto Autobahn A-25 for the final run to Wels. From Salzburg, head east on Autobahn A-1 before turning north on Route 138.

VISITOR INFORMATION The **tourist office,** Kaiser-Josef-Platz 22 (✆ **07242/43495;** www.austria-trips.com/wels/wels.htm), is open Monday to Friday 9am to 6pm.

WALKING AROUND WELS

Beautifully decorated facades of old houses, an intricately carved fountain, and a broad, cobbled pavement make **Stadtplatz** one of the most architecturally harmonious town squares in Austria. Most of the houses date from the 16th to the 18th centuries. The baroque **Rathaus,** built in 1748, is one of the most ornate buildings in the Old Town. The **Ledererturm,** dating from 1618, is the only tower remaining of those that once studded the town walls. Many homes or shops in the Old Town are supported by arches and passageways with vaulted ceilings.

Emperor Maximilian I died in Wels in 1519, stricken as he was traveling from the Tyrolean country to Wiener Neustadt. The house in which he died, **Kaiserliche Burg,** is on Burggasse, and has been turned into a museum of minor importance. You can see the room in which the emperor took his last breath.

The **Stadtpfarrkirche (Town Parish Church)** has a 14th-century Gothic chancel and three stained-glass windows from that same century. The entire church was once Gothic until baroque architects went to work on it. The Romanesque inner doorway is surmounted by a tower with a bulbous dome, dating from 1732.

Across from the church stands the privately owned **Salome Alt House.** Salome Alt was the mistress of Prince-Archbishop Wolf Dietrich, so frequently encountered in Salzburg history, and mother of 15 of his children. Following Wolf Dietrich's disgrace and overthrow, she retired to Wels.

On Ringstrasse, you can see what's left of **Schloss Pollheim,** where, the story goes, the shoemaker-poet Hans Sachs lived. Wagner is said to have based his character in *Die Meistersinger von Nürnberg* on Sachs.

NEARBY ABBEYS

Benediktinerstift Lambach ★ Founded in 1056, this Benedictine abbey lies in Lambach, 16km (10 miles) southwest of Wels and about 24km (15 miles) north of the Traunsee, where the Traun River meets its tributary, the Ager. Drive southwest for 16km (10 miles) along Highway 1 (referred to on some maps as Hwy. 144), following signs to Lambach.

The once Romanesque monastery, which stands on Marktplatz (Market Square) of the old market town, now sports a baroque exterior. A towering marble gateway from 1693 leads into the first courtyard.

In the so-called ringing chamber, you can see one of the abbey's major attractions, 11th-century Romanesque frescoes. These works of art were once hidden but later discovered. They were restored in 1967 and put on public view, an event hailed by the Austrian press.

The abbey's other attractions include a richly decorated library and a rather sumptuous refectory from the 18th century. The abbey church was built in the 1650s, and it is believed that its main altar was designed by the celebrated baroque architect J. B. Fischer von Erlach. The only surviving monastic theater in Austria, built in 1770, is reached by a stairway.

Marktplatz, in Lambach. ✆ **07245/28355** (Lambach tourist office). Admission 7€ ($11) adults, 4€ ($6.40) children. Mon–Sat 10–11am; Sun 2:30–5pm.

Stiftskremsmünster ★ The Benedictine Kremsmünster Abbey, near Bad Hall, between the emerging hills of the Alps and the Danube River, overlooking the Valley of Krems, was founded in A.D. 777. Two domed towers of the church dominate the local skyline. According to a 14th-century legend, Tassilo III, a Bavarian duke, had the abbey built to honor his son Gunther, who was killed by a wild boar during a hunt. The abbey's design was Romanesque, but in the 17th and 18th centuries, it was given the baroque treatment.

The most outstanding feature of a tour through Kremsmünster is the **Fischbehalter,** a fish pond made by the noted architect Carlo Antonio Carlone. It has five basins, each encircled by arcades, with statues that spout water. Figures depict everybody from Samson to Neptune.

In the cluster of abbey buildings, the **Kaisersaal (Hall of the Emperors)** has a portrait collection of the Holy Roman emperors, painted by Altomonte at the end of the 17th century. One of the most outstanding works of art is the *Crucifixion,* by Quentin Massys. The abbey still owns the chalice of Tassilo that was presented to the monks by the founding duke. It's the most ancient piece of goldsmith's work in either Austria or Bavaria, the duke's home. The library houses the priceless *Codex Millenarius,* an 8th-century translation of the Gospels.

An observatory tower, called the first skyscraper in Europe, rises nearly 61m (200 ft.) and has an exhibition on astronomy and other sciences. Many noted men have been pupils at the abbey school, including novelist Adalbert Stifter. The observatory tour (more about natural science) lasts 1½ hours and includes the fish pond.

To reach the abbey, take a train departing from the Linz Hauptbahnhof (Main Railway Station) for Graz, which leaves every 40 to 60 minutes (trip time: 45 min.). The train stops at either Kremsmünster Markt or Kremsmünster Bahnhof, which are very close to one another. Once you exit, you'll see many signs pointing toward the Stift Kremsmünster. It's a well-marked ramble eastward for 20 minutes. From Bad Hall, buses depart from Bad Hall's railway station approximately every 90 minutes throughout the day for the 15-minute ride to Kremsmünster. Driving from Wels, take Route 138 south and then Route 122 east to Kremsmünster.

In Kremsmünster. ✆ **07583/7212** (Kremsmünster tourist office). Admission 5€ ($8), plus another 4.80€ ($7.70) for the observatory tour. Abbey: Easter–late Oct daily 10am–4pm; Nov–Easter daily 11am–2pm. Observatory open for tours only May–Oct daily at 10am, 2, and 4pm. Tours in German or in English if reserved in advance; an English-language pamphlet explaining the tour is available. The observatory is closed Nov–Apr. The abbey is located 32km (20 miles) southwest of Linz and 26km (16 miles) west of Bad Hall.

WHERE TO STAY

Avalon Hotel Greif The Greif's simple exterior hides a nicely decorated, cozy interior with origins dating from 1561. This hotel is one of the best members of an Austrian hotel chain. Rooms are equipped with neatly kept bathrooms containing tub/shower combinations. The atmosphere is richly traditional, and if you stay here you'll be following in the footsteps of politicians, artists, kings, and emperors. After a beer in the Greif Café and Bar, you can enjoy American food in the Restaurant Steak.

Kaiser-Josef-Platz 50–51, A-4600 Wels. ✆ **07242/453610.** Fax 07242/44629. 56 units. 90€–120€ ($144–$192) double; 110€–140€ ($176–$224) triple. Rates include breakfast. AE, DC, MC, V. **Amenities:** Breakfast room; bar; lounge; room service. *In room:* TV, Wi-Fi, minibar, hair dryer.

WHERE TO DINE

Cafe-Konditorei Urbann PASTRIES/SNACKS Offering a shady summer garden, this cafe near the train station is the best-known in town. You'll see all kinds of people here, including the many local residents who show up every day for their usual cup of coffee and favorite pastry. The cafe prepares freshly made specialties such as handmade chocolate truffles, marzipan and nut *Kugeln* (balls), homemade gingerbread (winter only), and homemade jams and ice creams.

The Urbann family has owned this place since 1853, and there was a candle and gingerbread shop on the premises from as early as 1630. The place prefers not to be classified as a restaurant, but nonetheless it serves sandwiches, toast, and eggs. Coffee costs 2.90€ ($4.70), with pastries going for 3.50€ ($5.60).

Schmidtgasse 20. ✆ **07242/46051.** No credit cards. Mon–Fri 8:30am–6:30pm; Sat 8am–11pm.

Restaurant Wirt am Berg ★ Finds AUSTRIAN/INTERNATIONAL Established in 1630, this restaurant, about 4km (2½ miles) outside Wels, has been owned by the same family since 1881. Follow the signs toward Salzburg. Prominent diners have included the royal family of Monaco. The three-story restaurant, painted a deep yellow-orange, opens into a series of rustically decorated dining rooms with hunting trophies.

On warm days you might prefer to dine under the chestnut trees on the brick-covered terrace. Wild game is the most popular item on the menu in hunting season, although at any time of year you can enjoy an appetizer of carpaccio of venison with fresh fine herbs and a special salad marinated in walnut oil, or consommé of pheasant. This could be followed by venison ragout or *tafelspitz* (boiled beef). Dessert might be curd dumplings with buttered bread crumbs and stewed plums. The restaurant also offers more than 3,000 kinds of wine.

Salzburger Strasse 227. ✆ **07242/45059.** www.wirtamberg.at. Reservations recommended. Main courses 11€–30€ ($17–$48); 4-course fixed-price menu 43€ ($69); 6-course fixed-price dinner menu 56€ ($90). DC, MC, V. Tues–Sat noon–2pm and 6pm–midnight. Closed for lunch Fri.

12

Innsbruck & Tyrol: The Best of Scenic Austria

Tyrol is a land of ice and mountains, dark forests and alpine meadows full of spring wildflowers, Hansel and Gretel villages, summer holidays, and winter sports. One of the greatest sightseeing attractions in Europe is the Tyrolean Alps, and the mountain scenery is beautiful and panoramic at any time of year. In addition to being famous for its skiing, this spectacular alpine region offers travelers a host of other outdoor activities year-round, such as wonderful hiking and mountain climbing, glacier tours, and trout fishing. July and August bring the most visitors to the province, many of them North Americans, so reservations are essential.

If you're heading for Tyrol and want to travel around the region, Innsbruck is the best place to situate yourself. Several major roads (A12, A13, and 171) merge at Innsbruck, and you can easily reach most of the major ski resorts, as well as the Ötz Valley, Arlberg, and the Kitzbühel area. Parking is rarely a problem in these places, and, unless otherwise noted, you park for free. In addition to offering visitors a great location, Innsbruck has a great deal to offer, including a wonderful Alpenzoo, home only to animals indigenous to the Alps, and several great palaces, including Hofburg and Schloss Ambras.

Tyrol and its capital, Innsbruck, were centers of power at the end of the Middle Ages, when the Hapsburg Holy Roman Emperor, Maximilian I, ruled from here. Many of the wonderful castles that were scattered across the medieval countryside are only ruins today.

With a population of more than half a million Austrians occupying some 12,489 sq. km (4,822 sq. miles), Tyrol was a much larger district until South Tyrol was lost to Italy in 1919. South Tyrol was a large wine-producing area and the wealthiest part of Tyrol; its loss was a great blow for the Tyrolean people who remained in Austria, as it separated many of them from relatives, friends, and sometimes livelihood.

By the same post–World War I treaty, East Tyrol, whose capital is Lienz, was divided from North Tyrol, where Innsbruck is the capital. The two are separated by the portion of Tyrol given to Italy, which connects with a strip of Land Salzburg border. East of North Tyrol, the larger portion of the split province, lies Land Salzburg. To its west is the Austrian province of Vorarlberg (covered in chapter 13), to the north is Germany, and to the south are Italy and a small part of Switzerland. East Tyrol is bordered by Carinthia on the east, Land Salzburg on the north, and Italy.

Tyrol lies at the junction of several transcontinental links. The Valley of the Inn River cuts across the northern part of the province, and there are many other valleys connecting with that major artery. In addition to its famous mountains, the province is known for its deep-blue alpine lakes, such as the Achensee and the Walchsee. The Drau River, rising in the Höhe Tauern Alps, runs through East Tyrol. The Kaisergebirge is a nature reserve of Tyrol, with coniferous forests and meadowlands. And the Ötz Valley extends for 56km (35 miles) from the south bank of the Upper Inn.

Tyrol is a province of colorful folklore and customs, including *Schuhplatter* (a folkloric style) dancing, brass bands, and yodeling. Today Tyrol is a popular tourist spot, especially favored by Americans who, to an extent, have supplanted the once firmly entrenched British vacation crowds. It didn't become a mecca for American tourists until shortly before World War I, when rail magnate J. Pierpont Morgan spent time in Innsbruck and publicized the area upon returning home.

Tyrol is Austria's most frequented winter playground, and many prefer its ski slopes to those of Switzerland. Skiers and snowboarders flock here from mid-December until the end of March (when reservations at the most fashionable resorts are tight). And Seefeld, near Innsbruck, is one of Austria's "Big Three" rendezvous points for the international ski crowd. Kitzbühel ranks as one of the world's most fashionable ski resorts, and at the Kitzbühel Ski Circus, it's possible to ski downhill for 80km (50 miles). Skiers also head for St. Anton am Arlberg, the birthplace of modern skiing techniques.

TIPS FOR ACTIVE TRAVELERS

There's plenty to do outdoors in the dramatic high-altitude landscapes in Tyrol. If you don't want to make plans until you arrive, that's fine: Every hotel, inn, and pension in the region is well versed in where, when, and how you can fish, swim, ski, play tennis, or work out at a local spa. But if you want to plan in advance, here's a list of specialists who can help you plan your outdoor adventure and, in some cases, link you with specialized tours.

The best outfitter for arranging specialized tours, such as mountain climbing and hiking, is **David Zwilling,** Waldhof 64, A-5441 Abtenau (© **06243/30690;** www.outdoorconsulting.com). This outfitter will also arrange other tours including white-water rafting, biking, and even paragliding.

BIKING Many areas of Tyrol are simply too rocky and steep for cycling. With a bit of planning, however, you can usually limit your cycling to trips up and down valleys that separate the region's many mountains. You can arrange rentals at **Sport Kaserer,** Bilgeristrasse 18, Innsbruck (© **0512/377247;** www.tirol.at), and at **Schönherr Sport,** Stubaitalstrasse 79, at Neustift (© **05226/369043;** www.schoenherr.cc).

CANOEING & RAFTING For canoeing and white-water rafting, contact either branch of **Sportschule Fankhauser** (www.tirolrafting.at), and a specialist in conducting waterborne excursions. The company's branches consist of one at A-6382 Kirchdorf (© **05352/62101**), 35km (22 miles) from Innsbruck, and one at A-6425 Haiming (© **05266/88116**), 40km (25 miles) from Innsbruck.

CROSS-COUNTRY SKIING In winter, you can check with the tourist offices to find out about snow conditions. The staff will also tell you how to get to the major ski areas. One of the top three outfitters is **Schischule Seefeld,** 6100 Seefeld (© **05212/2412;** www.schi-seefeld.at). The other two are in the nearby alpine hamlet of Igls: **Platzer Wolfgang Jun KEG,** Eichlerstrasse 16 (© **0512/377377;** www.snowsport-igls.com), and **Schischule Igls-Patscherkofel,** Bilgeristrasse 18 (© **0512/377383**).

FISHING Some of the best trout and carp fishing in Austria is in the streams and lakes near the town of **Kössen,** about a 30-minute drive north of Kitzbühel. A fishing license is priced at 28€ ($45) per day for the Kolhbach or Weissenbach Rivers, or 12€ ($19) per day for the Taubensee. Licenses are for sale at the **Kössen Tourist Office** (© **05375/62870**), which is open Monday to Friday 9am to noon and 2 to 4pm, Saturday 9am to noon.

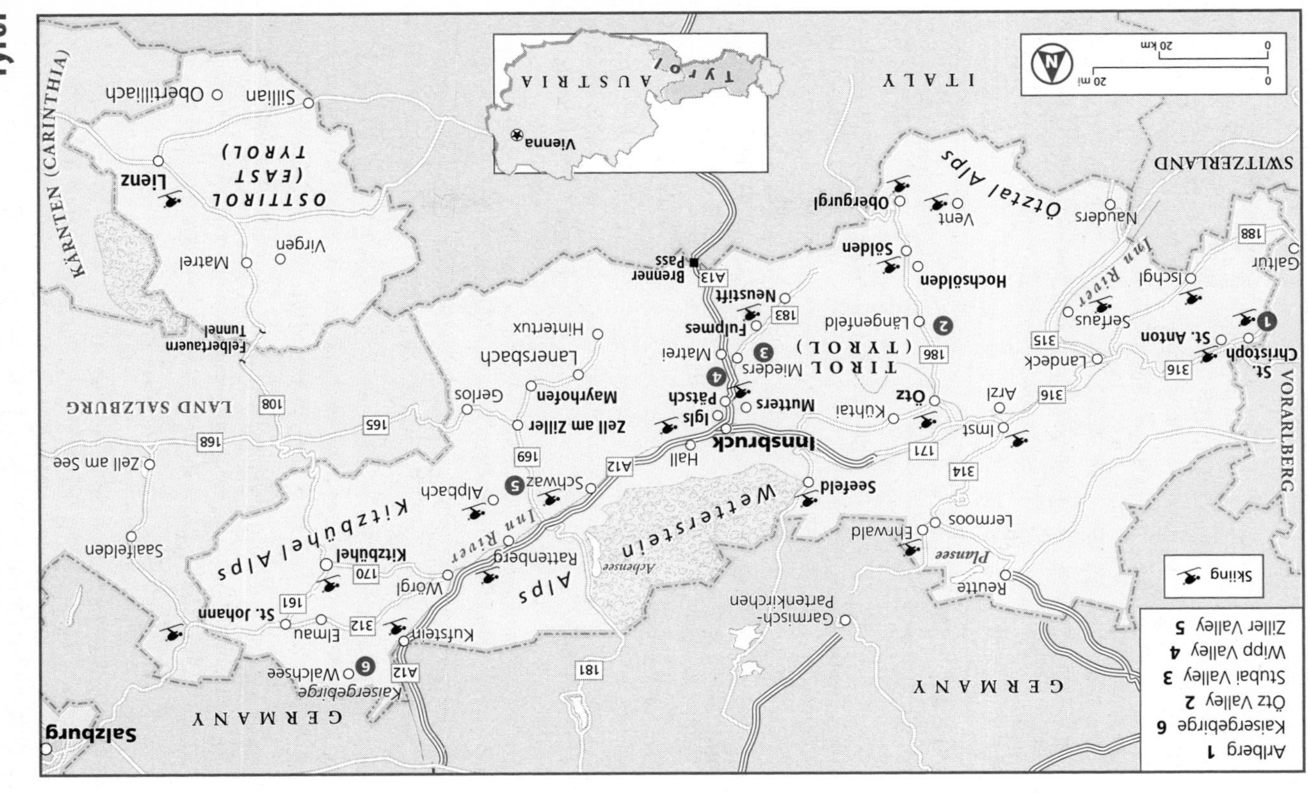
Arlberg 1
Kaisergebirge 6
Ötz Valley 2
Stubai Valley 3
Wipp Valley 4
Ziller Valley 5
Skiing
GERMANY
LAND SALZBURG
KÄRNTEN (CARINTHIA)
OSTTIROL (EAST TYROL)
TIROL (TYROL)
ITALY
SWITZERLAND
VORARLBERG
AUSTRIA
Tyrol
Vienna
Salzburg
Kaisergebirge
Walchsee
Kufstein
Elmau
St. Johann
Wörgl
Kitzbühel
Kitzbüheler Alps
Saalfelden
Zell am See
Rattenberg
Inn River
Alpbach
Schwaz
Alps
Achensee
Wetterstein
Hall
Innsbruck
Seefeld
Garmisch-Partenkirchen
Zell am Ziller
Gerlos
Mayrhofen
Lanersbach
Hintertux
Igls
Pätsch
Mutters
Mieders
Matrei
Fulpmes
Neustift
Brenner Pass
Felbertauern Tunnel
Virgen
Lienz
Sillian
Obertilliach
Kühtai
Ötz
Längenfeld
Hochsölden
Sölden
Obergurgl
Vent
Ötztal Alps
Imst
Arzl
Ehrwald
Lermoos
Plansee
Reutte
Landeck
Serfaus
Nauders
Ischgl
St. Anton
St. Christoph
Galtür
A12
A13
181
312
161
170
168
165
108
169
183
186
171
314
316
315
188
0
20 mi
20 km
N

GOLF Many of the golf courses in Tyrol are private, but at some, you can call in advance to reserve a tee time. Well-respected courses that welcome newcomers include the **Golfclub Rinn,** A-6074 Rinn (✆ **05223/78177;** www.alpinegolf.com), 10km (6 miles) south of Innsbruck, and **Golfclub Lans,** A-6072 Lans (✆ **0512/377165**), 8km (5 miles) south of Innsbruck. A bit farther afield is **Golfacademy Seefeld,** Reitherspitz-strasse, A-6100 Seefeld (✆ **05212/3797;** www.golfacademy-seefeld.at).

MOUNTAIN CLIMBING Austria's most dramatic mountain climbing occurs on the rocky (and sometimes icebound) slopes of Tyrol, particularly at **St. Anton, Mayrhofen, Kitzbühel,** and **Saalbach/Hinterglemm.** One of the best outfitters is Martin Ripfl-Marx, owner of **Tirolalpin Berg-Sport-Zentrum,** Seewald 11, A-6105 Leutasch (✆ **05214/515210;** www.tirolalpin.at). Set in an alpine hamlet 5km (3 miles) northwest of Seefeld, this outfitter offers physically fit adventurers a series of climbing excursions in the Tyrolean Alps. Trips range from a half-day initiation course for beginners (42€/$55 per person), to weeklong, high-endurance exposures to such alpine activities as rock and ice climbing, and "canyoning" down streambeds deeply eroded into layered bedrock. A worthy competitor closer to Innsbruck is the **Alpinschule,** In der Stille, A-6161 Natters (✆ **0512/546000;** www.alpinschule.com).

SAILING If the idea of navigating the tricky and oft-changing winds from the deck of a sailing craft appeals to you, the best and most comprehensive sailing school in the region is **Segelschule Tirol,** A-6213 Pertisau (✆ **650/5155850;** www.diesegelschule.eu). Headquartered in the lakefront hamlet of Maurach, adjacent to one of the Tyrol's largest lakes (a long and narrow body of water, the Achensee), it offers sailing instruction for all levels of sailors (beginners and advanced) as well as for children and teens. The Achensee, which measures 10km (6 miles) from end to end, lies 35km (22 miles) east of Innsbruck via the A12 superhighway.

SNOWBOARDING & SKIING Your best bet for snowboarding is to call **Austro Tours/Austria Ski** (✆ **800/333-5533** in the U.S., or 0664/2004655). This organization also arranges ski trips and winter hiking tours.

TENNIS There are many tennis courts in Innsbruck, but since they are so popular, you should reserve court time in advance. The best courts are at **Tennis & Squash Hallen,** Fürstenweg 172 (✆ **0512/284364;** www.burkia.at).

1 INNSBRUCK ★★★: THE CAPITAL OF TYROL

489km (304 miles) SW of Vienna; 159km (99 miles) S of Munich; 360km (224 miles) SW of Linz; 190km (118 miles) SW of Salzburg; 204km (127 miles) SE of Bregenz

The capital of Tyrol, Innsbruck (elevation 575m/1,880 ft.) is one of Europe's most beautiful cities. It has long been a center of commerce and traffic, as it lies at the junction of two important routes across the central Alps. In the eastern Alps, Innsbruck is about 30 minutes from the Italian border and 45 minutes from the German border.

Today Innsbruck's beauty is protected by town planners who ensure that any new structures built in the inner city harmonize with the preexisting Gothic, Renaissance, and baroque buildings. Modern urban development exists, away from the historic areas, spreading along the Inn River.

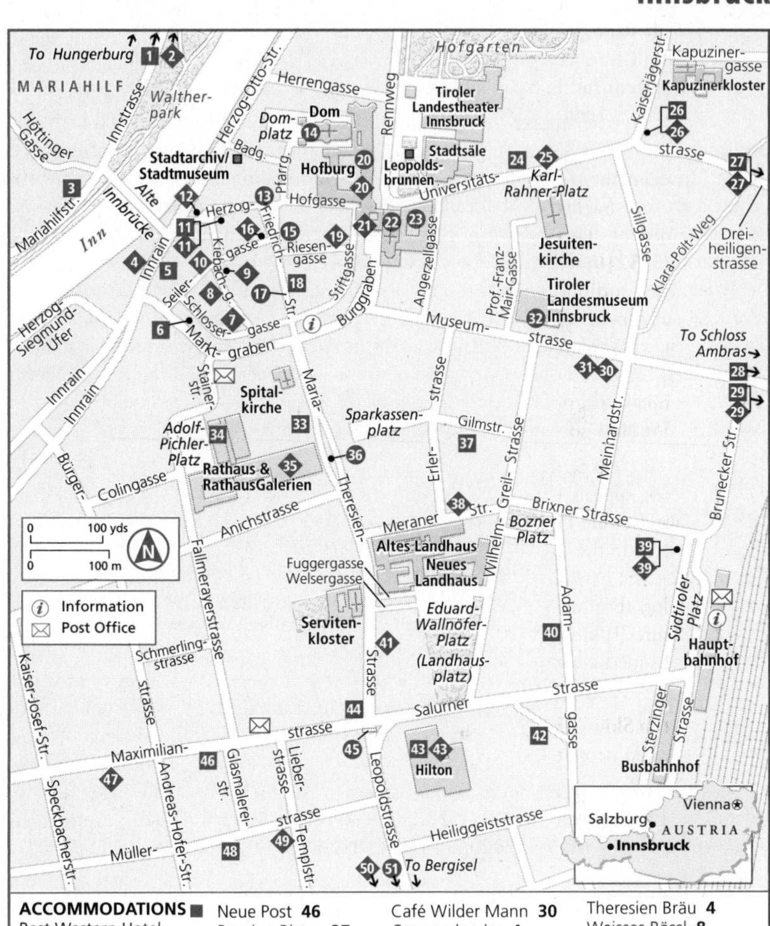

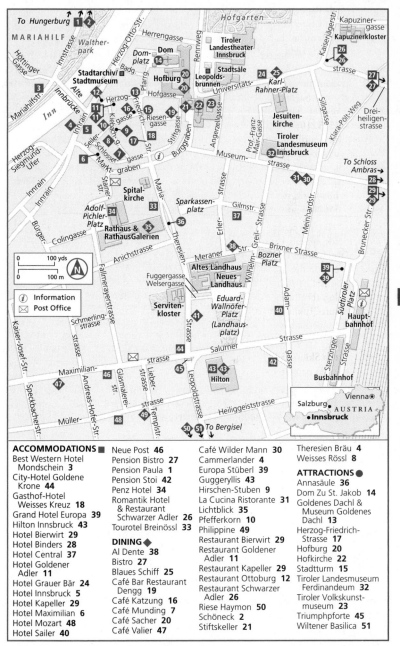

ACCOMMODATIONS ■

Best Western Hotel Mondschein **3**
City-Hotel Goldene Krone **44**
Gasthof-Hotel Weisses Kreuz **18**
Grand Hotel Europa **39**
Hilton Innsbruck **43**
Hotel Bierwirt **29**
Hotel Binders **28**
Hotel Central **37**
Hotel Goldener Adler **11**
Hotel Grauer Bär **24**
Hotel Innsbruck **5**
Hotel Kapeller **29**
Hotel Maximilian **6**
Hotel Mozart **48**
Hotel Sailer **40**
Neue Post **46**
Pension Bistro **27**
Pension Paula **1**
Pension Stoi **42**
Penz Hotel **34**
Romantik Hotel & Restaurant Schwarzer Adler **26**
Tourotel Breinössl **33**

DINING ◆

Al Dente **38**
Bistro **27**
Blaues Schiff **25**
Café Bar Restaurant Dengg **19**
Café Katzung **16**
Café Munding **7**
Café Sacher **20**
Café Valier **47**
Café Wilder Mann **30**
Cammerlander **4**
Europa Stüberl **39**
Guggeryllis **43**
Hirschen-Stuben **9**
La Cucina Ristorante **31**
Lichtblick **35**
Pfefferkorn **10**
Philippine **49**
Restaurant Bierwirt **29**
Restaurant Goldener Adler **11**
Restaurant Kapeller **29**
Restaurant Ottoburg **12**
Restaurant Schwarzer Adler **26**
Riese Haymon **50**
Schöneck **2**
Stiftskeller **21**
Theresien Bräu **4**
Weisses Rössl **8**

ATTRACTIONS ●

Annasäule **36**
Dom Zu St. Jakob **14**
Goldenes Dachl & Museum Goldenes Dachl **13**
Herzog-Friedrich-Strasse **17**
Hofburg **20**
Hofkirche **22**
Stadtturm **15**
Tiroler Landesmuseum Ferdinandeum **32**
Tiroler Volkskunst-museum **23**
Triumphpforte **45**
Wiltener Basilica **51**

The name Innsbruck means "bridge over the Inn," which is the river that flows through the city. The city lies at a meeting place of the Valley of the Inn and the Sill Gorge. As long ago as 1180, a little settlement on the river was moved from the northern bank to the site of the present Altstadt (Old Town). In 1239, as a part of Swabia Bavaria, it was granted its own "rights and privileges," and in 1420, Innsbruck became the capital of Austria.

The city was celebrated throughout Europe under the Hapsburg Holy Roman Emperor Maximilian I. Under Maximilian, whose reign (1490–1519) signaled the end of the Middle Ages, Innsbruck reached the height of its cultural and political importance (it's still the cultural center of Tyrol). The city had a second imperial heyday some 300 years later, during the 40-year reign of Maria Theresia. Much later, in 1945, Innsbruck became the headquarters of the French zone of occupation.

Twice in a dozen years—in 1964 and 1976—the eyes of the world turned to Innsbruck when it hosted the Winter Olympics. It's now a winter sports center with modern facilities. Skiers who come to Innsbruck benefit twice: They stay in a cosmopolitan city called the jewel of the Alps, and they ski on some of the world's choicest slopes. Nonskiers and summer visitors enjoy the sights of the medieval Old Town, the shops with Tyrolean specialties, and the many other outdoor activities that Tyrol offers.

ESSENTIALS

Getting There

BY PLANE Innsbruck's airport, **Flughafen Innsbruck-Kranebitten,** Fürstenweg 180 (✆ **0512/22525;** www.Innsbruck-airport.com), is 3km (2 miles) west of the city. It offers regularly scheduled air service from all major Austrian airports, as well as from Amsterdam, Frankfurt, London, Paris, and Zurich. **Tyrolean Airways** (✆ **51789**) serves the airport exclusively, although some foreign carriers will charter flights.

The best gateways from New York are Frankfurt and Vienna (from there to Innsbruck on Tyrolean Airways). Flying time from Zurich and Frankfurt is 50 to 70 minutes. From the airport, bus F leads to the city center. Tickets cost 1.80€ ($2.90). Taxis take about 10 minutes and cost 10€ ($16) or more.

There are six car-rental kiosks at the Innsbruck Airport: Budget (✆ **0512/588468**); ARAC Autovermietung (✆ **0512/206360**); Avis (✆ **0512/5717540**); Denzeldrive-National-Alamo (✆ **0512/582060**); Hertz (✆ **0512/580901**); and Sixt GmbH (✆ **0512/2929390**).

To drive from the airport to downtown Innsbruck, take the Fürstenweg (which becomes Mariahilfstrasse) for 2km (1¼ miles), following the signs to Innsbruck Centrum.

BY TRAIN Innsbruck is connected with all parts of Europe by railway links. Trains arrive at the main railway station, the **Hauptbahnhof,** Südtiroler Platz (✆ **05/1717,** www.oebb.at). There are at least five daily trains from Munich (trip time: 3 hr.) and eight daily trains from Salzburg (1 hr.).

BY BUS Bus service to all Austrian cities is provided by both **Postal Buses** and **Federal Railway Buses.** You can take a bus from Salzburg, although the train is quicker. For information about various bus routings through Tyrol, call ✆ **0512/585155.**

BY CAR If you're **driving** down from Salzburg in the northeast, take Autobahn A8 west, which joins Autobahn A93 (later it becomes the A12), heading southwest to Innsbruck. This latter Autobahn (A93/A12) is the main artery from Munich. From the south, you can take the Brenner toll motorway.

Innsbruck's Open Sesame Card

To attract more visitors to Innsbruck, the city has come up with the **Innsbruck Card** (www.innsbruck-tourismus.com), granting you a number of discounts to attractions, including 18 museums and all city-operated public transportation. The card even entitles you to a visit to the Swarovski Crystal Worlds, including transport on a shuttle bus specifically designed for cardholders. Free visits to the Alpenzoo are also included. The card costs 25€ ($40) for 1 day, 30€ ($48) for 2 days, or 35€ ($56) for 3 days. The card is half-price for children under 15.

Getting Around

A network of three **tram** and 25 **bus lines** covers all of Innsbruck and its close environs, and buses and trams use the same tickets. Single tickets in the central area cost 1.70€ ($2.70), and a booklet of four tickets goes for 5.70€ ($9.10). The tram is called either *Strassenbahn* or *Trambahn.* On the left bank of the Inn, the main tram and bus arteries are Museumstrasse and Mariahilfstrasse. On the right bank, trams and buses aren't routed into the pedestrian zone, but to their main stop in Marktgraben. For information about various routes, call the **Innsbrucker Verkehrsbetriebe** (✆ **0512/5307102;** www.ivb.at). Most tickets can be purchased at the Innsbruck tourist office, tobacco shops, and automated vending machines. A ***tageskarte*** **(day pass)** is available only from the tourist information office, tobacco shops, and cafes. A 24-hour pass costs 3.80€ ($6.10).

Postal Buses leave from the Autobushof (Central Bus Station), adjacent to the Hauptbahnhof. Here buses head for all parts of Tyrol. The station is open Monday through Friday from 7:30am to 6pm and Saturday from 7am to 1pm. For information about bus schedules, call ✆ **0512/585155.**

Taxi stands are scattered at strategic points throughout the city, or you can call a radio car (✆ **0512/5311**). For a nostalgic ride, you can hire a *fiaker* (horse-drawn carriage) from a spot adjacent to the **Tiroler Landestheater,** Rennweg; clip-clopping along costs around 30€ ($48) for 30 minutes.

You might consider renting a **bike** at the Hauptbahnhof. Rentals cost 24€ ($38) per day. You can return these bikes to any rail station in Austria if you don't plan on returning to Innsbruck. Rentals are available from April to early November only. For more information, call **Radsport Neuner** (✆ **0512/561501;** www.radsport-neuner.com).

Although you can make a better deal renting a car before leaving North America, it's also possible to rent cars in Innsbruck. You might try **Avis,** Salurner Strasse 15 (✆ **0512/571754**), or **Hertz,** Südtirolerplatz 1 (✆ **0512/580901**), across from the Hauptbahnhof. Although paperwork and billing errors are harder to resolve whenever you rent from a non-U.S.-based car rental outfit, you might also check the rates at local car outfitter, **Ajax,** Defreggerstrasse 8 (✆ **0512/341385**). See also "Getting There," above, for information on renting cars at the airport.

The center of Innsbruck is peppered with parking lots, many concealed underground. One of the largest and best positioned is at the **Tourist Center,** Salurnerstrasse 15 (✆ **0512/572353**). It charges 2.20€ ($3.50) per hour, day and night. Otherwise, parking in the city center's short-term parking zones (marked by special signs) is 1.10€ ($1.80) for each 30 minutes. Parking within these zones is limited to a maximum of 120 minutes. If you're parking in a limited-parking zone, you must purchase a voucher (sold at banks, gas stations, or tobacconists). Write down the time you parked the car, and place the voucher on the dashboard inside the windshield.

City Layout

The main street of the **Altstadt (Old Town)** historic district is Herzog-Friedrich-Strasse, which becomes Maria-Theresien-Strasse, the main axis of the postmedieval **New Town.** Altstadt developed on the right bank of the River Inn, site of the baroque and medieval buildings that give the city its architectural flair. To the south, Altstadt's boundaries end at Burggraben and Marktgraben. After 10:30am, it becomes strictly pedestrian, but that's all right, since the best way to see that part of Innsbruck is on foot.

Most of your explorations will be in Altstadt because (with a few exceptions) the New Town contains mostly residential neighborhoods. The dividing line between the old and new towns is Egger Lienz Strasse.

The Inn River divides this historic city into left- and right-bank districts, and many of the attractions, including the Hofkirche and the Goldenes Dachl, are on the right bank (in Altstadt). There are two major crossing points over the river: the **Universitätssbrücke** and the **Alte Innsbrücke.**

If you arrive at the **Hauptbahnhof (main railway station),** take Salurner Strasse and Brixner Strasse to Maria-Theresien-Strasse, which will take you into the very heart of Innsbruck.

Visitor Information

The **Innsbruck Tourist Office,** Burggraben 3 (✆ **512/59850;** www.innsbruck-tourism.at), is open daily 8am to 6pm. You can stock up on printed information about Innsbruck (and other parts of Tyrol) and ask questions about virtually any touristic feature of the town.

Fast Facts Innsbruck

Babysitters For an English-speaking babysitter, most hotel concierges will make arrangements for you.

Consulates Visitors from the U.S., Canada, New Zealand, and Australia have to use their respective consulates in Vienna. British citizens can go to the **British Consulate,** Kaiser Jägerstrasse 1, Top B9 (✆ **0512/588320**), open Monday to Friday 9am to noon.

Currency Exchange You can exchange money at any of the dozens of banks that line Innsbruck's commercial areas. Banks are usually open Monday to Thursday 7:45am to 12:30pm and 2:30 to 4pm, and Friday 7:45am to 3pm. There are also exchange facilities at Innsbruck's tourist office (above) and at the Hauptbahnhof. The branch at the Hauptbahnhof maintains automated currency exchange facilities available 24 hours a day. They accept American dollars in denominations of $20, $50, and $100.

Dentists & Doctors Check with the tourist office for a list of private English-speaking dentists and doctors, or contact the **University Clinic,** Anichstrasse 35 (✆ **0512/504**).

Drugstores **St.-Anna Apotheke,** Maria-Theresien-Strasse 4 (✆ **0512/585847**), is open Monday to Friday 8am to 12:30pm and 2:30 to 6pm, and Saturday 8am to noon. As required by law, the pharmacy posts addresses of other pharmacies open on weekends or at night.

Emergencies Call ✆ **133** for the police, **122** for the fire department, or **144** for an ambulance.

Hospitals Try the **University Clinic,** Anichstrasse 35 (✆ **0512/504**).

Internet Access You can check e-mail or access the Internet at the **Modern Internet Café,** Maria-Theresien-Strasse 16 (✆ **0512/584848;** tram 3). For a fee of 12€ ($16) an hour, you can Web-surf to your heart's content. Platters of simple food and drinks are available. It's open Monday to Saturday 10am to midnight.

Luggage Storage & Lockers At the Hauptbahnhof, on Südtirolerplatz (✆ **0512/930002409**), you can rent small lockers for 2.50€ ($3.25), or larger ones for 3.50€ ($4.55), for 48 hours.

Police Call ✆ **133** for the police.

Post Offices The **Hauptpostamt (Central Post Office),** Maximilianstrasse 2 (✆ **0512/5000**), is open daily from 8am to 9pm. The post office at the **Hauptbahnhof,** Bruneckstrasse 1–3 (✆ **0512/5000**), is open Monday to Saturday 6:30am to 9pm.

Safety Innsbruck has a low crime rate, but that doesn't mean you shouldn't take the usual precautions.

Taxes Innsbruck levies no special city taxes other than the value-added tax imposed on all goods and services in Austria.

Toilets These are found at the airport, bus and rail stations, and various cafes and museums scattered throughout the city. Public restrooms in the city center are labeled WC: Some require a .50€ (80¢) coin for access to a sit-down toilet.

Transit Information For information about local buses and trams, call the **Innsbrucker Verkehrsbetriebe** (✆ **0512/5307102**).

Useful Telephone Numbers For the airport, call ✆ **0512/22525;** for train information, call ✆ **05/1717.**

WHAT TO SEE & DO

Exploring the Town

Maria-Theresien-Strasse ★★, Innsbruck's main street, cuts through the heart of the city from north to south, and it's a good place to begin your exploration. It's fascinating just to watch the passersby, especially when they're attired in Tyrolean regional dress. Once, this street was traversed by wayfarers heading over the Brenner Pass from Italy and on to Germany. Today many 17th- and 18th-century houses line the street.

On the south end of this wide street, a **Triumphpforte (Triumphal Arch),** modeled after those in Rome, spans the shopping street. Maria Theresia ordered it built in 1765 with a twofold purpose: to honor the marriage of her son, the Duke of Tuscany (later Emperor Leopold II), to a Spanish princess, and to mourn the death of her beloved husband, Emperor Franz I. From this arch southward, the street is called Leopoldstrasse.

Traveling north from the arch along Maria-Theresien-Strasse, you'll see **Annasäule (St. Anna's Column),** a much-photographed attraction. It enjoys the same renown in Innsbruck as the Eros statue does in London's Piccadilly Circus. A statue of the Virgin Mary stands on a crescent moon atop this Corinthian column, which has statues of saints Cassianus, Virgilius, George, and Anna surrounding the base. Standing in front of the 19th-century **Rathaus (Town Hall),** the column was erected in 1706 to celebrate the withdrawal, in 1703, of invading Bavarian armies during the War of the Spanish Succession.

Not far north of the Annasäule, the wide street narrows and becomes **Herzog-Friedrich-Strasse,** running through the heart of the Altstadt. This street is flanked by a number of well-maintained burghers' houses with their turrets and gables. Look for the dormer windows and oriels. Most buildings here are overhung with protective roofs to guard them against snowfalls.

More Sights

Alpenzoo ★ (Kids) From this zoo, lying on the southern slope of the Hungerburg plateau, you'll get a panoramic view of Innsbruck and the surrounding mountains. The zoo contains only those animals indigenous to the Alps. Sheltered within are more than 800 creatures, belonging to more than 140 different and sometimes rare species, including otters, eagles, elk, rabbits, vultures, wildcats, bison, and wolves.

Weiherburggasse 37. ✆ **0512/292323.** www.alpenzoo.at. Admission 7€ ($11) adults, 5€ ($8) students, 3.50€ ($5.60) children 6–15, 2€ ($3.20) children 4–5, free for children 3 and under. Winter daily 9am–5pm; other seasons daily 9am–6pm. Tram: Hungerburgbahn (cog railway).Bus: 2 (May 15–Sept only) or 4, C, D, or E.

Dom zu St. Jakob Based on designs by the baroque architect Johann Jakob Herkommer, the Cathedral of St. James was rebuilt between 1717 and 1724. It is roofed with domes and has a lavish baroque interior, part of which was executed by the Asam brothers. Unfortunately, the church was heavily damaged during World War II. One of its chief treasures is the *Maria Hilf* (Mary of Succor), painted by Lucas Cranach the Elder, on the main altar. In the north aisle, look for a 1620 monument honoring Archduke Maximilian III, who died in 1618. Visits are prohibited during Mass.

Domplatz 6. ✆ **0512/583902.** www.sacred-destinations.com. Free admission. Winter daily 6:30am–6pm; summer daily 7:30am–7:30pm. Closed Fri noon–3pm. Tram: 1 or 3.

Goldenes Dachl & Maximilianeum ★ The Golden Roof is Innsbruck's greatest tourist attraction, and is certainly its most characteristic landmark. It's a three-story balcony on a house in the Old Town; the late-Gothic oriels are capped with 2,657 gold-plated tiles. It was constructed for Emperor Maximilian I to serve as a royal box where he could sit in luxury and enjoy tournaments in the square below. Completed at the dawn of the 16th century, the Golden Roof was built in honor of Maximilian's marriage, his second, to Bianca Maria Sforza of Milan (Maximilian was a ruler who expanded his territory through marriage, not conquest). Not wishing to alienate the allies gained by his first marriage, to Maria of Burgundy, he had an image of himself between the two women painted on his balcony. However, he is looking at his new wife, Bianca.

In 1996, the city of Innsbruck added a small museum, the **Maximilianeum,** to the second floor of the municipal building that's attached to the Goldenes Dachl. Inside you'll find exhibits that celebrate the life and accomplishments of this Innsbruck-based Hapsburg emperor who bridged the gap between the Middle Ages and the Northern Renaissance. Look for costumes, silver chalices and coins, portraits, and a video that depicts his era and personality.

You can also visit the **Stadtturm (City Tower),** Herzog-Friedrich-Strasse 21 (✆ **0512/587113**), nearby. Formerly a prison cell, the tower dates from the mid-1400s and stands adjacent to the Rathaus. From the top, there's a panoramic view of the city rooftops and the mountains beyond. It's open daily 10am to 5pm (July–Sept to 8pm). Admission is 3€ ($4.80) for adults and 1.50€ ($2.40) for children.

While you're here, take a look at the **Helblinghaus,** Herzog-Friedrich-Strasse, opposite the Goldenes Dachl. It's a Gothic structure to which a rococo facade was added.

Herzog-Friedrich-Strasse 15. ✆ **0512/581111.** Admission to the Maximilianeum 3.60€ ($5.80) adults, 2.70€ ($4.30) seniors and students, 1.45€ ($2.30) children 17 and under. Goldenes Dachl is closed to visitors. Summer daily 10am–6pm; winter Tues–Sun 10am–12:30pm and 2–5pm. Tram: 1 or 3.

Hofburg ★ The 15th-century imperial palace of Emperor Maximilian I was rebuilt in the baroque style (but with rococo detailing) during the 18th century on orders of Maria Theresia. The palace, flanked by a set of domed towers, is a fine example of baroque secular architecture. The structure has four wings and a two-story *Riesensaal* (Giant's Hall) painted in white and gold and filled with portraits of the Hapsburgs.

Also of compelling interest within the Hofburg are the State Rooms, the chapel, and a scattering of private apartments. You can wander at will through the rooms, but if you want to participate in a guided tour, management conducts two a day, at 11am and 2pm, in a multilingual format that includes English. Each tour lasts 30 to 45 minutes and costs 29€ ($46).

Rennweg 1. ✆ **0512/587186.** www.hofberg-innsbruck.at. Admission 5.50€ ($8.80) adults, 4€ ($6.40) students, 1.10€ ($1.75) children under 12. Daily 9am–5pm. Tram: 1 or 3.

Hofkirche Ferdinand I built this Gothic royal court church and tomb in 1553. Its most important treasure is the cenotaph of Maximilian I, although his remains are not in this elegant marble sarcophagus glorifying the Holy Roman Empire. He was never brought here from Wiener Neustadt, where he was entombed in 1519. This tomb, a great feat of the German Renaissance style of sculpture, has 28 bronze 16th-century statues of Maximilian's real and legendary ancestors and relatives surrounding the kneeling emperor on the cenotaph, with 24 marble reliefs on the sides depicting scenes from his life. Tyrol's national hero, Andreas Hofer, is entombed here.

The Hofkirche has a lovely Renaissance porch, plus a nave and a trio of aisles in the Gothic style. One gallery contains nearly two dozen small statues of the saint protectors of the House of Hapsburg. The wooden organ, dating from 1560, is still operational.

Another chapel, the **Silberne Kapell (Silver Chapel),** was constructed between the church and the palace in 1578. Archduke Ferdinand II of Tyrol had it constructed as the final resting place for him and his wife, Philippine Welser. The chapel takes its name from a large embossed silver Madonna in the center of the altarpiece (made of rare wood). The silver reliefs surrounding the Madonna symbolize the Laurentanian Litany. Alexander Colin designed the sarcophagi of Ferdinand and Philippine. The Tiroler Volkskunst-Museum (see below) is reached through the same entranceway. You can purchase a combined ticket to the church and the museum for 6.50€ ($10) for adults and 3€ ($4.80) for children.

Universitätsstrasse 2. ✆ **0512/584302.** Admission 4.45€ ($7.10) adults, 1.50€ ($2.40) students or children, free for children 5 and under. Mon–Sat 9am–5pm (museum only Sun 9am–noon). Tram: 1 or 3.

Swarovski Kristallwelten ★★★ Kids If Disney created a magical Kingdom of Crystal, he would surely have used the fabled "Crystal Worlds" as his role model. In just

15 minutes (by taking the Wattens bus from the Busbahnhof, next to the Hauptbahnhof), you are delivered to a fantasy world, a man-made hill where you'll see a giant face spouting a waterfall. This bizarre fantasy sets the theatrical stage for what's hidden inside and below. Deep inside the hill is a wonder world of crystal—an underground fantasy with seven linked chambers. Designed by the Viennese multimedia artist Andrew Heller, the kingdom is dedicated to the vision of Daniel Swarovski, founder of the world's leading producer of full crystal. Since it opened in 1995, millions of visitors have descended on the site.

After entering the giant head with its glittering eyes and waterfall, you'll immediately see a long wall of crystal with 12 tons of some of the finest cut stones in the world. In other chambers, you can wander into the "Planet of the Crystals," with a 3-D light show. Crystalline works of art on display were designed by everybody from Andy Warhol to Salvador Dalí. In the Crystal Dome, you get an idea of what it's like being inside a crystal, and in the Crystal Theater, a fairytale world of color, mystery, and movement unfolds.

After your visit, purchases can be made from the mammoth range of Swarovski products at the on-site shop. These range from detailed crystal items such as tiny musical instruments to depictions of animals. There's also a wide selection of crystal jewelry such as necklaces and earrings. The Crystal World also contains an alpine garden with rare and indigenous plants, plus an adventure playground for children. You can easily spend 2 hours here.

Kristallweltenstrasse 1. ✆ **05224/51080.** www.swarovski.com. Admission 9.50€ ($15), free for children under 12. Daily 9am–6pm.

Tiroler Landesmuseum Ferdinandeum ★ This celebrated gallery of Flemish and Dutch masters also traces the development of popular art in Tyrol, with highlights from the Gothic period. You'll also see the original bas-reliefs used in designing the Goldenes Dachl.

Museumstrasse 15. ✆ **0512/59489.** www.tiroler-landesmuseum.at. Admission 8€ ($10) adults, 4€ ($6.40) students and children. June–Sept Fri–Wed 10am–6pm, Thurs 10am–9pm; Oct–May Tues–Sat 10am–noon and 2–5pm, Sun 10am–1pm. Tram: 1 or 3.

Tiroler Volkskunst-Museum ★★ This museum of popular art is in the **Neues Stift (New Abbey),** which dates from the 16th and 18th centuries, and adjoins the Hofkirche on. The museum contains one of the largest and most impressive collections of Tyrolean artifacts, ranging from handicrafts and religious and profane popular art to furniture and national costumes. The three floors house a collection of Tyrolean mangers, or Christmas cribs, some from the 18th century. The *Stuben* (the finest rooms) are on the upper floors. Displays include styles ranging from Gothic to Renaissance to baroque, as well as a collection of models of typical Tyrolean houses.

Universitätsstrasse 2. ✆ **0512/584302.** Admission 8€ ($13) adults, 4€ ($6.40) children and students. Mon–Sat 9am–5pm; Sun 10am–5pm. Tram: 1 or 3.

Outdoor Activities

Ski areas around Innsbruck are excellent for winter activity or for summer mountain walks. Five cableways, 44 chairlifts, and surface lifts allow access to the five sunny, snow-covered areas around Innsbruck. In winter, the city is also known for bobsled and toboggan runs and ice-skating rinks.

In summer, you can enjoy tennis at a number of courts, golf on either a 9- or an 18-hole course, and go horseback riding, mountaineering, gliding, swimming, hiking, and shooting.

The **Hofgarten,** a public park containing lakes and many shade trees, lies north of Rennweg. Concerts are often presented at the Kunstpavillon in the garden in summer.

Nearby Attractions

Many satellite resorts, such as Igls (see section 2, later in this chapter), are good for day trips from Innsbruck. Below we've offered highlights of those attractions on the outskirts of the city.

Hungerburg ★★

The Hungerburg mountain plateau (872m/2,861 ft.) is the most beautiful spot in Tyrol, affording the best view of Innsbruck, especially on summer nights when much of the city, including fountains and historic buildings, is brightly lit. Some of the most scenic hotels in the Innsbruck area are here.

You can drive to the plateau. At press time, the cable cars that serve the area were under reconstruction, so check with the tourist office to see if they are up and running at the time of your visit.

Schloss Ambras ★★

This Renaissance palace, 3km (2 miles) southeast of the heart of Innsbruck on the edge of the Mittelgebirgsterrace, was built by Archduke Ferdinand II of Austria, Count of Tyrol, in the 16th century. It's divided into a **lower** and an **upper castle** set in the remains of a medieval fortress. This was Ferdinand's favorite residence and the center of his court's cultural life. The lower castle was planned and constructed by the archduke as a museum for his various collections, including arms and armor, art, and books, all of which can be seen today. The **Spanish Hall,** one of the first German Renaissance halls, was built to house the portraits of the counts of Tyrol.

The upper castle has a small but fine collection of medieval sculpture, black-and-white frescoes on the wall of the inner courtyard, and a portrait gallery hung with dynastic paintings from the 14th to the 18th centuries. In some of the living rooms, you can see 16th-century frescoes, late-16th-century wooden ceilings, and 17th-century furniture.

After viewing the interior, walk through the castle grounds. April through October, **Schloss Ambras,** Schloss Strasse 20 (✆ **0152/5244802;** www.khm.at), is open daily 10am to 5pm (Dec–Mar daily 2–5pm). It's closed in November. Admission is 5€ ($8) for adults, 3€ ($4.80) for students and children, December to March; 8€ ($13) for adults, 6€ ($9.60) for students and children, April to October. There are no guided tours. To reach the palace, you can take tram no. 3 or 6 from Innsbruck's Hauptbahnhof. The castle also maintains its own shuttle bus, a white-sided vehicle with the words SCHLOSS AMBRAS written on its sides, which departs from a point adjacent to the Landhaus on the Maria-Theresien-Strasse every 30 minutes in summer, every hour in winter, during the palace's open hours. Service runs less frequently December through April. Round-trip costs 4€ ($6.40) adults and 2€ ($3.20) children.

The Wiltener Basilica ★

In the southern district of Innsbruck, where the Sill River emerges from a gorge, Wilten is one of the most dramatic landscapes around the city. This ancient spot was once the Roman town of Veldidena.

Wilten's parish church, the **Wiltener Basilica,** Haymongasse 6 (✆ **0512/583385**), is one of the most splendid houses of worship in the Tyrolean country. Built between 1751 and 1755 in a rich rococo style with twin towers, the church did not become a basilica until 1957. Wiltener Basilica is noted for its stuccowork by Franz Xaver Feichtmayr. The ceiling frescoes are by Matthäus Günther. A sandstone figure depicting Our Lady under the Four Columns has been the subject of pilgrimage since the Middle Ages. Both the church and the basilica are open daily from 9am to dusk.

Across from the basilica is a cluster of baroque buildings that belonged to an abbey founded here in 1138. The abbey church, the **Stift Wilten,** Klosterg 7 (**© 0512/5830480**), merits a visit. Dating from the 1650s, the church has two stone giants guarding the porch and a grille from 1707 in the narthex (entranceway). This church was damaged by World War II bombings. To reach the site, take tram no. 1 to Stubaitalbahnhof/Bergisel.

Bergisel

If you're driving, head out the Brenner road to Bergisel (747m/2,451 ft.), a lovely wooded section just outside Innsbruck that's ideal for leisurely strolls in warmer weather. It lies near the gorge of the Sill River on the southern outskirts of Innsbruck, about a 20-minute walk from the Wiltener Basilica. Here you'll see the ski jumps built for the 1964 and 1976 Olympic Winter Games, and there's a great panoramic view from the top of the jumps.

The hill is a historic site, scene of the 1809 battles in which Andreas Hofer led some Tyrolean peasants against French and Bavarian forces (he was later shot to death on orders of Napoleon). Below the ski jump is the Andreas Hofer monument erected in 1893 to commemorate the battle. Tyroleans speak of this as their "field of remembrance," and it's filled with memorials and visitors. Heroic though the local deeds might be, they might not interest North Americans. Visit this place simply for the views and the relaxing walks.

WHERE TO STAY

Always arrive with a reservation, as Innsbruck is never out of season. Accommodations are particularly scarce from June until the end of summer and from mid-December to mid-April. Hotel information is available at the tourist office (see "Visitor Information," p. 344).

Very Expensive

Grand Europa Tyrol ★★ Opposite Innsbruck's railway station, in the heart of the city, the Europa is the best hotel in Innsbruck (it's also part of the Steigenberger Reservations System). Dating from 1869, this very formal but friendly hotel has hosted Queen Elizabeth II, the shah of Iran, General Patton, and the crew of *Apollo 14.* Rooms and suites are handsomely furnished with modern conveniences and Tyrolean or Biedermeier-style decorations. Each room offers a comfortable bed and a bathroom with a neatly kept tub/shower combination. The uniformed staff is helpful in every way and will usually be willing to show you the ornate yellow-and-white Barock Saal, which the Tyrolean government uses for its most important functions. The ballroom was constructed by King Ludwig's Bavarian architects and builders. The restaurant, **Europastüberl** (p. 356), is the finest in Tyrol.

Südtirolerplatz 2, A-6020 Innsbruck. **© 800/223-5652** in the U.S. and Canada, or 0512/5931. Fax 0512/587800. www.grandhoteleuropa.at. 122 units. 183€–314€ ($293–$502) double; 333€–504€ ($533–$806) suite. Rates include buffet breakfast. AE, DC, MC, V. Parking 20€ ($32). **Amenities:** Restaurant; bar; sauna; room service; babysitting; laundry service; dry cleaning; nonsmoking rooms; solarium. *In room:* A/C, TV, Wi-Fi, minibar, hair dryer, trouser press (some), safe.

The Penz Hotel ★★ This glittering structure that makes much use of glass may stand in the Altstadt but is has little in common with most of the district's buildings. The Penz is as modern as tomorrow, housed in the Rathausgalerie shopping mall, with a panoramic American Bar on its rooftop. You can drink and take in views of the old town and the Tyrolean Alps. Rooms are ultramodern and elegantly decorated, with the minimalist's eye for comfort. From the hardwood floors to the streamlined furnishings, to the discreet introduction of modern technology, everything is coordinated.

Adolf Pichler Platz 3, A-6020 Innsbruck. ✆ **0512/5756657-0.** Fax 0512/575657-0. www.the-penz.com. 96 units. 180€–260€ ($288–$416) double; 250€–420€ ($400–$672) junior suite. MC, V. Parking 15€ ($24). **Amenities:** Restaurant; bar; room service; health club; laundry service/dry cleaning; nonsmoking rooms; rooms for those with limited mobility. *In room:* A/C, TV, Wi-Fi, minibar, hair dryer, safe.

Expensive

Hilton Innsbruck ★ Erected in the mid-1980s and located 2 blocks from the railway station, this is the largest hotel and the tallest building (14 stories) in Innsbruck. Its contemporary comfort and capacity for large-scale conferences have made it very popular. Rooms, especially those on the upper floors, provide a view over the baroque spires of Innsbruck and its mountains. All contain built-in furniture and extras you'd expect of a government-rated four-star hotel. The **Jackpot Bar** provides slot fixes and drinks, depending on your whim and the time of day. Its restaurant, **Guggeryllis,** is well-recommended (see "Where to Dine," later in this chapter).

Salurner Strasse 15, A-6020 Innsbruck. ✆ **0512/59350.** Fax 0512/5935220. www.hilton.com. 176 units. 107€–194€ ($171–$310) double; 309€–380€ ($494–$608) suite. AE, DC, MC, V. Parking 11€ ($14). Tram: 1 or 3. **Amenities:** Restaurant; bar; fitness center; sauna; tour desk; room service; babysitting; laundry service; dry cleaning; nonsmoking rooms; 1 room for those w/limited mobility. *In room:* A/C, TV, Wi-Fi, minibar, hair dryer, trouser press, safe.

Hotel Grauer Bär ★ This hotel, located in the center of Innsbruck, is next to the Imperial Gardens, the most interesting sights, and the shopping area. "The Gray Bear" (its English name) has long been a family favorite. The good-size rooms are well maintained and traditionally furnished, with thick carpeting and built-in furnishings. Bathrooms have showers and tubs. Front rooms are the most comfortable and the best appointed, but they also suffer from the most traffic noise. To the side of the large lobby is the dining room, **Galerie,** with an ornate ribbed and vaulted white ceiling supported by a central stone column. Well-prepared international, Austrian, and Tyrolean specialties are served.

Universitätsstrasse 7, A-6021 Innsbruck. ✆ **0512/5254-2564.** Fax 0512/5254-2564-66. www.grauer-baer.com. 194 units. 108€–192€ ($173–$307) double; 175€–215€ ($280–$344) suite. Rates include buffet breakfast. AE, DC, MC, V. Parking 10€ ($16). **Amenities:** Restaurant; bar; fitness center; sauna; room service; massage; babysitting; laundry service; dry cleaning; nonsmoking rooms; solarium; rooms for those w/limited mobility. *In room:* TV, Wi-Fi, minibar, hair dryer, safe.

Hotel Innsbruck ★ This modern, streamlined, and comfortable hotel facing the Inn River is favored by upscale tourists and international business travelers. The staff is hardworking and multilingual. The furnishings in the rooms aren't remarkable, but all the beds are firm and the neatly kept bathrooms contain tub/shower combinations. The best rooms are on an upper floor and have small balconies; the dormer rooms on each floor are also superior. If you're stuck in one of the accommodations in the back, you'll do fine—in some respects, these are the coziest and most romantic rooms, opening onto vistas of the Altstadt.

The hotel contains two restaurants, one outfitted in a woodsy Tyrolean style with plenty of paneling, rustic accessories, and dirndl-clad waitresses. Unfortunately, most of the year, the restaurants cater to groups by reservation only. In such times, the hotel staff will recommend a nearby dining choice, even offering car service upon request. There's also a glassed-in winter garden for drinks, light meals, and coffee.

Innrain 3, A-6020 Innsbruck. ✆ **0512/598680.** Fax 0512/572280. www.hotelinnsbruck.com. 114 units. 155€–215€ ($248–$344) double. Rates include buffet breakfast. Half-board (winter only) 18€ ($29) per person extra. AE, DC, MC, V. Parking 14€ ($22). Tram: 1 or 3. **Amenities:** 2 restaurants; bar; lounge; indoor heated pool; sauna; room service; massage; babysitting; laundry service; dry cleaning; nonsmoking rooms; winter garden; rooms for those w/limited mobility. *In room:* TV, Wi-Fi, hair dryer, safe.

Hotel Maximilian ★ Built in 1982 and renovated in 1992, this inner-city hotel rates as one of the most attractive and up-to-date in Innsbruck. Possessing an antique charm, it offers modern and convenient accommodations. Rooms are rather small yet exceedingly up-to-date, with very firm beds. The most desirable ones look out over the back, where you'll have a close-up view of the shingled onion dome of the oldest church in Innsbruck (now used as the headquarters of a company that makes keys). Parking is sometimes available for free on the street; otherwise, it costs 11€ ($18) per day in a nearby public garage. The hotel's restaurant, serving mainly Austrian dishes, is open only to hotel guests.

Marktgraben 7–9, A-6020 Innsbruck. ✆ **0512/59967.** Fax 0512/577450. www.hotel-maximilian.com. 40 units. 110€–200€ ($176–$320) double. Rates include buffet breakfast. AE, DC, MC, V. Tram: 1. **Amenities:** Restaurant; bar; room service; babysitting; laundry service; dry cleaning; nonsmoking rooms. *In room:* TV, hair dryer, minibar, safe.

Neue Post ★ In the heart of the city, opposite the main post office, this building began life in 1902 when it was constructed as an apartment house. In the 1960s it was turned into a hotel. After growing tired and seedy, it was given a new lease on life in 2006, and we're recommending it for the first time. Today a Best Western, it offers rooms in two different categories—standard doubles or superior or deluxe doubles. It also has some of the best suite accommodations in Innsbruck. Some of its imperial architectural grandeur from the turn-of-the-20th-century remains, but everything has been modernized with all the latest gadgets. Its most elegant grace note is its Winter Garden Restaurant, serving a first-rate cuisine. The public rooms are imbued with an Art Nouveau style, and all the bedrooms, ranging from midsize to spacious, have fine furnishings, using high-quality fabrics.

Maximilianstrasse 15, A-6010 Innsbruck. ✆ **0512/594760.** Fax 0512/581818. www.hotel-neue-post.at. 50 units. 126€–190€ ($202–$304) double; 250€ ($400) suite. AE, DC, MC, V. Parking: 17€ ($22). **Amenities:** Restaurant; bar; coffee shop; room service; laundry service; dry cleaning. *In room:* A/C, TV, Wi-Fi, minibar, safe.

Romantik Hotel & Restaurant Schwarzer Adler ★★ An appealing alternative to Innsbruck's modern hotels, the Romantik Hotel lies behind an antique facade of stucco and shutters, and a big-windowed tower. The Ullrich family, the owners, furnished the interior in an authentic style with aged paneling, hand painted regional furniture, antiques, and *gemutlich* clutter that make for a cozy and inviting ambience. Rooms are virtually one of a kind, each with its special character and period decor. Persian carpets cover parquet floors, and the bathrooms have dual basins, powerful showerheads, and large tubs. We prefer the older accommodations, which are more spacious and have more Tyrolean character. The two suites are even more luxurious. Restaurant Schwarzer Adler is reviewed under "Where to Dine," below.

Kaiserjägerstrasse 2, A-6020 Innsbruck. ✆ **0512/587109.** Fax 0512/561697. www.deradler.com. 39 units. 165€–225€ ($264–$360) double; 290€–480€ ($464–$768) suite. Additional person 50€ ($80). Rates include breakfast. AE, DC, MC, V. Parking 12€ ($19). Tram: 1 or 3. **Amenities:** Restaurant; bar; fitness center; spa; room service; massage; laundry service; dry cleaning; nonsmoking rooms. *In room:* A/C, TV, Wi-Fi, minibar, hair dryer, safe (in some).

Moderate

Best Western Hotel Mondschein ★ Value This is one of four Best Western hotels in Innsbruck. It occupies a pink-fronted antique building that was originally erected in 1473 and that later functioned as a relay station for the Austrian (then horse-drawn) postal service. The antique integrity of its exterior has been carefully preserved, complete with its bay windows and solid proportions. Inside, however, it has been thoroughly modernized, with sturdy furniture and decor, and bedrooms that correspond to a modern international aesthetic of smooth lines, wood-grained furniture, and standardized comforts. Most have views of the river Inn or of Innsbruck's Old Town, whose northern edge lies within about 180m (591 ft.) of the hotel.

Mariahilfstrasse 6, A-6020 Innsbruck. ✆ **0512/22784.** Fax 0512/2278490. www.mondschein.at. 34 units. 115€–182€ ($184–$291) double; 230€–280€ ($368–$448) apt. Rates include buffet breakfast. AE, DC, MC, V. Free parking. Tram: 1. **Amenities:** Bar; babysitting; laundry service; dry cleaning; nonsmoking rooms. *In room:* TV, Wi-Fi, minibar, hair dryer, safe.

Hotel Central ★ One of the most unusual hotels in Innsbruck, Hotel Central was originally built in the 1860s, but from its very modern exterior you might not realize it. Throughout, you'll see a high-tech composition of textured concrete and angular windows. The comfortable rooms have an Art Deco design that evokes an almost Japanese sense of simplicity. Most are quite spacious, with excellent beds. In total contrast to the simplicity of the rest of the hotel, the ground floor contains a grand Viennese cafe with marble columns, sculpted ceilings, and large gilt-and-crystal chandeliers.

Gilmstrasse 5, A-6020 Innsbruck. ✆ **0512/5920.** Fax 0512/580310. www.central.co.at. 85 units. 125€–170€ ($200–$272) double. Rates include breakfast. AE, DC, MC, V. Parking 12€ ($19). Tram: 1 or 3. **Amenities:** Restaurant; bar; fitness center; sauna; laundry service; dry cleaning; nonsmoking rooms. *In room:* TV, Wi-Fi, minibar, hair dryer.

Hotel Goldener Adler ★★ Even the phone booth near the reception desk of this 600-year-old family-run hotel is outfitted in antique style. Famous guests have included Goethe, Mozart, and the violinist Paganini, who cut his name into the windowpane of his room. Rooms are handsomely furnished and vary in size and decor. Some have decorative Tyrolean architectural features such as beamed ceilings. Others are furnished more modernly. The size of your bathroom depends on your room assignment.

Herzog-Friedrich-Strasse 6, A-6020 Innsbruck. ✆ **0512/571111.** Fax 0512/584409. www.goldeneradler.com. 35 units. 150€–210€ ($240–$336) double; from 260€ ($416) suite. Rates include buffet breakfast. AE, DC, MC, V. Parking 11€ ($18). Tram: 1 or 3. **Amenities:** Restaurant; bar; babysitting; laundry service; dry cleaning; nonsmoking rooms. *In room:* TV, Wi-Fi, minibar, hair dryer, safe.

Hotel Kapeller Set within a 5-minute drive east of Innsbruck's historic core, this establishment is centered on a 500-year-old house and a 1960s four-story hotel. They're interconnected with a greenhouse-style reception area and bar. Rooms are outfitted in artfully rustic reproductions of Tyrolean-style furniture. Many overlook the mountains and the hotel's garden. Staff is attentive, English-speaking, and cooperative. Restaurant Kapeller is recommended under "Where to Dine," below. The hotel derives its name, incidentally, from a small Romanesque-era chapel that lies nearby.

Philippine-Welser-Strasse 96, A-6020 Innsbruck. ✆ **0512/343101.** Fax 0512/34310668. www.kapeller.at. 36 units. 140€ ($224) double; 165€ ($264) suite for 2–4 occupants. Rates include buffet breakfast. AE, DC, MC, V. Tram: 3. **Amenities:** Restaurant; bar; room service; laundry service; dry cleaning. *In room:* TV, Wi-Fi, minibar, hair dryer, safe.

Hotel Sailer ★ Now into a family management that has stretched over five generations, this is one of the best and more affordable hotels of Innsbruck, lying a short walk west of the Hauptbahnhof. A trio of antique buildings were joined together to form this welcoming hotel. Even though it's in the city, you feel like you're in an alpine retreat because of the use of woodwork on every floor. The public rooms are warm and inviting. Guest rooms are small to medium in size and lack the character and taste of the public rooms, but they're well maintained and beautifully kept with mainly built-in pieces. The best views, as would be expected, are on the upper floors. In a series of rustically decorated restaurants, Tyrolean specialties are served, and the intimate and wood-paneled bar is a retreat after you return from the slopes. In winter, folkloric shows are often presented.

Adamgasse 8. ✆ **0512/53630.** Fax 0512/53637. www.sailer-innsbruck.at. 86 units. 65€–110€ ($104–$176) double; 85€–160€ ($136–$256) suite. AE, DC, MC, V. Tram: Hauptbahnhof. **Amenities:** Restaurant; bar; sauna; laundry service; dry cleaning; nonsmoking rooms. *In room:* TV, Wi-Fi, hair dryer.

Tourotel Breinössl Constructed about a century ago and recently renovated, this building was originally erected as an oversize private home with enough bedrooms to double as a boardinghouse. Flowered loggias and bay windows protrude from the ocher-colored facade. The inside is tastefully woodsy, with touches of wrought iron and regional sculpture in the public areas. The comfortable rooms have attractively modern furniture and good beds. The hotel is owned and operated by a nationwide restaurant chain, Wienerwald, which also operates a restaurant on the hotel's ground floor.

Maria-Theresien-Strasse 12, A-6020 Innsbruck. ✆ **0512/584165.** Fax 0512/58416526. www.hotel-breinoessl.at. 41 units. 129€–139€ ($206–$222) double. Rates include breakfast. AE, DC, MC, V. Bus: R or O. Parking 15€ ($23). **Amenities:** Restaurant; bar; room service (7am–midnight); nonsmoking rooms. *In room:* TV, Wi-Fi.

Inexpensive

City-Hotel Goldene Krone Near the Triumphal Arch on Innsbruck's main street, this baroque house has a green-and-white facade. Rooms are modern, comfortable, well maintained, and, for the most part, spacious with plenty of light filtering through the many windows. Most have a table with chairs, and all have firm mattresses and triple-glazed windows to cut down on noise. The hotel offers good comfort: an elevator, soundproof windows, and a Viennese-inspired coffeehouse/restaurant, the **Art Gallery-Café.**

Maria-Theresien-Strasse 46, A-6020 Innsbruck. ✆ **0512/586160.** Fax 0512/5801896. www.goldene-krone.at. 37 units. 87€–106€ ($139–$170) double; 112€–144€ ($179–$230) suite. Rates include buffet breakfast. AE, MC, V. Parking 10€ ($16). Tram: 1. Bus: A, H, K, or N. **Amenities:** Restaurant; cafe; lounge; babysitting. *In room:* TV.

Gasthof-Hotel Weisses Kreuz ★ (Value This atmospheric inn, located in the center of Innsbruck, has not changed much during its lifetime, with the exception of the elevator that now carries newcomers up two flights to the reception area. In 1769, 13-year-old Wolfgang Mozart and his father, Leopold, stayed here, and in recent times, locally famous German-speaking actors and actresses have made it their temporary home. The reception area features carved stone columns, a TV room with an arched, wood-covered ceiling, a collection of massive Tyrolean chests, and a carved balustrade worn smooth by the palms of countless visitors. Rooms are cozy and atmospheric, either small or medium in size, with comfortable furnishings. Some have private bathrooms with neatly kept shower units.

Herzog-Friedrich-Strasse 31, A-6020 Innsbruck. ✆ **0512/594790.** Fax 0512/5947990. www.weisses kreuz.at. 40 units, 31 with bathroom. 63€–66€ ($101–$106) double without bathroom; 93€–118€

($149–$189) double with bathroom. Rates include buffet breakfast. AE, MC, V. Parking 10€ ($16). Tram: 3. **Amenities:** Bar; nonsmoking rooms. *In room:* TV.

Hotel Bierwirt This hotel consists of a pair of buildings that face each other across a busy street on the southern outskirts of town, about a 15-minute walk from the historic core. The older section dates from 1615 and benefits from a 1998 renovation that brought the cozy interior up to modern standards. The restaurant and all but a dozen of the rooms are in the original building, but regardless of their location, each room has a modern bathroom with a tub/shower combination and many contemporary comforts. Restaurant Bierwirt is recommended separately in "Where to Dine," below.

Bichlweg 2. A-6020 Innsbruck. ✆ **0512/342143.** Fax 0512/3421435. www.bierwirt.com. 50 units. 127€–164€ ($203–$262) double. MC, V. Parking 10€ ($16). Tram: 3. Bus: K. **Amenities:** Restaurant; bar; tennis court; sauna; children's playroom; airport shuttle service; massage; nonsmoking rooms; rooms for those w/limited mobility; tanning beds. *In room:* TV, Wi-Fi, hair dryer, safe.

Hotel Binders (Value) This is an unusual hotel, crafted and managed with a bit more imagination than equivalently priced inns within its immediate, somewhat remote, neighborhood. It presents a utilitarian, white-stucco facade to a suburban neighborhood southwest of Innsbruck's center, near the town's Olympic stadium, about a 20-minute walk from the center. Inside you'll find a carefully organized and thrifty interior, wherein a bar and cafe near the reception area function as the hotel's social center. Members of the Binder family recently installed an elevator in this older building; they've also renovated its public areas so frequently that not many traces remain to hint at the building's original construction. In distinct opposition to this, bedrooms run the gamut of stylishness. Most desirable are the "space-age" modern rooms, with names like Maple, Aluminum, Pink, and Turquoise. Older rooms still retain a dark-paneled, somewhat dowdy '70s version of an alpine-rustic decor.

Dr.-Glatz-Strasse 20, A-6020 Innsbruck. ✆ **0512/33436.** Fax 0512/3343699. www.binders.at. 50 units. 78€–130€ ($125–$208) double with bathroom. Rates include breakfast. AE, DC, MC, V. Parking garage 9€ ($14). Tram: 3. **Amenities:** Bar; sauna; nonsmoking rooms. *In room:* TV, Wi-Fi, minibar.

Hotel Mozart This renovated hotel has a central location and offers small rooms, including the family rooms (which have 3 or 4 beds). The beds aren't the town's most comfortable, but the price is right. Bathrooms are very small but do contain tub/shower combinations. You don't get a lot of frills here, but you do receive good, solid comfort at a reasonable price. From the railway station, walk down Salurner Strasse, crossing Leopoldstrasse, which leads you to Müllerstrasse and the hotel in about 10 minutes.

Müllerstrasse 15, A-6010 Innsbruck. ✆ **0512/595380.** Fax 0512/595386. www.mozarthotel.com. 42 units. 80€–95€ ($128–$152) double. Rates include buffet breakfast. Half-board 12€ ($19). AE, DC, MC, V. Parking outdoors 6€ ($9.60); garage 9€ ($14). Closed Dec 13–26. Tram: 1. **Amenities:** Breakfast room; lounge; nonsmoking rooms; rooms for those w/limited mobility. *In room:* TV, Wi-Fi, hair dryer, safe.

Pension Bistro This is a simple but engaging government-rated two-star hotel that occupies a building from around 1955 and is located within a 15-minute walk of the city center. Rooms are relatively spacious, albeit blandly decorated. Double-paned windows block out most of the noise from the busy street, and some have views of the nearby mountains. The restaurant is recommended separately in "Where to Dine," below.

Pradler Strasse 2, A-6020 Innsbruck. ✆ **0512/346319.** Fax 0512/36025252. www.tiscover.at/hotel-bistro. 11 units. 68€–70€ ($109–$112) double. Rates include breakfast. No credit cards. Bus: O or R. **Amenities:** Restaurant; bar. *In room:* TV, hair dryer.

Pension Paula ★ Finds Set on a hillside above Innsbruck and surrounded with greenery, this hotel evolved during the 1950s from the core of a 17th-century farmhouse. Today it's still maintained by the grandson (Wolfgang Gunsch) of the matriarch (Paula) who founded the place, and still retains reminders on the ground floor of the building's original function. Rooms are cozy but simple, with a bare-boned but comfortable ambience that's permeated with personalized attention. Half of the rooms contain well-kept private bathrooms with shower units. The two rooms (especially no. 15) under the sloping eaves of the third floor are among the most sought-after, partially because of their sense of privacy and romance. Panoramic views are available from the porch and terrace that extend out from the two lower floors of the building, and overall there's a sense of cordiality and friendliness.

Weiherburggasse 15, A-6020 Innsbruck. ✆ **0512/292262.** Fax 0512/293017. www.pensionpaula.at. 14 units, 7 w/private bathroom. 52€–57€ ($83–$91) double w/shared bathroom; 62€ ($99) double w/private bathroom; 80€ ($128) triple w/private bathroom. No credit cards. Bus: D. **Amenities:** Lounge. *In room:* No phone.

Pension Stoi Kids This pension is 3 minutes from the train station. The rooms are comfortable, with good beds and hallway showers. Because some rooms have three or four beds, this pension has long been a favorite of families on a budget. No breakfast is served, but there are several cafes nearby.

Salurner Strasse 7, A-6020 Innsbruck. ✆ **0512/585434.** Fax 05238/87282. 18 units, 7 w/private bathroom. 54€ ($86) double w/shared bathroom; 65€ ($104) double w/private bathroom; 70€ ($112) triple w/shared bathroom; 75€ ($120) triple w/private bathroom. No credit cards. Tram: 1 or 3. **Amenities:** Lounge. *In room:* No phone.

WHERE TO DINE

Dining is never a problem in Innsbruck, as this alpine town has more than 200 restaurants, inns, and cafes, some of which offer evening entertainment. If you're going to be in Austria for only a short time, we suggest that you stick to original Tyrolean specialties. However, if that doesn't suit you, there are restaurants serving international cuisine.

Expensive

Europastüberl ★★ AUSTRIAN/INTERNATIONAL The hotel that hosts this distinguished restaurant, with a delightful Tyrolean ambience, has the finest address in Innsbruck. Traditional regional and creative cooking is the chef's goal, and he achieves this exceedingly well. Diners can choose from both warm and cold appetizers, ranging from iced angler fish with Chinese tree morels to a small ragout of crayfish in a spicy biscuit with kohlrabi. Soups might include lobster minestrone with basil oil or cream of spinach and potato. Main dishes are served only for two people, such as roast pike perch with vegetables and buttery potatoes, and Bresse guinea hen roasted and presented with an herb sauce. Fresh Tyrolean trout almost always appears on the menu, or you might prefer the meat dishes, ranging from red deer ragout to fried jelly of calves' head Vienna style with a lamb's tongue salad. Many dishes, including *tafelspitz,* represent traditional Austrian cuisine. Desserts are often lavish, or you can settle for a Tyrolean apple strudel.

In the Hotel Europa Tyrol, Brixner Strasse 6. ✆ **0512/593-01.** Reservations required. Main courses 18€–30€ ($29–$48); fixed-price menu 48€–79€ ($77–$126). AE, DC, MC, V. Daily noon–2pm and 6:30–10pm. Bus: F.

Guggeryllis SCANDINAVIAN/INTERNATIONAL Located one flight above the lobby level of a government-rated four-star hotel, this popular restaurant is a favorite of the international business community, and it's romantic enough for intimate celebrations as well. In an attractive setting with potted palms, the restaurant is named for Emperor Maximilian's best-known and most popular court jester. Menu items emphasize a combination of Scandinavian, Austrian, and international foods, some of the best examples of which appear at the lunchtime buffet. We consider it, with its trio of meats and large array of salads, one of the most appealing options in town. A la carte items include such Nordic specialties as noisettes of reindeer with forest mushrooms and braised red cabbage, and such Austrian dishes as Wiener schnitzels, *tafelspitz,* saddle of veal steak in a morel-studded cream sauce, and a perfectly prepared version of grilled sole with lemon butter.

In the Hilton Innsbruck, Salurner Strasse 15. ✆ **0512/5935308.** Reservations recommended. Main courses 14€–28€ ($23–$45); lunch buffet 16€ ($26). AE, DC, MC, V. Daily noon–3pm and 6–11pm. Tram: 1 or 3.

Lichtblick ★★ INTERNATIONAL This chic dining spot on the seventh floor of the Rathausgalerie takes its name "bright spot" or Lichtblick from its location, but also from the dining experience. The vistas over the Altstadt are without precedent in Innsbruck and are especially dramatic at night. The restaurant overflows into the panoramic Café Bar Lounge 360, which you can visit even if you're not having dinner in the main restaurant.

Chef Andreas Zeindlinger is a whiz, using market-fresh ingredients to concoct sublime dishes on his constantly changing menu. Whether he's making such classics as risotto or a creamy polenta, he gives each dish an original touch. From poultry to beef and pork dishes, his bright ideas and sure technique are almost guaranteed to give you one of your finest meals in town.

Maria-Theresienstrasse 18, 7th floor Rathausgalerie. ✆ **0512/566550.** Reservations required. Fixed-price menus 39€–45€ ($62–$72). AE, DC, MC, V. Mon–Sat noon–2:30pm and 6:30–10pm. Bus: Ror F.

Pfefferkorn INTERNATIONAL The first thing you'll see within the thick walls of this hundred-year-old stone building is a bar, which focuses on drinks, a sense of conviviality, and a roster of simple, well-prepared platters. Upstairs there's a more formal and somewhat more sedate dining room, where the Austrian and International cuisine includes a wide choice of vegetarian dishes, fresh fish, pastas, and thick cuts of steaks and chops. Consider dishes from an "around the world" repertoire that includes sushi and "fingerfood" platters; a *pot-au-feu* of seafood served with *rouille* (spicy garlic-flavored mayonnaise); a rich assortment of meat, fish, and vegetarian fondues; *vitello tonnato* with field-green salads and parmesan-flavored vinaigrette; and eggplant cordon bleu with tomato-mozzarello sauce.

Seilergasse 8. ✆ **0512/565-444.** www.pepper.at. Reservations recommended. Main courses 11€–32€ ($18–$51); bar platters 8€–18€ ($13–$29); set menus 33€–57€ ($53–$91). AE, DC, MC, V. Wed–Sat 3pm–1am, Sun 10am–1am. Closed Feb. Tram: 3.

Restaurant Goldener Adler ★ AUSTRIAN/TYROLEAN/INTERNATIONAL Richly Teutonic and steeped in the decorative traditions of alpine Tyrol, this restaurant has a deeply entrenched reputation and a loyal following among local residents. The menu includes hearty fare based on cold-weather outdoor life—the chefs aren't into delicate subtleties. Examples include Tyrolean bacon served with horseradish and farmer's bread, cream of cheese soup with croutons, and Tyroler *Zopfebraten,* a flavorful age-old specialty consisting of strips of veal steak served with herb-enriched cream sauce and spinach dumplings. A well-regarded specialty is a platter known as *Adler Tres,* containing spinach dumplings, stuffed noodles, and cheese dumplings, all flavorfully tied together with a brown butter sauce and a gratin of mountain cheese.

Herzog-Friedrich-Strasse 6. ✆ **0512/5711110.** Reservations recommended. Main courses 12€–25€ ($19–$40). AE, DC, MC, V. Daily noon–10:30pm in summer; otherwise noon–2:30pm and 6–10:30pm. Tram: 1 or 3.

Restaurant Schwarzer Adler ★★ AUSTRIAN Even if you're not a guest at the richly atmospheric Romantik Hotel Schwarzer Adler (above), you might appreciate a meal within its historic premises. If you do, you'll follow in the footsteps of the 18th-century Kaiser Maximilian, who housed one of his mistresses in one of the lodgings within this building and who used to entertain her in one or another of these dining rooms. You'll have the option of dining within one of three cozily wood-paneled *stubes* (parlors) near the reception desk, on the hotel's ground floor, or within the more stately looking cellar, beneath the soaring vaulted ceilings of a dining room (Spiesesaal K&K—*Kaiser und Königlich*) that honors its long-ago associations with royalty. Cuisine is elaborate and intricate, the product of a management that's proud of the hotel's status as a member of Europe's Romantik Hotel chain. The finest examples include a salad of wild quail served with lentils, strips of braised goose liver, and a sauce that's enhanced with apple liqueur. There's also a divine smoked venison with a terrine of wild grouse and black bread; grilled filets of wild boar served with roasted potatoes; a gratin of wild mushrooms; and a salad of wild and mixed baby greens. Dessert might include a selection of sorbets flavored with wild alpine berries. As you'd expect, the wine list is long, broad, and impressive.

In the Hotel Schwarzer Adler, Kaiserjägerstrasse 2. ✆ **0512/587109.** Reservations recommended. Main courses 15€–29€ ($24–$46). AE, DC, MC, V. Mon–Sat 10am–1am; Sun 5pm–1am. Tram: 1 or 3.

Schöneck ★★★ AUSTRIAN/TYROLEAN The cozy premises of this restaurant were once devoted to cheap but cheerful old-fashioned food that was usually consumed by students and youth hostelers. All of that changed, however, when culinary entrepreneur Alfred Miller shut the place down for almost a year of painstaking renovations, inserted a new kitchen, and reconfigured the place into tastefully *gemütlich* and upscale enclave of elegant Tyrolean dining. Today, within a quartet of wood-paneled dining rooms, he serves arguably the finest cuisine in Innsbruck. From at least one of these, diners appreciate a view that sweeps out over the town, bringing in views of the nearby peaks as well. Menu items change with the season and the inspiration of the chef, but might include a carpaccio of salmon; grilled octopus with fish roe and fresh noodles; filet of Tyrolean venison with juniper-berry sauce and pepper-laced polenta; a tantalizing dish of braised scallops with fresh lobster and risotto flavored with squid ink; and grilled sea bass with an herb-flavored vinaigrette. Dessert? Consider the chocolate-stuffed cannelloni with fresh strawberries and house-made mango sorbet.

Weiherburggasse 6. ✆ **0512/272728.** www.wirtshaus-schoeneck.com. Reservations required. Main courses 28€ ($45); set-price menus 54€–79€ ($86–$126). AE, DC, MC, V. Thurs–Sat noon–2pm; Tues–Sat 6pm–midnight. Closed 2 weeks in Aug, 1 week in early Jan. Bus: W.

Moderate

Cammerlander ★ AUSTRIAN/INTERNATIONAL This is a spacious cafe/bar and a more formal dining area on two levels directly along the banks of the Inn River. In fair weather, nearly all guests, both locals and visitors, prefer the covered terrace with its river views. The restaurant is for people who like to eat well but shun flashiness or menus too innovative. You can start with one of the soups, perhaps a tomato and chili bowl or else a cream of lemongrass soup with curry. Serrano ham is one of the more delectable appetizers, as are the salads, particularly the sesame chicken.

Some of the best steaks in town are offered here, especially the tenderloin or rumpsteak. The menu also offers several versions of pizza. The fresh catch of the day is featured, as are several versions of chicken, including one savory version in a chili sauce.

Most guests order the *apfelstrudel* for dessert but for a change of pace you might opt for the green tea cake.

Innrain 2. ✆ **0512/586398.** www.cammerlander.at. Reservations recommended. Main courses 12€–18€ ($19–$29); lunch buffet 8.50€ ($14). AE, MC, V. Daily 11:30am–midnight. Tram: 1 or 2.

Hirschen-Stuben ★★ AUSTRIAN/ITALIAN Beneath a vaulted ceiling in a house built in 1631, this restaurant is charming, well established, and well recommended. You'll see hand-chiseled stone columns, brocade chairs, and a short flight of stairs leading down from the historic pavement of the street outside. The establishment, by its own admission, is at its best in spring, autumn, and winter, since it lacks a garden or terrace for outdoor summer dining. The food is well prepared, the staff is charming, and the ambience is appropriately welcoming. Menu items include steaming platters of pasta, fish soup, trout meunière, sliced veal in cream sauce (Zurich style), beef Stroganoff, pepper steak, stewed deer with vegetables, and filet of flounder with parsley and potatoes. The kitchen staff is equally familiar with the cuisine of both Austria and Italy.

Impressions

The chief crop of provincial Austria is scenery.

—John Gunther, *Inside Europe* (1938)

Kiebachgasse 5. ✆ **0512/582979.** Reservations recommended. Main courses 9€–23€ ($14–$37). AE, DC, MC, V. Tues–Sat 11:30am–2pm and Mon–Sat 6–10:30pm. Tram: 1 or 3.

Inexpensive

Al Dente ITALIAN/VEGETARIAN Part of the Italian craze sweeping Innsbruck, this modern restaurant turns out an array of reasonably priced and good-tasting Italian and Mediterranean-style dishes that are based on market-fresh ingredients. There's a beer garden and a terrace (May–Oct) for your added enjoyment. The salads are freshly made, with crisp lettuce, and served with creamy dressings. You can order your pastas with such zesty sauces as marinara, or perhaps a creamy carbonara or a well-flavored ragout. They do not serve meat of any kind. A casual, relaxed ambience prevails, and the trattoria is suitable for everyone from singles to families. For the most part, waiters are fluent in English, and a welcoming atmosphere prevails.

Meraner Strasse 7. ✆ **0512/584947.** www.restaurant-aldente.at. Reservations recommended. Main courses 7€–9.80€ ($11–$16). MC, V. Mon–Sat 11am–11pm. Tram: 1 or 3.

Bistro AUSTRIAN/INTERNATIONAL Within one large and paneled dining room, you'll find hints of folkloric charm, a loyal lunchtime clientele from surrounding office buildings, and a well-prepared menu that reflects the changing seasons. During springtime, expect creative uses of asparagus; during autumn and early winter, look for venison prepared in a variety of different ways. There's a year-round emphasis on fish that include Atlantic versions of turbot and sole, and such local freshwater varieties as *saibling,* pike-perch, zander, and trout. As its name suggests, this is an unpretentious affair with solid, generous portions.

Pradler Strasse 2. ✆ **0512/346319.** Reservations not necessary. Main courses 8€–17€ ($13–$27). AE, DC, MC, V. Tues–Sun noon–3pm; daily 6–11pm (last order). Bus: O or R.

Blaues Schiff MEDITERRANEAN/ITALIAN This place takes five different components and rolls them into rolled one: Restaurant, pizzeria, pub, bistro, and bar. It's also one of the most affordable dining outlets in a city long known as pricey. What's served here is standard grub along with beer and wine. The cooks don't muck about with nouvelle cuisine but concentrate on crowd-pleasers such as pastas and pizza. There is also the usual repertoire of standard south-of-the-border dishes (in this case, sunny Italy).

Universitätsstrasse 13. ✆ **0512/565410.** www.blauesschiff.com. Reservations not necessary. Main courses 5.90€–12€ ($9.50–$19). AE, DC, MC, V. Daily 10am–3pm and 6pm–midnight. Tram: 1 or 3.

Café Bar Restaurant Dengg AUSTRIAN/INTERNATIONAL A combined restaurant/cafe/bar with sophisticated modern furnishings forms the backdrop for one of the most up-to-date gathering places in Innsbruck. Though it's in the old part of town, it's contemporary as tomorrow. It has one of the most well-rounded menus in the heart of the city, with something for almost every palate. The cooks roam the world for inspiration. For example, instead of the usual spinach salad, you get additions such as pistachio nuts, squid, prawns, and a black ginger-laced sesame dressing. Dim sum arrives in steamy baskets with vegetables, and sea bass is served with a perfect accompaniment: a warm mushroom tartar from the forest. Suckling pig cutlets served Cantonese style with cabbage spring rolls are a delight, and veal liver saltimbocca is served with a salad of arugula and radicchio. Homemade sorbets are featured, although we prefer something more exotic from the chef's repertoire—perhaps homemade black sesame ice cream with marinated rhubarb.

Riesengasse 11–13. ✆ **512/582347.** Reservations recommended. Main courses 8.40€–22€ ($13–$36). AE, DC, MC, V. Mon–Fri 8am–1am. Tram: 1 or 3.

La Cucina Ristorante ITALIAN This trattoria continues the Italian "invasion" of Innsbruck. More and more of the townspeople, especially the young, are preferring the lighter and often more flavorful cuisine of Italy than more heavily laden Austrian dishes. This place is especially festive in summer, when action overflows onto a patio and beer garden setting. Fresh fish is always on the menu, and it's grilled and spiced to perfection. There's also an array of succulent homemade pastas, and the pizza oven is kept busy at night. Many guests begin with one of the freshly tossed salads. A selection of veal, poultry, and beef dishes round out the well-chosen menu, which is backed up by a varied wine list and an extensive range of beers.

Museumstrasse 26. ✆ **0512/584229.** Reservations recommended. Main courses 8.40€–22€ ($13–$34). AE, DC, MC, V. Daily 11am–1am. Tram: 1 or 3.

Philippine VEGETARIAN/FISH/INTERNATIONAL The inspiration for the mostly vegetarian food here derives from around the world, including India and Mexico, but the origins of its name are purely Austrian: It refers to Philippine Welser, wife of the 16th-century overlord of the Tyrol, Ferdinand II, and author of a book on the healing power of herbs. Positioned one floor above street level, with somewhat anonymous decor that might remind you of an airport waiting lounge, it was established as a public works project about a decade ago as a means of feeding and employing the city's homeless. All of that changed, however, in 2000, when members of the Puffing family took over its administration and whipped it into cracking good shape as a privately operated restaurant. Cuisine is tasty and flavorful, most of it focusing on all-vegetarian presentations of salads, lasagnas, curries, polenta with Gorgonzola, cannelloni with tofu, and pumpkin risotto with ginger and Parmesan cheese. There is a limited array of fish dishes, including stir-fries of shrimp with vegetables, braised salmon with a wine-flavored herb sauce, and zander (pikeperch) with an herb-flavored butter sauce. As lunches here are more popular than evening meals, lunch is served both on the street level and in the upstairs dining room; dinners are served only in the dining room upstairs.

Templstrasse 2 at Müllerstrasse. ✆ **0512/589157.** Reservations recommended. Main courses 8€–19€ ($13–$31). AE, DC, MC, V. Mon–Sat 11:30am–2pm and 6:30–10pm. Tram: 1.

Restaurant Bierwirt Value AUSTRIAN Antique-looking, with an architectural pedigree that goes back 300 years, this cozy alpine-style restaurant has lots of Tyrolean artifacts, carefully oiled paneling, and an excellent reputation for good food. Menu items include most of the traditional Tyrolean specialties, rib-sticking fare that goes down well in chilly weather. Examples include ragout of venison in a port-wine sauce, a savory version of *kasfarfeln* (thick consommé with cheese, onions, chives, and dumplings), savory stews, Wiener schnitzels, *tafelspitz,* roasts, and sausages.

Bichlweg 2. ✆ **0512/342143.** www.bierewirt.at. Reservations recommended. Main courses 7€–20€ ($11–$32). Mon–Fri noon–2pm; Mon–Sat 5–11pm. MC, V. Tram: 3. Bus: K.

Restaurant Kapeller AUSTRIAN/CONTINENTAL This restaurant occupies a 500-year-old house that was expanded into a hotel in the 1960s. Cozy and welcoming, it includes three paneled dining rooms, an attentive staff, and plenty of Tyrolean artifacts and charm. Savory menu items vary with the season, but are likely to include braised lamb with vegetables and a gratin of potatoes, duck with honey-flavored croutons and potato croquettes, and filets of sole with salmon mousse served with grape sauce and asparagus-flavored risotto. Die-hard regionalists sometimes appreciate an age-old Tyrolean dish, *peuscherl,* composed of the tongue, hearts, and offal of beef and sheep, served with an herb-flavored sauce.

Philippine-Welser-Strasse 96. ✆ **0512/343101.** Reservations recommended. Main courses 14€–30€ ($22–$48). AE, DC, MC, V. Tues–Sat 11am–2pm; Mon–Sat 6–10pm. Tram: 3.

Restaurant Ottoburg ★ AUSTRIAN/INTERNATIONAL This historic restaurant, established around 1745, occupies a 13th-century building that some historians say is the oldest in Innsbruck. Inside, four intimate and atmospheric dining rooms with "19th-century neo-Gothic decor" lie scattered over two different floors. Hearty dishes include venison stew, "grandmother's mixed grill," pork chops with rice and carrots, and fried trout. The international menu emphasizes Tyrolean specialties, best seen in the dessert list, which offers two kinds of strudel and several other pastries. In summer, a beer garden operates in the rear, open daily from 10:30am to 11:30pm.

Herzog-Friedrich-Strasse 1. ✆ **0512/584338.** www.ottoburg.at. Reservations recommended. Main courses 12€–25€ ($19–$40). AE, DC, MC, V. Tues–Sun 11am–2:30pm and 6pm–midnight. Tram: 1 or 3.

Riese Haymon TYROLEAN/AUSTRIAN Inside this 400-year-old building in the heart of the old city, you'll find an intensely Tyrolean ambience that includes four separate dining rooms, each paneled and accessorized with old-time artifacts, plus an attentive staff. Menu items include old-fashioned but flavor-filled dishes that rely on the seasonality of the ingredients and that often come with one of the restaurant's specialties, dumplings. Look for a changing menu that usually includes such local freshwater fish as *saibling,* pikeperch, salmon, and trout; veal and chicken dishes in wine sauce or brown stocks; Wiener schnitzel; braised liver; herb-flavored terrines of freshwater crayfish; and an especially savory version of braised oxtail.

Haymongasse 4. ✆ **0512/566800.** Reservations recommended. Main courses 9.80€–19€ ($16–$30); fixed-price lunch (Mon–Fri only) 6.60€–8.50€ ($11–$14); fixed-price dinner 28€–36€ ($45–$58). DC, MC, V. Daily 11:30am–2pm and 6–9:30pm. Tram: 1 or 3.

Stiftskeller AUSTRIAN/INTERNATIONAL The baroque detailing on this 18th-century yellow-and-white palace-turned-restaurant across from the Hofburg can be admired from the street-side beer garden (at night, lights illuminate the garden). In cold weather, you can dine inside, where there are several dining rooms. Meals are posted on a blackboard, and typical menu items include spaghetti carbonara and venison schnitzel in a pheasant-flavored cream sauce, followed by fresh homemade apple strudel. This place can get rowdy at night. During the warm summer months, folk music and oldies are played in the beer garden, starting at 7:30pm.

Burggraben 31. ✆ **0512/583490.** Reservations required. Main courses 13€–25€ ($21–$39). AE, DC, MC, V. Daily 9am–midnight. Closed Jan 8–Feb 20. Tram: 1 or 3.

Theresien Bräu AUSTRIAN/INTERNATIONAL There's a lot of energy, ambience, and goodwill associated with this place, which is reflected in the fact that it has become one of its neighborhood's most popular dining and drinking venues since it was established in 1996. It's the newest brewery in Tyrol and the only one that's based within the city limits of Innsbruck. The setting is on two floors of what was originally built in the 1940s as a movie theater. Today, you'll find all the apparatus and paraphernalia of a brewery (including big copper and stainless steel vats), artfully positioned in full view of the bar and the dining tables. The theme of the place doesn't evoke alpine Austria, as so many other restaurants in Innsbruck rather shamelessly do. Instead, you can expect a nautical motif of fish nets, brass and mahogany navigational instruments, rowboats, and old-fashioned steamer trunks. All of this is peripheral, of course, to the beer, which comes in as many as four different varieties that vary with the season and the whims of the brewmaster. Regardless of the color and flavor of the brew you select, it costs about 4€ ($6.40) for a foaming half-liter, or 8.50€ ($14) for an American-style 1.4-liter pitcher. Menu items might include everything from a small platter of beer-compatible sausages, a snack that management prices at 8.50€ ($14), to more substantial platters of meat, potatoes, or noodle-based dishes.

Maria-Theresien-Strasse 51–53. ✆ **0512/5875800.** www.brauwirtshaus.at. Reservations not necessary. Main courses 12€–22€ ($19–$35). AE, DC, MC, V. Mon–Wed 10am–1am; Thurs–Sat 10am–2am; Sun 10am–midnight. Tram: 3.

Weisses Rössl ★ AUSTRIAN/TYROLEAN You'll enter this time-honored place through a stone archway opening onto one of Old Town's most famous streets. At the end of a flight of stairs, marked with a very old crucifix, you'll find a trio of dining rooms with red-tile floors and a history of welcoming guests that stretches from 1590. One of the dining rooms (the Nebenstube) has what might be the most extensive set of stag horns (complete with the initials of the hunter and the date of the shooting) in Innsbruck. At first glance, the menu appears simple, listing such dishes as a Tiroler *Grüstl* (a kind of hash composed of sautéed onions, sliced beef, alpine herbs, and potatoes cooked and served in a frying pan), *saftgoulash* with polenta, several kinds of schnitzels, and a grilled platter *Alt Insprugg* for two diners. A dish the restaurant is especially proud of fresh blood and liver sausages with sauerkraut—is served only in midwinter and usually evokes vivid childhood memories for many of this restaurant's Tyrolean clients. In summer, the establishment expands onto an outdoor terrace. They also rent rooms; a double costs 120€ to 130€ ($192–$208), including breakfast.

Kiebachgasse 8. ✆ **0512/58305-07.** Reservations recommended. Main courses 18€–29€ ($29–$46). MC, V. Mon–Sat 11:30am–2pm and 6–10pm. Closed 2 weeks after Easter and 2 weeks in Nov. Tram: 1 or 3.

Cafes

Within a Bordeaux-red decor that closely emulates the rich cafe life of its mother-lode original in Vienna, you can visit the Innsbruck branch of the **Café Sacher,** Rennweg 1 (✆ **0512/565626;** www.sacher.com; tram: 1 or 3; bus: H or Y). Rip-offs and unauthorized copies of this chain's most famous pastry, the Sachertorte, have cost contestants millions in litigation over the years, and the holders of the original 19th-century recipes (the owners of the Hotel Sacher in Vienna) have clung ferociously to their property. You can order coffee, priced around 3.50€ ($5.60), and the famous pastry, at 4.95€ ($7.90) per slice. And if you're in the gift-giving mode, you can haul a Sachertorte, attractively boxed in a wooden container, away with you for between 10€ ($16) and 42€ ($67), depending on the size. Any of these carries a "certificate of authenticity," adding to the experience's somewhat pompous charm. The place is open daily 8:30am to midnight.

If you're tired of too-constant a diet of Austrian pastries, or if you want an insight into the way other countries create fattening between-meal treats, head for the **Café Valier,** Maximilianstrasse 27 (✆ **0512/586180;** tram: 1). Here, within a pink, mostly Jugendstil decor, you'll choose from French and Italian (not Austrian) pastries that—according to the owners—are unique in Innsbruck. Forget about *apfelstrudels* and *Salzburger Nockerl* here, since they simply don't exist. Instead, look for French-inspired *tarte aux framboises; tarte tatin, mousse à l'orange,* or *mousse au chocolat;* a light and airy *gâteau au chocolate avec mousse à l'orange;* and chestnut creams and chestnut sauces that, while all the rage in France, aren't really understood (except here) within the rest of Austria. There's been a bakery on-site here for at least a century, but the sit-down cafe didn't get set up till 1964. Don't expect full-fledged meals here, as most of the menu is devoted to pastries, most of which sell for around 3€ ($4.80) each, and sandwiches, toasted or otherwise. It's open Monday to Friday 8am to 7pm and Saturday 8am to 1pm.

One of the best views of the exterior of the Goldenes Dachl is available from the front terrace of the **Café Katzung,** Herzog-Friedrich-Strasse 16 (✆ **0512/586183;** www.cafe-katzung.at; tram: 1 or 3), a time-tested cafe whose interior was ripped apart and rebuilt during a 5-month period in 2002. The decor today is more streamlined and a bit more modern-looking than the cranky, faux-baroque decor it replaced, but the medley of international newspapers (at least 10 of them) is still available, suspended vertically on rods, in a style you'd associate with a library. Within a decor of wooden floors and a color scheme of pale green and cream with touches of red, you'll select from a full range of whiskeys, coffees, Austrian wine, and light platters that consist mostly of sandwiches, soups, and salads. More impressively, there's an in-house pastry chef who concocts tray after tray of strudels and tortes, all the Austrian staples, priced at 3.50€ to 5€ ($5.60–$8) each. It's open Monday to Saturday 8am to midnight and Sunday 9am to midnight.

On a quiet corner in the Old Town, **Café Munding★**, Kiebachgasse 16 (✆ **0512/584118;** www.nepomuks.at; tram: 1 or 3), is in a comfortable-looking house built in 1720 that has baroque frescoes, carved bay windows, and Tyrolean detailing. Although it's the oldest cafe in Tyrol, the interior has been modernized, offering an interconnected series of rooms. The first thing you'll see when you enter is a pastry and chocolate shop. Food is served in the inner rooms; in addition to coffee priced from 2.75€ ($4.40), the menu includes typical Tyrolean dishes, *toasts* (sandwiches), plus a vast selection of wine by the glass. Hours are daily from 8am to 11:30pm in summer (until 8pm winter).

One of the most colorful and artfully ethnic cafes along Museumstrasse, **Café Wilder Mann** (✆ **0512/583295**), was once part of a famous hotel that moved out of town, leaving only its cafe behind. The building that contains it is an antique in its own right, and the rustic and woodsy-looking decor seems to celebrate the alpine rusticity that such "Wild Men" (its English name) of the Tyrolean high Alps would have preferred. Come here for tea, coffee, ice creams, pastries, and such platters of rib-sticking food as crepes stuffed with filets of pork; Greek-style gyros with herb-flavored cream sauce; piccata of turkey with spaghetti; and such vegetarian dishes as all vegetable strudel. Dessert crepes, especially the versions with strawberries and/or chocolate, or the concoction with walnut-flavored ice cream and caramel sauce, are especially popular. This cafe is not to be confused with the more elaborate restaurant and hotel in the nearby suburb of Lans with the same name. Snacks and platters cost from 7.20€ to 11€ ($12–$17). It's open Monday to Friday 7am to 8pm (tram: 3).

SHOPPING

In Innsbruck, you can buy Tyrolean specialties such as lederhosen, dirndls, leather clothing, woodcarvings, loden cloth, and all sorts of skiing and mountain-climbing equipment. Stroll around **Maria-Theresien-Strasse, Herzog-Friedrich-Strasse,** and **Museumstrasse,** ducking in and making discoveries of your own. Stores are generally open from 9am to 6pm on weekdays and from 9am to noon on Saturday. Here are a few recommendations to get you going.

Lodenbaur Lodenbaur, similar to a department store, is devoted to regional Tyrolean dress. Most goods are made in Austria, including lederhosen, coats, dresses, dirndls, and accessories for men, women, and children. Be sure to check out the basement. Brixner Strasse 4. ✆ **0512/580911.** Tram: 1 or 3.

Tiroler Heimatwerk This is one of Innsbruck's best stores for handcrafted Tyrolean items such as sculpture, pewter, textiles, woolen goods, hand-knit sweaters, and lace. Do-it-yourselfers can buy regionally inspired fabrics and dress patterns, and whip them into a dirndl (or whatever). Also for sale are carved chests, mirror frames, and furniture. The store's elegant decor includes ancient stone columns and vaulted ceilings. Meraner Strasse 2. ✆ **0512/582320.** www.tirolerheimatwerk.at. Tram: 1 or 3.

INNSBRUCK AFTER DARK

Innsbruck is more lighthearted about its nightlife than Vienna. If you're in luck, you'll get to attend a summer concert in the park or perhaps take in an operetta at the theater. You might retire to a beer hall to listen to brass bands and yodeling, or be lulled by zither music at a restaurant. Best of all, you can attend a Tyrolean folkloric evening or retreat to a local wine tavern offering entertainment. Many restaurants offer Tyrolean evenings (featuring evergreen music and dancing) in addition to food.

Ask the tourist office about current events. In summer, a Tyrolean brass band often parades in costume, with a concert at the Goldenes Dachl. There are also often concerts at Schloss Ambras, ecclesiastical music at Wilten Basilica, and organ concerts at the Igls parish church.

In the center of the Altstadt, across from the Hofburg, the 170-year-old **Landestheater,** Rennweg 2 (✆ **0512/52074,** www.landestheater.at), is the major venue for theatrical or operatic presentations. The box office is open daily from 9:30am to 7pm, and performances usually begin at 7:30 or 8pm. Ticket prices are 9€ to 53€ ($14–$85) for most operas or operettas, and 4€ to 53€ ($6.40–$85) for theater seats. It's also the showcase for musicals and light operetta. For tickets, call ✆ **0512/512520744.**

Concerts are presented at the Kunstpavillon in the Hofgarten in summer.

If you want to gamble, you have to drive to the resort of Seefeld, where the **Spiel-Casino** offers roulette, baccarat, and blackjack daily from 5pm. Or you can try your luck on the slot machines at the **Hilton Hotel Innsbruck.**

The Bar & Club Scene

Hofgartencafe Just north of Altstadt, this is perhaps the most popular place in Innsbruck. Lying in Hofgarten, it's especially packed in summer, and offers not only live music, but also indoor and outdoor seating. A lively crowd of young people is attracted to these precincts where more beer is consumed than anywhere else in town. You can opt for the home-brewed beer or else a wide selection of wines, many from such South American countries as Chile and Argentina. Long drinks cost from 7€ ($11), and you can also order platters for 7.40€ to 20€ ($12–$31). It's open in summer daily from 11am to 4am. In winter, hours are Tuesday to Thursday 6pm to 2am, and Friday and Saturday 6pm to 4am. Hofgarten, Rennweg 6. ✆ **0512/588871.** www.der-hofgarten.at. Tram: 1 or 3.

Jackpot Bar The attractive bar near the Hilton Hotel lobby is one of the best places in Innsbruck to meet for a drink. Beer costs 4€ ($6.40) and up, and there are slot machines. It's open Monday to Friday from noon to 1am. In the Hilton Hotel Innsbruck, Salurner Strasse 15. ✆ **0512/59350.** Tram: 3.

Jimmy's Bar This bar lies in a modern building in the center of town, and is a bustling hangout in Innsbruck among young people, often university students. There's no dance floor and no live music, but it's something of an Innsbruck tradition to stop off here for a drink either early in the evening or later at night. Food is also served. The bar is open Monday to Friday 11am to 1am, Saturday and Sunday 7am to 2am. A large beer costs 2.50€ ($4). Wilhelm-Griel-Strasse 19. ✆ **0512/570473.** www.jimmys.at. Tram: 1 or 3.

Krah Vogel Lying off Maria-Theresien-Strasse, this bar attracts university students in droves who crowd its tables. In winter, when some of the patrons show up in Tyrolean dress, the place seems even livelier. In back is a small courtyard, and the overflow heads upstairs for more seating. The cafe has one of the most convivial atmospheres in town and is often crowded. Beer ranges for the most part from 2.50€ to 3.30€ ($4–$5.30), with sandwiches costing from 6€ ($9.60). Open Monday to Saturday 10am to 2am, and Sunday 5pm to 2am. Anichstrasse 12. ✆ **0512/580149.** Tram: 1 or 3.

Restaurant Fischerhausel Bar Although a lot of its business derives from its busy first-floor restaurant, the street-level bar also adds appeal. Rustically outfitted in a modernized version of the Tyrolean style, it's open Monday to Saturday from 10am to 11:30pm and Sunday 6 to 11:30pm. No one will mind if you remain in the bar, quaffing schnapps or suds or whatever, but if you opt to eventually migrate up to the dining room, a *tagesmenu* (fixed-price menu) will cost 8.40€ to 20€ ($13–$31). During warm weather, drinkers and diners tend to move out to the garden in back, soaking up the sunlight and the brisk alpine air. Herrengasse 8. ✆ **0512/583535.** Tram: 1 or 3.

Treibhaus Young people interpret this comprehensive and flexible gathering place as a combination of daytime cafe, snackish restaurant, concert hall, and dance club. Within its battered walls, you can attend a changing roster of art exhibits, cabaret shows, and protest rallies, all from a location within an alleyway about a block from Burggraben. A large beer costs 4.20€ ($6.70); snacks are priced from 3.20€ ($5.10). It's open Monday to Saturday 10am to 1am, with live music presented at erratic intervals. Angerzellgasse 8. ✆ **0512/586874.** Cover for live performances 10€–30€ ($16–$48). Tram: 1 or 3.

Gay Clubs

Gay people throughout the Tyrol tend to agree that the bars and dance clubs that cater to them are bigger, more fun, and a lot more spontaneous in Vienna or even better,

Berlin. If you're looking for a gay bar in the alpine fastnesses of Innsbruck, the options are extremely limited.

Bacchus Located across the street from Innsbruck's Holiday Inn, this is a cellar-level dance club that attracts a clientele composed of about 70% gay men, 25% gay women, and 5% interested and usually well-intentioned straight people. It's open nightly 9pm to 2am or later, depending on the crowd and the night of the week. Salurnerstrasse 18. ✆ **0512/940210.** www.bacchus.tirol.at. Tram: 1 or 3.

Folk Music

Throughout the Christmas season, Easter, and the high season, from 6 to 11pm, you can visit the **Goethe Stube,** in the Restaurant Goldener Adler, Herzog-Friedrich-Strasse 6 (✆ **0512/571111;** tram: 1 or 3), to hear authentic Tyrolean melodies, including the zither and yodelers. There's a one-drink minimum, and a large beer costs 3.50€ ($5.60). Meals start at 9€ ($14).

Another evening of authentic Tyrolean folk entertainment can be experienced courtesy of the shows of **Tiroler Alpenbühne/Geschwister Gundolf** (✆ **0512/263263**), who have been performing in Innsbruck for nearly 4 decades. While you have dinner, a brass band plays along with traditional Tyrolean instruments such as an alphorn, zither, singing saw, and Tyrolean folk harp. It's big, boisterous, and definitely unique. Shows are presented daily at 8:30pm at two locations (the **Gasthaus Sandwirt,** Reichenauerstrasse 151; bus: O or R; and **Messe-Saal,** Etzel-Strasse 33; tram: 1) in Innsbruck May through October. Tickets for the shows start at 15€ ($24). Dinner is optional but does complete the experience of the sounds of the region with the tastes of the region; it usually costs an additional 14€ ($22). For tickets and information, contact Tiroler Alpenbühne/Geschwister Gundolf daily from 8am to 11pm, or ask your hotel concierge if tickets are available. Tickets can be purchased on-site at both venues, but it's highly recommended that you secure a reservation. Scheduled performances are not held in November; from December to March, however, special shows will take place once a week for groups by request. If you're traveling alone or in a small group, call ahead to see if a show has been booked.

2 IGLS & THE ENVIRONS

This area, where many events of the Olympic Winter Games of 1964 and 1976 were held, might be called "Olympic Innsbruck." The cluster of resorts, the best known of which is Igls, puts each within easy reach of the Tyrol capital. A complete system of lifts opens up alpine scenery to everybody, from the beginner to the most advanced skier—or to the sightseer in warm weather. You might consider staying in one of these resorts instead of at an Innsbruck hotel.

IGLS ★

Lying on a sunny plateau in the alpine foothills at an elevation of 877m (2,877 ft.), Igls is the resort choice of many travelers who prefer staying here and driving into Innsbruck, which is 5km (3 miles) north (take Rte. 82). Although its numbers swell greatly with winter and summer visitors, the town has a population of fewer than 2,000. Long known as the "sun terrace" of Innsbruck, Igls is never likely to be too hot, even on the hottest day in Austria. Because it's so popular, Igls is certainly not the cheapest resort in Tyrol.

Essentials

GETTING THERE A streetcar from the **Berg Isel** station in Innsbruck will deliver you to Igls, 305m (1,001 ft.) higher than the capital, in about 30 minutes. Bus J leaves on the hour and the half-hour from the Innsbruck Hauptbahnhof. Tram no. 6 leaves Innsbruck at a quarter past each hour, and it leaves Igls at a quarter to each hour. For transportation information, call ✆ **0512/585155.**

VISITOR INFORMATION The **Igls tourist office** is on Hilberstrasse 15 (✆ **0512/377101;** www.tiscover.com/igls). It's open Monday to Friday 8:30am to 6pm, and Saturday 9am to noon Christmas to Easter and May to September.

Exploring "The Olympic Innsbruck"

Although much of its world renown has been based on winter sports, Igls is also a popular summer resort where you can wander along alpine trails, play golf, or enjoy tennis.

This is also Innsbruckers' favorite place to ski, and they're joined by throngs of visitors. Igls shared the Winter Olympics festivities and sporting competition with Innsbruck, and boasts a bobsled and toboggan run.

Where to Stay

Hotel Batzenhäusl ★ Only a 2-minute walk from the center, this traditional hotel/inn began as a winery in 1893. Its name derives from the Austrian word *batzen,* a silver coin commonly used in the late 19th century. The tavern's ornate paneling is carved from what the locals call "stone pine," the glow from which beautifully complements the flowered carpets, leaded windows, and hand-worked lamps. Other sections of this comfortable hotel are crafted in a more modern style. Rooms are medium in size and well furnished with alpine styling and wooden bed frames. Even if you don't stay here, you might want to consider having dinner in Restaurant Batzenhäusl (see "Where to Dine," below); it's great.

Lanserstrasse 12, A-6080 Igls. ✆ **0512/38618-10.** Fax 0512/386187. www.batzenhaeusl.at. 38 units. 92€–168€ ($147–$269) double; 145€–210€ ($232–$336) apt for 2. Rates buffet breakfast. AE, MC, V. Free parking outdoors; 5€ ($8) garage in summer, 7€ ($11) in winter. Closed late Oct–Dec 15. **Amenities:** Restaurant; bar; fitness center; spa; Jacuzzi; sauna; bike rentals; children's playroom; babysitting; laundry service; dry cleaning; nonsmoking rooms; library; solarium. *In room:* TV, Wi-Fi, minibar, hair dryer, safe.

Schlosshotel Igls ★★ The town's most historic and glamorous hotel, this baroque monument was built as a private castle in 1880 and converted into a small, plush hotel in the 1970s. It sits on its own grass-covered plateau at the end of a narrow street. Many famous guests to Tyrol have stayed here. Rooms are spacious and individually decorated with luxurious beds. Some rooms offer panoramic mountain views. The most renowned of the accommodations is the Rubino Suite, with a fireplace, terrace, and sauna. The hotel's excellent restaurant serves both traditional and international food in turn-of-the-20th-century surroundings. Guests also have access to the two tennis courts at the Schlosshotel's jointly owned hotel, the Sporthotel (below).

Viller Steig 2, A-6080 Igls. ✆ **0512/377217.** Fax 0512/377217-198. www.schlosshotel-igls.com. 18 units. 300€–400€ ($480–$640) double; 380€–880€ ($608–$1,408) suite for 2. Rates include half-board. AE, DC, MC, V. Free parking outdoors, garage 10€ ($16). Closed mid-Oct to Christmas. **Amenities:** Restaurant; bar; indoor heated pool; fitness center; sauna; room service; babysitting; laundry service; dry cleaning; solarium. *In room:* TV, Wi-Fi, minibar, hair dryer, safe.

Sporthotel Igls ★ Built in 1900, the Sporthotel is a fancifully designed establishment that's a cross between a baroque castle and a mountain chalet. Its details include jutting bay windows, at least three ornate hexagonal towers, and rows of flower-covered balconies. The spacious interior is dotted with antiques and conservative furniture, with plenty of *gemütlich* corners and sunny areas, both indoors and out. An annex handles the overflow. Rooms, which come in a variety of sizes, are cozily outfitted in the Tyrolean style, with lots of varnished pine and regional knickknacks. The owners also own an 18-unit Relais & Châteaux property, the Schlosshotel Igls (above).

The hotel has a large dining room where dinner is served to guests on the half-board plan. It also has an attractive a la carte restaurant for nonguests. Nonsmoking areas are provided. Tyrolean/Austrian cuisine is served, along with international and diet menus. In the evening, a one-man band plays in the hotel bar, and Tyrolean folkloric evenings are sometimes staged.

Hilberstrasse 17, A-6080 Igls. ✆ **0512/377241**. Fax 0512/378679. www.sporthotel-igls.com. 91 units. Winter 200€–374€ ($320–$598) double, 224€–438€ ($358–$701) suite for 2; summer 160€–224€ ($256–$358) double, 216€–284€ ($346–$454) suite for 2. Rates include breakfast. Half-board 18€ ($29) per person. AE, DC, MC, V. Parking 7€ ($11). Closed Oct 10–Dec 21 and 3 weeks after Easter. Bus: J. **Amenities:** Restaurant; bar; indoor heated pool; 2 tennis courts; fitness center; spa; Jacuzzi; sauna; room service; massage; babysitting; laundry service; dry cleaning; nonsmoking rooms; solarium; 1 room for those w/ limited mobility. *In room:* TV, Wi-Fi, minibar, coffeemaker, hair dryer, iron, safe.

Where to Dine

Gasthof Wilder Mann AUSTRIAN This place offers a breath of the Tyrolean mountains and country life in the Innsbruck suburb of Igls. Originally built in the 1600s, the building has been enlarged and modified over the years. If you appreciate architecture, you'll enjoy studying the stucco tower attached to the corner of this elongated building with a half-timbered triangular section just under the sloping roofline. The interior is spacious and rustic, with good service and a series of well-prepared traditional specialties such as wine soup, venison pâté with Cumberland sauce, and filet steak in a pepper-cream sauce. Dessert could be a *Salzburger Nockerl.*

Römerstrasse 12. ✆ **0512/379696.** http://wildermann-lans.at. Reservations recommended. Main courses 16€–280€ ($25–$45). AE, DC, MC, V. Daily noon–2pm and 6–10:30pm.

Restaurant Batzenhäusl Value AUSTRIAN In this carefully paneled antique-style dining room, the chalet chairs are intricately carved and the service is good. A house specialty is flambé filet steak "Didi," a popular creation prepared at your table. Other well-prepared Austrian dishes include three kinds of meat on the same platter (covered in a mushroom-cream sauce), *apfelstrudel,* and a series of savory meat-flavored soups. A favorite local dish is venison with cranberry sauce and wild mushrooms along with potato fritters and roast zucchini. You might prefer the outdoor veranda or the garden in summer, although the dining room inside is most attractive.

In the Hotel Batzenhäusl, Lanserstrasse 12. ✆ **0512/38618.** Main courses 9.90€–25€ ($16–$39); fixed-price menu 18€–36€ ($29–$57). AE, MC, V. Daily 11am–2pm and 6–10pm. Closed Apr and Nov.

PÄTSCH

This small village above Igls stands on the sunny western slope of the Pätscherkofel, with a panoramic view of the Stubai Glaciers. Lying on the old Roman road below the peak, Pätsch is only a short distance from the mountain's Olympics slopes.

In winter, Pätsch attracts visitors with its skiing (including cross-country runs), ice-skating, and curling; the resorts offer a ski school. Horse-drawn sleighs take you along snow trails. In summer, you can go on hikes, swim, or play golf and tennis. Summer skiing is also possible on the Stubai Glacier.

The most dramatic way to spend time in Pätsch involves taking a cable car, the **Patscherkofelbahn** ★ (✆ **0512/377234;** www.patscherkofelbahnen.at for information), up to the top of the Patscherkofel, a panoramic site at an elevation of 1,961m (6,434 ft.). From here, you'll have access to a cafe, a restaurant, and a network of hiking and ski trails. The cable car ride covers a distance of 4km (2½ miles) and takes about 18 minutes. Round-trip passage costs 10€ to 20€ ($16–$31) for adults and 5.70€ to 11€ ($9.10–$17) for children. Except for a closing during November, it operates year-round daily from 9am to 4pm.

Essentials

GETTING THERE There is no **train service** to Pätsch, but buses depart from Innsbruck's Hauptbahnhof for Pätsch usually once an hour (trip time: 20 min.). For **bus information,** call ✆ **0512/585155.** If you're **driving,** you can reach Pätsch by the Brennerbahn, via the Europabrücke; there's a 6€ ($9.60) toll. An alternate route is the road from Innsbruck going up through Vill and Igls.

VISITOR INFORMATION For **tourist information** in Pätsch, call ✆ **0512/377332.** The office is open Monday to Friday 8am to 12:30pm.

Where to Stay & Dine

Hotel Bär Sections of this amply proportioned hotel, specifically the reception area and the well-recommended Bauernstube, date from the 1200s, when they functioned as part of a simple inn. In 1970, a modern addition was built around the original core, turning the place into an unpretentious but worthwhile three-star hotel noted for its relatively reasonable rates. Today, you'll find public areas sheathed in pinewood paneling and stone. Big panoramic windows and an antique ceramic stove add to the cozy atmosphere. The snug and traditionally furnished rooms offer plenty of comfort, from the excellent beds to the well-polished bathrooms. Maintenance and housekeeping are first-rate, and Farbmacher family members are your hosts. Meals in the Bauernstube are served daily from noon to 2pm and 6 to 10pm. Main courses are 15€ to 18€ ($24–$29).

Römerstrasse 14, A-6082 Pätsch. ✆ **0512/38611.** Fax 0512/3861141. www.baerhotel.at. 39 units. Winter 106€–142€ ($170–$227) double; summer 88€–134€ ($141–$214) double. Rates include half-board. AE, DC, MC, V. Closed Nov 1–25 and Easter–May 8. **Amenities:** 2 restaurants; bar; lounge; indoor heated pool; sauna; children's playroom; room service; babysitting; solarium. *In room:* TV, hair dryer.

Hotel Grünwalderhof ★ (Finds) Once the private hunting lodge of the counts of Thurn and Taxis, members of the Seiler-Wanner family now operate this hotel. Standing on the site of an ancient Roman road, the hotel is in one of the town's prettiest chalets, with a natural-grained lattice relief under the slope of its gabled roof, striped shutters, and a modern extension stretching out the back toward the secluded outdoor swimming pool. Inside, the decor includes a scattering of antiques, paneling, and leather-upholstered chairs in the spacious and comfortable dining room. With their alpine coziness and good housekeeping, the rooms, which come in several sizes, are among the finest at the resort; some open onto private balconies with mountain vistas.

Römerstrasse 1, A-6082 Pätsch. ✆ **0512/377304.** Fax 0512/378078. www.gruenwalderhof.at. 26 units. Winter 88€–134€ ($141–$214) double; summer 100€–140€ ($160–$224) double; year-round from 156€ ($250) suite. Half-board 19€ ($30) per person extra. AE, DC, MC, V. Closed Apr and Nov. **Amenities:** Dining room; lounge; outdoor pool; tennis court; fitness center; sauna; room service; babysitting; laundry service; dry cleaning. *In room:* TV, hair dryer.

MUTTERS ★

On a sunny southern plateau above Innsbruck, Mutters—often called "the most beautiful village in Tyrol"—is just 10km (6½ miles) southwest of Innsbruck. You can drive to the center of the city from here in about 15 minutes along Mutters Strasse.

Mutters is in the skiing and recreation area of the Mutterer Alm and the Axamer Lizum, which were the central bases for the 1964 and 1976 Olympic Winter Games. Mutterer Alm is the place for easygoing skiers. It can be reached by cableway.

Essentials

GETTING THERE The **Stubaitalbahn tram** (✆ **0512/530712** for information) departs from Innsbruck's Hauptbahnhof 18 times a day, bound for Fulpmes and stopping at Mutters en route (trip time: 28 min.).

Buses from Innsbruck are infrequent (1 or 2 per day) and usually require a change in Götzens, Natters, and/or Axam. Transfers, however, tend to be so complicated that many people opt for the train. For **bus information,** call ✆ **0512/585155.** The village is separated from Innsbruck by a wide green section of forest lying above the city and the Inn Valley.

VISITOR INFORMATION For **tourist information** in Mutters, call ✆ **0512/548410** or go to **www.euroalps.eu**. The office is open Monday to Friday 8:30am to noon and 3 to 6pm.

Where to Stay & Dine

Hotel Altenburg ★ Local archives refer to a restaurant on this site in 1622. Later it became a farmhouse and then an annex of the nearby church. In 1910, it was transformed into a flower-bedecked chalet hotel. The ground floor is sheltered by a three-arched arcade, which serves as an attractive backdrop for the nearby greenhouse-style cafe. Each snugly furnished comfortable room has a small but spotlessly clean bathroom. The hotel's elegant restaurant is filled with upholstered banquettes and conservative furniture, with big windows overlooking the mountains. The **Restaurant Altenburg** serves first-rate Tyrolean and international cuisine. Occasionally, only hotel guests can dine here, so it's best to check. Evening entertainment is sometimes provided. The Wishaber family is your host.

Kirchplatz 4–6, A-6162 Mutters. ✆ **0512/548524.** Fax 0512/5485246. www.altenburg.com. 34 units. 88€–150€ ($141–$240) double. Rates include buffet breakfast. Half-board 14€ ($22) per person extra. AE, DC, MC, V. Closed Apr 1 to mid-May and Oct 10–Dec 10. **Amenities:** Restaurant; bar; indoor heated pool; sauna; room service; babysitting; laundry service; dry cleaning; solarium. *In room:* TV, Wi-Fi, minibar, hair dryer, safe.

Muttererhof ★ This government-rated three-star hotel, only a short walk from the village center, has a gabled roof and a dignified chalet facade—in season, its balconies are covered with flowers. The snug and comfortable rooms, in a variety of sizes, are furnished in a Tyrolean style; the best open onto private balconies with mountain vistas. The hotel has an elegantly paneled restaurant filled with carved chairs, leaded windows, and antiques, and a verdant lawn with cafe tables in summer.

Nattererstrasse 20, A-6162 Mutters. ✆ **0512/548491.** Fax 0512/5484915. www.hotel-muttererhof.at.tt. 20 units. 70€–96€ ($112–$154) double. Rates include breakfast. AE, DC, MC, V. Closed Oct 8–Dec 23 and Apr–May. Tram: STB from Innsbruck. **Amenities:** Restaurant; bar; babysitting; laundry service; dry cleaning; public Wi-Fi. *In room:* TV.

3 THE EASTERN SIDE OF THE ARLBERG: A SKIING MECCA

There's no such thing as a sacred ski (and snowboarding) mountain—as far as we know—but if there were, it would have to be the **Arlberg.** This is where alpine skiing began its conquest of the world. On the east side of the Arlberg, 114km (71 miles) west of Innsbruck, is what's known as the cradle of alpine skiing. Here the legends and stars known to all dedicated skiers were born: the Ski Club Arlberg, the early Kandahar races, and Hannes Schneider and his Arlberg method. (The west side of the Arlberg is covered in chapter 13.)

The Arlberg, with peaks that top the 2,745m (9,006-ft.) mark, lures skiers with its vast network of cableways, lifts, runs stretching for miles, a world-renowned ski school, and numerous sporting amenities. Runs begin at the intermediate level, reaching all the way to the nearly impossible.

The Arlberg is the loftiest mountain in the **Lechtral range,** and marks the boundary between the settlers of the Tyrolean country and the **Vorarlbergers,** who live in the extreme western province of Austria. One of the Arlberg's most celebrated peaks is the **Valluga,** at 2,812m (9,226 ft.).

In 1825, a road was opened, allowing traffic to travel to the **Arlberg Pass.** A 10km-long (6-mile) rail tunnel was opened in 1884, linking Tyrol and Vorarlberg. Finally, in 1978, a new road tunnel, Europe's third-longest, linked the two provinces. The toll for the **Arlberg Strassen Tunnel** is 9€ ($14) each way per car. If you're not driving, you'll find the area serviced by the well-known **Arlberg Express rail link.**

ST. ANTON AM ARLBERG ★★★

A modern resort has grown out of this old village on the **Arlberg Pass,** a place where ski history began. It also hosts some of the finest skiing in the Alps.

It was at St. Anton (1,289m/4,229 ft.) that Hannes Schneider developed modern skiing techniques and began teaching tourists how to ski in 1907. The Ski Club Arlberg was born here in 1901. In 1911, the first Arlberg-Kandahar Cup competition was held, with the best alpine skier winning a valuable trophy. Before his death in 1955, Schneider saw his ski school rated as the world's finest. Today, the ski school, still at St. Anton, is one of the world's largest and best, with about 300 instructors, most of whom speak English.

The little town is a compact resort village with a five-story limit on buildings. No cars are allowed in the business area, but sleds and skis are plentiful.

Essentials

GETTING THERE St. Anton is an express stop on the main **rail lines** crossing over the Arlberg Pass between Innsbruck and Bregenz. Just to the west of St. Anton, trains disappear into the Arlberg tunnel, emerging almost 11km (7 miles) later on the opposite side of the mountain range. About one train per hour arrives in St. Anton from Innsbruck (trip time: 75–85 min.) and from Bregenz (trip time: 85 min.). For rail information, contact ✆ **05/1717** (www.oebb.at).

Because of St. Anton's good rail connections to eastern and western Austria, most visitors arrive by train. From the city, however, many travelers take the **bus** on to other resorts such as **Zürs** and **Lech.**

St. Anton is 599km (372 miles) west of Vienna and 100km (62 miles) west of Innsbruck. If you're **driving** from Innsbruck, take Route 171 west.

VISITOR INFORMATION The **tourist office** in the **Arlberghaus** lies in the town center (© **05446/2269-0**; www.stantonamarlberg.com). In winter, hours are Monday to Friday 8am to 7pm, Saturday 9am to 6pm, and Sunday 9am to noon and 2 to 5pm. In summer, hours are Monday to Friday 8am to 6pm, Saturday and Sunday 9am to noon.

Skiing & More

The snow in this area is perfect for skiers, and the total lack of trees on the slopes makes the situation ideal. The ski fields of St. Anton stretch over some 16 sq. km (6 sq. miles). Beginners stick to the slopes down below, and for the more experienced skiers there are the runs from the **Galzig** and **Valluga** peaks. A cableway will take you to Galzig (2,092m/6,864 ft.), where there's a self-service restaurant. You go from here to Vallugagrat (2,649m/8,691 ft.), the highest station. The peak of the Valluga, at 2,812m (9,226 ft.), commands a panoramic view. **St. Christoph** (mentioned later in this chapter) is the mountain annex of St. Anton.

In addition to the major ski areas just mentioned, there are two other important sites. The **Gampen/Kapall** area is an advanced-intermediate network of slopes, whose lifts start just behind St. Anton's railway station. Also noteworthy is the **Rendl,** a relatively new labyrinth of runs to the south of St. Anton that offers many novice and intermediate slopes.

In winter, St. Anton am Arlberg is quite fashionable, popular with the wealthy—there's a more conservative segment of the rich and famous here than you'll see at other posh ski resorts. There are many other cold-weather pursuits besides skiing, including ski jumping, mountain tours, curling, skating, tobogganing, and sleigh rides, plus après-ski on the quiet side.

There's so much emphasis on skiing here that there's little talk of the summertime attractions. In warm weather, St. Anton is tranquil and bucolic, surrounded by meadowland. A riot of wildflowers blooming in the fields announces the beginning of spring.

At any time of the year, you can visit the **Ski und Heimat Museum (Skiing and Local Museum),** in the Arlberg-Kandahar House (© **05446/2475**), where displays trace the development of skiing in the Arlberg, as well as the region's history from the days of tribal migrations in and around Roman times. The museum, in the imposing structure at the center of the Holiday Park in St. Anton, is open in summer Wednesday to Sunday noon to 8pm, and in winter Tuesday through Sunday 3 to 10pm. Admission is 2€ ($3.20) for adults and 1€ ($1.60) for children.

The local library is also housed in the Arlberg-Kandahar House, and the park provides a variety of leisure activities, including minigolf, a woodland playground, a fishing pond, table tennis, open-air chess, and a curling rink.

Where to Stay

Expensive

Hotel Alte Post ★ This rambling four-story building with ocher-colored walls, green shutters, and jutting gables was built in the 17th century as a postal station, and can easily be reached from the town's rail station. Renovations retained most of the thick-timbered beauty, and rooms combine old-fashioned paneling with tiled and timbered private bathrooms that have tub/shower combinations and sometimes very elegant accessories. Members of the Tandl family are your hosts.

Since it became a hotel in the 1920s, some prominent skiers and show-business personalities have relaxed with lesser-known clients in the hotel's cozy niches, some of which are warmed with crackling fires. The hotel contains an excellent restaurant (see "Where to Dine," below).

A-6580 St. Anton am Arlberg. ✆ **05446/25530.** Fax 05446/255341. www.hotel-alte-post.at. 56 units. Winter 248€–462€ ($397–$739) double, 297€–610€ ($475–$976) junior suite for 2; summer 137€–185€ ($219–$296) double, 149€–240€ ($238–$384) junior suite for 2. Rates include half-board. AE, DC, MC, V. Closed late Apr–late May and late Oct–Dec 1. **Amenities:** Restaurant; bar; indoor heated pool; fitness center; Jacuzzi; sauna; massage; room service; babysitting; laundry service; dry cleaning; solarium. *In room:* TV, Wi-Fi, minibar, hair dryer, safe.

Hotel Neue Post ★ In the 1990s, a large and sprawling hotel complex was divided into two smaller (and adjacent) properties, the Hotel Alte Post (above) and the Hotel Neue Post. The Neue Post is not as new as its name implies. Built in 1896 and noteworthy because of its sprawling dimensions and wood-and-stucco facade, it has established a reputation as one of the resort's most sports-oriented hotels. It offers appealing rooms comfortably equipped with medium-size bathrooms. Housekeeping and general maintenance here are state-of-the-art.

The hotel contains a dimly lit and woodsy series of spacious public rooms, two dining rooms, and two of the most popular nightlife facilities in St. Anton, the Postkeller and Piccadilly Pub (see "St. Anton am Arlberg After Dark," below).

A-6580 St. Anton am Arlberg. ✆ **05446/22130.** Fax 05446/2343. www.st-anton.co.at. 66 units. Winter 222€–472€ ($355–$755) double; summer 118€–158€ ($189–$253) double. Rates include half-board. AE, DC, MC, V. Parking 7€ ($11) per day. Closed Apr 21–July 20 and late Sept–early Dec. **Amenities:** 2 restaurants; bar; 2 nightclubs; sauna; Jacuzzi; room service; laundry service; dry cleaning; nonsmoking rooms. *In room:* TV, Wi-Fi, minibar, hair dryer, safe.

Hotel St. Antoner Hof ★★ The only government-rated five-star hotel in St. Anton, the St. Antoner Hof is a bit more posh and a bit more attentive than other hotels in town. Built in the early 1980s and run by a group of enthusiastic skiers (the Raffl family), it rises in severe dignity about a block from the resort's historic center. Rooms, in a variety of sizes, are plush and fastidiously maintained, all with thick carpeting, fireplaces, and the most comfortable beds at the resort. Guests enjoy the public rooms, each of which seems awash in Tyrolean accessories, thick timbers, and collections of rustic implements. Blazing fireplaces and good cuisine are all part of the experience here; the restaurant, **Raffl Stube,** is recommended below.

A-6580 St. Anton am Arlberg. ✆ **05446/2910.** Fax 05446/3551. www.antonerhof.at. 37 units. 330€–720€ ($528–$1,152) double; 370€–840€ ($592–$1,344) suite for 2. Rates include half-board. DC, MC, V. Closed Apr 17–early Dec. **Amenities:** Restaurant; bar; indoor heated pool; fitness center; Jacuzzi; Turkish bath; sauna; children's playroom; room service; massage; babysitting; laundry service; dry cleaning; solarium. *In room:* TV, Wi-Fi, minibar, hair dryer, safe.

Hotel Schwarzer Adler ★★ In the center of St. Anton, this hotel has been owned and operated by the Tschol family since 1885. The beautiful fresco-covered building was constructed as an inn in 1570. The inn became known for its hospitality to pilgrims crossing the treacherous Arlberg Pass, and was eventually declared an "officially registered" hotel by Empress Maria Theresia. The hotel's interior contains several blazing fireplaces, Tyrolean baroque armoires, and oriental rugs. Rooms are handsomely furnished and well-equipped. All rooms have exceedingly comfortable beds. Nearly all bathrooms have big bathtubs, although a few singles offer only showers.

A-6580 St. Anton am Arlberg. ✆ **800/780-7234** in the U.S., or 05446/22440. Fax 05446/224462. www.schwarzeradler.com. 70 units. Winter 103€–273€ ($165–$437) per person double, 185€–337€ ($296–$539) per person suite; summer 60€–120€ ($96–$192) per person double, 112€–140€ ($179–$224) per person suite. Rates include half-board. AE, DC, MC, V. Closed Apr 20–June and Oct–Nov. **Amenities:** Restaurant; bar; indoor heated pool; fitness center; sauna; room service; massage; babysitting; laundry service; dry cleaning; all nonsmoking rooms. *In room:* TV, Wi-Fi, hair dryer, safe.

Sporthotel St. Anton ★ This sprawling government-rated four-star 1974 hotel sits on the main pedestrian thoroughfare of St. Anton. Ideal for shopping, it's a good choice for skiers too, since it's a 3-minute walk from the chairlifts. In winter, you're greeted at the entrance with the sight of a bar and the music of a full-time organist, whose melodies add to the feeling that a happy ski vacation involves at least several cocktails per day. Rooms are medium-size, comfortable, and contemporary, each with a balcony. Many patrons come to this hotel just to enjoy its food and drink (see "Where to Dine," below).

A-6580 St. Anton am Arlberg. ✆ **05446/3111.** Fax 05446/311170. www.sporthotel-st-anton.at. 53 units. 262€–404€ ($419–$646) double. Rates half-board. DC, MC, V. Free parking outside, 10€ ($16) garage. Closed May and Oct–Nov. **Amenities:** Restaurant; bar; indoor heated pool; sauna; massage; room service; babysitting; laundry service; dry cleaning; solarium. *In room:* TV, Wi-Fi, minibar, hair dryer, safe.

Moderate

Hotel Kertess ★ **Finds** Located in a quiet residential section named Oberdorf, this hotel is an address jealously guarded by its devotees. It lies on a hillside above the main tourist district of St. Anton, a steep 12-minute climb up the hill (and then only if you're hale and hearty). As you approach, you'll recognize the hotel by its country-baroque window trim. The hotel is family run, owned by Maria Kertess, a former ski instructor. In winter, you register near a blazing corner fireplace whose cheer permeates even the stylish Tyrolean bar a few steps away. Each snug and cozy room offers plenty of exposed wooden trim, functional if not stylish furniture, and, if you're lucky, a view of the Rendl ski slope. Even if you're not a guest here, consider the hotel's restaurant (see "Where to Dine," below). Because it's located in a residential neighborhood away from the town center, the hotel runs a shuttle bus service to St. Anton and its ski areas.

A-6580 St. Anton am Arlberg. ✆ **05446/2005-0.** Fax 05446/200556. www.kertess.com. 56 units. Winter 170€–440€ ($272–$704) double; summer 90€–100€ ($144–$160) double. Rates include half-board. AE, DC, MC, V. Closed Nov. **Amenities:** Restaurant; bar; indoor heated pool; fitness center; sauna; massage; Wi-Fi in lobby. *In room:* TV, safe.

Hotel Montjola Lying less than a kilometer (1/2 mile) west of the resort's center, about a 10-minute uphill walk, this hotel is rustically appealing. Most rooms are in a comfortable annex built in 1991, although the reception desk, restaurant, and bar are in the original core—a carefully preserved wood-and-stone structure dating from the 1930s. Rooms come in a variety of sizes, and decor ranges from traditional to contemporary; each has a good bed plus a small but efficient bathroom with a tub/shower combination. Throughout both sections, you'll see heavy ceiling beams, a stone-rimmed fireplace, rustic knickknacks, and immaculately set dining room tables. Fondue is a specialty of the in-house restaurant.

A-6580 St. Anton am Arlberg. ✆ **05446/2302.** Fax 05446/23029. www.montjola.com. 42 units. Winter 85€–157€ ($136–$251) per person double; summer 54€–66€ ($86–$106) per person double. Rates include half-board. AE, DC, MC, V. Closed Apr 18–May 12 and Oct 2–Nov. **Amenities:** Restaurant; bar; fitness center; sauna; room service; massage; babysitting; laundry service; dry cleaning; nonsmoking rooms; solarium. *In room:* TV, Wi-Fi, hair dryer, safe.

Where to Dine

Expensive

Raffl Stube ★★ Finds AUSTRIAN This restaurant didn't exist until 1982, when members of the Raffl family enclosed a corner of their lobby. The place contains only eight tables, and in the peak of the season, reservations are imperative, especially if you're not staying here. Overflow diners are offered a seat in a spacious but less special dining room across the hall. The hotel has long enjoyed a favored reputation for its cuisine, but somehow the food in the *stube* (tavern) tastes even better. Quality ingredients are always used, and the kitchen prepares such tempting specialties as roast goose liver with salad, cream of parsley soup with sautéed quail eggs, filet of salmon with wild rice, trout "as you like it," and roast filet of pork, along with the ever-popular fondue bourguignonne.

In the Hotel St. Antoner Hof, St. Antonam Arlberg. ✆ **05446/2910.** Reservations required. Main courses 20€–21€ ($31–$34); fixed-price menu 68€–78€ ($109–$125). AE, DC, MC, V. Daily 11:30am–2pm and 7–9:30pm. Closed mid-Oct to mid-Dec and mid-Apr to mid-June.

Steakhouse ★ STEAKHOUSE The Steakhouse occupies part of the street level of the Sporthotel St. Anton on the resort's main pedestrian thoroughfare. Here you can watch your steak sizzling as you sip a drink in warm comfort. Some guests prefer to sit on a barstool; perched here, you can talk directly to the chef at the nearby grill about the preferred degree of doneness of your dish. The steaks are just as good at a table in the wood-trimmed dining room. Menu selections include Lyons-style onion soup, small and "giant" salads, grilled crayfish, filet of veal in mushroom sauce, filet of pepper steak, and, if cholesterol is a problem, sliced roast turkey with pineapple on toast. Beer comes in foam-covered mugs, and wine is served in bottles as well as less expensive carafes.

In the Sporthotel St. Anton, St. Anton am Arlberg. ✆ **05446/3111.** Main courses 15€–37€ ($23–$59). DC, MC, V. Daily 11am–11pm in winter. Otherwise 11:30am–2pm and 5–9:30pm. Closed May and Oct–Nov.

Moderate

Hotel Alte Post Restaurant ★ AUSTRIAN Outsiders are welcomed into this historic establishment's five small antique dining rooms, where green ceramic stoves and intricately crafted wrought iron lend a mellow and graceful accent. The chefs cook with flair, turning out such classic dishes as rack of lamb, filet of beef, delightful sweetbreads, venison goulash, fresh duckling, and fondue Bacchus. Although traditional, the chefs are quite skillful. They might be using old recipes, but they give you lots of flavor and first-rate ingredients. You'll be guided through the menu by an attentive staff.

St. Anton am Arlberg. ✆ **05446/25530.** Reservations recommended. Main courses 12€–25€ ($19–$39). AE, DC, MC, V. Daily 7–9pm. Closed late Apr–June and late Oct–Dec 1.

Hotel Kertess Restaurant ★★ AUSTRIAN Some of the area's finest food—some say the best in St. Anton—is served at this restaurant. It lies in the suburb of Oberdorf, high on a slope. Guests dine in one of a trio of alpine rooms, with ceramic tile stoves, oriental rugs, and views of a snow-covered ski slope. Specialties include filet of venison in port-wine sauce, stuffed squab, salmon in Riesling sauce, and, for dessert, apple fritters in beer-flavored pastry with cinnamon. The cooking is delicious, sometimes even inspired. The hotel's bar, warmed by a blazing fire in the nearby reception area, is open throughout the afternoon. The restaurant is known to serve only hotel guests—check when you make table reservations.

St. Anton am Arlberg. ✆ **05446/2005.** Reservations required. Main courses 9.90€–25€ ($16–$40). MC, V. Winter daily 11am–10pm; summer daily 11am–10pm (but hot food only 6:30–9:30pm). Closed May–June and Oct–Nov.

Hotel Schwarzer Adler Restaurant ★★ AUSTRIAN/INTERNATIONAL This restaurant prides itself on its Tyrolean authenticity, which reaches its zenith in one of its two wood-paneled *stubes* (parlors), the preferred place to dine here. The darker of the *stubes* boasts paneling said to be 4 centuries old. Here, the lighting fixtures are especially noteworthy, each designed from raw horns and fashioned into some mythical or allegorical figure from a Teutonic legend. Atmosphere aside, the real reason patrons come here is the food. The kitchen brigade displays outstanding skills, which are best shown at one of the buffets. The menu tempts at every turn with such dishes as homemade salmon ravioli with a chervil-flavored cream sauce or medallions of anglerfish with ratatouille. The *tafelspitz* is another favorite. Deer and local fish are served in season.

St. Anton am Arlberg. ✆ **512/587109**. www.deradler.com. Reservations required. Main courses 13€–27€ ($21–$44); fixed-price menu 19€–37€ ($30–$60); summer-only fixed-price menu 37€ ($60). MC, V. Daily 7–9pm. Closed May–June and Oct–Nov.

Restaurant Ferwall ★★ Finds AUSTRIAN/INTERNATIONAL Set in the high-altitude region approaching the Arlberg Pass, this restaurant is isolated, rustic, and very famous. Ideal for a snowy night, it has entertained guests from the royal families of both Britain and the Netherlands, such musical luminaries as the late Herbert von Karajan, and scores of local residents who appreciate its romantic nostalgia for the Tyrol of myth and legend. The restaurant was established in 1972 in what was then an 11-year-old chalet. Some of the dining areas rely exclusively on candlelight—romance seems rampant, especially on cold winter nights. Menu items are based on traditional recipes that management considers a closely guarded secret. Venison frequently appears on the menu, often grilled and served with any of a wide choice of sauces, baked into casseroles, or ground and pressed into sausages and served with sauces and sauerkraut. The entire experience is a celebration of the virtues of Tyrolean country life.

Most visitors reach the restaurant by car or taxi, although in winter many opt for a ride in a horse-drawn sleigh, which costs about 75€ ($120) each way for six occupants. (If this is your intention, inform the restaurant when you book a table, and they'll make the arrangements for you.) Sleighs depart from the base of the three-star Mooserkreuz hotel, which lies on a very steep hillside less than 1.5km (1 mile) west of St. Anton.

Verwallwegasse 123. ✆ **05446/3249.** Reservations required. Main courses 8€–24€ ($13–$39). AE, DC, MC, V. Winter daily 10am–midnight; summer daily 10am–6pm. Closed Apr–June and Oct–Nov. Take Rte. 197 to St. Christoph and the Arlberg Pass 5km (3 miles) west of the center of St. Anton.

Cafes & Stubes

The popular **Café Aquila** (✆ **05446/2217**) achieved a certain kind of fame in the ski world as the Café Tschol. Now under another name, it lies just across the street from its founder, the Hotel Schwarzer Adler. Light meals, pastries, beer, wine, tea, and several varieties of coffee are served here. Dishes include spaghetti, goulash soup, spinach-stuffed ravioli, and a self-serve buffet of appetizers. Simple, uncomplicated meals begin at 12€ ($19), although snack food is also available. It's open daily from 10am to midnight.

Our favorite cafe in St. Anton, **Café Haeferl** (✆ **05446/3988**), seems more animated and more folkloric than any of its competitors, thanks to a decor that's rich with Tyrolean artifacts and the glow of varnished pine. Inside you'll find a crowd that includes dedicated hipsters, as well as long-time seniors looking for a caffeine fix and a midmorning pastry. Don't expect full meal service—only salads, platters, and small portions of such foods as goulash soup and *toasts* (sandwiches) are served. It's open daily from 8:30am to 10pm. You might want to drink or eat all day at **Fuhrmannstube** (✆ **05446/2921**).

Conveniently located near the town church on the main street, this rustic cafe and restaurant serves reasonably priced meals starting at 7.90€ ($13). It has a predictable but well-prepared array of such Teutonic specialties as *rösti* (hash browns), *spätzle* (pasta), goulash, and venison (in season). It's open daily from 10am to midnight; closed in May, June, October, and November.

St. Anton am Arlberg After Dark

St. Anton's after-dark spots are among the most frequented in Tyrol. It'll be best if you like your fellow skiers; in season you're likely to be knocking elbows (or whatever) in most places.

Krazy Kanguruh This restaurant/bar, originally built as a stable, attracts the resort's restless and reckless. To reach it, you'll either have to ski from the resort's uppermost slopes, walk breathlessly up the steep hill from the village, or drive your car via the suburb of Moos along a winding and treacherously narrow road. A phone call in advance will apprise you of driving conditions and directions, whose complexity you'll appreciate only after you get here.

Owned and operated by a dashing Swede, Gunnar Munthe, the place serves different functions depending on the hour of the day. From 11am to 2pm, lunches consisting of hamburgers, Wiener schnitzels, and such are served by some of the most attractive employees in Tyrol. Happy hour is raucous, rowdy, and loud. Be sure to ask for a shot of the pear-and-plum schnapps that a local farmer distills, especially for the Krazy Kanguruh. Lunches begin at 8€ ($13). No dinner is served. Beer costs 3.20€ ($5.10) and up. It's closed from April 15 to December 10. Moos 113. ✆ **05446/2633.**

Piccadilly Pub As its name suggests, this is an English-style pub. Lined with photos of happy revelers enjoying snow and suds, the place offers rowdy fun and loud music. Special tongue-in-cheek events such as Australia Day feature icons made of stuffed koala bears. The place is off the main pedestrian thoroughfare behind etched-glass swinging doors. A large beer begins at 4€ ($6.40). It's open from January to April daily from 9am to 2am; December Thursday to Saturday 9am to 2am. In the Hotel Neue Post. ✆ **05446/2213.**

Platz'l Bar Set in the heart of town, adjacent to the Hotel Alte Post, this warm and rustic hangout features a live pianist whose soothing tones create an ambience more sophisticated than the rock-'n'-roll mode of other bars nearby. Later in the evening, it usually offers recorded dance music as the town's nightlife begins to heat up. Beer costs 3.80€ ($6.10) for a large mugful. The bar's open only during the ski season, when fires inside burn brightly, December through April daily from 4pm to 3am. St. Anton. ✆ **05446/2169.**

Postkeller This energetic and bubbly winter-only nightspot is in the basement of the Hotel Neue Post, with a decor of pinewood paneling, unbreakable chairs and banquettes, and a long bar area. Live music is occasionally offered. The management creates an array of midwinter theme parties from time to time, including toga contests, beach parties, and carnival Rio parties. A large beer begins at 4€ ($6.40). The only food offered is an array of simple platters and snacks. November through April, it's open daily from 4:30 to 7pm for après-ski fun; then it reopens as a nightclub from 9pm to 3am. In the Hotel Neue Post. ✆ **05446/2213.** Cover 5€ ($8).

Rodelhütte Open only in winter, this après-ski hangout offers the chance to combine a drink or two beside a blazing fire and finish with a flourish—a zesty downhill run by toboggan. You can reach the place only after a brisk 20-minute uphill climb from St. Anton, as it lies less than 1km (1/2 mile) from the center. It's open daily December through April from 11:30am to around 9pm, depending on business; it's at its most convivial and crowded beginning around 5pm, as night falls over the nearby mountains. It is also open in July and August daily from 9am to 9pm. At the top of the town's toboggan run. ✆ 069910/858855.

St. Anton Bar This place is the most popular and energetic bar in town. The bar is round, allowing drinkers to casually check out their fellow imbibers. The music is imported, and its decor makes absolutely no concessions to Tyrolean *gemütlichkeit;* instead, it's international. The professional staff adeptly handles "fancy drinks." Access is directly from Hauptstrasse, not from inside the hotel. It's open from December to April daily from 9pm to 4am. In the Sporthotel St. Anton. ✆ **05446/3111.**

Sennhütte Cozy, charming, and artfully rustic, this wood-sided structure is most appropriately reached by ski or snowboard from higher elevations along the Galzig ski slope. As shadows lengthen on winter afternoons, skiers gravitate toward the blazing fireplace and the stiff drinks that make après-ski here unusually convivial. It's an event only during ski season and doesn't last as long as some other venues at lower altitudes that rock on into the wee hours. (It's at its peak only around 4–7:30pm.) Know in advance that after a day on the slopes and after some drinks here around dusk, maneuvering your way downhill on skis might break a leg, as has often happened. It's open in winter, when the skiers descend daily, from 10am to 8:30pm. It is also open from late June to late September, keeping the same hours. On the lower elevations of the Galzig ski slopes. ✆ **0663/2048.**

Vino Bar Hidden behind the Hotel Schwarzer Adler's 400-year-old exterior frescoes lies a bar where holiday-makers dance the night away after a day on the slopes. A large beer begins at 4€ ($6.40). It's open daily from 8pm to 3am, but in winter only. In the Hotel Schwarzer Adler. ✆ **05446/2244606.**

ST. CHRISTOPH ★★

The mountain way station of St. Anton, **St. Christoph** (1,784m/5,853 ft.) is linked to the St. Anton terrain by a cableway at Galzig. It's on the road to the Arlberg Pass and has essentially the same ski facilities available as St. Anton, only here you're closer to the action.

A hospice was originally established here in 1386 by a now-legendary saintlike mountain man, Heinrich of Kempten, whose self-imposed duty was to bury the remains of pilgrims who froze to death in the treacherous snowdrifts of one of the world's most unpredictable and temperamental mountain passes.

Because the Arlberg was the single most important route for commerce between northern Italy and the Teutonic world throughout the Middle Ages, literally hundreds of pilgrims froze to death at the pass or died of hunger, exposure, or avalanches. Kempten single-handedly founded the Order of Saint Christopher, a church-related society and monastery that has evolved into one of the most beneficent monastic orders of Europe. The monastery has accumulated some famous artistic treasures, many donated by grateful merchants whose caravans were sheltered and saved.

Appropriately, the monastery was built on the uppermost heights of the frequently snowbound pass, on the Tyrolean side. The land the monastery was built on was so hostile that after the surrounding trees were felled for fuel, large carts were required to bring all the basic necessities into the community.

Throughout the Age of Enlightenment, the hospice continued to recruit new members, who would patrol the pass every morning and evening. The members searched for frozen bodies, assisted wayfarers in trouble, and provided desperately needed accommodations for the thousands of caravans carrying goods across the pass.

By the late 19th century, honorary membership in the Order of St. Christopher was granted to VIPs and charitably minded individuals around the world, frequently by request of the Austrian government. Today members are initiated with pomp, ceremony, and good humor, and include such personalities as King Juan Carlos of Spain, the village postman, and Queen Juliana and Prince Bernhard of the Netherlands.

As roads, phone lines, and helicopter rescue teams made passage over the Arlberg less treacherous, the Arlberg Pass developed into one of the world's leading ski resorts. In the 1950s, the monastery, which had had difficulty recruiting new members, sold the complex to members of the Werner family. Under the guidance of the family patriarch, the monastery was brought into the 20th century with the addition of electricity and many of the era's creature comforts.

Tragically, only a few weeks after the completion of the improvements, a fire destroyed all but a portion of the ancient monastery. The fire provided the opportunity to rebuild the Arlberg Hospiz hotel, recommended below.

Essentials

GETTING THERE Few commercial rail lines could negotiate the steep and winding slopes leading up to the Arlberg Pass and St. Christoph. Passengers usually take the **train** to St. Anton and then board one of the five daily **buses** traveling north over the mountain passes to St. Christoph (trip time: 15 min.). Contact **St. Anton's tourist office** (✆ **05446/22690**) for bus and train schedules.

Motorists can continue west from St. Anton am Arlberg (above), following Route 316. The location is 8km (5 miles) west of St. Anton and 35km (22 miles) west of Landeck.

VISITOR INFORMATION The **tourist office** in the village center (✆ **05446/22690;** www.stantonamarlberg.com) is open Monday to Friday 8am to 6pm, Saturday 9am to noon.

Where to Stay & Dine

Arlberg Hospiz ★★★ This world-class winter-only hotel contains as much mystery, legend, and romance as any Austrian hotel. Many of its most charming touches were painstakingly re-created from old photographs. Visitors are welcomed into a luxurious world with more style and plush antique comfort than the medieval monks could have imagined. An equally luxurious annex is connected to the main building by an underground passageway. The plush accommodations are well furnished, with a host of extras and the finest service in Tyrol. Rooms are beautifully maintained and have double-glazed windows, working fireplaces, walk-in dressing areas, and balconies. The beds are some of the most luxurious in the area, and the spacious bathrooms have big tubs, powerful showerheads, and robes.

The Arlberg Hospiz offers superb food and an array of in-house entertainment. The party room changes its decor from year to year: Once it was transformed into an ancient Roman tavern.

Even if you don't stay here, consider having a meal in the hotel's "farmhouse"—but reserve in advance.

A-6580 St. Christoph. ✆ **05446/2611.** Fax 05446/3545. www.hospiz.com. 99 units. 540€–1,230€ ($864–$1,968) double; 670€–1,630€ ($1,072–$2,608) suite for 2. Rates include half-board. AE, DC, MC, V. Parking 15€ ($24). Closed May–Nov. **Amenities:** Restaurant; bar; nightclub; indoor heated pool; Jacuzzi; sauna; game room; room service; massage; babysitting; laundry service; dry cleaning; nonsmoking rooms. *In room:* TV, Wi-Fi, minibar, hair dryer, safe.

Gasthof Valluga This is the least expensive hotel on the Arlberg Pass, a simple chalet-style guesthouse with cramped but clean rooms and impressive views from the windows of its dining room and bar. The German-speaking owner, Lydia Haueis, maintains impeccably proper rooms, two suitable for up to four occupants. Each has thick carpeting, good beds, and cozy charm, although the bathrooms with tub/shower combinations are a bit cramped. The restaurant is warmly accommodating, serving reasonably priced meals. It's open in winter daily 8am to 10pm. Menu items include Tyroler crusted dumplings with bacon and cream sauce.

A-6580 St. Christoph. ✆ **05446/2823.** Fax 05446/2823160. www.arlberg.com/gasthof-valluga. 10 units. 180€–276€ ($288–$442) double. Rates include half-board. MC, V. Free parking. Closed June–late Nov. **Amenities:** Restaurant; bar; sauna; massage; room service; babysitting; laundry service; dry cleaning. *In room:* TV, minibar, hair dryer, safe.

Hotel Arlberghöhe Simple and unpretentious to the point of being almost bareboned, this hotel stands across from the more glamorous, prestigious, and expensive Arlberg Hospiz. It was built around 1940 but has been modernized several times since. Its rustic interior and heavy ceiling beams give the impression of far greater age. Skiers take warm refuge here, enjoying the well-scrubbed comfort as the gales blow around the chalet's dark-stained balconies. Many guests come here year after year, requesting a favorite chamber. Many rooms are quite spacious and heavy on wood tones, and they have beautiful tile bathrooms. The wooden beds are exceedingly comfortable and cozy, especially on a wintry alpine night. The food is good and there's plenty of it, a combination of classic Austrian dishes, Tyrolean specialties, and international offerings.

A-6580 St. Christoph. ✆ **05446/2635.** Fax 05446/263544. www.arlberghoehe.at. 17 units. 192€–332€ ($307–$531) double, 262€–398€ ($419–$637) suite. Rates include half-board. MC, V. Closed Oct–Nov and late May to mid-July. **Amenities:** Restaurant; bar; sauna; massage; babysitting; solarium. *In room:* TV.

4 SEEFELD ★★

24km (15 miles) NW of Innsbruck

Seefeld, a member of Austria's "Big Three" international rendezvous points (along with Arlberg and Kitzbühel) for winter-sports crowds, lies on a sunny plateau some 1,052m (3,451 ft.) above sea level. This is the town that hosted the Nordic events for the 1964 and 1976 Olympic Winter Games and the 1985 Nordic Ski World Championships.

ESSENTIALS

GETTING THERE More than a dozen trains per day depart from Innsbruck for the 40-minute trip to Seefeld. Other trains leave from Munich and pass through the Bavarian resort of Garmisch-Partenkirchen before arriving in Seefeld. For rail information, contact ✆ **05/1717** (www.oebb.at).

Despite its position on several different bus routes heading up into the nearby valleys, most visitors arrive here by train. However, you can take one of the dozen or so buses departing daily from Innsbruck's Hauptbahnhof for the 45-minute trip. For **bus information,** call ✆ **0512/585155** in Innsbruck.

If you're **driving** from Innsbruck, head west along Route 171 until you reach the junction with Route 313, at which point you go north.

VISITOR INFORMATION The Seefeld **tourist office,** Klosterstrasse 43 (✆ **0508/800;** www.seefeld.com), is open Monday to Saturday 8:30am to 6:30pm, and Sunday 10am to noon.

WINTER & SUMMER SPORTS

The slopes are served by one cable car railway, two cable cars, three chairlifts, and 14 drag lifts. The beginner slopes lie directly in the village center, and the base stations for ski lifts leading to Seefeld's main skiing areas lie less than 1km (1/2 mile) north of the resort (for the **Gschwandtkopf runs**) and less than 1km (1/2 mile) south of the resort (for the **Rosshütte/Seefelder Joch runs**). They, and virtually everything else in town, are served throughout the winter by the free shuttle buses that operate at 20- to 30-minute intervals during daylight hours. In addition to its downhill runs, Seefeld has more than 200km (124 miles) of well-maintained cross-country tracks.

Other winter activities offered here include curling, horse-drawn sleigh rides, ice-skating (**Eislaufplatz Olympia Sportzentrum; ✆ 05212/3050**) on artificial and natural ice rinks, horseback riding, indoor tennis (**Estess Academy; ✆ 05212/4515**), tube sliding, indoor golf, parasailing, bowling, squash, hiking (97km/60 miles of cleared paths), fitness workouts, swimming, and sauna sessions.

Summer visitors can enjoy swimming in three lakes, a heated open-air swimming pool near Seefeld Lake, or the Olympia indoor and outdoor pools. Other summer sports include tennis on 18 open-air and 8 indoor courts (Swedish Tennis School), riding (two stables with indoor schools), and golf on the 18-hole course, which has been rated by golf insiders as one of the 100 most beautiful courses in the world. There are 200km (124 miles) of walks and mountain paths to hike, as well as cycling, minigolf, parasailing, and rafting.

Whatever time of year it is, you can try your luck at the casino (**Bahnhofstrasse; ✆ 05212/2340**), where roulette, baccarat, blackjack, seven-card stud poker, and slot machines are played.

While based in Seefeld, you'll find it relatively easy to explore part of Bavaria, in Germany (see our companion guide, *Frommer's Germany*). You might or might not get to see little Wildmoos Lake. It can, and sometimes does, vanish all in a day or so, and then there may be cows grazing on what has become meadowland. However, the lake will suddenly come back again, and if conditions are right, it will become deep enough for swimmers. Wildmoos Lake comes and goes a lot more frequently than Brigadoon. You might also visit the little German town of Mittenwald, an easy day trip from Seefeld.

For more information about these destinations, call the **tourist information** number in Seefeld (✆ **0508/800**). Hours are Monday to Saturday 8:30am to 6:30pm, and Sunday 10am to noon.

WHERE TO STAY

Expensive

Hotel Astoria ★★ This luxurious, government-rated five-star choice stands on a beautiful elevated position in a large park with panoramic views of the surrounding mountain ranges. It's a 5-minute walk northwest of Seefeld's center. Because of its sunny and sheltered ambience, it's a favorite with well-heeled visitors in both summer and winter. Summer brings flowered terraces and gardens; winter brings the open fireplace in the lounge bar. The attractively furnished rooms have exceedingly comfortable beds and medium-size bathrooms. Saturday evenings are gala nights here, with candlelit dinners and music from the house band. Once a week, a Viennese *heurige* (wine tavern) or a Tyrolean evening with traditional buffet is presented.

Geigenbühel, A-6100 Seefeld. ✆ **05212/22720.** Fax 05212/2272100. www.astoria-seefeld.com. 56 units. Winter 254€–520€ ($406–$832) double, 400€–620€ ($640–$992) suite; summer 198€–338€ ($317–$541) double, 294€–460€ ($470–$736) suite. Rates include half-board. AE, DC, MC, V. Free outdoor parking; indoor parking 12€ ($19). Closed Apr–May 20 and Oct–Dec 20. **Amenities:** Restaurant; bar; indoor heated pool; outdoor pool; fitness center; spa; sauna; room service; massage; babysitting; laundry service; dry cleaning; solarium. *In room:* TV, Wi-Fi, minibar, hair dryer, safe.

Hotel Klosterbräu ★★★ The town's most unusual and elegant hostelry is constructed around a 16th-century cloister. The interior contains soaring vaults supported by massive columns. Rooms are encased in a towering chalet behind the front entrance, and windows look out over the midsummer buffet set up near the outdoor sun terrace. They come in a variety of sizes, but all are beautifully kept, with antiques and comfortable mattresses. Some rooms contain balconies opening onto mountain vistas. In the evening, chicly dressed patrons often drop in at Die Kane nightclub, whose comedians and musical revues provide a high spot in the village's nightlife. A daily afternoon tea dance in winter allows hotel guests to meet one another. Hotel Klosterbräu features two excellent restaurants; see "Where to Dine," below.

Klosterstrasse 30, A-6100 Seefeld. ✆ **05212/26210.** Fax 05212/3885. www.klosterbraeu.com. 120 units. Winter 270€–730€ ($432–$1,168) double, from 410€–2,700€ ($656–$4,320) suite; summer 218€–358€ ($349–$573) double, 428€–2,128€ ($685–$3,405) suite. Rates include breakfast. AE, DC, MC, V. Free parking on street; garage parking 15€ ($24). Closed Apr–May and Oct to mid-Dec. **Amenities:** 3 restaurants; bar; nightclub; 2 heated pools (1 indoor, 1 outdoor); fitness center; Jacuzzi; sauna; room service; babysitting; laundry service; dry cleaning; nonsmoking rooms; solarium. *In room:* TV, Wi-Fi, minibar, hair dryer, safe.

Moderate

Alpenhotel Lamm ★ The cozy interior of this 1940s hotel is decorated with ceiling beams, rural artifacts, and baroque sculpture. The best rooms are fairly elegant and spacious; all have balconies. The hotel's restaurant, Zum Kirchenwirt, enjoys a good reputation among visitors, and dancing and music are offered daily in the Lammkeller beginning around 8:30pm.

Dorfplatz 28, A-6100 Seefeld. ✆ **05212/2464.** Fax 05212/283434. www.alpenhotel.com. 88 units. 180€–310€ ($288–$496) double; 250€–380€ ($400–$608) apt for 2. Rates include breakfast. MC, V. Closed late Mar–Apr and Nov–Dec 15. Parking 6€ ($9.60). **Amenities:** Restaurant; bar; fitness center; Jacuzzi; sauna; room service; massage; laundry service; dry cleaning; nonsmoking rooms; rooms for those w/ limited mobility. *In room:* TV, Wi-Fi, minibar, hair dryer, safe.

Karwendelhof ★ The Wilberger family runs one of the most elegant hotels in Tyrol. The century-old Tyrolean parlors have parquet floors, beamed ceilings, and antique accents. The personalized, rustically furnished rooms are elegant yet simple. Some have balconies opening onto mountain vistas, but all are immaculately maintained and have bathrooms, some with bidets.

The hotel restaurant, Alte Stube, is completely covered in old paneling burnished to a rich mellow glow. Dishes include well-prepared beef, veal, and pork, accompanied by fresh vegetables and followed by regional cheeses and home-baked pastries. Reservations are necessary. The hotel's K-Keller is one of the village's social centers. It's open only in winter 9pm to 2:30am. A casino in an adjoining building opens at 3pm every day in winter.

Bahnhofstrasse 124, A-6100 Seefeld. ✆ **800/780-7234** in the U.S., or 05212/26550. Fax 05212/265544. www.karwendelhof.at. 42 units. Winter 122€–250€ ($195–$400) double, 189€–320€ ($302–$512) suite for 2; summer 116€–175€ ($186–$280) double, 172€–199€ ($275–$318) suite for 2. Rates include half-board.

AE, DC, MC, V. Free parking on street; garage parking 10€ ($16) in summer, 12€ ($19) in winter. Closed Apr and Nov. **Amenities:** Restaurant; bar; beer cellar; fitness center; sauna; room service; babysitting; laundry service; dry cleaning; casino. *In room:* TV, Wi-Fi, minibar, hair dryer, safe.

Waldhotel (Kids) One of the oldest hotels in Seefeld, the Waldhotel has been fully renovated. Its location, at the edge of the resort adjoining the woods surrounding Seefeld, is about a 7-minute walk from the village center. All of the well-appointed rooms have balconies and terrific beds. The very best rooms have sitting areas; some of the smaller doubles are a bit cramped. A panoramic garden restaurant and a terrace are favorite spots for lunch or tea. Dinners include a choice of four-course menus, and breakfast is a buffet. In winter, there's a curling rink, and the hotel is just a 3-minute walk from the cable cars leading to the slopes. Year-round, the place offers a variety of entertainment, such as a live Dixieland band or Tyrolean music.

Römerweg 106, A-6100 Seefeld. ✆ **05212/22070.** Fax 05212/200130. www.waldhotel-seefeld.at. 50 units. Winter 106€–180€ ($170–$288) double, 158€–250€ ($253–$400) suite for 2; summer 96€–130€ ($154–$208) double, 110€–184€ ($176–$294) suite for 2. Rates include half-board. AE, MC, V. Parking garage 10€ ($16). Closed Apr and 2 weeks in Nov. **Amenities:** Restaurant; bar; sauna; babysitting; children's playroom; nonsmoking rooms; rooms for those w/limited mobility. *In room:* TV, hair dryer.

Inexpensive

Hotel Christina A 5-minute walk from the town center is this comfortable, contemporary chalet with exposed wood and a rustic, homey character. It has an indoor pool accessible through big glass doors in the cellar. Many of the comfortably furnished rooms have balconies, and, after renovations, the rooms are better than ever, with excellent beds.

Reitherspitzstrasse 415, A-6100 Seefeld. ✆ **05212/2553.** Fax 05212/255332. 14 units. Winter 102€–120€ ($163–$192) double, 160€ ($256) suite for 2; summer 78€–92€ ($125–$147) double, 130€ ($208) suite for 2. Rates include buffet breakfast. DC, MC, V. **Amenities:** Breakfast room; lounge; indoor heated pool; fitness room; sauna; solarium. *In room:* TV, hair dryer.

WHERE TO DINE

Most guests book into a Seefeld hotel on the half-board plan, and most of the hotels listed above have excellent dining facilities, although you should call ahead to make reservations.

Gourmet Restaurant Ritter Oswald/Bräukeller ★★ CONTINENTAL/TYROLEAN There are two restaurants of charm and historic importance within the most legendary hotel of Seefeld. The more expensive of the two is the Ritter Oswald. Set on the hotel's lobby level and outfitted with Tyrolean artifacts, richly oiled paneling, hunting trophies, and alpine mementos, it's small (60 seats), intimate, and cozy, with elaborate service rituals and food that mimics the grand cuisine you'd expect in, say, Salzburg or Vienna. Menu items change with the seasons but might delectably include filets of venison with a morel and port-wine sauce, strips of filet of veal served with herb-flavored cream sauce and spinach, and sophisticated variations on local freshwater trout. The less expensive and larger (150 seats) of the two is the cellar-level Bräukeller, which is capped with a 500-year-old vaulted stone ceiling that originally functioned as part of a monastery. Earthier and a bit more swashbuckling than the Ritter Oswald, it focuses on the hearty, folkloric cuisine of the Austrian Alps, with menu items that include *tafelspitz,* liver-and-noodle soup, grilled lake char with seasonal vegetables, Wiener schnitzel, and braised beef with wild mushrooms. There's live Tyrolean-style music performed nightly in the Bräukeller. Whereas you might be subtly steered into buying wine with your meal in the Ritter Oswald, no one will object if you opt for beer as accompaniment for your meal in the Bräukeller.

In the Hotel Klosterbräu, Klosterstrasse 30. ✆ **05212/26210.** www.klosterbraeu.com. Reservations recommended in Ritter Oswald, not necessary in the Bräukeller. Ritter Oswald main courses 13€–29€ ($21–$46); Bräukeller main courses 8.50€–19€ ($14–$30). AE, DC, MC, V. Both restaurants daily 11am–2pm and 6–11pm. Closed mid-Mar to mid-June and Oct to mid-Dec.

Restaurant Vorspiel ★ INTERNATIONAL/AUSTRIAN In this previously recommended hotel, vorspiel is the casino restaurant and one of the most fashionable in town. Top-quality service and a first-rate cuisine delight visitors flocking to this chic resort. You will smack your lips over the harmonious selections that appear on the ever-changing menu, based for the most part on market-fresh ingredients. The restaurant is especially known for its fish and pork dishes, although it also does a fine turn with succulent steaks, roast duck, and the classic Austrian veal dishes. Its fixed-price menu is among the best in town.

In the Hotel Karwendelhof, Bahnhofstrasse 125. ✆ **05212/2655.** Reservations required. Main courses 16€–24€ ($26–$38); 4-course set menu 55€ ($88). MC, V. Wed–Mon 6–10pm.

SEEFELD AFTER DARK

Seefeld has plenty of nightlife options to keep you entertained after a day in the alpine outdoors. Consider a drink at a glass-sided, oversize replica of an Eskimo's igloo, **Bar Siglu,** Klosterstrasse (✆ **05212/2621186**), where live music is presented in the early evening in ways that somehow makes the drinks taste better.

The town is filled with cafes and bars; take your pick, as they are similar. One particular favorite, which also serves Tyrolean dishes, is **Sportcafe Sailer,** Innsbruckerstrasse 12 (✆ **05212/2005**), which has a real local atmosphere and outdoor setting. If you like the beer and companions, you can order full meals here. Freshly made soups are popular in winter, and the most ordered main dish—soul food to the Austrians—is *gröstli* (made with potatoes, eggs, and bacon). In summer and winter, it's open daily from 11:30am to 10pm; in the spring and fall, daily 11:30am to 2pm and 6 to 10pm.

In season, Seefeld bustles with typical wine and beer cellars, along with nightclubs and dance clubs that come and go. However, the major nighttime attraction is the **Spiel-Casino Seefeld,** at the Hotel Karwendelhof, Bahnhofstrasse (✆ **05212/2340**). It offers baccarat, blackjack, seven-card stud poker, a money wheel, American and French roulette, and 70 slot machines. Your admission is 21€ ($34)—but that gives you the equivalent of 25€ ($40) in chips. It's open daily from 3pm to 3am.

Hotel Klosterbräu, Klosterstrasse 30, is the most sophisticated nightspot in town; its nightclub, **Die Kane,** presents an international orchestra and a floor show daily in winter and 3 nights a week in summer from 9pm to 3am. In winter, the club opens at 5pm for a *tans-tee* (tea dance). The hotel also features international specialties in its restaurant, **Ritter Oswald Stube,** and a gemütlich atmosphere in its **Bräukeller,** open from 11am to midnight, presenting *stemming* (folk) music after 8pm

5 THE ZILLER VALLEY ★★

Zillertal is the German name for the Ziller Valley east of Innsbruck, a resort mecca in summer and winter. Some say that this is the most beautiful valley in all of Tyrol. You might doubt this claim as you go through the first stretches of the Zillertal, but don't turn back. It gets more impressive as you travel deeper into the valley.

When you first enter the Zillertal during the warmer months, you'll pass rich meadowlands and sleek, healthy grazing cows. To the west are the **Tux Alps** and to the east are the **Kitzbühel Alps,** covered later in this chapter. As tempting as it might be to head for these alpine areas, continue farther into the Ziller Valley, which will suddenly grow narrower, with the scenery becoming more dramatic.

The people of the Zillertal are the finest singers in Austria, as generation after generation of valley families inherited magnificent voices and made use of their talents. Pass through the first of the little villages and resorts, since we think better ones lie ahead.

ZELL AM ZILLER

Zell am Ziller lies 479km (298 miles) west of Vienna and 60km (37 miles) east of Innsbruck. This is the first town that merits a stop, but don't confuse this resort with Zell am See in Land Salzburg. Zell am Ziller is the major town of the lower section of the Ziller Valley, and inns here are reasonably priced. Once it was a gold-mining town, but those days are long gone.

Essentials

GETTING THERE If you're coming directly to Zell am Ziller, you can **fly** to the nearest international airport, in Munich, and arrange further transportation from there.

Trains from Innsbruck travel frequently to **Jenbach,** which sits on the main rail line to Salzburg (trip time: 20 min.). At Jenbach, trains depart every hour for Zell am Ziller (trip time: 45 min.). For rail information, contact ✆ **05/1717** (www.oebb.at).

Most **bus lines** servicing Zell am Ziller originate in nearby towns and villages. However, three buses per day depart from Innsbruck's Hauptbahnhof for Zell am Ziller (trip time: 1¾ hr.). For **bus information** in Zell am Ziller from other parts of Austria, call ✆ **05282/2211.**

If you're **driving** from Innsbruck, head east along Autobahn A12 to the junction with Route 169, and cut south.

VISITOR INFORMATION The **tourist office** in the town center (✆ **05282/2281;** www.zell.at) is open Monday to Friday 8:30am to 12:30pm and 3 to 6pm, Saturday 9am to noon and 4 to 6pm, and Sunday 4 to 6pm. Closed on Sunday in summer.

Exploring Zell am Ziller

Like many other Austrian villages, Zell has a **Pfarrkirche (Parish Church)** ★, this one dating from 1782. A huge dome tops its octagonal design.

Once this village was known only as a summer holiday site, but more recently it has also become a winter sports resort. In 1978, the Kreuzjoch area was opened to skiers, and Zell am Ziller took its place on the tourist ski maps of Europe. In season, a free ski bus stops at the major hotels to transport guests to the slopes.

You can travel by gondola to a restaurant with a view of the **Gründalm** (1,022m/3,353 ft.) and then continue by chairlift to **Rosenalm** (1,761m/5,778 ft.), where another restaurant opens onto a panoramic view. From Rosenalm, a surface lift can take you to a lofty citadel 2,266m (7,434 ft.) above sea level.

Another ski area, the **Geriosstein,** more than 5km (3 miles) from Zell am Ziller, also has bus service, but not as frequently. From the bottom station, a cableway will lift you to 1,647m (5,404 ft.), where you can take a chairlift up to 1,836m (6,024 ft.).

Where to Stay

Hotel Bräu At the edge of the town's most important crossroads, this ample chalet was originally built in the 15th century, and an extra wing was added in 1985. Rising five balconied stories, its ocher-colored facade is embellished with *trompe l'oeil* frescoes.

Inside, it contains three different dining rooms (see "Where to Dine," below). Each comfortable guest room is outfitted with wood trim and plenty of Tyrolean charm. Modern extras have not been ignored. Rooms are a bit small, however.

Dorfplatz 1, A-6280 Zell am Ziller. ✆ **05282/2313.** Fax 05282/231317. www.hotel-braeu.at. 36 units. Winter 128€–196€ ($205–$314) double, 150€–216€ ($240–$346) suite; summer 104€–120€ ($166–$192) double, 132€–138€ ($211–$221) suite. Rates include half-board. No credit cards. Closed Apr and Oct 15–Dec 20. **Amenities:** Restaurant; bar; sauna; room service; massage; laundry service; dry cleaning; nonsmoking rooms; rooms for those w/limited mobility. *In room:* TV, Wi-Fi, minibar, hair dryer, safe.

Where to Dine

Hotel Bräu Restaurant AUSTRIAN Lined up side by side on the street level of the Hotel Bräu, this trio of authentic Tyrolean dining rooms competes with one another for the most regional charm. You might want to check out each of them before deciding. They're called **Speisezimmer, Bräustübl,** and **Casino.** Full meals cost around 35€ ($46) and include solid Teutonic dishes, suitable for cold-weather days.

Dorfplatz 1. ✆ **05282/2313.** Reservations required. Main courses 11€–28€ ($17–$44). No credit cards. Daily 11:30am–2pm and 6–9pm. Closed Apr and Oct 15–Dec 10.

MAYRHOFEN ★

The road divides at Zell am Ziller, and to reach Mayrhofen, head southwest on Route 169 to the popular resort. This resort, standing at 633m (2,077 ft.), enclosed by towering alpine peaks and lying at the foot of the glaciers crowning the adjacent Alps, is a premier summer holiday spot and winter playground, the finest in the valley in terms of facilities and accommodations. Some of the area's best food is served here. After a visit here, we recommend that you return to Zell and then go southeast to **Gerlos.**

Essentials

GETTING THERE Following the routes used to reach Zell am Ziller, travelers from Innsbruck transfer at the railway junction at Jenbach. From Jenbach, **trains** depart every hour for the 1-hour ride south to Mayrhofen. From Mayrhofen many bus lines fan out into the nearby valleys. Unless you're coming from one of those obscure valleys, it's easier to take the train. Mayrhofen is 76km (47 miles) southeast of Innsbruck. For **bus and rail information,** call ✆ **05282/2211.**

VISITOR INFORMATION The **tourist office** in the town center (✆ **05285/6760;** www.mayrhofen.com) is open Monday to Friday 8am to 6pm, Saturday 9am to noon, and Sunday 10am to noon.

Summer Sports, Skiing & More

For decades, Mayrhofen has drawn summer holiday crowds with its endless **opportunities** for mountaineering, hang gliding, shooting, tennis, fishing, swimming in a heated outdoor pool, minigolf, cycling, and even summer skiing in the **Hintertux glacier area** at the top of the valley. Mayrhofen is also a mecca for mountain climbers during the nonskiing seasons.

In recent years, the resort village has become more a ski center. Starting from scratch, you can learn to ski at the resort school: The children's ski training is especially good here, and a kindergarten makes this an ideal family resort. Slopes for advanced skiers are available in the **Penkenjoch** section to the west of Mayrhofen, with a cableway taking you to nearly 1,830m (6,004 ft.). From the top, you'll be rewarded with one of the most panoramic views of the Zillertal alpine range; there's also a restaurant, also with quite a view.

You can also take a cableway (departs south of Mayrhofen) up to ski in the **Ahorn** area (1,906m/6,253 ft.). There are seven surface lifts at the top, as well as another restaurant with a panoramic view.

Other winter activities include sledding on a natural toboggan run, curling, ice-skating, horse-drawn sleigh rides, horseback riding, and playing sports in an indoor arena.

After your outdoor fun, you can spend your evening attending a tea dance or eating fondue. You can also hear some of that famous Ziller Valley singing at folk festivals in July and August. The dates change every year, so check with the tourist office. Another popular summer diversion is taking a ride on the narrow-gauge steam train between Zell am Ziller and Mayrhofen.

Venturing into the Alps

From Mayrhofen you can also venture into the Alps around the Zillertal, where you'll be rewarded with some of the most spectacular scenery in Tyrol. By the time you reach Mayrhofen, the trail through the Zillertal that you've been following will have split into four different parts, each of which runs through a valley radiating off the Zillertal. Three of the valleys have the suffix *grund* (German for "ground") on their names: the **Stillupgrund,** the **Zemmgrund,** and the **Zillergrund.**

You might not have time to explore all these valleys, but if you can make time for one, make it the fourth and loftiest valley, the **Tuxertal,** or Tux Valley, which cuts like a deep slash through the mountains. This valley reaches its end point at several glaciers, including the **Olperer,** 3,477m (11,407 ft.) high. You can take a bus from Mayrhofen to either the village of **Lanersbach** or on to **Hintertux,** both in the Tuxertal. The road runs west from Mayrhofen for some 21km (13 miles) to the end of the valley, where ski lifts branch off in several directions.

You come first to Lanersbach, the largest village in the Tuxertal, lying in a sunny, sheltered spot. From here you can take a chairlift to the **Eggalm plateau,** which has a restaurant at 2,001m (6,565 ft.) and offers one of the most scenic panoramas the Ziller Alps has to offer.

Hintertux, your ultimate destination, lies at the top of the valley, virtually on the doorstep of the towering glaciers. Because of thermal springs, Hintertux also enjoys a reputation as a spa. You might want to buy some woodcarvings from the skillful craftspeople here.

You can ski on the glaciers in summer. A chairlift or a gondola from Hintertux will transport you to **Sommerbergalm** (2,074m/6,804 ft.), and once here, you can take a surface lift west to **Tuxer-Joch Hütte** (2,531m/8,304 ft.).

Where to Stay

Alpenhotel Kramerwirt (Kids) This hotel's facade has green shutters, a painted illustration of a medieval figure, and a towerlike construction high above the roofline. The rustic interior contains a scattering of oriental rugs and antique chests. Some rooms have romantic four-poster beds and big bathrooms; others are designed in a more functional style with less spacious bathrooms. Additional but less desirable rooms are located in a 1980s annex a short walk away. A folkloric nightclub, the **Götestube,** is in the cellar. Live musicians entertain the drinkers and diners.

Am Marienbrunnen 346, A-6290 Mayrhofen. ✆ **05285/6700.** Fax 05285/6700502. www.kramerwirt.at. 80 units. Winter 144€–228€ ($230–$365) double, 194€–260€ ($310–$416) suite; summer 132€–156€ ($211–$250) double, 164€–194€ ($262–$310) suite. Rates include half-board. MC, V. Closed Nov 20–Dec 10. **Amenities:** Restaurant; bar; nightclub; 2 Jacuzzis; sauna; children's playrooms; room service; babysitting. *In room:* TV, Wi-Fi, hair dryer, safe.

Elisabethhotel ★★ Kids Named after the young matriarch of the Thaler family, the owners, this stylish and luxurious hotel is a 3-minute walk from the village center. Its chalet-style facade is accented with carefully detailed balconies, heavy overhanging eaves, painted designs, and a tower. Rooms, the resort's finest, have charming Tyrolean motifs. Bathrooms are generally spacious and equipped with charming appointments, large tubs, showers, and cosmetic mirrors. On the premises are a cozy restaurant, Sissi Stube, and an elegant bar named after one of Mozart's most memorably comic characters, Papageno. There's also a large terrace with a coffee shop and an Italian restaurant, Mamma Mia. In winter, a dance club operates in the basement, and in summer there's a large garden to use, plus a children's playground.

Einfahrt Mitte 432, A-6290 Mayrhofen. ✆ **05285/6767.** Fax 05285/676767. www.elisabethhotel.com. 32 units. Winter 329€–347€ ($526–$555) double, from 450€ ($720) suite; summer 204€–245€ ($326–$392) double, 340€–580€ ($544–$928) suite. Rates include half-board. AE, DC, MC, V. Closed Nov and May. **Amenities:** Restaurant; bar; nightclub; indoor heated pool; fitness center; Jacuzzi; sauna; children's playground; room service; massage; babysitting; laundry service; dry cleaning; nonsmoking rooms; solarium; rooms for those w/limited mobility. *In room:* TV, Wi-Fi, minibar, hair dryer, safe.

Where to Dine

Wirtshaus Zum Griena ★ Finds AUSTRIAN/TYROLEAN This restaurant, strong on regional charm and cuisine, sits in a meadow above Mayrhofen's main colony of resort hotels. The two dining rooms are covered with pinewood planks that everyone claims were installed about 400 years ago. Even the tables are an unfinished series of smoothly sanded planks. Even if you read German, you might find the menu tough going, as it's written in a little-used Tyrolean dialect. Many dishes are based on butter-and-egg alpine recipes, sometimes laden with cream from high-altitude cows. Several involve baking in a ceramic pot, including noodles layered with cream and cheese. Ever had beer soup? You might opt for the cheese platter, a bowl of polenta, or one of the meat dishes. The Wiener schnitzel, in the words of the apron-clad waitress, comes "fresh from the veal" and is "very, very pretty."

Dorfhaus 768. ✆ **05285/62778.** Reservations recommended. Main courses 8€–13€ ($13–$20). MC, V. June–Oct Tues–Sun 11am–10pm; Dec–May daily 11am–11pm. Closed Nov. Drive uphill (north) from the town center for 10 min. to the secluded suburb of Dorfhaus; turn left at a fountain and head several hundred feet down a 1-lane road flanked with a fence.

6 THE KITZBÜHEL ALPS ★★★

Hard-core skiers and the rich and famous are attracted to this old region. Such a dense network of lifts covers the Kitzbühel Alps that they're Austria's largest skiing area, with a series of superlative runs. The action centers on the town of Kitzbühel, but there are many satellite resorts that are much less expensive, including **St. Johann** in Tyrol. Kitzbühel is, in a sense, a neighbor of Munich, 130km (81 miles) to the northeast: Most visitors to the Kitzbühel Alps use Munich's international airport.

KITZBÜHEL ★★★

Edward, Prince of Wales (you might remember him better as the Duke of Windsor), might have put Kitzbühel on the international map with his 1928 "discovery" of what was then a town of modest guesthouses. Certainly his return a few years later with Mrs. Simpson caused the eyes of the world to focus on this town, and the "upper crust" of England and other countries began flocking here, placing a stamp of elegance on Kitzbühel.

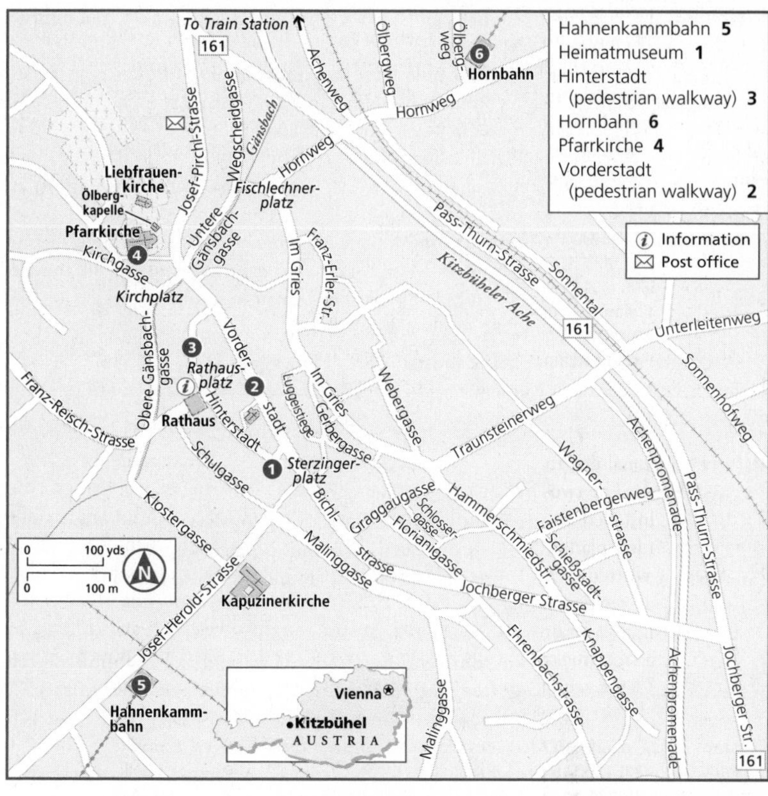

At the time of this 20th-century renaissance, however, Kitzbühel was already some 8 centuries old by documented history, and a settlement existed here much, much longer than that. Archaeological finds have shown that during the Bronze Age—and until the 9th century B.C.—copper was mined and traded in nearby mountains. The settlement *Chizbühel* is first mentioned in documents of 1165, the name derived from the ruling family of Chizzo. Kitzbühel was a part of Bavaria until 1504, when it came into the hands of Holy Roman Emperor Maximilian I of Austria and was annexed to Tyrol.

A second mining era began in Kitzbühel in the 15th century—this time copper and silver—and the town became fat and prosperous for many decades. Numerous buildings from the mining days are still here, as are remnants of the town walls and three of the gates. In what used to be the suburbs of Kitzbühel, you'll see some of the miners' cottages still standing.

Kitzbühel is not a cheap place to stay, but to make things easier on your pocketbook, the local tourist office has come out with a **Guest Card** for summer visitors. This card is valid after being stamped at your hotel or guesthouse and entitles you to discounts, some quite substantial, on the price of many activities, plus some freebies.

Essentials

GETTING THERE Two and three **trains** per hour (many express) arrive in Kitzbühel from Innsbruck (trip time: 60 min.) and Salzburg (trip time: 2½ hr.). For rail information, contact ✆ **05/1717** (www.oebb.at).

Although it's serviced by at least nine local **bus lines** running into and up the surrounding valleys, most visitors arrive in Kitzbühel by train. The most useful of these bus lines runs every 30 to 60 minutes between Kitzbühel and St. Johann in Tyrol (trip time: 25 min.). In addition, about half a dozen buses travel every day from Salzburg's main railway station to Kitzbühel (trip time: 2¼ hr.). For **regional bus information,** call ✆ **05356/62715.**

Kitzbühel is 449km (279 miles) southwest of Vienna and 100km (62 miles) east of Innsbruck. If you're **driving** from Innsbruck, take Autobahn A12 east to the junction with Route 312 heading to Ellmau. After bypassing Ellmau, continue east to the junction with Route 342, which you take south to Kitzbühel.

VISITOR INFORMATION The **tourist office,** Hinterstadt 18 (✆ **05356/777;** www.kitzbuehel.com), is open Monday to Friday 8:30am to 6pm, Saturday 9am to 6pm, and Sunday 10am to noon and 4 to 6pm.

What to See & Do

Exploring the Town

The town has two main streets, both pedestrian walkways: **Vorderstadt** and **Hinterstadt.** Along these streets, Kitzbühel has preserved its traditional architectural style. You'll see three-story stone houses with oriels and scrollwork around the doors and windows, heavy overhanging eaves, and gothic gables.

The **Pfarrkirche (Parish Church)** was built from 1435 to 1506 and was renovated in the baroque style during the 18th century. The lower part of the **Liebfrauenkirche (Church of Our Lady)** dates from the 13th century; the upper part dates from 1570. Between these two churches stands the **Ölbergkapelle (Ölberg Chapel)** with a 1450 "lantern of the dead" and frescoes from the latter part of the 16th century.

Heimatmuseum, Hinterstadt 32 (✆ **05356/67274;** www.museum-kitzbuehl.at), is the town's most visible showcase of its own culture and history. It lies within what was originally the town granary, constructed in the city's center on the site of an early medieval castle. In 1998, it was enlarged with the incorporation of the town's oldest extant tower, a 14th-century stone structure once part of Kitzbühel's medieval fortifications. Inside you'll see artifacts based on the town's legendary mines, from prehistoric times and the Bronze Age through the Middle Ages, as well as trophies of the region's skiing stars with lots of emphasis on its 19th- and early-20th-century development into a modern-day ski resort. The museum is open March 11 to July 9 and September 21 to December 5 Tuesday to Saturday 10am to 1pm; July 10 to September 20 daily 10am to 6pm. Admission is 5€ ($8) for adults and 2€ ($3.20) for persons under 18.

Skiing Galore at the Kitzbühel Ski Circus

In winter, the emphasis in Kitzbühel, 702m (2,303 ft.) above sea level, is on skiing, and facilities are offered for everyone from novices to experts. The ski season starts just before Christmas and lasts until late March. With more than 62 lifts, gondolas, and mountain railroads on five different mountains, Kitzbühel has two main ski areas, the **Hahnenkamm** and the **Kitzbüheler Horn** ★★. *Hahnenkammbahn* (cable cars) are within easy walking distance, even in ski boots.

Skiing became a fact of life in Kitzbühel as long ago as 1892, when the first pair of skis was imported from Norway and intrepid daredevils began to slide down the snowy slopes at breakneck speeds. Many great names in skiing have since been associated with Kitzbühel, the most renowned being town native Toni Sailer, triple Olympic champion in the 1956 Winter Games in Cortina.

The linking of the lift systems on the Hahnenkamm has created the celebrated **Kitzbühel Ski Circus ★★★**, which makes it possible to ski downhill for more than 80km (50 miles), with runs that suit every stage of proficiency. Numerous championship ski events are held here, such as the World Cup event each January, when top-flight skiers pit their skills against the toughest downhill course in the world, a stretch of the Hahnenkamm especially designed for maximum speed. Its name, Die Strief, is both feared and respected among skiers because of its reputation as one of the world's fastest downhill racecourses. A ski pass entitles the holder to use all the lifts that form the Ski Circus.

More Winter & Summer Pursuits

Skiing, of course, is not the only winter activity here—there's also curling, ski-bobbing, ski jumping, ice-skating, tobogganing, hiking on cleared trails, and hang gliding, as well as indoor activities such as tennis, bowling, and swimming. The children's ski school, **Schischule Rote Teufel,** Museumkeller, Hinterstadt (✆ **05356/62500**), provides training for the very young skier. And don't forget the après-ski, with bars, nightclubs, and dance clubs rocking from teatime until the wee hours.

Kitzbühel has summer pastimes, too, with activities including walking tours, visits to the **Wild Life Park at Aurach** (3km/2 miles from Kitzbühel), tennis, horseback riding, golf, squash, brass-band concerts in the town center, cycling, and swimming. For the latter, there's an indoor swimming pool, but we recommend going to the **Schwarzsee (Black Lake).** This *see,* about a 15-minute walk northwest of the center of town, is an alpine lake with a peat bottom that keeps the water relatively murky. Covering an area of 6.5 hectares (16 acres), with a depth that doesn't exceed about 8m (26 ft.), it's the site of beaches and **Seiwald Bootverleitung,** Schwarzsee (✆ **05356/62381**), an outfit that rents rowboats and putt-putt electric-driven engines in case you want to fish or sunbathe from within a boat. Rowboats rent for 8€ ($13) per hour, and small-scale electric engines rent for 15€ ($24) per hour. Obviously, everything is shuttered down tight from September to mid-May.

One of the region's most exotic collections of alpine flora is clustered into the jagged and rocky confines of the **Alpine Flower Garden Kitzbühel,** where various species of gentian, gorse, heather, and lichens are found on the sunny slopes of the Kitzbüheler Horn. Set at a height of around 1,830m (6,004 ft.) above sea level, the garden—which is owned and maintained by Kitzbühel as an incentive to midsummer tourism—is open from late May to early September daily from 8:30am to 5:30pm, and it's most impressive during June, July, and August. Admission is free, and many visitors see it by taking the Seilbahn Kitzbüheler cable car to its uppermost station and then descending on foot via the garden's labyrinth of footpaths to the gondola's middle station. (You can also climb upward within the garden, reversing the order of the gondola stations, although that would require a lot more effort.) The **Seilbahn Kitzbüheler cable car** (✆ **05356/6951**), 16€ ($25) round-trip, departs from the Kitzbühel at half-hour intervals daily but only operates in the summer.

Where to Stay

Although there's a wide range of hotels in Kitzbühel, reservations are mandatory in the high-season winter months, particularly the peak ski times such as February. As for Christmas in Kitzbühel, someone once wrote, "It's best to make reservations at birth."

Very Expensive

Romantik Hotel Tennerhof ★★★ High in the foothills of the mountains near the Hornbahn cable cars, and less than 1km (1/2-mile) west of the town center, this comfortable, government-rated five-star chalet hotel evolved from a 17th-century farmhouse. The whole place is furnished in a Tyrolean style with great care and taste, offering good living and complete relaxation in a garden setting. The views from the outdoor cafe encompass the pool and the village. The owners, the Pasquali family, take a personal interest in their guests and see that a high standard of service is maintained. If you're a traditionalist, try one of the rooms in the original building, as they're the most intimate and cozy. All rooms are beautifully furnished.

The hotel restaurant (see "Where to Dine," below) offers wholesome food, with vegetables and herbs straight from the hotel's garden.

Griesenauweg 26, A-6370 Kitzbühel. ✆ **05356/63181.** Fax 05356/6318170. www.tennerhof.at. 48 units. Winter 271€–645€ ($434–$1,032) double, 387€–1,128€ ($619–$1,805) suite; summer 225€–344€ ($360–$550) double, 321€–580€ ($514–$928) suite. Rates include breakfast. Half-board (granted with a stay of 3 or more days) 30€ ($48) per person extra. AE, DC, MC, V. Closed Apr 12–May 14 and Oct–Dec 18. **Amenities:** Restaurant; bar; 2 heated pools (1 indoor, 1 outdoor); Jacuzzi; sauna; steam room; room service; massage; babysitting; laundry service; dry cleaning; solarium. *In room:* TV, Wi-Fi, minibar, hair dryer, safe.

Expensive

Hotel Goldener Greif ★ The ancestor of this hotel was built in 1271, and parts of it still remain within the massive walls of this well-known establishment. The hotel, next to the Spiel-Casino and 180m (591 ft.) from the Hahnenkamm cable-car station, has many balconies and elaborate shutters. Owner Josef Harisch (his daughter, Maria Harisch, runs the hotel now) likes traditional charm with a good dose of luxury thrown in. The interior contains fireplaces, antique furniture, oriental carpets, Tyrolean paintings, and The Greif Keller in, of course, the cellar. The comfortable, attractive rooms have firm beds. Most rooms are quite spacious, and many have alpine oak furnishings, alcove seats, nonworking fireplaces, parquet floors, double-glazed windows, and (in some cases) a whirlpool. If you want to splurge a bit, you can request one of the deluxe suites, many with a hunting-lodge motif and their own Jacuzzis, private steam baths, and fireplaces.

The superb **Restaurant Goldener Greif** (see "Where to Dine," below) serves Austrian and regional cuisine.

Hinterstadt 24, A-6370 Kitzbühel. ✆ **05356/64311.** Fax 05356/65001. www.hotelgoldenergreif.at. 56 units. Winter 152€–252€ ($243–$403) double, 220€–290€ ($352–$464) suite; summer 132€–166€ ($211–$266) double, 160€–182€ ($256–$291) suite. Rates include breakfast. Half-board available for a supplement of 12€–18€ ($19–$29) per person. AE, DC, MC, V. Free parking on street. Closed Apr–May and Oct–Nov. **Amenities:** Restaurant; bar; indoor heated pool; fitness center; sauna; room service; massage; laundry service; dry cleaning; solarium. *In room:* TV, Wi-Fi, hair dryer.

Hotel Schloss Lebenberg ★★ The core of this hotel is a medieval castle whose walls and turrets have been covered with stucco, and a modern extension has been added nearby. The entire complex sits on a hill looking over the village, less than 1.5km (1 mile) from Kitzbühel, with dozens of mountain paths originating at its door. Rooms are elegantly furnished and come in a wide range of sizes, including some spacious enough for sitting areas with wrought-iron coffee tables. Many beds are canopied. French doors lead to private patios or balconies. The dozen or so large, Gothic-style castle rooms are the most sought after. The hotel restaurant serves lunch and dinner, and provides a lavish breakfast buffet for guests.

Lebenbergstrasse 17, A-6370 Kitzbühel. ✆ **05356/69010.** Fax 05356/6901-404. www.austria-trend.at/leb. 120 units. Winter 172€–330€ ($275–$528) double, from 405€ ($648) suite; summer 212€ ($339) double, 228€ ($365) suite. Rates include half-board. AE, DC, MC, V. Free outside parking; garage parking 14€ ($22). Hotel bus picks up guests at train station. **Amenities:** Restaurant; bar; indoor heated pool; fitness center; sauna; room service; babysitting; laundry service; dry cleaning; nonsmoking rooms. *In room:* TV, Wi-Fi, hair dryer, safe.

Hotel Weisses Rössl ★ This hotel was originally built in the 19th century as an inn for the merchants passing through Kitzbühel by coach. Today it's impeccably maintained by the Klena family and its fine staff. Dozens of seating niches offer cozy intimacy, and a fireplace provides midwinter cheer a few paces from the heavily trafficked lobby. The fourth floor contains a panoramic terrace with one of the best mountain views in town. A 2-minute walk from the ski lifts, the hotel offers snugly equipped rooms with comfortable furniture and neatly kept bathrooms. An a la carte restaurant serves well-prepared Austrian and international dishes.

Bichlstrasse 3–5, A-6370 Kitzbühel. ✆ **05356/71900.** Fax 05356/71900-99. www.roesslkitz.at. 65 units. Winter 448€–820€ ($717–$1,312) double, 740€–962€ ($1,184–$1,539) suite for 2; summer 238€–570€ ($381–$912) double, 405€ ($648) suite for 2. Rates include half-board. Closed Easter to late May and mid-Oct to mid-Dec. AE, DC, MC, V. **Amenities:** Restaurant; bar; indoor heated pool; health club; sauna; room service; babysitting; laundry service; dry cleaning. *In room:* TV, Wi-Fi, minibar, hair dryer, safe.

Hotel Zur Tenne ★★ A sophisticated family from Munich operates this hotel, one of the resort's best. It combines Tyrolean *gemütlichkeit* with urban style and panache, and the staff shows genuine concern for its clientele. The hotel was created in the 1950s by joining a trio of 700-year-old houses. Rooms are as glamorous as anything in Kitzbühel: wood trim, comfortable beds, eiderdowns, and copies of Tyrolean antiques. Many have working fireplaces and canopied beds for a romantic touch.

In addition to intimate lounges and niches and nooks, the hotel sports the most luxurious health complex in town, complete with a tropical fountain, two hot tubs, and a hot-and-cold foot bath.

The Zur Tenne Restaurant offers international cuisine with a Tyrolean flair (see "Where to Dine," below).

Vorderstadt 8–10, A-6370 Kitzbühel. ✆ **05356/644440.** Fax 05356/6480356. www.hotelzurtenne.com. 50 units. Winter 289€–310€ ($462–$496) double, 362€–485€ ($579–$776) suite for 3; summer 161€–229€ ($258–$366) double, 390€ ($624) suite for 3. Rates include breakfast. Half-board 42€ ($67) per person extra in winter, 38€ ($61) in summer. AE, DC, MC, V. Free parking outdoors, 12€ ($19) in covered garage nearby. **Amenities:** 2 restaurants; bar; lounge; fitness center; 2 Jacuzzis; sauna; room service; massage; babysitting; laundry service; dry cleaning; solarium. *In room:* TV, Wi-Fi, minibar, hair dryer, safe.

Sporthotel Bichlhof ★ Slightly more than 3km (2 miles) south of the resort's center, this 1970s hotel offers panoramic views over most of the valley. This tasteful chalet complex surrounds you with a decor of exposed paneling and patterned carpeting. The spacious rooms sometimes look Japanese in their simplicity. The most desirable ones open onto private balconies with views of the surrounding mountains. The hotel's restaurant serves authentic Tyrolean cuisine, specializing in fish caught in its own lake. As part of its weekly programs, the hotel offers guided torchlit walks, Tyrolean buffets, and fondue evenings or barbecues.

Bichlnweg 153, A-6370 Kitzbühel. ✆ **05356/64022**. Fax 05356/63634. www.bichlhof.at. 47 units. Winter 225€–300€ ($360–$480) double, from 375€ ($600) suite for 2; summer 190€–265€ ($304–$424) double, from 220€ ($352) suite for 2. Rates include half-board. MC, V. Closed Apr–May and Oct 15–Dec 15. **Amenities:** Restaurant; bar; indoor pool; 18-hole golf course; 2 tennis courts; fitness center; Jacuzzi; sauna; room service; massage; babysitting; laundry service; dry cleaning; nonsmoking rooms. *In room:* TV, Wi-Fi, minibar, hair dryer, safe.

Moderate

Hotel Bruggerhof ★ (Finds Less than 1.5km (1 mile) west of the town center, near the Schwarzsee, is this countryside chalet with a sun terrace. Originally built as a farmhouse in the 1920s, it later gained local fame as a restaurant. The interior has massive ceiling beams and a corner fireplace. The owners, the Reiter family, run a well-maintained hotel. Rooms are comfortable, cozy, and decorated in an alpine style. All have a well-lived-in look, although housekeeping is attentive. Don't expect the smooth-running efficiency of a large-scale chain hotel, as everything here is family managed, idiosyncratic, and personalized—sometimes to the point of eccentricity.

Reitherstrasse 24, A-6370 Kitzbühel. ✆ **05356/62806.** Fax 05356/6447930. www.bruggerhof-camping.at. 25 units. Winter 228€–434€ ($365–$694) double; summer 180€–246€ ($288–$394) double. Rates include half-board. AE, DC, MC, V. Closed Apr and Oct 15–Dec 15. **Amenities:** Restaurant; bar; minigolf; 2 tennis courts; fitness center; Jacuzzi; sauna; room service; babysitting; laundry service; dry cleaning; nonsmoking rooms; solarium. *In room:* TV, Wi-Fi, minibar, hair dryer, safe.

Hotel Schweizerhof ★ (Kids This hotel is a well-designed cross between a chalet and a mountain villa. The interior has some attractive antiques, oriental rugs, and beamed and paneled ceilings. The generally spacious rooms have terraces and lovely interiors; those in the newer wing are more up-to-date. Management has tried to create the aura of a "living room" in the bedrooms, making you want to linger instead of using it just as a crash pad for the night. Of course, nothing in the room can compete with the private balcony overlooking the Stein or the imposing Kaiser Mountains. The hotel restaurant's food is Tyrolean and international, and the menu is varied and interesting. On some winter evenings, the public rooms seem more like a house party than a hotel. Summer brings tables and umbrellas out on the lawns. The hotel overlooks the children's ski school next to the Hahnenkamm cableway. It prides itself on its beauty center and health club, which is very much a part of its allure.

Hahnenkammstrasse 4, A-6370 Kitzbühel. ✆ **05356/62735.** Fax 05356/62735-57. www.hotel-schweizerhof.at. 42 units. Winter 190€–318€ ($304–$509) double, 232€–348€ ($371–$557) suite for 3; summer 120€–156€ ($192–$250) double, 144€–180€ ($230–$288) suite for 3. Rates include half-board. AE, DC, MC, V. Closed Apr 5–May 18 and Oct–Dec 20. **Amenities:** Restaurant; bar; 18-hole golf course; spa; Jacuzzi; sauna; children's playroom; room service; massage; nonsmoking rooms; rooms w/ limited mobility. *In room:* TV, Wi-Fi, hair dryer.

Hotel Zum Jägerwirt ★ The name of this place means "Hunter's Inn," and even if you don't like to hunt wild animals, you'll love the blazing fires and mellow paneling of this rustic hotel. The inn was indeed a hotel once catering to hunters, who are known in Austria for their appreciation of good food and atmosphere. The government-rated four-star hotel, 180m (591 ft.) west of the town center, was recently enlarged and renovated. It has a bar area with hewn overhead beams. Double rooms are spacious and well furnished, while singles are rather small and might not be large enough to handle all your ski equipment. Heavy pine furniture, oriental rugs, and good beds make the place inviting, although time has taken its toll on the decor.

The hotel restaurant, Jägerwirt, serves both Austrian and international specialties. In addition to an ample breakfast buffet, guests are treated in the evening to a large salad buffet, plus a bountiful dinner. The chef can cater to special diets.

Jochbergerstrasse 12, A-6370 Kitzbühel. ✆ **05356/69810.** Fax 05356/64067. www.hotel-jaegerwirt.at. 78 units. Winter 160€–276€ ($256–$442) double, 258€–420€ ($413–$672) suite for 2; summer 112€–180€ ($179–$288) double, 210€–340€ ($336–$544) suite for 2. Rates include breakfast. AE, DC, MC, V. Closed Apr–May and Oct–Dec 20. **Amenities:** Restaurant; bar; indoor heated pool; Turkish bath; children's pool; fitness room; sauna; room service; massage; laundry service; dry cleaning; nonsmoking rooms; solarium. *In room:* TV, Wi-Fi, minibar, hair dryer, safe.

Inexpensive

Gasthof Eggerwirt (Value) Lying in Kitzbühel's lower altitudes, this lodging sits next to a gurgling alpine stream. Today, country-baroque designs highlight the traditional stucco facade of a remodeled and much enlarged hotel, whose structure was actually built in 1658. Inside, the Gasthof is clean, with well-maintained standards of simple, solid comfort in its rooms. Decor is functional, and all rooms have neatly kept bathrooms; some units contain a private balcony. Considering the location, however, pricing is very good. There's a charming dining room, Florianistube (see "Where to Dine," below).

Goensbachgasse 12, A-6370 Kitzbühel. ✆ **05356/62455.** Fax 05356/6243722. www.eggerwirt-kitzbuehel.at. 20 units. Winter 116€–164€ ($186–$262) double; summer 84€–116€ ($134–$186) double. MC, V. Rates include breakfast. Parking garage 10€ ($16). Closed Easter–May 20 and Nov. **Amenities:** Restaurant; bar. *In room:* TV, Wi-Fi, minibar, safe.

Where to Dine

Many guests stay at Kitzbühel on the half-board plan. It's also fashionable to dine around, checking out the action at the various hotels. With one or two exceptions, most notably the Wirtshaws Uterberger-Stuben, all the best restaurants are in hotels.

Expensive

Hotel Restaurant Zur Tenne ★★ INTERNATIONAL Large, elegantly paneled, and accented with a corner bar, this is one of the top restaurants of Kitzbühel. The light Tyrolean atmosphere invites you to relax and enjoy traditional dishes. A cooperative and polite young staff sees to your dining needs. Depending on the amount of sunlight streaming in, the most popular seating area is often the glass-sided extension. The restaurant's cachet and cuisine have improved dramatically in recent years. The delectable menu is likely to include carpaccio, a salad of juniper-smoked trout, filet of roast saddle of hare, medallions of venison, Hungarian goulash, and chateaubriand. A popular favorite is the Tenne special steak, served with Idaho baked potatoes and sour cream. A dessert specialty is an iced soufflé flavored with Grand Marnier.

Vorderstadt 8–10. ✆ **05356/644440.** Reservations recommended. Main courses 12€–31€ ($19–$50). AE, DC, MC, V. Daily 11:30am–1:30pm and 6:30–10pm.

Restaurant Goldener Greif ★★ TYROLEAN The setting is cozy and warm, and the cuisine is some of the best at the resort, with a menu that includes everything from a simple goulash to caviar. The dining room features vaulted ceilings, intricate paneling, ornamental ceramic stoves, 19th-century paintings, and, in some cases, views out over the base of some of Kitzbühel's busy cable cars. Menu items are savory and designed to satisfy appetites heightened by the bracing alpine climate. You might order veal steak with fresh vegetables, pepper steak Madagascar, or venison. Many kinds of grilled steaks are regularly featured. A "Vienna pot" is one of the chef's specials, and fresh Tyrolean trout is offered daily. Begin with a Serbian bean soup or decide on a fondue bourguignonne. All the meat, sausages, and smoked meat come from the hotel's own butcher.

Hinterstadt 24. ✆ **05356/64311.** Reservations recommended. Main courses 12€–30€ ($18–$48); fixed-price menu 16€–35€ ($26–$56). AE, DC, MC, V. Daily 11am–2pm and 6–10pm. Closed mid-Apr to late May and mid-Oct to mid-Dec.

Romantik Hotel Tennerhof Restaurant ★★★ TYROLEAN You'll walk a short distance from the town center before reaching this well-run hotel, which looks like a balconied hunting lodge. Rated by some critics as one of Austria's best restaurants, it has huge windows with views that just might stop you between courses. House specialties include mushroom tarts; crayfish soufflé; tomato-cream soup; rabbit bouillon; saddle of lamb with polenta; veal medallions and asparagus; and, for dessert, curd-cheese dumplings and strawberries, freshly made sorbets, or a lemon soufflé that's renowned throughout the region. The kitchen staff is dedicated, talented, and hardworking, comfortable with both regional dishes and international specialties. You'll have a delightful time—and so will your palate.

Griesenauweg 26. ✆ **05356/63181.** Reservations required. Jacket required for men. Main courses 25€–34€ ($40–$54); fixed-price 5-course menu 48€ ($77). AE, DC, MC, V. Daily noon–2pm and 7–9:30pm. Closed Oct–Dec 16 and Tues Mar–June and Apr 12–May 14.

Moderate

The Dining Rooms in the Schloss Lebenberg ★ AUSTRIAN/INTERNATIONAL Although this hotel offers comfortable rooms, we actually prefer the Schloss Lebenberg for its well-managed restaurant and its sense of history. Originally built in 1548, it was transformed in 1885 into Kitzbühel's first family-run hotel. Since then, the royal family of Monaco has graced the dining room, along with thousands of other lesser luminaries who have appreciated the savory cuisine. The most elegant of the hotel's three dining areas is the Gobelins Room, although the other dining rooms are equally appealing and a bit less intimidating. Always reliable specialties include cream of tomato soup with gin, Tyrolean-style calves' liver, Wiener schnitzels, roulades of beef, and many desserts, which often feature mountain berries.

Lebenbergstrasse 17. ✆ **05356/69010.** Reservations required. Main courses 15€–27€ ($24–$43); 4-course fixed-price menu 45€ ($72). AE, DC, MC, V. Daily 6:45–8:45pm.

Florianistube (Value) INTERNATIONAL/TYROLEAN Named after St. Florian, patron saint of the hearth, this restaurant is in one of the less ostentatious guesthouses at the resort, and welcomes outsiders. You dine in a cozy Tyrolean *stube* (tavern), and the menu is comprehensive for a restaurant in an inn—it might include typical Austrian or Tyrolean dishes, or tournedos with mushroom sauce, spaghetti with clam sauce, or fondue bourguignonne. Cooking is reliable and the ingredients are fresh, but don't expect a lot of imagination from the kitchen staff or finesse in the service rituals. In summer, a lunch or dinner buffet is served outside in the rear garden.

In the Gasthof Eggerwirt, Goensbachgasse 12. ✆ **05356/62437.** Reservations recommended. Main courses 10€–22€ ($16–$35). AE, MC, V. Daily 11am–2pm and 6–10pm.

A Cafe: The Hottest Rendezvous Spot

Even before night falls, people make a mad dash for a seat at **Café Praxmair,** Vorderstadt 17 (✆ **05356/62646**). One of the most famous pastry shops in Austria, it's known for its Florentine cookies. Later in the evening, the Praxmair Keller offers the town's most permissive nightlife. It remains open all night, summer and winter. If it's before 5 o'clock, the item to order is hot chocolate with a "top hat" of whipped cream. Coffee costs from 3€ ($4.80); pastries go for 2.50€ to 3.25€ ($4–$5.20). The cafe is open daily from 10am to 1am; the cellar bar is open daily from 10pm to dawn.

Shopping

A promenade around the resort's center reveals shops containing all the luxury goods and sporting equipment a shopper could need to satisfy even serious binges of acquisitive lust. But if you're looking specifically for sporting goods, consider dropping into **Kitz Sport,** Jochbergerstrasse 7 (✆ **05356/62504**) or **Country Classics-Driendl-Schulze Hinmüller OEG,** Jochbergerstrasse 21 (✆ **05356/66808**), where you'll find locally handcrafted pewter, ironwork, ceramics, woodcarvings, and a small selection of folkloric clothing for men and women. For an outlet with even greater amounts of women's *trachten* (traditional clothing such as dirndls), head to **Sport Alm,** Josef Pirchl Strasse 9 (✆ **05356/71038**). Traditional clothing for men, women, and children, as well as modern, conventional clothing for all occasions, is available at **Eden,** Vorderstadt 22 (✆ **05356/62656**).

Kitzbühel After Dark

If you're lucky enough to be in Kitzbühel during July or August, you can schedule your nightly promenade to coincide with the open-air concerts that begin every Tuesday, Thursday, and Friday at 8:30pm. Musicians position themselves against one edge of the Vorderstadt, whose edges are sealed off against motorized traffic. The result is an open-air all-pedestrian party with lots of folkloric and alpine overtones. Expect alpine folk music every Tuesday and Friday, and a roster of more international music (Dixieland or free-form jazz, or perhaps a New Orleans–style blues concert) every Thursday.

Even if you arrive when a concert isn't scheduled, you can always enjoy Kitzbühel's collection of nightlife and drinking options, most of which line either edge of the resort's two most central avenues, Vorderstadt and Hinterstadt. A site whose decor you might immediately recognize as inspired by 1950s America (it contains an antique car and a replica of an old-fashioned gasoline station) is **Highways Pub,** Im Gries 20 (✆ **05356/75350**). A watering hole with a theme like that of a Victorian pub is **The Londoner,** Franz-Reisch-Strasse 4 (✆ **05356/71427**), where old-fashioned paneling and hot music sometimes have late-night clients up and dancing on the tables. A conventional dance club, usually brimming with high-altitude energy, is **Python Club,** Hinterstadt 6 (✆ **05356/63001**). A more glamorous address, with a more aggressive policy about screening rowdies from the lines that sometimes form on weekends, is **Take Five Disco,** Hinterstadt 22 (✆ **05356/71300**). Here, within a mostly black and artfully lit interior, you'll find one of the biggest settings for a dance club in town.

In winter, every Thursday from 5:30pm to around 1am, the **Alpenhotel Kitzbühel Annemarie Hirschhuber** (✆ **05356/64254**) sponsors live music that usually transforms the place into a fun and convivial dance. Admission is free at this party, held about 2km (1¼ miles) northwest of Kitzbühel's center, beside the lake.

Local residents who want to escape too constant a diet of evergreen music and ski-related raucousness head for the cool and quiet enclaves of Kitzbühel's most appealing piano bar, **The Piano Place,** in the Hotel Tennerhof, Griesenauweg 26 (✆ **05356/63181**). It features live music in winter (Dec–Apr) every Wednesday to Sunday 6pm to midnight; and in summer (late June–late Aug) every Thursday to Sunday during the same hours. The music is very, very conducive to drinking. Whiskey with soda costs around 7€ ($11); beer costs 4€ ($6.40).

A Casino

Casino Kitzbühel Although it offers a less ambitious roster of entertainment options than it did in years gone by, this remains the only (legal) gambling venue in Kitzbühel. You'll be required to show a passport before entering, after which you can wander among machines and croupiers devoted to roulette, blackjack, baccarat, poker, and slot machines. There's also a bar on-site, where you might eventually search out a perch for the observation of the sometimes-sleepy gambling action at the tables.

It's open only about 6 months out of the year, from July 1 to mid-September, and from about a week before Christmas to the end of March. During those periods, it's open daily 3pm to 3am. Unlike some other Austrian casinos, men are not required to wear jackets or ties. In the Hotel Goldener Greif, Hinterstadt 24. ✆ **05356/62300.** 20€ ($32) buys 25€ ($40) of welcome chips.

ST. JOHANN IN TYROL

St. Johann has neither the chic reputation nor the high prices of Kitzbühel. You'll save money if you stay here and go to Kitzbühel, 10km (6 miles) to the south, to enjoy the facilities there.

Essentials

GETTING THERE One **train** per hour (some express) arrives in St. Johann by way of Kitzbühel from Innsbruck (trip time: 1¼ hr.) and Salzburg (trip time: 2¾ hr.). Some trains from Salzburg require a transfer in the railway junction of Schwarzach–St. Veit. For rail information, contact ✆ **05/1717** (www.oebb.at). You can also take one of the half-dozen **buses** that run every day between St. Johann and Kitzbühel (30 min.). For **bus or train information** in Kitzbühel, call ✆ **05356/64055.** Buses also pull into St. Johann from Salzburg several times a day, stopping first at Kitzbühel (trip time: 1¾ hr.).

St. Johann lies 399km (248 miles) west of Vienna, 90km (56 miles) east of Innsbruck, and 90km (56 miles) southwest of Munich. If you're **driving** from Innsbruck, follow the A12 east to the junction with Route 312, which you take east to St. Johann.

VISITOR INFORMATION The **tourist office,** Poststrasse 2 (✆ **05352/633350;** www.st.johann.tirol.at), in the town center, is open Monday to Friday 8:30am to noon and 2 to 6pm, and Saturday 9am to noon.

Exploring St. Johann

Lying between two mountains, the **Wilder Kaiser** and the **Kitzbüheler Horn,** this village is both a summer vacation center and a winter ski resort. In summer, it has a busy open-air swimming pool, and in winter, the good ski runs appeal to both beginners and experts. A ski school and ski kindergarten, plus cross-country ski trails, add to the attractions. Bars in the snow are also popular.

Many old Tyrolean houses fill the little town with charm, and some of the traditional inns have musical evenings.

The Kaisergebirge, near St. Johann, also draws many mountain climbers.

Where to Stay

Gasthof Post ★ Gasthof Post, in the town center adjacent to the village church, is about as solid a building as you'll find in Tyrol. It was first constructed in 1224, and parts of its original wooden ceiling beams are still in place. The interior is replete with stone and wood columns and bucolic charm. Rooms range from large to intimately small and are well furnished with good beds and small private bathrooms; many open onto balconies. There's a large dining room for hotel guests and an a la carte restaurant.

Speckbacherstrasse 1, A-6380 St. Johann in Tyrol. ✆ **05352/62230.** Fax 05352/622303. www.hotel-post.tv. 45 units. Winter 154€–182€ ($246–$291) double; summer 86€–96€ ($138–$154) double. Rates include half-board. AE, DC, MC, V. Closed Apr and Nov 16–Dec 18. **Amenities:** 3 restaurants; bar; free access to nearby public indoor heated pool; room service; massage; babysitting; 1 room for those w/limited mobility. *In room:* TV, Wi-Fi.

Hotel Fischer In the village center, this solidly built four-story chalet was erected in 1972 with wooden balconies and a sun terrace framed by cascading vines. The sunny rooms are comfortable and cozy, although in some cases they're a bit on the small side. Housekeeping rates an A. The elaborately paneled dining room is open only to hotel residents, a fact that permeates it with the atmosphere of a private club. The Grander family is helpful and glad to point out nearby bars and clubs that might supplement the diversions available within the house cocktail lounge.

Kaiserstrasse 3, A-6380 St. Johann in Tyrol. ✆ **05352/62332.** Fax 05352/62332100. www.hotel-fischer.com. 36 units. Winter 114€–170€ ($182–$272) double, 180€–200€ ($288–$320) suite; summer 86€–132€ ($138–$211) double, 136€–158€ ($218–$253) suite. Rates include half-board. AE, MC, V. **Amenities:** Restaurant; bar; fitness center; sauna. *In room:* TV, Wi-Fi, hair dryer.

Hotel Park ★ **Kids** Well-scrubbed and appealing, this modern, government-rated four-star hotel made few attempts to emulate the chalet-style architecture of many of its competitors when it was built in 1973. The result is an angular, well-accessorized hotel that's among the least expensive, with a hardworking family-derived staff. Skiers appreciate its easy access to the lifts, close to the larger of the town's two gondola stations. Most rooms look out over either the ski slopes or the mountains; the others overlook a pleasant garden. All have a cozy, warm feeling, although they are not overly large. Our favorite feature in the sitting room is the copper-sheathed bonnet over the fireplace, built into a corner of two stucco walls. There's an attractive restaurant, The Park, serving Tyrolean and Austrian dishes. In summer, guests gravitate to the beer garden. The hotel is a good choice for families because it has a playground, and a supply of bicycles and mountain bikes.

Spechbacherstrasse 45, A-6380 St. Johann in Tyrol. ✆ **05352/62226.** Fax 05352/622266. www.park.at. 54 units. Winter 140€–178€ ($224–$285) double; summer 104€–114€ ($166–$182) double. Rates include half-board. AE, DC, MC, V. Parking garage 6€ ($9.60). Closed mid-Oct to mid-Dec and late Mar–late May. **Amenities:** Restaurant; bar; free access to the nearby public indoor heated pool; sauna; bike rentals; playground; babysitting. *In room:* TV, Wi-Fi, hair dryer, safe.

Where to Dine

La Rustica ITALIAN The decor is solidly elegant yet rustic, a play on both the restaurant's name and its position within a building from the 1850s in the center of the resort. But unlike many restaurants, its menu incorporates a wider-than-expected gamut of food that includes two dozen kinds of pizzas, about 20 kinds of main-course pastas, and about 20 hearty meat dishes that go well with the bracing alpine air. Most are inspired by the culinary tenets of northern (usually alpine) Italy, with the exception of a pizza Margherita, whose simple tomato-with-basil-and-garlic ingredients derive from pure Neapolitan models. Desserts are made on the premises. The clientele seems about evenly divided in its preference for either Chianti or beer.

Spechbacherstrasse 31. ✆ **05352/62843.** www.larustica.at. Reservations recommended. Main courses 6€–20€ ($9.60–$32). Pizza 6.50€–12€ ($10–$18). AE, DC, MC, V. Tues–Sun 11am–2pm and 5pm–midnight. Closed 3 weeks in Apr and 3 weeks in Oct and Nov.

7 EAST TYROL ★★★

East Tyrol (known as Österreich in German) is not geographically connected to North Tyrol. When South Tyrol was ceded to Italy in 1919 in the aftermath of World War I, East Tyrol was cut off from the rest of the province by a narrow projection of Italian land that borders Land Salzburg.

Italy, including what used to be South Tyrol, lies to the south and west, with Land Salzburg to the north and Carinthia to the east. The little subprovince, of which Lienz is the capital, is cut off from its neighbors on the north by seemingly impenetrable Alps.

Because of its isolated position, East Tyrol tends to be neglected by the average North American tourist, which is a shame. The grandeur of its scenery and the warm hospitality of its people make it worth visiting. It's crowned by the towering peaks of the **Lienz Dolomites★★**, which invite exploration. The scenery along the **Drau** and the **Isel** valleys is spectacular. These two main valleys have many little side hollows worth exploring, especially the **Virgental.** You'll see alpine pastureland, meadows, relatively undiscovered valleys, and beautiful lakes.

The Romans occupied East Tyrol in ancient times. Later the Slavs moved into the area as settlers and made it a section of Carinthia. It has known many rulers, from the Bavarians to the French. Even Great Britain had a hand in running things here, when the Allies made East Tyrol a part of the British-occupied sector of Austria from 1945 to 1955.

Since 1967, it has been possible to reach East Tyrol by taking the 5km-long (3-mile) **Felbertauern Tunnel,** a western route through the Alps. If you're driving, you can come from the east or the west. From the **Grossglockner Road,** you take the Felbertauern Road and the tunnel. If you're driving from the north to Lienz, East Tyrol's capital, you can take the Felbertauern Road from Land Salzburg, passing through the tunnel. In summer, you might want to take the Grossglockner Road and the Iselberg Pass. This road runs along the boundary between East Tyrol and Carinthia.

It's also possible to take a train from Italy to East Tyrol. Corridor trains operate between Innsbruck and Lienz as well. As you pass through Italy on this trip, the trains are locked and you don't have to show your passport or clear Italian Customs.

Woodcarving, long a pursuit in East Tyrol, is still practiced in tranquil chalets during the long winter months. You might want to shop for some pieces while you're here.

LIENZ ★

Don't confuse this city with Linz, the capital of Upper Austria. This **Lienz,** with an *e,* is the capital of East Tyrol. It sits at the junction of three valleys—the Isel to the northwest, the Puster to the west, and the Drau to the east. The old town of Lienz stretches along the banks of the Isel River, with Liebburg Palace, a 16th-century building, now the seat of local government, overshadowing Hauptplatz (Main Square).

Essentials

GETTING THERE From Innsbruck, Lienz-bound travelers can take the direct **Korridorzug train,** which involves no border formalities with Italy. The **Val Pusteria** is another connection, going via Italian territory to Lienz (trip time: 3½ hr.). From Salzburg, you'll have to change trains in the rail junction at **Spittal-Millstattersee** (3½ hr.). The **railway station** can be reached by calling ✆ **05/1717** (www.oebb.at).

A confusing array of **buses** travels among the various villages of East Tyrol. One daily bus, after many stops, travels to Lienz from Innsbruck, and another travels from Zell am See. For **bus information** in Lienz, call ✆ **04852/64944.**

From Kitzbühel (see section 8, earlier in this chapter), you can **drive** to Lienz by traveling southeast along Route 161, which becomes Route 108. From Salzburg, take the A10 southeast to the junction with Route 100 near Seeboden and follow the signs west to Lienz. Lienz lies 434km (270 miles) southwest of Vienna, 180km (112 miles) south of Salzburg, and 222km (138 miles) southeast of Munich.

VISITOR INFORMATION The **tourist office,** Europaplatz (✆ **04852/65265;** www.lienz-tourismus.at), is open Monday to Friday 8am to 6pm, and Saturday 9am to noon. In July and August it's open Monday to Friday 8am to 7pm, Saturday 9am to noon and 5 to 7pm, and Sunday from 10am to noon.

What to See & Do

Outdoor Activities

In winter, Lienz, at an elevation of 869m (2,851 ft.), attracts skiers to its two major ski areas: the **Hochstein** and the **Zertersfeld,** serviced by chairlifts and drag lifts. The height of the top station is 2,204m (7,231 ft.).

In summer, the town fills up with mountain climbers, mainly Austrians, who come to scale the Dolomites. This is a good base for many excursions in the area. For example, from Schlossberg you can take a chairlift up to **Venedigerwarte** (1,017m/3,337 ft.). You can explore the excavations of **Aguntum,** the Roman settlement, 5km (3 miles) east of Lienz, or swim in **Lake Tristacher,** 5km (3 miles) south of the city.

The Dolomites, actually the northwestern part of the Gailtal alpine range, lie between the Gail Valley and the Drau Valley: Their highest peak is the **Grosse Sandspitze** at more than 2,745m (9,006 ft.).

Exploring Lienz

Schloss Bruck and Osttiroler Heimatmuseum The showcase of Lienz, and the focal point of its civic pride, is this former stronghold of the counts of Gorz, who controlled vast medieval estates from this strategically located castle that dominated most of the access routes to the Isel Valley. In the early 1500s, it fell to the Hapsburgs. It rises impressively less than 1km (1/2 mile) west of the town center and contains a museum devoted to the history, culture, sociology, and artifacts of the region. The **Rittersaal (Knight's Hall)** shows how the castle looked in the Middle Ages. The **Albin Egger-Lienz gallery** contains an art collection of the outstanding native painter Egger-Lienz (1868–1926). Another section displays artifacts unearthed at the archaeological site of the Roman town of Aguntum.

Iseltaler Strasse. ✆ **04852/62580.** www.museum-schlossbruck.at. Admission 7€ ($11) adults, 5€ ($8) students and seniors, 2.50€ ($4) children under 16. May–Oct daily 10am–6pm. Closed Oct–May.

St. Andrä If you have time, visit the Church of St. Andrew, with its outstanding collection of 16th-century tombstones carved of marble quarried outside Salzburg. The last Gorz count is buried here. The church, consecrated in 1457, was restored in 1968. During the restoration, workmen uncovered murals, some dating from the 14th century. The church is the finest example of Gothic architecture in East Tyrol. A **memorial chapel** honors the Lienz war dead. The renowned painter Egger-Lienz is entombed here.

Patriasdorfer Strasse. Free admission. Daily 9am–5pm.

Gasthof Goldener Fisch ★ Well-maintained, carefully designed, and with an interior that was radically upgraded, this government-rated three-star hotel occupies what was originally built in the 1880s as the solid, four-story home of a prosperous local landowner. Michael and Daniela Vergeiner are the hardworking owners of a hotel whose beige-fronted facade wasn't altered during the renovations, and which, in summer, is still accented with window boxes filled with seasonal flowers. Bedrooms are monochromatic and painted in tones of beige and off-white, with shower stalls and a sense of cozy efficiency. An on-site cafe and restaurant, whose location less than 180m (591 ft.) from the town center encourages lots of local traffic, serves traditional platters of food, coffee, and drinks daily from 7am to midnight.

Kärntnerstrasse 9, A-9900 Lienz. ✆ **04852/62132.** Fax 4852/6213248. www.goldener-fisch.at. 30 units. 86€–84€ ($138–$134) double. Rates include breakfast. AE, DC, MC, V. Closed Nov. **Amenities:** Restaurant; bar; health club; sauna; children's playground; massage. *In room:* TV, Wi-Fi, hair dryer.

Gasthof-Hotel Haidenhof This appealing hotel looks like a cross between an alpine chalet and a Mediterranean villa. The windows of the hotel's central section are bordered with painted Tyrolean designs, whereas on either side, symmetrical wings stretch toward the surrounding forest. Views from the balconies of the well-furnished rooms encompass most of Lienz. Rooms are exceedingly comfortable, if a bit old-fashioned, with well maintained small bathrooms. On the premises are a sun terrace and a paneled restaurant serving regional specialties.

Grafendorferstrasse 12, A-9900 Lienz. ✆ **04852/62440.** Fax 04852/624406. www.haidenhof.at. 25 units. 120€–164€ ($192–$262) double. Rates include half-board. MC, V. Closed mid-Oct to mid-Nov. Drive 10 min. north of Lienz to the suburb of Gaimberg. **Amenities:** Restaurant; bar; lounge; fitness room; sauna; massage; nonsmoking rooms; solarium. *In room:* TV, Wi-Fi, hair dryer.

Hotel Sonne This hotel's modernized mansard roof rises from one end of Südtirolerplatz. In addition to a helpful staff, the hotel has terra-cotta floors, oriental rugs, a roof garden, and a sun-flooded restaurant with an outdoor terrace. The reservations system is tied in to the Best Western network. The cozy rooms have modern furniture and good beds. The hotel maintains a very good restaurant, the Restaurant Sonne (daily 11am–2pm and 6–10pm).

Südtirolerplatz, A-9900 Lienz. ✆ **800/780-7234** in the U.S., or 04852/63311. Fax 04852/63314. www.hotelsonnelienz.at. 62 units. 116€–138€ ($186–$221) double. Rates include breakfast. Half-board 20€ ($32) per person extra. AE, DC, MC, V. Free parking outside; garage parking 8€ ($13). **Amenities:** 2 restaurants; bar; sauna; room service; laundry service; dry cleaning; nonsmoking rooms; solarium; rooms for those w/limited mobility. *In room:* TV, Wi-Fi, minibar, hair dryer.

Romantik Hotel Traube ★★★ This hotel's location, in the very heart of town on a tree-lined street, couldn't be more ideal. The facade is painted a vivid red, with forest-green shutters and a canopy covering part of the ground-level cafe. Furnishings in the public areas are elegant and comfortable. The hotel was demolished in World War II but rebuilt in the 1950s. Rooms contain either antique furnishings or copies of traditional pieces. The comfort level is greater here than anywhere else in East Tyrol. Beds are luxurious and the bathrooms come in a range of sizes. Many windows open onto views of the nearby mountains. On the premises are a well-furnished bar and two restaurants. One restaurant is quite formal (see below); the other, less expensive one offers Italian food.

Hauptplatz, A-9900 Lienz. ✆ **04852/64444.** Fax 04852/64184. www.tiscover.at/romantikhotel-traube. 55 units. 124€–198€ ($198–$317) per person double. Rates include breakfast. AE, DC, MC, V. **Amenities:** 2 restaurants; bar; indoor heated pool; squash; tennis court; sauna; bike rental; room service; massage; babysitting; laundry service; dry cleaning. *In room:* TV, Wi-Fi, minibar, hair dryer, safe.

Where to Dine

Romantik Hotel Traube ★ AUSTRIAN/TYROLEAN/ITALIAN Amid Tyrolean accents of flowered banquettes, gilded wall sconces, and big arched windows, this airy restaurant offers elegant meals in comfortable surroundings. The cuisine here is the best in town, based on fresh ingredients deftly handled in the kitchen. Menu items run an artful line between experimental dishes and tried-and-true Tyrolean favorites. Examples include a terrine of smoked salmon with a honey-mustard sauce, an autumn salad that's dressed with olive oil and air-dried chunks of smoked lamb, filet of venison wrapped in bacon with potato terrine and Brussels sprouts, and braised joint of lamb with a gratin of leeks and braised vegetables. A fish dish that's considered a delicacy of the house, despite the unappetizing translation of its name, is *setauket* (frogfish), served on a bed of stewed tomatoes with risotto.

Hauptplatz 14. ✆ **04852/64444.** Reservations required. Main courses 9€–25€ ($14–$40); fixed-price 3-course menu 18€ ($29). AE, DC, MC, V. Tues–Sun 11am–2pm and 6–11pm. Closed Nov 1–Dec 22.

Shopping

More energy seems to be devoted to folkloric clothing in Lienz than to virtually any other product in town. Consequently, you'll find lots of outlets scattered throughout the tourist zone, one of the best of which is **Krismer,** André-Kranz-Gasse 4 (✆ **04852/62497**). The store has stacks of old-fashioned clothes (dirndls, lederhosen, loden coats, alpine hats with pheasants' feathers, embroidered suspenders) that correspond to East Tyrolean traditions. And if you're hankering for a sampling of the local breads, cheeses, sausages, and *bundnerfleisch* (air-dried alpine beef that's reminiscent of beef jerky), consider dropping into any of the well-stocked local delicatessens, a particularly worthwhile example of which is **Feinkost Zuegg,** Rechteiselkai (✆ **04852/669930**).

Lienz After Dark

No one ever seems to get thirsty in Lienz, where virtually every hotel and guesthouse has a *gemütlich*-looking *stube* (tavern) lined with varnished pine that's ready, willing, and eager to dispense steins of beer and East Tyrolean folklore. But if you're interested in equivalent bars that play dance music, consider **Life,** within the Dolomite hotel, Dolomitenstrasse 2 (✆ **04852/62962**). It features a woodsy, alpine-derived decor where dozens of steins of beer have been spilled over the years, and has been known to extend the dancing even onto the tabletops.

Incidentally, if your visit to Lienz happens to fall between early July and late September, at least part of your evening entertainment will be free. Every Saturday, Sunday, and Wednesday, beginning at 8pm, the city sponsors a 75-minute concert of traditional Tyrolean music, performed by musicians in *trachten* (traditional Tyrolean garb), from a perch within the **Hauptplatz.** The only problem with these love fests of Tyrolean nostalgia is that they simply don't last long enough.

The second weekend in August in Lienz is the scheduled time for **Stadtfest,** a public celebration of the contributions of Lienz to East Tyrolean culture. Expect kiosks scattered throughout the town's historic center selling food, wine, beer, and enough sausages to ring the city. There's also an ongoing series of afternoon and evening concerts by singers and musicians in folkloric garb, warbling away—a la Maria von Trapp—their odes to Tyrolean nostalgia.

13

Vorarlberg

Austria's westernmost province is Vorarlberg, a land of mountain villages, lakes, deep valleys, and meadowlands. In autumn, one of the most beautiful spots on the continent is the plain of the Rhine Valley near Dornbirn. This region is a mini Switzerland, and there are things to do here year-round. The three biggest attractions are the ski slopes that rival Switzerland's, the gorgeous Lake Constance, and the lush forests of the Bregenzerwald. The region's two best-known tourist centers, Lech and Zürs, are very expensive, but prices in the rest of the province are quite reasonable.

Vorarlberg's mountains make for great skiing, and slopes are linked together, offering miles and miles of trails. The Bregenz Forest, on the northern part of the Vorarlberg alpine range, has every bit as much charm and character as the Black Forest.

Two annual special events take place in Vorarlberg during the summer: the Music Festival at Hohenems, in the second half of June, which focuses on the works of Franz Schubert; and the Bregenz operas, presented on a large stage floating in Lake Constance.

From Tyrol, you head west to reach Vorarlberg: The best gateways to the province are Zürs or Lech, which are both on Route 198, north of the Arlberg Tunnel. Parking in the Vorarlberg region is rarely a problem, and, unless otherwise noted, you park for free.

1 THE WESTERN SIDE OF THE ARLBERG

We visited the east side of Arlberg in chapter 12 (Innsbruck and Tyrol), so it's time for us to tell you the "west side story" of this massif that separates Vorarlberg from Tyrol. This part of Austria is one of the major winter-sports meccas in Europe. The leading resorts on the Arlberg massif, the highest mountain range in the Lechtal Alps, include **Lech** and **Zürs.** With an **Arlberg ski pass,** you can use the 85 ski tows, chairlifts, and cable cars located in the entire Arlberg region. The Arlberg ski pass costs 46€ ($73) for adults, 27€ ($43) for children under 16, and 42€ ($67) for seniors.

Up through the **Flexen Pass,** you come to Zürs, a chic, elegant, refined resort with skiing at **Trittkopf** and **Madloch.** Lech is larger, with easier skiing on the **Kriegerhorn** and **Mohnenfluh.**

SKIING IN ZÜRS & LECH Part of the Vorarlberg's popularity stems from its two most visible and stylish resorts, **Zürs** and **Lech.** Both resorts boast lofty altitudes that are high even by central European ski-resort standards; they enjoy access to more than 1,000m (3,281 ft.) of skiable hillside above Lech and almost 700m (2,297 ft.) of carefully maintained hillsides above Zürs, where midwinter snows accumulate in deep billowing drifts.

Zürs boasts straight downhill runs that have tested the skills of Olympic champions, as well as gracefully sculpted runs that pass rocky outcrops and thickets of trees. Lech, positioned in the center of a roster of north- and east-facing bowls and slopes, offers a greater number of ski options that challenge intermediate skiers as well as the experts.

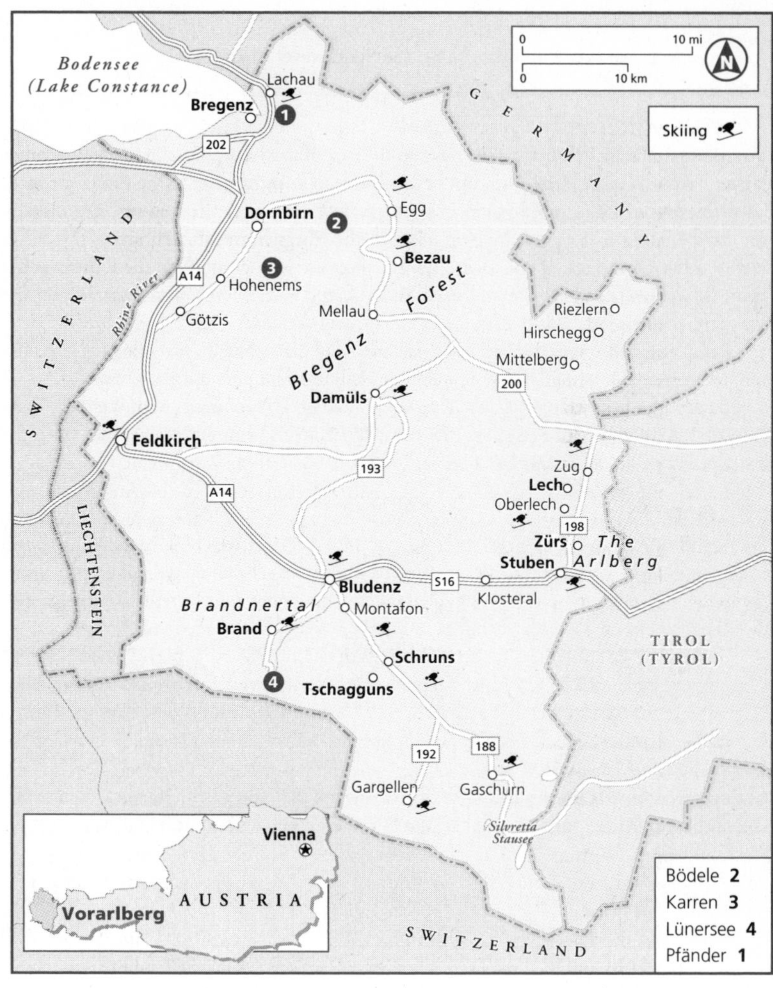

Although they are competing resorts, Zürs and Lech cooperate with each other. Chances are that the ski pass you buy will allow you access to the slopes and chairlifts of both resorts.

The 20km ($12^1/_2$ miles) of ski trails running between the two resorts offer experiences on four different mountains, and there's enough variety to qualify the area as one of the most exciting ski transits in Austria. If there are complaints about the resorts (and they certainly don't involve a lack of snow), it's only because you have to ski back into one of the villages for lunch: Dining options on the slopes are limited.

Favorite ski venues around Lech include the **Kriegerhorn** and the less-popular **Rüfikopf,** which has perilously steep slopes and is subject to avalanche danger after

Did You Know?

Local legend has it that Vorarlberg—not Mount Ararat in the Middle East—is where Noah landed with his ark after the flood waters receded.

snowstorms. In Zürs, the best skiing lies to the east of the resort, in regions known as the **Hexenboden** and the **Trittkopf,** but because of the morning glare, these slopes are most appealing in the afternoon. Morning skiers usually head out to the **Seekopf** and **Zürsersee** areas or the slopes running downhill from the **Muggengrat chairlift.**

Regardless of the resort you select, trails usually are impeccably groomed, the evening après-ski venues are the most stylish in Austria, and Vorarlberg's scenery is among the most appealing in the world.

Zürs, Lech, and the nearby ski resort Oberlech are linked by 34 lifts (the whole region has 88 lifts), all of which can be traveled on only one ski pass. Lifts and runs are close together, and it's possible to ski between Lech and Zürs. A cable car, running daily from 7am to 1am, connects Oberlech to the heart of Lech: You can take a cable car from the heart of the resort to **Rüfikopf** (2,329m/7,641 ft.).

LECH ★★

Founded in the 14th century by émigrés from the Valais district of Switzerland, Lech still has its original *Pfarrkirche* (parish church) from that era. This archetype of a snug alpine ski village is practically joined to Oberlech, a satellite resort a little farther up the mountain. Lech stands at 1,440m (4,724 ft.); Oberlech is at 1,710m (5,610 ft.).

Zürs is more fashionable, but Lech has its own claim to fame: It played host to Prince Charles and his future wife, Princess Diana. Despite its reputation as a ski resort, Lech offers some great warm-weather activities, too. In summer, visitors come here to tour the **Upper Lech Valley,** which stretches for 56km (35 miles) to a scenic valley between the Lechtal and the Allgäu Alps.

Regardless of which resort you stay in, we suggest that you go to Oberlech on a sunny day and find yourself a spot in one of the big sun-terrace restaurants.

Essentials

GETTING THERE Set in the upper regions of the Arlberg Pass, Lech has no railway connections. Visitors are best advised to take the **train** to the rail stations at either end of the Arlberg Tunnel and then transfer to a bus that winds its way up the mountain passes to Lech. Passengers from either Vorarlberg or Tyrol should get off at Langen am Arlberg, the closest station to Lech. All Zurich-Vienna express trains stop here. Passengers then transfer to one of the half-dozen daily **buses** that depart for Lech (trip time: 25 min.). For bus information and schedules, call the Lech tourist office (below).

Lech is 90km (56 miles) southeast of Bregenz, 648km (403 miles) west of Vienna, and 200km (124 miles) east of Zurich. If you're **driving** from Tyrol, take Route 198 north after you pass through the Arlberg Tunnel.

VISITOR INFORMATION The **tourist office** (✆ **05583/21610**) is in the town center. It's open in winter Monday to Saturday 8am to 6pm, Sunday 8am to noon and 3 to 5pm; in summer Monday to Saturday 8am to noon and 2 to 6pm, Sunday 8am to noon and 3 to 5pm.

Snowboarding in the Arlberg

Snowboarding techniques are taught at each of the ski schools in Arlberg's resorts. Shredders have free access to all of the region's slopes, and Lech even has several slopes that allow *only* snowboarders.

Warm-Weather Expeditions

From Mid-June to mid-September, Lech offers an **Activ-Inclusiv Program.** As part of this program, any hotel guest in Lech gains automatic free access to the five cable cars that run in the summer, tennis courts, and the indoor pool. Daily guided hikes (of various difficulties) covering 5 to 11km (3–7 miles) are also included in the program.

Where to Stay

Hotel Berghof (see "Where to Dine in Lech," below) also rents rooms.

Very Expensive

Gasthof Post ★★★ Queen Beatrix of the Netherlands frequently visited this establishment, but even without its royal clientele, it's the noblest hotel in town. Behind the hotel's chalet facade ornamented with *trompe l'oeil* murals, the Moosbrugger family displays many 18th-century items, including alpine painted chests and baroque sculpture. Rooms come in a variety of sizes, but all contain rustic decorations, double-glazed windows, beamed ceilings, and excellent beds.

The hotel's convivial gathering places include a popular sun terrace and several bars. Zither and Austrian folk music are often presented in the peak winter months.

Dorf 11, A-6764 Lech. ✆ **05583/22060.** Fax 05583/220623. www.postlech.com. 39 units. Winter 480€–680€ ($768–$1,088) double, from 750€ ($1,200) suite; summer 260€–340€ ($416–$544) double, from 400€ ($640) suite. Rates include breakfast. Half-board 30€ ($48) per person. MC, V. Parking 12€ ($19). In winter minimum stay of 7 days required. Closed late Apr to mid-June and late Sept–Nov 30. **Amenities:** 2 restaurants; bar; indoor heated pool; tennis court; fitness center; spa; Jacuzzi; sauna; children's playroom; room service; massage; babysitting; laundry service; dry cleaning; nonsmoking rooms; solarium. *In room:* TV, Wi-Fi, minibar, hair dryer, safe.

Hotel Kristiania The most advanced skiers are often attracted to this tranquil retreat because it was built by the family of Othmar Schneider, the Olympic ski champion. The many amenities make this a worthy government-rated four-star hotel. Rooms facing south have balconies and mountain views, while north-facing rooms have views of the village and the valley, but no balconies. The Kristiania is a 3- to 5-minute walk above the resort's center. Most guests leave their ski equipment at the Skiraum in the center of town, where someone will wax their skis for the following day, so that they don't have to lug them uphill to the hotel. The hotel contains a restaurant for half-board guests, and another one for a la carte diners who call and reserve a table. Austrian and international cuisine is served.

Omesberg 331, A-6764 Lech. ✆ **05583/25610.** Fax 05583/3550. www.kristiania.at. 34 units. Winter 470€–780€ ($752–$1,248) double, 840€–1,150€ ($1,344–$1,840) suite; summer 340€–360€ ($544–$576) double, 800€ ($1,280) suite. Half-board 35€ ($56) per person. AE, DC, MC, V. Parking 15€ ($24). Closed Apr 25–Dec 1. **Amenities:** 2 restaurants; bar; indoor heated pool; Jacuzzi; sauna; concierge; room service; massage; babysitting; laundry service; dry cleaning; nonsmoking rooms. *In room:* TV, Wi-Fi, minibar (in some), hair dryer, safe.

Hotel Krone ★★ (Kids) One of the two oldest and most historic hotels in Lech, this is the resort's only member of the Romantik chain, and as such it features large doses of genuine history and folkloric charm. Designed like a chalet in 1741, it was acquired by descendants of its present owners, the Pfefferkorn family, in 1865. The hotel's interior is attractively woodsy, with ceramic-tile stoves, oriental rugs, beamed ceilings, a spacious sun deck, and comfortable fireside chairs. Rooms are elegantly furnished, with exceedingly comfortable beds. Many have balconies, and the best of the doubles contain sitting rooms. Hotel guests enjoy the evening dance club, which is located in an adjoining wing to avoid disturbing the rest of the guests. Sometimes Tyrolean evenings are staged.

A-6764 Lech. ✆ **05583/2551.** Fax 05583/255181. www.kronelech.at. 51 units. Winter 300€–650€ ($480–$1,040) double, from 980€ ($1,568) suite; summer 174€–252€ ($278–$403) double, 288€–412€ ($461–$659) suite. Rates include half-board. 7-night minimum in winter. MC, V. Parking 11€ ($18) in winter, free in summer. Closed Apr 30–late June and Sept 27–late Nov. **Amenities:** Restaurant; 2 bars; dance club; indoor heated pool; fitness center; spa; Jacuzzi; sauna; children's playroom; room service; babysitting; laundry service; dry cleaning; solarium. *In room:* TV, minibar, hair dryer, safe.

Expensive

Hotel Arlberg ★★★ Built in 1965, the Hotel Arlberg is a sprawling chalet well equipped for an alpine vacation in any season, and it's one of the only government-rated five-star hotels open during the summer in Lech. The interior offers regional antiques, crafted paneling, elegant accessories, and a baronial fireplace. Rooms are excellently furnished with antiques, rugs over thick carpeting, luxuriously comfortable beds, and double-glazed windows. Most are spacious and open onto big picture windows and individual balconies. Medium-size bathrooms are done in marble with corner tubs and dual basins.

The food served in the richly outfitted dining room is as generous as the decor itself. The Schneider family directs a team of chefs who prepare a daily European specialty, as well as Austrian-inspired foods—a wide variety of game and fish dishes, cream-flavored goulash, and cream schnitzels. Guests appreciate the intimate lighting in the bar after a day in the brilliant sunshine. Meals are also served, in season, on a flower-bedecked sun terrace. The hotel is entirely nonsmoking.

A-6764 Lech. ✆ **05583/21340.** Fax 05583/213425. www.arlberghotel.at. 58 units. Winter 396€–678€ ($634–$1,085) double, 594€–816€ ($950–$1,306) suite; summer 252€–308€ ($403–$493) double, 362€–468€ ($579–$749) suite. Rates include half-board. MC, V. Free parking. Closed Apr 20–June 1 and Sept 22–Dec 1. **Amenities:** 2 restaurants; 2 bars; 2 pools (1 indoor heated, 1 outdoor available only in summer); tennis court; fitness center; spa; sauna; room service; massage; babysitting; laundry service; dry cleaning. *In room:* TV, minibar, hair dryer, safe.

Moderate

Hotel Lech and Pension Chesa Haña This very pleasant establishment, open year-round, is 5 minutes from the ski lifts. The interior of the two-chalet complex is handsomely paneled and accented with soft lighting. The recently renovated, medium-size rooms are comfortably furnished and have small but tidy bathrooms with tub/shower combinations. At the hotel restaurant, you can enjoy a fondue evening and a rustic dinner with zither music (Austrian and international cuisine is served). It is open only to hotel guests. Special events include toboggan games at night, horse-drawn sleigh rides with torches, and even cocktail parties in cable cars.

A-6764 Lech. ✆ **05583/22890.** Fax 05583/2727. www.hotel-lech.info. 40 units. 300€ ($480) double. Rates include half-board. MC, V. **Amenities:** Restaurant; bar; sauna; massage; babysitting; laundry service; dry cleaning; nonsmoking rooms; tanning beds. *In room:* TV, hair dryer, safe.

Places to Stay in Nearby Oberlech

Whereas Lech boasts medieval roots and a status as a bona-fide alpine village, Oberlech is a relatively recent creation of modern tourism, and most of the hotels here are open only in winter. Some hardy souls struggle about a kilometer (½ mile) uphill on foot from Lech to reach Oberlech, site of about 10 hotels and a grocery store. The situation is complicated by the fact that Oberlech's streets are reserved for pedestrians. The best way to reach Oberlech is to ride the **Bergbahn Oberlech cable car,** which operates daily from 7am to 1am (✆ **05583/2350** for information), from the center of Lech to Oberlech. Those with ski passes ride free. Otherwise, the roundtrip ticket costs 5.80€ ($9.30) for adults, 3€ ($4.80) for children.

If your hotel is in Oberlech, park your car at the base of the Bergbahn Oberlech (the cost of which is usually included in the price of your hotel), and carry your luggage to the cable car, whose operator will phone ahead to your hotel. An employee will usually meet you at the top to assist with your luggage.

Hotel Montana ★ *Finds* Above the village, this government-rated four-star hotel opens onto a large sun terrace looking out over Lech. The light-grained chalet has a stylish interior. Its cafe/bar area is an attractive place for an afternoon drink. Furnished in an alpine style, the rather small rooms are exceedingly cozy on long, wintry alpine nights. Bathrooms are also small but have tub/shower combinations and adequate shelf space. Owner Guy Ortlieb, an expatriate Frenchman, organizes weekly farmer buffets and cocktail parties, and does what he can to make guests feel at ease. The hotel restaurant, **Zur Kanne,** serves a high-quality French cuisine and is reviewed below (see "Places to Dine in Nearby Oberlech & Zug").

A-6764 Oberlech. ✆ **05583/2460.** Fax 05583/246038. www.montanaoberlech.at. 43 units. 280€–410€ ($448–$656) double; 600€ ($960) suite for 2. Rates include half-board. AE, MC, V. Parking 11€ ($18). Closed May-Oct. **Amenities:** Restaurant; cafe/bar; indoor heated pool; sauna; room service; babysitting; laundry service; dry cleaning. *In room:* TV, minibar, hair dryer, safe.

Sonnenburg Built as one of the first hotels in Oberlech, and opening onto the village square, this large double chalet has wood-trimmed balconies, a sun terrace looking down the hillside, and a warm, intimate, and woodsy decor. The well-maintained rooms have modern comforts, though they lack alpine charm. Nonetheless, the hotel is a welcome retreat on a snowy night, and the bathrooms, though small, are equipped with tub/shower combinations and are handsomely cared for by the bevy of maids. A short distance away—connected by an underground passage—stands the hotel's annex, Landhaus Sonnenburg, whose pleasantly furnished rooms rent for slightly less than those in the main building.

A-6764 Oberlech. ✆ **05583/2147.** Fax 05583/214736. www.sonnenburg.at. 83 units. 245€–420€ ($392–$672) double; 338€–506€ ($541–$810) suite for 2. Rates include half-board. MC, V. Closed May–Nov. **Amenities:** 3 restaurants; 2 bars; indoor heated pool; fitness center; sauna; room service; babysitting; laundry service; dry cleaning; nonsmoking rooms. *In room:* TV, minibar, hair dryer, safe.

Where to Dine

Expensive

Bauernstube/Johannisstube ★★ AUSTRIAN/INTERNATIONAL These restaurants are the best recommended and most legendary in Lech, partly because of their age and partly because of their superb cuisine. The older of the two, Bauernstube, is reportedly the oldest building in Lech, a weathered and nostalgically evocative chalet from the 1400s that serves such traditional recipes as fondues (five different kinds),

Swiss-style *raclettes* (a melted cheese dish served on bread), and T-bone steaks. The culinary star of the place, the Johannisstube, lies within the main body of the Goldener Berg Hotel, in a room that was dismantled from a 200-year-old chalet and reinstalled in this more modern building. Here, in a setting that's among the most glamorous in an admittedly glamorous town, you can enjoy carefully prepared international dishes that change according to the season and the chef's inspiration. Examples include turbot with fennel and herb sauce, grilled sea bass with saffron sauce, filets of roebuck in port-wine sauce, and homemade pâté of foie gras studded with truffles.

In the Hotel Goldener Berg, Oberlech 117. ✆ **05583/2205.** Reservations required. Main courses 28€–35€ ($45–$56). AE, DC, MC, V. Bauernstube mid-Dec to mid-Apr and late June–mid-Sept daily 11am–11pm; Johannisstube Dec to mid-Apr daily 7–11pm.

Gasthof Post Restaurant ★★ AUSTRIAN/NOUVELLE The Moosbrugger family, owners of the previously recommended Gasthof Post hotel, also presides over the restaurant, a member of Relais & Châteaux. Step into an old-fashioned imperial world of antiques, alpine paneling, and tile stoves. Many guests are on half-board, but nonresidents can select from two dining salons and an a la carte menu or, perhaps more recommendable, a fixed-price menu. The latter is expensive, but you get top-quality ingredients prepared with care and flair. Game is featured in season, and Austrian classics, including *tafelspitz,* are always served. Other delicacies include lamb, fresh fish, venison, rabbit pâté, international specialties, and an impressive dessert list.

Dorf 11, A-6764 Lech. ✆ **05583/22060.** Reservations recommended. Main courses 25€–35€ ($40–$56); fixed-price menu 45€–85€ ($72–$136). DC, MC, V. Daily 7–9pm. Closed mid-Apr to June 24 and Oct 1–Nov 30.

Hotel Berghof Restaurant ★ AUSTRIAN/INTERNATIONAL Peter Burger and his family run this popular government-rated four-star hotel dining room with white walls and wood trim. Big windows look out over the "baby lift" and the ski slopes. You might enjoy cream of cauliflower soup, saddle of lamb, *tafelspitz,* a filet of chamois with salad greens and a red-wine dressing, or medallions of veal in calvados with curried potatoes. For dessert, perhaps you'll sample a soufflé of curd cheese. Year after year, this kitchen turns out respectable and well-prepared food that has pleased some of the most demanding palates in Europe.

The Berghof is also a good place to stay. Built in 1960 and enlarged in 1995, it offers 45 rooms, each comfortably and attractively furnished. Rates for half-board are 264€ to 518€ ($422–$829) for a double room. Each room is equipped with TV, minibar, hair dryer, and safe.

A-6764 Lech. ✆ **05583/2635.** Fax 05583/26355. Reservations required. Main courses 20€–27€ ($32–$43); 5-course fixed-price dinner 28€–40€ ($45–$64). MC, V. Daily 10am–10pm. Closed Apr 20–June 1 and Sept 20–end of Nov.

Restaurant Walserstuben ★ AUSTRIAN You might want to escape your hotel dining room for at least one meal at this august establishment. The most elegant of the hotel's restaurants is in a fine dining citadel, the Walserstuben, and its smaller and more intimate salon is the Stube. Both rooms open onto a view of the mountains and contain antiques and well-oiled paneling. Prices in both are the same. Guests might begin with snails in wine sauce with garlic butter or a creamy garlic soup with bread croutons. The chef invariably prepares homemade al dente noodles, and you can count on such Austrian classics as Wiener schnitzel and *tafelspitz;* game is featured in season. You might interrupt your repast with a palate-cleansing sorbet and later follow with a walnut parfait.

The menu is well balanced and full of flavor, and you know that well-trained professionals are manning the stoves in the kitchen.

In the Hotel Schneider Almhof, Tannberg 59, A-6764 Lech. ✆ **05583/3500.** Reservations required. Main courses 28€–35€ ($45–$56). AE, DC, MC, V. Daily 12:30–2pm and 6:30–11pm. Closed Apr 24–Dec 9.

Moderate

Restaurant Panorama ★ AUSTRIAN Located in the previously recommended Hotel Krone, this a la carte restaurant is patronized by many nonguests. The Pfefferkorns are your charming hosts. The restaurant affords views of the mountains or of the village center; many diners prefer a table in the main part of the restaurant, which has a row of large windows overlooking the river and, beyond it, the rendezvous point for the ski school. You could also sit in an additional pair of smaller and more intimate *stubes* (taverns). Chef specialties include roast veal in a chicken-liver sauce and several regional recipes. One dish that invariably pleases is alpine trout from local streams prepared virtually any way you desire. A mixture of innovative and traditional dishes keeps satisfied clients coming back for more. Dishes are rich in flavor and texture, and the chefs try to use very fresh ingredients.

In the Hotel Krone, A-6764 Lech. ✆ **05583/2551.** Reservations recommended. Main courses 23€–30€ ($36–$48). MC, V. Daily noon–2pm and 7–9:30pm. Closed mid-Apr to early July and Sept 17–Dec 8.

Places to Dine in Nearby Oberlech & Zug

Auerhann ★ (Finds) AUSTRIAN/INTERNATIONAL This restaurant prides itself on its role as the oldest dining spot in and around Lech. Set on the outskirts of town, in the hamlet of Zug, the 17th-century building was originally a farmhouse. The ambience is warm, woodsy, and undeniably authentic to alpine Austria's traditions. The restaurant serves large quantities of homemade noodle dishes (studded with ham, cheese, and herbs, among other things), four kinds of fondue (Chinese, bourguignonne, cheese, and in summer, chocolate for dessert), game dishes (such as venison in red-wine sauce), plus wine and beer. Desserts tend toward traditional favorites such as strudel smothered in vanilla sauce. The kitchen seems immune to passing fads and fancies in cuisine, and turns out consistently reliable dishes based on tried-and-true methods.

Zug, A-6764. ✆ **05583/275414.** Reservations recommended. Main courses 15€–30€ ($24–$48). No credit cards. Winter Mon–Sat 11am–midnight; summer Tues–Sun 11am–midnight. Closed late May–June 30 and Oct 1–Dec 15.

Gasthof Rote Wand ★ AUSTRIAN/INTERNATIONAL Lying in the hamlet of Zug (3km/2 miles north of Lech) near the onion-domed village church, this pleasantly old-fashioned place serves meals in an unpretentious *beisl* (bistro) tradition. Prince Rainier and Caroline of Monaco, King Hussein of Jordan, and Princess Diana all dined at this rustic restaurant. A specialty of the house is *spätzle* (pasta) with cheese; roast veal and pork, warm cabbage salad, and *tafelspitz* (boiled beef) are also available. Some diners come for the fondue bourguignonne or *chinoise,* which you could precede with a soup made from puree of venison. If you're up for dessert, the hot curd strudel is heavenly.

The Gasthof Rote Wand now offers 26 rooms and in 1998 they built 12 apartments. A standard room costs 322€ to 462€ ($515–$739) per person including half-board. Apartments cost 420€ to 600€ ($672–$960) per person including half-board.

Zug, A-6764. ✆ **05583/3435.** Reservations required. Main courses 18€–36€ ($29–$58). MC, V. Mon–Sat 6–9pm. Closed late Apr–Nov 30.

Zur Kanne FRENCH/ALSATIAN/AUSTRIAN This restaurant is run by Alsace-born Guy Ortlieb, who operates the previously recommended Hotel Montana and sets very high standards. It's known for serving the best fish in the valley, including a filet of freshwater *fera* from Lake Constance. You might begin with homemade foie gras and then follow with filet of roebuck in red-wine sauce. The waiter presents a menu with no prices—the fixed-price menus are best. Many customers prefer to dine on the sun terrace, even during the chilly winter months when electric heaters are strategically placed.

In the Hotel Montana, Oberlech, A-6764. ✆ **05583/2460.** Reservations required for dinner. Main courses 28€–38€ ($45–$61); fixed-price dinner 46€–58€ ($74–$93). MC, V. Daily noon–6pm and 7–9:30pm. Closed Apr 27–Nov 27.

Shopping

Most of the shops in Lech line the resort's main thoroughfare, the **Hauptstrasse,** and all steadfastly refuse to identify themselves with an individual street number. Lech offers sporting equipment from almost every important manufacturer in Europe. Three of the most impressive shops include **Sportalp** (✆ **05583/2110**), **Sporthaus Strolz** (✆ **05583/2361**), and **Pfefferkorn** (✆ **05583/2224**), all on Hauptstrasse. If you're interested in souvenirs or folkloric clothing, Sporthaus Strolz and Pfefferkorn both offer Austrian handicrafts, lederhosen, and traditional Austrian clothing.

Lech Après-Ski & After Dark

Lech has the finest après-ski life in Vorarlberg, and if you ever get bored here, you can check out the action at the satellite resorts or go over to Zürs.

The evening begins with a tea dance at the **Hotel Tannbergerhof** (✆ **05583/2202**), where Veronica Heller welcomes you; later in the evening you can enjoy disco music. It's open from December to April 14 daily from 9pm to 5am. Beer starts at 4.50€ ($7.20); hard drinks start at 10€ ($16).

The previously recommended **Hotel Krone** (✆ **05583/2551**) is a major nightlife spot in Lech. Its magnet in winter is the **K Bar,** where there's live music from the 1950s through the 1980s, and evergreen music is often featured. Beers cost 4.50€ to 8€ ($7.20–$13). It's open daily from 10pm to 4am, and there's no cover. The hotel lounge also occasionally has a zither player. In summer, about twice a week, depending on demand, folkloric evenings are presented for free.

Oberlech's **Red Umbrella,** operated by the December-to-April **Petersboden Sport Hotel** (✆ **05583/3232**), is the most famous afternoon rendezvous for skiers in the Lech area. The hydraulically operated red umbrella, approximately 36 feet wide, is set on an elevated wooden deck. It's raised at 10am each morning and lowered each afternoon at 4 or 5pm, depending on business. Under the umbrella there's a circular bar where you can sit on a stool and order drinks such as *Jägertee* (laced with rum) or vodka *feigen* (with figs floating in it). Of course, in this cold, schnapps remains the favorite drink. The food here is simple and filling; a popular item is *germknödel,* a jam-stuffed steamed dumpling covered with poppy seeds. Meals begin at 12€ ($19). If the weather is bad, you can retreat to the hotel to eat, drink, and warm yourself by a log fire.

STUBEN

This little village and winter resort is almost a suburb of Lech, lying on the southern fringes of the larger village on the west side of the Arlberg Pass. Stuben can be reached by bus, but the most romantic way to go from Lech is by horse-drawn sleigh.

The hamlet has been a way station for alpine travelers for many centuries, but in recent years, it has become a modern ski area with its own lift station on **Albona.** (It was the birthplace of Hannes Schneider, the great ski instructor.) Stuben is not as glamorous as Zürs, but its prices are much more reasonable and its location is just fine for skiers. Stuben has links with St. Anton in the Tyrol, as well as with Lech and Zürs.

Stuben is especially geared for family enjoyment, with children's ski courses, special meals, and hosts who help the small fry feel at home.

The helpful tourist office (✆ **05582/3990**) is inside the Hotel Post (under separate management) in the Village center. It's open in winter daily 9am to noon and 3 to 6pm; in summer Monday to Friday 9am to noon.

Essentials

GETTING THERE Although a casual glance at some maps might lead newcomers to believe that Stuben lies on the main rail lines between Innsbruck and Bregenz, this is not the case. Stuben-bound passengers must get off the **train** at the tunnel's western mouth, **Langen am Arlberg,** and then take one of the dozen or so daily **buses** that wind their way upward during the 10-minute ride to Stuben. For rail information, contact ✆ **05/1717** (www.oebb.at).

Drivers should follow the directions to Lech and then follow signs to Stuben, which is 10k (6 miles) south of Lech and 24km (15 miles) east of Bludenz.

Where To Stay

Hotel Mondschein ★★ This building dates from 1739, when it was constructed as a rambling private home near the village church. Today it's the second-oldest hotel in Stuben, and its antique accents include forest-green shutters and weathered siding. The snug and cozy rooms have alpine accents and comfortable beds. Crackling fires add to the ambience (and warmth), and secondary heating is provided by traditional ceramic-tile stoves. The hotel is a well-recommended government-rated three-star choice.

A-6762 Stuben. ✆ **05582/511.** Fax 05582/736. www.mondschein.com. 46 units. 170€–270€ ($272–$432) double. Rates include half-board. MC, V. Parking 8.50€ ($14). **Amenities:** Restaurant; bar, indoor heated pool; fitness center; sauna; babysitting; laundry service; dry cleaning; nonsmoking rooms; après-ski parties in mountain hut; solarium. *In room:* TV.

Hotel Post ★ When it was built in 1608, this comfortable, government-rated three-star hotel served as a shelter for tired mail-coach drivers. Most of the rustically attractive public rooms have fireplaces and deep-seated chairs. On the premises are a dining room and two old *stubes,* or taverns, where people can drink and dine a la carte. In 1997, a third *stube* was added to the existing two, using old timbers and antique panels removed from an older site for authenticity. The hotel is just at the edge of the village. Accommodations are spacious and decorated in a bright alpine style. Rooms at the nearby Hunting Lodge Post, or Jägdhaus (which is part of the hotel), cost the same but are slightly less desirable.

A-6762 Stuben. ✆ **05582/761.** Fax 05582/762. 40 units. Winter 170€–280€ ($272–$448) double; summer 94€–130€ ($150–$208) double. Rates include half-board. One week minimum stay in winter. DC, MC, V. Parking 8.50€ ($14) in garage, free outside. Closed May–June and Oct–Nov. **Amenities:** Restaurant; bar; sauna; steam bath; room service (7am–10pm); massage; nonsmoking rooms; solarium. *In room:* TV, minibar.

ZÜRS ★

An immaculate resort lying 4km (2½ miles) south of Lech in a sunny valley, Zürs (1,708m/5,604 ft.) consists of about 1km (½ mile) of typical white stucco Vorarlberger buildings with carved-wood balconies. The resort, really a collection of extremely expensive hotels, is reached via the scenic **Flexen Road.**

Zürs is strictly a winter resort, and nearly all hotels close in summer. Because of its location, Zürs is avalanche prone, but these potential snowslides do not deter the loyal Zürs clientele.

Zürs (pronounced *Seurs*) is one of the world's most elegant resorts (more formal than Lech), and it's a favorite of royalty and film stars. Although Zürs is far more elite than either St. Moritz or Gstaad, it lacks their ostentatious attitudes. The resort has 130 ski instructors, and the snow here has been compared to talcum powder. Wealthy guests, many from South America, often have their own personal teachers.

A chairlift east of Zürs takes you to **Hexenboden** (2,349m/7,707 ft.), and a cable lift goes to **Trittkopf** (2,402m/7,881 ft.), which has a mountain restaurant and sun terrace.

In the west, a chairlift will take you to **Seekopf** (2,188m/7,179 ft.), and from the windows and terrace of the restaurant here, you can see the frozen **Zürser Lake.** A chairlift travels from Seekopf to the top station at 2,451m (8,041 ft.).

The year-round population of Lech is 1,000 people, but the year-round population of Zürs is just 100: Zürs is almost dead in the summer. Guests to Zürs are smug about returning season after season, some for as many as 30 years in a row, and it seems like everyone knows everyone else. Every hotel in Zürs has facilities that let guests ski directly up to a point near the hotel's entrance.

Essentials

GETTING THERE The **buses** described in the Lech section (p. 406) stop in Zürs about 10 minutes before their scheduled arrival in Lech. Likewise, if you're **driving,** follow the same directions for Zürs as for Lech (p. 406). Zürs is 90km (56 miles) southeast of Bregenz, 34km (21 miles) east of Bludenz, and 43km (27 miles) west of Landeck in Tyrol. If you're arriving at the Zurich airport, as many do, Zürs is 240km (149 miles) east. Many of the hotels offer shuttle bus service from the airport to Zürs.

The nearest **railway station** is in the town of **Langen,** 14km (9 miles) away. It receives six or seven direct trains a day from Innsbruck (trip time: 1 1/3 hours). For rail information, contact ✆ **05/1717** (www.oebb.at). From Langen, yellow postal buses and taxis make frequent runs to and from Zürs.

VISITOR INFORMATION The **tourist office** (✆ **05583/2245**) is in the town center. It's open Monday to Saturday 8am to 6pm, Sunday 8am to noon and 3 to 5pm.

Where to Stay

This is one of the most expensive ski resorts in the world—*prices are loaded.* If you're seeking bargains, you'll have to go to a more modest resort. The Hotel Hirlanda (see "Where to Dine," below) also rents rooms.

Very Expensive

Central Sporthotel Edelweiss ★ One of the genuinely "picturesque" hotels of Zurs, with balconies and an old-fashioned look that corresponds to its role as one of the two oldest hotels in town, this hotel has kept up with modern tastes and a kind of urban-hipster mode that corresponds well with upscale clients from Munich and Vienna. Bedrooms are spacious yet cozy and brightly painted, with handsome furniture and comfy beds, and throughout there's a staff with advice about nearby ski trails and outdoor diversions. The hotel has an elegant dining room reserved for residents on half-board, as well as an additional two eateries, the ultra-upscale gourmet venue known as Chesa, with seating for a maximum of only 30 diners at a time, and the more democratic (and cheaper) Flexenhäusl, a mountainside affair specializing in fondues, which is open to the general public.

A-6763 Zürs. ✆ **05583/2662.** Fax 05583/3533. www.edelweiss.net. 65 units. 190€–351€ ($304–$562) per person double; 219€–450€ ($350–$720) per person suite. Rates include half-board. MC, V. Parking 15€ ($24). Closed May–early Dec. **Amenities:** 2 restaurants; bar; nightclub; fitness center; sauna; boutiques; room service; massage; babysitting; laundry service; dry cleaning; solarium. *In room:* TV, minibar, hair dryer, safe.

Hotel Zürserhof ★★★ An exclusive and private world unto itself, this hotel—the most luxurious of mountain refuges—consists of five interconnected chalets in the shelter of an alpine valley. Some of its more generous competitors cite it as the best hotel in central Europe, with virtually everything under one roof, and it really is a small, self-sufficient city in its own right. The hotel grew out of a house erected by the Count and Countess Valley Tattenbach in 1927. Film stars, royalty, and various VIPs from around the world have long been attracted to this destination, the hotel that put Zürs on the tourist map.

Accommodations consist of private apartments, many of which have stone fireplaces, bars, double-glazed windows looking out onto mountain views, and other opulent comforts. Rooms blend contemporary and rustic features perfectly. The spacious bathrooms have plenty of shelf space, robes, and tub/shower combinations. Suites have Roman-style baths. The public areas are decked out with old panels, antiques, and Persian carpets.

There's music almost every night in the cellar bar. The hotel's restaurant is reviewed below (see "Where to Dine").

A-6763 Zürs. ✆ **05583/2513.** Fax 05583/3165. www.zuerserhof.at. 81 units. 410€–825€ ($656–$1,320) per person double, 900€–3,400€ ($1,440–$5,440) suite. Rates include full board. MC, V. Free parking. Closed mid-Apr to early Dec. **Amenities:** Restaurant; bar; indoor heated pool; 4 tennis courts; fitness center; Jacuzzi; sauna; room service; massage; babysitting; laundry service; dry cleaning; solarium. *In room:* TV, minibar, hair dryer, safe.

Sporthotel Lorunser ★★★ The late Princess Grace of Monaco used to send her children to this luxurious five-star hotel, and Queen Beatrix of the Netherlands sometimes stays here during her winter holidays. Designed with cedar shingles, stucco, and regional paintings around the windows, the five-story hotel has intricately carved ceiling beams, open fireplaces, and elegant accessories and furnishings. Most accommodations have one spacious bedroom with ample and rather luxurious beds topped with eiderdowns, plus a sofa and a painted armoire. Some of the junior suites also have a separate sitting area.

The hotel serves some of the best food in Zürs, but the dining room is open only to hotel guests. In the right sunny weather, lunch can be served on a spacious terrace with an "ice bar." The constantly changing dinner menu features five courses served in a series of interconnected dining rooms. From the poultry liver parfait with apple-nut salad to the main course of succulent stuffed breast of farmer's chicken flavored with tarragon, the cuisine is scrumptious. The chef has a motto: Serve only what's fresh, never repeat the menu, and always be inventive. Men most often wear jackets in the evening at the height of the season.

A-6763 Zürs. ✆ **05583/22540.** Fax 05583/225444. www.lorunser.at. 60 units. 338€–562€ ($541–$899) double; 590€–698€ ($944–$1,117) suite for 2. Rates include full board. MC, V. Parking 10€ ($16). Closed mid-Apr to mid-Dec. **Amenities:** Restaurant, bar; fitness rooms; spa; Jacuzzi; sauna; room service; massage; babysitting; laundry service; dry cleaning; nonsmoking rooms. *In room:* TV, hair dryer, safe.

Expensive

Hotel Enzian ★ Set above the bustle of Zürs, this symmetrical chalet offers a tasteful combination of wood walls, coffered ceilings, and fireplaces where you can snuggle up après-ski, plus a sauna where you can relax your tired muscles. Your sports-loving hosts do everything they can to create an informal ambience. The well-appointed rooms and suites have many modern extras. The hotel's newer rooms (added in the early 1990s) are more luxurious and have more amenities than the rooms in the hotel's older core. Bathrooms are spacious, with towel warmers and tubs (except for eight rooms, which have showers). The hotel is at the edge of the village, on a hill behind a church and near the cable-car station—you can ski from the front door to all the lifts. You'll enjoy a glass of Glühwein in the international alpine *stube* (tavern). On the premises are two dining rooms, a cozy bar, and a sun terrace with waiter service.

A-6763 Zürs. ✆ **05583/22420.** Fax 05583/3404. www.hotelenzian.com. 36 units. 228€–246€ ($365–$394) double; 300€–398€ ($480–$637) suite for 2. Rates include half-board. MC, V. Parking 9€ ($14) in garage, free outside. Closed May–Nov. **Amenities:** 2 restaurants; bar; high-tech indoor golf course; squash court; fitness center; spa; sauna; game room; room service; massage; babysitting; laundry service; dry cleaning; nonsmoking rooms. *In room:* TV, minibar, hair dryer, safe.

Hotel Erzberg ★★ (Finds) Within its category, this is one of the most appealing hotels in Zürs. The hotel's location, close to the ski lifts, is ideal. Built in 1972, the comfortable interior features wrought iron, soft lighting, and softly burnished paneling crafted from local pines. Rooms are cozy and warm, and each contains a good bed and a well-equipped private bathroom. Much of the bar's charm derives from the live music provided by the Wolff family.

Although there's a separate restaurant on the premises that's open to the public, hotel residents dine in their own dining room. Regardless of where it's consumed, the food is well prepared, flavorful, and served in generous quantities. The day begins with a buffet breakfast, and dinner is four courses, including a big salad buffet. Sometimes the hotel arranges special events, such as candlelight dinners and welcome cocktail parties.

A-6763 Zürs. ✆ **05583/26440.** Fax 05583/264444. www.hotel-erzberg.at. 26 units. 176€–324€ ($282–$518) double; 280€–416€ ($448–$666) junior suite. Rates include half-board. MC, V. Free parking outdoors, 13€ ($21) in covered garage. Closed late Apr–Nov. **Amenities:** Restaurant; bar; sauna; room service; babysitting; laundry service; dry cleaning; nonsmoking rooms. *In room:* TV, hair dryer, safe.

Where to Dine

Hotel Hirlanda ★ AUSTRIAN This hotel, originally built as a small inn in the 1920s, houses a popular restaurant frequented by ski instructors. The kitchen prepares hearty Vorarlberg fare as well as gastronomically delicate dishes. The grill uses different kinds of wood, which gives meat a pungent and savory flavor; the wine cellar is impressive as well. You might begin with onion soup served with cheese and croutons, or perhaps lobster-stuffed ravioli. Spicy seasoned filet steaks are prepared on the wooden charcoal grill. Barbary goose with orange sauce is another delectable main course. The pastry chef concocts different surprises every night, perhaps Málage sabayon with mango slices. The owners keep the fireplace blazing to take the chill off the coldest winter night.

Twenty-nine cozy, alpine-style bedrooms are also rented. On the half-board plan, doubles cost 240€ to 380€ ($384–$608), and suites are 320€ to 450€ ($512–$720). The minimum stay is 5 days. Parking costs 11€ ($18).

A-6763 Zürs. ✆ **05583/2262.** Reservations required. Lunch main courses 17€–30€ ($27–$48); dinner main courses 22€–30€ ($35–$48). MC, V. Daily 11am–2pm and 7–11pm. Closed mid-Apr to early Dec.

Hotel Zürserhof Restaurant ★★★ INTERNATIONAL A rich and famous clientele dines here, occasionally in black tie in season, especially for the twice-a-week galas. Though dress codes have been relaxed, few other hotels within central Europe match the Zürserhof's glamour and sophistication. The cuisine is of the finest international standard, and the service is the best at the resort. Even the unpretentious cuisine of rural Austria is expensive here (although well prepared). Main courses might include a delectable roast suckling pig, Viennese roast chicken, roast veal, bratwurst, and roast pork. Many guests prefer to dine in the *stube,* which has a traditional alpine decor. The kitchen also prepares the most beautiful cheese buffet in town.

Zürs, A-6763. ✆ **05583/2513.** Reservations required. Main courses 25€–35€ ($40–$56). MC, V. Daily noon–2pm and 7:30–9pm. Closed mid-Apr to Oct.

Restaurant Chesa INTERNATIONAL This sporty, elegant place is run by the Strolz family. The restaurant is decorated in Kaiser gold, yellow, and green, and its ambience is stimulating on a winter's night. Main courses include zander filet with a warm vinaigrette sauce, or beef filet stuffed with goose liver and served with a sabayon of chives and quickly sautéed vegetables. The cheese board is impressive, as is the wine list. A fresh salad buffet is offered daily, along with whole-food selections for health-conscious guests. After dinner, many guests head to the basement dance club for late-night entertainment.

In the Central Sporthotel Edelweiss, Zürs, A-6763. ✆ **05583/2662.** Reservations required. Main courses 12€–26€ ($19–$42). MC, V. Tues–Sun noon–2pm and 7–9:30pm. Closed May–Nov.

Zürs After Dark

After dinner, many hotel guests retreat to their hotel bars—or even up to their rooms—for privacy and R&R before braving the wilds of the Tyrolean Alps for another day of skiing. But if you're tempted to go dancing, the resort's two dance clubs are **Vernissage,** in the Robinson Club Alpenrose (✆ **05583/2271**), and the **Disco Zürserl,** in the Hotel Edelweiss (✆ **05583/2662**). Neither charges any cover; beers cost around 4.50€ ($7.20) each. Of the two, Vernissage is likely to be more crowded because of its location within the largest hotel in Zürs. Both open for business at 10pm and continue until the last client staggers home.

2 THE MONTAFON VALLEY ★★

Montafon is a high alpine valley known for its sun and powdery snow. It stretches some 42km (26 miles) at the southern tip of Vorarlberg, with the Ill River flowing through on its way to join the Rhine. The valley, filled with mountain villages and major winter recreation areas, is encircled by the mountain ranges of Rätikon, Silvretta, and Verwall.

Montafon has been called a "ski stadium" because of its highly integrated ski region. One ski pass covers unlimited use of 70 cable cars, chairlifts, and T-bars in all four of the valley's main ski areas, as well as transportation among the resorts.

Hochjoch-Zamang offers skiing in the back bowls and down the front, and is the main mountain at Schruns (of Hemingway fame). Tschagguns has **Grabs-Golm** for some easier runs. **Silvretta-Nova** at Gaschurn and St. Gallenkirch is a superb ski circus on several mountains, and the **Schafberg** of Gargellen is secluded in a side valley.

EXPLORING SCHRUNS & TSCHAGGUNS ★

Schruns is the largest resort in the Montafon Valley, lying on the right bank of the Ill River. Tschagguns (a smaller resort) is on the left, and the hamlets are so close (less than 1.5km/1 mile apart) that they can be treated as one.

Although known for their winter sports, these towns are also popular in summer. The warm-weather allure here revolves around walking, hiking, and climbing in the alpine majesty of the Vorarlberg. Locals pride themselves on the nearness of **Pizbuin,** the highest peak in the Vorarlberg (more than 3,660m/12,008 ft. above sea level). Throughout the Montafon Valley, yellow-and-black signs point out natural attractions and destinations, and how long it will take to get there. For more information about climbing and hiking, call **Bergfuhrer Montafon** (**© 066443/11445;** www.montafon.bergfuhrer.at), a local climbing club. Ski lift passes are also sold in the summer (for hiking and climbing, not skiing). These passes include unlimited lift rides as well as free access to all the valley's public pools. For more information, call the tourist office.

Above Tschagguns, at Latschau, you can take a cable railway or chairlift to **Grabs-Golm** at 1,388m (4,554 ft.), a small but fascinating ski region with several lifts, including a four-person lift going up to 2,135m (7,005 ft.). These slopes attract both beginners and experts alike, and are known for World Cup races. While you're at Golm, you can stop at a rustic little restaurant or a modern self-service one, and then take the surface lift to Hochegga at 1,587m (5,207 ft.).

Ernest Hemingway spent winters at Schruns writing *The Sun Also Rises.*

Essentials

GETTING THERE Almost two dozen **trains** depart from Bludenz every day for Schruns (trip time: 22 min.). Schruns is the last stop on this line, and several buses head into the nearby valleys from Schruns. For rail information, contact **© 05/1717** (www.oebb.at).

About two **buses** per day depart from Bludenz's railway station and arrive at Schruns in around 20 minutes. From the railway station in Schruns, about a dozen buses per day make the 3-minute trip to Tschagguns's main square, **Dorfplatz.** If you are laden with luggage, you might want to take a taxi.

Schruns is 698km (434 miles) west of Vienna and 63km (39 miles) southeast of Bregenz. From Bregenz, **drive** southeast along Autobahn A14 until you reach Bludenz. At Bludenz, follow the MONTAFON signs and head up the valley until you reach Schruns.

VISITOR INFORMATION The **tourist office** (**© 05556/721660**) is located at Postfach 145, in the village center of Schruns. Open Monday to Friday 8am to 6pm, Saturday 8am to noon and 4 to 6pm, and Sunday 11am to noon and 4 to 6pm.

WHERE TO STAY

In Schruns

Hotel Krone Value Owned by members of the Gmeiner family since 1847, this yellow baroque building has white trim, black shutters, and a hipped roof with at least one pointed tower. It's one of the few baroque structures in a resort loaded with chalets. The hotel has a shaded beer garden, a collection of rustic artifacts, and ornate paneling whose rich glow is reflected in the leaded windows. Rooms are pleasantly furnished, comfortable, and snug, with excellent beds and small shower-only bathrooms. The in-house restaurant, the Montafoner Stube, offers well-prepared and beautifully served cuisine. It's open daily for lunch and dinner, and welcomes everyone.

Ausserlitz 2, A-6780 Schruns. ✆ **05556/72255.** Fax 05556/7225522. www.austria-urlaub.com. 12 units. Winter 142€–164€ ($227–$262) double; summer 116€–122€ ($186–$195) double. Rates include half-board. MC, V. Closed 3 weeks in May and 3 weeks in Nov. **Amenities:** Restaurant; bar; sauna; room service. *In room:* TV, minibar, hair dryer, safe.

Löwen Hotel Schruns ★★ Built in 1974, this is the most lavish hotel in Schruns. The hotel's creative designers decided to give guests the best of both the alpine and modern worlds. The rambling chalet sits back on a large lawn in the center of town. The shrub-dotted lawn, however, actually rests on top of a modern steel, glass, and concrete construction. In many ways, this is a town social center and, except for outdoor recreation, it provides almost everything you need. Rooms are imaginatively designed and well furnished, with good, comfortable beds and small bathrooms.

The hotel contains the upscale Restaurant Edel-Weiss, which serves nouvelle cuisine, and the more casual and more *gemütlich* Restaurant Barga. The most desirable corner of the Restaurant Barga is the Montafoner Stube, where wood paneling and alpine accessories foster warmth and a sense of well-being. The hotel is the major after-dark venue in the area (see "Schruns & Tschagguns after Dark," below).

Silvrettastrasse 8, A-6780 Schruns. ✆ **05556/7141.** Fax 05556/73553. www.loewen-hotel.com. 85 units. Winter 260€–420€ ($416–$672) double, 360€–510€ ($576–$816) suite; summer 230€–310€ ($368–$496) double, 350€–410€ ($560–$656) suite. Rates include half-board. AE, DC, MC, V. Parking 6€ ($9.60). Closed Apr 20–May 16 and late Oct to mid-Dec. **Amenities:** 2 restaurants; bar; dance club; 2 heated pools (1 indoor, 1 outdoor); fitness center; Jacuzzi; sauna; salon; room service; massage; babysitting; laundry service; dry cleaning; nonsmoking rooms; rooms for those w/limited mobility. *In room:* TV, minibar, hair dryer, safe.

In Tschagguns

Hotel Montafoner Hof ★★ This government-rated four-star hotel, run by the Tschohl family, is the premier resort at Tschagguns. A striking peach color on the outside, the Montafoner Hof is decorated inside with Austrian woods to lend it an authentic alpine atmosphere; however, the hotel (built in 1987) is completely modern in other respects. All of the well-furnished rooms come with good beds, lounge corners, and balconies with mountain views, plus small but well-organized bathrooms with ample shelf space and tub/shower combinations.

The Montafon Stube offers a rather glamorous fixed-price menu. The lobby bar and a hideaway near it, the Kaminstube, offer comfortable armchairs and sofas positioned in front of a blazing fireplace with lots of alpine artifacts. This is a popular après-ski venue.

Finds The Gathering Place of Town

Café Feuerstein, Dorfstrasse 6, Schruns (✆ **05556/72129**), is the best-known place in town for ice cream and pastries. Housed in an antique building in the town center, the establishment serves attractively decorated pastries—some are miniature works of art. Coffee begins at 2.50€ ($4); pastries start at 2.60€ ($4.20), and individual pizzas range from 6€ to 12€ ($9.60–$19). It's open noon to 9pm. Closed Easter to June and late October to mid-December.

Across the street, less expensive meals are served in the 4-century-old **Gasthof Löwen,** operated by the hotel's owner and closed mid-June to July 7. The *tagesmenu* (day's menu) costs 16€ ($26) and because of its reasonable prices, the restaurant is also popular with local residents.

Kreuzgasse 9, A-6774 Tschagguns. ✆ **05556/71000.** Fax 05556/71006. www.montafonerhof.com. 50 units. Winter 232€–346€ ($371–$554) double, 246€–372€ ($394–$595) suite for 2; summer 130€–248€ ($208–$397) double, 174€–274€ ($278–$438) suite for 2. Rates include half-board. DC, MC, V. Closed Easter–May 12 and Oct 26–Dec 10. **Amenities:** Restaurant; bar; inside-outside heated pool; fitness center; Jacuzzi; sauna; room service; babysitting; laundry service; dry cleaning; rooms for those w/limited mobility. *In room:* TV, minibar, hair dryer, safe.

SCHRUNS & TSCHAGGUNS AFTER DARK

Be aware that Schruns offers a wider range of nightlife than the smaller and sleepier Tschagguns, where a drink or two beside a flickering fire in any of the resort's hotels might be the most popular after-ski activity.

In Schruns, the previously recommended Löwen Hotel offers more energy and a greater number of options than anything else in town. Its dance club, **Löwen Grube,** is open nightly from 9pm to at least 3:30am from December to late April. The evening invariably begins with a spate of live Montafon Valley evergreen music that's performed from 9 to 11pm. After that, disco rules till closing. Entrance is free. A calmer, more contemplative bar that's undeniably cozy is the Löwen Hotel's **Kamin Bar.**

There are no equivalent dance clubs in Tschagguns, although if you prefer something a bit quieter—or a bit earlier in the afternoon—there's a fire blazing in the Montafoner Hof's rustically appointed and very charming **Kaminstube** whenever temperatures justify it. It's open in winter daily 3pm to 3am.

3 THE BRAND VALLEY ★★

Often visited from Bludenz, the Brand Valley (Brandnertal in German) is one of Austria's most scenic valleys, a place of rare beauty surrounded by glaciers. The valley runs for about 15km (10 miles) before reaching Brand, and along the way are romantic little villages and lush pastureland set against a panoramic alpine backdrop. This valley offers a wealth of inns and hotels, especially at Brand, and skiers are drawn to the mountain ranges, namely **Niggenkopf** and **Palüd.**

ESSENTIALS

GETTING THERE No rail lines run into Brand. The easiest way to reach the resort is by taking the **train** to Bludenz, from which about a dozen **buses** per day make the 30-minute trip to Brand. Each bus makes at least five different stops in Brand, whose city limits sprawl for several miles beside the valley's main highway.

Brand is 69km (43 miles) south of Bregenz, 10km (6 miles) southwest of Bludenz, and 171km (106 miles) east of Zurich. To reach it by **car,** follow the directions to Bludenz (see above) and then cut southwest along the road that's marked BRAND.

VISITOR INFORMATION The **tourist office** (✆ **05559/555**) is in the town center. It's open in winter Monday to Friday 9am to noon and 2 to 5pm.

EXPLORING BRAND

A few centuries ago, exiles from the Valais, in Switzerland, settled this village at the mouth of the Zalimtal, near the Swiss border. At an elevation around 1,035m (3,396 ft.),

Brand has long been a popular mountain health resort spread out along a mile-long stretch at the base of the Scesaplana mountain range. It's now a much-visited winter-sports center, the main resort of the **Rätikon district** of Vorarlberg.

You can take a cableway to the top of the **Tschengla,** at 1,250m (4,101 ft.), as well as a chairlift to **Eggen,** at 1,270m (4,167 ft.). From Eggen, it's easy to make connections to **Niggenkopf,** at 1,600m (5,249 ft.).

About 6km (4 miles) south of Brand, beside the only road leading south of town (it's an extension of the Hauptstrasse and is marked LUNERSEE), you'll find the **Lunersee Talstation.** Here, hardy souls can start a 1-hour climb leading steeply uphill to the **Lunersee (Lake Luner) ★★**, a glacial lake whose size has been increased with the construction of a dam and whose western edge abuts the frontier of Switzerland. If you find the climb daunting, you can take a cable car, Bergbahnen Brandnertal. It operates from May 5 to October 26 daily from 8:30am to noon, and then from 1:30 to 4:30pm. The cost roundtrip for adults is 9.50€ ($15), 7.50€ ($12) for students and persons under 18, free for children under 5 when accompanied by a parent. Once you're there, you might opt for a relatively flat walk around the austere-looking lake, a trek that takes most hikers about 2 hours. Remember that the last cable car downhill departs at 5pm.

WHERE TO STAY & DINE

Hotel Scesaplana ★ In the resort's center, this hotel has been tastefully modeled after a chalet, with wood accents, accommodating sun terraces, and balconied extensions. The hotel offers attractively furnished rooms in two categories. Type A includes cheerful twin rooms with modern furniture in the new part of the hotel (a third bed can be added) and semi-suites in the building's old section. Type B includes standard rooms in the old building, most of which have balconies and sitting areas.

There are three restaurants, a pub, and a cigar bar named Havana. A range of other sports is within easy reach, including riding, fishing, skiing, a 9-hole golf course, and carriage drives (many of them at an additional fee). The hotel restaurants are quite pleasant, and guests on the half-board plan receive a wide choice of specialties included with the evening meal.

A-6708 Brand. ✆ **05559/221.** Fax 05559/445. www.tiscover.at/scesaplana. 62 units. Winter 180€–308€ ($288–$493) double; summer 120€–186€ ($192–$298) double. Rates include half-board. DC, MC, V. Free parking. Closed Oct 20–Dec 20. **Amenities:** 3 restaurants; 2 bars; 2 heated pools (1 indoor, 1 outdoor); 9-hole golf course; 4 outdoor and 2 indoor tennis courts; Jacuzzi; sauna; room service; massage; babysitting; laundry service; dry cleaning; nonsmoking rooms; tanning beds. *In room:* TV, minibar, hair dryer, safe.

BRAND AFTER DARK

Nightlife is very casual in Brand, but when there are enough visitors in town, bars usually throw their doors open for a sometimes rollicking good time. The resort's nightlife centerpiece is the lobby level of the **Hotel Scesaplana** (✆ **05559/221**), where two bars divert and amuse the resort's many outdoor-loving visitors.

4 EN ROUTE TO BREGENZ: FELDKIRCH & DORNBIRN

If you're heading for Bregenz, Vorarlberg's capital, the Bregenz Forest, or Switzerland, you really should stop at Feldkirch and Dornbirn along the way. Arrive in Feldkirch in the morning, wander through the old town and castle, and stay the night before continuing on to Bregenz.

This venerable town, "the gateway to Austria," lies on the western edge of Vorarlberg. Unfortunately, many people rush on to other destinations, but we think this town, dating back to medieval times, is worth exploring. Feldkirch was once a fortified town that grew up at the "heel" of Schattenburg Castle, on a tributary of the Ill River.

Essentials

GETTING THERE Feldkirch sits atop an important junction in the Austrian railway network, with lines to Innsbruck and Bregenz, as well as a line running into Liechtenstein and Switzerland. Dozens of **trains** arrive every day from Innsbruck (trip time: 1¾–2½ hr.) and Bregenz (trip time: 35 min.). It's easier to arrive by train, but many local bus lines connect in Feldkirch. For rail information, contact © **05/1717** (www.oebb.at).

Passengers who opt to fly to a point near Feldkirch usually land in Zurich. From the **Hauptbahnhof** in Zurich, trains depart every 2 hours, stopping at Feldkirch en route to either Innsbruck or Vienna.

By car, Feldkirch is 35km (22 miles) south of Bregenz (take the A14 south to reach it) and 121km (75 miles) east of Zurich (the nearest airport), from which it can be reached by taking Swiss motorway N13 to the Feldkirch exit.

VISITOR INFORMATION The **tourist office** (© **05522/73467**) is at Herrengasse 12. It's open year-round Monday to Saturday 8am to 7pm.

Exploring the Old Town & Castle

The **Old Town** ★, which can be explored in about an hour, is the attraction here—the New Town lies to the northeast. The heart of the Old Town is **Marktgasse (Market Street)**, a rectangle with arcades. Many of the old houses facing Marktgasse are graced with oriels (large bay windows) and frescoed facades. A popular wine festival is held here on the second weekend of July, and the town fills up with revelers.

Among the curiosities of the Old Town is the **Katzenturm**, or Tower of the Cats, named for a defense cannon adorned with lion heads. The **Churertor (Chur Gate)** is another Feldkirch landmark. Sights include the **Domkirche**, a cathedral known for its 15th-century double nave, where you should stop in and see the *Descent from the Cross*, a 1521 painting by Wolf Huber of the Danube school.

Schattenburg Schloss (Schattenburg Castle), at Neustadt, can be reached by car (by heading up Burggasse), or you can climb the steps by the **Schloss-Steig.** The castle was once a fortress, and parts of it date from the turn of the 16th century. It's now a museum and restaurant. From the castle precincts, you have a panoramic view of the Valley of the Rhine.

The Heimatmuseum (© 05522/71982; www.heimatmuseum.com), in Schattenburg Schloss, exhibits a wealth of furnishings of the region, ranging from those you might have found in a farmer's shack to pieces that graced noblemen's halls. Also displayed are large collections of art and armor. The museum is open Tuesday to Sunday 9am to noon and 1 to 5pm. Admission is 3€ ($4.80) for adults and 2€ ($3.20) for children.

Where to Stay

Hotel Alpenrose ★ *Finds* In the heart of the Old Town and only a few minutes' walk from the pedestrian precinct, this hotel appeals to traditionalists. With a history going back 5 centuries, it has been run by the Gutwinski family since 1896. The nonsmoking accommodations come in various sizes and are quite stylish, with most containing small private bathrooms with shower units. Run with charm and flair, the hotel has an elevator, and there's a Biedermeier lounge for guests. The hotel's featured restaurant, Rosenbar, serves regional cuisine.

Rosengasse 4–6, A-6800 Feldkirch. ✆ **05522/72175.** Fax 05522/721755. www.hotel-alpenrose.net. 29 units. 122€ ($195) double; 140€ ($224) suite. Rates include buffet breakfast. AE, DC, MC, V. **Amenities:** Restaurant; bar; lounge; room service; massage; laundry service; dry cleaning; 1 room for those w/limited mobility. *In room:* TV, minibar, hair dryer, safe.

Where to Dine

Landgasthof Schäfle (Value) AUSTRIAN/CONTINENTAL One of the coziest and best-recommended restaurants in Feldkirch is associated with a 24-room hotel that's 3km (1.8 miles) north of the town center, in a verdant residential district. The building that contains it dates from around 1906, although extensive renovations brought it up to date in 2008. During clement weather, you'll dine beneath canvas parasols in a manicured garden, with the venue moving indoors whenever the weather is bad. Bread is fresh made on site every day, and the wine list focuses on little-known vintages from the region. Schnitzels are scrumptious here, as is the goulash and the roster of freshwater fish. If you need a room for the night, there are 24 brightly painted, decent, and cozy bedrooms upstairs, each with light-grained wooden furniture but very few frills other than telephone, TV, private bathroom, and plug-in Internet connections. With breakfast included, doubles cost 90€ ($144) each.

Naflastrasse 3, 6800 Feldkirch-Altenstadt. ✆ **05522/72203.** Fax 05522/72203-17. www.schaefle.cc. Reservations recommended for dinner, not for lunch. Main courses 12€–22€ ($19–$35); set-price menus 15€ ($24). AE, MC, V. Mon–Fri 11am–2:30pm and 5pm–midnight.

DORNBIRN

In the heart of Vorarlberg, Dornbirn, the "city of textiles," is the province's largest town and commercial center. Only 11km (7 miles) south of the provincial capital, it sits on the outskirts of the Bregenz Forest, at the edge of a broad Rhineland Valley.

The city center, Marktplatz (Market Square), is graced by a 19th-century neoclassical parish church and by the Rotes Haus (Red House), a 1639 building that's now a restaurant.

Essentials

GETTING THERE Dornbirn is an express stop on the rail lines connecting Innsbruck with Bregenz. **Trains,** both local and express, arrive from either direction at 30-minute intervals throughout the day. For rail information, contact ✆ **05/1717** (www.oebb.at). It's easier to get here by train, but there's also a **bus** that travels from the railway station at Bregenz to Dornbirn about nine times throughout the day (trip time: 26 min.).

If you're **driving** from Bregenz, head south along the A14 until you reach the signposted junction with Route 190, where you'll head east for Dornbirn.

VISITOR INFORMATION There's a **tourist office** (✆ **05572/22188**) in the center at Rathausplatz 1. It's open year-round Monday to Friday 9am to noon and 1 to 6pm, Saturday 9am to noon.

Seeing the Sights

If you're a car buff, you shouldn't pass up a visit to the **Rolls-Royce Museum** ★, 11A Gütle (✆ **05572/52652;** www.rolls-royce_museum.at), the world's largest museum dedicated to the world's most illustrious cars. Rolls-Royce collector Frank Vonier assembled the collection, and many of the swanky cars were once owned by celebrities, including such pop icons as John Lennon or such horrors as Generalissimo Francisco Franco, the longtime Spanish dictator. Many of the vehicles were also owned by members of the British royal family, including Queen Elizabeth and the late Queen Mother. The exhibition room is a converted old spinning mill built in 1862. The vehicles are spread over three floors, where you can learn everything you need to know about the history of Rolls-Royce.

The most impressive vehicles are a seven-seater 1926 Phantom III, a continental 1933 Phantom II, and a 1936 Phantom III. Take the A14 motorway to Dornbirn, exiting at Dornbirn Süd. Drive along Lustenauerstrasse, passing the Dornbirn Hospital, and follow the signs to Gütle. By public transport, take bus no. 4 from the center of Dornbirn. Admission is 8€ ($13) for adults and 4€ ($6.40) for ages 6 to 16. It's open Tuesday to Sunday 10am to 6pm.

The most exciting excursion in the area is to **Karren** (976m/3202 ft.), about 2km (1½ miles) from the heart of town. If you're pretty fit, you can make the climb in about 2 hours, but you can also take a cable car and get there in 5 minutes. From Karren, you can hike down to the **Rappen Gorge** ★, with the Ache River flowing through it.

Where To Stay

Gesundheitszentrum Rickatschwende ★ This large, modern, renovated hotel lies on a steeply sloping hillside overlooking Dornbirn. It's composed of two interconnected buildings; one houses the restaurant, the other contains the bedrooms. The atmosphere here is calm and quiet, and guests opt for walks in the nearby forest or in grassy meadows, or for any of the various spa cures offered by the on-site health therapists. Rebuilt in 2000, the building has rooms outfitted with warm colors, exposed wood, big windows, balconies, excellent beds, and small but efficiently arranged bathrooms with tub/shower combinations.

Rickatschwende 1, A-6850 Dornbirn. ✆ **05572/25350.** Fax 05572/2535070. www.rickatschwende.com. 47 units. 150€–194€ ($240–$310) double; 290€–388€ ($464–$621) suite. Rates include breakfast. Half-board 30€ ($48) per person extra. MC, V. From the center of town, drive west toward Bödele for 5km (3 miles). Closed Nov 29–Jan 4. **Amenities:** Restaurant; bar; indoor heated pool; fitness center; spa; sauna; whirlpool; room service; massage; laundry service; dry cleaning; nonsmoking rooms; 1 room for those w/ limited mobility. *In room:* TV, hair dryer, safe.

Where to Dine

Das Rotes Haus ★★ AUSTRIAN/VORARLBERG No other restaurant in the region offers such a historic setting for a meal. It was originally built in 1639 as a tavern and has functioned in the same role ever since. Its owners proudly define it as the oldest building that's open to the public in the Austrian Rheintal (this part of the Rhine Valley), and as such, strenuous efforts are made to preserve and protect the antique quality of its setting. You'll dine within one of five cozy dining rooms, each rustic and charming, but each with a slightly different decor. We prefer the Jagdstube, outfitted with hunting trophies, and the Ammannstube, which displays political memorabilia. Don't worry if these rooms are full: All five dining rooms are richly nostalgic. Local menu items include schnitzels, *tafelspitz,* a main-course version of veal goulash, and *kässpaetzle,* a noodle dish crafted from local cheeses and herbs. A note about the building's facade: In the 17th century, the dark red color of the exterior was created by mixing cow's blood or bull's blood with binders to create the dark red that—with some assistance from modern paint—still adorns the building's facade today.

Marktplatz 13, Dornbirn A-6850. ✆ **05572/31555.** www.roteshaus.at. Reservations recommended. Main courses 9.50€–22€ ($15–$35). AE, DC, MC, V. Tues–Sat 11am–2pm and 6–10pm (last order). Closed Dec 25–Jan 6.

5 BREGENZ ★★

658km (409 miles) W of Vienna; 130km (81 miles) E of Zurich; 11km (7 miles) S of Lindau (Germany)

Bregenz, the capital of Vorarlberg, sits on terraces rising above the water at the eastern end of Bodensee (Lake Constance). Once the Roman town of Brigantium, Bregenz is now a major tourist spot that's both modern and historic. The modern part of town lies along the lake's shore, and the old town rises above it. In summer, the promenade along the Bodensee's shoreline is popular.

ESSENTIALS

GETTING THERE Bregenz is the most important railway station in western Austria, where dozens of **trains** arrive from Zurich, Munich, Innsbruck, and Vienna throughout the day. The trip from Innsbruck takes about 3 hours and occasionally requires a change of train at Feldkirch. Although it's easier to arrive here by train, several bus lines make the trip to Bregenz. For **train and bus information,** call ✆ **05/1717** (www.oebb.at).

If you're **driving** from Innsbruck, take Route 171 west (passing through the Arlberg Tunnel) into Vorarlberg, and then follow the S19 west until you hook up with the A14 Autobahn going north.

VISITOR INFORMATION At the **tourist office,** Bregenz-Tourismus, Bahnhofstrasse 14 (✆ **05574/49590**), you can pick up a map for a walking tour of the Old Town. It's open year-round Monday to Friday 8:30am to 5pm, Saturday from 9am to noon.

SEEING THE SIGHTS

You can travel the Bodensee district by boat, venturing into Germany and Switzerland, which share Bodensee with Austria. For a panoramic view of the lake and the town, with Switzerland looming in the background, take a cable car to **Pfänder** (see "Up the Mountain to Pfänder," below).

The **Unterstadt (Lower Town)** is Bregenz's shopping district, with traffic-free malls along the shore. In spring, the flower beds along the quays of the Unterstadt blaze with color.

The Bregenz Music Festival

Bregenz is at its liveliest during the annual **Bregenz Music Festival.** This festival, held during a 4-week period in mid-July to mid-August, was established in 1946. Open-air and indoor concerts are given (some at the acoustically sophisticated Festspiele-und-Kongresshaus), but the most appealing productions are the lavish operas, operettas, and musical comedies. The more elaborate shows—with their ornately dressed actors and singers—are presented on a stage floating on the Bodensee. The audience looks on from a shoreside amphitheater that seats 6,500. Some of the latest productions have included *Death in Venice* by British composer Benjamin Britten. Tickets, from 15€ to 280€ ($24–$448), are available at the Bregenzer Festspielhaus, Platz der Wiener Symphoniker 1 (✆ **05574/4076;** www.bregenzerfestspiele.com).

The Upper Town is called both **Oberstadt** and **Altstadt**. Once the stronghold of the counts of Bregenz and Montford, this area is great for history buffs. If you're driving from the Lower Town, head up Kirchstrasse, Thalbachgasse, and Amstorstrasse; park; and then stroll back into the Middle Ages as you wander through the old quarter's quiet squares and narrow streets. Even before it was the Roman town of Brigantium, the Upper Town was the site of a Celtic settlement.

The **Pfarrkirche (Parish Church),** dedicated to St. Gall, stands on a hill south of the Upper Town. This 15th-century sandstone structure has a sunken nave from the 18th century.

Martinsturm On the upper floor of the 13th-century Tower of St. Martin is a local military museum. St. Martin's Chapel (founded in 1362), at the base of the tower, features 14th-century murals. Far more interesting than the art, however, is the view of the surrounding area from the top of the tower, which is capped with one of the largest all-wood cupolas in Austria.

Graf-Wilhelm-Strasse. ✆ **05574/46632.** Admission 1€ ($1.60) adults, .50€ (80¢) children. Easter–Oct 15 daily 9am–6:30pm.

Vorarlberger Landesmuseum ★ You'll find a rich collection of artifacts from throughout the province in the Vorarlberg Regional Museum. Exhibits include relics from prehistoric and Roman days. You'll see Romanesque and Gothic ecclesiastical works of art from the churches in the district. Also make time to see the so-called portrait of the Duke of Wellington by Angelica Kauffmann.

Kornmarktplatz 1. ✆ **05574/46050.** www.vlm.at. Admission 6€ ($9.60) adults, 1.50€ ($2.40) children. Tues–Sun 9am–noon and 2–5pm.

WHERE TO STAY

For the most luxurious accommodations in the area, stay at Deuring Schlössle (see "Where to Dine," below).

Hotel Mercure Near the Festspielhaus, in the center opening onto the lake, this hotel, a member of a popular French hotel chain, is one of the town's most up-to-date. And it's in the same building as the local casino. The small rooms are of the bland hotel-chain variety but are comfortable. Some have balconies. The hotel's specialty restaurant, Symphonie, also operates an inexpensive cafeteria. Summer guests enjoy sitting out on the large umbrella-shaded terrace for drinks and food.

Platz d. Wiener Symphoniker 2, A-6900 Bregenz. ✆ **05574/461000.** Fax 05574/47412. www.accorhotel.com. 94 units. 198€–338€ ($317–$541) double. Rates include buffet breakfast. Half-board 20€ ($32) per person extra. AE, DC, MC, V. **Amenities:** Restaurant; bar; 18-hole golf course; fitness center; sauna; room service; babysitting; laundry service; dry cleaning; nonsmoking rooms; solarium; rooms for those w/limited mobility. *In room:* TV, Wi-Fi, minibar, hair dryer, safe.

Schwarzler Hotel ★ One of the best hotels in Bregenz, the elegant Schwärzler Hotel is a 5-minute drive east of the town center. Completely renovated, it has hosted famous visitors such as the late Arthur Ashe and José Carreras. Most of the handsomely furnished rooms are spacious and have balconies. Bathrooms are small but efficiently organized with a shower. The restaurant, **Schwärzler,** is one of the most respected in the area, serving Swiss, Austrian, and international dishes. The hotel is known for its candlelight dinners and farmer buffets.

Landstrasse 9, A-6900 Bregenz. ✆ **05574/4990.** Fax 05574/47575. www.schwaerzler-hotels.com. 82 units. 130€–270€ ($208–$432) double. Rates include breakfast. Half-board 28€ ($45) per person extra. AE,

DC, MC, V. Free parking. **Amenities:** Restaurant; bar; indoor heated pool; sauna; bike rental; room service; massage; babysitting; laundry service; dry cleaning; nonsmoking rooms; solarium. *In room:* TV, Wi-Fi, minibar, hair dryer, safe.

WHERE TO DINE

Deuring Schlössle ★★ AUSTRIAN In the center of Bregenz, at the highest point in the Old Town, this restaurant is one of Austria's finest. Through the efforts of its owners, the Huber family, the imposing, ivy-covered 600-year-old castle has provided exceptional food (and hotel rooms) since 1987. The establishment contains half-timbered detailing, a Renaissance-era fireplace, and an impressive wine list. Menu items are seasonal, varied, and thoughtful, such as cream soup with exotic fruits and pikeperch with crab sauce, spinach, and buttered noodles; roasted breast of duck with wine sauce, ginger-flavored cabbage, and potato pancakes; and marinated whitefish from nearby lakes served with apple-cucumber salad and blinis.

Some guests opt to spend the night in one of the 15 rooms. Accommodations are spacious and contain antiques, Persian carpets, parquet floors, and panoramic views of Lake Constance. Modern comforts have been added, and rooms come in a variety of sizes, with great beds and luxurious bathrooms with both tubs and showers. Our favorite guest room is "Gott im Epona" in the tower, which is surrounded with windows. With its garden ambience, the place is both stylish and relaxing. Doubles with half-board included are 330€ to 460€ ($528–$736), and suites run 480€ to 660€ ($768–$1,056). Rooms contain minibars, TVs, and phones.

Ehre-Guts-Platz 4, A-6900 Bregenz. ✆ **05574/47800.** Fax 05574/4780080. Reservations required. Main courses 24€–34€ ($38–$54); fixed-price menus 52€ ($83) for 4 courses, 57€–65€ ($91–$104) for 5 courses, 75€–80€ ($120–$128) for 6 courses. AE, DC, MC, V. Mon–Sat 6–9pm.

Golden Hirschen ★ AUSTRIAN One of the most "folklorically conscious" dining rooms in town occupies an old-world building that was originally built as a tavern around 1800 and has functioned in that capacity ever since. Inside, you'll find one very large dining room whose seating expands during clement weather onto an outdoor terrace, where the views extend out over the other historic buildings of Bregenz's historic core. Come here for the kind of cuisine that many Austrians associate with their grandmothers. Examples include giant Wiener schnitzels; *tafelspitz;* local fish served with herbs and a white-butter sauce; variations on noodle dishes, including versions with creamy ham and mushroom sauce; roasted beef with onions; and creamy goulash. Dishes that are a bit less obviously associated with the region include grilled turkey in a tomato-flavored Gorgonzola sauce and well-prepared pastas, some made with spinach-flavored tagliatelle. A particular specialty favored by residents of these parts is *kisselfleisch,* composed of roasted pork served with sauerkraut, braised onions, and herbs.

Kirchstrasse 8, A-6900 Bregenz. ✆ **05574/42815.** Reservations recommended. Main courses 10€–24€ ($16–$38). AE, DC, MC, V. Wed–Mon 11am–midnight.

SHOPPING

Nose-to-the-grindstone Bregenz doesn't have a lot of shopping options, but you'll find a scattering of outlets within the Lower Town that might appeal to you. Foremost for sporting goods is **Sport Christian,** Römerstrasse, 2 (✆ **05574/42234;** www.sportchristian.at), where you'll find every type of equipment and clothing you'd need for every imaginable summer and winter sport. And noteworthy for traditional alpine clothing—lederhosen, dirndls, and woolen clothing suitable for men, women, and children in any season—is **Sagmeister,** Römerstrasse 10 (✆ **05574/43190**).

BREGENZ AFTER DARK

If you're in Bregenz on a summer night, you don't need nightlife: Few smoke-filled clubs could compete with a walk along the lakeshore and a visit to a cafe. However, if you'd like another diversion, you can visit the **Spiel-Casino Bregenz,** Platz der Wiener Symphoniker 3 (✆ **05574/45127;** www.casinos.at), where roulette, baccarat, and blackjack are played daily from noon to 3am (Friday to Saturday until 4am). Parking in the garage is free, as is entrance to the casino. Entrance is 25€ ($40). Men must wear jackets and ties. The in-house restaurant, **Falstaff,** offers a fixed-price four-course menu (it includes the admission charge) for 52€ ($83).

UP THE MOUNTAIN TO PFÄNDER

Almost 300,000 visitors a year make the uphill trek to the mountain observation station of Pfänder, west of Bregenz. Pfänder is accessible by road (a meandering distance of 10km/6½ miles) or via the **Pfänderbahn cable car** (a straight-line transit of 4km/2½ miles) from the center of Bregenz. Celebrated as the second-oldest cable car in Austria, it was originally built in 1927 and was massively upgraded with almost double its original capacity in 1994. Operating year-round daily from 8:30am to 7pm, it departs from its lowest station, about 460m (1,509 ft.) east of the **Kornmarkt I Bregenz,** and takes about 7 minutes to reach its summit. Round-trip fare is 10€ ($17) for adults or 3€ ($4.80) for ages 6 to 15. Call ✆ **05574/42160** for information about departure times.

At the summit, you'll find a scattering of shops and restaurants along with the **Pfänder Wildlife Park** ✆ **0664/9053040.** The owners emphasize that it is not a zoo. The park's large fenced-in areas are devoted to herds of red deer, wild boar, mountain goats, and wild sheep. Access to the Wildlife Park is free; it takes about 20 minutes to wander through its 10 hectares (26 acres) of rocky terrain. One of the highlights of the park is the twice-daily ***Greifvogel-Flugschau*** **(Birds of Prey Show),** during which ornithologists display the age-old hunting techniques of trained falcons, eagles, owls, and vultures. The 45-minute shows are presented from May to early October at 11am and 2:30pm. Tickets to the show are 4.80€ ($7.70) for adults and 2.40€ ($3.90) for children.

To get to this alpine complex by car from Bregenz, travel east of town (toward Lindau, Germany) along a narrow, twisting road through the mountains. Turn right, toward Lochau, where you'll pass a parish church, and turn right onto a secondary road leading to Pfänder. Cars usually park at a large lot near the summit. From here, you'll walk about 10 minutes to reach the panorama from the Berghaus Pfänder. From the Berghaus, an additional 15-minute walk leads to another, much smaller, alpine house with its own simple restaurant and a different panorama, the **Schwedenschanze Belvedere.**

6 THE BREGENZ FOREST ★

From Bregenz, you can make one of the most interesting scenic excursions in Vorarlberg—or in Austria, for that matter—deep into the **Bregenzerwald,** or Bregenz Forest. It's not as well known as Germany's Black Forest, but it has just as much charm and character.

The forest takes up the northern part of the Vorarlberg alpine range. A state highway splits the valley of the Bregenzer Ache River, making driving easy, but the true charm of the forest lies off the beaten path in the little undiscovered valleys cut by the river's tiny tributaries. Don't expect a proliferation of trees in the Bregenz Forest: The Austrians have cleared a lot of the woodlands to make meadows, where you'll see contented cows grazing and the Alps towering in the background.

Factoid

If you're passing through the valley on a Sunday, you'll see an occasional Vorarlberger going to church in his or her traditional garb. The headdress of the women is often striking, ranging from small crowns to wide-brimmed black straw hats. Unlike most of the rest of Europe, the people of this area wear white for mourning rather than black.

One of the most frequented areas for sports and recreation is the Bödele, which lies between the Valley of the Ache and the Valley of the Rhine. Skiers are drawn to the highlands in winter.

BEZAU

The best-known village of the Bregenz Forest, Bezau is surrounded by a landscape that's scenic in any season. Be careful not to confuse Bezau with a village nearby, at the end of the neighboring valley, named Bizau.

In the spring, summer, and autumn, you can hike, go mountaineering, swim, fish for trout, or play tennis or minigolf. In winter there's alpine skiing, with the **Hinter-Bregenzerwald ski ticket** covering a range of more than 50 lifts and cable railways. There are some 56km (35 miles) of cross-country ski trails, and you can also go tobogganing. A cableway from here will take you to the **Baumgartenhöhe,** at 1,632m (5,354 ft.).

Essentials

GETTING THERE Bezau has no railway connections. Most travelers take one of the many daily **trains** to Dornbirn, a 15-minute ride south of Bregenz. Around 20 **buses** depart every day from Dornbirn; the trip to Bezau takes about 50 minutes.

If you're **driving** from Bregenz, head south on the A14 to the junction with Route 200. Cut east along this winding road to Bezau, which lies 36km (22 miles) from Bregenz.

VISITOR INFORMATION The **tourist office,** Platz 39 (✆ **05514/2295**), is in the center of town. It's open year-round Monday to Friday from 9am to noon and 1:30 to 5:30pm, Saturday 9am to noon.

Where to Stay & Dine

Gasthof Gams This dignified hotel has a facade of cedar shingles, white stucco, gables, and balconies. Although the core was built in 1648, guests will find an abundance of modern comforts, including a big garden and several antique-style sitting rooms. Rooms are well furnished and come in a variety of sizes; each year a few units are renovated. The most desirable rooms open onto private balconies with scenic views. Beds are first-rate, and the small bathrooms have tub/shower combinations. The restaurant specializes in game, particularly venison. You'll also be offered seafood, such as a well-prepared filet of sole, along with filet steak, curry dishes, and desserts with fresh mountain berries.

Platz 44, A-6870 Bezau. ✆ **05514/2220.** Fax 05514/222024. www.hotel-gams.at. 41 units. 142€–220€ ($227–$352) double; 260€–280€ ($416–$448) suite for 2. Rates include half-board. V. **Amenities:** Restaurant; bar, lounge; outdoor heated pool; fitness room; spa; Jacuzzi; sauna; room service; massage; babysitting; laundry service; dry cleaning; solarium. *In room:* TV, hair dryer, safe.

DAMÜLS

At an elevation of 1,427m (4,682 ft.), this town is one of the best places to ski in the Bregenz Forest. One skier who goes here every year describes it as a place "for connoisseurs." Hotels organize weekly après-ski programs, so check to see what's going on during your stay. Damüls, the loftiest village in the forest, is an area of great scenic beauty, so a summer visit is also pleasant.

Essentials

GETTING THERE From Bregenz, visitors should take a southbound 15-minute **train** to Dornbirn and then board one of the **buses** to Damüls. Buses depart around six times a day (trip time: 1½ hr.).

To get to Damüls from Innsbruck, you have to take a 2-hour train ride west to Bludenz and then board one of the nine daily buses that depart for the 90-minute ride to Damüls.

Damüls is 60km (37 miles) southeast of Bregenz, and a long 698km (434 miles) west of Vienna. To get to Damüls by **car** from Bezau, drive southeast along Route 200 until you come to the junction with Route 193, and head southwest to Damüls.

VISITOR INFORMATION The **tourist office** (✆ **05510/6200**) is in Kirchdorf, at the edge of the village center. It's open year-round Monday through Friday from 8:30am to noon and 1:30 to 6:30pm; in winter it's also open Saturday 10am to noon and 4 to 6pm, Sunday 10am to noon.

Where to Stay & Dine

Hotel Damülser Hof This collection of modern chalets, each connected by covered passageways, sits in an alpine meadow a 5-minute walk uphill from the village church. Built in 1963 and partially renovated virtually every year since then, it boasts an elegant interior with enough variety in its decor to please most guests. The cozy public areas have intimate niches, soft lighting, and several fireplaces. Rooms are medium-size, comfortable, and well furnished, if rather impersonal.

A-6884 Oberdamüls. ✆ **05510/2100.** Fax 05510/543. www.damuelserhof.at. 50 units. Winter 170€–232€ ($272–$371) double; summer 140€–160€ ($224–$256) double. Rates include half-board. MC, V. Parking 8€ ($13) indoors, free outdoors. Closed Nov. **Amenities:** Breakfast room; 2 bars; indoor heated pool; fitness center; spa; sauna; room service; massage; babysitting; nonsmoking rooms; bowling alley; solarium; rooms for those w/limited mobility. *In room:* TV, hair dryer, safe.

14

Carinthia

If you like hiking, watersports, or just lazing in the sun, Carinthia's beautiful countryside—gentle hills and steep mountains scattered with idyllic lakes—makes it a wonderful area to explore during the warmer months; it's also an ideal stopping point if you're heading to Italy.

The high mountains ringing Carinthia (or Kärnten, in German) create the province's natural borders, and the area has been likened to a gigantic amphitheater. Mountainous Upper Carinthia lies to the west, and the Lower Carinthia Basin region slopes to the east. The province is bisected by the east-flowing Drau River, which becomes the Drava when it enters Slovenia. Villach is the biggest road and rail junction in the eastern Alps, and Klagenfurt is the capital of Carinthia.

If you're athletic, climb the gentle *nocken* (hills), or head for the more demanding mountains. The region boasts more than 200 warm, clean lakes, and fishing is a popular pastime here, either in the lakes or in the colder mountain streams. The "Carinthian Riviera" is the name given to the main lake area, including the Wörther See, not far from Klagenfurt. Lake Ossiacher and Lake Millstatter are also in this area. Weissensee, another big lake, is less well known than the other three, but it's really the most scenic. The best way to see the lakes is to take one of the boats that operate from April to mid-October.

If you want to enjoy the lakes, visit Carinthia from mid-May to September, although the first 2 weeks in October are ideal, too. Hordes of visitors flock here in July and August, so make reservations in advance if you plan on visiting during those months.

Although the warm lakes are Carinthia's main attraction, the province also attracts some skiers to its mountains in winter. However, Carinthia's relatively mild winters don't always make for the best ski conditions. The ski season here lasts only from December to March. As a ski center, this province is much less expensive than Tyrol or Land Salzburg. Regardless of the season you visit, if you're driving, parking is rarely a problem: Unless otherwise noted, you park for free.

Archaeological discoveries prove that Carinthia was inhabited by humans far back in unrecorded time, and the Romans didn't overlook the area, either—their legions marched in to conquer alpine Celtic tribes in the kingdom of Noticum, establishing it as a Roman province.

For centuries, this area was home to ethnic groups from Slovenia, belonging to the kingdom of Germany and Avar-dominated Slavs from the east. Hoping to fend off invasions, the populace eventually invited Bavaria to become Carinthia's protector, and so it became part of the Holy Roman Empire.

When the Hapsburgs took Kärnten as a part of their rapidly expanding empire, it was a duchy of the Holy Roman Empire under the Bohemian aegis. To secure his control over the area, Ferdinand I of Hapsburg, soon to become emperor, married the heiress to Bohemia and made Carinthia an imperial duchy. Later, Carinthia was designated a province of Austria.

The former country of Yugoslavia claimed southern Carinthia after World War I. During this time, some territory was ceded to Yugoslavia, and more was given to Italy, but all this land was later restored. In 1920, after the collapse of the Hapsburg Empire, the Slovenian minority in the south, along the Yugoslav border, voted to remain with Austria. Today, a sizable minority of Carinthia's population is Slovenian, but the majority of it is German.

If you spontaneously decide to spend a day boating, bicycling, or fishing, the staff at any local hotel should be able to tell help you out. Here's a list of outfitters who can help with advance planning and, in some cases, link you with a choice of specialized tours.

BIKING Carinthia's gentle contours are ideal for cyclists. The tourist office in the **Rathaus** (✆ **0463/5372223**) in Klagenfurt rents bicycles for 10€ ($16) per day.

BOATING The reception staff at virtually any lakeside hotel can arrange boating lessons and boat rentals, but two local experts are **Segel-und-Surfschule Wörthersee/Berger,** Seecorso 40, Velden (✆ **04274/26910**), and **Flaschberger Georg,** Seeuferstrasse 130, Pörtschach (✆ **04272/2743**). These two outfits or any of the dozens of other *bootverleih* (boat-rental agencies) can help you arrange windsurfing, canoeing, or sailing, and, where it's allowed, even rent you a motorized craft for fishing.

FISHING Any local tourist office can provide you with the worthwhile pamphlet *"Kärnten Fischen,"* which explains the rules and procedures involved with a fishing expedition. Some hotels adjacent to important lakes offer fishing packages that include rooms, boat rentals, guides, and equipment in one price, and most hotel staff are well versed.

GOLF Some of the most appealing golf games in Austria are configured at sites that are relatively close to Carinthia's most beautiful lakes. From May to October, Carinthian golf is in full swing. The best of the district's golf courses include **Golfanlage Moosburg-Pörtschach,** A-9062 Moosburg (✆ **04272/83486;** www.golfmoosburg.at). A nearby golf academy, **Golfakademie Moosburg-Pörtschach,** A-9062 Moosburg (✆ **04272/82302**), offers lessons on the same course. Another fine course is **Golfclub-Austria Wörthersee,** Golfstrasse 2, A-9062 Moosburg (✆ **04272/83486**). Each of the courses mentioned above has 18 holes, a par of 72, and greens fees of 65€ ($104).

HIKING Every lakeside resort has marked trails branching out over the mountains or through valleys. In summer, Carinthia is host to hordes of hikers. The Ossiacher See area is especially suited for hiking, as are Hochosterwitz and Friesach. Some of the best hiking is possible from the towns of **Bad Kleinkirchheim, Feld am See,** and **Millstatt.** Ask at the local tourist office for information and maps.

SKIING Carinthia doesn't have the mountains or facilities for skiing like Vorarlberg or Tyrol, but **Friesach** is emerging as a major ski area, attracting cross-country skiers in particular. The top ski resort is Bad Kleinkirchheim.

SWIMMING & WATERSPORTS All the major lakes contain public beaches, and the waters are among the purest in Europe. You can drink from them safely, although we don't recommend this. In late summer, lake temperatures reach about 75°F (24°C), making them ideal for swimmers. If you'd like to combine your swimming with more serious watersports, check with such outfitters as **Segel-und-Surfschule Wörthersee/Berger,** Seecorso 40, Velden (✆ **04274/26910**), or **Flaschberger Georg,** Seeuferstrasse 130, Pörtschach (✆ **04272/2743**).

TENNIS Most major resorts have their own courts; we particularly like Villach and its satellite areas. Try the courts at **Tennisplätz-ASKÖ, Landskron, Süduferstrasse** at Villach (✆ **04242/41879**), or **Tenniscamp Warmbad** at Warmbad-Villach (✆ **04242/32564**).

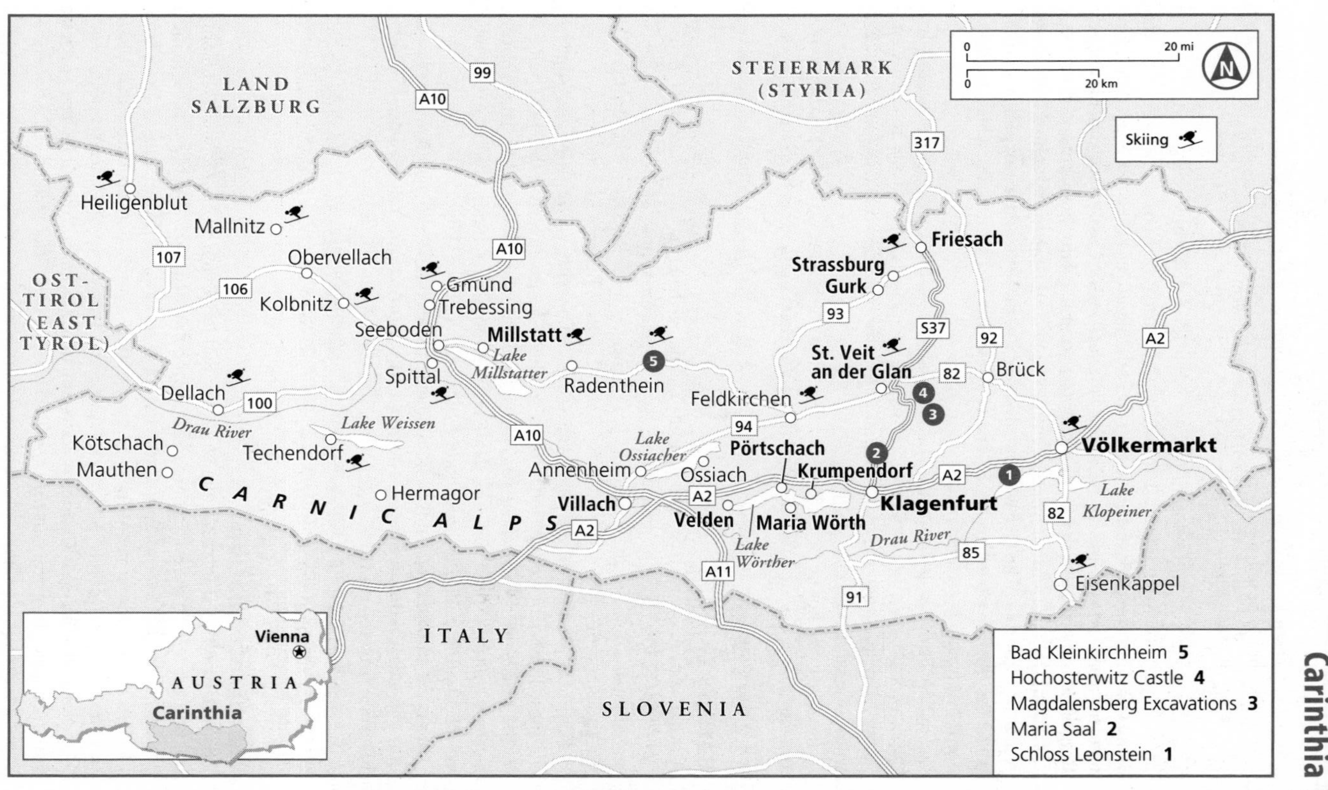
LAND SALZBURG
STEIERMARK (STYRIA)
OST-TIROL (EAST TYROL)
0 20 mi
0 20 km
Skiing
Heiligenblut
Mallnitz
Obervellach
Kolbnitz
Gmünd
Trebessing
Seeboden
Millstatt
Lake Millstatter
Spittal
Radenthein
Dellach
Drau River
Lake Weissen
Kötschach
Mauthen
Techendorf
Hermagor
CARNIC ALPS
Villach
Annenheim
Lake Ossiacher
Ossiach
Feldkirchen
Pörtschach
Krumpendorf
Velden
Maria Wörth
Lake Wörther
Klagenfurt
Friesach
Strassburg
Gurk
St. Veit an der Glan
Brück
Völkermarkt
Lake Klopeiner
Eisenkappel
Drau River
ITALY
SLOVENIA
Vienna
AUSTRIA
Carinthia
99
A10
107
106
100
317
93
S37
92
82
94
A2
A11
85
91
Bad Kleinkirchheim 5
Hochosterwitz Castle 4
Magdalensberg Excavations 3
Maria Saal 2
Schloss Leonstein 1

1 KLAGENFURT

61km (38 miles) NE of Italy; 31km (19 miles) N of Slovenia; 309km (192 miles) SW of Vienna; 140km (87 miles) SW of Graz; 209km (130 miles) SE of Salzburg

Klagenfurt is not an attraction in its own right; it's a sleepy city that's a great stopover point if you're driving around Carinthia's lakes. Arrive in Klagenfurt, get settled, and wander around the city's historic center. Stay the night, and then use Klagenfurt as the base for your explorations to **St. Veit, Hochosterwitz Castle, Magdalensberg,** the **Cathedral of Gurk,** and the region's lakes (see section 2, later in this chapter).

Klagenfurt, a university town dating from 1161, is the provincial capital and cultural center of Carinthia. The city was destroyed by fire in 1514 and was rebuilt and designated the duchy's capital in 1518. The city was fortified with walls, which were torn down during the Napoleonic invasions in 1802.

The city center is quadrangular and rimmed with streets that were laid down where the city's walls once stood. The center of this quadrangle, and of the modern city, is **Neuer Platz,** presided over by a fountain in the shape of a ferocious dragon called Lindwurm, the city's symbol.

It can get very hot in the peak of summer, but if you're here, do as the Klagenfurters do and retreat to the nearby **Wörther See (Lake Wörther)** in the western sector of the city.

ESSENTIALS

Getting There

Austrian Airlines serves Carinthia from Vienna, arriving at the **Klagenfurt Airport** (✆ **0463/41500** for flight information; www.klagenfurt-airport.at), northeast of the city, several times a day. Because Klagenfurt is a popular summer lakeside resort, **Austrian Airlines** adds summer flights from Zurich, Rome, London, Berlin, and Frankfurt.

Klagenfurt, located on the lines connecting Vienna with Venice, Italy, and Zagreb, is the most important railway junction in southern Austria. It's also the focal point for several smaller rail lines whose passengers are eventually transferred to larger lines to Salzburg, Innsbruck, and Bregenz. **Trains** arrive from several different directions at intervals of 30 minutes or less throughout the day; call ✆ **05/1717** for schedules.

It's easier to take the train, but from Klagenfurt at least 20 different **bus** lines fan out into the surrounding region. For regional **bus information,** call ✆ **0463/54340** in Klagenfurt.

If you're **driving** from Vienna, head south on Autobahn A2, cut southeast at the junction with Route 17, and go through the Semmering mountain pass. Then follow Route 83 into Klagenfurt.

Visitor Information

The **tourist office** is in the **Rathaus,** or city hall (✆ **0463/5372223;** www.klagenfurt.at); to reach it from the rail station, head down Bahnhofstrasse. Open May to September Monday to Friday 8am to 8pm, Saturday 10am to 7pm, Sunday 10am to 3pm. From October to April, hours are Monday to Friday 10am to 6pm, Saturday and Sunday 10am to 1pm.

If you're driving into Klagenfurt and want to leave the car, this city offers restricted parking zones where you can park for 90 minutes in specially marked "blue zones," so-called because of blue lines on the road. You have to use a parking voucher to stop in limited-parking zones. Vouchers can be purchased at banks, gas stations, or tobacconists. When you park, you must write in the time you arrived and display the voucher on the dashboard, inside the windshield.

EXPLORING KLAGENFURT

Alter Platz, both a broad thoroughfare and a square, is lined with many baroque mansions. It's a pedestrian zone that's the center of the **Altstadt (Old Town),** and many crooked, narrow little streets and alleys open off the square.

The **Trinity Column** in Alter Platz dates from 1681; it was built to commemorate those who died from the plague. One of the most interesting buildings on the square is the 17th-century **Altes Rathaus (Old Town Hall).** It has a three-story arcaded courtyard. The **Haus zur Goldenen Gans (House of the Golden Goose),** on Alter Platz, dates from 1599.

The **Domkirche (Cathedral) of Klagenfurt** lies to the southeast of Neuer Platz. Construction on this building began in 1578, and the interior is richly adorned in stucco and has ceiling paintings from the 18th century. Next door to the cathedral, **Diozesanmuseum** ★, Lidmanskyg 10 (✆ **0463/577701064**), is a small, often overlooked, museum containing a remarkable collection of **religious art** ★★ from the 12th to the 18th centuries. Sculpture, tapestries, jewelry, artwork, and stained glass are on display here, including the oldest extant stained-glass window in the country, a portrait of Mary Magdalene from 1170. Some works of art in the museum are truly remarkable, including one-of-a-kind pieces such as a rare processional cross made of iron with traces of gilt dating from the 12th century. Diozesanmuseum is open June 1 to June 14 and from September 15 to October 15, Monday to Saturday 10am to noon; from June 15 to September 14, Monday to Saturday 10am to noon and 3 to 5pm. Admission costs 4€ ($6.40) for adults and 2€ ($3.20) for children.

If you're traveling with children, consider an excursion to a nearby theme park, **Minimundus,** Villacherstrasse 241 (✆ **0463/21194;** www.minimundus.at). Here, scaled-down versions of the world's most famous buildings are artfully arranged in a layout that incorporates flower beds and whimsical interpretations of some of the buildings. Examples include small-scale versions of the Eiffel Tower, the Great Wall of China, Big Ben, and various European castles and Asian temples. Every model within the park measures approximately 1/25 the size of the original. Minimundus is open April to October. In April and October, it's open daily from 9am to 6pm; in May, June, and September, it's open daily 9am to 7pm; in July and August, it's open daily 9am to 8pm. Admission costs 12€ ($19) for adults and 7€ ($11) for children under 16.

Landesmuseum ★ At this provincial museum, you can see Roman artifacts gleaned from excavations in Carinthia. Exhibits display art and artifacts from prehistoric times to the present. The most outstanding feature is a display of ecclesiastical art. See the skull of a rhinoceros, said to have been a model for the renowned Dragon Fountain in Neuer Platz.

Museumgasse 2. ✆ **050536/30599.** www.landesmuseum-ktn.at. Admission 5€ ($8) adults, 3€ ($4.80) seniors and children. Apr–Oct Tues–Sun 10am–6pm (until 8pm on Thurs); Nov–Mar Tues–Sun 10am–4pm (until 8pm on Thurs).

Landhaus Originally an arsenal and later Carinthian state headquarters, this structure now houses the offices of the provincial government. Building began in 1574 and finished in 1590. The courtyard of the present building has two-story arcades, and the set of staircase towers has bulbous caps. Its **Grosser Wappensaal (Great Blazon Hall)**, dating from 1739, was handsomely decorated by Josef Ferdinand Fromiller. The painting on the hall's ceiling depicting 665 heraldic shields is executed in *trompe l'oeil.*

Landhaushof 1. ✆ **0463/577570.** Admission 5€ ($8) adults, 3€ ($4.80) ages 6–18. Apr–Oct 9am–noon and 12:30–5pm. Closed Nov–Mar.

WHERE TO STAY

Arcotel Hotel Moser Verdino ★ In the town center north of the Domkirche, the jutting tower of this hotel's elaborate pink-and-white facade was built in 1890 in a rich Art Nouveau design. For more than a century, it has been the town's leading hotel. Bedrooms are comfortable, mostly midsize, and attractively furnished and well maintained. The most popular cafe in town, Café Moser Verdino, is near the oak-trimmed lobby.

Domgasse 2, A-9020 Klagenfurt. ✆ **0463/57878.** Fax 0463/516765. www.arcotel.at. 71 units. 105€–180€ ($168–$288) double. AE, DC, MC, V. **Amenities:** Restaurant; bar; room service; babysitting; laundry service; dry cleaning; rooms for those w/limited mobility. *In room:* TV, Wi-Fi, minibar, hair dryer, safe.

Das Salzamt Palais Hotel Landhaus An offbeat boutique hotel of considerable charm, this restored Renaissance palace in the heart of Klagenfurt dates from the Renaissance era. Until 1935, it was the "Salzamt" or town salt tax office. Today, it has emerged as a fashionable hotel with lots of camp in some bedrooms, where you are likely to find red velvet, gilt, and leopard skin "hearts." There is much comfort here, ranging from the heavenly beds to the padded headboards. The bathrooms are equally luxurious, some with whirlpool baths. In a small but cozy spa area, overlooking the rooftops of the city, you can use the Finnish sauna, a vapor bath, or else take a hot and cold Kneipp shower. The sun might be shining in the hotel solarium even in the winter months.

Landhaushof 3, A-9020. ✆ **0463/590959**. Fax 0463/590-9590-9. www.landhaushof.at. 27 units. 200€–230€ ($320–$368) double; 300€ ($480) junior suite; 390€ ($624) suite. Rates include breakfast. AE, DC, MC, V. **Amenities:** Restaurant; bar; public Internet; room service; spa; solarium; laundry service. *In room:* A/C, TV, minibar, safe.

Hotel Garni Blumenstöckl Centrally located off Neuer Platz, this old-fashioned hotel (with a history that goes back 4 centuries) tends to be heavily booked in summer, so reservations are needed as far in advance as possible. One of this establishment's finest features is its elegant courtyard, where ornate wrought-iron balconies are supported by chiseled stone columns. The hotel offers peaceful and simply furnished rooms in a wide variety of sizes. Only breakfast is served here, and parking is free on the street after 6pm.

10 Oktober-Strasse 11, A-9020 Klagenfurt. ✆ **0463/57793.** Fax 0463/577935. 12 units. 76€–80€ ($122–$128) double. Rates include buffet breakfast. No credit cards. Closed 1 week at Christmas. **Amenities:** Breakfast room; lounge. *In room:* TV.

Hotel Sandwirt All Austrian presidents elected since 1945 have stayed in this historic hotel. This centrally located neoclassical building was constructed in the 1650s. Rooms vary widely in style and size, but are usually high-ceilinged and comfortably old-fashioned; some, however, are very modern. Most contain double beds, and each is equipped with a tub/shower bathroom.

Pernhartgasse 9, A-9020 Klagenfurt. ✆ **0463/56209**. Fax 0463/514322. www.sandwirt.at. 40 units. 149€–174€ ($238–$278) double. Rates include buffet breakfast. AE, DC, MC, V. Free parking. **Amenities:** Restaurant; bar; cafe; fitness center; sauna; steam room; nonsmoking rooms; rooms for those w/limited mobility. *In room:* TV, minibar.

Goldener Brunnen Value Set nearly adjacent to Klagenfurt's cathedral, within a yellow-fronted antique building that still belongs to the local Catholic diocese, this hotel took most of its present form around 2000, when a team of entrepreneurs upgraded the then-creaky building's interior into a streamlined, mostly white collection of pleasant-looking bedrooms. There's no full-fledged restaurant on the premises, but there's a cafe, known mostly for its lunch business, within the hotel's cobble-covered courtyard, which closes between 7 and 8pm every day, depending on the season. Come here for solid dependability and its boutiquey-style—there's nothing flashy about the place.

Am Domplatz, A-9020 Klagenfurt. ✆ **0463/57380.** Fax 0463/516520. www.goldener-brunnen.at. 26 units. 110€–140€ ($176–$224) double; 160€ ($256) junior suite. Rates include breakfast. Free parking. AE, DC, MC, V. **Amenities:** Cafe; bar; limited room service; nonsmoking rooms. *In room:* A/C, TV, Wi-Fi, minibar, safe.

Palais Porcia ★★★ This pocket of posh is installed in a former town palace dating from the 1700s that once belonged to Italian princes. The stylish boutique hotel, filled with Baroque embellishments and Biedermeier antiques, is still so opulent you'd think the nobles were still in residence. Modern hotel comforts have been discreetly installed. The spacious bedrooms are lavishly decorated, filled with art work that seemingly belongs in a museum, and much use made of four-poster beds, velvet sofas, and brocaded wallpaper. The most spectacular bedroom is called Himmelbett Room or "Heaven's Bed," although the Rose Room and the Blue Room are also lavishly decorated.

Neuerplatz 13, A-9020. ✆ **0463/511590-30**. www.hotel-palais-porcia.com. 35 units. 113€–197€ ($181–$315) double; 197€–349€ ($315–$558) suite. AE, DC, MC, V. Parking: 11€ ($17). **Amenities:** Bar; sauna; public Internet. *In room:* A/C, minibar, hair dryer, safe.

Roko-Hof ★ Finds A very small corner of this cozy, yellow-fronted hotel dates from the 1600s, when the site was used as the headquarters for a Venetian merchant. About 70 years ago, a small hotel was established on the site, but much of what you'll see now dates from the late 1990s, when Roswitha Reichmann-Kollman expanded her premises into the government-rated four-star hotel you'll see today. Bedrooms are each contemporary looking and comfortable, all with a nearly identical color scheme of yellow and blue. The in-house restaurant serves well-prepared continental and Austrian cuisine, and the lakefront is about 1km (.6 mile) away.

Villacher Strasse 135, A-9020 Klagenfurt. ✆ **0463/21526.** Fax 0463/2152634. www.hotel-rokohof.at. 58 units. 130€–150€ ($208–$240) double. AE, DC, MC, V. Rates include breakfast. Free parking. Bus: 10, 11, or 12. **Amenities:** Restaurant; cafe/bar; room service; laundry service; dry cleaning. *In room:* TV, Wi-Fi, hairdryer.

Schloss Hotel Wörthersee ★ Despite its limited number of rooms, this is the most internationally famous hotel in Klagenfurt. Set across the road from the Wörthersee, it was originally built as a private villa in 1845 by a distant relative of Germany's counts of Thurn und Taxis. In 1892, a railway station (since demolished) was constructed nearby, and the building was bought and enlarged into a hotel. In 1982, the hotel was purchased by its present owners, the Strohschein family, who added what became the most popular restaurant in the region. In 1990, a German television series *(Schloss-Hotel Wörthersee)* filmed its most melodramatic scenes here.

Today the hotel is a combination of an Edwardian villa and a Teutonic castle, and a tunnel beneath the road leads to the hotel's private beach and a lakeside promenade that stretches for several miles. Most rooms have balconies and wood trim or paneling. The kitchens for the in-house restaurant, **Strohschein's Heuriger,** are supervised by the family matriarch, Hildstraud, and they produce some of the region's finest cuisine.

Villacher Strasse 338, A-9020 Klagenfurt. © **0463/21158.** Fax 0463/211500. www.schloss-hotel.at. 34 units. 64€–98€ ($102–$157) double; from 118€ ($189) suite for 2. Rates include buffet breakfast. MC, V. Closed Dec 23–28. Head west from the center of Klagenfurt for 3km (2 miles) toward Villach. **Amenities:** Restaurant; bar; indoor heated pool; sauna. *In room:* TV, Wi-Fi.

WHERE TO DINE

Da Luigi ★ (Finds ITALIAN/SEAFOOD One of the best restaurants in Klagenfurt focuses on dishes you'd expect to find in an upscale resort along the Adriatic, served with Italian panache in a mostly pink setting near Klagenfurt's Stadtstheater. Examples include grilled sea bass with balsamic vinegar and olive oil, and grilled daurade (a type of bream) served with a fresh tomato, white wine, and cognac sauce. The array of fresh shellfish, including crabs, oysters, clams, and about a half dozen other mollusks, is one of the best in town. The chefs always try to secure the freshest ingredients on the market. The wines come from throughout Europe, but there's a special emphasis on Austrian and Italian vintages.

Khevenhüllerstrasse 2. © **0463/353453.** Reservations recommended. Main courses 12€–24€ ($19–$38); fixed-price menu 45€–70€ ($72–$112). MC, V. Mon–Sat 11:30am–2pm and 6–10pm.

Felsenkeller AUSTRIAN Set less than a kilometer (1/2 mile) north of town, this restaurant features a sophisticated, elegant, and relatively inexpensive set of menu items that are served within a big-windowed building with views that sweep from the dining room out over the Ossiacher See. Menu items rely on fresh seasonal ingredients and change with the inspiration of the chef. Good-tasting examples include a gourmet version of fish and chips wherein mussels are deep-fried and served with a pinot wine sauce. Other choices include game, especially venison (in season), partridge, veal, pork, and usually at least one vegetarian dish a day.

Feldkirchner Strasse 141. © **0463/420130.** Reservations recommended. Main courses 10€–20€ ($16–$32). AE, DC, MC, V. Mon–Sat 9:30–12:30am.

Hamatle (Value CARINTHIAN There's been a popular restaurant in this century-old building since the 1950s, and present management, in place since around 1995, does everything it can to preserve the nostalgia. The result is a cozy restaurant with *grossmutter art* (grandmother-style) cuisine and an obvious allegiance to the traditions of Carinthia. (Its name is the equivalent, in local dialect, of *heimat,* which translates as "homeland.") There are two dining rooms, one on each of two floors, outfitted in a country-comfortable lake-district style. Menu items focus on noodles (usually in a creamy sauce and dotted with, among other things, ham, onions, and/or mushrooms); braised trout with butter sauce and herbs; succulent schnitzels of pork, chicken, or veal; and beefsteaks.

Linsengasse 1. © **0463/555700.** www.kaerntnerhamatle.at. Reservations recommended. Main courses 10€–20€ ($16–$32). AE, DC, MC, V. Tues–Sat 10am–11pm, Sun 10am–4pm.

Maria Loretto ★★ SEAFOOD This is the kind of long-established restaurant where an extended local family might migrate for a breath of fresh air, a view over the lake, and a well-prepared roster of mostly fish dishes. The setting is directly beside the lake, within a pair of pale blue, vaguely baroque dining rooms whose style is best described as *romantische-gemütlich* (romantic and cozy). Menu items include a small selection of meats (especially Wiener schnitzels and grilled filet steak), and lots and lots of fish. Raw ingredients are hauled in from the North and Mediterranean seas, the Atlantic Ocean, and the freshwater lakes and streams of the surrounding region. Most of these are prepared in the simplest way possible: lightly grilled and seasoned with a garlic-flavored butter sauce, served with salad and boiled new potatoes, and accompanied with a young and fruity white wine, preferably Austrian or Italian. Consider prefacing any main course with such starters as onion or garlic soup; a carpaccio of tuna, whitefish, or beef; smoked trout; or perhaps succulent snails cooked in garlic-butter sauce with a gratin of cheese.

Lorettoweg 54. ✆ **0463/24465.** www.maria-loretto.at. Reservations recommended. Main courses 11€–24€ ($18–$38). V. Daily 11am–10pm. Closed Jan 6–Feb 28. From Klagenfurt's center, take bus marked STRANDBAD KLAGENFURT/KLAGENFURT SEE.

Restaurant Lido AUSTRIAN/MEDITERRANEAN Although it originated in the 1980s as a rather grand and elegant restaurant, Lido has devolved into a much simpler, less pretentious bistro. Three kilometers (2 miles) west of the town center, beside the road leading to Villach, it offers simple but well-prepared fare: Wiener schnitzel; cold platters of smoked fish, including local salmon and whitefish; crayfish salads; roasted lamb with rosemary and thyme; cold sliced beef in aspic; and an assorted roster of grilled fish.

Friedelstrand 1. ✆ **0463/210712.** Reservations recommended. Main courses 20€–25€ ($32–$40). AE, DC, MC, V. Daily 12:30–2:30pm and 6:30–10:30pm. Closed 3 weeks in Nov.

Restaurant Oscar ★ AUSTRIAN/ITALIAN Stalwart and reliable, with a reputation for solid, well-prepared Italian and Austrian food, this restaurant lies on the northern edge of Klagenfurt's commercial core near the local hospital. The dining room is large but cozy, trimmed with dark-stained wood and furnished with modern-looking tables and chairs and high-tech lighting. Menu items lean toward Italy, with touches of Austrian specialties thrown in as well, and include homemade pastas; schnitzels; a savory roasted goose; hearty soups; crepes (including flavorful versions with spinach and/or mushrooms); risottos; roasted pork served with local cheeses and sage; and a rich focus every autumn on game dishes. The choice of fish is wide, with an emphasis on meaty "noble" fish that include sea bass and sea trout.

Sankt Veiter Ring 43. ✆ **0463/500177.** Reservations recommended. Main courses 12€–24€ ($19–$38); fixed-price lunch 18€ ($29); fixed-price dinner 35€ ($56); fixed-price dinner w/wine 48€ ($77). AE, DC, MC, V. Mon–Sat 11am–2pm and 6–11pm.

SHOPPING

The capital of Carinthia might surprise you with its quiet sense of prosperity and genteel good taste. Many of the interesting shops lie beside the **Bahnhofstrasse** and the pedestrian-only streets that radiate outward from the Alterplatz. Among the most appealing shops, you'll find **Kastner & Öhler,** Priesterhausg 7 (✆ **0463/56568**), where you'll see virtually every piece of equipment you'd need for the pursuit of sports in any season.

Kärntner Heimatwerk, Herrengasse 2 (✆ **0463/55575**), is housed on the street level of a pink-and-white baroque building in the center of town. It offers the best collection of locally made handicrafts in Klagenfurt. Merchandise includes a selection of embroidery, ceramics, wrought iron, glassware, and textiles sold by the meter. It's open Monday to Friday 8:30am to 6pm, and Saturday 8:30am to noon.

KLAGENFURT AFTER DARK

The largest, grandest, and most formal theater in Klagenfurt is the **Stadttheater,** Theaterplatz 4 (✆ **0463/540640;** www.stadttheater-klagenfurt.at), which presents opera, classics of German theater, and chamber and orchestral music performed by visiting groups. Built in 1910, this building went through a 2-year renovation (ending in 1998) that has given it a new state-of-the-art interior.

If you're lucky enough to arrive in Klagenfurt between mid-July and late August, make a point of strolling through the Neuerplatz every evening after 9:30pm. Here, open-air movies of famous cultural events (from virtually everywhere) are presented without charge. Past presentations have included filmed concerts by Billy Joel, Liza Minnelli, Montserrat Caballé, Bruce Springsteen, Tina Turner, and the Vienna Opera's presentation of various operas by Verdi. Kiosks around the square's perimeter offer snacks and drinks.

The rest of the year, take an evening stroll around the neighborhood of the **Pfarr-platz,** where you'll find most of Klagenfurt's nightlife options. The best of the lot includes **Bar Gallo Nero,** Pfarrhofgasse 8 (✆ **0463/512780**), where there's live music that never dips into anything too loud, too metallic, or too abrasive. Nostalgic references to Ireland pour out of **Pub Molly Malone,** Theatergasse 7 (✆ **0463/57200**), where pints of Irish, German, and Austrian beer make the traditional ballads and fiddle music more appealing.

2 CATHEDRALS, CASTLES & MORE: SIDE TRIPS FROM KLAGENFURT

ST. VEIT AN DER GLAN

The capital of Carinthia from 1170 until 1518, St. Veit an der Glan was where the dukes of Carinthia held power when the province was an imperial duchy. In the 15th century, high walls were built to fortify the city. To reach the town from Klagenfurt, drive 14km (9 miles) north on Route 83.

In the rectangular **Hauptplatz (Main Square)** at the center of town is a **Trinity Column** dating from 1715, erected to mark the town's deliverance from the plague. Also in this square is the fountain called **Schüsselbrunnen.** It is believed that the bottom part of this fountain was excavated at the old Roman city of Virunum. A bronze statue crowning the fountain depicts a 16th-century miner, which St. Veit has adopted as its symbol.

The **Rathaus (Town Hall)** has a baroque exterior, although the building dates from 1468, and an arcaded courtyard. Guided tours are conducted through the great hall Thursday to Tuesday 8am to noon and 1 to 4pm, and on Wednesday 8am to noon (closed Sat–Sun Nov–Apr).

Where To Stay & Dine

Hotel Ernst Fuchs Palast ★★★ Finds This is Carinthia's first art hotel, designed by Ernst Fuchs, doyen of Austria's Fantastic Realists. With a Tiffany-glass exterior, it's a luxurious, government-rated four-star establishment. This former ducal town has long been in need of accommodations to match its charm, and now it has a suitable hotel. The hotel is often a venue for seminars and conferences.

The public rooms are filled with art, and each of the bedrooms is decorated in a different color scheme. All bathrooms come with new equipment, each with a shower unit. The restaurant offers impressive Styrian and continental cuisine, and there is grand comfort throughout the place.

Prof. Ernst Fuchs Platz 1, A-9300 St. Veit an der Glan. ✆ **04212/4660.** Fax 04212/4660660. www.hotel-fuchsplalast.at. 60 units. 150€ ($240) double. Half-board 15€ ($24) per person extra. Rates include buffet breakfast. AE, MC, V. **Amenities:** Restaurant; bar; room service; babysitting; laundry service; dry cleaning; nonsmoking rooms; 1 room for those w/limited mobility. *In room:* TV, Wi-Fi, minibar, hair dryer, safe.

HOCHOSTERWITZ CASTLE ★

St. Veit an der Glan stands at the center of the most castle-rich section of Austria, with more than a dozen of the fortress complexes lying within a 10km (6½-mile) radius of

St. Veit. The best-known and most visited is **Hochosterwitz Castle** in Laundsdorf-Hochosterwitz (✆ **04213/2020**), about 10km (6¼ miles) to the east of St. Veit. The castle was first mentioned in documents of 860; in 1209, the ruling Spanheims made the Osterwitz family hereditary royal cupbearers and gave them Hochosterwitz as a fiefdom. When the last of that line was a victim of a Turkish invasion, the castle reverted to Emperor Frederick III, who bestowed it upon the area's governor, Christof Khevenhuller. In 1570, Baron Georg Khevenhuller, also the governor, purchased the citadel and fortified it against the Turks, providing it with an armory and adding the gates, a task completed in 1586. Since that time, the castle has been the property of the Khevenhuller family, as shown on a marble plate in the yard dated 1576.

The castle—the most striking in the country—stands in a scenic spot on a lonely, isolated hilltop 160m (525 ft.) above the valley. From the castle, you get an eagle's-eye view of the surrounding area, and to reach it you go up a 16th-century approach ramp and through a total of 14 fortified gates. You can look at the armor collection, visit a number of rooms, and wander through the portrait gallery.

Hochosterwitz Castle is open only Easter to October daily 8am to 6pm. Admission is 7.50€ ($12) for adults and 4.50€ ($7.20) for ages 6 to 18. A regional cafe and restaurant are located in the inner courtyard.

THE EXCAVATIONS AT MAGDALENSBERG ★

You can also strike out from St. Veit and head south, back to Klagenfurt, on Route 83. If you turn left after 6km (4 miles) on a road marked MAGDALENSBERG and travel east, you'll reach the **Ausgrabungen (Excavations) at Magdalensberg** (✆ **04224/2255**). About 14km (9 miles) from St. Veit, Magdalensberg was a Celto-Roman settlement site and the oldest Roman habitation north of the Alps. The Romans built a town here when they came to trade in the final century before the birth of Christ. In 1502, a farmer made the first discovery of a settlement here when he found a bronze statue, now called the **Magdalensberg Youth** (on display in Vienna).

However, it was not until the late 19th century that excavation work began, and even then, collectors were mainly interested in discovering valuable Roman art objects. Serious archaeologists began to work the site during the Allied occupation of Austria after World War II.

As you explore the ruins, you can see the foundations of a temple, as well as public baths and some mosaics. Tours are conducted only May to October daily 9am to 7pm. Admission is 5€ ($8) for adults and 3€ ($4.80) for children under 16.

A celebrated ritual (which has pagan origins), the "Four Hills Pilgrimage," starts from here every April. Participants race over four hills with burning torches, and must complete the run within 24 hours.

At the summit of the mountain, the Austrians have erected a shrine honoring two saints: Mary Magdalene and Helen. From it, a panoramic view of the encircling mountain range and the Klagenfurt basin unfolds.

STRASSBURG

Returning once more to St. Veit, you can head northeast along Route 83, which becomes the E7. When you reach the junction with Route 93, turn west along the upper Gurk Valley road, passing through the hamlet of Strassburg, which was a walled town in the Middle Ages. There is a Gothic **Pfarrkirche (Parish Church)** here, and the **Heilig-Geist-Spital Church,** dating from the 13th century, has some well-preserved frescoes. Dominating the village is a castle built in 1147, but it's changed over the centuries. This once was the headquarters of the powerful prince-bishops of Gurk. It has been turned into a local museum.

THE CATHEDRAL OF GURK ★★

A major pilgrimage site lies 3km (2 miles) to the west of Strassburg: the **Cathedral of Gurk Pfarramt Gurk** (**✆ 04266/8236**). The cathedral is the principal feature of the little market town of Gurk, and from 1072 until 1787, this area was the bishop's see. The *dom* (cathedral) is a three-aisled basilica erected between the mid-12th and early 13th centuries, and it's one of the best examples of Romanesque ecclesiastical architecture in the country. A set of towers with onion-shape domes rises nearly 43m (140 ft.).

The cathedral is rich in artwork, including the **Samson doorway** ★, an excellent example of Romanesque sculpture dating from 1180. Some **16th-century carved panels** ★ tell the story of St. Emma, an 11th-century countess who was canonized in 1938. The main 17th-century altar has dozens of statues, and there's a **1740 baroque pulpit** ★. In the bishop's chapel you can see **Romanesque murals** ★—other than the main altar, these are the most important art objects in the cathedral.

The cathedral is open daily 9am to 6pm. You can take a guided tour in English of both the cathedral and the crypt for 4.60€ ($7.40). For 6.20€ ($9.90), you can include a visit to the bishop's chambers. Guided tours are conducted at 10:30am, 1:30, and 3pm daily.

FRIESACH

After visiting the Cathedral of Gurk, you can take the same road east, back through Strassburg. Back on the E7, and depending on your time and interest, you can either turn north to visit the town of Friesach or else travel south again, passing through St. Veit en route to Klagenfurt.

If you opt for the Friesach detour, you'll find an interesting old town worth exploring. If you came from Vienna, Friesach might be your gateway to Carinthia. This is an ancient town whose first mention in historic annals occurred in the mid-9th century. The town once belonged to the prince-archbishops of Salzburg, who held on to it until the beginning of the 19th century. Lying in the broad Valley of Melnitz, this was once a major stopover for traders between Venice and Austria's capital.

In the historic center of town, you can see part of the 12th-century town walls and the remains of a water-filled moat. The Romanesque **Stadtpfarrkirche (Town Parish Church),** Wiener Strasse, was constructed in the 13th century and is noted for its stained glass in the choir. The town has a number of other interesting buildings, including a **Dominican monastery** from 1673, built on the site of a much older structure and containing a 14th-century church. The monastery lies north of the moat, and in summer, open-air plays are performed here. You can also visit the 13th-century **Heiligblutkirche (Church of the Holy Blood)** south of Hauptplatz.

West of Friesach, a 1.5km-long (1-mile) road or footpath takes you to the hill **Petersberg,** where the 10th-century **Church of St. Peter** stands. Here you can visit a watchtower to see 12th-century frescoes, and you can also see the ruins of a castle that belonged to the prince-archbishops of Salzburg. North of the town, on **Geiersberg,** is a second 12th-century castle, partially reconstructed but still mostly in ruins.

MARIA SAAL ★

Just outside of Klagenfurt, you can visit the pilgrimage church of **Maria Saal,** on a hill overlooking the Zollfeld Plain, some 10km (6¼ miles) north of the provincial capital along Route 83.

Maria Saal was first built by Bishop Modestus around the mid-8th century. The present church, which dominates the valley with its twin towers made of volcanic stone, dates from the early part of the 15th century, when a defensive wall was constructed to ward off attacks from the east. In the latter part of that century, the Magyars tried to take the fortress-church, but, like the Turks in later years, they were unable to conquer it.

One of the church's most outstanding features is a "lantern of the dead" in the late-Gothic style. There are some marble Gothic tombstones on the church grounds, and there's the *karner* (charnel house), an octagonal Romanesque building with two tiers of galleries. The church has many objets d'art, but it's the 1425 image of the Virgin that has made it a pilgrimage site.

An excursion to take from Maria Saal is to the **Herzogstuhl,** or Carinthian Ducal Throne, 1.5km (1 mile) to the north. A double throne on this ancient site was constructed from stones found at the Roman city of Virunum. The dukes of Carinthia used the throne to grant fiefs in medieval days.

THE VELLACH VALLEY

Southeast of Klagenfurt, the Vellach Valley leads to the Slovenian border, and your fellow visitors here are likely to be Slovenians. **Eisenkappel** is the major stopover in the valley. This town is surrounded by centuries-old forests and mineral springs, and because of its position as a frontier town only 15km (10 miles) from the Austro-Slovenian border's Jezersko Pass, it also offers many cultural and historical attractions.

The southernmost of all Austria's market villages, Eisenkappel, also known as Selezna Kapla, its Slovenian name, is home to a large Slovenian ethnic population. It lies at the foot of Karawanken, 39km (24 miles) from Klagenfurt (or Celovec, as you're likely to hear it called in this valley).

From Klagenfurt, drive south along Route 91 to the junction with Route 85. Cut east until you reach the junction with Route 82, and then head south to Eisenkappel.

There are many sky-blue lakes and white mountain peaks near Eisenkappel. **Lake Klopeiner** (below), to the north of this town, is the warmest lake in Carinthia, and 8km (5 miles) to the southwest you'll see **Trögerner Gorge.**

LAKE KLOPEINER

Surrounded by woodlands and shaped like an amphitheater, Lake Klopeiner lies south of the market town of Volkermarkt. To get there, drive east along Route 70.

The lake's waters sometimes reach 82°F (28°C) in summer, and the lake is fairly small—only 2km ($1^1/_2$ miles) long and less than a kilometer (about $^1/_2$ mile) wide at its broadest point. In summer, it's flooded with fun-loving Austrians. To keep the sky-blue water free of pollution, the government does not permit motor-powered craft on the lake. The resorts that ring the lake are part of the community of **St. Kanzian.**

LAKE OSSIACHER

Follow Route 95 northwest of Klagenfurt, passing through Moosburg and Feldkirchen to reach Ossiacher See (Lake Ossiacher). This body of water, some 11km (7 miles) long, is the province's third-largest lake. Its water temperature during the summer is only slightly cooler than that of Lake Wörther—a comfortable 79°F (26°C).

The lake is ringed with little villages that have become resorts by attracting summer visitors, mainly Austrians, who come to enjoy the sun and the water.

Our first stop, **Feldkirchen,** is an old town that once belonged to the Bamberg bishops. Located at a major crossroads, Feldkirchen grew and prospered from traders passing through the area, and pieces of the Middle Ages live on here, especially in the patrician houses and narrow streets. Visit the old quarter to see the Biedermeier facades that were added in the first part of the 19th century. The village has a Romanesque **Pfarrkirche (Parish Church)** with a Gothic choir and frescoes from the 13th century. Some small lakes near the town are worth visiting, if time permits.

Ossiach, a resort on the lake's south side, is small (pop. 650), but it's still the biggest settlement on the Ossiacher See. Ossiach has an 11th-century Benedictine abbey that was reconstructed in the 1500s. The monastery was dissolved a century or so ago, and **Carinthian Summer Festival** special events take place here.

On the lake's north shore are the **Sattendorf** and **Treffen** resorts, which are open year-round. Here you can breathe the pure mountain air and wander across alpine meadows deep into the forest. Vacationers can splash around in Ossiacher See or in indoor pools.

From the lake, you can make several easy excursions; take the **Kanzelbahn cable car** (10 min. from the resort) or drive to either Italy or Slovenia (20 min. to either destination). You can also make day trips to Klagenfurt (p. 434) or Villach (p. 447).

The little lakeside resort of **Annenheim** is on the north side of the Ossiacher See, near the end of the lake. From here, a cable car, the **Kanzelbahn,** takes you to **Kanzelhöhe** at 1,488m (4,882 ft.), where an observatory tower offers a panoramic view of the surrounding country.

3 LAKE WÖRTHER

The province's biggest alpine lake, 15km (10 miles) long, is the Wörther See, or Lake Wörther, lying west of Klagenfurt and linked to the city by a channel. In summer, it's a mecca for watersports enthusiasts.

This alpine lake's waters are quite warm—their temperature often exceeds 80°F (27°C) in midsummer. Beginning in May, Austrians swim here, something that rarely occurs in alpine lakes of most other provinces. The little villages around Wörther See are flourishing summer resorts, especially **Maria Wörth** and **Velden.**

VELDEN ★★: THE HEART OF THE AUSTRIAN RIVIERA

Velden, at the western end of the Wörther See, is the most sophisticated resort in Carinthia, and it's known as the heart of the Austrian Riviera. The resort has many landscaped parks that sweep down to the lakeside, and from most hotel rooms you'll have views of the sparkling blue lake with the peaks of **Karawanken** in the background.

Essentials

GETTING THERE Velden sits astride the main routes that connect Klagenfurt with Villach, Salzburg, and Innsbruck. Dozens of trains stop throughout the day, and the trip from Klagenfurt takes 14 to 21 minutes. For information about **train schedules,** call ✆ **05/1717** (www.oebb.at).

Velden has bus lines extending north and south, into small nearby villages, and east and west, paralleling the railway tracks to Klagenfurt and Villach. For **bus information,** call ✆ **0463/54340** in Klagenfurt.

If you're **driving** from Klagenfurt, head west along Route 83 for 23km (14 miles).

VISITOR INFORMATION The **tourist office** in the village center (✆ **04274/2103**) is open Monday to Thursday 8am to 6pm, Friday and Saturday 8am to 8pm, and Sunday 9am to 5pm.

What to Do in Velden

Naturally, the big attraction here is watersports, ranging from swimming in the warm alpine lake to surfing. The long swimming season begins May 1 and continues until the end of October. Instruction is available for all water activities. The most respected watersports outfitter in Velden is **Segelschule und Surfschule Berger,** Seecorso 40, Velden (✆ **04274/2691**). They rent equipment—Windsurfers, small boats, and canoes or kayaks—and give instruction. Many resort hotels have tennis courts, and you can also play golf at an 18-hole course 6km (4 miles) from Velden in a hilly landscape.

Most guests spend their time playing in the lake during the day and dancing the night away. Five o'clock tea dances are popular, and you can also trip the light fantastic to the orchestral music on the lake terraces. Summer festivals are often staged in Velden, and balls and beauty contests keep the resort's patrons amused. Contact the tourist office for more information about events and schedules. Also, this is a fine area for taking scenic country drives.

Where to Stay & Dine

Golf Park Hotel ★★ This grand hotel attracts Viennese celebrities, members of the Saudi Arabian royal family, tennis and ski stars, and film crews shooting movies at the region's historic monuments. Originally built in 1968, it has been enlarged and renovated since. The hotel sits in its own park beside the lake, offering peace, quiet, and impressive views of the valley below. Rooms are tastefully modern, each well furnished with comfy beds.

The heart and soul of the hotel is the restaurant, where a verdant terrace opens up in warm weather. The chef concocts a tempting array of frequently changing specialties, which might include a mousse of smoked trout with caviar in a champagne-flavored gelatin, river crayfish in a dill-flavored yogurt, and a supreme of freshwater char with tarragon and fresh asparagus.

Seecorso 68, A-9220 Velden. ✆ **04274/22980.** Fax 04274/22989. www.hotelgolf.com. 90 units. 198€ ($317) double; from 228€ ($365) suite for 2. Rates include half-board. AE, DC, MC, V. **Amenities:** Restaurant; bar; indoor heated pool; 9-hole putting course; 3 tennis courts; fitness center; sauna; massage; babysitting; laundry service; dry cleaning; solarium. *In room:* TV, Wi-Fi, minibar, hair dryer, safe.

Hotel Alte Post-Wrann ★ For many years, this hotel was the provincial headquarters for the postal routes from Vienna to Venice. Renovated, enlarged, and improved many times since, the hotel retains its stone-trimmed arched windows. Unlike many of the region's hotels, this one is open year-round. The sunny rooms are comfortable and conservatively furnished, and come in a variety of sizes—some quite large. All beds are excellent. Bathrooms generally have tubs or showers.

The entrance to the hotel's **Wrann** restaurant is marked by massive beams; during summer, seating is in the garden. Here, under a canopy of trees, you can order a range of traditional Austrian and regional recipes. The summer-only restaurant, **Vinoték,** is fashioned after a Viennese *heurige* (wine tavern) and specializes in local wines.

Europaplatz 4–6, A-9220 Velden. ✆ **04274/2141.** Fax 04274/51120. www.wrann.at. 36 units. 110€–146€ ($176–$234) double; 144€–190€ ($230–$304) suite. Rates include buffet breakfast. DC, MC, V. Parking 7€ ($11). **Amenities:** Restaurant; bar; fitness center; sauna; room service; babysitting; laundry service; dry cleaning; nonsmoking rooms; 1 room for those w/limited mobility. *In room:* TV, Wi-Fi, minibar, hair dryer, safe.

Shopping

Despite its relatively small size, Velden has some cosmopolitan shopping options. Its boutiques reflect trends in Vienna, Paris, and, to some extent, Milan. The main shopping thoroughfare is **Am Corso** (the end of Am Corso closest to the lake is called **See Corso**);

in addition to being the address of several of the town's bars and nightclubs, it's home to the best shops. For sporting goods of every conceivable type, stop in **Kretschman.** If you're searching for glamorous evening gowns, head for **Tschebull,** Am Corso 21 (© **04274/4947**).

Velden After Dark

The most visible and (on weekends) busiest nightlife spot is the **Casino Velden,** Am Corso 17 (© **04274/2064**). Built in the 1980s with lots of glass overlooking the lake and the busy boulevard that fronts it, the casino contains a series of roulette, blackjack, and baccarat tables, jangling slot machines, and a convention center. There are also two bars and a restaurant where you can lick your wounds after losing at the gambling tables.

You must be at least 18 years old and present your passport to enter; men must wear a jacket and tie. The complex is open daily from noon to 3am. Games of chance include blackjack, baccarat, stud poker, and American and French roulette, as well as slot machines. You pay 23€ ($37) at the door, but you're granted 30€ ($48) worth of chips, so entrance is essentially free.

Don't think, however, that you have to enter the precincts of the casino to be amused and entertained. The **American Bar** (also known as the **Schinackl Bar,** Am Corso 10; © **04274/51233**) is the de facto social centerpiece for the town. Here you'll see virtually everyone, either drinking at the bar with you or during their promenades up and down the lakefront. Set almost adjacent to the casino, it's open May to mid-September nightly from 8pm to 4am, features both indoor and outdoor areas, and presents live music from Monday to Saturday beginning at 10pm. A *schinackl,* incidentally, is a vernacular name for a style of rowboat used to catch fish in Carinthia.

If you're young at heart, you might enjoy the **Crazy Bull Disco,** Klagenfurter Strasse 17 (© **4274/2034**), where high-volume music, sometimes heavy metal, brings influences from faraway London and Los Angeles to otherwise sleepy Velden. The Crazy Bull is open nightly 10pm to around 4am, usually without any charge.

MARIA WÖRTH ★

Maria Wörth is one of the best bases for visiting Carinthia's largest alpine lake, the Wörther See. Part of this village, on the southern side of the lake across from Pörtschach, juts out into the lake on a rocky peninsula, providing a good view of the area. In addition to enjoying the lake, you can visit the golf courses in the nearby hamlet of Dellach.

The village's Gothic **Pfarrkirche (Parish Church)** has a baroque interior and a Romanesque crypt. It's noted for its 15th-century main altar. The circular *karner* (charnel house) in the yard was built in 1278.

Nearby is another noted church, the **Rosenkranzkirche,** from the 12th century, often referred to as "the winter church." It has some Romanesque frescoes of the Apostles from that century.

Essentials

GETTING THERE To reach Maria Wörth, take the **train** to either Velden or Klagenfurt, and then board one of the dozens of buses that depart throughout the day for Maria Wörth (trip time: 25–45 min.). For rail information, contact © **05/1717** (www.oebb.at). For bus information, call © **0463/54340** in Klagenfurt. If you're **driving** from Klagenfurt, head south on Route 91 and take the first exit marked MARIA WÖRTH. Follow an unclassified road running along the southern tier of the lake. The drive takes about 15 to 20 minutes.

VISITOR INFORMATION The **tourist office** in the town center (✆ **04273/2240**) is open Monday to Friday 8am to 12:30pm and 1 to 5pm, and Saturday and Sunday 10am to 12:30pm and 1:30 to 4pm.

Where to Stay & Dine

Aenea ★★★ This startlingly modern hotel is designer chic. In all the province of Carinthia there is nothing so stylishly minimalist, so trend-setting, rising five floors in a glass-and-concrete structure that evokes an avant-garde museum of art. The location is in the village of Reifinitz, opening onto the southern tier of Lake Wörthersee, 2 miles (3km) from Maria Wörth.

The interior is designed for complete relaxation, management boasting "maximum individual freedom—with no preordained hotel rhythm." On the fourth floor is a sun terrace with a Finnish sauna, aroma steam bath, solarium, fitness center, massage room, and even a tennis court, plus a panoramic pool. An elevator takes you down to the lake pavilion with its bathing beach. Bedrooms are stunning in design, the bold, super-cool creation of Rodolfo Dordoni, the Italian designer with Philippe Starck bathrooms. Each room is a suite with a good-sized terrace opening onto Wörthersee.

Wörthersee Süduferstrasse 86, A-9081, Reifinitz (Maria Wörth). ✆ **04273/26220.** Fax 04273/26220-10. www.aenea.at. 15 suites. July–Aug 550€ ($880) suite; off-season 350€ ($560) suite. Rates include breakfast. AE, DC, MC, V. Closed Nov–Mar. **Amenities:** Restaurant; 2 bars; pool; tennis court; fitness center; spa; sauna; steam bath; room service; massage; laundry service; bathing beach; solarium; sun terrace. *In room:* A/C in some, TV, Wi-Fi, hair dryer, safe.

4 VILLACH

48km (30 miles) W of Klagenfurt; 140km (87 miles) SE of Salzburg

Villach, in the center of the Carinthian lake district in a broad basin along the Drau River, is a great place from which to explore the rest of the district. It's also the gateway to the south, and it's easy to make day trips to Slovenia or Italy from here. If you were planning on continuing south anyway, this is also a good stopover point. There was a settlement here in Roman times, and Villach belonged to the bishops of Bamberg (a distant lake near Nürnberg, Germany) from the 11th century until Maria Theresia acquired it for the Hapsburgs. Today it's an industrial town.

ESSENTIALS

GETTING THERE Villach is a railway junction for four different lines connecting central and southern Austria with Italy, and **trains** arrive throughout the day from Vienna (trip time: 4½ hr.) and Klagenfurt (trip time: 25 min.). Although it's easier to take the train, several different bus lines fan out into the surrounding countryside. For **train information,** call ✆ **05/1717;** for **bus information,** call ✆ **04242/44410.** If you're **driving** from Klagenfurt, Villach is about 56km (35 miles) west on the Autobahn A2.

VISITOR INFORMATION The **tourist office,** Rathausplatz 1 (✆ **04242/2052900**), is open Monday to Friday 9am to 6pm, and Saturday 10am to 5pm.

EXPLORING VILLACH & THE VILLACHER ALPS ★

At the center of the Altstadt (Old City) is **Hauptplatz (Main Square).** There's a bridge over the Drau at Hauptplatz's north end, and the **Pfarrkirche (Parish Church)** is at the south end. The church is a mixture of styles, with a baroque altar and Gothic choir stalls.

Thermal Waters to Keep You Young

From the heart of the Old Town in Villach, it's a 4km (2½-mile) drive to **Warmbad-Villach,** a town known for its thermal swimming pools and mineral springs. This spa, on the southern fringe of Villach, is the only place where visitors can swim at the source of the thermal waters, which are supposed to counteract the aging process.

The warm springs at Warmbad were used by the ancient Romans, and there was a road that passed through Warmbad en route to Italy. During the Middle Ages, Villach became a thriving market town.

Beginning with Europe's spa craze in the late 19th century, a handful of spa hotels sprung up around Warmbad-Villach, the first of which was the Kurhotel Warmbaderhof. We've recommended a few spa hotels below.

Hotel Warmbaderhof, Kadischenallée, Warmbad Villach (✆ **04242/30010;** fax 04242/30011309; www.warmbad.at), is the largest and most dignified of the hotels that have sprung up near Warmbad's famous springs. Built 200 years ago, and enlarged and modernized since, it boasts a covered passageway leading directly to the town's spa facilities. Set amid gardens in the town center, the hotel offers its own heated swimming pool with a ceiling shaped like a continuous barrel vault, and an angular outdoor pool connected with the indoor pool. The two hotel restaurants serve well-prepared food. Most of the 116 rooms and 12 suites are in a modern wing attached to the establishment's historic core and are conservatively furnished. The double rate is 246€ to 402€ ($394–$643); a suite runs 460€ to 490€ ($73–$784). Rates include half-board, and there's free parking. The hotel is closed 3 to 4 weeks in November and December.

Standing in a large park, **Der Karawankenhof,** Kadischenallée (✆ **04242/300220;** fax 04242/30022061; www.warmbad.at), offers a battery of health

Like most towns of its size, Villach has a **Trinity Column,** dating from 1739, commemorating deliverance from the plague.

In the **Schillerpark,** on Peraustrasse, there's a large panoramic relief of the province, the **Relief von Kärnten,** that's on view from May 2 to the end of October (except Fri, Sun, and holidays) from 10am to 4:30pm.

Villach is a good center from which to explore the Carinthian lake district, including the **Villacher Alps,** an 18km (11-mile) journey via the Villacher Alpenstrasse toll road (12€/$19 each way). There are panoramic views in many directions, and the best viewing spots are marked. At the end of the road you'll find a chairlift that will take you to the summit of **Dobratsch** (2,166m/7,106 ft.), which offers one of the most famous views in Austria. At the top, a network of hiking paths fans out.

If you're in Villach in summer, you might want to drive southeast to **Faaker See (Lake Faaker),** a small body of water that's popular with swimmers and water-skiers. This lake's waters frequently reach 79°F (26°C) in July and August. From Villach, follow the signs to Faak.

and spa facilities. The "bath world," as they call it, consists of whirlpools, indoor and outdoor swimming pools, rapids, a fitness center, a gym, a sauna, massage treatments, and other facilities. The restaurant serves excellent food. This sizable four-star modern hotel, open all year, rents 70 well-furnished rooms and 10 suites; the double rate is 150€ to 184€ ($240–$294) or 216€ ($346) in a suite. Rates include half-board.

Josefinenhof Hotel ★, Kadischenallée 8 (✆ **04242/30030;** fax 04242/30033089; www.warmbad.com), functions as a government-rated four-star hotel with its own spa, fitness, and conference facilities. Although much of this hotel was built in the 1960s, its original core was established in the 1700s as a hospital. Its sun terrace stretches toward the hotel's private park. You can enjoy treatment at the hydrotherapy and beauty center, or partake of a host of health and medical services. The 52 comfortable rooms and nine suites have rows of sun-flooded windows and balconies. Bathrooms are well equipped with robes and hair dryers. The double rate is 135€ ($216). Rates include full board, and there's free parking.

GETTING THERE Warmbad, no more than a cluster of buildings on routes heading into Italy, is 4km (2½ miles) south of Villach, and virtually everything in town stems from tourism. A **red bus** (marked WARMBAD when it goes to Warmbad and BAHNHOF as it heads back to Villach) runs between the towns at 30-minute intervals all day long; the trip takes 10 to 12 minutes. In Villach, the railway station acts as the stop for the red bus, although it stops almost everywhere else in between the towns. There are also trains that come from Villach's main railway station at 30-minute intervals. For information about train schedules and fares, call ✆ **05/1717.**

WHERE TO STAY

Romantik Hotel Post ★★ Rich in Carinthian history, this hotel was built in 1500, and some original elements, like the rich vaulted ceilings, have been incorporated into the hotel. The facade is a Teutonic fantasy of carved stone detailing, Ionic columns, and intricately patterned wrought iron. Between 1548 and 1629, this was the town palace of one of Carinthia's richest families. During that period, the house hosted an emperor, a king, an archduke, and later an empress (Maria Theresia). Later still, the nephew of Napoleon I dropped in and signed a registration slip that still belongs to the hotel. On the premises is a baronial fireplace, an arcaded courtyard shielded from the sun by an ancient collection of chestnut trees, and a host of elegantly furnished rooms. Rooms come in various sizes and have marvelously comfortable beds.

The establishment pays special attention to its traditional cuisine, much of which is heavily laced with cheese, butter, and cream. These include *tafelspitz;* schnitzels (sometimes stuffed with cheese and ham); and recipes with local venison, including soups, pâtés, and stews. The hotel also offers health-conscious cuisine. In July and August, piano music and candlelit dinners are offered in the garden courtyard.

Hauptplatz 26, A-9500 Villach. ✆ **04242/261010.** Fax 04242/26101420. www.romantik-hotel.com. 67 units. 130€–170€ ($208–$272) double; 225€–250€ ($360–$400) suite. Rates include buffet breakfast. AE, DC, MC, V. **Amenities:** Restaurant; bar; fitness center; sauna; massage; laundry service; dry cleaning; nonsmoking rooms; solarium. *In room:* TV, Wi-Fi, minibar, hair dryer, safe.

WHERE TO DINE

Stadt Restaurant ★★ AUSTRIAN/CARINTHIAN Acclaimed for its cuisine and highly rated in European gourmet guides, this restaurant is a traditional favorite. Wolfgang Puck was an apprentice chef at The Post before heading to Los Angeles, where he eventually opened his well-known restaurant, Spago. In summer, tables are placed outside in fair weather in a part of the hotel known as The Orangerie, with its wild roses and climbing ivy. If there's a celebrity visiting in summer, chances are you'll find them dining here. The menu is seasonally adjusted to take advantage of the best produce. Freshly caught fish, especially in summer, is the local favorite, and it's grilled to your preference. Many Carinthian specialties based on recipes from long ago are also served here, including *kärtner käsnudeln,* which are large, round ravioli stuffed with savory cheese. In summer the herbs used in many of the dishes come straight from the hotel garden, as do many of the fresh vegetables. In the evening, live piano music entertains diners.

Hauptplatz 26. ✆ **04242/261010.** Reservations required. Main courses 15€–24€ ($24–$38) AE, DC, MC, V. Daily 11:45am–2:30pm and 6:30–10:30pm.

5 LAKE MILLSTATTER

The second-largest lake in the province, Millstatter See is 13km (8 miles) long, 2km (1 mile) wide, and 140m (459 ft.) deep. This beautiful blue lake, east of Spittal, is set against a backdrop of the forested **Seerücken** (866m/2,841 ft.) to the south and **Nockberge** to the north.

MILLSTATT AM SEE

About midway along the lake's northern rim, **Millstatt am See** and **Seeboden** are the principal lake resorts. Most hotels here are open only during the warmer months, and prices are highest in July and August, when reservations are mandatory. Prices are often reduced in late spring and early autumn, when it's easier to find a room. An **organ-music festival** is held May to September.

Essentials

GETTING THERE Because Millstatt has no train connections, most travelers take a train to Spittal an der Drau from Klagenfurt (trip time: 1 hr.) or Salzburg (trip time: 2 hr.). (On many maps and timetables, this railway junction is referred to as Spittal-Millstattersee.) From Spittal's railway station, passengers catch one of the **buses** that depart around 16 times a day for the 20-minute trip to Millstatt am See.

Millstatt is 299km (186 miles) southwest of Vienna and 90km (56 miles) west of Klagenfurt. To **drive** here from Villach, head northwest along the A10, bypassing Spittal. At the turnoff for Seeboden, head east along the northern perimeter of the lake, following Route 98.

VISITOR INFORMATION The **tourist office** in the village center (✆ **04766/2022**) is open daily 9am to 7pm.

Visiting the Abbey

Other than the lake, Millstatt's main attraction is the ***Stift* (Abbey)** ★, which was founded in 1080 as a Benedictine monastery. Near the end of the 15th century, it was taken over by Jesuits. One part of the monastery has been used as a hotel (the **Hotel Lindenhof**) since 1773, and it was once the mansion of the Grand Master of the Knights of St. George.

In the abbey courtyard stands a 1,000-year-old "Judgment" lime tree. The cloister, which has Gothic vaulting and Romanesque arches, is reached from the east side of the court. The abbey contains a fresco of the Last Judgment, a masterpiece of Austrian Renaissance art. The Stiftskirche (Abbey Church) has a Romanesque doorway that is the complex's major architectural attraction.

Where to Stay & Dine

Hotel Alpenrose ★ (Finds) Enjoying a splendid scenic setting with a view of the valley and the mountains, the Hotel Alpenrose is in the tiny alpine village of Obermillstatt, 2km (1½ miles) from the center of Millstatt. This is the first "biohotel" to open in Austria, and the Theuermanns (your hosts) are involved in holistic medicine, macrobiotic diets, and yoga. They run a good hotel and restaurant in a chalet-inspired building that contains well-furnished rooms, each with a balcony. There are no radios or TVs "to ensure tranquillity," but you will find good beds and small bathrooms with well-kept shower units. On the premises is an array of new-age programs, including yoga. Smoking is not permitted.

Obermillstatt, A-9872 Millstatt am See. ✆ **04766/2500.** Fax 04766/3425. www.biohotel-alpenrose.at. 30 units. 96€–111€ ($154–$178) per person. Rates include vegetarian half-board. No credit cards. **Amenities:** Restaurant; lounge; heated outdoor pool; spa; sauna; laundry service; dry cleaning; rooms for those w/limited mobility. *In room:* Hair dryer, safe.

Hotel am See Die Forelle ★ This attractive, four-story hotel has a history dating from around 1900, when a private villa and an unpretentious guesthouse were combined to form one building. Today, much enlarged and improved over the years, the hotel has a lakeside terrace sheltered by chestnut trees and a reputation as one of the finest hotels on the Millstatter See. The hotel's interior contains bright, medium-size rooms (all but 10 have lake views) equipped with good beds. The small bathrooms have tubs or shower stalls. There's a big, well-maintained lawn that leads down to the lakefront beach. The Aniwanter family serves excellent cuisine, with fixed-price four-course meals and a la carte dishes.

A-9872 Millstatt am See. ✆ **04766/2050.** Fax 04766/205011. www.hotel-forelle.at. 126€–280€ ($202–$448) double. Rates include half-board. MC, V. Closed mid-Oct to early May. **Amenities:** Restaurant; bar; outdoor heated pool; whirlpool; Jacuzzi; sauna; room service; nonsmoking rooms. *In room:* TV, hair dryer, safe.

15

Styria

In Styria, the "green heart of Austria," forests cover about half the country, and grasslands and vineyards blanket another quarter. This is one of Austria's bargain provinces—even its top hotels charge only moderate prices. Trout fishing, mountain climbing, and hiking are popular summer activities, and in the past decade Styria has been emerging as a ski area. (It has a long way to go before it will rival Land Salzburg or Tyrol, however.) Schladming/Rohrmoos is a skiing center of Dachstein-Tauern, in the upper valley of the Enns River.

Interesting areas to visit in Styria include Bad Gleichenberg, the most important summer spa in South Styria, set among parks and mineral waters; and Bad Aussee, an old market town and spa in the heart of the lush Salzkammergut. Also worth a visit are Murau, a winter ski region and a good center for driving tours of the surrounding countryside, and Mariazell, Austria's pilgrimage center. If you're driving around this area, you should know that parking is free unless otherwise noted, and is rarely a problem.

Styria ("Steiermark" in German) is the second-largest province in the country. It borders Slovenia and Hungary, as well as the Austrian provinces of Burgenland, Lower Austria, Upper Austria, Land Salzburg, and Carinthia. Northwestern Styria includes the alpine ranges of the Salzkammergut, while its eastern section resembles the steppes of Hungary. The Dachstein features mammoth glaciers.

Throughout history, this rich land of valleys, rivers, mountain peaks, and glaciers has been sought after. It was greedily attacked by Huns, Hungarians, and Turks, and even in Celtic times people knew that the mountains of Upper Styria were a valuable source of iron ore, which the tribes used for weapons and other goods. The Romans also exploited the rich deposits, and the Crusaders used armor made from Styrian iron to fight the "infidel" in the East. Iron resources shaped Styria's economy, and today it's Austria's leading mining province.

Styria is a province deeply steeped in tradition, and the costume that some of the men still occasionally wear demonstrates this point. Derived from an original peasant costume, it's made of stout greenish-gray cloth with Styrian green material used for the lapels and the stripe along the side of the pant legs.

Graz, the capital of Styria, is the second-largest Austrian city, and in imperial times it was known as the place to which state officials retired—the city even acquired the nickname Pensionopolis (City of the Retired).

TIPS FOR ACTIVE TRAVELERS

Within Styria's borders are the alpine ranges of the Salzkammergut and steppe country that resembles that of the Great Hungarian Plain. This conglomerate of river valleys, mountain peaks, glaciers, and verdant sun-drunk vineyards is a great place to pursue outdoor activities. Graz serves as a good base for stockpiling supplies and planning your excursions. Here are the essentials for planning an outdoorsy vacation in Styria.

BALLOONING Styria is home to several hot-air ballooning outfits. Ask a local entrepreneur to take you up for a 90- to 120-minute escapade over the region's rooftops and lakes, preferably with a bottle of champagne and a good companion. The oldest outfitter

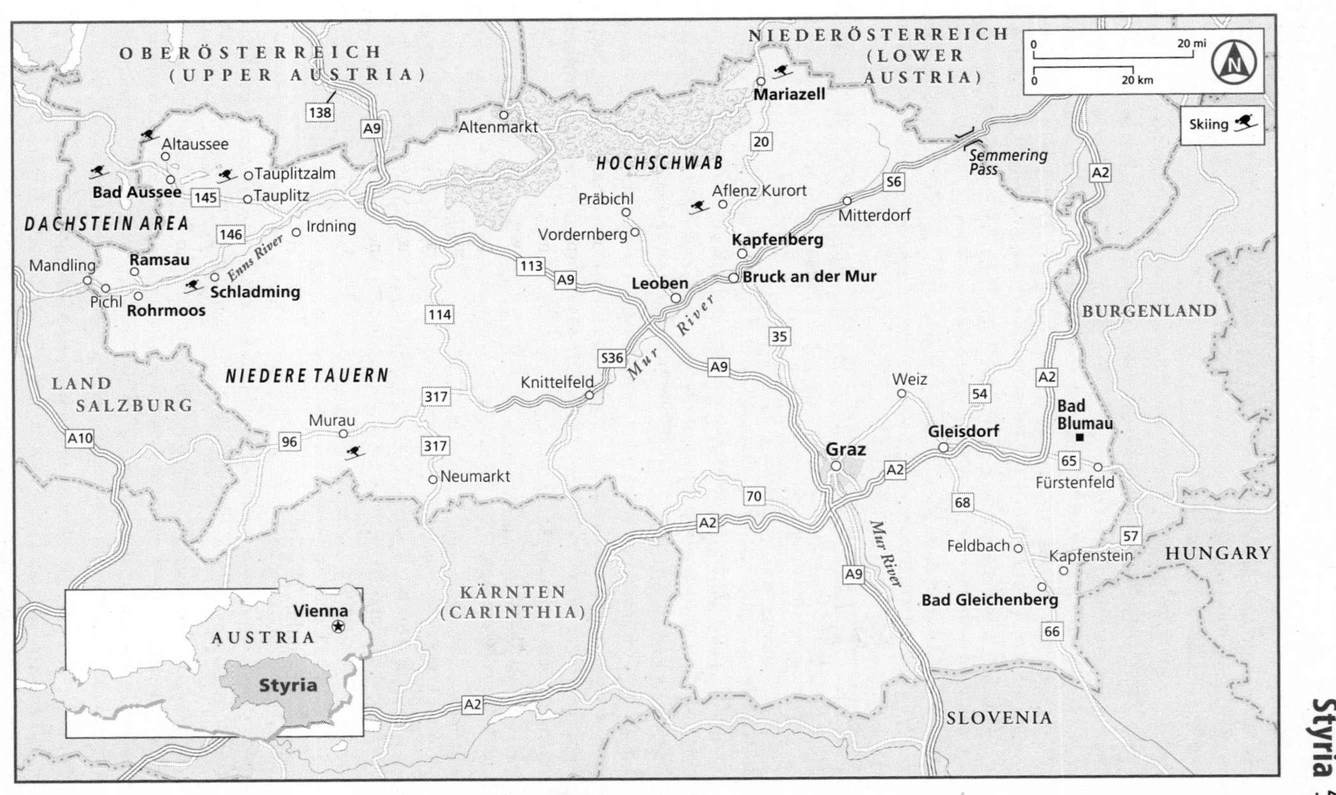

STYRIA

15

TIPS FOR ACTIVE TRAVELERS

in Styria (established in 1976) is **Gerd Skreiner's Union Aeronautic Styria,** Postfach 68A, A-8182 Puch bei Weiz (✆ **06645/456941**). Located in a village adjacent to the Stubenbergsee (a local lake), 40km (25 miles) east of Graz, it maintains six balloons. Excursions cost 230€ ($368) per person for the first flight and 140€ ($224) for subsequent flights. Flights can be conducted, weather permitting, in any season. Each balloon holds a pilot and up to three passengers.

BIKING Cycling enthusiasts will be pleased by Styria's terrain. The gentle undulations of the eastern plain and the historic scenery make for a pleasant ride. You can rent a bike through an independent operator, **Bicycle,** Kaiser-Franz-Josef-Kai 66 (✆ **0316/8213570**), near Graz's town center for 10€ ($16) per day. Contact **Eurobike,** Mühlstrasse 20, A-5162 Oberturn (✆ **06219/74440**), to arrange bike tours through some of the most scenic regions of Austria and Italy. A particularly appealing trip is an excursion known as the Muradweg, a week-long trek along the Mur River. The average age of participants in this tour ranges from 50 to 60, and cost is between 490€ to 610€ ($784–$976), depending on the hotel you choose. Overnight accommodations, some meals, equipment rental, and luggage transfers are included in the price. You pay extra, however, for breakfast and dinner, costing 100€ to 120€ ($160–$192) per person.

BOATING The region's many lakes are great places for experienced and novice boaters. **Hotel Backenstein,** Braühof 156, A-8993 Grundlsee (✆ **03622/8545;** www.backenstein.at), offers packages that include boat rentals, lessons, and accommodations.

CANOEING White-water enthusiasts will be enchanted by the clean, crisp waters of the glacial runoff. Although water temperatures can be brisk, any hearty paddler will tell you the best way to stay warm is to paddle furiously. **Sportagentur Strobl,** Ausseer Strasse 2–4, A-8940 Liezen (✆ **03612/25343**), will help set you adrift.

FISHING If you want to spend an afternoon fishing, cast your luck with one of the guide services that can be arranged for you by the **Tourismusver Ausseer Land,** Bahnhustrasse 132, A-8990 Bad Aussee (✆ **03622/54040**), or Tourismusverband **Murau,** Bundesstrasse 13A (✆ **03532/2720**).

GOLF Styria's gently undulating landscapes are well suited for golf courses, many of which allow nonmembers to reserve tee-off times if the course isn't too busy. Two of the region's most appealing golf courses are **Golfclub Gut Murstätten,** A-8403 Lebring (✆ **03182/3555;** www.gcmurstaetten.at), a half-hour drive south of Graz; and the **Golfclub Murhof,** A-8130 Frohnleiten (✆ **03126/3010;** www.murhof.at), a half-hour drive north of Graz. Additionally, any hotel or tourist office can point you to other golf courses.

HIKING Alpinists who toil for their highs will want to experience some of the climbs in the Dachstein-Tauern region. It's best to scale the steep rock faces of the Alps with an experienced guide. A guide (or just some climbing buddies) can be located for you by **Alpin- und Abenteuerclub Dachstein,** Schilldletten 88, A-8972 Ramsau (✆ **03687/815980**).

SKIING The Dachstein glacier enables year-round skiing in Styria. Cross-country skiers will find this a great diversion in summertime. For general and booking information, contact **Tourismusverband Ramsau** (✆ **03687/81833**). The Dachstein-Tauern (see later in this chapter) and Salzkammergut regions have winter ski facilities.

TENNIS If you want to play tennis, **Sporthotel Matschner** in Ramsau (✆ **03687/817210**) offers guests hotel and tennis packages, as do many other hotels with courts (see hotel reviews throughout this chapter).

1 GRAZ ★★

200km (124 miles) SW of Vienna; 138km (86 miles) NE of Klagenfurt; 285km (177 miles) SE of Salzburg

Graz, Styria's capital, blends modern life and historical architecture. The city's legacy dates from prehistoric times, when its location at a ford across the Mur River was a major factor in its development. Romans, Slavs, and Bavarians all had a hand in shaping the town.

Graz is a great place to stay because it's easy to make day trips into the countryside from here, and there's plenty to see and do. Visit the Schlossberg (castle), go hiking or hot-air ballooning, or visit one of the museums. If you're here in the fall, you might want to attend the **Steierischer Herbst (Styrian Autumn)** festival, which features contemporary art, music, and literature. The arts festival has a reputation for being avant-garde, presenting everything from jazz to mime.

Fearing floods, early settlers established fortifications on the steep dolomite hill overlooking the river's ford. The city's name is derived from the Slavic word *gradec,* meaning "little fortress." A small castle was built on the hill, which is now the Schlossberg. Graz has been ruled by many governments, including those of Germany, Bohemia, Hungary, the Babenbergs, and the Hapsburgs.

The medieval town developed at the foot of the Schlossberg and some of the late-Gothic period structures remain. These buildings were constructed when Emperor Frederick III used Graz as a capital after the Hungarians forced him out of Vienna. The castle and the cathedral, along with the city's narrow-gable roofs and arcaded courtyards, all contribute to its charm.

Life wasn't always kind to the people of Graz. In 1480, the little town was afflicted by the "Plagues of God"—locusts, the Black Death, the Turks, and a threat from the Hungarians.

When the Hapsburg inheritance was divided into Austrian and Spanish branches in 1564, Graz became the prosperous capital of "Inner Austria" and the residence of Archduke Carl, who ruled Styria, Carinthia, and Italian Hapsburg lands. Carl had the town's fortifications strengthened in the Italian style, with bastions and moats.

A Jesuit college and Lutheran school were both active by the end of the 16th century. The astronomer Johannes Kepler (1571–1630) began his teaching career at the Lutheran school. Fine arts and commerce flourished in Graz, bringing honor and riches to the city, and that prosperity is reflected in palaces and mansions built during that period. Italian Renaissance architects were making their impact here around the time Emperor Ferdinand II moved his court to Vienna in 1619.

The city walls were demolished in 1784, and the slopes they'd stood on were planted with trees. Napoleon's armies made three appearances here, and Austria's defeat by his forces at the Battle of Wagram (1809) resulted in a treaty that forced Graz to level the Schlossberg's battlements. Only the **Uhrturm (Clock Tower)** and the **bell tower** were saved, rescued by payment of a high ransom by the citizens of Graz. The Schlossberg became the beautiful park you see today.

During World War II, the city saw much bombing and devastation. However, in 1945, Graz was allotted to the British, and reconstruction began.

Today, Graz has some 250,000 inhabitants, and it supports thriving breweries, machine factories, trading companies, and service industries. The **Graz Fair** is an important commercial and industrial event in southeastern Europe. Graz's three universities, opera house, theater, museums, concert halls, and art galleries comprise Styria's cultural center.

Getting There

By Plane

Austrian Airlines (© **05176/67200**) offers daily flights from Vienna to **Thalerhof International Airport** (© **0316/2902;** www.flughafen-graz.at), 18km (11 miles) south of Graz. **Tyrolean Air** and **Lufthansa** also serve the airport. There's a white-sided, 15-passenger minivan that makes six trips a day between Graz's airport and the city center. A one-way trip costs 5€ ($6.50) per person. Departures coincide with the arrival of incoming flights, but the trips aren't frequent enough. The much more convenient cab ride from the airport to the city center (for up to four passengers) costs around 20€ ($26).

By Train

Graz is Austria's southern center for rail lines between Vienna and Slovenia. It's also the junction for secondary rail lines that extend to Budapest and a series of valleys in western Styria. At least 10 trains depart every day from Vienna's Südbahnhof for Graz (trip time: 2½ hr.). Through connections, it's easy to get here from other Austrian cities such as Innsbruck, Salzburg, and Klagenfurt. In addition, about one local train per hour arrives in Graz from minor rail lines in western Styria's isolated valleys and from the more populated areas of eastern Styria and the Hungarian border. For **rail information,** call © **05/1717** (www.oebb.at).

By Bus

Graz is also the departure point for about 100 different bus lines, most of which head toward hamlets and small villages. For bus information, call © **0316/5987.** Because of its excellent train connections, however, most travelers arrive by rail.

By Car

If you're driving from Vienna, take Autobahn A2 south. The Autobahn doesn't stretch all the way to Graz; part of it is Route 54, which becomes Autobahn A2 again northeast of Graz.

Getting Around

Graz City Transport, Jakoministrasse 1 (© **0316/820606**), operates streetcar and bus service throughout the city. **Jakominiplatz,** on the river's eastern bank, and **Griesplatz,** on the western bank, are the points where most streetcar lines intersect. The Graz City Transport office at Jakoministrasse 1 is open Monday to Friday 8am to 6pm, Saturday 9am to 1pm.

For information on Postal Buses, contact the **Graz City Tourist office,** Herrengasse 16 (© **0316/80750**).

The city's largest underground parking lot is the **Tiefgarage Andreas Hofer Platz,** on the Andreas-Hofer-Platz (© **0316/829191**). Parking costs 32€ ($51) for a full day or 4€ ($6.40) per hour. Within the city's historic center, you can park in the blue zones—indicated by a blue line painted beside the curb—for up to 3 hours. Parking costs .60€ ($1) per half-hour. You can either put coins in a parking meter or buy parking vouchers from tobacco shops or post offices. To use the voucher, fill in the blanks with the date and the time you parked in a spot, and leave it on the dashboard so it's visible through the windshield.

Major car-rental agencies in Graz (all also represented at the airport) include **Avis,** Schlögelgasse 10 (© **0316/812920**); **Budget,** Europaplatz 12 (© **0316/722074**); and **Hertz,** Andreas-Hofer-Platz (© **0316/825007**). These offices are open Monday to Friday 8am to 5pm, Saturday 9am to noon.

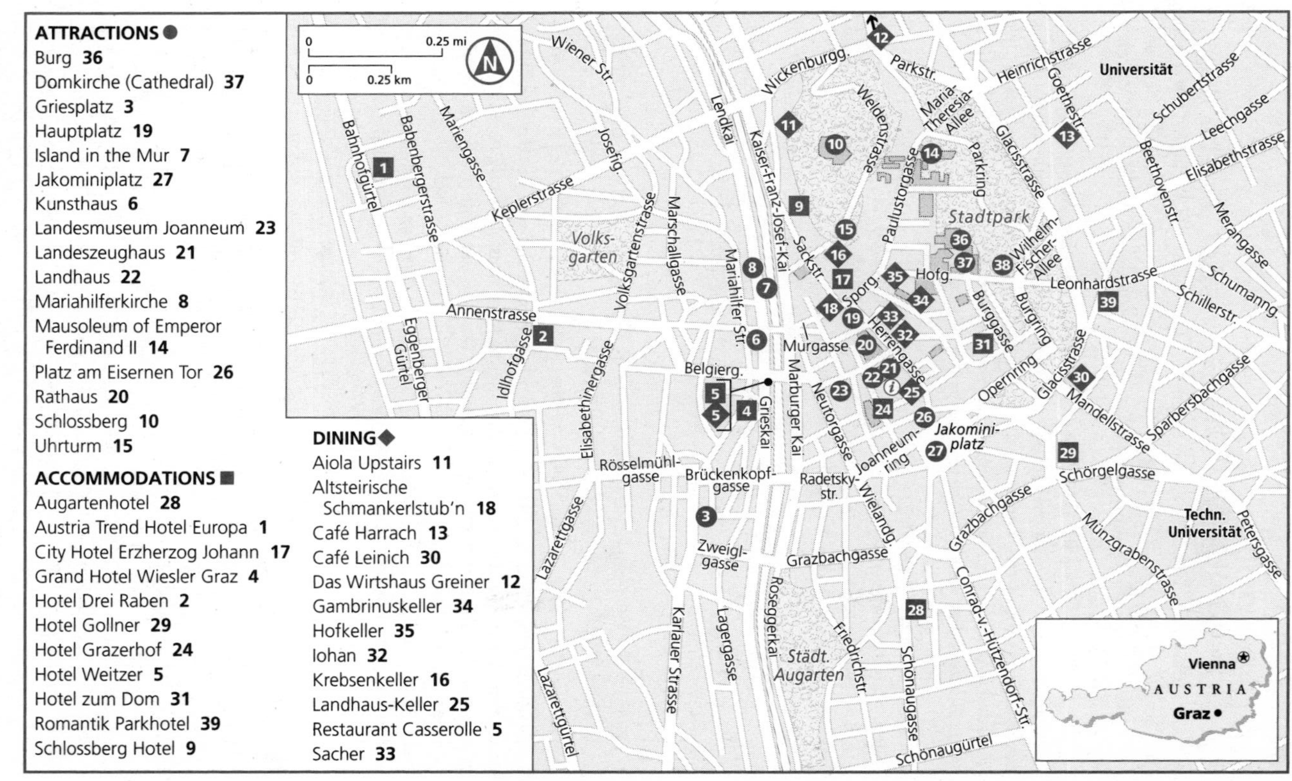
ATTRACTIONS ●
Burg 36
Domkirche (Cathedral) 37
Griesplatz 3
Hauptplatz 19
Island in the Mur 7
Jakominiplatz 27
Kunsthaus 6
Landesmuseum Joanneum 23
Landeszeughaus 21
Landhaus 22
Mariahilferkirche 8
Mausoleum of Emperor Ferdinand II 14
Platz am Eisernen Tor 26
Rathaus 20
Schlossberg 10
Uhrturm 15
ACCOMMODATIONS ■
Augartenhotel 28
Austria Trend Hotel Europa 1
City Hotel Erzherzog Johann 17
Grand Hotel Wiesler Graz 4
Hotel Drei Raben 2
Hotel Gollner 29
Hotel Grazerhof 24
Hotel Weitzer 5
Hotel zum Dom 31
Romantik Parkhotel 39
Schlossberg Hotel 9
DINING ◆
Aiola Upstairs 11
Altsteirische Schmankerlstub'n 18
Café Harrach 13
Café Leinich 30
Das Wirtshaus Greiner 12
Gambrinuskeller 34
Hofkeller 35
Iohan 32
Krebsenkeller 16
Landhaus-Keller 25
Restaurant Casserolle 5
Sacher 33
0 0.25 mi
0 0.25 km
Vienna
AUSTRIA
Graz
Universität
Techn. Universität
Stadtpark
Volksgarten
Städt. Augarten
Jakominiplatz
Wiener Str.
Wickenburgg.
Parkstr.
Heinrichstrasse
Goethestr.
Schubertstrasse
Leechgasse
Elisabethstrasse
Merangasse
Schumanng.
Schillerstr.
Beethovenstr.
Glacisstrasse
Parkring
Maria-Theresia-Allee
Weldenstrasse
Paulustorgasse
Wilhelm-Fischer-Allee
Leonhardstrasse
Hofg.
Sporg.
Herrengasse
Burggasse
Burgring
Opernring
Mandellstrasse
Sparbersbachgasse
Schörgelgasse
Münzgrabenstrasse
Petersgasse
Grazbachgasse
Conrad-v.-Hötzendorf-Str.
Schönaugasse
Schönaugürtel
Friedrichstr.
Roseggerkai
Marburger Kai
Grieskai
Neutorgasse
Joanneumring
Radetskystr.
Wielandg.
Murgasse
Sackstr.
Kaiser-Franz-Josef-Kai
Lendkai
Mariahilfer Str.
Belgierg.
Brückenkopfgasse
Zweiglgasse
Lagergasse
Karlauer Strasse
Rösselmühlgasse
Elisabethinergasse
Lazarettgasse
Lazarettgürtel
Marschallgasse
Volksgartenstrasse
Josefig.
Keplerstrasse
Mariengasse
Babenbergerstrasse
Bahnhofgürtel
Annenstrasse
Idlhofgasse
Eggenberger Gürtel

Taxi service is available by hailing a cab on the street, lining up at any of the city's clearly designated taxi stands (the largest is in front of the main railway station), or calling ✆ **878** (which gains access to the biggest company in Graz), 983, or 889.

City Layout

The **Altstadt (Old Town)** lies on the left bank of the Mur, centered on **Hauptplatz (Main Square).** To the south of this landmark plaza looms the **Rathaus (Town Hall).** Southeast of Hauptplatz is **Herrengasse,** a pedestrian area used by local shoppers, which comes to an end at **Platz am Eisernen Tor,** with its column mounted by a 17th century figure of the Virgin.

At the eastern end of the **Opernring** is the municipal park, **Stadtpark,** dating from the 19th century. Northeast of Hauptplatz looms the **Burg,** a 15th-century imperial stronghold. South of the Burg rises the late-Gothic **Graz cathedral,** and south of the cathedral is the baroque **mausoleum** of Emperor Ferdinand II. Rising above the Altstadt is the **Schlossberg,** which can be reached by the cable railway.

Visitor Information

The **Graz City Tourist Office,** Herrengasse 16 (✆ **0316/80750;** www.graztourismus.at), will book hotel rooms and provide information about the area. Hotels throughout Styria can be booked here. It's open September to June, Monday to Friday 10am to 5pm, Saturday and Sunday 10am to 4pm; July and August, Monday to Friday 10am to 7pm, Saturday 10am to 6pm, and Sunday 10am to 4pm.

Fast Facts Graz

Babysitters Most hotels will set up visitors with a qualified babysitter, or call **UNIKID,** Maxmellallee 11 (✆ **0316/3801064**).

Currency Exchange The best rates are offered at the main post office (see below).

Dentists & Doctors Your hotel will provide the name of one, but if you call the local hospital, **Landeskrankenhaus,** Auenbruggerplatz 1 (✆ **0316/3850**), you can also get the names of English-speaking doctors and dentists on call for local emergencies.

Drugstores The biggest and most central store is **Kastner & Öhler,** Sackstrasse 7–13 (✆ **0316/8700**). Hours are Monday to Friday 9am to 6:30pm and Saturday 9am to 7pm.

Emergencies Call ✆ **133** for the police, **122** for the fire department, or **144** for an ambulance.

Hospitals The two best medical facilities in Graz include the **Krankenhaus der Elisabethinen,** Elisabethinergasse 14 (✆ **0316/70630**), and the larger **Landeskrankenhaus,** Auenbruggerplatz 1 (✆ **0316/3850**). Both have emergency rooms, and many staff members speak English.

Internet Access The most convenient location is **Café Zentral,** Andreas-Hofer-Platz 9 (✆ **0316/832468**), open Monday to Friday from 7am to 10pm, Saturday 7am to noon. It charges 4.50€ ($7.20) per hour.

Luggage Storage There are luggage-checking facilities on the main floors of both the railway station and the bus station. Depending on the size of your luggage, you can either store your luggage at the storage office for 3€ ($4.80) per day, or you can rent lockers for 2€ to 5€ ($3.20–$8). The service is available daily 6am to midnight.

Police Call ✆ **133** for the police.

Post Office The main post office, **Neutorgasse** 46 (✆ **0316/8808425**), is open Monday to Friday 8am to 8pm and Saturday 8am to 1pm. There's also a post office next to the Hauptbahnhof (main railway station).

Restrooms Restrooms in the city center are labeled WC (water closet). Toilets are also found at bus, rail, and air terminals; at major museums; and in cafes, where it's polite to buy some small item such as coffee.

Safety Graz traditionally has been one of Europe's safest cities. However, crime is rising, so take the usual precautions.

Taxes Graz imposes no special city taxes other than the value-added tax imposed on all goods and services in Austria.

Transit Information Call ✆ **0316/820606.**

Useful Telephone Numbers For the airport, call ✆ **0316/2902;** for train information, call ✆ **05/1717.**

WHAT TO SEE & DO

Exploring the Town

Much of Graz's Old Town has been well preserved, and many visitors take tours through this section of town. Major sights include **Hauptplatz (Main Square),** in the heart of the city, surrounded by ancient houses with characteristic brown-tile roofs and narrow gables. The most notable house is the **House of Luegg** at the corner of Sporgasse, known for its arcades and facade dating from the 17th century.

A few steps down Herrengasse, the wide shopping and business street, is the **Landhaus,** seat of the provincial government, a 1565 Renaissance masterpiece. An especially prominent window above the main gate intensifies the gate's effect, and the arched Renaissance fountainhead was poured in bronze. The south side of the courtyard ends in an arcade that runs the length of the court.

Paulustor (Paul's Gate), set between the remnants of Graz's rampart, dates from the time Italian architects fortified the city. The side of the gate facing the city is plain, but the other side is decorated with the large coats-of-arms of Archduke Ferdinand and his first wife, Anne of Bavaria.

To escape from the monumental historic core of Graz for a few hours, visit the little-known neighborhood of **Gries,** lying across the River Mur from the old town. This is where a vast army of immigrants have settled, forming Graz's multi-ethnic sector. The center of Gries is the aptly named **Griesplatz,** where vendors sell mainly handicrafts from such countries as South Korea, Vietnam, the Philippines, Thailand, and China. There's also a large settlement of Turks and Lebanese who live here. You can sit in a cafe that evokes Beirut, listening to Middle Eastern music pour out.

Burg One of the most visible buildings in town, the castle was built in 1499 for Emperor Maximilian I. The Burg is devoted exclusively to offices of the Austrian and Styrian provincial governments and is not open to visitors. However, it does contain an unusual winding staircase, the **Wendeltreppe,** whose corkscrew (helix) shape is a marvel of medieval stonework. The concierge will usually allow visitors in for a peek.

Northeast of Hauptplatz in the Old Town. Free admission. Mon–Fri 9am–5pm. Tram: 3 or 6.

Domkirche This cathedral was originally the Romanesque Church of St. Aegydius. It was a fortified structure outside the town walls that was first referred to in a late-12th-century document. In the 15th century, Frederick III had the church converted into a spacious three-bayed city parish church in the late-Gothic style, although it ended up with a wooden turret instead of a gothic spire. Archduke Carl of Inner Austria attached the church to his residence, the Burg, and later entrusted it to the Jesuits. After the dissolution of that order in Austria, it became the cathedral church of the bishops of Seckau. Inside you'll see two shrines (ca. 1475) made in Mantua, and a baroque high altar, the 18th-century creation of Franz Georg Kraxner.

Burggasse 3. © **0316/821683.** Free admission. Mon–Sat 6:30am–7:45pm; Sun 7am–7pm. Tram: 3 or 6.

Island in the Mur ★ For Graz's designation as Europe's Cultural Capital for 2003, the **Island in the Mur** (© **0699/13090013**) was created in the shape of a dome and a bowl. The "isle" appeals to locals and visitors alike, and its glass and metal structure features an amphitheater, playground, and cafe/bar, called Insel. In the words of its Brooklyn-based architect, Vito Acconci, the island "takes the city into the river and the river into the city." Frankly, we think the whole attraction evokes a utopian spaceship. The cafe/bar, for example, is submerged under a water roof and reached through a spiraling pathway that includes two access ramps and tubes linking the island with both riverbanks. The island rests on a floating platform.

Kunsthaus ★★ It looks like a blue-skinned blob plopped down in Graz. The denizens of Graz call it the "Friendly Alien," and even its British architects, Colin Fournier and Peter Cook, pronounced it a "Spacelab." One art critic said the building resembled "nothing so much as a bodily organ that's outgrown its hosts," with 16 tubercles or light nozzles illuminating the art galleries inside. Regardless of what the building looks like—and there's nothing like it in all of Austria—Kunsthaus is a showcase of modern art on the banks of the River Mur. Look for a series of changing and always cutting-edge exhibitions. These might include everything from "Videodreams: Between the Cinematic and the Theatrical," or "Living in Motion: Design and Architecture for Flexible Dwelling."

Corner of Südtirolerplatz and Lendkai. © [illegible]. [illegible]. Admission 7€ ($11) adults, 5.50€ ($8.80) seniors, 3€ ($4.80) students, 14€ ($22) family ticket. Tues–Sun 10am–6pm (Thurs until 8pm). Closed Dec 24–25. Tram 1, 3, 6, or 7 to Station Kunsthaus Graz.

Landesmuseum Joanneum This major attraction has galleries at different locations. The natural history displays—geology, botany, zoology—are at the **old Joanneum building,** Raubergasse 10 (© **0316/80179730**). The Old Gallery—with collections of paintings from medieval times to the 18th century, and a large arts and crafts department—has moved to **Schloss Eggenberg** at Eggenberger Allée 90 (below). The **New Gallery,** on the third floor of the former Heberstein town house, Sackstrasse 16 (© **0316/829155**), shows art from the 19th century to the present.

The changing exhibits in this gallery are what might intrigue you most. For example, one temporary exhibition, "The Phantom of Desire," was devoted to the images of masochism in art. It was inspired by the fact that Leopold von Sacher-Masoch, who gave his name to this sexual predilection, was a former resident of Graz. Surprisingly for such a culturally conservative city, the exhibition featured images of everything from a man pleasuring himself to scenes of fetishism ranging from bondage to whipping. We can't promise you anything that erotic at the time of your visit, but check to see what's on.

At the **Eggenberg Palace** (see Schloss Eggenberg, below), you'll find the prehistory and early history departments, including an extensive collection of Roman stones in an open-air pavilion in the park, the **Münzenkabinett,** a coin collection, and the **Styrian Hunting Museum.**

Departments at various addresses. Admission 7€ ($11) adults, free for children under 14. Geology, botany, and zoology section Mon–Sat 9am–4pm; Old Gallery Apr–Oct Tues–Wed and Fri–Sun 10am–6pm, Thurs 10am–8pm; Nov–Mar Tues–Sun 10am–6pm; New Gallery Tues–Wed and Fri–Sun 10am–6pm, Thurs 10am–8pm. Tram: 1, 3, 4, 5, or 6. Bus: 31.

Landeszeughaus As the capital, Graz has always been militarily important, and for more than 2 centuries it was a bulwark against the Turks. The armory, built between 1642 and 1645 by Anton Solar, dates from the Turkish wars. The early baroque gate, created by Giovanni Mamolo, is flanked by statues of Mars and Minerva (war deities), and the building's four upper floors are separated by their original wood-beam ceilings. There's also a vaulted cannon hall on the ground floor.

Now a museum displaying 3 centuries of weaponry, the Landeszeughaus contains some 30,000 harnesses, coats of mail, helmets, swords, pikes, muskets, pistols, harquebuses, and other implements of war. In 1749, Empress Maria Theresia, in recognition of Styrian military service and strategic significance, allowed this arsenal to remain when the others in her empire were destroyed. This is part of the Landesmuseum Joanneum (above).

Herrengasse 16. ✆ **0316/80179810.** www.zeughaus.at. Admission 7€ ($11) adults, 5.50€ ($8.80) seniors, 3€ ($4.80) students, free for children under 6. Apr–Oct Tues–Sun 10am–6pm (until 8pm on Thurs); Nov–Mar Tues–Sun 10am–3pm. Tram: 3 or 6.

The Governor: From Graz Muscle Man to Movie Star

Born Arnold Alois Schwarzenegger (the last name, in German, means "black plowman") on July 30, 1947, in Thal, a suburb of Graz, Arnold is now the governor of California—and the home folks are sure proud. So proud, in fact, that many of them wanted to build a $5-million, 24m-tall (79-ft.) steel statue of him, until local media convinced residents the money should be better spent on local charities. In Graz, Arnold began lifting weights at age 15. By 20, he was named Mr. Universe and went on to win 13 titles, including Mr. Olympia and Mr. World.

Locals call him *Sterische Eiche,* or the Styrian Oak. His name is now so big he's causing hundreds upon hundreds of visitors to flock to see his hometown. Naturally, all the aspirant young bodybuilders in Graz use Arnold as their role model and collect pictures of him, showing how "Li'l Arnie" (his young nickname in Graz) went from girlie man to burly man.

Mariahilferkirche Built for the Minorite brothers, the Church of Our Lady of Succor sits on the right bank of the Mur River. Pietro de Pomis carried out its reconstruction in the early 17th century and painted the celebrated altarpiece depicting St. Elizabeth interceding with the Virgin Mary. This painting made the church a pilgrimage site.

Mariahilferplatz 3. ✆ **0316/713169.** Free admission. Daily 7am–8pm. Tram: 3 or 6.

Mausoleum of Emperor Ferdinand II Next to the Domkirche is one of Graz's most remarkable buildings. Begun in 1614 and completed in 1638, this structure was intended as the tomb of the emperor and his first wife. The church, with a crossing cupola and a vaulted tomb chapel, is regarded as the best example of mannerism in Austria. The high altar is an early work of J. B. Fischer von Erlach, done from 1695 to 1697. The tomb's central sarcophagus, intended for Ferdinand's parents, contains only his mother's remains.

On Bürgergasse. ✆ **0316/821683.** Admission 4€ ($6.40) adults, 3€ ($4.80) children. May–Oct daily 10am–noon and 1–4pm; Nov–Apr daily 10:30am–noon and 1:30–3pm. Tram: 3 or 4.

Schlossberg Overlooking Graz, this formerly fortified hill rises to a height of 473m (1,552 ft.) above sea level. As mentioned above, in 1809 the fortifications were leveled as part of the terms of Austria's treaty with Napoleon. You can take a **cable railway** (✆ **0316/887413**) to the restaurant on top of the hill, or you can climb the winding stairs. From the top, you'll be able to look down on the city and its environs. Guided tours of the citadel start from the bell tower opposite the upper station of the cable railway. Although you can visit the Schlossberg year-round, no guided tours are offered from November to April.

During the summer, concerts are held on a wooden stage constructed within the castle's ramparts. Tickets are not cheap—from 12€ to 75€ ($19–$120). Upcoming concerts are announced every season. For more information about schedules, call the tourist office.

The **Uhrturm (Clock Tower)** on the citadel is a curiosity; it rises above the walls of the former **Citizens' Bastion.** It acquired its appearance between 1555 and 1556, when the original Gothic tower was remade in the Renaissance style: The builders added a circular wooden gallery with oriels and four huge clock faces.

✆ **0316/8724902.** Round-trip cable car fare 3€ ($4.80) adults, 1€ ($1.60) children under 16. Admission to tours 3€ ($4.80) adults, 1.50€ ($2.40) ages 6–15, free for children 5 and under. Cable car operates Apr–Sept daily 9am–11pm; Oct–Mar daily 10am–10pm. Tours given daily on the hour 9am–5pm. No tours Nov–Apr. Take the Zahnradbahn from Kaiser-Franz-Josef-Kai 38; departs every 15 min. The ascent takes 5–10 min.

Nearby Attractions

Piber Stud Farm The most important stud farm in Austria lies some 24km (15 miles) west of Graz. Lipizzaner horses are bred and trained here, and the result is quite magnificent. General Patton rescued these horses and their very special lineage from doom during a daring raid to retrieve them from behind Soviet lines at the end of World War II. When their early training is complete, the horses raised on this farm are sent to the Spanish Riding School in Vienna.

Piber Bundesgestvet, Piber, near Koeflach. ✆ **03144/3323.** www.piber.com. Admission 11€ ($18) adults, 9€ ($14) seniors, 6€ ($9.60) students, free 6 and under. 75-min. tours given Nov–Mar daily 2:30pm; Apr–Oct daily 11am. Drive west from Graz on Rte. 70 until the marked turnoff onto an unclassified road to Piber. Call for an appointment before visiting and verify times.

Schloss Eggenberg About 3km (2 miles) west of the center of Graz, this square 17th-century palace has towers at its four corners and an accentuated facade over the main gate. The building sits in a large park that's now used as a game preserve. The four wings of the baroque structure surround a large court with arched arcades and two smaller courts separated by the palace church. You can take guided tours of the baroque state apartments on the second floor.

The ground floor of the south wing houses the Landesmuseum Joanneum's Old Gallery, plus the department of prehistory and early history, with a good collection of Styrian antiquities and coin collections.

Eggenberg Allée 90. ✆ **0316/5832640.** Admission 6€ ($9.60) adults, 3€ ($4.80) children under 14. Palace tours Apr–Oct daily 10 and 11am, noon, and 2, 3, and 4pm; no tours Nov–Mar. Landesmuseum collections daily 9am–1pm and 2–5pm. Tram: 1.

An Open-Air Museum

Österreichisches Freilichtmuseum ★ (✆ **03124/53700**), about 16km (10 miles) north of Graz in Stübing, is set in a wooded valley branching off the Mur Valley. Here you'll find buildings, some of which are 400 years old, from all the Austrian provinces. The 85 authentic structures include a Rauchstubenhaus (smokeroom house) from East Styria, a Rauchhaus (smokehouse) from Land Salzburg, and circular, triangular, and rectangular houses. All the houses are maintained by the Styrian provincial and Austrian national governments.

Architectural enthusiasts will find that this museum has an intriguing display of the regional variations of building traditions. Because of the park's sprawling size (around 40 hectares/100 acres), the buildings—mostly farmhouses, barns, and farm-related storage or food-processing sheds—are set within the rural habitats that originally produced them. Despite its location in the verdant heart of Styria, the curators have tried to showcase buildings that derived throughout the country—from Vorarlberg in the west to Burgenland, a marshy low-lying province similar to the plains of neighboring Hungary.

The museum is open from early April to late October Tuesday to Sunday 9am to 5pm. Admission is 8€ ($13) for adults and 4.50€ ($7.20) for children. You can take a train from Graz toward Bruck an der Mur and get off at the station marked STÜBING, a local (*not* express) stop. After that, it's a 40-minute walk, or you can take a taxi. About 10 buses head to Stübing each day from Graz's Lendplatz (on the western bank of the Mur River, a 5-min. walk west of Old Town); the trip takes 35 minutes.

WHERE TO STAY

Accommodations range from first-class hotels to camping sites. There are many reasonably priced family hotels and inexpensive lodgings in Graz, and even the top hotels will seem surprisingly inexpensive.

Expensive

Grand Hotel Wiesler Graz ★★ On the River Mur, this historic hotel, built in a classic Art Nouveau style, is the most desirable hotel in town. It's the choice of Arnold Schwarzenegger whenever he comes back home to visit Graz. After you register, an employee brings fruit and tea to your room. The view from the neoclassical windows encompasses many of the medieval city's baroque spires that soar toward the mountains on the opposite side of the river. The comfortable medium-size rooms come with wide, firm beds, thick carpeting, and wooden furnishings, many of which are original, dating from 1910. The Wiesler's restaurant offers good food and an attractive decor. There's an informal snack bar for sit-down food, plus the Grand Café, where you can read international newspapers while enjoying fresh pastries and rich coffee. The bar serves up piano music and special drinks.

Grieskai 4–8, A-8010 Graz. ✆ **0316/7066-0.** Fax 0316/706676. www.hotelwiesler.com. 98 units. 99€–199€ ($158–$318) double; 199€–399€ ($318–$638) suite. Children under 12 stay free in parents' room. AE, DC, MC, V. Parking 12€ ($19). Tram: 3 or 6. **Amenities:** Restaurant; cafe; bar; sauna; room service; babysitting; laundry service; dry cleaning; nonsmoking rooms; solarium. *In room:* A/C, TV, Wi-Fi, minibar, hair dryer, trouser press (some), safe.

Schlossberg Hotel ★★ Finds Housed behind a beautifully embellished cerulean facade, this 15th-century baroque inn is both unusual and charming, and it's our favorite hotel in town. (It has more atmosphere than the Grand Hotel Wiesler Graz.) The owner's wife decorated this formerly decrepit rooming house herself in 1982 with 19th-century furniture. There's an early Biedermeier ceramic stove in the bar area, several pieces of baroque sculpture set in well-placed niches, and a courtyard with a lion's-head fountain. The medium-size rooms are among the town's most inviting, and many open onto private balconies.

Guests can enjoy drinks 24 hours a day on a terrace with a panoramic view of Graz from the banks of the River Mur. Breakfast is the only meal served, and it's offered in a beautiful winter garden.

Kaiser-Franz-Josef-Kai 30, A-8010 Graz. ✆ **0316/80700.** Fax 0316/807070. www.schlossberg-hotel.at. 54 units. 190€–235€ ($304–$376) double; 380€ ($608) suite. AE, DC, MC. Parking 15€ ($24). Tram: 4 or 5. **Amenities:** Breakfast room; bar; outdoor heated pool; fitness center; sauna; room service; massage; babysitting; laundry service; dry cleaning; nonsmoking rooms; solarium. *In room:* TV, Wi-Fi, minibar, hair dryer, safe.

Moderate

Augartenhotel ★★ This is one of the best hotels in Graz, offering both regular doubles and apartments with kitchens for those desiring longer stays. Only a few steps from the heart of town, it combines a modern interior with a glass-and-metal facade. Its rooftop terrace with panoramic views over the city is reason alone to like this place. If it's available, ask for room 501, which offers the most spectacular views. Wooden floors and warm interiors are found in the beautiful bedrooms, which are decorated in part with glass and metals in gray, silver, and white. The restaurant, adorned with modern art, serves a modern cuisine with an emphasis on fresh fish and vegetables produced in the region. The hotel is both sophisticated and down-home friendly with a most helpful staff.

Schönaugasse 53A, A-8010 Graz. ✆ **0316/208000.** Fax 0316/2080080. www.augartenhotel.at. 56 units. 140€ ($224) double, 180€ ($288) apt. AE, DC, MC, V. **Amenities:** Restaurant; bar; indoor pool; gym; sauna. *In room:* A/C, TV, Wi-Fi, minibar, hair dryer.

Austria Trend Hotel Europa Opened in 1986, this five-story hotel is the largest and, in many ways, the most convenient in Graz. It lies adjacent to the railway station, a 20-minute walk south of the town's medieval center. The medium-size rooms are comfortably modern. After you arrive, you can relax at the intimate bar, Bella Grazia, where snacks and drinks are served. A covered shopping center is attached to the hotel. There's also a restaurant, Vier Jahreszeiten, located on the second floor. It serves regional specialties and offers a selection of Styrian wines.

Bahnhofgürtel 89, A-8020 Graz. ✆ **0316/70760.** Fax 0316/7076606. www.austria-trend.at. 121 units. 190€–200€ ($304–$320) double; 220€–284€ ($352–$454) suite. Rates include breakfast. AE, DC, MC, V. Parking 11€ ($18). Tram: 1, 3, 6, or 7. **Amenities:** Restaurant; bar; sauna; laundry service; dry cleaning; nonsmoking rooms; solarium; 1 room for those w/limited mobility. *In room:* TV, Wi-Fi, minibar, hair dryer.

Best Western Hotel Pfeifer Kirchenwirt ★ Finds Motorists are especially attracted to this restored 1695 inn, lying 6km (3.7 miles) northeast of Graz next to the Maria Trost Pilgrimage church painted in "Maria Theresa ocher." Set in the lush "green heart" of Styria, this is a classic inn with the finest meals and the most comfortable rooms in the area. Even if you can't stay over, consider driving here for a meal in summer. Tables are placed under the old chestnut trees with a view of the church. Meals are traditional, and the wine cellar is especially rich in Styrian vintages. Accommodations are spacious and all of them have been upgraded to the standard of a government-rated four-star hotel.

Kirchplatz 9, A-8044 Graz. ✆ **0316/3911120.** Fax 0316/3911-1249. www.bestwestern.at. 31 units. 140€–180€ ($224–$288) double. AE, DC, MC, V. **Amenities:** Restaurant; bar; sauna; room service; public Internet. *In room:* TV, fridge, hair dryer.

City Hotel Erzherzog Johann Standing near the Old Town's pedestrian zone, this hotel dates from the 16th century. It was built as a *gasthof* (inn) and named after the most powerful figure (Erzherzog Johann) in Styria at the time. The elegant establishment arranges its rooms around a skylit atrium surrounded by curving wrought-iron balconies and plants. The newer rooms tend to be more spacious and tranquil, while the others (especially the singles) are rather standardized and a bit small.

Sackstrasse 3–5, A-8010 Graz. ✆ **0316/811616.** Fax 0316/811515. www.erzherzog-johann.com. 64 units. 148€–240€ ($237–$384) double; 295€–360€ ($472–$576) suite. Rates include breakfast. Half-board 24€ ($38) per person extra. AE, DC, MC, V. Parking 15€ ($24). Tram: 3 or 6. **Amenities:** Restaurant; bar; sauna; fitness center; room service; babysitting; laundry service; dry cleaning; nonsmoking rooms. *In room:* TV, Wi-Fi, minibar, hair dryer, trouser press (some).

Hotel Gollner Although the Gollner was originally built in the late 1800s, renovations have created an ambience of bland modernity and dependable comfort. This hotel is popular with the artists performing at the opera house next door. The comfortable, high-ceilinged rooms are filled with contemporary furniture and come in a variety of sizes. The hotel has a garden terrace on its rooftop and another garden in back. In the historic heart of the town, the hotel stands adjacent to the opera, near Herrengasse. Breakfast is the only meal served.

Schlögelgasse 14, A-8010 Graz. ✆ **0316/8225210.** Fax 0316/8225217. www.hotelgollner.at. 50 units. 155€–240€ ($248–$384) double. Rates include breakfast. AE, DC, MC, V. Parking 11€–13€ ($18–$21). Tram: 3 or 6. **Amenities:** Breakfast room; bar; sauna; room service; laundry service; dry cleaning; nonsmoking rooms. *In room:* TV, Wi-Fi, minibar, hair dryer, safe.

Hotel Weitzer Standing on the River Mur, the largest hotel in Graz (not to be confused with the Grand Hotel Wiesler) consists of two buildings connected by an overhead glass tunnel. The same family has run the whole complex for four generations. Behind soundproof windows, rooms are well-lit and comfortably furnished. Some of the more spacious accommodations offer queen-size beds, whereas a dozen corner rooms are filled with paired double beds. The third floor is the nonsmoking floor. For the best views, ask for one of the fifth-floor rooms. Restaurant Casserolle, on the ground floor, is one of the best restaurants in town (see "Where to Dine," below). The hotel also offers the Café Weitzer, in typical Viennese style, along with a lobby bar for cocktails and after-dinner drinks. The hotel is a member of the Steigenberger Reservations System.

Grieskai 12–14, A-8011 Graz. ✆ **800/223-5652** in the U.S., or 0316/7030. Fax 0316/70388. www.weitzer.com. 200 units. 99€–205€ ($158–$328) double; 150€–399€ ($240–$638) suite. AE, DC, MC, V. Parking 13€ ($21). Tram: 1, 3, 6, or 7. **Amenities:** Restaurant; wine tavern; bar; sauna; room service (7am–10pm); massage; babysitting; laundry service; dry cleaning; nonsmoking rooms; solarium; rooms for those w/limited mobility. *In room:* A/C (some), TV, minibar, hair dryer.

Hotel zum Dom ★ **Finds** In the heart of the medieval core, close to the cathedral, this converted palace has been turned into a hip little hotel with individually designed bedrooms. The former Palais Inzaghi, constructed in 1775 in the rococo style, was converted into an inn with modern amenities, yet with the basic architecture left intact. Each room has its own fragrance, its own music, and even its own unique door sign. Furnishings are both contemporary designer objects and antiques or old artifacts. Breakfast is a buffet served in the winter garden, or else you can patronize Restaurant MOD, with its sophisticated elegance, specializing in such dishes as wild garlic cappuccino or shrimp-stuffed sole. Perhaps you'll end your repast with a rhubarb tart with sour cream ice.

Bürgergasse 14. ✆ **0316/824800.** Fax 0316/8248008. www.domhotel.co.at. 28 units. 170€–220€ ($272–$352) double; 227€–332€ ($363–$531) suite. Rates include breakfast. AE, DC, MC, V. Parking 12€ ($19). Bus: 30. **Amenities:** Restaurant; wine bar; 24-hr. room service; laundry service; dry cleaning; nonsmoking rooms; rooms for those w/limited mobility. *In room:* TV, Wi-Fi, minibar, coffeemaker (some), hair dryer, iron, safe.

Romantik Parkhotel ★ Finds Although it was built in 1574, this hotel looks much newer because of frequent renovations. It lies within a 10-minute walk east of the city center, near the opera house. The interior is filled with baronial accessories, including suits of armor, hanging tapestries in the beamed dining room, and a scattering of antiques. Rooms are comfortable and traditionally furnished with double-glazed windows, plush carpeting, antiques, good beds, and small bathrooms. A garden in back provides a midsummer escape.

Leonhardstrasse 8, A-8010 Graz. ✆ **0316/36300.** Fax 0316/363050. www.parkhotel-graz.at. 67 units. 155€–205€ ($248–$328) double; 199€–330€ ($318–$528) suite. Rates include buffet breakfast. AE, DC, MC, V. Parking 8€ ($13). Tram: 1, 3, 6, or 7. **Amenities:** Restaurant; bar; indoor heated pool; fitness room; spa; sauna; room service; laundry service; dry cleaning. *In room:* TV, minibar, hair dryer, safe.

Inexpensive

Hotel Drei Raben Value This five-story hotel was originally built as an apartment house around 1900, and was later modernized and transformed into a hotel. Within a 5-minute walk from the railway station and a 10-minute walk from the Old Town, the hotel offers modern comfort and well-furnished, medium-size rooms. Housekeeping rates a plus here. On the premises is a local branch of Wienerwald, a chain restaurant specializing in all-day dining, roast chicken, and reasonable prices aimed at the family trade.

Annenstrasse 43, A-8020 Graz. ✆ **0316/712686.** Fax 0316/7159596. www.dreiraben.at. 51 units. 121€ ($194) double; 147€ ($235) triple. Rates include buffet breakfast. AE, DC, MC, V. Parking 8.10€ ($13). Tram: 3 or 6. **Amenities:** Restaurant; bar. *In room:* TV, Wi-Fi (in some), hair dryer.

Hotel Grazerhof This four-story hotel in a central location boasts a congenial atmosphere. Many Austrian visitors stay here. Rooms are simple and comfortable, but since there's no elevator, you might huff and puff a bit to reach those on the uppermost floor. Each year a selection of rooms is renovated. Accommodations are a bit small, but each room has a neatly kept bathroom. Corridor bathrooms are adequate and well maintained. On the premises is a very popular restaurant favored by locals, with set menus that range from 12€ to 23€ ($19–$36).

Stubenberggasse 10, A-8010 Graz. ✆ **0316/824358.** Fax 0316/81963340. www.grazerhof.at. 25 units. 90€ ($144) double; 120€ ($192) triple. Rates include breakfast. AE, DC, MC, V. Parking 22€ ($35). Tram: 3 or 6. **Amenities:** Restaurant; bar. *In room:* TV.

WHERE TO DINE

The variety of restaurants in Graz is enormous. Prices in even the top restaurants are moderate. You can dine in the hotels (which have some of the best food in town) or in cozy pubs and intimate bistros.

We suggest skipping typical international cuisine and concentrating on genuine Styrian specialties such as *wurzelfleisch,* a kind of stew, or the different kinds of *sterz,* a German version of kasha (made with cracked buckwheat or corn). The homemade sausages are generally excellent. Vienna is noted for its *hendl* (chicken) dishes, but Graz chefs also do chicken extremely well.

The art of beer brewing is cultivated in Graz. Residents especially like the local Puntigam or Reininghaus beer, as well as the Gösser beer, brewed in Upper Styria.

You might want to try Styrian wine, whose grapes grow on steep, sunny slopes. Important varieties such as Welschriesling, Muskat-Sylvaner, Traminer, and the Schilcher (which grows in a limited area in West Styria) have received international recognition. Many wine restaurants provide background music in the evening.

Expensive

Iohan ★★ CONTINENTAL/NEW AUSTRIAN Although it's set on the ground floor of a medieval building behind the Rathaus (Town Hall), you might get the feeling that you're in an underground cellar here, thanks partly to a majestic-looking vaulted stone ceiling and some very impressive masonry. Long, narrow, vaguely monastic, and permeated with a sense of the Middle Ages, it's the premier and most stylish restaurant of Graz, with a clientele whose names appear in the society section of the local newspaper. Its sophisticated touches of postmodern design put the place firmly in the 21st century. There's an elongated bar—almost 30m (100 ft.) of it—crafted from beechwood, theatrical lighting, and food that's on the nouvelle side of the culinary equation. Menu items are much worked over, frequently adapted to the seasons. The best examples, depending on the time of year you arrive, include a divine breast of wild goose glazed with Pinot Grigio and a confit of goose liver; a mélange of sweet potatoes, Jerusalem artichokes, and poached carp dumplings; a platter containing three different preparations of veal served with a parsley and salsify *rösti* (a patty sautéed to crispy golden brown) and a creamy version of red lentils; and filet of beef with crabmeat, roast onions, and white-bread dumplings. You'll recognize the outside of this place thanks to a baroque overlay that was added to the building's original medieval core, and a flickering torch that blazes near its entrance.

Landhausgasse 1. ✆ **0316/8213120.** Reservations required. Main courses 16€–23€ ($26–$36); 3-course menu 33€ ($52). AE, DC, MC, V. Tues–Sat 6pm–1am. Tram: 1, 3, 4, 5, 6, or 7.

Landhaus-Keller ★ AUSTRIAN This restaurant is in one of the most historic buildings in Graz, in the city center near the casino. (Its entrance is at the rear side of the Landhaus; its neighbor is the Zeughaus, the Armory.) In summer, outdoor tables are set up in a flowered courtyard with a view of a baroque church's arcade. The building was constructed in the early 16th century, and since then the cellars have hosted such famous guests as Metternich, Franz and Eduard Sacher, and the Duke of Wellington. A dimly lit corridor passes three rustic and authentically Teutonic dining areas (there are six if you count the nooks and crannies), ranging from the Hunters' Room to the Knights' Room.

A wide and well-prepared selection of seafood, veal, beef, pork, and chicken dishes is served. Specialties are usually based on old Styrian recipes. You might begin with sour-cream soup with scorched polenta, meatballs with sauerkraut, Styrian cheese dumplings in beef broth, and browned omelets with blueberries. Specialties of which the chef is particularly proud include Styrian beef with chanterelles and smoked *saebling* (salmon trout) with horseradish sauce.

Schmiedgasse 9. ✆ **0316/830276.** www.landhaus-keller.at. Reservations recommended. Main courses 11€–25€ ($17–$39); fixed-price menu 35€–45€ ($56–$72). DC, MC, V. Mon–Sat 11:30am–midnight. Closed holidays. Tram: 1, 3, 4, 5, 6, or 7.

Restaurant Casserolle ★ AUSTRIAN One of the finest hotel dining rooms in Graz, this prestigious restaurant on the banks of the Mur offers a "taste of Styria." To go completely local, ask the waiter to bring you a Styrian Old Slivovitz, a schnapps made from plums. You can follow with a selection of hot or cold appetizers, perhaps Styrian *speck* (delicately cured and finely sliced ham garnished with grated horseradish). A homemade chicken-liver pâté with Cumberland sauce is also recommended, or you could begin with one of the day's soups, perhaps a clear oxtail broth laced with sherry. Both freshwater and sea fish are offered, ranging from John Dory to grilled filet of pikeperch. One of the chef's specialties is veal served in a casserole with Swiss-style sautéed potatoes. One entire section of the menu is taken up with Austrian beef specialties, not just the typically Viennese *tafelspitz,* but tournedos with a truffle-cream sauce and even chateaubriand (which requires two diners). Boiled beef *Goldener Ochs* (a slice of boiled prime beef) is even better than the *tafelspitz.* You can have a sweet dessert, such as a traditional apple strudel, or finish your meal, as many locals do, with a small cheese plate, perhaps Austrian Emmentaler, a mild nut-flavored cheese.

In the Hotel Weitzer, Grieskai 12–14. ✆ **0316/7030.** www.weitzer.com. Reservations recommended. Main courses 12€–35€ ($19–$56). AE, DC, MC, V. Daily noon–2pm and 6–10pm. Tram: 1, 3, 6, or 7.

Moderate

Das Wirtshaus Greiner AUSTRIAN About 1.5km (1 mile) north of the town's center, this cozy and historic setting occupies an old-fashioned building whose foundations date back to the early 1600s. Inside, you'll find a light and well-maintained set of dining rooms where the staff prepares meticulous parfaits of venison with orange and pistachio marmalade; roasted quail with alpine berries; filet of zander with a wine, butter, and herb sauce; and roasted goose with caramelized onions.

Grabenstrasse 64. ✆ **0316/685090**. www.wirtshaus-greiner.at. Reservations recommended. Main courses 11€–20€ ($17–$32). MC, V. Mon–Fri 11:30am–2pm and 6–10pm. Tram: 4, 6, or 7.

Hofkeller ★★ MEDITERRANEAN The best of Graz's new crop of hip and trend-conscious restaurants contains only 40 seats, each laid out under the ochre-painted 400-year-old vaults of a historic building in the town center. Your host, and the resident chef, is Norbert Kabelka, a 40-something wunderkind who has managed to attract whatever Austrian celebrities happen to be visiting Graz at the time, along with a regular crowd of food-loving locals. Menu items vary with the seasons, but are usually devoted to a local reinterpretation of the classics of the Mediterranean world. The finest examples include a succulent version of octopus salad, a salad of orange and fennel in an herb-laced vinaigrette; grilled lamb chops with rosemary sauce and potatoes; grilled sea bass with lemon sauce and fresh spinach; and a tempting array of pastas—one of the best of which is a delightfully simple version prepared with fresh tomatoes, olive oil, herbs, and capers.

Hofgasse 8. ✆ **0316/832439.** www.hofkeller.at. Reservations recommended. Main courses 10€–19€ ($16–$30). DC, MC, V. Mon–Sat noon–2pm (last order) and 6pm–midnight. Bus: 3, 6.

Sacher ★ AUSTRIAN The Sacher Hotel is the most famous in Vienna, and in modern times Sacher cafes are appearing in some of the country's leading cities. Graz is no exception. This chic cafe, patronized by both visitors and locals, lies in the center at the intersection of Herrengasse and Hauptplatz. With its sparkling chandeliers, glittering gilt, and red upholstery, it is the most fashionable of all the cafes of Graz.

Of course, you can order the legendary rich chocolate Sachertorte here, but you can also enjoy full meals as well. From breakfast specialties, including fluffy omelets, to the final desserts of the evening, including perhaps *apfelstrudel,* you can sample Viennese classics here, such as a Wiener schnitzel or *tafelspitz* (boiled cuts of beef), and most definitely Anna Sacher's legendary fried chicken. Sweet and savory snacks are also served in the adjacent Sacher Wien-Snackbar.

Herrengasse 6. ✆ **0316/8005-0.** www.sacher.com. Reservations not required. AE, DC, MC, V. Main courses 11€–16€ ($17–$26). Mon–Sat 8:30am–8pm; Sun 10am–7pm.

Inexpensive

Altsteirische Schmankerlstub'n ★ STYRIAN The most authentic recipes of the Styrian kitchen are served here, the cuisine often compared to "granny's home cooking." The stube is the local favorite, using local products of good quality for classic meals. Theresia Oberländer and her daughters launched this restaurant in 1995, dedicating it to the serving of traditional family-style meals in a friendly, inviting atmosphere. Their salads are the best in town, perhaps because they use a local pumpkin seed oil, which comes from a nearby mill at Leitinger where the Oberländer family was born. Their organic juices are also from a local farmer. The chef's specialty is *Rinderschulterscherzl*, boiled beef served with a pumpkin purée. Desserts are made fresh daily and are among the richest and best tasting in town.

Sackstrasse 10. ✆ **0316/833211.** Reservations recommended. Main courses 7.90€–19€ ($13–$30). No credit cards. Daily 11am–11pm.

Gambrinuskeller INTERNATIONAL The decor, like the menu, combines elements from rustically conservative Austria with overtones of the Middle East and the Balkans. A stainless-steel deli-style case separates the busy kitchen from the dining areas. The unusual menu offers Brazilian, Persian, and Italian foods, too. You might enjoy *churrasco* (Brazilian barbecue) of pork, Iranian-style kabobs, Italian pasta dishes, and grilled steaks. Dessert could be anything from baklava to apple strudel. The cuisine is marvelous change-of-pace fare, although the chefs perhaps extend themselves too much by offering such widely varied menus. In summer, the garden attracts diners and drinkers. Menu items include rump steak from South America and boiled shin of pork with root vegetables and horseradish.

Färbergasse 6–8. ✆ **0316/81018-01.** Reservations not required. Main courses 8.50€–21€ ($14–$33). AE, DC, MC, V. Tues–Sat 10am–11:30pm. Tram: 1, 3, 4, 5, 6, or 7.

Krebsenkeller (Value) AUSTRIAN/INTERNATIONAL Many diners select this restaurant as much for its architecture as for its simple, wholesome food. Built in 1538, Krebsenkeller's entrance lies beneath a covered passageway that ends in an enclosed courtyard. Cafe tables spill from beneath a grape arbor into the courtyard-style garden. There's ample seating indoors in a series of dining rooms, including an underground *keller* (cellar), a street-level *stüberl* (tavern), and a *gemütlich* room known locally as the Osteria. Menu items include grilled dishes prepared in varying degrees of spiciness, a variety of homemade soups, fresh salads, fresh fish, and wild game. Dine as the residents do and order the savory kettle of goulash or the boiled pork with a cabbage salad. For dessert, the best choice is a crepe stuffed with marmalade, chocolate, or ice cream and covered with a hot strawberry or cranberry sauce.

Sackstrasse 12. ✆ **0316/829377-0.** Reservations recommended. Main courses 8.90€–18€ ($14–$28); fixed-price menus 9€–21€ ($14–$34). DC, MC, V. Daily 10am–midnight. Tram: 1, 3, 4, 5, 6, or 7.

CAFES

Aiola Upstairs ★, Schlossberg 2 (✆ **0316/818797**), is the trendy bar in Graz, attracting hip young things to its precincts with its striking architecture and its inventive menu. Its greatest asset is a spectacular view of Graz. "Our guests come here to enjoy chill-out grooves," the manager told us. When the weather allows, the cafe turns into one huge patio. The location is beside the Uhrturm and elevator. The food is mainly Italian, with a typical meal of pasta, wine, and coffee costing less than 20€ ($32). Open Monday to Saturday 9am to 2am, Sunday 9am to midnight.

Café Harrach, Harrachgasse 26 (© **0316/322671**), is the most arts-oriented cafe in Graz, attracting lots of students. Because Styria is known for its wine, more spritzers are consumed here than beer. Harrach is like an old Viennese coffeehouse, and local cafe culture at its best is seen here. Many patrons come here and make a night of it. It's open Monday to Friday 9am to midnight, Saturday 5pm to midnight, and Sunday 4pm to midnight.

With a view looking over the open-air market (perfect on a summer day), the popular **Café Leinich,** Kaiser-Josef-Platz 4 (© **0316/830586;** tram: 3 or 6), has served good coffee and homemade pastries (rich concoctions using an abundance of fresh fruit and berries) since 1891. Coffee and pastries start at 2.90€ ($4.70). It's open Monday to Friday 7am to 7pm and Saturday 7am to 2pm.

SHOPPING

You might begin your shopping expedition at Hauptplatz, the main square in the center of town. The major shopping streets, including the wide, elegant **Herrengasse,** branch off from here. The second major shopping street is the also elegant and car-free **Sporgasse,** which is lined with upscale shops and sidewalk cafes. In the heart of the old city, Sporgasse runs along the River Mur's Left Bank. The major item to buy here is Styrian clothing in its famous gray-and-green hues. Stores offer a good selection of dirndls and hats in particular, as well as local handicrafts and leather clothing. Stores are generally open Monday to Friday 9am to 6pm and on Saturday 9am to noon.

Brühl and Söhne You'll find high-quality, but also high-priced, Styrian clothing for men, women, and children here. The inventory includes fashionable dirndls, coats, skirts, hats, vests, suits, and accessories. Schmiedgasse 12. © **0316/8216160.** www.bruhl.at. Tram: 1, 3, 4, 5, 6, or 7.

Steirisches Heimatwerk This large store sells only Austrian-made items, a big selection of regional clothing, fabrics, shoes, and cookbooks, as well as objects made from glass, ceramics, and wood. Some more unusual items include depictions of the local saints hand-painted in small wooden frames. Paulustorgasse 4. © **0316/8271060.** Bus: 30.

GRAZ AFTER DARK

One of the most visible and frequently showcased buildings in Graz is the **Opernhaus (Opera House),** Opernring (© **0316/8000-0**; www.buehnen-graz.com; tram: 1 or 7). It's the year-round home of Graz's opera company, of which local residents are justifiably proud. The faux-baroque theater was designed "in the style of Fischer von Erlach" at the end of the 19th century. Recent performances have included *Lucia de Lammermoor, Cavelleria Rusticana, Tosca, Rigoletto,* and even Broadway musicals. Depending on the event and your seat, tickets are 10€ to 75€ ($16–$120).

The Bar & Club Scene

Sometimes restaurants combine dancing and nightclub shows, so you might be able to spend an entire evening at one address. The cafes often have music as well.

The area around **Farbergasse-Mehlplatz** is the most popular place for people from all walks of life, and the city's greatest cluster of bars and restaurants is here. Locals refer to it as their *Bermuda Dreleck* (Bermuda Triangle).

The city often offers some excellent jazz; but performances are not always rigidly scheduled, and certainly not every night of the week. It's best to call to find out if a jazz program is being presented at the time of your visit. Your best bet is **Das Neue Wist,** Mosterhofgasse 34 (✆ **0316/8366660**).

Bang The hottest gay bar in town is this neon-lit temple of gaiety that jumps to a disco beat on Friday and Saturday nights. The music's loud and the men are hot; after midnight only men are allowed in. The bar is open Wednesday, Thursday, and Sunday from 9pm to 2am. The dance club on Friday and Saturday rocks from 9am to 4am. Dreihackeng 4–10. ✆ **0316/719549.** No cover in bar; 5€ ($8) in dance club.

Gamlitzer Weinstube This is the most visible *weinstube* (wine tavern) in town, established 300 years ago. The food is plentiful, inexpensive, and designed to accompany the wines (many from Styria) served here. Meals begin at around 6€ ($9.60) each, and wine sells for 2.80€ ($4.50) and up per glass. In summer, most of the establishment's business is conducted at tables and chairs outdoors. It's open Monday to Friday 9am to 11pm. Mehlplatz 4. ✆ **0316/828760;** www.gamlitzer.com.

M-1 One of the most desirable bars in Graz, M-1 is located behind large glass windows on the rooftop of a historic building in the town's nightlife district. Views from the comfortable chairs encompass a postmodern design and breathtaking scenery. The crowd is congenial, and recorded music evokes the place's big-city style. Beer costs 4€ ($6.40). It's open daily from 9am to 2am. Färberplatz 1. ✆ **0664/3924729.**

Stargayte ★ You don't even have to be gay to appreciate the fun patrons at this club. It has the best drag shows in town and even fetish parties to bring out the leather set, some of whom wear knee-high black boots and nothing else. A waiter tells guests to dress "like a bitch or a pimp—or perhaps an Austrian soldier—to enjoy the fun more." This is a bar, lounge, and dance club, and every Thursday night it's for women only. Open Monday to Thursday and Sunday 8pm to 6am, Friday and Saturday 8pm "until the last customer leaves" long after sunrise. Keesgasse 3. ✆ **0664/5162522;** www.stargayte.at.

A Casino

One of the premier nightlife venues in Graz is contained within **Casino Graz,** Landhausgasse 10 (✆ **0316/832578**). Set at the corner of the Schmiedgasse, in the historic core of town, the casino is housed in a modern (ca. 1984) building, its chief draw being the availability of its slot machines (daily 11am–3am) and its roulette wheels and blackjack tables (daily 3pm–3am). To enter, you'll have to be over 18 and present appropriate ID (bring your passport). Jackets and ties are usually required for men, although ties are optional June to September. Entrance is free, although you'll be offered the opportunity to buy 25€ ($40) worth of chips for the price of 23€ ($37). On the premises are a restaurant and a piano bar; within one of the building's many meeting rooms, cabaret shows are occasionally presented.

2 BAD GLEICHENBERG ★

195km (121 miles) S of Vienna; 64km (40 miles) SE of Graz

The oldest and most important summer spa in South Styria (with a history of water treatments dating from Roman times), Bad Gleichenberg lies southeast of Graz. The countryside here, near Slovenia's border, is relatively flat, a low-altitude setting of rolling hills and vineyards. This is one of the most interesting and least-known parts of Austria to explore.

Untersteienmark, or Lower Styria, where this spa is located, was much larger in the days of the Hapsburgs. Much of its territory was lost to Yugoslavia following the breakup of the empire after World War I.

Bad Gleichenberg sits in a scenic valley opening to the south. In the area's landscaped parks you'll see exotic plants, including the giant sequoia. You can partake of the mineral waters of the Emma, Konstantin, and Johannisbrunnen springs and even take a bottle home with you. The spa has flourished for 160 years, longer than any other spa in Styria. The clientele here tends to be middle-aged or elderly, and there's an emphasis on low-key activities. The calm is punctuated with an entertainment program and special tours in the environs. Hotels ring the spa facilities, which mark the resort's center. Mud baths and long soaks in the thermally heated waters are big here, along with rest and relaxation.

ESSENTIALS

Getting There

By Train

Bad Gleichenberg lies at the end of a minor rail line stretching eastward from Graz. Passengers board an eastbound train in Graz and head toward the Hungarian border town of Szentgotthárd, changing trains at Feldbach (trip time: 50–60 min.). From Feldbach, about five trains a day continue to the Bad Gleichenberg. Fortunately, because rail connections from Feldbach to Bad Gleichenberg aren't always convenient, passengers can also board one of the eight Bad Gleichenberg–bound buses that depart from Feldbach's railway station every day. The trip from Feldbach to Bad Gleichenberg by bus or train takes an additional 30 to 35 minutes. For rail information, contact © **05/1717** (www.oebb.at).

By Bus

There's one early morning bus, departing daily at 7:30am for Bad Gleichenberg from Vienna's Wien Mitte bus station (trip time: 3 hr.). From Graz, four buses depart Monday through Saturday at 8:25am, 10:30am, 12:15pm, and 4:35pm from in front of the main railway station for Bad Gleichenberg (trip time: 2 hr.).

By Car

If you're driving from Graz, take the A2 east to the junction with Route 68, which you take south to the junction with Route 66. Continue south on Route 66 to Bad Gleichenberg.

Visitor Information

The tourist office in the town center (© **03159/2203;** www.bad-gleichenberg.at) is open Monday to Friday 8am to 5pm and Saturday 9am to noon.

WHERE TO STAY & DINE

Hotel Gleichenberger Hof ★ Value This cozy 1970s chalet is set in a forested area with a masonry sun terrace stretching below the facade. It's located in the town's center near the spa facilities. The interior has rustic yet modern accessories, including a piano bar and an open fireplace, and all rooms have balconies. The medium-size rooms are furnished tastefully and comfortably. Bathrooms are small but tidily maintained, with tub/shower combinations and adequate shelf space. The restaurant is open to nonguests for lunch only.

Bergstrasse 27, A-8344 Bad Gleichenberg. © **03159/2424.** Fax 03159/29556. www.gleichenbergerhof.at. 27 units. 120€–150€ ($192–$240) double; 147€–177€ ($235–$283) suite for 2. Rates include half-board. MC, V. Closed Nov 26–Jan 18. **Amenities:** Restaurant; bar; 24-hr. room service; babysitting; laundry service; dry cleaning. *In room:* TV, Wi-Fi, minibar, hair dryer, safe.

Schloss Kapfenstein ★ Finds As an alternative to staying in Bad Gleichenberg, you can go east to Kapfenstein and its Schloss hotel near the Slovenian border. The 10km (6-mile) trip takes 20 minutes. Drive south from Bad Gleichenberg along Highway 66, and then cut east along the unnumbered *bundesstrasse* (provincial highway) that's marked KAPFENSTEIN. This solidly built castle has a hipped roof and a curving extension that's almost as old as the main building itself. Set in the middle of forests and rich fields, the castle offers rooms filled with antique furniture and all the modern comforts.

If you want, you can dine on the castle's terrace, which offers a view of the village below. Specialties are based on regional dishes such as roast hen, homemade *blutwurst* (blood sausage) and other sausages, and apple strudel. The Winkler family makes its own wine, a very delicate and famous vintage.

A-8353 Kapfenstein. ✆ **03157/300300.** Fax 03157/3003030. www.schloss-kapfenstein.at. 14 units. 130€–170€ ($208–$272) double. Rates include half-board. MC, V. **Amenities:** Restaurant; bar; breakfast-only room service; laundry service; dry cleaning. *In room:* TV, minibar, hair dryer, safe.

3 MARIAZELL ★

150km (93 miles) SE of Vienna; 140km (87 miles) N of Graz

Mariazell is the most celebrated pilgrimage center in Austria, in addition to being a winter playground and a summer resort. It's the national shrine of Austria, Hungary, and Bohemia.

ESSENTIALS

Getting There

By Train

Mariazell is at the terminus of a secondary train line that originates in the capital of Lower Austria, St. Pölten, 84km (52 miles) to the north. St. Pölten, which sits astride the main rail lines connecting Vienna and Salzburg, receives dozens of trains from Vienna (trip time: 45 min.) and Salzburg (trip time: 2½ hr.) throughout the day. From St. Pölten, about half a dozen trains head south to Mariazell (trip time: 2½ hr.). For rail information, contact ✆ **05/1717** (www.oebb.at).

By Bus

About half a dozen buses depart every day from Vienna's Wien Mitte bus station for their final destination at Mariazell (trip time: 2¼–4 hr.).

If the train schedule between St. Pölten and Mariazell is inconvenient, you can take one of the several daily buses that parallel the same route (trip time: 1½ hr.). In addition, two buses depart daily from the Graz railway station to Mariazell (trip time: 3 hr.). For bus information, call ✆ **0316/820606.**

Finally, buses depart several times a day for Mariazell from the important railway junction of Mürzzuschlag (trip time: 1½ hr.), which is set on the main rail lines between Vienna and Graz.

By Car

If you're driving from Graz, head north along Autobahn A9 until you reach the junction with the S35 north. Continue north to the junction with Route 20, which leads into Mariazell.

Bad Blumau: Austria's Most Whimsical Spa

If you make the 90-minute trip south from Vienna to Blumau, or the slightly shorter trip from Graz, through the green rolling hills and blond fields of Styria, you'll come to a dip in the road, a little town, and one of the most marvelous sights you have ever seen: **Bad Blumau** ★★★.

Imagine this: trees bubbling out of rooftops, mad yellow and white towers topped with onion domes, a lake-size pool with hidden fountains spraying thermal waters at random, hallway floors canted like coffee mugs turned on their sides. It's the world's largest inhabitable artwork, a 271-room spa with the sort of architecture you might expect if you hired a creative child. In this case, the "child" just turned 70. Friedensreich Hundertwasser he has littered Austria with his creations, among them the gaily colored Hundertwasserhaus at the edge of the Ring in Vienna. (See "Other Top Attractions," in chapter 6.)

Although it's a work of art, Bad Blumau is also a functioning spa. The rooms are comfortable, with minibars and safes; bathrooms are well maintained with tub/shower combos. The suites have just about the only level floors in the place.

The therapies here tend to drift toward the new age. Although you can happily glut yourself on shiatsu and Swedish massage, try having an attendant dip you in mare's milk, whey, or the essence of evening primrose, and then suspend you in a heat box for a good half-hour. The 3-hour "resurrection therapy" session involves gongs, a box of pebbles, hypnotism, and more than a few euros.

The saunas are co-ed and naked—don't be ashamed, no one else is—and are the best part of the complex. You can choose from Roman and Finnish saunas, Turkish baths, the Aromasauna, and the Bio-sanarium, which involves gassy peppermint and blinking lights. Likewise, in the health areas, you're apt to receive treatments from an attendant who is young, of the opposite sex, and utterly professional. The pool has lockers for day-trippers and overnight guests alike.

You'll eat well, if not entirely healthfully: The buffet is full of meat and cheese, all delicious, but doubtless engineered to fatten all the happy Germans who fill the place. The a la carte menu advertises itself as "international," but let's just say it never made it to California.

The spa also offers child care, shopping, a hairdresser, laundry service, and parking. Conference and fitness rooms are also available. Blumau and the baths, A-8283 Blumau 100, are about 130km (81 miles) south of Vienna and 50km (37 miles) east of Graz (✆ **03383/51000;** fax 03383/5100805; www.blumau.com). Rates are 250€ to 288€ ($400–$461) for a double and 300€ to 404€ ($608–$646) for a suite; half-board is 25€ ($40) extra. Rates include half board and free use of all thermal bath and sauna facilities, service charge, and tax. Spa treatments and visitor tax are not included.

To get from Graz to Bad Blumau, take the Autobahn (A2) east and follow the signs to the spa (it's well marked).

Visitor Information

The **tourist office,** Hauptplatz 13 (✆ **03882/2366;** www.mariazell.at), is open Monday to Friday 9am to 5:30pm, Saturday 9am to 4pm, and Sunday 9am to 12:30pm. It is closed on Sunday in October and November.

WHAT TO SEE & DO

Seeing the Shrine

The pilgrimage destination **Mariazell Basilica,** on Hauptplatz (✆ **03882/2595**), dates from the early 13th century, and has three prominent towers. The goal of the pilgrimage, however, was to come and pray and make votive offerings to the statue of the Virgin, which is mounted on the altar.

The church was originally constructed in the Romanesque style, and then a Gothic choir was added in the late 14th century. The bulbous domes are baroque, a style added to most of Austria's churches in the 17th century. Both Fischer von Erlachs, senior and junior, aided the Mariazell transformation. The grave of the world-famous Hungarian Cardinal Mindszenty is in the church; there's also the Mindszenty Museum. In 1983, Pope John Paul II visited Mariazell and the cardinal's burial place.

In the treasury are votive offerings accrued over some 600 years. The Chapel of Grace is the national shrine of Austria. Miracles are attributed to its statue of the Virgin, giving rise to fame that has spread all over Europe. The altar on which the statue is mounted was designed by the younger von Erlach. In summer, large groups gather on Saturday night for torchlight processions to the church.

The treasury is open May to October Tuesday to Friday from 10:30am to noon and 2 to 3pm, and Saturday and Sunday from 10am to 4pm. Admission is 3€ ($4.80).

Outdoor Activities

Mariazell is a winter vacation center for the whole family. Here you'll find all the components of a modern winter-sports and recreation center: avalanche-controlled grounds for skiers of all skill levels, a cableway, a chairlift, numerous surface lifts, a natural toboggan run, a skating rink, a ski school, and a ski kindergarten.

Its high altitude and good, brisk climate also make this a favored summer vacation site. You can go walking on some 200km (125 miles) of footpaths or go mountaineering, swimming, rowing, sailing, windsurfing, canoeing, fishing, horseback riding, glider flying, and camping. You can also play tennis or golf.

For the area's most dramatic views, you can take the **Seilbahn Mariazell-Bürgeralpe,** Wienerstrasse 28 (✆ **03882/2555**), to the Bürgeralpe at 1,270m (4,167 ft.). Leaving from the center of town, cable cars depart about every 20 minutes. They run in July and August daily from 8:30am to 5:30pm; in September daily from 8:30am to 5pm; in May, June, October, and November daily 9am to 5pm; in December daily from 8am to 4pm; and from January to April daily from 8am to 4pm. A round-trip costs 11€ ($18).

WHERE TO STAY & DINE

Hotel Goldene Krone Next to the basilica is a well-managed, government-rated three-star hotel that was established as an inn in the 1300s. Rebuilt several times and renovated again in 1991, the Goldene Krone is in a substantial old Styrian house with stone trim. The interior has a contemporary bar area with decorative masonry. Rooms are a bit small, but they're well maintained and equipped with good, firm beds and small bathrooms. The restaurant, which serves Austrian national dishes along with Styrian specialties, is open to nonguests daily from 7am to 11pm.

Grazerstrasse 1, A-8630 Mariazell. ✆ **03882/2583.** Fax 03882/258333. 20 units. 75€ ($120) double. Rates include breakfast. Half-board 54€ ($86) per person extra. AE, DC, MC, V. Closed Nov 10–17 and 2 weeks in Mar. **Amenities:** Restaurant; lounge; room service; laundry service; dry cleaning. *In room:* TV, Wi-Fi.

4 BAD AUSSEE ★

196km (122 miles) NW of Graz; 299km (186 miles) SW of Vienna; 80km (50 miles) SE of Salzburg

Surrounded by a lake, mountains, and woods, **Bad Aussee** is an old market town and spa in the "green heart" of the Salzkammergut. Unlike spa towns such as Bad Gleichenberg, Bad Aussee has developed into a resort relatively recently. It also doesn't place much emphasis on the medical/recuperative therapies that are all the rage at other resorts. Instead, most of the clientele comes here for its high altitude—650m (2,133 ft.) above sea level, nearly twice that of Bad Gleichenberg—and its profusion of hiking trails that are clearly marked with green-and-white signs. Guests here tend to be younger and more vigorous than those at the more sedentary Bad Gleichenberg.

From this spa, you can explore the **Altaussee,** one of the most beautiful bodies of water in Styria, which faces the Totes Gebirge.

Bad Aussee lies amid a network of lakes in the Valley of Traun, with the peaks of the Totes Gebirge and the Dachstein massif visible in the distance. The best time to visit is in June, when fields of narcissus burst into bloom, one of the most spectacular signs of spring coming to Europe.

Despite the relative lack of interest in spa rituals here, Bad Aussee does emphasize the saltwater and freshwater springs that are tapped by many of the town's hotels. Waters from the Bad Aussee Glaubersalt spring are said to be effective for losing weight, partly because a pint or so will usually manage to curtail the most stalwart of appetites. Salt mined in the nearby hills, it is added to bathwater and is said to relieve aches and pains.

Bad Aussee, at the confluence of a pair of upper branches of the Traun River, is the capital of the Styrian section of the Salzkammergut. Only 5km (3 miles) north is the Altaussee, with the spa town of Altaussee on its shore.

One of Austria's most beautiful areas, the town is a good center for walking and climbing in summer. Although Bad Aussee has long been known as a summer spa resort, it has also developed into a winter ski center. Several ski lifts are located nearby, making it attractive to ski enthusiasts.

Bad Aussee's best-known association is with Archduke Johann of the House of Hapsburg. In 1827, he married the daughter of a local postmaster, a cause célèbre rivaling the later romance of the Duke and Duchess of Windsor. There's a statue of the "Prince of Styria," Johann, in the Kurpark.

ESSENTIALS

Getting There

By Train

Bad Aussee sits astride a secondary rail line running between the Austrian junctions of Stainach-Irdning (which services passengers arriving from Graz and Vienna) and Attnang-Puchheim (which services passengers arriving from Salzburg and Linz). The trip from Graz to Stainach-Irdning takes about 2½ hours. At Stainach-Irdning, passengers transfer onto any of a dozen northbound trains for Bad Aussee (trip time: 40 min.).

Passengers starting in Salzburg or Linz can take any of the dozens of daily trains to Attnang-Puchheim and then transfer to a southbound train. This train passes through several resorts in Upper Austria—most notably Bad Ischl and Bad Goisern—before reaching Bad Aussee (2½ hr.). For rail information, contact ✆ **05/1717** (www.oebb.at).

By Bus

Because of its good (albeit complicated) rail connections, most visitors arrive in Bad Aussee by train. The most useful of the handful of bus lines running into Bad Aussee, however, is the one that runs from Styria across the border of Upper Austria into the resort of Bad Ischl several times a day (trip time: 45 min.).

By Car

Driving from Graz, take Autobahn A9 northwest and continue in the same direction as it becomes Route 113. Follow that highway's extension, which becomes Route 146, and cut west at the junction of Route 145 toward Tauplitz.

Visitor Information

The **tourist office** in the village center at Bahnhofstrasse 132 (✆ **03622/540400;** www.ausseerland.at) is open Monday to Friday 9am to 7pm and Saturday 9am to 4pm.

WHERE TO STAY & DINE

Erzherzog Johann ★★ This government-rated four-star hotel in the town's center is the resort's finest. The conservatively designed building has stone detailing, and its rustic interior offers fireplaces, beamed ceilings, and comfortable furniture. Rooms are a bit small, with a balcony, good beds, and small bathrooms. Housekeeping gets high marks. The hotel restaurant serves a sampling of excellent Austrian and international dishes, with fresh ingredients used whenever possible. Main courses are served daily from noon to 2pm and 6:30 to 9:30pm. The area's sporting facilities are easily accessible from here.

Kurhausplatz 62, A-8990 Bad Aussee. ✆ **03622/52507.** Fax 03622/52507680. www.erzherzogjohann.at. 62 units. 174€–202€ ($278–$323) double. Rates include half-board. AE, DC, MC, V. Free parking. Closed Nov 14–Dec 5. **Amenities:** Restaurant; bar; indoor heated pool; fitness center; spa; sauna; room service; massage; babysitting; laundry service; dry cleaning; nonsmoking rooms. *In room:* TV, Wi-Fi, minibar, hair dryer.

Hotel-Pension Villa Kristina ★ Value This charming and personal establishment was built in 1892 as a simple inn for the many hunters who frequented the region. Friedl Raudaschl bought the place in the 1970s, updated its plumbing and electricity, and named it after his wife, Krista, who continues to manage it with him today. The hotel lies on ample private grounds beside the River Traun and the road leading to Altaussee, about a 10-minute walk from Bad Aussee. Inside and out, the steep-roofed, wood-trimmed house is loaded with handcrafted details. Medium-size rooms are filled with a certain Eastern Austrian charm, although modern luxuries, including efficiently organized bathrooms are present. The best rooms have private balconies with great views. The hotel has a home library and a piano, and meals are served only to guests who request them in advance.

Altauseerstrasse 54, A-8990 Bad Aussee. ✆/fax **03622/52017.** www.villakristina.at. 12 units. 80€–98€ ($128–$157) double. Rates include breakfast. AE, DC, MC, V. Closed Apr and Nov–Dec 22. **Amenities:** Restaurant; bar; room service; laundry service; dry cleaning. *In room:* TV, Wi-Fi.

5 DACHSTEIN-TAUERN

The province's major ski area, Dachstein-Tauern, lies in northwest Styria. The Dachstein, in the Salzkammergut, is a gigantic alpine mountain range cutting across Land Salzburg, Upper Austria, and Styria, with mammoth glaciers lying between its peaks. The Enns River separates the Dachstein and the Tauern massifs. Championship ski races are held here, and it's a great place for powder skiing.

SCHLADMING & ROHRMOOS

To see more of West Styria, stay in either Rohrmoos or Schladming, south of Bad Aussee, and use these resorts as a center for exploring the alpine mountain range of Dachstein-Tauern.

Essentials

GETTING THERE This skiing center is in the Dachstein-Tauern recreation and winter-sports area on Route 308 and the Vienna-Bruck/Mur-Graz rail line. It's easy to reach. The center of Rohrmoos is 2km (1 mile) south of the center of Schladming, but the edges of the two resorts touch one another; for most practical purposes, they are considered one.

At least one **train** per hour reaches Schladming from Graz (trip time: 2½ hr.) or Salzburg (trip time: 1¼ hr.). Some trains from Graz might require a transfer at Selzthal, and some trains from Salzburg require a transfer in Bischofshofen. For rail information, contact © **05/1717** (www.oebb.at).

Many **bus routes** begin in Schladming and wind into the surrounding hills and valleys; many of the town's residents use these buses. Rohrmoos has no rail connections, but many buses travel along the northeast to southwest stretch of the valley between Schladming and Rohrmoos, making frequent stops at the hotels that line the valley's main road.

In the northwestern corner of Styria, Schladming/Rohrmoos is often visited by people **driving** from Land Salzburg. To get here, take the A10 south from Salzburg to the junction with Route 308, heading east. Schladming is 299km (186 miles) southwest of Vienna and 203km (126 miles) northwest of Graz.

VISITOR INFORMATION The **tourist office** in Schladming (© **03687/23310;** www.schladming-dachstein.at) is open Monday to Friday 9am to 6pm and Saturday 9am to noon.

Skiing, Hiking & More

The **Planai** (1,900m/6,234 ft.) and the **Hochwurzen** (1,850m/6,070 ft.) have fast downhill runs and ski slopes, equipped with a cableway, five double chairlifts, a connecting three-seat chairlift, ski buses, and 15 surface lifts, at all altitudes. Some 22,000 people per hour can be transported. The **Dachstein-Südwand cableway** makes skiing at 2,704m (8,871 ft.) possible in summer. There are ski schools, and you can leave children at the ski kindergarten, which has a children's surface lift.

Miles of winter footpaths make for good, invigorating walking. You can also enjoy horse-drawn sleigh rides, tobogganing, ski-bobbing, curling, game-feeding trips, and many other winter activities. Cafes and bars offer lively après-ski activities, as do the hotels. In summer, you'll enjoy mountaineering, swimming, tennis, bowling, and top-quality entertainment, along with warm Styrian hospitality. Golf, rafting, and parasailing are available in nice weather.

Schladming is an ancient town in the upper valley of the Enns River, lying between Dachstein to the north and Schladminger Tauern to the south. It was a silver- and copper-mining town in medieval times. Old miners' houses are still standing. The Pfarrkirche (Parish Church) is late Gothic, and the town's 1862 church is the largest Protestant church in Styria.

Where to Stay & Dine in the Area

Alpenhotel Schwaigerhof (Kids) Located on a hillside with a mountain view, this five-story chalet, built in stages from 1975 to 1981, is attractively embellished. The comfortably furnished rooms, decorated with modern pieces, are either small or medium in size. A host of sporting facilities is available nearby.

A-8970 Rohrmoos. ✆ **03687/614220.** Fax 03687/6142252. www.schwaigerhof.at. 42 units. Winter 134€–140€ ($214–$224) double, 146€–190€ ($234–$304) suite; summer 142€–154€ ($227–$246) double, 154€–206€ ($246–$330) suite. Rates include half-board. AE, MC, V. Parking 10€ ($16). **Amenities:** 2 restaurants; bar; indoor heated pool; fitness center; Jacuzzi; sauna; children's playground; massage; laundry service; dry cleaning; nonsmoking rooms; solarium; rooms for those w/limited mobility. *In room:* TV, Wi-Fi, minibar, hair dryer, safe.

Gasthof Sonneck This chalet has white walls, big windows, wooden balconies, and a flagstone-covered terrace. The interior is rustically outfitted with glowing pine and tasteful furniture. The comfortable small rooms—furnished with modern, built-in pieces—look out over the mountains and have balconies. Bathrooms are also small but efficiently organized with tub/shower combinations and more than enough shelf space.

Rohrmoos 112, A-8970 Schladming. ✆ **03687/61232.** Fax 03687/612326. www.sonneck.at. 20 units. Winter 94€–135€ ($122–$176) double; summer 75€–82€ ($98–$107) double. Rates include half-board. MC, V. Closed Oct–Nov. **Amenities:** Restaurant; bar; lounge; sauna; solarium. *In room:* TV, Wi-Fi, hair dryer, safe.

Hotel Alte Post ★★ This chalet-style, government-rated four-star establishment has a center-of-town location, a history that dates from 1618, and a popular restaurant with a nouvelle/traditional Austrian cuisine menu. Rooms are among the finest in town, although only moderate in size. Each is traditionally furnished with many modern touches. Bathrooms, though small, are neatly arranged with shower/tub combos. In the restaurant, hot food is served daily from 11:30am to 2pm and 6 to 10pm. Less-formal meals and afternoon snacks are available in the rustic Knappenstube. Even if you're staying at the hotel, reservations in the formal dining room are advised.

Hauptplatz 10, A-8970 Schladming. ✆ **03687/22571.** Fax 03687/225718. www.alte-post.at. 40 units. Winter 158€–248€ ($253–$397) double; summer 126€–160€ ($202–$256) double. Rates include breakfast. AE, DC, MC, V. Closed Nov and 2 weeks in Apr. **Amenities:** Restaurant; bar; sauna; room service; laundry service; dry cleaning; nonsmoking rooms. *In room:* TV, Wi-Fi, minibar, hair dryer.

RAMSAU

At the foot of the mighty Dachstein massif, which reaches a height of nearly 3,050m (10,006 ft.), Ramsau is an emerging ski resort, rivaling but not yet surpassing Schladming. Ramsau is completely devoted to skiing in winter and, to a lesser extent, trekking and climbing in summer. Trails are clearly marked with white-and-green signs. The prices here are, in general, lower than at Schladming.

Essentials

GETTING THERE Ramsau has no train connections, but about two **buses** per hour from Schladming arrive here throughout the day. The trip up the valley roads takes about

20 minutes. If you're **driving,** you can take a winding, unclassified, but signposted road north from the center of Schladming.

Where to Stay & Dine

Almfrieden Wander- und Langlauhofhotel Value Set at the base of a rock-strewn mountain, this government-rated three-star hotel is rustically paneled with pine boards and dotted with open fireplaces and mountain chairs. The cozy rooms are equipped with comfortable wooden beds and a table where breakfast can be served. Many open onto private balconies that catch the sun. The cuisine served here is among the finest in the area, with good Austrian and Italian wines and both Styrian and continental dishes. Guests can also try marksmanship on the indoor rifle range.

A-8972 Ramsau. ✆ **03687/81753.** Fax 03687/817536. www.almfrieden.at. 36 units. Winter 122€–164€ ($195–$262) double; summer 96€–112€ ($154–$179) double. Rates include half-board. MC, V. Closed Easter–May 15 and Oct–Dec 18. **Amenities:** Restaurant; bar; lounge; fitness room; Jacuzzi; sauna; room service; laundry service; dry cleaning; nonsmoking rooms; 1 room for those w/limited mobility; solarium; internet room. *In room:* TV.

Sporthotel Matschner Built in 1967 and much improved since then, the Matschner is one of the resort's largest hotels. Located in the town center, it's a double chalet with many flowered balconies. The hotel offers cozy, beautifully maintained, well-furnished rooms with good beds. All rooms are nonsmoking and open onto private balconies with a view. The hotel provides easy access to many nearby sporting facilities. No smoking is allowed.

A-8972 Ramsau. ✆ **03687/817210.** Fax 03687/82666. www.matschner.at. 60 units. Winter 158€–242€ ($253–$387) double, 222€–306€ ($355–$490) suite; summer 134€–178€ ($214–$285) double, 166€–212€ ($266–$339) suite. Rates include half-board. MC, V. Closed Easter–May 15 and Nov 15–Dec 5. **Amenities:** Restaurant; bar; indoor heated pool; tennis court; Jacuzzi; sauna; children's playroom; massage; babysitting; laundry service; dry cleaning; rooms for those w/limited mobility. *In room:* TV, Wi-Fi, minibar, hair dryer, safe.

Appendix A: Fast Facts, Toll-Free Numbers & Websites

1 FAST FACTS: AUSTRIA

AMERICAN EXPRESS This company has agents in Vienna and Salzburg. See "Fast Facts" under the individual cities, or check its website (www.americanexpress.com) for office locations and hours.

AREA CODES The country code for Austria is **43;** the city code for Vienna is **1,** if you're calling from outside the country. Within the country use **01.**

ATM NETWORKS/CASHPOINTS See "Money & Costs," p. 50.

BUSINESS HOURS In the federal provinces, banking hours vary according to the region. The exchange counters at airports and railroad stations are generally open from the first to the last plane or train, usually from 8am to 8pm daily. Many stores are open 8am to 6pm Monday to Friday, and 8am to noon on Saturday; they close for 2 hours during the middle of each day.

CAR RENTALS See "Toll-Free Numbers & Websites," p. 486.

DRINKING LAWS Upper Austria, Salzburg, and Tyrol prohibit the consumption of distilled beverages below the age of 18, while Carinthia and Styria prohibit drinks containing more than 12% or 14% of alcohol respectively in this age bracket. Carinthia additionally requires adolescents to maintain a blood alcohol level below 0.05%, while Upper Austria prohibits "excessive consumption," and Salzburg prohibits consumption that would result in a state of intoxication. Prohibitions in Vienna, Burgenland, Lower Austria, and Vorarlberg apply only to alcohol consumption *in public*. Enforcement in supermarkets is quite strict, while in restaurants and bars enforcement is quite lax especially for beer and wine.

DRIVING RULES See "Getting There and Getting Around," p. 44.

DRUG LAWS Penalties for violations are severe and could lead to imprisonment or deportation. Selling drugs to minors is dealt with particularly harshly.

DRUGSTORES In Austrian cities, at least one pharmacy stays open 24 hours. If a particular pharmacy is closed, a sign on the door will list the address and phone number of the nearest one that is open.

ELECTRICITY Austria operates on 220 volts AC (50 cycles). That means that U.S.-made appliances that don't come with a 110/220 switch will need a transformer (sometimes called a converter). Many Austrian hotels stock adapter plugs but not power transformers.

EMBASSIES & CONSULATES The main building of the **Embassy of the United States** is at Boltzmanngasse 16, A-1090, Vienna (© **01/313390**). However, the consular section is at Parkring 12,

A-1010 Vienna (✆ **01/3125035**). Lost passports, tourist emergencies, and other matters are handled by the consular section. Both the embassy and the consulate are open Monday to Friday 9 to 11:30am. Emergency services 8:30am to 5pm.

The **Canadian Embassy,** Laurenzerberg 2 (✆ **01/531383000**), is open Monday to Friday 8:30am to 12:30pm and 1:30 to 3:30pm; the **British Embassy,** Jauresgasse 12 (✆ **01/716130**), is open Monday to Friday 9:15 to 10:15am and 2 to 3pm; **Australian Embassy,** Mattiellistrasse 2-4 (✆ **01/506740**), is open Monday to Friday 8:30am to 4:30pm. The nearest **New Zealand Embassy** is located in Berlin, Germany, Friedrichstrasse 60 (✆ **030/206210**), and is open Monday to Friday 9am to noon. The **Ireland Embassy,** Rotenturmstrabe 16–18 (✆ **01/7154246**), is open Monday through Friday 8:30 to 11am and 1 to 4pm.

EMERGENCIES Emergency phone numbers throughout the country (no area code needed) are as follows: ✆ **133** for the police, **144** for accident service, **122** to report a fire, and **120** to report a car breakdown on the highway.

GASOLINE See "Gasoline," p. 49.

HOLIDAYS Bank holidays in Austria are as follows: January 1, January 6 (Epiphany), Easter Monday, May 1, Ascension Day, Whitmonday, Corpus Christi Day, August 15, October 26 (Nationalfeiertag), November 1, December 8, and December 25 and 26. Check locally when you arrive in Austria. Some of these holidays fall on different days every year.

INSURANCE When traveling, any number of things could go wrong—lost luggage, trip cancellation, a medical emergency—so consider the following types of insurance.

Travel Insurance Check your existing insurance policies and credit card coverage before you buy travel insurance. You may already be covered for lost luggage, canceled tickets, or medical expenses. The cost of travel insurance varies widely, depending on the cost and length of your trip, your age and health, and the type of trip you're taking, but expect to pay between 5% and 8% of the vacation itself. You can get estimates from various providers through **InsureMyTrip.com**. Enter your trip cost and dates, your age, and other information for prices from more than a dozen companies.

Medical Insurance For travel overseas, most health plans (including Medicare and Medicaid) do not provide coverage, and the ones that do often require you to pay for services up front and reimburse you only after you return home. Even if your plan does cover overseas treatment, most out-of-country hospitals make you pay your bills upfront, and send you a refund only after you've returned home and filed the necessary paperwork with your insurance company. As a safety net, you may want to buy travel medical insurance, particularly if you're traveling to a remote or high-risk area where emergency evacuation is a possible scenario. If you require additional medical insurance, try **MEDEX Assistance** (✆ **410/453-6300;** www.medexassist.com) or **Travel Assistance International** (✆ **800/821-2828;** www.travelassistance.com). For general information on services, call the company's **Worldwide Assistance Services, Inc.** (✆ **800/777-8710;** www.worldwideassistance.com).

Lost Luggage Insurance On international flights (including U.S. portions of international trips), baggage coverage is limited to approximately $9.07 per pound, up to approximately $635 per checked bag. If you plan to check items more valuable than the standard liability, see if your valuables are covered by your homeowner's policy and get baggage insurance as part of your comprehensive travel-insurance package. Don't buy insurance at the airport, as it's usually overpriced. Be sure to take any valuables or irreplaceable items with you in your carry-on luggage, as many valuables (including books, money, and electronics) aren't covered by airline policies.

If your luggage is lost, immediately file a lost-luggage claim at the airport, detailing the luggage contents. For most airlines, you must report delayed, damaged, or lost baggage within 4 hours of arrival. The airlines are required to deliver luggage, once found, directly to your house or destination free.

Trip Cancellation Insurance Trip-cancellation insurance helps you get your money back if you have to back out of a trip, if you have to go home early, or if your travel supplier goes bankrupt. Allowed reasons for cancellation can range from sickness to natural disasters to the Department of State declaring your destination unsafe for travel. For information, contact one of the following recommended insurers: **Access America** (✆ **800/284-8300;** www.accessamerica.com), **AIG Travel Guard International** (✆ **800/826-4919;** www.travelguard.com), **Travel Insured International** (✆ **800/243-3174;** www.travelinsured.com), and **Travelex Insurance Services** (✆ **800/228-9792;** www.travelex-insurance.com).

INTERNET ACCESS It's hard nowadays to find a city that *doesn't* have a few cybercafes. Although there's no definitive directory for cybercafes—these are independent businesses, after all—two places to start looking are at **www.cybercaptive.com** and **wwws.cybercafe.com**.

LEGAL AID Your embassy (see above) will give you advice if you run into trouble abroad. They can advise you of your rights and can even provide a list of attorneys (for which you'll have to pay if services are used). But they cannot interfere on your behalf in the legal process of Austria. For questions about American citizens who are arrested abroad, including ways of getting money to them, telephone the **Citizens Emergency Center** of the Office of Special Consulate Services in Washington, D.C. (✆ **202/647-5225**). Citizens of other nations should go to their Vienna-based consulate for advice.

LANGUAGE German is the official language of Austria, but because English is taught in the high schools, it's commonly spoken throughout the country, especially in tourist regions. Certain Austrian minorities speak Slavic languages, and Hungarian is commonly spoken in Burgenland. See Appendix B for a glossary of common and useful German words and phrases.

LOST & FOUND Be sure to call all of your credit card companies the minute you discover your wallet has been lost or stolen. Your credit card company or insurer may also require you file a police report and provide a report number or record of the loss. Most credit card companies have an emergency toll-free number to call if your card is lost or stolen; they may be able to wire you a cash advance immediately or deliver an emergency credit card in a day or two. Visa's emergency number outside the U.S. is ✆ **410/581-3836;** call collect. American Express cardholders should call collect ✆ **336/393-1111.** MasterCard holders should call collect ✆ **314/542-7111.**

MAIL Post offices *(das postamt)* in Austria are usually located in the heart of the town, village, or urban district they service. If you're unsure of your address in any particular town, correspondence can be addressed care of the local post office by labeling it either POST RESTANTE or POSTLAGERND. If you do this, it's important to clearly designate the addressee, the name of the town, and its postal code. To claim any correspondence, the addressee must present his or her passport.

As an alternative to having your mail sent *post restante* to post offices, you might opt for the mail services offered in Salzburg, Innsbruck, and Vienna by American

Express (see above). There's no charge for this service to anyone holding an American Express card or American Express traveler's checks.

The postal system in Austria is, for the most part, efficient and speedy. You can buy stamps at a post office or from the hundreds of news and tobacco kiosks, designated locally as *Tabac/Trafik.* Mailboxes are painted yellow, and older ones are emblazoned with the double-headed eagle of the Austrian Republic. Newer ones usually have the golden trumpet of the Austrian Postal Service. A blue stripe on a mailbox indicates that mail will be picked up there on a Saturday.

NEWSPAPERS & MAGAZINES In major cities, you'll find the *International Herald Tribune* or *USA Today,* as well as other English-language newspapers and magazines, including the European editions of *Time* and *Newsweek,* at hotels and news kiosks.

PASSPORTS Allow plenty of time before your trip to apply for a passport; processing normally takes 3 weeks but can take longer during busy periods (especially spring). And keep in mind that if you need a passport in a hurry, you'll pay a higher processing fee.

For residents of Australia: You can pick up an application from your local post office or any branch of Passports Australia, but you must schedule an interview at the passport office to present your application materials. Call the **Australian Passport Information Service** at ✆ **131-232,** or visit the government website at **www.passports.gov.au**.

For residents of Canada: Passport applications are available at travel agencies throughout Canada or from the central **Passport Office,** Department of Foreign Affairs and International Trade, Ottawa, ON K1A 0G3 (✆ **800/567-6868;** www.ppt.gc.ca).

For residents of Ireland: You can apply for a 10-year passport at the **Passport Office,** Setanta Centre, Molesworth Street, Dublin 2 (✆ **01/671-1633;** www.irlgov.ie). Those under age 18 and over 65 must apply for a 12€ 3-year passport. You can also apply at 1A South Mall, Cork (✆ **021/494-4700**) or at most main post offices.

For residents of New Zealand: You can pick up a passport application at any New Zealand Passports Office or download it from the website. Contact the **Passports Office** (✆ **0800/225-050** in New Zealand or 04/474-8100; www.passports.govt.nz).

For residents of the United Kingdom: To pick up an application for a standard 10-year passport (5-year passport for children under 16), visit your nearest passport office, major post office, or travel agency, or contact the **United Kingdom Passport Service** (✆ **0870/521-0410;** www.ukpa.gov.uk).

For residents of the United States: Whether you're applying in person or by mail, you can download passport applications from the U.S. Department of State website at **http://travel.state.gov**. To find your regional passport office, either check the U.S. Department of State website or call the **National Passport Information Center** toll-free number (✆ **877/487-2778**) for automated information.

POLICE Dial ✆ **133** anywhere in Austria to summon the police.

SAFETY No particular caution is needed other than what a careful person would maintain anywhere. Austria is a very safe country in which to travel.

SMOKING Many Austrians are heavy smokers, and unlike in the United States, smoking is not prohibited in many restaurants. If you're sensitive to smoke, ask the headwaiter to sit you in a nonsmoking section, if possible. If not, ask to be seated away from the smoke or outside on a terrace.

TAXES In 1993, all countries belonging to the European Union became a single market by enforcing the Single European Act and merging into a common customs and Value Added Tax (VAT) zone. VAT is a special tax applied to goods and services alike. The rates vary from country to country; in Austria the rate is 20%.

You can arrange for a refund of VAT if you can prove that the goods on which you paid tax were carried out of Austria. To get the refund, you must fill out Form U-34, which is available at most stores (a sign will read TAX-FREE SHOPPING). Get one for the ÖAMTC (Austrian Automobile and Touring Club) quick refund if you plan to get your money at the border. Check whether the store gives refunds itself or uses a service. Sales personnel will help you fill out the form and will affix the store-identification stamp. You show the VAT *(MWSt)* as a separate item or state that the tax is part of the total price. Keep your U-34 forms handy when you leave the country, and have them validated by the Viennese Customs officer at your point of departure.

Know in advance that you'll have to show the articles for which you're claiming a VAT refund. Because of this, it's wise to keep your purchases in a suitcase or carry-on bag that's separate from the rest of your luggage, with all the original tags and tickets, and the original receipts nearby. Don't check the item within your luggage before you process the paperwork with the Customs agent. In some instances, if your paperwork is in order, you'll receive a tax refund on the spot. If your point of departure is not equipped to issue cash on the spot, you'll have to mail the validated U-34 form or forms back to the store where you bought the merchandise after you return home. It's wise to keep a copy of each form. Within a few weeks, the store will send you a check, bank draft, or international money order covering the amount of your VAT refund. Help is available from the ÖAMTC, which has instituted methods of speeding up the refund process. Before you go, call the Austrian National Tourist Office for the ÖAMTC brochure "Tax-Free Shopping in Austria."

TELEPHONE Never dial abroad from your hotel room unless it's an emergency. Place phone calls at the post office or some other location. Viennese hotels routinely add a 40% surcharge, some as much as 200%. For help dialing, contact your hotel's operator, or dial ✆ **09** for placement of long-distance calls within Austria or for information about using a telephone company credit card; dial ✆ **1611** for local directory assistance; ✆ **1613** for European directory assistance; ✆ **1614** for overseas directory assistance; and ✆ **08** for help in dialing international long distance. Coin-operated phones are all over Vienna. To use one, pick up the receiver, insert a minimum of .10€ (20¢), wait for the dial tone, then dial the number. Know in advance that .10€ (20¢) will allow no more than about 2 minutes of talk time even to a number within Vienna. When your talk time is finished, a recorded German telephone announcement instructs you to put in more coins. To avoid this unwelcome interruption, most Viennese insert up to .40€ (70¢) at the beginning of their call. In theory, the phone will return whatever unused coins remain at the end of your call, although this doesn't always happen. On some older phones, you need to push a clearly designated button before the coins drop into the phone and the call is connected.

Avoid carrying lots of coins by buying a ***Wertkarte*** at tobacco/news kiosks or at post offices. Each card is electronically coded to provide 3€ ($4.80), 7€ ($11), 14€ ($22), or 35€ ($56) worth of phone calls. Buyers receive a slight discount because cards are priced slightly lower than their face value.

AT&T's USA Direct plan enables you to charge calls to your credit card or to call collect. The access number, ✆ **0800/200288,** is a local call all over Austria. For **Sprint,** dial ✆ **0800/200236;** for **World-com,** dial ✆ **0800/200235;** for **British Telecom,** dial ✆ **0800/200209;** and for **Canada Direct,** dial ✆ **0800/200217.**

The international access code for both the United States and Canada is **001,** followed by the area code and the seven-digit local number.

TIME Austria operates on central European time, which makes it 6 hours later than U.S. Eastern Standard Time. It advances its clocks 1 hour in summer, however.

TIPPING A service charge of 10% to 15% is included on hotel and restaurant bills, but it's a good policy to leave something extra for waiters and 2€ ($3.20) per day for your hotel maid.

Railroad station, airport, and hotel porters get 1.50€ ($2.40) per piece of luggage, plus a 1€ ($1.60) tip. Your hairdresser should be tipped 10% of the bill, and the shampoo person will be thankful for a 1.50€ ($2.40) gratuity. Toilet attendants are usually given .50€ (80¢), and hat-check attendants expect .50€ to 1.50€ (80¢ to $2.40), depending on the place.

TOILETS All airport and railway stations have restrooms, rarely with attendants. Bars, nightclubs, restaurants, cafes, and hotels have facilities as well. You'll also find public toilets near many major sights.

2 TOLL-FREE NUMBERS & WEBSITES

MAJOR AIRLINES

Aeroméxico
✆ 800/237-6639 (in U.S.)
✆ 020/7801-6234 (in U.K., information only)
www.aeromexico.com

Air France
✆ 800/237-2747 (in U.S.)
✆ 800/375-8723 (U.S. and Canada)
✆ 087/0142-4343 (in U.K.)
www.airfrance.com

Air India
✆ 212/407-1371 (in U.S.)
✆ 91 22 2279 6666 (in India)
✆ 020/8745-1000 (in U.K.)
www.airindia.com

Alitalia
✆ 800/223-5730 (in U.S.)
✆ 800/361-8336 (in Canada)
✆ 087/0608-6003 (in U.K.)
www.alitalia.com

American Airlines
✆ 800/433-7300 (in U.S. and Canada)
✆ 020/7365-0777 (in U.K.)
www.aa.com

British Airways
✆ 800/247-9297 (in U.S. and Canada)
✆ 087/0850-9850 (in U.K.)
www.british-airways.com

China Airlines
✆ 800/227-5118 (in U.S.)
✆ 022/715-1212 (in Taiwan)
www.china-airlines.com

Continental Airlines
✆ 800/523-3273 (in U.S. or Canada)
✆ 084/5607-6760 (in U.K.)
www.continental.com

Delta Air Lines
✆ 800/221-1212 (in U.S. or Canada)
✆ 084/5600-0950 (in U.K.)
www.delta.com

EgyptAir
✆ 212/581-5600 (in U.S.)
✆ 020/7734-2343 (in U.K.)
✆ 09/007-0000 (in Egypt)
www.egyptair.com

El Al Airlines
✆ 972/3977-1111 (outside Israel)
✆ *2250 (from any phone in Israel)
www.el.co.il

Finnair
✆ 800/950-5000 (in U.S. and Canada)
✆ 087/0241-4411 (in U.K.)
www.finnair.com

Iberia Airlines
✆ 800/722-4642 (in U.S. and Canada)
✆ 087/0609-0500 (in U.K.)
www.iberia.com

Japan Airlines
✆ 012/025-5931 (international)
www.jal.co.jp

Lufthansa
✆ 800/399-5838 (in U.S.)
✆ 800/563-5954 (in Canada)
✆ 087/0837-7747 (in U.K.)
www.lufthansa.com

Olympic Airlines
✆ 800/223-1226 (in U.S.)
✆ 514/878-9691 (in Canada)
✆ 087/0606-0460 (in U.K.)
www.olympicairlines.com

Qantas Airways
✆ 800/223-1226 (in U.S.)
✆ 084/5774-7767 (in U.K. or Canada)
✆ 13 13 13 (in Australia
www.qantas.com

Swiss Air
✆ 877/359-7947 (in U.S. and Canada)
✆ 084/5601-0956 (in U.K.)
www.swiss.com

Turkish Airlines
✆ 90 212 444 0 849
www.thy.com

United Airlines*
✆ 800/864-8331 (in U.S. and Canada)
✆ 084/5844-4777 (in U.K.)
www.united.com

U.S. Airways*
✆ 800/428-4322 (in U.S. and Canada)
✆ 084/5600-3300 (in U.K.)
www.usairways.com

CAR RENTAL AGENCIES

Auto Europe
✆ 888/223-5555 (in U.S. and Canada)
✆ 0800/2235-5555 (in U.K.)
www.autoeurope.com

Avis
✆ 800/331-1212 (in U.S. and Canada)
✆ 084/4581-8181 (in U.K.)
www.avis.com

Budget
✆ 800/527-0700 (in U.S.)
✆ 087/0156-5656 (in U.K.)
✆ 800/268-8900 (in Canada)
www.budget.com

Dollar
✆ 800/800-4000 (in U.S.)
✆ 800/848-8268 (in Canada)
✆ 080/8234-7524 (in U.K.)
www.dollar.com

Enterprise
✆ 800/261-7331 (in U.S.)
✆ 514/355-4028 (in Canada)
✆ 012/9360-9090 (in U.K.)
www.enterprise.com

Hertz
✆ 800/645-3131
✆ 800/654-3001 (for international reservations)
www.hertz.com

Kemwel (KHA)
✆ 877/820-0668
www.kemwel.com

Appendix B: Language Lessons

English is widely spoken throughout Austria, especially in cities such as Vienna and Salzburg and at all the major resorts. However, when you encounter someone who doesn't speak English, the following might be useful. Even attempting to use a little German is a nice sign of respect toward your hosts.

1 BASIC PHRASES & VOCABULARY

English	German	Pronunciation
Hello	Guten Tag	goo-ten-*tahk*
How are you?	Wie geht es ihnen?	vee *gayt* ess ee-neen
Very well	Sehr gut	zayr *goot*
Thank you	Danke schön	dahn-keh-*shern*
Good-bye	Auf Wiedersehen	owf *vee*-dayr-zayn
Please	Bitte	*bit*-tuh
Yes	Ja	yah
No	Nein	nine
Excuse me	Entschuldigen sie	en-*shool*-di gen zee
Give me	Geben Sie mir	*gay*-ben zee meer
Where is . . .	Wo ist . . .	*voh* eest
the station?	der bahnhof?	dayr *bahn*-hoft
a hotel?	ein hotel?	ain *hotel?*
a restaurant?	ein restaurant?	ain res-tow-*rahng*
the toilet?	die toilette?	dee twah-*let*-tuh
To the right	Nach rechts	nakh *reshts*
To the left	Nach links	nakh *leenks*
Straight ahead	Gerade aus	goh *rah* deh ows
I would like . . .	Ich möchte . . .	ikh *mersh* ta
to eat	essen	*ess*-en
a room	ein zimmer	ain *tzim*-mer
for one night	für eine nacht	feer *ai-neh* nakht
How much is it?	Wieviel kostet?	vee-*feel* kaw-stet
The check, please	Zahlen, bitte	*tzah*-len bit-tuh
When?	Wann?	vahn

English	German	Pronunciation
Yesterday	Gestern	*geh*-stern
Today	Heute	*hoy*-tuh
Tomorrow	Morgen	*more*-gen
Breakfast	Frühstück	*free*-shtick
Lunch	Mittagessen	*mi*-tahg-gess-en
Dinner	Abendessen	*ah*-bend-ess-en

2 NUMBERS

1	Eins	aintz)
2	Zwei	tzvai
3	Drei	dry
4	Vier	feer
5	Fünf	fewnf
6	Sechs	zex
7	Sieben	*zee*-ben
8	Acht	akht
9	Neun	noyn
10	Zehn	tzayn
11	Elf	ellf
12	Zwölf	tzvuhlf
13	Dreizehn	*dry*-tzayn
14	Vierzehn	*feer*-tzayn
15	Fünfzehn	*fewnf*-tzayn
16	Sechzehn	*zex*-tzayn
17	Siebzehn	*zeeb*-tzayn
18	Achtzehn	*akh*-tzayn
19	Neunzehn	*niyn*-tzayn
20	Zwanzig	*tzvahn*-tzik
30	Dreissig	*dry*-tzik
40	Vierzig	*feer*-tzik
50	Fünfzig	*fewnf*-tzik
60	Sechzig	*zex*-tzik
70	Siebzig	*zeeb*-tzik
80	Achtzig	*akht*-tzik
90	Neunzig	*noyn*-tzik
100	Hundert	*hoon*-dert

3 MENU TERMS

SOUPS (SUPPEN)

Erbsensuppe pea soup
Gemüsesuppe vegetable soup
Gulaschsuppe goulash soup
Kartoffelsuppe potato soup
Linsensuppe lentil soup
Nudelsuppe noodle soup

MEAT (WURST, FLEISCH & GEFLÜGEL)

Aufschnitt cold cuts
Brathuhn roast chicken
Bratwurst grilled sausage
Deutsches beefsteak, hamburger
Ente duck
Gans goose
Geflügel poultry
Kalb veal
Kassler Rippchen pork chops
Lamm lamb
Leber liver
Ragout stew
Rinderbraten roast beef
Rinderfleisch beef
Schinken ham
Schweinebraten roast pork
Truthahn turkey
Wurst sausage

FISH (FISCH)

Aal eel
Forelle trout
Hecht pike
Karpfen carp
Kerbs crayfish
Lachs salmon
Makrele mackerel
Rheinsalm Rhine salmon
Schellfisch haddock
Seezunge sole

VEGETABLES (GEMÜSE)

Blumenkohl cauliflower
Bohnon beans
Bratkartoffeln fried potatoes
Erbsen peas
Grüne Bohnon string beans
Gurken cucumbers
Karotten carrots
Kartoffelbrei mashed potatoes
Kartoffelsalat potato salad
Kohl cabbage
Rote rüben beets
Rotkraut red cabbage
Salat lettuce
Salzkartoffeln boiled potatoes
Spargel asparagus
Spinat spinach
Tomaten tomatoes

BEVERAGES (GERÄNKE)

Bier beer
  ein dunkles a dark beer
  ein helles a light beer
Milch milk
Schokolade chocolate
eine Tasse Kaffee a cup of coffee
eine Tasse Tee a cup of tea
Wasser water

CONDIMENTS

Brot bread
Brötchen rolls
Butter butter
Eis ice
Eissig vinegar
Knödel dumplings
Pfeffer pepper
Reis rice
Sahne cream
Salz salt
Senf mustard
Zucker sugar

COOKING TERMS

blutig rare
gebacken baked
gebraten fried
gefüllt stuffed
gekocht boiled
geröstet roasted
gut durchgebraten well-done
heiss hot
kaltes cold

INDEX